WALLS AND MIRRORS

MODULA-2 EDITION

Benjamin/Cummings Series in Structured Programming

WALLS AND MIRRORS

INTERMEDIATE PROBLEM SOLVING AND DATA STRUCTURES

MODULA-2 EDITION

Paul Helman

Robert Veroff

University of New Mexico

THE BENJAMIN/CUMMINGS PUBLISHING COMPANY, INC.

Menlo Park, California · Reading, Massachusetts · Fort Collins, Colorado ·
Don Mills, Ontario · Wokingham, U.K. · Amsterdam · Sydney ·
Singapore · Tokyo · Madrid · Bogota · Santiago · San Juan

Sponsoring Editor: Alan Apt
Production Coordinator: Pat Waldo, Partners in Publishing
Cover Designer: Gary Head
Book Designer: Christy Butterfield
Artist: Kelly Solis-Navarro

Photograph of The Great Wall of China opening Part III by Steven Edelman.
Photograph of Stanford University opening Part II by Larry Olsen.
Cover photograph courtesy The Bettmann Archive.

Library of Congress Cataloging-in-Publication Data

Helman, Paul. Walls and Mirrors Modula-2
    Intermediate problem solving and data structure.

    Includes index.
    1. Electronic digital computers—Programming.
2. Data structures (Computer science)   3. Modula-2
(Computer program language)   I. Veroff, Robert.
II. Title.
QA76.6.H453 1988   005.13′3   88-2869
ISBN 0-8053-8945-8

ABCDEFGHIJ-DO-898

The Benjamin/Cummings Publishing Company, Inc.
2727 Sand Hill Road
Menlo Park, California 94025

PREFACE

This book is intended primarily for the intermediate-level problem-solving course in a computer science curriculum. We have tried to cover thoroughly all the topics in the ACM's 1984 guidelines for such a course (CS-2). However, with undergraduate computer science education in its current state of flux, it is common to see great diversity in computer science curricula. Our book includes comprehensive coverage of enough topics to make it appropriate for courses with several different foci, including advanced programming and problem solving, software engineering, and elementary data structures courses.

In our opinion, the most important role of the second course is to help the student learn to integrate problem solving and programming abilities. We emphasize both the thought processes and the methods used by the computer scientist. It is just as important that the student learn how a computer scientist develops, analyzes, and implements a method as it is to learn the mechanics of the method. A computer science major cannot learn the subject from a cookbook approach to the material.

The book is divided into four parts: *Review of Structured Programming and Problem Solving, Recursion, Data Abstraction as a Problem Solving Tool*, and *Advanced Techniques for the Management of Data*. This division allows the instructor to easily tailor the book to a particular course. In most cases, Parts II and III will form the core of a one-semester course. The coverage given to Parts I and IV will depend on what role the course plays in your curriculum. A course that is primarily designed to teach structured programming and software engineering techniques should emphasize the material in Part I; a data structures course should emphasize the end of Part III and all of Part IV. More detailed suggestions for use in different courses appear later in the Preface.

COVERAGE OF TOPICS

The book contains classic computer science topics and problem areas that are consistent with the ACM's 1984 recommendations for CS-2. In addition, the latter sections of Part III together with Part IV contain the material necessary to satisfy the needs of a traditional lower-division data structures course.

We attempt to present analytical tools for the development of solutions within the context of example problems. Top-down design and the successive refinement of algorithms and data structures (through data abstraction) are applied to problems throughout the book, including two large case studies. We continually emphasize the value of recursive thinking and the tradeoffs between potential solutions. Similarly, the use of good documentation, debugging aids, and loop invariants to develop and verify solutions is part of our problem-solving methodology.

We introduce linked-list processing early and use the techniques in building data structures. This allows the consideration of the tradeoffs between sequential and linked data structures to be developed into a central problem-solving theme. These tradeoffs are at first considered at an informal level and are gradually viewed more and more quantitatively.

Classic application areas arise in the context of the major topics of the book. For example, searching and sorting are discussed in the context of both recursion and the abstract data type table. Binary search, Quicksort, and Mergesort, being naturally recursive algorithms, are first introduced in Part II. In the context of the ADT table (Parts III and IV), we introduce binary search trees, 2–3 trees, hashing, and file indexing. Sorting is again considered in the context of external files and also in the last chapter as a way of introducing order-of-magnitude analysis.

Algorithms for recognizing and evaluating algebraic expressions are first introduced in Part II in the context of recursive grammars, and are again considered in Part III as an application of stacks. Graph searching and traversals are two other important applications of stacks. Event driven simulation is introduced as an application of queues.

ORGANIZATION

Part I of the book is titled *Review of Structured Programming and Problem Solving*. We call the first part a *review*, not so much because we expect the students to have a thorough knowledge of the material but rather because its emphasis is more on programming than on the earlier stages of the problem solving process. In this sense, much of Part I will resemble an extension of an introductory course. The topics "reviewed" in this part include structured programming with Modula-2, pointer variables, and linked lists. The presentation of pointer variables and linked lists does not assume any previous knowledge of the material. Part I concludes with a case study in which we design and implement an interactive inventory system.

Part II is about *Recursion*. The ability to think recursively is one of the most useful skills that a computer scientist can possess. The insights into a concept, problem, or algorithm gained through a recursive approach are often of great value in helping to better understand its nature.

Our treatment of recursion emphasizes intuition over mechanics. We believe that a true understanding of recursion comes from repeated encounters with recursive definitions of both concepts and problems. We include examples ranging from simple recursive definitions to recursive algorithms for searching and sorting. We hope that when students complete this part of the book, recursion will be an integral part of their problem-solving repertoire.

Part III introduces the student to *Data Abstraction as a Problem-Solving Tool*. We focus on data abstraction's role in the problem-solving process along with the successive refinement of algorithms. We present the basic abstract data types and the data structures used to implement them. We emphasize the importance of weighing tradeoffs when selecting a data structure for a particular application. The choice of a data structure is often between a sequential (array-based) implementation and a linked implementation.

The abstract data types fall into two categories, those that organize their data by position and those that organize their data by value. The abstract data types in the first category are stacks, queues, and ordered lists. Those in the second category are tables and priority queues. The discussions of the abstract data type table constitute a key element of the book. A table must efficiently support the classic information storage and retrieval operations of *insert data by value, remove data by value*, and *search for data by value*. Our exploration of the various implementations of a table leads us to consider issues of efficiency. This introduces the student, at an informal level, to the notion of order-of-magnitude analysis. The application of this analysis to the linear implementations of tables (arrays and linked lists) motivates the need for the binary search tree implementation.

Part IV presents *Advanced Techniques for the Management of Data*—more advanced data structures and sorting algorithms. We develop 2–3 trees and hashed table implementations and analyze which operations each supports best. We then consider the problem of sorting and indexing data stored in direct-access external files. We show how Mergesort can be generalized to work on external files, and how hashing and B-tree indices are generalizations of the internal hashing schemes and 2–3 trees already developed. The final chapter introduces the student to "big-O" notation and applies it to the comparison of four sorting algorithms.

COMMENTS ON THE MODULA-2 EDITION OF *WALLS AND MIRRORS*

The primary topics of Walls and Mirrors are program design, recursion, data abstraction, and elementary data structures. Since these are essentially language independent topics, what is the rationale behind this new Modula-2 version of *Walls and Mirrors*? The answer is that while the book's major themes indeed are language independent, we have made an effort to illustrate most concepts with working programs. We feel that many of these concepts can be embodied more cleanly in Modula-2 programs than in Pascal programs.

Modula-2's advantages over Pascal materialize in many different facets of programming, including modular program development, data abstraction, and the implementation of many simple yet fundamentally important algorithmic concepts. Specifically, Modula-2 improves on Pascal in the following respects, each of which impacts the program-level realization of many of the concepts presented in *Walls and Mirrors*.

Support of Abstract Data Types.   The syntax of Pascal forces an ADT's type definition to be at the global program level. The spirit of data abstraction, however, mandates that an ADT's type definition be "packaged" with the functions and procedures that implement the ADT operations. This package, as much as possible, should be independent of the remainder of the program. For example, one should be able to replace one ADT implementation package with another without affecting the remainder of the program. In addition, portions of the program outside of the ADT package should not be able to access directly any ADT variables (this convention is commonly referred to as **data hiding**). While it is impossible to cleanly implement ADT packages in Pascal, Modula-2's support of independent program modules can be used to realize many aspects of the package perspective. Modula-2 allows type definitions to be local to the ADT module (rather than being global, as in Pascal) and allows ADT variables to be defined as a hidden type, thereby denying portions of the program outside of the ADT module access to these variables.

Separate Compilation of Program Units.   Even if one never were to use abstract data types, the ability to compile a program whose source code is spread across many files is essential in any large software development project. Separate compilation allows members of a programming team working on different logical units of a program to debug and test conveniently each individual program unit. This software engineering tool tends to promote a high degree of independence between program units.

Control Structures.   Pascal's AND and OR operators are unguarded. That is, when either of the logical expressions

```
E1 AND E2
E1 OR E2
```

is evaluated, both E1 and E2 will be evaluated, even when the value of one of these operands is sufficient to establish the value of the logical expression (e.g., in the expression E1 AND E2, E2 will be evaluated even when E1 evaluates to FALSE). This convention convolutes many simple yet fundamentally important algorithms. For example, consider a loop to search the array A[1..Max] for the value V. The pseudocode algorithm is simply

```
WHILE (i <= Max) AND (A[i] # V)
 i := i+1

IF (i > Max)
 THEN V is not present
 ELSE V is at location i of array A
```

This loop does not translate directly into Pascal because Pascal's AND is not guarded, thus leading to a subscript out of range error when V is not present in A. To implement this loop in Pascal, one has to choose between several unattractive alternatives (e.g., an artificial Boolean variable controlling the termination of the loop, a GOTO out of the loop). In contrast, Modula-2's AND and OR operators are guarded, thus allowing the above loop to be implemented directly. Algorithmic structures requiring guarded AND and OR operators occur time and time again, making such operators an important feature of a programming language.

Open Arrays. In Pascal, when an array is passed to a subprogram, the array must have a predefined size. This makes it impossible to implement in Pascal general purpose library routines, such as a sort procedure for an arbitrarily sized array of integers. Modula-2 supports open arrays as subprogram parameters, allowing arrays of any size to be passed to a single subprogram.

PROGRAMMING WITH ADT'S IN MODULA-2

Modula-2 is a relatively young language and, as a consequence, no universally accepted conventions yet exist for how Modula-2 best can be utilized to realize many important concepts. A prime example of this is the Modula-2 realization of abstract data types. While one might think that data abstraction in Modula-2 is a natural, we have spent a good deal of time grappling with the problem of how best to use the language to implement the principles of data abstraction.

Before outlining our Modula-2 programming conventions for abstract data types, we discuss briefly what we feel are the most crucial principles of data abstraction as it relates to CS-2 and software engineering.

The Wall. There must be a clear separation of an ADT's definition from its implementation. The user's portion of a program must have access only to an ADT's definition and not to any aspects of its implementation. In particular, the data structures used to implement an ADT should be hidden completely from the user's portion of the program.

The Contract. There should exist a precise, written contract between the user and the ADT implementor. This contract should contain:

1. A complete definition of the ADT, including the calling sequence for each operation.

2. A message from the user to the ADT implementor describing aspects of the program's utilization of the ADT that might be relevant to a choice of implementation. Such aspects might include, for example, an estimate of the maximum number of items that can be stored in the ADT at any point in time, and the frequency with which each ADT operation will be performed.

Program Modifiability.   It should be extremely simple to change from one ADT implementation to another. Ideally, it would be possible to replace the module implementing a given ADT with another module implementing the same ADT without requiring any changes to, or recompilation of, the other modules in the program.

Generality of the ADT Implementation.   The implementation of an ADT should be as generic as possible. For example, it should be possible to use a single implementation of the ADT stack, regardless of whether the stack is to contain integers, characters, or even some user-defined record type. The concept of a generic ADT implementation supports the construction of ADT implementation libraries.

Modula-2 allows us to achieve almost all of these principles if we adopt programming conventions such as the following.

1. An ADT's data structure always is defined as a hidden pointer type. This achieves the objective of hiding from the user's modules the implementing data structures.

2. A contract is in two pieces—the ADT's definition file and a "user message" file. The former file contains the ADT definition, while the latter file contains a message to the implementor that aids her or him in the selection of an implementation. Separating the message to the implementor from the ADT's definition file allows a single definition file to be associated with the ADT, even if the ADT is used in many different contexts.

3. The calling sequence for an ADT operation is independent of the ADT's implementation. This implies, for example, that we include "success flags" on some operations, even when an implementation ensures that the operation cannot fail. Also, if an implementation with a fixed maximum size is used to implement an ADT, the constant that represents this maximum size appears only in the ADT's implementation file (although the ADT implementor might well utilize the user's message contained in the ADT contract to select this value). These conventions allow a single definition file for an ADT to be associated with any number of different implementations of the ADT, thus allowing an ADT's implementation module to be replaced without requiring a recompilation of any of the program's other modules.

4. The type definition for the items to be stored in an ADT is imported from a user module into the ADT's definition and implementation modules. This allows the same implementation module to be applicable to many different instances of the ADT, even when the instances contain items of different user-defined types.

MODULA-2'S TYPE WORD AND FILE HANDLING

We have avoided the use of Modula-2's type WORD. We realize that some instructors will advocate using the type WORD in the context of an ADT's definition and implementation modules. This use of the type WORD allows a single pair of definition and implementation modules to support simultaneously instances of the ADT containing (logically) different types of items (for example, a stack of integers and a stack of characters). Our alternative convention of importing the (true) item type from a user module necessitates multiple copies of the ADT definition and implementation modules when such ADT instances must be supported simultaneously. Our objection to the WORD approach is that it leads to a large amount of "bit-level" detail, which obscures the algorithms and data structures that have been developed to implement the ADT. Since the study of these algorithms and data structures is central to the book, we believe that the WORD approach would be counterproductive. See Chapter 6 for a full discussion of our conventions for implementing ADT's in Modula-2.

Modula-2 does not include any I/O routines as part of the language, but rather assumes the existence of standard I/O library modules. Many of these standard modules (for example, FileSystem) interact with files at a relatively low level. The philosophy is that a programmer easily can use these standard modules to build whatever file-handling packages are appropriate for a given application. Whereas this approach certainly is sound in practice, it is a bit inconvenient in the context of a book such as ours. Our interest in files is in the algorithms that interact with them, rather than the details and quirks of file-handling operations. Consequently, we shall assume the existence of a collection of useful file-handling operations (for example, operations that support record-oriented I/O). The definition modules describing these operations appear in the Appendix.

USE IN YOUR CURRICULUM

By appropriately choosing which parts to emphasize, the instructor can easily *tailor* the book to fit a particular curriculum. Here are a few suggestions.

Courses Closely Following ACM's CS-2. If your introductory course emphasizes structured programming and covers the advanced Modula-2 topics presented in Chapter 2, then students can be left to review most of the first two chapters on their own. On the other hand, if the introductory course manages to cover only the basics of the Modula-2 language, then a fair amount of class time should be devoted to Chapters 1 and 2. In either case, the development of linked lists in Chapter 3 should be covered well in class. Also, the case study in Chapter 3 should be used to reinforce the concepts discussed in Chapters 1 and 2, even if the students have already studied this material in the introductory course.

The course should cover the material through Chapter 10, at least. Topics from Chapters 11 through 13 may be chosen selectively, as time permits. Our coverage of 2–3 trees, hashing, external sorting, and the comparison of sorting algorithms can be presented in any order or omitted completely.

CS-2

Part I: moderate to heavy coverage
Part II: complete coverage
Part III: complete coverage
Part IV: light to moderate coverage

Lower Division Data Structures Courses. At many schools, the primary undergraduate data structures course comes early in the curriculum. You can use our book in such a course by giving high priority to the material in Chapters 6 through 13. This means that you should spend as little time as possible on Chapters 1 and 2, and you may even find it necessary to omit some of the material on recursion. You should assign projects, such as those suggested in Chapter 11, in which the students develop programs for 2–3 trees and hashing.

Lower Division Data Structures

Part I: light coverage
Part II: light to moderate coverage
Part III: complete coverage
Part IV: complete coverage

Second and Third Quarter Courses. The book should work very well for schools on the quarter system. If the first quarter is an introductory Modula-2 course, then Parts I, II, and the beginning of Part III would constitute a reasonable second quarter. This would leave the remainder of Part III and all of Part IV for the third quarter.

Second Quarter

Part I: complete coverage
Part II: complete coverage
Part III: complete coverage of first half

Third Quarter

Part III: complete coverage of second half
Part IV: moderate coverage

SPECIAL FEATURES

- Case Studies
- Chapter Previews
- Chapter Summaries
- Common Pitfalls/Debugging
- Exercises
- Instructor's Guide
- Software Support
- Class Tested

In an attempt to illustrate "real-world programming," we develop and later modify a large interactive inventory program. The goal is to demonstrate that top-down design and modularity are invaluable aids in the development and modification of a large program. We attempt to make this and other problems more realistic by requiring the solutions to use external files. Many of our programs interact with Modula-2 files, and in Chapter 12 we also consider generic direct-access files.

Each chapter begins with a Preview and is followed by a Summary. The Previews are designed to orient students toward the material in the chapter. The Summaries attempt to place the chapters in proper perspective and alert the student to common misconceptions about the concepts and techniques presented. A collection of Exercises is included in each chapter to reinforce points from the text. A few are simple "self-check" type exercises, but most are thought questions and programming Projects. The most challenging exercises are labeled with asterisks.

Accompanying the text is an *Instructor's Guide,* which contains solutions to Exercises and programming Projects as well as suggestions for additional projects. Also available is a machine-readable copy of all the programs that appear in the book.

ACKNOWLEDGMENTS

We would first like to thank our editor, Alan Apt. He got us started on this project, and his confidence in us kept us going. Alan always provided us with invaluable guidance and assistance. We would also like to thank his most delightful and able assistant, Mary Ann Telatnik, and our production coordinator, Pat Waldo, who has been a real pleasure to deal with.

During the development of this book, the following people used our manuscript and made several useful suggestions and contributions. Thanks to Sto Bell, Kris Jensen, Sue Medeiros, Cleve Moler, John Rowe, and all of the students at the University of New Mexico who had to suffer through the early drafts. Our appreciation also goes to Stephanie Horoschak, who drew the diagrams used in these drafts.

Finally, we would like to thank our reviewers:

Richard Botting, California State University, San Bernardino
Jeffrey Brumfield, University of Texas, Austin
Philip Carrigan, Northeastern University
Michael Clancy, University of California, Berkeley
Shaun Cooper, University of New Mexico
Charles Engelke, University of Florida, Gainesville
Ken Lord, Queens College, New York
Andrew Oldroyd, Washington University, St. Louis

Rich Pattis, University of Washington, Seattle
David Radford, University of Illinois, Chicago
Richard Snodgrass, University of North Carolina
Paul Spirakis, New York University
Clinton Staley, University of California, Santa Barbara
Laurie White, University of Florida, Gainesville
Brad Wilson, Western Kentucky University

Paul Helman
Robert Veroff

BRIEF CONTENTS

For my Steffie, too   P.H.

Hey, Jude   R.V.

DETAILED CONTENTS

PART III DATA ABSTRACTION AS A PROBLEM-SOLVING TOOL: THE WALLS   249

CHAPTER 6   DATA ABSTRACTION   250

DATA ORGANIZED BY POSITION

DATA ORGANIZED BY VALUE

CHAPTER 10   VARIATIONS OF THE ADT TABLE   466

PART IV   ADVANCED TECHNIQUES FOR THE MANAGEMENT OF DATA   519

CHAPTER 11   ADVANCED IMPLEMENTATIONS OF THE ADT TABLE   520

CHAPTER 12   EXTERNAL METHODS   560

CHAPTER 13   A COMPARISON OF SORTING ALGORITHMS   598

MAJOR PROBLEMS SOLVED

WALLS AND MIRRORS

MODULA-2 EDITION

PART I

REVIEW OF
STRUCTURED PROGRAMMING
AND PROBLEM SOLVING

CHAPTER 1

REVIEW OF STRUCTURED PROGRAMMING WITH MODULA-2

PREVIEW   This chapter summarizes several fundamental principles that serve as the basis for dealing with the complexities of large programs. The discussion reinforces the basic principles of structured programming, which are further illustrated by the case study in Chapter 3. We demonstrate that writing well-structured and well-documented programs is cost effective. We also present a brief discussion of algorithms and data structures, and we indicate how these topics tie together the book's main theme of developing problem-solving and programming skills. As we move into Parts II, III, and IV, the focus will shift from discussions of programming principles to the development and use of new problem-solving tools. Even when the focus of discussion is on these new tools, you should note how our solutions adhere to the basic principles discussed in this chapter.

PROBLEM SOLVING AND PROGRAMMING

Computer science is, in part, the study of methods for effectively using a computer to solve problems. A first course in computer science typically emphasizes programming issues. Our focus in this book will be on the broader issues of problem solving. We begin with a brief overview of the problem-solving and programming processes and their close relationship.

What Is Problem Solving?

We use the term **problem solving** to refer to the entire process of taking the statement of a problem and developing a computer program that solves that problem. This process requires us to pass through many phases, from gaining an understanding of the problem to be solved, through the design of a conceptual solution, to the implementation of the solution with a computer program.

Let us be a bit more specific about what a solution is. We typically view a solution as consisting of two components: algorithms and data structures. An **algorithm** is a concise specification of a method for solving a problem. One type of action that an algorithm often must perform is to operate on a collection of data. An algorithm may, for instance, have to put new data into a collection, remove data from a collection, or ask questions about a collection of data. A **data structure** is a means of storing a collection of data. When constructing a solution, we must choose data structures that allow the data to be operated on easily in the manner required by the algorithm.

The above description of algorithms and data structures may perhaps leave the false impression that all the cleverness in problem solving goes into devel-

4

CHAPTER 1
REVIEW OF
STRUCTURED
PROGRAM-
MING WITH
MODULA-2

oping the algorithm and that data structures play only a supporting role. This is far from the truth. A data structure is really far more than "a means of storage." It should be viewed as also consisting of a set of algorithms for performing operations on the data it stores. For example, suppose that we need to store a collection of names in a manner that allows us to search rapidly for a given name. One solution to this problem is to store the names sorted in an array and to use a binary search algorithm to search the array for a specified name. We can view the *sorted array together with the binary search algorithm* as a data structure that solves this problem.

Thus, the view that data structures support algorithms is only one side of the story. The other side is that algorithms are part of what constitutes a data structure. One of the points we stress in this book is that, as we design a solution, algorithms and data structures should be developed in tandem. The global algorithm for solving a problem suggests operations that need to be performed on the data, which in turn suggest data structures (including their algorithms) for performing the operations on the data. The development of the solution may, however, proceed in the opposite direction as well. The kinds of data structures that we are able to construct can influence the strategy of our global algorithm for solving a problem. That is, our knowledge of which data operations are easy to perform and which are difficult can have a large effect on how we approach a problem.

As you have probably surmised from the above discussion, there is frequently not a sharp distinction between an "algorithms problem" and a "data-structures problem." It is often possible to look at a solution from one perspective and feel that the data structures are supporting a clever algorithm and then to look at the same solution from another perspective and feel that the algorithms are supporting a clever data structure.

Problem-Solving Tools

The design of a solution requires the careful development of both algorithms and data structures. In this book we shall study several tools to aid in this development. Three of these tools are top-down design, data abstraction, and recursion.

The problem-solving methodology we attempt to teach in this book applies **top-down design** in a manner that simultaneously develops algorithms and data structures. Both algorithms and data structures begin as "black boxes." Each black box specifies what it does but not how it does it. As the problem-solving process proceeds, the black boxes are gradually refined, until eventually their actions are realized by Modula-2 code. An extremely important rule in this problem-solving process is that no one black box may "know" how any other black box performs its task—it may know only what that task is. For example, if one part of a solution is to sort some data, one of the black boxes will be a sorting algorithm. The other black boxes will know that the sorting black box can be used to sort, but they will not know how it does it. In this way the various components of a solution are kept isolated from one another.

This strategy of dividing a solution into isolated components should be fairly familiar to you. You are perhaps most familiar with the strategy when it is

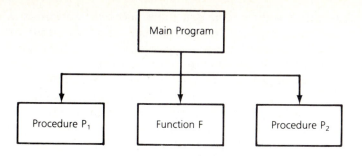

Figure 1–1

*Partitioning a
program into
independent
modules*

applied to programming. A program should be partitioned into independent **modules**—functions, procedures, and other blocks of code.* (See Figure 1–1.)

A modular program has many advantages, several of which we discuss in the following sections. One of the major tenets of our problem-solving philosophy is that modularity should be practiced at all points of the problem-solving process. The various parts of a solution, though developed together, should interact as little as possible. This method helps to simplify the problem-solving process. It also allows us to modify one part of the solution without significantly affecting the other parts. In the sorting example cited above, we should be able to change the sorting algorithm without affecting the rest of the solution.

Most introductory courses stress the modular development of algorithms, and we shall attempt to illustrate this technique further with many examples. For most of you, however, the modular development of data structures will be a new concept. **Data abstraction** is a tool that allows each data structure to be developed in relative isolation from the rest of the solution. The other modules of the solution will "know" what operations the data structure is capable of performing (such as put new data into the collection, remove data from the collection, or search for some data), but these other modules should not depend on how the data is stored or how the operations are performed. Data abstraction is thus a natural extension of modularity to data structures. This problem-solving tool is the topic of Part III.

Recursion is another extremely powerful problem-solving tool. Problems that at first appear to be very difficult are often solved very simply with a recursive approach. Like top-down design, recursion breaks a problem into several smaller problems. What's striking about recursion is that these smaller problems are of *exactly the same type* as the original problem. That is, a recursive solution solves a problem by solving smaller instances of the same problem! This might sound a bit magical to you, but as you will see in Part II, recursion is a very real and important problem-solving tool.

What Is a Good Solution?

Before we ask you to devote your time and energy to the study of problem-solving tools, it seems only fair that we indicate at the outset why we believe that mastery of these tools will help to make you a good problem solver. An

*When we speak of modules, we are generally referring to the abstract concept as opposed to Modula-2's language construct.

6

CHAPTER 1
REVIEW OF
STRUCTURED
PROGRAM-
MING WITH
MODULA-2

obvious statement is that the use of these tools has been demonstrated to produce good solutions. This statement, however, leads us to the more fundamental question, what *is* a good solution? We conclude our introductory comments with a brief attempt at answering this question.

Since a computer program is the final form our solutions will take, let us begin by considering what constitutes a good computer program. A program presumably is written to perform some task. In the course of performing that task, a real and tangible **cost** is incurred. This cost includes such factors as the computer resources (computing time and memory) the program consumes, the difficulties encountered by those who use the program, and the consequences of a program that does not behave correctly.

The costs just mentioned do not, however, give the whole picture. They pertain only to one phase of the life cycle of a solution—the phase in which it is an operational program. In assessing whether or not a solution is good, we must also consider the phases during which the solution was developed and the phases that follow the initial implementation of the solution with a program. Each of these phases incurs costs, too. The total cost of a solution must take into account the value of the time of the people who developed, refined, coded, debugged, and tested it. A solution's cost must also include the cost of maintaining, modifying, and expanding it.

Thus, when calculating the overall cost of a solution, we must include a diverse set of factors. If we adopt such a multidimensional view of cost, it is reasonable to evaluate a solution against the following criterion:

A solution is good if the total cost it incurs over all phases of its life cycle is small.

It is interesting to consider how the relative importance of the various components of this cost has evolved since the early days of computing. In the beginning, the cost of computer time relative to human time was extremely high. In addition, programs tended to be written to perform very specific, narrowly defined tasks. If the task changed somewhat, a new program was written. Program maintenance was probably not much of an issue, and thus there was little concern if a program was hard to read. It was common for a program to have only one user, its author. As a consequence, programmers tended not to worry about reducing the likelihood of their programs being misused; a program's interface generally was not considered to be important.

In this type of environment, one cost clearly overshadowed all others: computer resources. If two programs performed the same task, the one that was more resource efficient (required less time and memory) was better. How things have changed! Since the early days of computers, computing costs have dropped dramatically, thus making the value of the problem-solvers' and programmers' time a much more significant factor in the cost of a solution. Another consequence of the drop in computing costs is that computers are being used to perform tasks in a wide variety of areas, many of them nonscientific. People who interact with computers often have no technical expertise and no knowledge of the workings of programs. People want their software to be easy to use.

Today, programs are larger and more complex than ever before. They are often so large that many people are involved in their design, use, and maintenance. Good structure and documentation are thus of the utmost importance.

As programs are used to perform more highly critical tasks, the prices for malfunctions will soar. Techniques for formally verifying the correctness of a program will be used, and well-structured programs will be required. People will not and should not entrust their livelihoods (or their lives) to a program that only its authors can understand and maintain.

These developments have made obsolete the notion that the most efficient solution is always the best. If two programs perform the same task, it is no longer true that the faster one is necessarily better. Programmers who use every trick in the book to save a few microseconds of computing time at the expense of clarity are not in tune with the cost structure of today's world. Programs must be written with people as well as computers in mind.

At the same time, we do not wish to give the false impression that the efficiency of a solution is no longer important. To the contrary, there are many situations where a solution's efficiency is the prime determinant of whether or not it is even usable. Our point is that a solution's efficiency is only one of many factors that must be considered. If two solutions have approximately the same efficiency, then other factors should dominate the comparison. However, when the efficiencies of solutions differ *significantly*, this can be the overriding concern. The stages of the problem-solving process at which we should be most concerned about efficiency are those at which we develop the underlying methods of solution—the algorithms and the data structures. It is the choice of the algorithms and data structures, far more than the manner in which they are coded, that leads to significant differences in efficiency.

The problem-solving philosophy we advocate in this book reflects the view of the multidimensional cost of a solution. We believe that the philosophy is reasonable in today's world and that it will be reasonable in the years to come.

A SUMMARY OF PROGRAMMING ISSUES

Given that a good solution is one that, in the course of its life cycle, incurs a small cost, the next questions to ask are, what are the characteristics of good solutions and how can we construct good solutions? In this section we summarize the answers to these very difficult questions. More complete answers are to be found by observing the principles of problem solving that are practiced throughout the book. In Chapter 3, for instance, we present a large case study. A major goal of the case study is to demonstrate how a formidable problem can be solved by carefully following a few key programming principles. Throughout the remainder of the book, even as our emphasis shifts from programming to the earlier stages of the design of a solution, you should note how our programs attempt to adhere to these principles.

Our presentation makes the following assumptions about your knowledge of Modula-2.

1. **Elementary data constructs.** You should be expert in the use of the five basic data types: integer, cardinal, real, character, and Boolean. Fluency is also assumed in the syntax and semantics of **TYPE** definitions. These include enumerated, subrange, and ordinal types as well as single and multidimen-

8

CHAPTER 1
REVIEW OF
STRUCTURED
PROGRAM-
MING WITH
MODULA-2

sional arrays of each of these types. We recognize, however, that many of you will need to develop the ability to sense which types are appropriate in a particular situation. For example, when does the use of a subrange add to the readability of a program, and when does it detract from it? How does the use of a subrange interact with program debugging and the handling of "bad input"? When is an array the most efficient data structure (as opposed to, say, a linked list—a structure you will soon encounter)?

2. **Program execution constructs.** You are assumed to be familiar with the way Modula-2 evaluates expressions and executes statements. Also, you should have good judgment in choosing between control structures: **WHILE** versus **FOR** versus **REPEAT**; **IF-THEN** versus **IF-THEN-ELSE** versus **CASE**. There are, however, some subtleties in these matters that we shall explore. Similarly, you are assumed to be well versed in the mechanics of subprograms (such as parameter passing and scope rules for variables), but we shall continually attempt to demonstrate the role of modularity as perhaps the single most important factor contributing to good program development, readability, and modifiability. We assume no experience with recursive subprograms, which are the topic of Part II.

The programming issues discussed in this section should also be familiar to you. It is usually the case, however, that the beginning student does not truly appreciate their importance. After the first course in programming, many students still just want to "get the thing to run." We hope that the discussion to follow and the case study in Chapter 3 will help to emphasize just how important these issues really are.

One of the most widespread misconceptions held by beginning students is that a computer program is "read" only by a computer. As a consequence, the beginning student tends to consider only whether or not the *computer* will be able to "understand" the program—that is, will the program compile, execute, and produce the correct output? The truth of the matter is, of course, that programs often must be read and modified by other people. In a typical programming environment, a program is shared by many individuals. It may be written by one person, used in conjunction with other programs written by other people, and modified by a different person a year later. It is therefore essential that great care be taken to design the program so that it is easy to read and understand.

You should always keep in mind the following six issues of program structure and design:

KEY CONCEPTS

Six Key Programming Issues

1. Modularity through top-down design
2. Modifiability
3. User interface
4. Fail-safe programming
5. Style
6. Debugging

Modularity Through Top-Down Design

When you begin to write programs of moderate size and complexity, you will find that it is not possible for the human mind to cope with the entire program at once. This is true of the human minds writing the program and of the human minds reading the program. Modularity through top-down design is a solution to this and other problems associated with large programs. Furthermore, as we shall continually emphasize, modularity through top-down design should be practiced at all phases of the problem-solving process, beginning with the initial design of a solution. A modular implementation is generally derived naturally from a solution that was developed through top-down design.

What is meant by top-down design and modularity? The philosophy of top-down design is that a task should be addressed at successively lower levels of detail. This approach leads to the partitioning of a solution into many independent **modules.** At first, each module is little more than a statement of what needs to be solved and is devoid of detail. Each module is refined, in turn, by partitioning it into additional modules. The result is a hierarchy of modules; each module is refined by its children, which solve smaller problems and contain more detail than their parent. The refinement process continues until the modules at the bottom of the hierarchy are simple enough to be translated directly into procedures, functions, and isolated blocks of code that solve very small, independent problems. Such a program is said to be **modular.**

To illustrate the concept of a modular solution, consider a very simple example. We wish to find the median among a collection of test scores. We can break the solution into three independent tasks:

```
read the test scores into an array
sort the array
get the "middle" element of the array
```

The module for solving each of these tasks can be developed in virtual isolation from the other modules. If the three modules perform their tasks, then calling them in the above order will correctly find the median, regardless of *how* each task is performed.

The process of developing each module proceeds by dividing it into subtasks. For example, the task of reading the test scores into an array can be refined into the following two modules:

```
prompt the user for a score
place the score into the array
```

The solution process continues by developing, in a similar manner, modules for each of these two tasks. Figure 1–2 illustrates the hierarchy of modules for solving this problem.

What are the advantages of a modular program? As the size of a program grows, so too does the difficulty of many programming tasks. Modularity is a means of slowing down the growth rate of the level of difficulty. The primary difference between a small modular program and a large modular program is

10

CHAPTER 1
REVIEW OF
STRUCTURED
PROGRAM-
MING WITH
MODULA-2

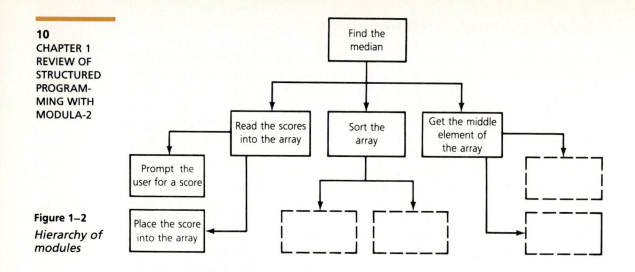

Figure 1–2

Hierarchy of modules

simply the number of modules each contains. Since the modules are independent, working on one large modular program is not very different from working on lots of small, independent programs. On the other hand, working on a large nonmodular program is more like working on lots of interrelated programs simultaneously.

More specifically, modularity has a favorable impact on the following aspects of programming:

1. **Constructing the program.** The complexity of a program (in the sense of keeping track of what's going on) can quickly get out of hand. By restricting attention to small, independent tasks, *writing a large program is reduced to writing lots of small programs*. This approach also permits team programming, where several programmers work independently on their own modules.

2. **Debugging the program.** Debugging a large program could be a monstrous task. Imagine typing in a 10,000-line program all at once, eventually getting it to compile (neither of these first two steps would be a whole lot of fun), and watching your program execute. After a few hundred lines of output, you get the message

```
subscript value of 34 is out of range at line 5679
```

You quickly turn to line 5679, and sure enough there's the assignment statement

```
A[place] := A[place+1];
```

How did that subscript get out of range? You should anticipate spending the next day or so tracing through the intricacies of your program before discovering what has gone wrong.

A great advantage of writing modular code is that debugging a large program is reduced to debugging lots of small programs. When coding begins on a group of modules, you can be (almost) certain that all other modules coded so far are correct. That is, before you consider the coding of a group of modules to be finished, you should extensively test the modules by executing them with a wide range of data values carefully chosen to induce all possible behaviors. If this testing is done thoroughly, you can have a high degree of certainty that any problem is a result of an error in the last group of modules added. *Modularity isolates errors.*

More theoretically, there are formal methods for proving properties of programs that can be used to establish the correctness of a program. Modular programs are amenable to the verification process.

3. **Reading the program.** A person reading a large program may have trouble seeing the forest for the trees. Just as top-down design helps the programmer cope with the complexities of solving a problem, so will the reader of a program usually find a top-down approach very helpful in understanding how a program works. A modular program is easy to follow because the reader can get a good idea of what's going on without reading any of the code. A well-written module can be understood fairly well from only its name, header comment, and the names of the subprograms that it calls. The reader of a program needs to study actual code only if one requires a detailed understanding of how the program operates. This is discussed further in the section on style later in this chapter.

4. **Modifying the program.** This is the topic of the next section, but as the modularity of a program has a direct bearing on its modifiability, we also briefly mention it here. A small change in the requirements of a program should require only a small change in the code. If this is not the case, it is likely that the program is poorly written and, in particular, that it is not modular. To accommodate a small change in the requirements, a modular program usually requires a change in only a few of its modules. *Modularity isolates modifications.* A simple example is presented in the discussion of modifiability in the next section.

5. **Eliminating redundant code.** Another advantage of modular design is that operations performed in many different parts of the program are identified and implemented as subprograms. This means that the code for the operation will appear only once, resulting in an increase in both readability and modifiability (see the example in the next section).

Modifiability

Imagine that the specification for a program changes after some period of time. It is not at all uncommon for a program to be required to do something in a different manner than was originally specified or even for it to do more than was originally specified (that is, the program must be *expanded*).

Subprograms. Suppose, for instance, that a library has a large program that catalogues its books. The program represents a book with a record defined as follows:

12

CHAPTER 1
REVIEW OF
STRUCTURED
PROGRAM-
MING WITH
MODULA-2

```
CONST

    maxsize = 20;

TYPE

    string = ARRAY [0..maxsize-1] OF CHAR;

    book = RECORD
                callno : REAL;
                author : string;
                title  : string;
            END;
```

At several points, the program needs to print out the information about a requested book. The program could include, at each of these points, the sequence of statements

```
WITH request DO

    WriteString('Call number : ');
    WriteReal(callno,6);
    WriteLn;

    WriteString('Author : ');
    WriteString(author);
    WriteLn;

    WriteString('Title  : ');
    WriteString(title);
    WriteLn;

END; (* WITH *)
```

Alternatively, this sequence could be replaced by a call to the procedure *PrintInfo*, defined by

```
PROCEDURE PrintInfo(request : book);
BEGIN

    WITH request DO

        WriteString('Call number : ');
        WriteReal(callno,6);
        WriteLn;

        WriteString('Author : ');
        WriteString(author);
        WriteLn;
```

```
          WriteString('Title  : ');
          WriteString(title);
          WriteLn;

    END;  (* WITH *)

END PrintInfo;
```

Not only does the use of the procedure have the obvious advantage of eliminating redundant code, it also makes the resulting program more modifiable. Suppose that, after the library's program has been running for a year, it is realized that the library's patrons often wish to know the length of a given book. This requires changing only the type definition of *book* to

```
book = RECORD
          callno : REAL;
          author : string;
          title  : string;
          length : CARDINAL;  (* new field *)
       END;
```

and redefining the procedure *PrintInfo* to

```
PROCEDURE PrintInfo(request : book);
BEGIN

   WITH request DO

      WriteString('Call number : ');
      WriteReal(callno,6);
      WriteLn;

      WriteString('Author : ');
      WriteString(author);
      WriteLn;

      WriteString('Title  : ');
      WriteString(title);
      WriteLn;

      (* print out the new field *)
      WriteString('Length : ');
      WriteCard(length,1);
      WriteLn;

   END;  (* WITH *)

END PrintInfo;
```

14

CHAPTER 1
REVIEW OF
STRUCTURED
PROGRAM-
MING WITH
MODULA-2

If the procedure had not been used, the modification would have required that the corresponding change be made at each point in the program where the information is printed. Simply finding each of these points could be difficult, and a few would probably be overlooked.

In this simple example, the advantages of using procedures should be clear. For a slightly more subtle illustration, recall our discussion of modularity in the design of a solution. There we used the example of a solution that, as one of its tasks, needs to sort some data. Developing the sorting algorithm as an independent module and eventually implementing it as a procedure would make the program more modifiable. If the sorting algorithm were implemented as a procedure, it could be changed (if, for instance, the sorting algorithm was found to be too slow) without even looking at the rest of the program. The old procedure could be "cut out" and the new one "pasted in." If the sorting instead had been integrated into the program, the required surgery might be quite intricate.

In general, it is a very bad sign if a program needs to be rewritten to accommodate small modifications; a well-structured program is usually easily modified to solve similar problems. Since each module solves only a small part of the overall problem, a change in problem specifications usually affects only a few of the modules.

User-Defined Constants.   The use of *user-defined constants* is another way to enhance the modifiability of a program. For example, Modula-2's restriction that an array must be of a predefined, fixed size causes a bit of a difficulty. Suppose that a program uses an array to process the SAT scores of the computer science majors at your university. At the time the program was written, there were 202 computer science majors, so the array was defined by

```
TYPE
    scores = ARRAY [1..202] OF INTEGER;
```

The program processes the array in several ways (reads in the scores from a file, prints out the scores, averages the scores) using a construct such as

```
FOR i := 1 TO 202 DO
   process the score
END
```

If the number of majors should change, not only does the type *scores* need to be redefined, but each loop that processes the array must also be changed to reflect the new array size. In addition, there may be other references in the code that depend on the size of the array. A 202 here, a 201 there—which to change?

On the other hand, if the program utilizes a constant

```
CONST
    size = 202;
```

the array is defined by

```
TYPE
    scores = ARRAY [1..size] OF INTEGER;
```

and the processing loops have the form

```
FOR i := 1 TO size DO
   process the score
END
```

References that depend on the size of the array are in terms of the constant $size$ ($size$, $size - 1$, and so on). To change the array size, only the definition of the constant $size$ needs to be changed.

User Interface

Another area where programs should be written with people in mind is the user interface. The data that a program takes as input and produces as output is often processed by humans. A few obvious points are:

1. In an interactive environment, the user should always be prompted for input in a manner that makes it quite clear what is expected. For example, the prompt "?" is not nearly as enlightening as the prompt "Enter account number for deposit." A program should never be written with the assumption that its users will know what responses are required.

2. The input should always be echoed. Whenever data is input to a program (either from a user at a terminal or from a file), the values read should always be output. This serves two purposes. First (primarily in the case of interactive input), it gives the user a check on the data entered—a guard against typos and errors in data transmission. Second, the output is more meaningful, as it will be self-explanatory when there is a record of what input generated the output.

3. The output should be well labeled and easy to read. An output of

```
Jones, Q.   223 2234.00 1088.19  X, Y  Smith, T.  111 110.23
L,  Harris, V.  44  44000.00 22222.22
```

is more prone to misinterpretation than is

```
CUSTOMER ACCOUNTS AS OF 1800 HOURS 3/20/87

status codes: X = new account
              Y = joint account
              L = inactive more than 30 days
```

NAME	ACC#	CHECKING	SAVINGS	STATUS
Jones, Q.	223	$ 2234.00	$ 1088.19	X, Y
Smith, T.	111	$ 110.23	-----	L
Harris. V.	44	$44000.00	$22222.22	-----

16

CHAPTER 1
REVIEW OF
STRUCTURED
PROGRAM-
MING WITH
MODULA-2

These are the obvious aspects of a user interface. Several more subtle points separate a program that is only usable from one that is user friendly. Students tend to ignore a good user interface, but the relatively little time that is invested here makes a big difference between a good program and one that merely solves the problem.

For example, consider a program that requires a user to input a line of data in some fixed format, with exactly one blank between the fields. It would be much more convenient for the user to use a free-form input that would alleviate the need for concern about the number of blanks between the fields. It takes so little time to add a loop that skips blanks, so why require the user to follow an exact format? Once this small amount of effort is made, it is a permanent part of a program (in fact, it is a permanent part of the programmer's library), and the user never has to think about it (as opposed to having every user worrying about it every time the program is used).

Fail-Safe Programming

A fail-safe program is one that will perform reasonably no matter how it is used. Unfortunately, this is, in general, an unattainable goal. A more realizable goal is to anticipate the ways that the program might be misused and to guard carefully against these abuses.

We shall consider in this discussion two types of errors. The first type is an *error in data entry*. For example, a program expects a nonnegative integer and −12 is input. When this type of problem is encountered, the program should not abort without displaying some sort of useful message. The message

```
subscript out of range ... program terminated
```

is not as useful as the message

```
-12 is not a valid number of children.

Please reenter the number of children.
```

The second type of error is an *error in the program logic*. Although discussion of this type of error belongs in the debugging section at the end of this chapter, detecting errors in program logic is also an issue of fail-safe programming. A program that has been running (apparently) correctly may at some point behave unexpectedly, even if the data it is given is valid. One possible source of this problem is that although we tried our best to test the program, the data that elicited the surprise behavior was not accounted for by the program logic. A second possible source of the problem is that the program was modified, causing an assumption made by some part of the program to become invalid. Whatever the cause, a program should have built-in safeguards to watch out for these kinds of problems. It should monitor itself and be able to indicate *there's something wrong with me and my results shouldn't be trusted.*

To illustrate these points we consider a small problem. We are computing statistics about the people in income brackets between $10,000 and $100,000. The brackets are rounded to the nearest thousand dollars: $10,000, $11,000, ..., $99,000, $100,000.

The raw data is a file of zero or more pairs of numbers of the form:

<G> <Q>

where Q is the quantity of people with an income that falls into the G-thousand-dollar group. The data was compiled by several people, so there may be several entries for the same value of G. As we input the data, we need to add up and record the number of people for each value of G. From the problem's context, G is an integer in the range 10 to 100 inclusive, and Q is a nonnegative integer.

Guarding Against Errors in Input. We begin by constructing type definitions and an input procedure for the problem. The first solution presented illustrates several common ways in which a program can fall short of the fail-safe ideal. We then consider several possible modifications to the solution and develop some "do's and don'ts" about fail-safe programming in general and for the use of subrange types in particular. We eventually arrive at an input procedure that is much closer to the fail-safe ideal than the original.

Many of the points that we wish to make specifically concern Modula-2, so we shall analyze actual code rather than pseudocode. A first stab at a solution might be

```
CONST

    low = 10;      (* low end of incomes of interest *)
    high = 100;    (* high end of incomes of interest *)

TYPE

    thousands = [low..high];
    IncomeTable = ARRAY thousands OF INTEGER;

(* ------------------------------------------------------------
    InputData:  Read and tally the income statistics in
    IncomeData.
    ----------------------------------------------------------- *)
PROCEDURE InputData (VAR IncomeData : IncomeTable);

VAR

    group, quantity : INTEGER;    (* values input *)
    i               : thousands;  (* loop control variable *)
```

18

CHAPTER 1
REVIEW OF
STRUCTURED
PROGRAM-
MING WITH
MODULA-2

```
BEGIN

    (* zero out the array *)
    FOR i := low TO high DO
        IncomeData[i] := 0;
    END;

    ReadInt(group);
    WHILE (Done) DO

        ReadInt(quantity);

        WriteString('Income group = ');
        WriteInt(group,1);
        WriteString(' and quantity = ');
        WriteInt(quantity,1);
        Write('.');
        WriteLn;

        IncomeData[group] := IncomeData[group] + quantity;
        ReadInt(group);

    END;

END InputData;
```

What are some of the problems with this procedure? If an input pair contains unexpected data, the program will not behave reasonably. Consider two specific possibilities:

1. The program accepts a negative value for *quantity*. Though this is clearly an invalid value for *quantity* (you can't have a negative number of people in an income group), it will be added to the appropriate array entry, so the statistics produced by the other parts of the program will not be valid.

2. The first integer of a pair is not in the range *[low..high]*. The reference *IncomeData[group]* will then cause execution to terminate with a message such as

```
    subscript value of 9 is out of range at line ...
```

Let us now attempt to address these problems in our solution. We might first consider using Modula-2's facility for subrange types. We shall discover, however, that *it is not appropriate to use subrange types as a mechanism for catching errors in input.* This kind of mistake is commonly made by Modula-2 programmers. For example, since the number of people in any income group should never be negative, we might change the global type definitions to

```
thousands = [low..high];   (* remains the same *)
IncomeTable = ARRAY thousands OF CARDINAL;
          (* an array of this type can contain
             only nonnegative integers *)
```

Let us consider whether this change really addresses the concern about a negative input value for *quantity*. First notice that it is possible for a negative value to be added to an entry of *IncomeData* without that entry becoming negative (for example, *quantity* has the value −4000 and is added to an entry of *IncomeData* having the value 10,000). Thus a negative value for *quantity* could be accepted and added to an entry of the array *IncomeData*, invalidating the results of the rest of the program.

Not only would the subrange fail to catch many input errors, but even when it did catch errors it might well generate a very confusing message. For example, suppose that *quantity* is given the value −4000 and is added to an entry of *IncomeData* having the value 2143. The program would terminate with a message such as

```
value of -1857 is not in range
```

This is not the most useful of messages! It does not really help us find that the problem was caused because a value of −4000 appeared as the second integer in some input pair. This ungraceful termination caused by an error in input is not consistent with our goal of having a fail-safe program.

We thus conclude that making *IncomeData* an array of *CARDINAL* does not solve the problem of bad input values for *quantity*. There is, however, another reason for wanting *IncomeData* to be an array of this type, as we shall see in the next section, on guarding against errors in program logic.

Our next attempt at solving the problem of bad input might be to make the variable *quantity* itself type *CARDINAL*. This, however, is *not* at all a good idea because it too conflicts with the goal of a fail-safe program. If the data contains a negative value for *quantity*, the program would abort with a message such as

```
value of -4000 is not in range
```

A better solution is to leave *quantity* as an integer but always to check its value before updating the array:

```
ReadInt (group)
ReadInt (quantity)

  . . .

IF (quantity >= 0) THEN
   add to InputData
```

20

CHAPTER 1
REVIEW OF
STRUCTURED
PROGRAM-
MING WITH
MODULA-2

```
ELSE
    handle the error
END
```

Now that we have developed a satisfactory solution to the problem of a bad input value for *quantity*, it is clear how we can solve the problem of a bad input value for *group*. After a value for *group* is input, we check to see if it is in the range *[low..high]*. If the value is in range, we may use *group* to subscript the array *IncomeData*. If it is not in range, however, we must handle the input error.

There are several reasonable courses of action for the program to take after it has encountered an error in the input. One possibility is for the program to print out an informative message such as

```
The value 9 supplied for income group
is not in the required range of [10..100]
```

and terminate. Another possibility is to print out a similar message, ignore the bad input pair, and continue. Which action is correct really depends on how the program uses the data once it is input.

We illustrate these points with a solution that attempts to make the input procedure as universally applicable and the program that uses it as modifiable as possible. In the solution below, when the input procedure encounters an error, it will print out a message, ignore the data pair, and continue. If one or more invalid data pairs are encountered, the procedure sets a flag, leaving it to the calling routine to determine the appropriate action (such as abort or continue). Thus the same input procedure can be used in many contexts, and the action taken upon encountering an error is easily modified. Error handling is further discussed in the section on style later in this chapter.

```
CONST

    low = 10;      (* low end of incomes of interest *)
    high = 100;    (* high end of incomes of interest *)

TYPE

    thousands = [low..high];
    IncomeTable = ARRAY thousands OF CARDINAL;

(* ------------------------------------------------------------
    InputData:  Read the income data and store it in the array
    IncomeData of type IncomeTable.

    If erroneous data is encountered (first integer not in the
    range [low..high] or second integer negative) the pair is
    ignored, a message printed, and input is continued.  If one
```

or more errors are encountered, DataError is set to true by
the procedure and the calling routine is expected to take
appropriate action.

```
    ASSUMPTION:   The input file contains pairs of integers.
    ----------------------------------------------------------- *)
PROCEDURE InputData(VAR IncomeData : IncomeTable;
                    VAR DataError : BOOLEAN );

VAR

    group, quantity : INTEGER;     (* values input *)
    i               : thousands;   (* loop control variable *)

BEGIN

    DataError := FALSE;   (* haven't found a data error yet *)

    (* zero out the array *)
    FOR i := low TO high DO
        IncomeData[i] := 0;
    END;

    ReadInt(group);
    WHILE (Done) DO

        ReadInt(quantity);

        WriteString('Income group = ');
        WriteInt(group,1);
        WriteString(' and quantity = ');
        WriteInt(quantity,1);
        Write('.');
        WriteLn;

        IF ((group >= low) AND (group <= high)
                        AND (quantity >= 0)) THEN

            (* the input is valid - convert it to
               CARDINAL and add it to the tally *)
            IncomeData[group] := IncomeData[group]
                                + VAL(CARDINAL,quantity);

        (* error in input data *)
        ELSE
            WriteString('There is an error in the input.');
            WriteLn;
```

22
CHAPTER 1
REVIEW OF
STRUCTURED
PROGRAM-
MING WITH
MODULA-2

```
        IF ((group < low) OR (group > high)) THEN
          WriteString
            ('Income group is not in range [10..100].');
          WriteLn;
        END;

        IF (quantity < 0) THEN
          WriteString('Quantity is negative.');
          WriteLn;
        END;

        WriteString('This input pair will be ignored.');
        WriteLn;

        DataError := TRUE;

      END;  (* error in the input data *)

      ReadInt(group);

    END;  (* while there is more input *)

END InputData;
```

This input procedure will behave gracefully in the face of most common input errors. However, it is not completely fail safe. What happens if the last input pair is incomplete (containing only a single integer)? What happens if an input pair contains a noninteger? The procedure would be more fail safe if it read its input character by character, converted to integer, and checked for end of file. In most contexts, this processing would be a bit extreme. However, if the people who enter the data frequently make these types of errors, the procedure could easily be modified (note that the input procedure is an isolated module) to operate in this manner. In any case, the procedure's header comment should include any assumptions made about the data and an indication of what might make the program abort abnormally.

Guarding Against Errors in Program Logic.   Let us now turn to the second type of error that a program should guard against, errors in its own logic. Recall that these are errors that we perhaps did not catch when the program was debugged or that were introduced through program modification.

Unfortunately, there is no reliable way for a program to let us know when there is something wrong with it. (Could a program be relied upon to tell us that there is something wrong with its mechanism for telling us that there is something wrong?!) We can, however, build into a program checks that certain conditions always hold. Such checks would be conditions that are always satisfied when a program is correctly implementing its algorithm. Such conditions, called **invariants,** are very important in algorithm design and are discussed in Chapter 5.

As a simple example, consider again the array *IncomeData* from the previous example. Recall that we chose to leave *IncomeData* as an array of *CARDINAL* values. Although this choice does not help to guard against input errors, to some extent it does guard against errors in the program's logic. If at any time the program attempts to store a negative value in the array (this would clearly be an error), the program terminates. The termination is not very graceful, but it is far better for a program to terminate ungracefully than it is for it to continue to produce output that—unbeknownst to the users—is incorrect.

Modula-2's type checking should really be our last line of defense against errors in a program's logic. If, for example, the program computes a value to add to an entry of the array *IncomeData*, it might be reasonable for the program to check first that this computed value is within some range of believability. If the value is outside such a range, the program can terminate with a message alerting the users to a potential problem and requesting that debuggers be called in.

Another general way in which a program should be made fail safe is for its subprograms to check the values of the parameters that are passed to them. For example, consider the function *SumBetween*, which returns the sum of all the integers between integers x and y.

```
(* ------------------------------------------------------------
   SumBetween:  Return the sum of all the integers between
   x and y.

   ASSUMPTION:  The value of x is less than or equal to the
   value of y.
   ------------------------------------------------------ *)
PROCEDURE SumBetween(x, y : INTEGER) : INTEGER;

VAR

   sum, i : INTEGER;

BEGIN

   sum := 0;
   FOR i := x TO y DO
      sum := sum + i;
   END;

   RETURN (sum);

END SumBetween;
```

The header comment of this function contains information about what assumptions are made, *as should always be the case*. The value returned by this function is valid only if the assumption is met—if x is greater than y, then the

24

CHAPTER 1
REVIEW OF
STRUCTURED
PROGRAM-
MING WITH
MODULA-2

function will return the incorrect value of zero (whereas the sum of the integers between 10 and 5, for example, is 45).

In the context of the program for which this function was written, it may be reasonable to make the assumption that x will be less than or equal to y. That is, if the rest of the program is working correctly, then *SumBetween* will be called only with such values. Actually, this last observation gives us a good reason for *SumBetween* to check the relationship between the values of x and y. If it turns out that x is greater than y, then the result of the check indicates that there may be something wrong elsewhere in the program.

Another reason the function *SumBetween* should check whether x is less than or equal to y is that the function should be correct outside the context of its program. That is, if we borrowed the function for use in another program, we would like the function to warn us if it is being used incorrectly. For instance, this new program could call *SumBetween* with x greater than y. We would like a stronger check than simply the statement of the assumptions in the header comment. Thus *a subprogram should state its assumptions and, when possible, check that its parameters conform to these assumptions.*

Style

We consider seven issues of personal style in programming:

> *Seven Issues of Style*
>
> 1. Extensive use of subprograms
> 2. Avoidance of global variables in subprograms
> 3. Use of variable parameters
> 4. Use of functions
> 5. Error handling
> 6. Readability
> 7. Documentation

We readily admit that much of the following discussion reflects the personal taste of the authors and that there certainly are other good programming styles.

Extensive Use of Subprograms.   We are firm believers in the use of subprograms. We believe it to be very difficult to overuse subprograms. If a set of statements performs an identifiable, recurrent task, it should be a subprogram.

There are two arguments against the extensive use of subprograms. First, subprograms may incur a large overhead. A program with all its code in line runs faster than one that calls subprograms to execute the same statements. However, it is false to infer from this fact that it is cheaper to use programs that do not contain subprograms. The use of subprograms is cost effective if human time is considered to be a significant component of the program's cost. In addition to the consideration of the cost of human time, current research trends support extensive use of subprograms. Compilers are being written that reduce the penalties for subprogram calls. Transformation tools are being developed that take a program with subprograms and transform it for execution into an equivalent program with the subprograms represented in line.

A second objection to the extensive use of subprograms is that they can be difficult to read. Subprograms may be overused if they cause a reader constantly to flip back and forth through the program. If the subprograms implement recurrent tasks, however, the distraction they may cause is made up for by the increase in the program's modifiability. In short, it is possible to overuse subprograms, but it is far easier to underuse them.

Avoidance of Global Variables in Subprograms. One of the main advantages of subprograms is that they can implement the concept of an isolated module. This isolation is sacrificed when a subprogram accesses a global variable, since the effects of a subprogram's action are no longer self-contained or limited to variable parameters. Hence, the isolation of errors and modifications is greatly compromised when global variables appear in subprograms.

Should global variables ever be accessed by a subprogram? Yes, but only if the sacrifice of isolation is justifiable. Several programs in this book access global variables in subprograms, and our justification is readability. If some piece of data is so inherently important to a program that almost every subprogram must access it, then the data is *global in nature*. Allowing the subprograms to globally access the variables containing this data best reflects the relationship between the data and the program as a whole. We shall point out several examples of this situation as they arise.

Use of Variable Parameters. A subprogram does interact, in a controlled fashion, with the rest of the program via the use of parameters. Value parameters (the default, when the keyword **VAR** is not specified) pass values *into* the subprogram, but any change to these parameters made by the subprogram is not reflected in the actual parameters back in the calling routine. The communication between the calling routine and the subprogram is one-way. Since the restriction to one-way communication supports the notion of an isolated module, *value parameters should be used when possible.*

When is it appropriate to use variable parameters? The obvious situation is when a procedure needs to return values to the calling routine. However, if the procedure needs to return only a single value, it may be more appropriate to use a function (discussed in the next section). If a function is not appropriate, then variable parameters are probably in order.

There is another situation in which variable parameters might be in order, but the issues are very subtle. Suppose that a procedure has a parameter X whose value it does not alter. The natural choice is for X to be a value parameter. However, the invocation of a procedure with value parameter X causes the value

26

CHAPTER 1
REVIEW OF
STRUCTURED
PROGRAM-
MING WITH
MODULA-2

of the actual parameter corresponding to X to be copied into the temporary storage that is local to the procedure. This incurs very little overhead if X is a simple variable, but the time required to copy a large array (and the temporary storage required for it) might be significant. However, if X were a variable parameter, then no copy of it would be made, which could lead to significant savings in both computing time and storage.

The problem with making X a variable parameter is that it conveys misinformation about the procedure's relation with the rest of the program. By convention, a variable parameter is one used to communicate a value from the procedure back to the calling routine. Variable parameters make the program more difficult to read and more prone to errors if modifications are required. (The argument is analogous to the one justifying the use of a constant in place of a variable whose value is initialized and never altered.) Thus, there is a trade-off between readability and modifiability on the one hand and efficiency on the other. In this book, unless there is a significant difference in efficiency, we generally take the side of readability and modifiability. In the later parts of the book we explore such trade-offs more fully.

Use of Functions.   Since Modula-2 could not possibly include all potentially useful statements in its set of primitive statements, it provides the programmer with procedures, a mechanism for writing new statements out of the built-in primitives. The procedure can be called from anywhere in a program that the user-defined statement is needed. Similarly, a function is a mechanism by which the programmer can write new *expressions*. Any time a value needs to be calculated, the function can be called as if it were part of the language.

A function is to be used as an expression, and, like any other expression, it should be used only to compute a simple value. This corresponds to the mathematical notion of a function. It therefore would be very strange if invoking a function did *anything* other than return the required value. Imagine evaluating the expression $(2 * x)$ and having the values of five other variables change! *A function should never do anything but return the required value.* That is, a function should never have a **side effect**.

What functions have potential for side effects?

1. **Functions with global variables.** If a function references a global variable, it has the potential for a side effect—*in general, functions should not assign values to global variables.*

2. **Functions with variable parameters.** A variable parameter indicates that the function will change its value (recall the previous discussion on the use of variable parameters). This is a side effect—*in general, functions should not have variable parameters.*

3. **Functions that perform I/O.** I/O (input and output) is a side effect—*in general, functions should not perform I/O.*

Error Handling.   A fail-safe program checks for errors in its input and logic and attempts to behave gracefully when they are encountered. Error handling often necessitates exceptional actions that would constitute bad style in normal program execution. For example, error handling may involve the use of functions with side effects.

A subprogram should check for certain types of errors (for example, bad input or invalid parameter values). What action should a subprogram take when it encounters an error? The procedure *InputData* in the income statistics program earlier in this chapter printed an error message and returned a Boolean flag to the calling routine to indicate that bad data was encountered. Thus the procedure *InputData* left it to the calling routine to decide on the appropriate action. In some situations, however, it is more appropriate for the subprogram itself to take the action—for example, when the required action does not depend on the point from which the subprogram is called.

If a *function* handles errors as described above (it prints an error message or returns a flag), it is violating our rule against functions with side effects. Despite this fact, the above actions seem reasonable for functions as well as procedures.

Depending on context, the appropriate action in the face of an error can range from ignoring erroneous data and continuing execution to terminating the program. One possible course of action would be to call a diagnostics procedure. This procedure would print out as much information as possible to help the user determine why the program had to abort—including, for example, current values of variables and an echo of erroneous data. After the procedure has reported all this information, it could terminate the program by executing a *HALT* statement.

Readability.   For a program to be easy to follow, it should have good structure and design, good choice of variable names, good indentation and use of blank lines, and good documentation. Clever programming tricks that save small amounts of computer time at the expense of large amounts of human time should be avoided. Examples of these points are found in the programs throughout the book.

A good indentation style can be used to enhance the readability of a program. The layout of a program should make it easy for a reader to identify the program's modules. Blank lines should be used to offset each subprogram, and within a subprogram (and the main program) individual blocks of code should themselves be offset and visibly indented. These blocks are generally (but are not limited to) the actions performed within a control structure, such as a **WHILE** loop or an **IF-THEN-ELSE** statement.

There are several good indentation styles to choose from. The most important general requirements of an indentation style are that:

1. Blocks should be indented sufficiently so that they stand out clearly.
2. Indentation should be used consistently—the same type of construct should always be indented in the same manner.

Documentation.   A program should be well documented so that it can easily be read, used, and modified by others. There are many acceptable styles for

28

CHAPTER 1
REVIEW OF
STRUCTURED
PROGRAM-
MING WITH
MODULA-2

documentation, and just what should be included often depends on the particular program. We believe the following are the essential features that should be included in a program's documentation.

Documentation

1. A header comment for the program. This should include:
   a. Statement of purpose
   b. Author and date
   c. Brief description of the global algorithms and data structures
   d. Description of how to use the program
   e. Description of the key variables
   f. Assumptions such as what type of data is expected and what could go wrong. *This is very important!*
2. A "miniheader" comment in each module, similar to the program's header, containing information pertinent to that module
3. Comments in the body of each module to explain important and confusing parts of the program

---

Beginning programmers tend to downplay the importance of documentation because the computer doesn't read comments. We hope that by now you can anticipate that our answer to this is that people do read programs. There is also a tendency to document programs as a last step. Documentation should be used as the program is being developed. The task of writing a large program might extend over a period of several weeks. You may find that the procedure that seemed so obvious when you wrote and debugged it last week will seem so confusing when you try to debug it again next week.

Debugging

No matter how much care we take in writing a program, there will inevitably be bugs that need to be tracked down. Fortunately, programs developed under the guidelines presented in the previous sections are generally amenable to debugging. Programs that are modular, clear, and well documented are certainly easier to debug than those that are not. Fail-safe techniques that guard against certain errors and report them when they are encountered are also a great aid in debugging.

Many students seem to be totally baffled by bugs in their programs and have no idea how to proceed. These students simply have not learned to track down a bug systematically. Without a systematic approach, finding a small bug in a large program can indeed be a difficult task.

The difficulty that many people have in debugging a program is perhaps in part due to a desire to cling to the belief that their program is really doing what it's supposed to do. For example, on receiving the error message

```
subscript value of 11 out of range on line 1098
```

a student might say, "That's impossible. The statement at line 1098 isn't even being executed. That's in the **ELSE** clause, and I'm positive that the **THEN** clause is being executed."

What we would say to such a student is, "Don't tell us. Show us." The proper approach is to add *write* statements that show which branch has been taken and to verify the value of the Boolean condition. If the condition is false when we expect it to be true (as the error message indicates), then the next step is to determine how it became false.

How, then, can we find the point in a program where something becomes other than what it should be? The trick to debugging is simply to use a program's output to tell us what's going on. This may sound pretty mundane, but the real trick is to use the program's output in an effective manner. After all, you don't simply put *write* statements at random points of the program and have them report random information. The *effective use of output* is one of the keys to debugging.

What do we mean by the effective use of output? The main idea is to systematically use the output to zero in on the points of the program that are causing the problem. A program's logic implies that certain conditions should be true at various points in the program (recall that these conditions are called invariants). A bug means that a condition which we think ought to be true isn't. To correct the bug, we must find the first point in the program at which one of these conditions differs from expectation. By inserting *write* statements at strategic locations of a program (for example, at entry and departure points of loops and subprograms), we can systematically zero in on the bug.

The placement and content of each *write* statement should be such that its output informs us of whether things start going wrong before or after a given point in the program. Thus, after we run the program with an initial set of diagnostic *write* statements, we should be able to find two points that a bug occurs between. For example, things are fine before procedure *P1* is called, but something is wrong by the time *P2* is called. This kind of information allows us to concentrate the next batch of diagnostics between these two points. We continue the process until eventually the search is limited to just a few statements. There's really no place in a program for a bug to hide.

The ability to place *write* statements in appropriate locations and to have them report appropriate information comes in part from thinking logically about the problem and in part from experience. Here are a few general guidelines.

What a Write Statement Should Report.   A *write* statement should be used to report both the values of key variables and the location in the program at which the variables have those values:

30
CHAPTER 1
REVIEW OF
STRUCTURED
PROGRAM-
MING WITH
MODULA-2

```
WriteString('At point A in procedure Compute: ');
WriteLn;
WriteString('   x = ');
WriteInt(x,1);
WriteString('   y = ');
WriteInt(y,1);
WriteString('   z = ');
WriteInt(z,1);
WriteLn;
```

Write Statements in Subprograms. Two key locations to place *write* statements are at the beginning and end of a subprogram:

```
PROCEDURE P(...);
BEGIN

    WriteString('Parameter values on entering procedure P:');
        .
        .
    WriteString('Parameter values on leaving procedure P:');

END P;
```

Write Statements in Loops. *Write* statements should be placed at the beginnings and ends of loops. The values of the control variables should be reported:

```
WriteString('Before entering FOR loop A, ');
WriteString('the variables have the following values:');
WriteString('   start = ');
WriteInt(start,1);
WriteString('   stop = ');
WriteInt(stop,1);
WriteLn;

(* this is FOR loop A *)
FOR i := start TO stop DO
   WriteString('At the beginning of iteration when i = ');
   WriteInt(i,1);
   WriteString(' the variables have the following values:');

   WriteString('At the end of iteration when i = ');
   WriteInt(i,1);
   WriteString(' the variables have the following values:');
     .
     .
END;

WriteString('After exiting FOR loop A, ');
WriteString(' the variables have the following values:');
```

```
WriteString('   start = ');
WriteInt(start,1);
WriteString('   stop = ');
WriteInt(stop,1);
WriteLn;
```

Write Statements in IF-THEN-ELSE Statements.   *Write* statements should be placed before the test in an **IF-THEN-ELSE** statement and should be used to report the branch taken as a result of the test. The values of the variables involved in the test should be reported.

```
WriteString('Before IF-THEN-ELSE A, variables have values: ');
            .
            .
(* IF-THEN-ELSE A *)
IF <cond> THEN
    WriteString('Condition is true, so follow THEN branch');
         .
         .
ELSE
    WriteString('Condition is false, so follow ELSE branch');
         .
         .
END;
```

Special Dump Routines.   Often the variables whose values we wish to print are arrays or other, more complex data structures. If so, we should write dump routines to accomplish the task. The single statement required to call each dump routine can easily be moved from one point in the program to another as we track down a bug. The routines need to display the data structures in a highly readable manner. The time spent on these routines often proves to be worthwhile as they are called repeatedly while we debug different parts of the program.

  We hope that this discussion has conveyed the importance of the *effective use of output in debugging*. Even the best programmers have to spend some time debugging. Thus, to be a truly good programmer, you must be a good debugger.

EXPLOITING FEATURES OF MODULA-2 IN SOFTWARE ENGINEERING: INDEPENDENT PROGRAM MODULES AND SEPARATE COMPILATION

In this chapter we have emphasized that the technique of modular solution development should be practiced at all levels of the problem-solving process. The judicious application of this technique reliably produces highly readable and highly modifiable program-level implementations of solutions. Since most modern programming languages (for example, Modula-2, Pascal, C, Ada, and PL/1) support the constructs necessary for producing modular and modifiable

32
CHAPTER 1
REVIEW OF
STRUCTURED
PROGRAM-
MING WITH
MODULA-2

programs, much of the discussion of the previous sections is essentially language independent. We now turn our attention to a Modula-2 specific issue: the language's support of independent program modules. Modula-2's support of independent program modules is a powerful tool that can enhance greatly the modularity and modifiability of a program. In this section we shall discuss the value of independent program modules, and demonstrate that this value is increased when program modules are compiled separately.

Figure 1–3

Structure of a Modula-2 program

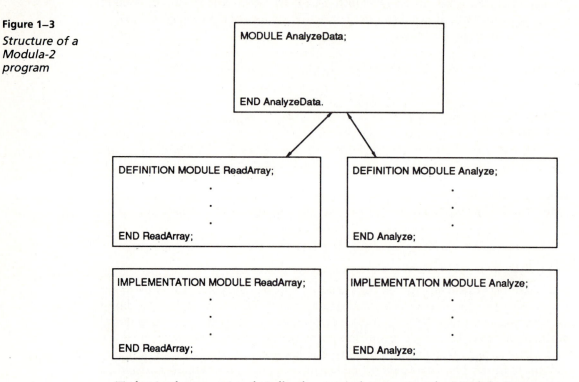

To begin, let us review briefly the general structure of a Modula-2 program. In Figure 1–3 we see a program that consists of a main program module, two implementation modules, and two definition modules. In abstract terms, we can think of each of the two implementation modules as implementing a set of supporting algorithms that the main algorithm needs to utilize. For example, one of the implementation modules might contain subprograms for reading values into an array, while the second implementation module might contain subprograms for analyzing the data stored in an array.

Associated with each implementation module is a definition module. A definition module is far more than a syntactic requirement of Modula-2. A definition module serves as a **contract** between the algorithms in the corresponding implementation module and the program modules that need to utilize these algorithms. That is, a definition module specifies how each subprogram is to be called (by specifying the number and types of parameters for each subprogram) and specifies via comments the effect of each subprogram call (every definition module should include, for each exported subprogram, comments that describe fully the action of the subprogram). This contract allows the algorithms themselves to remain as black boxes to the outside world—the contract specifies to the remainder of the program how to call the subprograms and what the subprograms will do, but keeps hidden how the subprograms are implemented. Further, each module of a program is forced to specify explicitly (by means of an **IMPORT** statement) which foreign subroutines, variables, and types it utilizes. These syntactical requirements of Modula-2 clearly have beneficial effects on program documentation.

The reader at this point might wonder how much modularity really is gained when algorithms are implemented as separate program modules rather than as well-documented subprograms within a single program module. While it is true that subprograms by themselves have many of the virtues of the black box concept, we observe that the use of separate program modules yields an additional benefit: each program module can reside in its own source file. Placing each program module in its own source file is a practice that creates impenetrable black boxes. When all subprograms and the main program reside together in the same source file, a programmer must resist the temptation of looking at the implementation details of the subprograms that she should be treating as black boxes. On the other hand, when program modules reside in separate source files, a programmer actually can be prevented from seeing the implementation details of the black boxes (for example, by denying her read access to the files containing certain implementation modules). The physical separation of program modules into individual source files reinforces the **walls** between the logical units of a program.

The physical separation of program modules has another key advantage, one that is especially valuable in the context of large software development projects. When program modules reside in separate files, the modules can be compiled independently. The separate compilation of independent program units is an extremely important software engineering technique that, we should point out, is not supported by Standard Pascal. Separate compilation greatly enhances many of the advantages of modular program development discussed earlier, including:

Independent Development of Modules.   Consider a large software development project involving several people. In such an environment it is common for each person to develop and implement algorithms addressing one aspect of the overall problem. For example, one of the programmers might be responsible for a sorting algorithm. Once the programming team constructs a definition module to act as the sorting algorithm's contract, the programmer responsible for the sorting algorithm can go off and work on the algorithm in virtual isolation from the rest of the team. The programmer can develop, debug, and test the sorting module without interacting with the modules being developed by the other team members. Such a practice fosters a high degree of independence between program modules. When the programmer finishes implementing the sorting algorithm, the final product is a compiled module. Assuming that the other programmers in the team also produce compiled modules, the final step in the program's development is simply to link together the modules to form an executable program. Not only does separate compilation make it convenient to develop a pro-

34

CHAPTER 1
REVIEW OF
STRUCTURED
PROGRAM-
MING WITH
MODULA-2

gram in pieces and foster module independence, it also has the potential of saving a great amount of computer resources. With separate compilation the entire program never needs to be compiled at once; without separate compilation the entire program would have to be compiled in order to test every small change that was made in the course of the program's development.

Program Modifiability.   We previously have spoken of how modularity leads to increased program modifiability. Placing a program's modules in separate source files enhances still further a program's modifiability. Continuing the example of the software development project, suppose that after the program is operational it is decided that the sorting algorithm must be improved (for example, because the original algorithm is too slow). Because the implementation module for the sorting algorithm is in its own source file, it is extremely easy to replace the module with one implementing a faster sorting algorithm. The original sorting algorithm's definition module serves as the contract for the new sorting algorithm, precisely specifying the required behavior of the new algorithm. This allows the new sorting algorithm to be developed and tested in isolation from the rest of the program and implies that no other source files (including the file containing the sorting algorithm's definition module) need be touched. Not only does this prevent errors from being introduced via careless changes to other modules of the program, it also implies that the other modules do not need to be recompiled. We need only compile the new sorting algorithm and link the compiled module to the rest of the program. Separate compilation once again has the potential of saving a great amount of computer resources.

The Use of Library Modules.   Over a period of time, a software development team will accumulate a library of useful program modules. For example, once the program described above is operational, the library will contain a completely tested sorting module. If at some time in the future the programming team needs to develop another program that requires a sorting algorithm, no new code needs to be written. The developers of the new program need only consult the contract (that is, the definition module) for the existing sorting algorithm and place the appropriate subroutine calls in the new program. Once this is done, the new program is ready for linkage with the sorting module. Observe that it is quite possible that many programs will be linked with the same sorting module. This sharing of the sorting module is far preferable to duplicating the source code of the sorting procedure in every program that utilizes it. The preference for a single, shared module is based on ease of program maintenance. To illustrate this point, suppose we discover that the sorting algorithm can be improved by means of a small modification. If the source code of the sorting procedure were duplicated in each program that utilized it, we diligently would have to make the same change in every program that contained the sorting procedure. With a shared module, however, we need make the change only once, and simply link each program to the new library module.

We conclude this section by previewing the connection between independent program modules and **data abstraction**. We already have seen that independent program modules greatly enhance the modularity of a program with respect to its algorithms. This same facility also can enhance the modularity of a program with respect to its data structures. As we shall see in Part III, the walls between a program's modules can be used to protect, or hide, the data structures defined within each logical program unit. Data hiding is achieved through a technique know as data abstraction, a conceptual problem-solving tool very much akin to modular algorithm development. Like modular algorithm development, data abstraction is greatly enhanced at the implementation level by Modula-2's support of the physical separation of program modules.

Throughout the book we shall use the terms *contract* and *wall* to describe the separation of a program's algorithms into independent modules. Beginning in Chapter 6, a program's data structures, as well as its algorithms, will be defined by contracts and hidden by walls.

SUMMARY

1. When evaluating the quality of a solution, we must consider a diverse set of factors. These include the solution's correctness, its efficiency, the time that went into its development, its ease of use, and the cost of modifying and expanding it.

2. When designing a solution, we should proceed in a top-down fashion. The tasks should be broken into independent modules, which are gradually refined. Some of these modules perform algorithmic-type tasks (for example, sort an array), and others perform data-management-type tasks (such as retrieve a data item). In either case, each module should be a "black box" from the perspective of the rest of the program.

3. Great care should be taken to ensure that the final solution is as easy to modify as possible. A modular program generally can be modified because changes in the problem's requirements frequently affect only a handful of the modules. The use of user-defined constants (as in the declarations of array bounds) is another factor that can greatly enhance a program's modifiability.

4. A program should be as fail safe as possible. Two ways that a program can be made fail safe are for it to guard against errors in input and errors in its own logic. Modula-2's facility for subrange types should be a last line of defense against errors in program logic and in general should not be used to guard against errors in input.

5. A subprogram should correspond to the notion of an isolated module as much as possible. To this end, global variables should not be overused, and functions with side effects should be avoided whenever possible.

6. A subprogram should always include a header comment that tells what it does and what assumptions it makes (such as about the values of its parameters).

36
CHAPTER 1
REVIEW OF
STRUCTURED
PROGRAM-
MING WITH
MODULA-2

COMMON PITFALLS / DEBUGGING

1. The effective use of output is one of the keys to debugging. *Write* statements should be used to report the values of key variables at key locations. These locations include the beginnings and ends of procedures and loops and the branches of conditional statements.

2. To facilitate the use of output in debugging, dump routines that display the contents of the data structures should be written. Calls to such routines can easily be moved as a bug is tracked down.

3. Programs should be written to be on guard against errors. A fail-safe program checks that an input value is within some acceptable range and reports if it isn't. An error in input should not cause a program to terminate before it clearly reports what the error was. A fail-safe program also attempts to detect errors in its own logic. For example, in many situations subprograms should check that the parameters have valid values (for example, the second parameter is larger than the first).

4. Subrange types should be used only as a last line of defense against errors. A variable into which data is read should not be of a subrange type, since an out-of-range value causes an ungraceful termination. A proper use of subrange types is to help enforce a condition in the program's logic.

EXERCISES

1. Consider the following program, which interactively reads and writes the identification number, name, age, and salary (in thousands of dollars) of a group of employees. How can we improve the program? Some of the issues are obvious. Others are more subtle. Try to keep in mind all the topics discussed in this chapter.

```
MODULE stats;

VAR

    x1, x2, x3, i : INTEGER;
    name : ARRAY [0..7] OF CHAR;
```

```
BEGIN

    ReadInt(x1);
    WHILE (Done) DO
        IReadString(name);
        ReadInt(x2);
        ReadInt(x3);
        WriteInt(x1,1);
        WriteString(name);
        WriteInt(x2,1);
        WriteInt(x3,1);
        WriteLn;
        ReadInt(x1);
    END;

END stats.
```

2. We have stressed the importance of adding fail-safe checks to a program wherever possible. What can go wrong with the following function? How can we protect ourselves?

```
PROCEDURE tan(x : REAL) : REAL;
BEGIN

    RETURN ( sin(x)/cos(x) );

END tan;
```

3. Write a program that will read employee information into an array of records, sort the array by employee identification number, write out the sorted array, and compute various statistics on the data, such as the average age of an employee. What subprograms did you identify during the design of your solution?

4. The following program is supposed to compute the floor of the square root of its input value *x* (the largest integer less than or equal to the square root of *x*).

```
(* compute floor(sqrt(x)) for x >= 0 *)
MODULE sqrt;

VAR

    x, ans, temp1, temp2 : INTEGER;
```

38
CHAPTER 1
REVIEW OF
STRUCTURED
PROGRAM-
MING WITH
MODULA-2

```
BEGIN

    (* initialize *)
    ReadInt(x);
    ans := 0;
    temp1 := 1;
    temp2 := 1;

    WHILE (temp1 < x) DO
        INC(ans);
        INC(temp2, 2)
        temp1 := temp1 + temp2;
    END;

    WriteString('The floor of the square root of ');
    WriteInt(x,1);
    WriteString(' is ');
    WriteInt(ans,1);
    WriteLn;

END sqrt.
```

There is a bug in this program.

a. What output will be produced for $x = 64$?

b. Debug the program on the computer. How did you choose the placement of extra *write* statements?

c. How can we make the program more user friendly and fail safe?

5. Sometimes, due to some severe error, we must abort a program from a location deep inside nested procedure calls, **WHILE** loops, and **IF-THEN-ELSE** statements. Write a diagnostics procedure that can be called from anywhere in a program. This procedure should take an error code as an argument (some mnemonic enumerated type), print an appropriate error message, and terminate the program.

PROJECTS

6. Write a program that sorts and evaluates bridge hands.

INPUT

The input is a stream of pairs of characters representing playing cards. For example,

        2C QD TC AD 6C 3D TD 3H 5H 7H AS JH KH

represents the 2 of clubs, queen of diamonds, 10 of clubs, ace of diamonds, and so on. Each pair consists of a rank followed by a suit, where rank is A,

2, . . . , 9, T, J, Q, or K and suit is C, D, H, or S. For this problem you are to form hands of 13 of these cards. You can assume that there will be no errors in the input and that there will be exactly 13 cards represented on each input line. Input is terminated by end of file.

As an optional exercise, see how much more flexible and fail safe you can make your program. That is, try to remove as many of the above assumptions as you can.

Each hand of 13 cards is to be printed out in a nice form arranged by suits and rank within suit (aces are high). The hand is then evaluated using the following standard bridge values.

> Aces count 4
>
> Kings count 3
>
> Queens count 2
>
> Jacks count 1
>
> Voids (no cards in a suit) count 3
>
> Singletons (one card in a suit) count 2
>
> Doubletons (two cards in a suit) count 1
>
> Long suits with more than 5 cards in the suit count 1 for each card
>   over 5 in number

For example, the above hand should produce the output

```
CLUBS       10   6   2
DIAMONDS     A   Q  10   3
HEARTS       K   J   7   5   3
SPADES       A
Points = 16
```

because there are 2 aces, 1 king, 1 queen, 1 jack, 1 singleton, no doubletons, and no long suits. (The singleton ace of spades counts as both an ace and a singleton.)

7. Write a program that will act as an interactive calculator capable of handling very large nonnegative integers. This calculator need perform only the operations of addition and multiplication.

In this program each input line is of the form:

```
<num1> <op> <num2>
```

and should produce output

```
        num1
op      num2
----------
        num3
```

40

CHAPTER 1
REVIEW OF
STRUCTURED
PROGRAM-
MING WITH
MODULA-2

where *num1* and *num2* are (possibly very large) nonnegative integers, *op* is the single character '+' or '*', and *num3* is the integer obtained by performing the desired calculation.

Design your program carefully! You will need the following.

a. A data structure for representing large numbers; for example,

```
ARRAY [1..maxsize] OF [0..9]
```

b. A procedure for reading in numbers: Skip leading 0's. Don't forget that 0 is a valid number.

c. A procedure for writing numbers: Do not print leading 0's, but if the number consists of all 0's, a single 0 should be printed.

d. A procedure for adding two numbers.

e. A procedure for multiplying two numbers.

In addition, you should:

f. Check for overflow (numbers with more than *maxsize* digits) when reading, adding, and multiplying numbers.

g. Have a good user interface.

Optional: Allow signed integers (negative as well as positive integers) and write a procedure for subtraction.

CHAPTER 2

REVIEW OF ADVANCED MODULA-2

PREVIEW   This chapter presents the Modula-2 data type pointer. We show the correct use of the type and discuss ways it is commonly misused. We give examples showing how the use of pointers can greatly improve a solution. The case study of Chapter 3 further illustrates the use of pointer variables in the solution to a large, real-world problem.

Every high-level programming language provides a collection of built-in data types. These are referred to as the language's **primitive data types**. Integers, reals, characters, and arrays are primitive data types supported by almost all high-level languages. Modula-2 is unusually rich in the data types it supports. In addition to the basic types, Modula-2 supports subrange types, enumerated types, and records. In this chapter we review an advanced data type built into Modula-2: pointers.

Not only does Modula-2 provide a rich set of built-in data types, it also provides a means for the programmer to define his or her own data structures. In Part III we discuss data structures not directly supported by Modula-2 and how they can be constructed out of Modula-2's primitives.

POINTERS

One of the most frequently performed computing tasks is the maintenance, in some specified order (such as alphabetical order), of a collection of data. Many examples immediately come to mind: students ordered by their names, baseball players ordered by their batting averages, and corporations ordered by their assets.

The problem of *maintaining* ordered data requires more than simply sorting the data. Often some new data item needs to be inserted into its proper, ordered place. Similarly, we often must delete some data item. For example, suppose your university maintains an alphabetically ordered list of the students who are currently enrolled. Insertion and deletion operations must be performed because students are constantly enrolling in and leaving school.

Suppose that the list of students is maintained in the array *Students*, as shown in Figure 2–1(a).

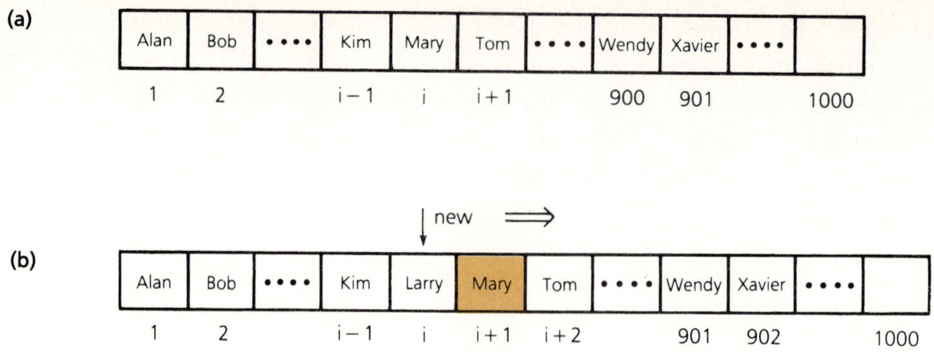

(a)

(b)

Figure 2–1

*(a) Array of
names;
(b) shifting
for insertion*

In Modula-2, we could implement the array of students with the following definition.

```
CONST

    maxstudents = 1000;
    maxsize     =   10;

TYPE

    string   = ARRAY [0..maxsize-1] OF CHAR;
    namelist = RECORD

                    (* number of names present *)
                 lastpos : [0..maxstudents];

                 names   : ARRAY [1..maxstudents] of string;
             END;

VAR

    Students : namelist;
```

To insert a new student name, we must find the position in the array where the name belongs, shift to the right the names from this position on, and insert the new name in the newly created opening. This is depicted in Figure 2–1(b). The following Modula-2 procedures perform the insertion. Note that procedure *Find* calls procedure *CompareStr*, which is imported from library module *Strings*. See the Appendix for the definition of *CompareStr*.

```
(* --------------------------------------------------------------
   Find:  Return the position of the first element of
   list.names (in the range [1..list.lastpos]) which is greater
   than or equal to target.  If there is no such element,
   value = list.lastpos+1 is returned.
   -------------------------------------------------------------- *)
```

```
PROCEDURE Find(target : string; list: namelist) : INTEGER;

VAR

    place : INTEGER;

BEGIN

    place := 1;

    (* find the proper position in the array - note that the
       second operand of the AND operator is not evaluated
       if place > list.lastpos, thereby avoiding a subscript
       out of bounds error *)
    WHILE ( (place <= list.lastpos)
            AND (CompareStr(target,list.names[place]) > 0) ) DO

        INC(place);

    END;

    RETURN (place);

END Find;

(* ------------------------------------------------------------
   Insert:  Insert newname into its proper place in
   list.names.  If the array is full, a message to this
   effect is printed.  If one or more elements identical to
   newname are already on the list, newname will be inserted
   in front of these elements.
   ------------------------------------------------------------ *)
PROCEDURE Insert(newname : string; VAR list : namelist);

VAR

    i, place : [1..maxstudents];

BEGIN

    IF (list.lastpos = maxstudents) THEN
        WriteString('Array is full--cannot insert new name.')
        WriteLn;

    ELSE

        place := Find(newname, list);
```

```
(* shift and insert *)
FOR i := list.lastpos TO place BY -1 DO
    list.names[i+1] := list.names[i];
END;

list.names[place] := newname;

INC(list.lastpos);

    END;

END Insert;
```

Let us now consider how to delete a student's name from the list. We could blank it out after finding the name in the list. However, this strategy can lead to gaps in the array, as illustrated in Figure 2–2(a).

Figure 2–2

*(a) Delete
causing a gap;
(b) fill gap by
shifting*

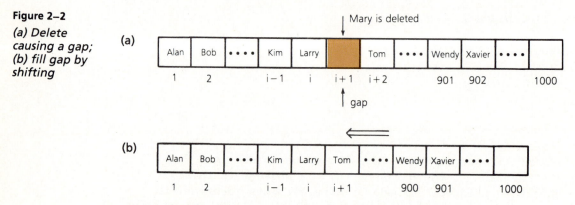

An array that is full of gaps has two significant problems:

1. Variable *list.lastpos* could have the value *maxstudents* even though there are empty cells in the array. As a consequence, it could become impossible to insert new names into the array even when there are fewer than *maxstudents* names present.

2. Because the names are spread out, the *Find* procedure might have to look at every cell of the array even when only a handful of names are present.

Thus, what we really need to do is shift the elements of the array to fill the gap left by the departed name, as shown in Figure 2–2(b).

The following Modula-2 procedure performs the deletion by shifting. The type definitions and function *Find* are the same as above.

```
PROCEDURE Delete(name : string; VAR list : namelist);

VAR

    i     : [1..maxstudents];
    place : [1..maxstudents+1];
```

```
    place := Find(name, list);

    (*  delete the item from the array if it has been found --
        note that the second operand of the OR operator is not
        evaluated if place > list.lastpos, thereby avoiding a
        subscript out of bounds error *)

    IF ( (place > list.lastpos) OR
         (CompareStr(name,list.names[place]) # 0) ) THEN
       WriteString(name);
       WriteString(' is not in the array.');
       WriteLn;
    ELSE
       (* name is present - shift to delete *)
       FOR i:= place TO (list.lastpos-1) DO
          list.names[i] := list.names[i+1];
       END;
       DEC(list.lastpos);
    END;

END Delete;
```

Using an array to maintain the sorted list of student names thus requires shifting of data for both insertions and deletions. Wouldn't it be nice if there were methods, which did *not* necessitate the shifting of data, for inserting a new data item between a specified pair of data items and for removing an item from a specified position? How can this be done? To get a conceptual notion of such a scheme, consider Figure 2–3.

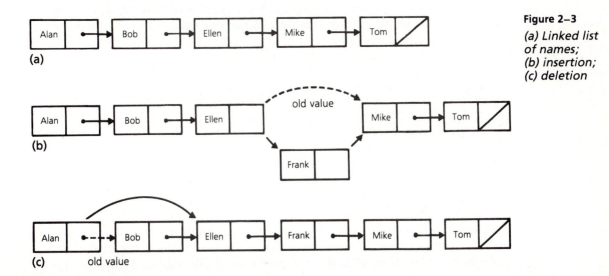

Figure 2–3

(a) Linked list of names;
(b) insertion;
(c) deletion

In these diagrams, each member of the list *points to* the next member. If a new member needs to be inserted, we simply find its place in the list and set two pointers. Similarly, if an item is to be deleted, we find the item and set a pointer so that the item is bypassed.

These diagrams should help free you from the notion that the only way to maintain a given order on the data is to store the data in that order. Although the most intuitive means of imposing an order on the data is to order it physically, it is possible to use other means. In a physical ordering, the data item that comes after some item x is the data item that happens to be "to the right" of x. In a **linked list,** however, x actually *points to* the next data item—and thus x's successor can be anywhere physically. This flexibility not only allows us to insert and delete data items without shifting data, it also allows us to increase the size of a linked list easily. That is, *while an array can hold only a fixed number of data items, a linked list is able to grow as needed.* In many applications, this flexibility gives a linked list a significant advantage.

This may all be well and good theoretically, but how can we get one data item to point to another? For this we introduce Modula-2's type **pointer.** Consider the following:

```
TYPE
    ptr = POINTER TO INTEGER;

VAR
    p : ptr;
```

The variable *p* is said to be an integer pointer because it can *reference a memory cell* that contains an integer. (Pointers to any other type, including user-defined types, are declared analogously.) What does it mean to *reference a memory cell*? When a variable such as

```
x : INTEGER;
```

is declared, a memory cell is allocated that is capable of holding an integer. The identifier *x* is used to refer to this cell. To put the value 5 in the cell, we say

```
x := 5;
```

To print out the value that is in the cell, we say

```
WriteString('The value of x is ');
WriteInt(x,1);
```

We use the declaration

```
p : ptr;
```

to allocate a memory cell capable of holding a reference to another memory cell that holds an integer. This reference that *p* can hold is the computer's representation of the location, or **address** in memory, of the cell (see Figure 2–4).

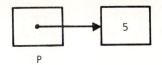

Figure 2–4

Pointer to an integer

P

The notion of one memory cell referencing another memory cell is a bit tricky. In the above example it is important to keep in mind that the content of *p* is not an integer in the usual sense. The content of *p* is of interest to us only because it tells us where in memory to look for the integer value. That is, we can get to the integer value *indirectly* by following the reference contained in *p*.

look in location 342 for what you want		....	26	10	5	9	....

P

340 341 342 343

"memory locations"

Figure 2–5

Indirect reference

Let us now consider how we can actually use *p* to get to the integer to which it points. In Modula-2 we are not allowed to look at the address contained in *p*; for example, we cannot say

```
WriteInt (p, 1) ;
```

How can we get to the integer in the memory cell that *p* is referencing? Suppose that *p* points to a memory cell that contains the value 5 (more precisely, *p* contains the address of a memory cell that contains the value 5). In Modula-2, *p*^ is an expression that has *the value in the memory cell to which p points.* Thus, in the situation depicted above, the expression *p*^ has the value 5.

A similar convention is used to store a value in the memory cell that *p* points to. For example, we can put the value 7 into the memory cell that *p* points to with the assignment statement

```
p^ := 7;
```

After this assignment, the expression *p*^ has the value 7, since 7 is now the value in the memory cell that *p* points to. Notice that the assignment statement

```
p := 7;
```

is illegal, since it is a type clash: *p* can contain a *reference* to (address of) a memory cell that contains an integer, while 7 *is* an integer.

If we also had the declaration

```
q : ptr;
```

we could assign to *q* the value in *p* with the assignment

```
q := p;
```

Pointer *q* now points to the same memory cell that *p* points to.

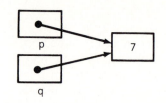

Figure 2–6

*Two pointers
referencing
the same
memory cell*

Now for the big question: How do we get a pointer variable to point to a memory cell in the first place? To begin, there is an important restriction on what a pointer variable can point to. If we had the declarations

```
VAR
    p :  POINTER TO INTEGER;
    x :  INTEGER;
```

we could *not* get *p* to point to the memory cell associated with *x*. (Consider what would happen if we tried *p : = x*.) All the variables declared via standard variable declarations are allocated **static** memory—static because the memory is allocated just before the program (or subprogram) is executed. The execution does not affect the memory requirements of such variables.

Pointer variables do not point to these statically allocated memory cells but rather to memory cells allocated **dynamically**. Until a memory cell is created for *p* to reference, it does not point to anything (its value is undefined), and it is in effect useless. Modula-2 allocates dynamic memory by means of the procedure *NEW*, which is defined when procedure *ALLOCATE* is imported from the library module *Storage*. In its simple form, *NEW* takes a pointer variable for its argument, for example,

```
NEW (p) ;
```

The result of this procedure call is that a new memory cell is created, and *p* is returned pointing to it. Since *p* is an integer pointer, only integers may be placed in this new cell. If *p* had been declared as

```
p :  POINTER TO CHAR;  { pointer to a character }
```

then *NEW (p)* would create a memory cell in which a character could be placed.

Observe that this newly created memory cell has no name in the usual sense. The only way to get at its contents or to put contents in it is indirectly via the pointer *p*. The following simple program should serve to illustrate these concepts.

```
MODULE PointerDemo;

(* memory management procedure NEW *)
FROM Storage IMPORT
```

```
    ALLOCATE;

(* standard I/O *)
FROM InOut IMPORT

    WriteInt, WriteLn;

TYPE

    ptr = POINTER TO INTEGER;

VAR

    p, q : ptr;

BEGIN
```

```
    NEW(p);              (* Allocate a cell of type integer.    *)
```

```
    p^ := 1;             (* Assign a value to the new cell.     *)
```

```
    NEW(q);              (* Allocate a cell of type integer.    *)
```

```
    q^ := 2;             (* Assign a value to the new cell.     *)

    WriteInt(p^,2);
    WriteInt(q^,2);
    WriteLn;             (* Output line contains: 1   2
                            These are the values of the integers
                            in the cells to which p and q point.  *)
```

```
    p^ := q^ + 3;        (* The assignment is performed as follows:
                            The right hand side of the assignment
                            operator is evaluated.  The value in
                            the cell to which q points, 2 in this
                            case, and 3 are added together.  The
                            result is assigned to the cell to
                            which p points.                      *)
```

```
                      WriteInt (p^, 2) ;
                      WriteInt (q^, 2) ;
                      WriteLn;              (* Output line contains:  5  2       *)

                      p := q;               (* p now points to the same cell as q.
                                               The cell p formerly pointed to is
                                               lost--it cannot be referenced.    *)

                      WriteInt (p^, 2) ;
                      WriteInt (q^, 2) ;
                      WriteLn;              (* Output line contains: 2  2        *)

                      p^ := 7;              (* The cell to which p points (which is
                                               also the cell to which q points) now
                                               contains the value 7.             *)

                      WriteInt (p^, 2) ;
                      WriteInt (q^, 2) ;
                      WriteLn;              (* Output line contains: 7  7         *)

                      NEW (p) ;             (* This changes what p points to but not
                                               what q points to.                 *)

                      q := p;               (* q now also points to the newly created
                                               memory cell.  The cell to which q
                                               previously pointed to is now lost--it
                                               cannot be referenced.             *)

                   END PointerDemo.
```

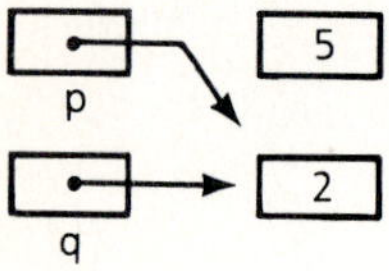

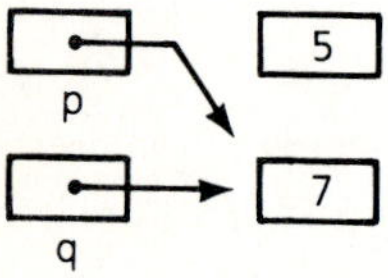

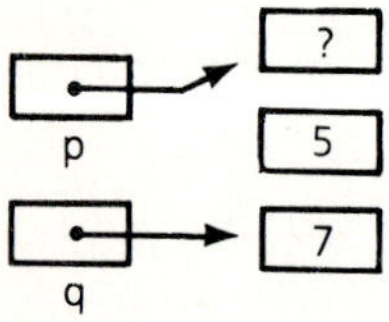

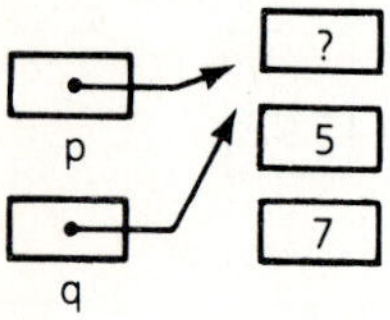

Figure 2–7   *Programming with pointer variables*

The last assignment statement illustrates the problem of what to do with a memory cell that is no longer needed. Simply removing all references to the cell is wasteful as it is no longer accessible, though it remains allocated to the program. The procedure *DISPOSE*, which is defined when the procedure *DEALLO-CATE* is imported from the library module *Storage*, is used to solve this problem. The call

DISPOSE (p) ;

deallocates the node pointed to by *p*, making the node available for future allocation. Note that in the above example, the call *DISPOSE (q)* would have to be made *before* the final assignment to *q*.

Although we have now illustrated most of the mechanics of pointers, it is not yet completely clear how they can be used to implement the concept of a linked list (as pictured in Figure 2–3). After all, each item on a linked list contains both a data value (for example, an integer) and a pointer to the next item. We begin to answer the questions of how we can set up such a list, how we can print out the information on a linked list, and how we can insert into and delete from a list. We postpone a full discussion until Chapter 3.

Since each item on the list must contain two pieces of information (the data value and a reference to the next item on the list), it is natural to conclude that the items on the list should be records. One field of the record is the data (an integer in our example), and the other is a pointer. But what type of pointer should it be—to what will it point? You might guess that the pointer should point to an integer, but actually it must point to a record, since the items of the list are indeed records and not integers. Thus a record of type *item* will have as one of its fields a pointer to type *item*. This is perhaps a difficult notion to comprehend: Each record of type *item* contains a pointer to another record of type *item*.

The type definitions are thus

```
TYPE

    ptr = POINTER TO item;   (* item is not yet defined *)
    item = RECORD
               data : INTEGER;
               next : ptr;
           END;
```

data   next

Figure 2–8
List node

It is common to call a record of this form a **node** (see Figure 2–8).

Here *ptr* is defined to be *POINTER TO item* before *item* is defined. In all other contexts Modula-2 does not allow a type to be used in a **TYPE** definition before it is itself defined. For pointers, however, this is legal syntax: The compiler flags *item* as a type it does not yet know about and comes back to it when it is eventually defined.

We need to consider two minor issues. First, what is the value of the *next* field in the last item on the list? Modula-2 provides the constant **NIL**, which can be assigned to a pointer of any type. By convention, a **NIL** pointer value means that the pointer does not point to anything. By setting the *next* field of the last record of the list equal to **NIL**, we can easily detect when we are at the end of the list. It is common to confuse a pointer variable whose value is **NIL** with one whose value is *uninitialized*. Until a pointer variable is explicitly assigned a value, its value (like that of any other variable) is undefined—it should not be assumed to be equal to **NIL**.

Second, nothing is pointing to the beginning of the list, and if we can't get to the beginning of the list, we can't get to the second item on the list—and if we can't get to the second item on the list, we can't get to the third item on the list, and so on. The solution is to have an additional pointer whose purpose is to point to the first item on the list.

Figure 2–9

*External
pointer to a
list*

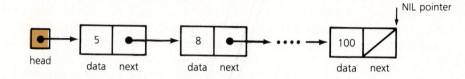

Observe that the pointer variable *head* is different from the other pointers in the diagram in that it is not part of a record. Rather, it is a simple pointer variable external to the list, and it serves as a way of getting to the list's beginning. Also, note that the variable *head* always exists, even at times when there are no items on the list. The declaration

```
VAR
    head : ptr;
```

creates the variable *head* whose value, like that of other uninitialized variables, is undefined. What value should *head* be initialized to (and changed to if a list ever becomes empty)? Assigning *head* the value **NIL** is a logical choice, as this indicates that *head* is not pointing to anything.

It is a common mistake to think that before *head* can be assigned a value, the call

```
NEW (head) ;
```

must be made. The misconception is rooted in the belief that the variable *head* does not exist before the call. This is not at all true: *head* is a declared variable, waiting to be assigned a value. Thus, for example, *head* can be assigned **NIL** without first calling

```
NEW (head) ;
```

In fact, the effect of the sequence

```
NEW (head) ;
head : = NIL;
```

is to cause the only reference to the newly created node to be lost (see Figure 2–10).

Figure 2–10

Lost cell

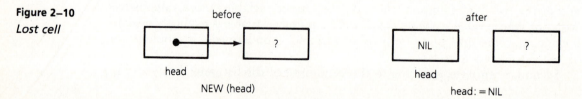

This takes care of how the list is structured, so now let's see how we can write out the contents of a list. Suppose we have a linked list, as pictured in Figure 2–9. A high-level solution is:

```
set the current position to the first record on the list
WHILE (NOT at the end of the list) DO
    write out the data field of the record at the current position
    advance the current position to the next record on the list
END
```

This solution makes it clear that we need to keep track of the current position on the list. That is, we need a pointer variable to point to the record that we are up to. We thus must have the following additional declaration.

```
VAR
    cur : ptr;
```

To initialize *cur* to point to the first record, we simply let *cur* point to the same record that *head* points to:

```
cur := head;
```

To print out the data field of the current record, we use the statement

```
WriteInt(cur^.data,1);
```

This makes sense, since *cur^* is referring to a record, which must be qualified by supplying a field name. Finally, to advance the current position to the next record, we assign:

```
cur := cur^.next;
```

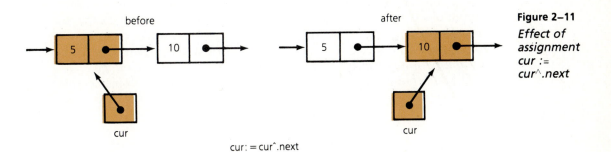

Figure 2–11
Effect of assignment
cur :=
cur^.next

If this is not clear, consider

```
temp := cur^.next;
cur  := temp;
```

and then convince yourself that the intermediate step is not necessary. Putting all this together, we get the *PrintList* procedure:

```
PROCEDURE PrintList(head : ptr);

VAR

    cur : ptr;

BEGIN

    cur := head;
    WHILE (cur # NIL) DO
        WriteInt(cur^.data,1);
        WriteLn;
        cur := cur^.next;
    END;

END PrintList;
```

Procedure *PrintList* is an instance of a **list traversal**, which is a common operation. A traversal sequentially visits each node on the list until the end is reached. In *PrintList*, the data field of each node is printed when the node is visited. In later examples, we shall see that there are other useful things that can be done to a node when it is visited.

We see that pointer variables can be used to implement the basic concept of a linked list. However, we have not yet seen how to perform operations that alter the structure of the list. These are developed in the next chapter. As we study the operations that alter the structure of a list in Chapter 3, the potential advantages of a linked list over an array will become more apparent. We have indicated that one of these advantages is that the data does not need to be shifted when items are inserted into and deleted from a linked list. A second advantage of perhaps more importance concerns the ability to use the Modula-2 procedure *NEW* to dynamically allocate memory cells for a program. Because *NEW* can be used to allocate memory cells as needed, we don't require an estimate of the amount of data that the program will have to handle. Contrast this with a static array. If we are going to use an array to store a list of student names, we would have to have an upper bound on the number of students that must be handled. *The ability of a linked list to grow as needed is a major advantage.*

Although pointer variables are the most natural means of implementing linked lists in Modula-2, it is also possible to implement linked lists with arrays.

ARRAY-BASED IMPLEMENTATIONS OF LINKED LISTS

In this section we shall consider array-based implementations of linked lists. In addition to presenting the mechanics of this alternative to the pointer-based implementation, we shall discuss further the general natures of sequential and linked data structures.

Mechanics of the Implementation

Several widely used programming languages (most notably FORTRAN) do not provide pointer type variables. Fortunately, linked lists can be implemented using a construct supported by virtually all high-level programming languages, the array. It may seem a bit odd that one would consider implementing a linked list with an array since our original motivation for linked lists was to overcome several disadvantages of arrays. However, many of the obstacles that led us to develop linked lists actually are inherent to sequential data structures rather than to arrays per se. As we shall see, arrays can be used to implement data structures that are not sequential. That is, arrays can implement data structures in which the item that follows item x is not necessarily "to the right" of item x in the array.

Consider a linked list, such as the linked list of names depicted in Figure 2–3. Each member of this list consists of two pieces of information: a data value and information that indicates where the next member of the list can be found. Modula-2's pointer variables provide a convenient means for representing this second piece of information. If we did not have pointer variables at our disposal, we would have to devise some other means of keeping track of this "who's next" information.

We can implement this linked list with an array of records.

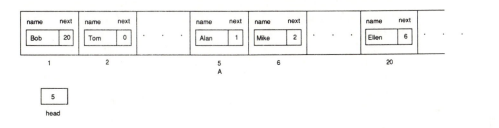

Figure 2–12
*Linked list as
array of
records*

Each record in the array has structure very similar to a node on the pointer-based list. The difference is that the *Next* field of each record in the array is an integer, rather than a pointer, variable. This integer field represents the array index corresponding to the location of the next record on the list. In Figure 2–12, for example, the *Next* field of the record contained in *A[6]* has value 2, indicating that on the linked list the record contained in *A[2]* follows the record contained in *A[6]*. (Note that if we were programming in a language such as FORTRAN that does not support records, we could implement the linked list of Figure 2–3 with a pair of arrays, an array *Names* containing strings and an array *Next* containing integers. Under this scheme, the name that follows on the linked list the name in *Names[i]* is stored in location *Next[i]* of the array *Names*.)

Recall that in the pointer-based implementation of a linked list there is an external pointer variable *head* that points to the first node on the list. Analogously, in the array-based implementation we must have an integer variable that indicates which array location contains the first record on the list. In Figure 2–12, for example, the integer variable *head* has value 5, indicating that the first record on the list is contained in A[5]. Recall also that in the pointer-based implementation, a special pointer value NIL is used to indicate that a pointer variable is not pointing to anything. The value NIL is placed in the *Next* field of the record at the end of the list and is also placed in *head* when the list is empty. When using the array-based implementation, we must select an integer value to play the same role as NIL. We can choose for this purpose any integer value that cannot represent an array location. If, for example, the array starts at location 1, the value 0 can play the role of the NIL pointer.

There is one final issue to discuss regarding the mechanics of the array-based implementation of linked lists. This issue concerns the management of the records in the array. Just as Modula-2 provides a procedure *NEW* for allocating a new linked list node, we must write our own procedure *ArrayNew* to allocate an available record from the array A for use on the linked list. That is, we require a procedure *ArrayNew(i)* that returns in *i* a value such that A[i] contains a record that can be added to the linked list. Further, since the number of records available for the linked list is limited by the size of array A, it is highly desirable to have a procedure *ArrayDispose(i)* that takes the record in A[i], which had been on the linked list, and makes the record available again for future allocations. In the remainder of this section we shall assume the existence of procedures such as *ArrayNew* and *ArrayDispose*. Exercise 2.5 discusses the implementation of such procedures.

With these conventions, the linked list operations described for the pointer-based implementation can be easily adapted to the array-based implementation. For example, the following pseudocode traverses the linked list shown in Figure 2–12.

```
cur := head
WHILE (cur # nil) DO   (* nil is a user-defined
                          constant with value 0 *)
    print A[cur].name
    cur := A[cur].next
END
```

Analysis of the Implementation

Now that we have seen the mechanics of implementing linked lists with arrays, let us consider the question of the implementation's utility. That is, let us ask if an array-based implementation of a linked list has the same benefits as a pointer-based implementation of a linked list. It should be clear from the above discussion that an item can be inserted into and deleted from an array-based linked list without shifting data. As with the pointer-based implementation, the insertion and deletion of a data item is accomplished by changing the value in the next fields of the appropriate records.

One of the major benefits of a linked list is thus preserved by the array-based implementation. The other major benefit of a linked list discussed in this chapter is that its size is dynamic. That is, while an array has a static maximum size, a pointer-based linked list can grow as needed by means of the dynamic allocation of nodes. Since an array is indeed static, it would appear that the advantage of dynamic storage allocation is lost when a linked list is implemented with an array. In fact, however, dynamic storage allocation is only partially sacrificed when a linked list is implemented with an array.

Compare the pointer-based implementation of the linked list of students (depicted in Figure 2–3) and the array-based implementation (depicted in Figure 2–12). It is clear that the array-based implementation is inferior to the pointer-based implementation in one key regard: When the array-based implementation is used, the maximum number of students enrolled in the university must be predicted in advance. The array-based implementation of a linked list thus appears to suffer from the same fixed-size limitation as does the more familiar sequential array implementation (see Figure 2–1). Consider, however, the following situation. Rather than maintaining a single list of students, we wish to organize students by their major department. That is, we wish to maintain one list of students for each department in the university.(For simplicity, we assume that each student in the university has exactly one major, though a student can change her major.) If we did not know about linked lists, we probably would maintain one array of names for each department in the university (see Figure 2–13).

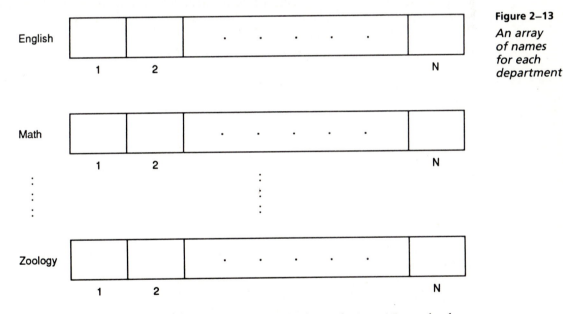

Figure 2–13

An array of names for each department

Observe that there is a severe problem with this solution. Not only do we need an estimate of the total number of students enrolled in the university, we also need an estimate of the number of students in each department. If our estimate of the number of students in each department is not accurate, a situation such as the one depicted in Figure 2–14 could well occur.

Here we see that computer science majors have filled the *CS* array, while the array *History* of history majors is only partially full. If a new student declares herself as a computer science major, there is no room in the *CS* array to place her name. Thus, even though we may have an accurate prediction of the total number of students in the university, and even though there is plenty of space

History	Aiken	Brock	. . .	White	. . . . UNUSED . . .
	1	2		K	N

Figure 2–14

Unbalanced arrays

CS	Allen	Brown	. . . . . .	Zucker
	1	2		N

available in the *History* array, the data structures cannot accommodate the new computer science major.

This example motivates the important technique of *sharing memory* between data structures. The technique can be implemented with linked lists—either pointer-based or array-based—but generally cannot be implemented with sequential data structures. The technique of sharing memory between data structures is based on maintaining a "common block" of memory, chunks of which are allocated to the data structures as needed. Returning to the problem of maintaining lists of majors, let us agree to implement each list of students as an array-based linked list. We will define a single array of records to be the common block of memory to be shared between the linked lists.

Figure 2–15

Array Univ shared between linked lists

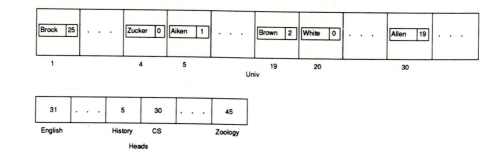

In Figure 2–15 the array *Univ* simultaneously contains the linked list of students for each department. Notice that each linked list must have its own head variable pointing to its beginning. A convenient way to implement these multiple heads is with an array *Heads* indexed with the enumerated type

```
Departments = (English, Math, ..., Zoology)
```

To traverse any one of the linked lists, we simply modify the pseudocode presented above so that the traversal starts at the record pointed to by the appropriate head pointer. For example, we can traverse the list of Math majors as follows.

```
cur := Heads[Math]
WHILE (cur # nil) DO   (* nil is a user-defined
                          constant with value 0 *)
```

```
        print Univ[cur].name
        cur := Univ[cur].next
    END
```

Convince yourself that so long as the linked lists are managed properly there is never any danger of entering the wrong list in the course of the traversal (or any other properly written operation), despite the fact that, physically, the lists are all contained in the same array *Univ*.

The primary advantage of sharing the array *Univ* among the many lists is that we need predict only the *total* number of students to be enrolled in the university. If we have done this correctly, we will never run out of memory for any departmental list, regardless of how many majors any particular department might have. When a new student enters the university and declares D as her major, we add her name to department D's list as follows.

```
ArrayNewU(i)  (* Procedure to allocate a
                  free record from array Univ *)
Univ[i].name := newname
insert into the list pointed to
    by Heads[D] the record in Univ[i]
```

Notice that since a record is allocated from the common array *Univ* regardless of the list on which the record is to be placed, the only time we will be unable to add a new name to a list is when the array *Univ* has no records available for allocation. This occurs only when our prediction of the total number of students enrolled in the university is exceeded. Note we are assuming the existence of a procedure *ArrayDisposeU* that can be called to make a student's record available for future allocation whenever a student leaves the university.(As an exercise, consider how to handle a student who changes her major.).

An Abstract Comparison of Sequential and Linked Data Structures

We conclude this section by comparing abstractly sequential and linked data structures. We shall identify the attribute of a data structure that is the prime determinant of whether the data structure should be considered sequential or linked. We also shall demonstrate that this same attribute determines the extent to which a data structure can share memory with other data structures.

We have characterized informally a sequential data structure as one in which the item that follows item x is "to the right" of item x in the data structure. We can generalize and formalize this concept in terms of the notions of **implicit next** and **explicit next**. Any time a collection of data is stored in an array-based or pointer-based data structure, the data becomes *ordered*. For example, in the data structures we have studied, there is a first item, a second item, and so on. This order implies that given any item in the structure (except the last item), there is a *next* item after it. If array A is used to implement a sequential data structure, the location of the next item after item $A[i]$ is *implicit*—it is in $A[i+1]$. In a linked list (whether it be pointer-based or array-based), however, the location of the next item after item x must be determined *explicitly*. The information as to where this next item can be found is stored explicitly in item x's *Next* field. *This notion of an implicit next versus an explicit next is the primary difference between a sequential and linked data structure.*

Earlier in this chapter we alluded to the fact that an explicit next is the characteristic that allows pointer-based linked lists to grow dynamically. Since the linked list utilizes an explicit next, the procedure *NEW* is free to allocate a new node for the list from anywhere in memory. In a very strong sense, the ability of a pointer-based linked list to grow dynamically, virtually without limit, is in fact a consequence of the data sharing that is made possible by the explicit next of *any* linked data structure, be it pointer-based or array-based. We can view all the memory available to a program as being shared among the program's data structures. When the program makes a call to the procedure *NEW*, a piece of available memory is allocated and can be added to a pointer-based linked list by setting the appropriate *Next* pointer. Therefore, a pointer-based linked list can grow to a limit determined only by the *total* amount of memory available to the program. Notice how this perspective of dynamic allocation to a pointer-based linked list is completely analogous to the sharing of the array *Univ* among several array-based linked lists. As with the pointer-based linked list, the characteristic of the array-based linked list that permits the sharing of memory is its utilization of an explicit next. As long as the array *Univ* contains an available record, that record can be added to any of the linked lists simply by setting the *Next* field of the appropriate record on the linked list.

In contrast, the implicit next of a sequential data structure generally makes impossible this type of memory sharing. Consider again the problem of maintaining a list of the majors for each department in a university. A sequential solution has the following form.

Figure 2–16

Array Univ divided into subarrays

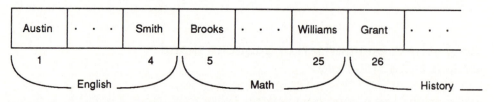

Because a sequential implementation, by definition, utilizes an implicit next, the students of any major department must be stored in a subarray consisting of consecutive locations of *A*. For example, the math majors are stored in *A[5]*, *A[6]*, ... , *A[25]*. Suppose that a new student declares herself to be a math major and thus the math subarray must grow. There are only two array locations that legitimately can be added to the math subarray—*A[4]* and *A[26]*. If we attempted to place a math major in any other array location, the math majors would no longer be "connected" by an implicit next. If, as in Figure 2–16, neither of the feasible array locations is available, the subarray cannot be expanded despite the fact that the array *Univ* contains unallocated memory locations. The above example also indicates why programming languages typically do not support the ability to increase the size of an array dynamically. An array *A* typically is stored in sequential cells of the computer's memory. Given this convention,

1. The value of a pointer variable *p* cannot be inspected. For example, $write(p)$ is an error.

2. An uninitialized pointer variable has an undefined value, not the value **NIL**.

3. An attempt to reference a pointer variable that has the value **NIL** is an error. For example,

    ```
    write(p^);
    write(p^.data);
    p := p^.next;
    ```

    all result in an error if *p* has the value **NIL**.

the only way the size of *A* can be increased while the program is executing is by allocating to *A* memory that is adjacent to it. However, at any point in the program's execution it is quite likely that this memory would have been allocated previously to other variables in this, or even other, programs.

In this chapter we have focused on the advantages that linked data structures enjoy over sequential data structures. Sequential data structures do have many advantages, however. One seemingly obvious advantage is that sequential data structures are more memory efficient, because they require no space for explicit next information. This advantage must be taken with a grain of salt, however. Sequential data structures are more memory efficient than linked structures only if we have an accurate estimate of the maximum amount of memory that will be required. Otherwise, we are likely to overestimate the amount of required memory and thereby waste space.

A major advantage that sequential data structures enjoy over linked data structures is **direct access**. Consider, for example, a situation that requires us to access the ith item on a list. If a sequential implementation is used, this item is stored in $A[i]$ and can be accessed directly. On the other hand, if a linked data structure is used, the list must be traversed from its beginning until the ith item is reached. For large lists, the ability to directly access an item can make a significant difference in a program's efficiency.

In conclusion, we cannot say that, in general, linked data structures are better than sequential data structures or vice versa. Rather, each has its own advantages and disadvantages. Therefore, when choosing between linked and sequential data structures, trade-offs must be weighed carefully in the context of the needs of each particular problem. Developing your ability to weigh these trade-offs is one of the major goals of this book.

SUMMARY

1. Pointer variables are an extremely useful data type. They can be used to implement the data structure known as a linked list by using a type declaration such as:

```
ptr  = POINTER TO node;
node = RECORD
            data : INTEGER;
            next : ptr;
         END;
```

2. An important advantage of a linked list over an array is that the size of a linked list can be increased dynamically. Also, items can be inserted into and deleted from a linked list without requiring that data be shifted.

3. Linked lists can be implemented using arrays. Although the overall size of an array is fixed, memory management techniques can be used to allow a list to grow dynamically. These same techniques allow several linked lists to share the memory of a single array.

4. A sequential implementation is one that utilizes an implicit ordering scheme— for example, the item that follows $A[i]$ is stored in $A[i+1]$. A linked implementation is one that utilizes an explicit ordering scheme—for example, the item that follows the one in node N is found by following node N's pointer.

EXERCISES

1. Eliminate the statements that are syntactically incorrect in this program and trace the execution by hand.

```
MODULE testptr;

(* memory management procedure NEW *)
FROM Storage IMPORT

    ALLOCATE;

(* standard I/O *)
FROM InOut IMPORT

    WriteInt, WriteLn;

TYPE

    intptr = POINTER TO INTEGER;
    intptrptr = POINTER TO intptr;

VAR

    p, q : intptr;
    pp : intptrptr;
```

```
        NEW (p) ;
        NEW (q) ;

        WriteInt (p, 5) ;
        WriteInt (q, 5) ;
        WriteLn;

        p^ := 7;
        q^ := 11;
        WriteInt (p^, 5) ;
        WriteInt (q^, 5) ;
        WriteLn;

        NEW (pp) ;
        pp^ := 20;
        pp^ := p;
        WriteInt (p^, 5) ;
        WriteInt (pp^^, 5) ;
        WriteLn;

        pp^^ := pp^^ + q^;
        WriteInt (p^, 5) ;
        WriteInt (pp^^, 5) ;
        WriteLn;

        NEW (pp^) ;
        pp^^ := -3;
        pp^^ := q^ + p^ + pp^^;
        WriteInt (p^, 5) ;
        WriteInt (q^, 5) ;
        WriteInt (pp^^, 5) ;
        WriteLn;

    END testptr.
```

2. Trace the execution of the given program by hand.

```
MODULE testptr;

(* memory management procedure NEW *)
FROM Storage IMPORT

    ALLOCATE;

(* standard I/O *)
FROM InOut IMPORT
```

```
                Write, WriteInt, WriteString, WriteLn;

CONST

    maxsize = 8;
    maxfamily = 100;

TYPE

    string = ARRAY [0..maxsize-1] OF CHAR;

    person = RECORD
                  name : string;
                  age : CARDINAL;
             END;

    family = ARRAY [1..maxfamily] OF person;

    personptr = POINTER TO person;
    familyptr = POINTER TO family;

VAR

    pptr : personptr;
    fptr : familyptr;
    i : INTEGER;

BEGIN

    NEW(pptr);
    pptr^.age := 25;
    pptr^.name := 'Fred     ';
    WriteString(pptr^.name);
    WriteString(' is ');
    WriteInt(pptr^.age,1);
    WriteString(' years old.');
    WriteLn;

    NEW(fptr);
    fptr^[10] := pptr^;
    WriteString(fptr^[10].name);
    WriteString(' is ');
    WriteInt(fptr^[10].age,1);
    WriteString(' years old.');
    WriteLn;

END testptr.
```

3. Write a function

```
PROCEDURE count(head : nodeptr) : INTEGER;
```

to count the number of records on the linked list pointed to by *head*. Assume the type definitions

```
nodeptr = POINTER TO node;
node = RECORD
          data : INTEGER;
          next : nodeptr;
       END;
```

4. Some programming languages (for example, FORTRAN) do not directly support the data types records and pointers. In these languages, structures such as records and linked lists have to be implemented with the structures that are available.

   a. How can we implement a record using only arrays and simple variables? How about an array of records?

   b. Devise a scheme to represent a linked list of integers using two integer arrays (called *Data* and *Next*) and a single integer-valued variable called *head*.

5. On the surface it seems that the implementation discussed in Exercise 4 sacrifices the primary motivation for having linked structures, which is dynamic allocation. In Chapter 9, however, we will see that dynamic allocation is not the only motivation for having linked structures (that is, a fixed-sized implementation can in fact be useful). Furthermore, as we have discussed, it's possible to share the *Data* and *Next* arrays between several linked lists. Implement the Modula-2 procedures *ArrayNew* and *ArrayDispose* discussed in this chapter. In this context you will see that a linked list that has been implemented with arrays can indeed be viewed as a dynamic structure.

6. Write a program that will read in English prose and list in alphabetical order all the words that occur in the prose, along with a count of the number of times each word occurs.

   The heart of this program will be a procedure that reads in a word. If we agree to treat any character other than the letters 'A'..'Z' as a delimiter, then we can define a word to be any string of up to 8 characters that is surrounded by delimiters. (If a string between delimiters is more than 8 characters, read the entire string but truncate it to 8 characters when you record it.)

   You can assume that there will be at most 100 distinct words in the text.

CHAPTER 3

LINKED LISTS

PREVIEW This chapter continues the discussion on linked lists begun in Chapter 2. We develop algorithms for inserting items into and deleting items from a sorted linked list. Following the discussion on linked lists, we present a large case study on the development of a computerized system for maintaining the inventory of a retail store. We follow the processes of designing and implementing the solution with the goal of seeing in action the principles and concepts of the previous two chapters. The problem also provides a natural application for linked lists.

The case study in this chapter illustrates the value of the tools and techniques discussed in the previous two chapters. The case study follows the design and implementation of a computer program that manages the inventory of a video-cassette dealer. The size and complexity of this problem make it essential that the solution be developed in a top-down fashion and that the program be highly modular.

Before presenting the case study, we resume the discussion of linked lists begun in Chapter 2. The techniques for performing some basic linked list operations, such as insertion into and deletion from a sorted linked list, play a central role in the case study, and they are also the basis of many of the data structures that appear throughout the remainder of the book. The material in this chapter is thus essential to much of the discussion in the following chapters.

PROGRAMMING WITH LINKED LISTS

In Chapter 2 we illustrated how pointer variables can be used to implement the basic concept of a linked list. Recall that by using the definitions

```
TYPE

    ptr = POINTER TO item;
    item = RECORD
                data : INTEGER;
                next : ptr;
          END;
```

and the declaration

```
VAR
    head : ptr;
```

we were able to implement a linked list of nodes such as the list shown in Figure 2–9.

The only task we performed in Chapter 2 on a linked list was to print its contents. Since we had not yet learned how to build a linked list, we had to assume that somehow it had been set up in advance for us. We shall now study ways to perform operations that actually alter the structure of a linked list. These operations allow us to build a linked list from scratch and to insert nodes into and delete nodes from an existing linked list.

Deleting a Specified Node from a Linked List

To address the problem of deleting a specified node from a linked list, we first assume that the list shown in Figure 3–1 is already in existence.

Figure 3–1

*Deleting a
node from
a linked list*

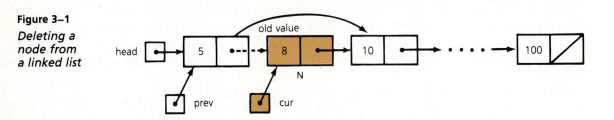

Notice that, in addition to *head*, the diagram includes two external pointer variables:

```
cur  : ptr;   (* pointer to current node *)
prev : ptr;   (* pointer to previous node *)
```

Our task is to delete the node pointed to by *cur*. The role of the pointer variable *prev* will become apparent in a moment.

As the diagram indicates, the deletion of the node N pointed to by *cur* can be accomplished by altering the value of the pointer field *next* in the node that precedes N. This pointer needs to be set so that it points to the node following N, thus bypassing N on the chain. Notice that this pointer change does not directly affect the node N. Node N remains in existence, and it points to the same node that it pointed to before the deletion. However, the node has been effectively deleted from the list. For example, notice that the procedure *PrintList* from Chapter 2 would not print the contents of the node N.

Thus, we see that the node N can be deleted from the list by changing the value of the pointer in the node that precedes it. To accomplish this in Modula-2, we see first that, if we had only the pointer *cur* (which points to N), there would be no direct way of getting to the node that precedes N. After all, the links on the list cannot be followed backwards. This is where the pointer variable *prev*, shown in Figure 3–1, comes into play. *If we are to delete the node N from a linked list, we need a pointer to the node that precedes N.*

If we do have the pointer variable *prev*, which points to the node preceding N, the pointer change suggested by Figure 3–1 is easy to implement in Modula-2. The following assignment statement is all that is required.

```
prev^.next := cur^.next;
```

There are two questions to be answered about the deletion of a node from a linked list:

1. How did the variables *cur* and *prev* come to point to the appropriate nodes?
2. Does the method described above work for any node N, regardless of where in the linked list it appears?

To answer the first question, consider the context in which we might expect to delete a node. In one common situation, we need to delete a node that contains a particular data value. In other words, the *Delete* procedure is not given the values of *cur* and *prev*, but instead it has to establish these values as its first step. That is, the *Delete* procedure must search the list for the node N that contains the data value to be deleted. Once the node N (and the node that precedes N) has been found, the deletion of N proceeds as described above. We present the details of such a *Delete* procedure later in this section.

In answer to the second question, the method described does not work if the node to be deleted is the *first* node on the list. If the node to be deleted is the first node on the list, then it certainly doesn't make sense to assert that *prev* points to the node that precedes this node! We are leading up to the fact that the *deletion of the first node on a linked list is a special case.* Consider Figure 3–2.

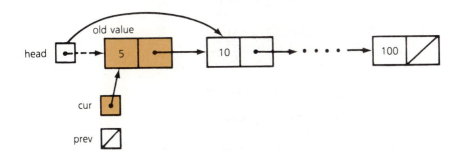

Figure 3–2

Deleting the first node

When we delete the first node of the list, the value of *head* must change. It must be made to reflect the fact that, after the deletion, there is a new first node on the list—that is, the node that was second prior to the deletion is now first. This is accomplished by the assignment statement

```
head := cur^.next;
```

As was the case for the deletion of an interior node, the old first node is now bypassed, although it still exists. Notice also that if the node to be deleted is the *only* node on the list (and thus it is also the first node), then the assignment statement

```
head := cur^.next;
```

assigns the value **NIL** to the variable *head*. Recall that an empty list is indicated by the value **NIL** in *head*, and thus the deletion of the only node on a list is handled correctly.

Note that it is really a bit wasteful that the node N still exists after its deletion from the linked list. If the value of *cur* is changed so that it no longer points to N, N will be in a state of limbo—it still requires storage space, even though it can no longer be accessed by the program. If a program were to accumulate many nodes in this limbo state, its storage requirements might become unreasonably high. As we discussed in Chapter 2, the procedure *DISPOSE* can be used to return to memory nodes that are no longer needed, thus alleviating this problem.

These are the mechanics of deleting a specified node from a linked list. Shortly, we shall incorporate the techniques into a procedure for deleting a node with a specified data value.

Inserting a Node into a Specified Position

Figure 3–3 illustrates the technique of inserting a new node into a specified position of a linked list. We wish to insert the new node pointed to by the variable *newitem* between the nodes pointed to by *prev* and *cur*. As the diagram suggests, the insertion can be accomplished by the pair of assignment statements

Figure 3–3

*Inserting a
new node
into a linked
list*

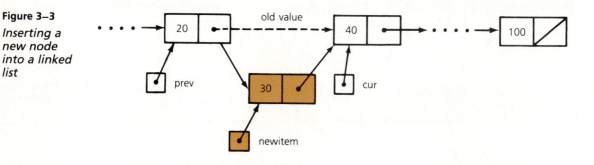

```
newitem^.next := cur;
prev^.next := newitem;
```

The following two questions are analogous to those asked about the deletion of a node:

1. How did the variables *newitem*, *cur*, and *prev* come to point to the appropriate nodes?

2. Does the method work for inserting a node into any position of a list?

The answer to the first question, like the answer to the corresponding question for the *Delete* operation, is found by considering the context in which the *Insert* operation will be used. In the case study in this chapter, for example, we maintain a sorted linked list of cassette titles. For that problem we want a procedure to insert a new title into its proper sorted position in the list. The first step of such an *Insert* procedure is to establish the values of *cur* and *prev*. This is done by traversing the list until the proper sorted position for the new title is found. Once this is accomplished, a new node is created by calling Modula-2's *NEW* procedure,

```
NEW(newitem);
```

The final step is to assign the two pointer values, as shown above. We fill in the details of this *Insert* procedure in the next section.

The answer to the second question is that *insertion, like deletion, must account for special cases*. First consider the insertion of a node at the beginning of the list, shown in Figure 3–4. To insert a node at the beginning, we must set *head* to point to the new node and the new node to point to the node that had been at the beginning of the list. This can be accomplished by

```
newitem^.next := head;
head := newitem;
```

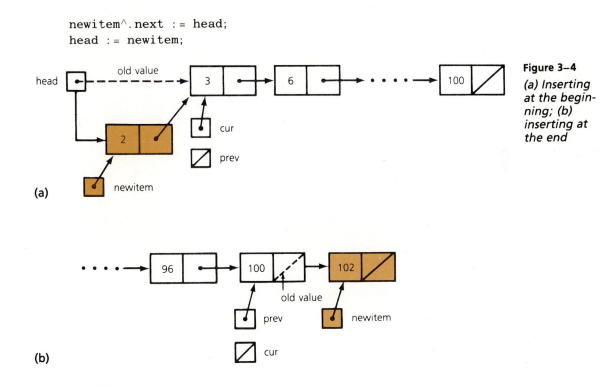

Figure 3–4

(a) Inserting at the beginning; (b) inserting at the end

Observe that if the list is empty before the insertion (*head* = **NIL**), the *next* field of the new item is set to **NIL**. This is correct since the new item is the last item (as well as the first item) on the list.

Inserting a new node at the *end* of a list (see Figure 3–4b) also must be viewed as a special case since the pair of assignment statements

```
newitem^.next := cur;
prev^.next := newitem;
```

is intended to insert the new node between the node pointed to by *cur* and the node pointed to by *prev*. If the new node is to be inserted at the end of the list, what node should *cur* be pointing to? In this situation it makes sense to view the value of *cur* as **NIL** (think of what happens as *cur* moves past the end of the list). Observe that if *cur* has the value **NIL** and *prev* points to the last node on the list, then the above pair of assignment statements will indeed insert the new node at the end of the list.

Insert and Delete Procedures for a Sorted Linked List

As we have mentioned, we often have a linked list sorted by its data values. The case study at the end of this chapter is an application that uses such a linked list. There are also many problems that require a linked list to be ordered in ways other than sorted by its data values. Examples of such problems and their solutions appear throughout Part III of this book.

We shall now use the techniques developed above to construct procedures to insert into and delete from a sorted linked list. To be more precise, we wish to implement the following two procedures.

```
Insert(head, X, success)
(* Insert X into its proper sorted position in the linked list
   pointed to by head.  If the list already contains an item
   with value X, the insertion is not allowed and the list
   remains unchanged.  The Boolean flag success indicates
   whether X was inserted. *)

Delete(head, X, success)
(* Delete the data item equal to X (if it is present) from the
   sorted linked list pointed to by head.  The Boolean flag
   success indicates whether X was present. *)
```

The specification of the `Insert` procedure does not allow the list to contain two items with the same value. This is an arbitrary decision, and, in fact, we might very well wish to allow duplicate values in some applications, in which case we would modify the `Insert` procedure accordingly. In the case study to follow, we do not wish to allow duplicates, so we choose to implement `Insert` as described above.

Let us now implement the `Insert` procedure. As we observed in the previous discussion, in order to insert the value *X* into a sorted list, we must traverse the list from its beginning until the appropriate place for *X* is found. The appropriate place for *X* in the sorted order is just before the node containing the first data item greater than *X*. We know that we will need a pointer *cur* to the node that is to follow the new node (to the node containing the first data item greater than X) and a pointer *prev* to the node that is to precede the new node (to the node containing the last data item smaller than X). Thus, as we traverse the list, we keep a *trailing* pointer. When we reach the node containing the first value larger than X, the trailing pointer points to the previous node. At this time, the new data item can be inserted between the nodes pointed to by *cur* and *prev* as described above. We shall not modify the procedure to prevent insertion of duplicate values until the final refinement of the solution.

A first attempt at the algorithm is thus:

```
(* initialize to start the traversal
    from the beginning of the list *)
prev := NIL
cur := head


(* advance so long as X > the current data item *)
WHILE (X > cur^.data) DO
    prev := cur
    cur := cur^.next
END


(* create a new node with newitem pointing to it *)
NEW(newitem)
newitem^.data := X


(* insert the node pointed to by newitem between
    the nodes pointed to by prev and cur *)
newitem^.next := cur
prev^.next := newitem
```

Our earlier discussion has alerted us to the fact that there are two special cases to watch for:

> the insertion of a node at the beginning of the list
> the insertion of a node at the end of the list

We have already seen how to handle these special cases, but in the context of this *Insert* procedure, the detection of the special cases is somewhat tricky.

First consider the insertion of a node at the beginning of the list. This arises when the value X to be inserted is *smaller* than all the values currently on the list. When this is the case, the **WHILE** loop,

```
WHILE (X > cur^.data) DO
    prev := cur
    cur := cur^.next
END
```

is never entered, so *prev* and *cur* maintain their original values. In particular, *prev* maintains its original value of **NIL**. Since this is the only situation where the value of *prev* is equal to **NIL** following the **WHILE** loop, we can use the condition

prev = NIL

to detect an insertion at the beginning of the list. We thus refine our insertion algorithm to:

```
(* initialize to start the traversal
   from the beginning of the list *)
prev := NIL
cur := head

(* advance so long as X > the current data item *)
WHILE (X > cur^.data) DO
    prev := cur
    cur := cur^.next
END

(* create a new node with newitem pointing to it *)
NEW(newitem)
newitem^.data := X

(* test for insertion at the beginning of the list *)
IF (prev = NIL) THEN
    (* insert at the beginning of the list *)
    newitem^.next := head
    head := newitem
ELSE
    (* insert between the nodes pointed to by prev and cur *)
    newitem^.next := cur
    prev^.next := newitem
END
```

The second special case, insertion at the end of the list, arises when the value *X* to be inserted is *greater* than all the values currently on the list. As we noted earlier, insertion at the end of the list can be handled with the standard pair of assignment statements

```
newitem^.next := cur
prev^.next := newitem
```

provided that *prev* is pointing to the last node on the list and that the value of *cur* is **NIL**.

The difficulty caused by insertion when *X* is greater than all the values in the list is in the behavior of the **WHILE** loop,

```
WHILE  (X > cur^.data)  DO
    prev := cur
    cur := cur^.next
END
```

Eventually, at the top of the loop, *X* is compared to the value in the last node. At the loop's next iteration, *cur* is assigned the value **NIL**. After this iteration, *X* is again compared to

```
cur^.data
```

This attempt at referencing the pointer *cur* when its value is **NIL** results in a program error.

To solve this problem, we need another test in the termination condition of the **WHILE** loop.

```
(* initialize to start the traversal
   from the beginning of the list *)
cur := head
prev := NIL

(* advance to X's proper sorted position *)
WHILE ((cur # NIL)  AND  (X > cur^.data))  DO
    prev := cur
    cur := cur^.next
END

(* create a new node with newitem pointing to it *)
NEW(newitem)
newitem^.data := X

(* test for insertion at the beginning of the list *)
IF  (prev = NIL)  THEN
    (* insert at the beginning of the list *)
    newitem^.next := head
    head := newitem
ELSE
    (* insert between the nodes pointed to by prev and cur *)
    newitem^.next := cur
    prev^.next := newitem
END
```

Notice how this solves the problem of inserting a node at the end of the list. In the case that *X* is greater than all the values on the list, *prev* points to the last node on the list and *cur* has the value **NIL** upon termination of the **WHILE** loop. This allows the new node to be inserted at the end of the list with the standard pair of assignment statements

```
newitem^.next := cur
prev^.next := newitem
```

Observe that the above solution correctly handles insertion into an empty list as a special case of insertion at the beginning of the list. When the list is empty, *cur* is assigned an initial value of **NIL** (by the statement *cur := head*), and thus the **WHILE** loop is never entered. Following the **WHILE** loop, *prev* has the value **NIL**, thus indicating an insertion at the beginning of the list. Since the new node's *next* field is assigned the value **NIL** (by the statement *newitem^.next := head*), it is correctly set up as the last node on the list as well as the first.

We now present our final refinement before going to actual code. The one issue that still remains is the procedure's handling of duplicates. Recall that the specification of the *Insert* procedure states that we are to disallow the insertion of a value that is already present in the list. The following procedure accomplishes this by checking, upon termination of the **WHILE** loop, whether *X* is equal to the value in the node pointed to by *cur*. If a duplicate is detected, the insertion is disallowed. Notice that we must be careful not to make this check if the value of *cur* is **NIL**. This can be handled naturally with the following test.

```
IF ((cur # NIL) AND (X = cur^.data)) THEN
   X is a duplicate value, disallow the insertion
ELSE
   X is not a duplicate value, insert it
END
```

The complete pseudocode procedure follows.

```
Insert(head, X, success)
(* Insert X into its proper sorted position in the linked list
   pointed to by head.  If the list already contains an item
   with value X, the insertion is not allowed and the list
   remains unchanged.  The Boolean flag success indicates
   whether X was inserted. *)

BEGIN

   (* initialize to start the traversal
      from the beginning of the list *)
   cur := head
   prev := NIL

   (* advance to X's proper sorted position *)
   WHILE ((cur # NIL) AND (X > cur^.data)) DO
      prev := cur
      cur := cur^.next
   END

   (* insert if there is no duplicate *)
   IF ((cur # NIL) AND (X = cur^.data)) THEN
```

```
    (* duplicate - disallow the insertion *)
    success := FALSE

ELSE
    (* create a new node with newitem pointing to it *)
    NEW(newitem)
    newitem^.data := X

    (* test for insertion at the beginning of the list *)
    IF (prev = NIL) THEN
        (* insert at the beginning of the list *)
        newitem^.next := head
        head := newitem
    ELSE
        (* insert between the nodes pointed to by prev and cur *)
        newitem^.next := cur
        prev^.next := newitem
    END

    success := TRUE

  END (* test for duplicate *)

END Insert
```

The procedure is now very close to code, and there is only one small Modula-2 issue that we must discuss. This has to do with how the pointer variable *head* should be passed to the procedure; we must decide if it should be a value or a variable (**VAR**) parameter. It must be a variable parameter, but the reasoning is complex. If your first instinct is that *head* must be passed as a variable parameter, since the nodes on the list to which it points will be altered by the procedure, you have reached the right conclusion but for the wrong reason.

Let us consider what would happen if the pointer were passed as a value parameter. Figure 3–5 illustrates that while the actual parameter *p* is copied into the formal parameter *head*, the list nodes themselves are *not* copied. Thus, if the procedure makes any changes to the nodes on the list, the changes are made to the actual nodes, not to local copies of the nodes; that is, *any changes the procedure makes to the list are not localized to the procedure.*

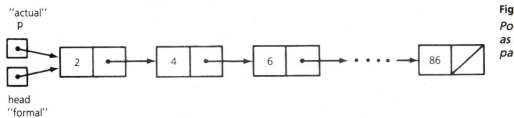

"actual"
p

head
"formal"

Figure 3–5

*Pointer head
as a value
parameter*

Passing the head of a list to a procedure as a value parameter thus allows the procedure to modify the nodes on the list (and even to insert and delete nodes).

Thus, it would now seem that *head* could be a value parameter in the *Insert* procedure. This would be correct if not for the possibility that the procedure will change the value of *head* itself. If the new node is inserted at the beginning of the list, the value of *head* changes, and this change must be reflected in the actual parameter corresponding to *head* (*p* in the above diagram). This is the only reason that *head* needs to be a variable parameter!

The Modula-2 version of the *Insert* procedure is as follows:

```
(* -----------------------------------------------------------
   Insert:   Insert X into its proper sorted position in the
   linked list pointed to by head.   If the list already
   contains an item with value X, the insertion is not allowed
   and the list remains unchanged.   The Boolean flag success
   indicates whether X was inserted.
   --------------------------------------------------------- *)
PROCEDURE Insert(VAR head : ptr; X : INTEGER;
                     VAR success : BOOLEAN);

VAR

    cur, prev, newitem : ptr;

BEGIN

    (* initialize to start the traversal
       from the beginning of the list *)
    cur := head;
    prev := NIL;

    (* advance to X's proper sorted position *)
    WHILE ((cur # NIL) AND (X > cur^.data)) DO
        prev := cur;
        cur := cur^.next;   (* note that cur is not NIL *)
    END;   (* while *)

    (* test for duplicate value *)
    IF ((cur = NIL) OR (X # cur^.data)) THEN

        (* create a new node with newitem pointing to it *)
        NEW(newitem);
        newitem^.data := X;

        (* test for insertion at the
           beginning of the list *)
        IF (prev = NIL) THEN

            (* insert at the beginning of the list *)
            newitem^.next := head;
            head := newitem;
```

```
        (* insert between the nodes
           pointed to by prev and cur *)
        ELSE
           newitem^.next := cur;
           prev^.next := newitem;
        END;


        success := TRUE;

     (* disallow the insertion *)
     ELSE
        success := FALSE;

     END;  (* test for duplicate *)

END Insert;
```

We now turn our attention to implementing the *Delete* procedure for a sorted linked list. Much of the reasoning for *Delete* is analogous to that for *Insert*, so we present only one level of pseudocode and leave the Modula-2 procedure as an exercise. You may wish to review the earlier discussion on the mechanics of deleting a specified node.

The algorithm for the *Delete* procedure can be stated at the pseudocode level as follows:

```
Delete(head, X, success)
(* Delete the data item equal to X (if it is present) from the
   sorted linked list pointed to by head.  The Boolean flag
   success indicates whether X was present. *)

BEGIN

    (* initialize to start the traversal
       from the beginning of the list *)
    cur := head
    prev := NIL

    (* advance to X's proper sorted position *)
    WHILE ((cur # NIL) AND (X > cur^.data)) DO
       prev := cur
       cur := cur^.next
    END

    (* if X is present delete it *)
    IF ((cur # NIL) AND (X = cur^.data)) THEN

        (* check for deletion from the beginning of the list *)
        IF (prev = NIL) THEN
           head := cur^.next
```

```
        ELSE
            prev^.next := cur^.next
        END

        DISPOSE(cur)
        success := TRUE

    (* X is not present *)
    ELSE
        success := FALSE

    END

END Delete
```

Dummy Head Nodes

Both the *Insert* and *Delete* procedures just presented require a special case
to handle action at the first position of a list. Although our procedures correctly
handle this case, many people would prefer a method that eliminates the need
for the special case. One such method is to add a dummy head node to the list
(see Figure 3–6). In this way, the item at the first position of the list is stored in
the second node. The dummy head node is always present, even when the list is
empty.

Figure 3–6

*Dummy head
node*

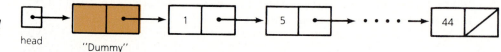

head   "Dummy"

When the dummy head node is used, the special case is eliminated from the
Insert and *Delete* procedures because these procedures will initialize *prev*
to point to the dummy head node (rather than to **NIL**). Thus, for example, in
the *Delete* procedure the statement

```
    prev^.next := cur^.next;
```

deletes the node pointed to by *cur* from the list regardless of whether or not
this node is the first (real) node on the list.

Despite the fact that the introduction of a dummy head node eliminates the
need for the special case, we do not, in general, advocate its use in a linked list.
We feel that handling the first list position separately is less distracting than
altering the list's structure by adding the dummy head node. (Chapter 10, in the
context of doubly linked lists, again considers the use of dummy head nodes.)

Some people like to put global information about the list (such as its length
or the smallest or largest value in the list) in a dummy head node (see Figure
3-7a).

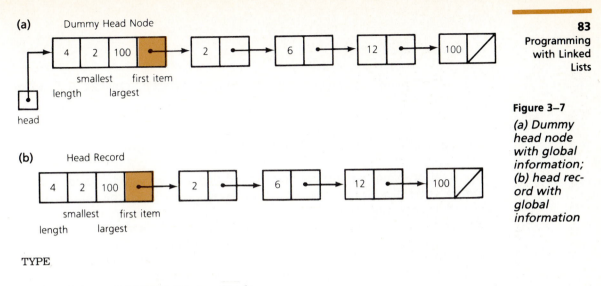

Figure 3-7

*(a) Dummy
head node
with global
information;
(b) head rec-
ord with
global
information*

```
TYPE

    headptr = POINTER TO headnode;
    headnode = RECORD
                    length,
                    smallest,
                    largest   : INTEGER;
                    firstitem : ptr;  (* pointer to first item *)
               END;


VAR

    head : headptr;
```

Unless the dummy head node is exactly the same type of record as the other nodes on the list, the list operations will still require a special case for the first position. This situation occurs because a Modula-2 pointer variable can point only to one type of record. Thus, the same pointer variable (for example, *prev*) could not be used to point both to the dummy head node and to a (real) list node. In particular, the same pointer *prev* could not be initialized to point to the dummy head node and then be advanced to traverse down the list. This problem can be overcome by using a variant record or Modula-2's type *ADDRESS*.

Our own preference for handling global information is to put the information in a record that contains the external pointer to the first node on the list (see Figure 3-7b).

```
TYPE

    headrecord = RECORD
                      length,
                      smallest,
                      largest   : INTEGER;
                      firstitem : ptr;
                 END;
```

```
VAR

    head : headrecord;
```

Whether or not to use a dummy head node is, however, a matter of personal taste.

Saving a Linked List and Restoring It from a File

As a final problem, we discuss how linked lists can be saved in and restored from external files so that the list can be preserved between the runs of a program. The case study in this chapter utilizes this technique in a business application. The program maintains a linked list of information about a retail store's inventory. Since the program is not continually running, we need a way to save the list in a file so that it can be restored each time the program is restarted.

We develop the technique here by saving and restoring a linked list of integers like the ones we have been using throughout this section. In the case study, we will need to save and restore lists of more complex items, necessitating the use of a more general type of file than that supported by library module *InOut*.

We start with the following definitions and declaration:

```
TYPE

    ptr = POINTER TO item;
    item = RECORD
                data : INTEGER;
                next : ptr;
            END;

VAR

    head : ptr;
```

Let us suppose that our program needs to write a linked list of integers to a file in a way that will allow us to later restore the list. What should we write to the file? We might think that we must save each node in its entirety— that is, save the entire record (which contains an integer and pointer field). However, saving the pointer field (even if we could) would serve no useful purpose because once the program has terminated, the pointer value saved for each record would be meaningless. The memory location referenced by a pointer field would be valid before the list was written out to a file, but once the program has terminated the saved pointer value would not be well defined (for example, it may reference a memory location allocated to some completely different structure within the program or even within another program altogether). Thus, the solution of writing out the entire node to a file would not be a good one.

It turns out that all we need to do is write the data portion of each node (in this case an integer) to the file because it is easy to restore the list structure from only this information (see Figure 3–8).

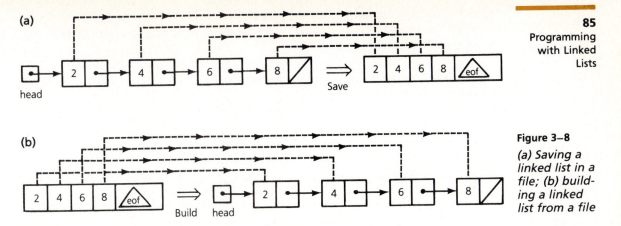

(a)

head

Save

(b)

Build   head

Figure 3–8

*(a) Saving a
linked list in a
file; (b) build-
ing a linked
list from a file*

The following procedure performs this task.

```
(* ------------------------------------------------------------
    SaveList:   Save in an external file the data in the
    linked list pointed to by head.
    ------------------------------------------------------- *)
PROCEDURE SaveList(head : ptr);

VAR

    cur : ptr;

BEGIN

    OpenOutput('');
    cur := head;

    (* traverse the list to the end, writing out each item *)
    WHILE (cur # NIL) DO
        WriteInt(cur^.data, 1);
        WriteLn;
        cur := cur^.next;
    END;

    CloseOutput;

END SaveList;
```

Once the integers on the list have been saved in the file, we can recreate the
list any time we wish. After the program that originally created the list has
terminated, the data endures in the file. Thus, for example, when the program
(or another program) is active again, it can restore the list by reading the data
from the file.

To develop a procedure to restore a linked list, we first notice that the procedure *SaveList* has written the integers to the file in the order that they

appeared on the list. Our `RestoreList` procedure thus must build the list by reading the file and placing each newly read integer at the end of the list.

A pseudocode solution is:

```
WHILE (not at the end of the file) DO
    read in the next integer
    place the integer at the end of the list
END
```

To add a new integer to the end of the list, we must:

1. Use *NEW* to allocate a new node for the list.
2. Set the pointer field in the last node on the list to point to the new node.
3. Put the integer in the new node.
4. Set the pointer field in the new node to **NIL**.

Each time we read a new integer, we must get to the last node on the list. One way to accomplish this is to traverse the list each time a new integer is read. A much more efficient method uses a pointer variable `tail` to remember where the end of the list is (just as *head* remembers where the beginning of the list is). Like *head*, `tail` is external to the list (see Figure 3–9).

Figure 3–9

Linked list with head and tail pointers

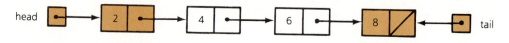

head → 2 → 4 → 6 → 8 ← tail

With `tail` pointing to the end of the list, Steps 1 and 2 can both be performed with the single statement

```
NEW(tail^.next);
```

This call to *NEW* allocates a new node and sets the *next* field of the node pointed to by `tail` (which is the last record on the list) to point to this new node. Notice that we could have accomplished the same task using a temporary pointer variable:

```
NEW(temp);
tail^.next := temp;
```

We thus have an easy method for adding a new integer to the end of the list. But what about the first integer on the list? Before it is inserted in the list, the list is empty and `tail` doesn't point to anything. One way to handle this is to treat the first insertion as a special case before the **WHILE** loop. This leads to the procedure `RestoreList`.

```
(* -------------------------------------------------------------
   RestoreList:  Restore the data in an external file to a
   linked list pointed to by head.
   ------------------------------------------------------------- *)
PROCEDURE RestoreList(VAR head : ptr);
```

```
VAR

    tail : ptr;
    num : INTEGER;

BEGIN

    OpenInput ('');

    ReadInt (num);

    (* test for an empty file *)
    IF (Done) THEN

        (* add the first integer to the list *)
        NEW (head);
        head^.data := num;
        head^.next := NIL;
        tail := head;
        ReadInt (num);

        (* add the remaining integers to the list *)
        WHILE (Done) DO

            NEW (tail^.next);
            tail := tail^.next;
            tail^.data := num;
            tail^.next := NIL;
            ReadInt (num);

        END;

    (* the file is empty, return the empty list *)
    ELSE
        head := NIL;

    END;

    CloseInput;

END RestoreList;
```

Let us consider one final task. Suppose a file contains integers that are not in the order we want them. For example, we want the integers to appear in ascending order on our linked list, but in the file they are in no particular order at all. We can easily solve this problem by using the *Insert* procedure that we developed earlier. Since the procedure inserts new items into their proper sorted order, the following algorithm will do the trick.

```
PROCEDURE BuildSortedList(f, head)
(* Construct a linked list pointed to by head which contains in
   sorted order the integers in the current input file.  For
   simplicity we will assume that the file contains no
   duplicates. *)

BEGIN

   head := NIL


   WHILE (NOT at end of file) DO
      read(x)
      Insert(head, x, success)
   END

END BuildSortedList
```

This type of sorting algorithm is known as an **Insertion sort** and is among the sorting algorithms studied in Chapter 13.

A CASE STUDY: MAINTAINING AN INVENTORY

The case study in this section helps illustrate the issues of program design and development discussed in the previous chapters. The particular problem that we solve, maintaining an inventory, is chosen because its solution nicely demonstrates how a complex problem can be effectively solved using principles of top-down design and modularity. The solution also illustrates Modula-2 list processing and file handling.

Statement of the Inventory Problem

Our object is to write an interactive program that will maintain an inventory for a video-cassette dealer. The inventory consists of a list of movie titles and the following inventory information associated with each title:

1. **Have count:** number of cassettes currently in stock
2. **Want count:** desired number to be kept in stock (for making decisions about purchase orders)
3. **Wait list:** list of names of people waiting for the title if it is sold out

Because the inventory program won't be running at all times, there should be a mechanism for saving the inventory in a file and for restoring the inventory when the program is run again.

There are three separate input files.

A file containing a previously saved inventory.

A file containing information on an incoming shipment of cassettes. (See command D below.)

Single letter commands (with arguments where necessary) to inquire about or modify the inventory. It is expected that these commands will be entered interactively.

A file with the saved inventory. Any inventory items with have value = 0, want value = 0, and an empty wait list should be deleted from the inventory (not saved in the file).

Output as specified by the individual commands.

The program should be able to execute the following commands:

INFORMATION COMMANDS

H	(help)	Print out a summary of the available commands.
I <title>	(inquire)	Print the inventory information for a specified title.
L	(list)	List out the entire inventory (in alphabetical order by title).

ACTION COMMANDS

A <title>	(add)	Add a new title to the inventory. Prompt for initial want value.
M <title>	(modify)	Modify the want value for a specified title.
D	(delivery)	Take delivery of a shipment of cassettes, assuming that the shipment information (titles and counts) has been entered into a file by our clerk. Read in the file, mail out cassettes to the people on the wait list, and update the have values in the inventory accordingly. Note that an item will have to be added to the inventory if a delivered title is not present in the current inventory.
O	(order)	Write a purchase order based on a comparison of the have and want values in the inventory. The object is to bring the have value up to the want value.
R	(return)	Write a return order based on a comparison of the have and want values in the inventory. Decrease the have values accordingly (the return is made). The object is to reduce the have value to the want value.

S <title>	(sell)	Decrease the count for the specified title by one. If the title is sold out, put a name on the wait list for the title.
Q	(quit)	

Solution to the Inventory Problem

In the last section, we presented a problem statement that we now use as a high-level specification for a computer program. In this section we describe the process of going from the statement of the problem to a program that effectively solves the problem (meets its specification). We can view this process as having three main steps. Although these steps are presented as isolated topics in the following discussion, we must always keep a global perspective.

Step 1: The top-down design of a solution.   We hope that you are well aware of the spirit of top-down design. Because the human mind is not capable of solving very large problems directly, we solve problems by breaking them into smaller problems and by adding successively finer levels of detail to their solutions. The end result of this process is a solution that is easy to translate into the control structures and data structures of a particular programming language.

Step 2: The bottom-up implementation of the solution with a program.   The solution produced by a top-down design is a hierarchy of subproblems that will correspond to modules in a program. In Figure 3–10, the solution to problem A is defined in terms of subproblems S_1, S_2, and S_3. Before we begin to code the module that solves problem A, it seems reasonable that we should first complete the implementations of the solutions to subproblems S_1, S_2, and S_3. This is a *bottom-up implementation*. Once we are confident that the modules for S_1, S_2, and S_3 are working, we can use them to continue the implementation of the solution to problem A.

Figure 3–10

Top-down design, bottom-up implementation

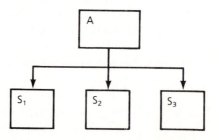

In some situations it might be reasonable to implement a module *before* implementing some of its submodules. For example, in Figure 3–10, we may choose to implement module A before module S_3. In this case we would write a dummy procedure for S_3 that does nothing but report that it has been called. These placeholders, which are often referred to as **stubs**, allow us to focus our attention on the central parts of the solution. We see examples of both of these strategies in this case study.

Step 3: The final set of refinements to the program. The result of the second step of the solution process is a correct program that has been tested extensively and debugged as necessary. If we have a program that solves our original problem, you might wonder about the significance of the third step of the solution process.

In Chapter 1 we talked about the issues of fail-safe programming and nice user interfaces. We believe that the best approach to solving a problem is very often to make some simplifying assumptions during the top-down design of the solution (for example, the input will be in a certain format and will be correct) and to develop a complete working program under these assumptions. More sophisticated input and output routines and additional fail-safe checks can then (often) be cleanly added to the working program. This is the intention of the third step of the solution process. The ability to proceed in this manner is one of the key advantages of having a modular design!

We believe that this approach makes a lot of sense. Of course, we must take care to ensure that the final refinements don't turn out to require an entire redesign of the solution. This is what we mean when we say that the three steps cannot really be done in complete isolation. In order to make realistic simplifying assumptions early in the design process, it is necessary to have some idea of how these assumptions will be accounted for later on.

Our solution strategy is, therefore, first to design and implement a solution with respect to some initial simplifying assumptions. The outcome (of the first two steps of our solution process) is a well-structured program that solves the original problem. The last step of the solution process takes a program that merely meets its specification and refines it into a "nice" program.

Top-Down Design of a Solution

In this section we describe the highlights of a methodical, top-down approach to the inventory problem. At many steps in the development of the solution, choices must be made. Although the following discussion may give the illusion that the choices are clear-cut, this situation is not always the case. In reality there are more trade-offs between the choices and more false starts (wrong choices considered) than we can possibly describe in a reasonable amount of space. We shall, however, try to convey as much as possible the spirit of the problem-solving process.

The discussion may also give the illusion that all subproblems are solved in complete isolation from other subproblems. In reality, as we have said, many are best solved with other subproblems and a perspective of the overall picture in mind. The methodology that we describe gives a framework for the systematic solution of large problems. Some of the more subtle aspects of weighing trade-offs and keeping the big picture in proper perspective are dealt with in Parts III and IV of this book.

We can now begin our discussion of the top-down design of a solution to the inventory problem. From the statement of the inventory problem, it is clear that at the highest level we can break the inventory problem into the following subtasks (see Figure 3–11):

I. Restore the current inventory from an external file.

II. Execute user commands to ask about or modify the inventory.

III. Save the current inventory in an external file.

Figure 3–11

*Division of
the problem
into
subproblems.*

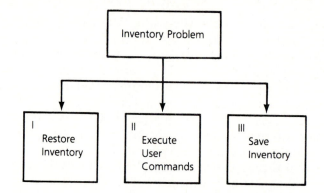

Before we proceed with the refinement of the three subproblems, we consider the choice of a data structure. In Part III of this text, we demonstrate that the choice of a data structure should be based on the operations that are expected to be performed on the data. We see that since the data structure is an integral part of all phases of the solution process, it should be refined in a top-down fashion along with the algorithm. At this time, however, the emphasis is on using the data structures rather than on developing and choosing between them.

The problem description suggests some common operations that will be performed on the inventory:

1. List the inventory in alphabetical order by title (L command).
2. Find the inventory item associated with a title (I, M, D, and S commands).
3. Insert new inventory items (A and D commands).

Recall that associated with each title there might be a list of people who are waiting for that title. We want to be able to add new people to the end of this list (when they want to buy a cassette that is sold out) and to delete people from the beginning of the list (when new cassettes are delivered).

In Part III of the book we discuss various data structures that support these kinds of operations in an efficient way. For now, we settle for a data structure that is both reasonable with respect to more advanced analysis and is consistent with the level of material that has so far been presented. In Chapter 10 we redo the solution so that it utilizes more sophisticated data structures.

We choose to represent the inventory as follows:

1. The inventory will be a linked list of data items, sorted by the title that each item represents.
2. Each item will contain a title, a have value (number in stock), a want value (number desired), and a pointer to the beginning of a linked list of people's names (the wait list).
3. Because we must be able to add new names to the end of an item's wait list, each item will also contain a pointer to the last name on its list. (Recall the

insert and delete operations for a linked list that we illustrated earlier in the chapter.)

These decisions can all be summarized by Figure 3–12 and the following Modula-2 type definitions.

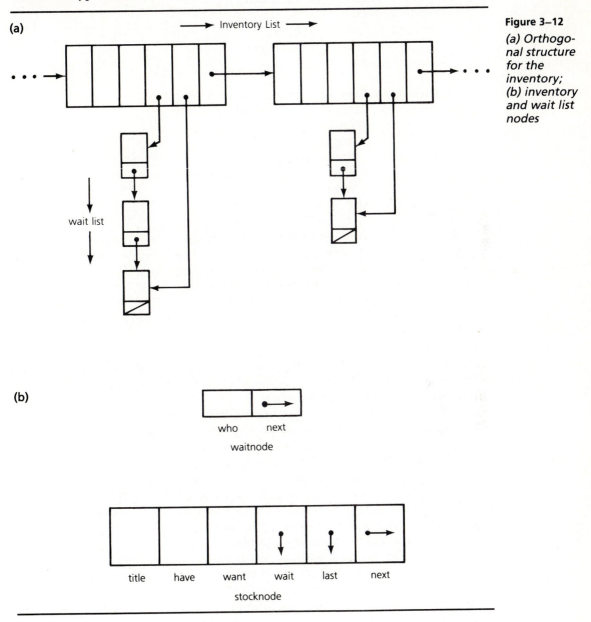

CONST

    maxstring = 15;

TYPE

```
(* titles and names *)
string = ARRAY [0..maxstring-1] OF CHAR;

(* wait list - people waiting for back orders *)
waitptr  = POINTER TO waitnode;
waitnode = RECORD
                who : string;
                next : waitptr;
           END;

(* inventory list - list of stock items *)
stockptr  = POINTER TO stocknode;
stocknode = RECORD
                title : string;
                have, want : INTEGER;
                wait, last : waitptr;
                next : stockptr;
            END;
```

Now, we need to consider how our data structures will interact with the rest of the program. In Chapter 1 we discussed reasons for avoiding global structures in general, but we did say that it might be appropriate to make a structure global if it is an integral part of all (or almost all) aspects of the program. If our inventory program is designed to operate on a single, fixed inventory, then it is reasonable to treat the inventory structure globally. However, if the program is designed to (or might later be modified to) manipulate more than one inventory (for example, if we want to look at saved histories of our inventory), then we want to have general subprograms that can be passed different inventory structures as arguments. We choose to take the second approach in anticipation of future modifications to our program.

With the data structure chosen, we continue with the design of solutions to Subproblems I, II, and III. We consider Subproblems I and III first. We choose to do these together because they are so closely associated—both dealing with communication between the internal data structure for processing the inventory and an external file for saving the inventory.

At the highest level, Subproblem I is to read the inventory from a file into our data structure. This means that for each inventory item, we must be able to read the title, have and want values, and the wait list. Similarly, Subproblem III requires us to write the inventory to a file.

Before we can proceed, we must consider how the inventory is going to be saved in a file. Because we can't save a linked list in a file (it doesn't make sense to read a record that has a pointer field in it), we have to save the inventory in such a way that we can reconstruct the inventory data structure as we read it in. Recall that this can be accomplished by saving just the data portion of the list items.

Up until this point, all of the input and output in the book has been limited to simple scalar and string types (for example, using the library module *InOut*). From the description of the inventory problem, however, it is apparent that a record-oriented file interface would be convenient. That is, we would like to be able to read and write as a single unit an entire record containing the data portion of an inventory list item.

Modula-2 supports a set of low-level operations for interfacing with files. These low-level operations easily can be used to build convenient user-level file interface subprograms such as those found in library module *InOut*. We have written a module, similar to *InOut*, that supports input and output for a file containing items of *any* single fixed type. This module allows several such files to be open simultaneously for reading or writing. We use this module, which we call *FileIO*, in our solution to the case study. The definition module for *FileIO* is found in the Appendix.

We utilize module *FileIO* in our solution by declaring two *FixedFiles* (the file type defined in *FileIO*): one to save inventory list items, the other to save the associated wait list items. Our use of two files is not a problem, but note that the original statement of the inventory problem must be modified to accommodate this change (it specifies "a file"). This change is not at all unreasonable given the spirit of the problem.

There is still one slight complication. In order to be able to restore the wait lists, we must know their lengths. In particular, since the names on all the wait lists are to be stored together in a single file, we must be able to determine where one list ends and the next begins.

To address this problem, recall that the have value of a stock item is the number of items currently in stock. It is reasonable to adopt the convention that a negative have value is the number of cassettes that we are short—the size of the wait list!

We can summarize this discussion with a slight modification to the above type definitions and the addition of the declarations for the two files:

```
(* external file operations *)
FROM FileIO IMPORT

    FixedFile;

CONST

    maxstring = 15;

TYPE

    (* titles and names *)
    string = ARRAY [0..maxstring-1] OF CHAR;

    (* wait list - people waiting for back orders *)
    waitptr  = POINTER TO waitnode;
    waitnode = RECORD
                    who : string;
                    next : waitptr;
               END;
```

```
                        (* data fields for a single stock item *)
                        stockinfo = RECORD
                                        title : string;
                                        want, have : INTEGER;
                                    END;


                        (* node on inventory list - includes
                           both data and pointer fields *)
                        stockptr  = POINTER TO stocknode;
                        stocknode = RECORD
                                        item : stockinfo;
                                        wait, last : waitptr;
                                        next : stockptr;
                                    END;

                VAR

                        (* file for saving inventory items *)
                        invfile : FixedFile;

                        (* file for saving names on the wait lists *)
                        waitfile : FixedFile;
```

Figure 3–13
*Modified
node
structure*

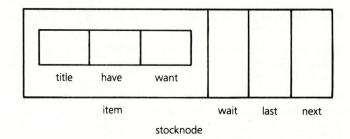

stocknode

The inventory record in Figure 3–13 has been redefined so that it contains a subrecord consisting of the title and the have and want values. This redefinition allows these items to be written to a file as a unit, thus addressing the above concern of saving and restoring a linked list.

With this data structure, we can attempt our first version of a solution to Subproblem I.

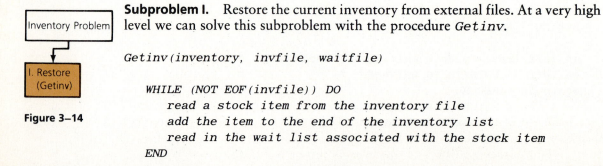

Figure 3–14

Subproblem I.   Restore the current inventory from external files. At a very high level we can solve this subproblem with the procedure *Getinv*.

Getinv(inventory, invfile, waitfile)

> *WHILE (NOT EOF(invfile)) DO*
>   *read a stock item from the inventory file*
>   *add the item to the end of the inventory list*
>   *read in the wait list associated with the stock item*
> *END*

As we have described, the addition of the first node to a linked list is a special case. We therefore refine the first attempt as follows:

```
Getinv(inventory, invfile, waitfile)

  IF (NOT EOF(invfile)) THEN

      (* get the first item for the inventory list *)
      read the first item from the inventory file
      add it as the first item on the inventory list
      Getwait(stock item, waitfile)   (Subproblem I.1)

      (* get the rest of the list *)
      WHILE (NOT EOF(invfile)) DO
         read the next item from the inventory file
         add it to the end of the inventory list
         Getwait(stock item, waitfile)
      END
  END
```

Subproblem I.1.   Read in the wait list for a stock item. This procedure uses the fact that wait list size can be determined by the have value of the stock item.

```
Getwait(stockitem, waitfile)

  IF (have value < 0) THEN
     size := negative of the have value
     FOR i := 1 TO size DO
        read a name from the wait file
        add the name to the end of the wait list
     END
  END
```

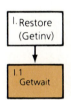

Figure 3–15

Subproblem III.   Save the current inventory in external files.

FIRST PASS

```
Putinv(inventory, invfile, waitfile)

  FOR (each item in the inventory) DO
     IF (the item is still part of the inventory) THEN
        save the item (and its wait list)
     END
  END
```

Figure 3–16

SECOND PASS

Recall that an item whose want value has been set to zero is removed from the inventory (by not saving it in the file) if its have value is zero and its wait list is empty. The following refinement implements this convention.

```
Putinv(inventory, invfile, waitfile)

    FOR (each item in the inventory) DO
        IF (the have value is not zero)
            OR  (the want value is not zero)
            OR  (the wait list is not empty) THEN

            (* write the wait list to waitfile *)
            Putwait(stock item, waitfile)   (Subproblem III.1)

            write out the stock item to the inventory file
        END
    END
```

Note that nodes are never actually deleted from the linked list of inventory items. Items are removed from the inventory simply by not writing them out to the file when the Q command is executed. Since this removal occurs just before the program terminates (and all memory is returned to the system), there is nothing gained by explicitly disposing of these nodes at this time.

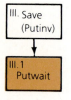

Figure 3–17

Subproblem III.1. Save the wait list for a stock item in an external file.

```
Putwait(stockitem, waitfile)

    trav := stockitem.wait
    WHILE (trav # NIL) DO
        write out the wait name to waitfile
        trav := trav^.next
    END
```

Note that we have assumed (for both saving and restoring the inventory) that the have value is a true indicator of the size of the wait list, which will be the case if all the program is working correctly. But what if something goes wrong? For example, if a later modification to the program causes a violation of this relationship, the inventory structure could become invalid or the program could abort in a very inelegant way—a way that would be very unsatisfactory to a user. For example, when restoring the inventory, we could attempt to read past the end of file if we expect some wait list to be longer than it is.

We should check that these values are in the correct relationship whenever we save or restore the inventory (recall the discussion of fail-safe programming in Chapter 1). We do not concern ourselves with this important detail now, however, but we view this as one of the refinements to the program to be made in Step 3 of the solution process.

With this portion of the problem out of the way, we can turn to the core of the inventory problem, Subproblem II. Many of the subproblems that we solve are very simple and have high-level solutions that are self-explanatory. We explain the solution only where it is necessary to support or clarify the refinements.

Subproblem II. Execute user commands to ask about or modify the inventory. We process user commands until the quit command is encountered. At a very high level, Subproblem II can be stated as follows.

FIRST PASS

main program

```
read the first command
WHILE (command is not a Q (for quit)) DO
    execute the appropriate command
    read the next command
END
```

SECOND PASS

main program

```
Getcmnd(command)    (Subproblem II.1)
WHILE (command # 'Q') DO
    CASE command OF
        'H' : Help                (Subproblem II.2)
      | 'I' : Inquire(inventory)  (Subproblem II.3)
      | 'L' : List(inventory)     (Subproblem II.4)
      | 'A' : Add(inventory)      (Subproblem II.5)
      | 'M' : Modify(inventory)   (Subproblem II.6)
      | 'D' : Delivery(inventory) (Subproblem II.7)
      | 'O' : Order(inventory)    (Subproblem II.8)
      | 'R' : Return(inventory)   (Subproblem II.9)
      | 'S' : Sell(inventory)     (Subproblem II.10)
    END
    Getcmnd(command)
END
```

As part of our final refinement of the user interface, we will want to test for undefined commands.

Subproblem II.1. Read the next command.

FIRST PASS

Getcmnd(command)

```
skip blanks in the input file
read the command
```

SECOND PASS

Getcmnd(command)

Figure 3–18

Figure 3–19

```
(* skip leading blanks and read command *)
read(command)
WHILE ((command = ' ') OR (command = EOL)) DO
   echo command
   read(command)
END
```

Figure 3–20

Subproblem II.2. Process command H. Summarize the available commands.

Help

  write out a summary of each command

Figure 3–21

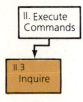

Subproblem II.3. Process command I. Print information on a specified title.

FIRST PASS

Inquire(inventory)

  read in a title argument
  find the title in the inventory
  write out the title, have, and want values
  write out the associated wait list

SECOND PASS

Inquire(inventory)

```
  (* get the title argument *)
  IReadString(title)

  (* find the title in the inventory *)
  loc := Find(inventory, title)   (Subproblem II.3.1)

  (* write out the information *)
  IF (loc # NIL) THEN
     WITH loc^.item DO
        Write(title)
        Write(have)
        Write(want)
     END
     Waitnames(loc^.wait)   (Subproblem II.3.2)
  END
```

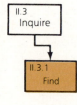

Figure 3–22

Subproblem II.3.1. Find a title in the inventory. Return **NIL** if the title is not found. Observe that this is very similar to the search portions of the *Insert* and *Delete* procedures discussed earlier in the chapter.

Find(inventory, title) : returns a pointer to a stock item

```
(* locate the title *)
cur := inventory
WHILE ((cur # NIL) AND (title > cur^.item.title)) DO
    cur := cur^.next
END


(* set the function value *)
IF ((cur # NIL) AND (title = cur^.item.title)) THEN
    RETURN (cur)
ELSE
    RETURN (NIL)
END
```

Subproblem II.3.2. Write out the names on the specified wait list.

```
Waitnames(ptr)

    WHILE (ptr # NIL) DO
        write out the name pointed to by ptr
        ptr := ptr^.next
    END
```

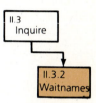

Figure 3–23

Subproblem II.4. Process command L. List the current inventory.

FIRST PASS

```
List(inventory)

    FOR (each item in the inventory) DO
        write out the title, have, and want values
        write out the associated wait list
    END
```

Figure 3–24

SECOND PASS

```
List(inventory)

    trav := inventory
    WHILE (trav # NIL) DO
        WITH trav^.item DO
            Write(title)
            Write(have)
            Write(want)
        END
        Waitnames(trav^.wait)
        trav := trav^.next
    END
```

Figure 3–25

Subproblem II.5. Process command A. Add a new title to the inventory. The A command is intended to be used to add a new title to the inventory. We define it to mean that a new title is added if the title does not already exist. If the title does already exist, then we prompt the user to modify the existing want value.

FIRST PASS

```
Add(inventory)

    read in a title argument
    insert the new title in the inventory (if it's not already there)
    read the want value
```

SECOND PASS

```
Add(inventory)

    (* get the title argument *)
    IReadString(title)

    (* insert a new stock item if necessary
       - return loc pointing to the item *)
    Insert(inventory, title, loc)   (Subproblem II.5.1)

    (* update the want value for the stock item *)
    read the want value
```

Subproblem II.5.1. Insert a new item in the inventory if it is not already present. Return a pointer to the item.

FIRST PASS

```
Insert(inventory, title, loc)

    locate where the title should go
    insert it if it's not already there
    return a pointer to the item
```

SECOND PASS

```
Insert(inventory, title, loc)

    (* locate where the title should go *)
    prev := NIL
    cur := inventory
    WHILE ((cur # NIL) AND (title > cur^.item.title)) DO
        prev := cur
        cur := cur^.next
    END
```

Figure 3–26

```
(* insert it if necessary *)
IF ((cur = NIL) OR (title # cur^.item.title)) THEN
    insert the new node between prev and cur
END

return loc pointing to the new node
```

Subproblem II.6. Process command M. Modify the want value for a specified title. The M command is to be used to modify the want value of an existing title. We define it to include the addition of a new title if it does not already exist. Note that *Add* and *Modify* are identical and can be combined into one routine, *AddModify*.

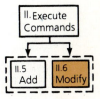

Figure 3–27

Subproblem II.7. Process command D. Take delivery of a shipment. The D command specifies that shipment information for a delivery will be in an external file. The routines in library module *InOut* will be sufficient to support this operation.

FIRST PASS

Delivery(inventory)

Figure 3–28

```
    open the delivery file
    WHILE (NOT at the end of the delivery file) DO
        read the delivery information (counts and titles)
        locate the title (insert it if it's not already there)
        update the have value for the title
        hold cassettes for people on the wait lists
    END
```

SECOND PASS

Delivery(inventory)

```
    open the delivery file
    WHILE (NOT at the end of the delivery file) DO
        (* read the count and title *)
        ReadInt(count)
        ReadString(title)

        (* update the have value in the inventory
           - create a new item if necessary *)
        Insert(inventory, title, loc)
        update the have value
```

```
(* process back orders if necessary *)
WHILE ((wait list is not empty) AND (count > 0)) DO
    hold one cassette for the first person on the wait list
    delete the first person from the wait list
    DEC(count)
END
```
END

Subproblem II.8. Process command O. Write a purchase order.

Order(inventory)

```
FOR (each item in the inventory) DO
    IF (have value < want value) THEN
        write a purchase order
    END
END
```

Figure 3—29

Subproblem II.9. Process command R. Write a return order.

Return(inventory)

```
FOR (each item in the inventory) DO
    IF (have value < want value) THEN
        write a return order
        decrease the have value accordingly
    END
END
```

Figure 3—30

Subproblem II.10. Process command S. Sell a cassette.

FIRST PASS

Sell(inventory)

```
read in a title argument
find the title in the inventory
IF (the title is not in the inventory) THEN
    write a message
ELSIF (the have value > 0) THEN
    decrease the have value by 1
ELSE
    read in a name for the wait list
END
```

Figure 3—31

```
Sell (inventory)

    (* get the title argument *)
    IReadString(title)

    (* find the title in the inventory *)
    loc := Find(inventory, title)

    (* decrease the have value by 1 if possible *)
    IF (loc = NIL) THEN
        write message
    ELSIF (have value > 0) THEN
        DEC(have value)
    ELSE
        (* get a name for the wait list *)
        IReadString(name)
        add the name to the end of the wait list
    END
```

We have now completed a top-down design of a solution to the inventory problem. This design is summarized by Figure 3–32.

Before we can implement our solution with a Modula-2 program, we must consider how to partition the data structures and subprograms into program modules. Later in the book (in the context of data abstraction) we'll see how the partition of a solution into program modules becomes an integral part of the solution process. For now, with the solution already laid out before us, the partition into program modules is fairly straightforward. We choose to have four program modules as follows:

Inventory

The main program module.

InvDataStruct

Type definitions for the primary inventory data structures together with the support operations for the data structures: *Find* and *Insert*.

InvProcs

The subprograms that execute the inventory commands: *Help*, *Inquire*, *List*, *AddModify*, *Delivery*, *Order*, *Return*, and *Sell*.

InvIO

The input and output procedures for the entire program: *Getinv*, *Putinv*, *Getwait*, *Putwait*, *Waitnames*, and *Getcmnd*.

The place at which the design of a solution ends and its implementation with a program begins is not at all clear. We could easily justify refining the solution further before turning to the coding. The intention of this discussion, however, is not to walk you through every detail of this particular problem but rather to give you a good feeling for the spirit of the solution process. With this in mind,

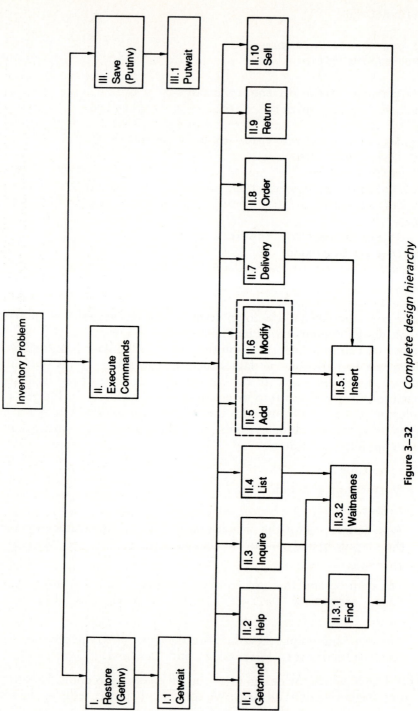

Figure 3–32   *Complete design hierarchy*

we turn to the second stage of the solution process, the implementation of the solution with a program.

Bottom-Up Implementation of the Solution with a Program

This stage of the process is intended to take our solution and produce a working Modula-2 program. Although there is a lot of coding detail in this step, we emphasize the organization rather than the details of the implementation process; that is, we demonstrate how to build a program systematically from the bottom up, adding a few new routines at a time until the program is complete.

We shall summarize here the major steps that we took to get from the pseudocode solution to a complete working program. Again, the emphasis of this discussion will be on the order that things were done rather than on the programming details.

The development of this program occurred in two main phases. In the first phase we essentially chose to ignore the wait lists by treating calls to the wait list operations (procedures *Getwait*, *Putwait*, and *Waitnames*) as stubs. Recall that stubs are placeholder procedures that simply report that they have been called. We chose this approach because the wait list operations are peripheral to the main focus of the problem. The second phase of the implementation consisted of replacing the stubs with the implementations of the corresponding modules. Within each phase, we added a few routines at a time, got them to work, and then added more routines.

Phase 1: Omit the wait list operations.   We have broken the discussion into the following five steps:

1. One of the most useful and important procedures that we can write is often not part of the solution at all. During the development of a large program, it is useful to have a special debugging procedure that writes out the status of our primary data structures and program variables. Having this as a separate procedure allows us easily to add diagnostics to or remove them from any place in the code during the remainder of the program development.

   In this particular program, the debugging routine also happens to be one of the routines for our program, procedure *List*. Procedure *List* was therefore one of our highest priorities. Note, however, that *List* cannot be tested unless some data has been put into the data structure. Our first coding task was to define and implement some minimal subset of the solution that would put something into the data structure and allow us to test *List*. This can be accomplished with the following procedures:

Getcmnd (Subproblem II.1)	Read in a command.
AddModify (II.5 and II.6)	Insert new items into the inventory.
Insert (II.5.1)	Insert a new node into the data structure (needed for *AddModify*).

2. After the procedures in Step 1 were working to our satisfaction, we turned our attention to adding a new set of routines to expand the scope of the program. We chose from among many possibilities and decided to write the routines for saving and restoring the inventory. One reason for this decision is that it allowed us to continue the development of the program over a series of runs without having to create a new inventory from scratch each time.

Getinv (I)	Restore the inventory from a file.
Putinv (III)	Save the inventory in a file.

We did not code the procedures *Putwait* and *Getwait* (for saving and restoring the wait lists) until Phase 2 of the program development.

3. At this point, our program was starting to look like a solution to the original problem. We chose to add the following routines next, primarily because they were easy to write.

Help (II.2)	Write out a summary of the commands.
Order (II.8)	Write a purchase order.
Return (II.9)	Write a return order.

4. The choices here were fairly arbitrary. We focused on the addition of procedure *Inquire*.

Inquire (II.3)	Write information on a specified title.
Find (II.3.1)	Locate a title in the inventory (needed for *Inquire*).

5. Finally, we added the last two procedures:

Delivery (II.7)	Process a delivery.
Sell (II.10)	Sell a cassette.

Phase 2: Implement the wait list operations.   At this point we had a working program that supported all the inventory commands but did not account for the wait lists. It was fairly easy to add the remaining subprograms:

Getwait (I.1)	Read in (from a file) the wait list for a stock item.
Putwait (III.1)	Write out (to a file) the wait list for a stock item.
Waitnames (II.3.2)	Write out the wait list for a stock item.

Final Set of Refinements to the Program

At the end of Step 2 (bottom-up implementation of the solution), we had a complete working solution to the original problem. The last step of the solution process was to refine the program into the "nice" program that appears at the end of this section. This included, for example, the following refinement: We added internal checks to the program to test for program errors. Given the nature of our program, it is reasonable to assume that other people might be modifying it in the future. These modifications might violate some of our assumptions about our data and data structures, and we would like to have the program help us avoid any serious consequences. This is in the spirit of the discussion on fail-safe programming in Chapter 1.

For example, consider the operations that restore and save the inventory. The correctness of the inventory program depends heavily on the integrity of these operations, and these operations in turn depend on the *have* value for each inventory item being a true indicator of the size of the associated *wait* list. If the program were to be modified in such a way that caused a violation of this relationship, the results could be severe—the entire inventory structure could lose its validity. One type of enhancement to this program was to include checks of this relationship in the places where the inventory structure could be ruined. We chose to build this extra testing into our procedures *Getinv* and *Putinv*, the procedures that restore and save the inventory structure.

The code should serve to illustrate many of these points. Before presenting the complete program, we wish to make one final comment. One of the reasons that we like this inventory problem is because there is so much room for growth. The exercises at the end of the chapter suggest modifications and enhancements. We hope that the ease of changing and adding to our program will help to convince you of the value and effectiveness of top-down design and modularity.

```
MODULE Inventory;
(*

    INTERACTIVE INVENTORY PROGRAM

    This program manages the inventory for a video-cassette
    dealer.  The basic organization is:

        1.   Read in the current inventory from a file.
        2.   Process commands for the day's activities.
        3.   Write out the current inventory to a file.

    The idea is that this is a program for an ongoing activity.
    By saving the inventory in a file, the program can be
    terminated (e.g., at the end of the day or to run other
    programs) without losing the data for the current inventory.

    INPUT

        Commands are single characters.  The user will be prompted
        for necessary arguments.

        The following commands are currently implemented (see the
        specified subprograms for details):

            Information Commands:

                H - summarize the available commands (Help)
                I - print data for a specified title (Inquire)
                L - list the current inventory (List)
```

Action Commands:

A - add a new title to the inventory (AddModify)
M - modify data for a specified title (AddModify)
D - take delivery of a shipment (Delivery)
O - write a purchase order (Order)
R - write a return order (Return)
S - sell one copy of a specified title (Sell)

Command "Q" saves the inventory and exits.

OUTPUT - as specified by the commands

DATA STRUCTURES

The data structures are defined and maintained in module InvDataStruct.

FILES

terminal - interactive input and output for inventory commands

invfile - save the inventory between program runs

waitfile - save the associated wait lists

In addition, the D (delivery) command reads delivery information from a file. The file name is supplied interactively.

ASSUMPTIONS

If a delivery is processed (D command), an external file name will be provided, and this file is complete and in the proper format.

FUTURE DEVELOPMENT

This is only the first crack at such a program. Suggestions for its enhancement will be made in the exercises. Such enhancements might include:

1. more flexible and sophisticated input of commands
2. more flexible use of external file names
3. keeping some statistics on sales
4. more commands
    ... etc.

*)

```
(* low-level system utilities *)
FROM SYSTEM IMPORT

    TSIZE;

(* inventory data structures *)
FROM InvDataStruct IMPORT

    string, stockptr, stockinfo;

(* save and restore the inventory *)
FROM InvIO IMPORT

    Getcmnd, Getinv, Putinv;

(* process the inventory commands *)
FROM InvProcs IMPORT

    Help, Inquire, List, AddModify, Delivery, Order, Return,
    Sell;

(* standard I/O *)
FROM InOut IMPORT

    Write, WriteString, WriteLn;

(* external file operations *)
FROM FileIO IMPORT

    CreateFile, FixedFile;

VAR

    (* file for saving inventory items *)
    invfile : FixedFile;

    (* file for saving names on the wait lists *)
    waitfile : FixedFile;

    (* inventory structure *)
    inventory : stockptr;

    cmnd : CHAR;

BEGIN   (* MAIN PROGRAM *)

    (* define the inventory files *)
    CreateFile(invfile,'invfile',TSIZE(stockinfo));
    CreateFile(waitfile,'waitfile',TSIZE(string));
```

```
(* initialize with the previous saved inventory *)
inventory := NIL;
WriteString('Restoring inventory ...');
WriteLn;
Getinv(inventory, invfile, waitfile);
WriteString('... inventory restored.');
WriteLn;

(* get the initial command *)
Getcmnd(cmnd);

(* process all commands *)
WHILE (cmnd # 'Q') DO

    (* process the current command *)
    CASE cmnd OF
        'H' : Help;                          (* help              *)
      | 'I' : Inquire(inventory);            (* print title data  *)
      | 'L' : List(inventory);               (* list inventory    *)

      | 'A',                                 (* add title         *)
        'M' : AddModify(inventory);          (* modify title      *)
      | 'D' : Delivery(inventory);           (* take delivery     *)
      | 'O' : Order(inventory);              (* write order       *)
      | 'R' : Return(inventory);             (* write return      *)
      | 'S' : Sell(inventory)                (* sell title        *)
    ELSE
        Write(cmnd);
        WriteString(' is not a recognized command.');
        WriteLn;
    END;

    (* get the next command *)
    Getcmnd(cmnd);

END;

(* save the current inventory *)
WriteLn;
WriteString('Saving inventory ...');
WriteLn;
Putinv(inventory, invfile, waitfile);
WriteString('... inventory saved.');
WriteLn;

WriteLn;
WriteString('Goodbye.');
WriteLn;
```

```
END Inventory.

DEFINITION MODULE InvDataStruct;
(*
    INVENTORY DATA STRUCTURES

    The inventory is kept as a linked list of stock items,
    sorted by title.

    Each stock item has a sublist of names of people waiting
    for the item if it is sold out (called the wait list).

    Each stock item contains the fields:

        item  - subrecord of data values
        wait  - pointer to the beginning of the wait list
        last  - pointer to the end of the wait list

    Item is a subrecord of data for the stock item.  It
    contains the fields:

        title - title of the video cassette
        have  - the number of cassettes currently in stock
        want  - the desired number to be kept in stock

    WARNING:  Program logic depends on the following assumption:

        A negative have value for a title indicates a backlog of
        orders.  In such cases the size of the corresponding wait
        list is given by the absolute value of the have value.
*)

(* external file operations *)
FROM FileIO IMPORT

    FixedFile;

EXPORT QUALIFIED

    maxstring, prompts, string, waitptr, waitnode, stockinfo,
    stockptr, stocknode, Find, Insert;

CONST

    maxstring = 15;

TYPE
```

```
(* prompt types *)
prompts = (titleprompt, nameprompt);

(* titles and names *)
string = ARRAY [0..maxstring-1] OF CHAR;

(* wait lists for back orders *)
waitptr  = POINTER TO waitnode;
waitnode = RECORD
                who : string;
                next : waitptr;
             END;

(* a single stock item *)
stockinfo = RECORD
                title : string;
                have  : INTEGER;
                want  : CARDINAL;
              END;

(* list of stock items *)
stockptr  = POINTER TO stocknode;
stocknode = RECORD
                item : stockinfo;
                wait, last : waitptr;
                next : stockptr;
              END;


(* -------------------------------------------------------
   Find:  Return a pointer to the item in inventory that
   contains title.  Return NIL if title is not present.
   ------------------------------------------------------- *)
PROCEDURE Find(inventory : stockptr;
               title : string) : stockptr;


(* -------------------------------------------------------
   Insert:  Insert title in inventory if it is not already
   present.

   On return, loc will point to the inventory item.
   ------------------------------------------------------- *)
PROCEDURE Insert(VAR inventory : stockptr; title : string;
                 VAR loc : stockptr);



END InvDataStruct.
```

```
IMPLEMENTATION MODULE InvDataStruct;
(*
    INVENTORY DATA STRUCTURES
*)


(* string comparison *)
FROM Strings IMPORT

    CompareStr;

(* memory management procedure NEW *)
FROM Storage IMPORT

    ALLOCATE;



(* -------------------------------------------------------
    Find:   Return a pointer to the item in inventory that
    contains title.   Return NIL if title is not present.
    ----------------------------------------------------- *)
PROCEDURE Find(inventory : stockptr;
               title : string) : stockptr;

VAR

    cur : stockptr;

BEGIN

    (* locate the title *)
    cur := inventory;
    WHILE ((cur # NIL) AND
           (CompareStr(title, cur^.item.title) > 0)) DO
        cur := cur^.next;
    END;

    (* set the function value *)
    IF ((cur # NIL) AND
        (CompareStr(cur^.item.title, title) = 0)) THEN
        RETURN (cur);
    ELSE
        RETURN (NIL);
    END;

END Find;
```

```
(* ------------------------------------------------------------
   Insert:   Insert title in inventory if it is not already
   present.

   On return, loc will point to the inventory item.
   ------------------------------------------------------------ *)
PROCEDURE Insert(VAR inventory : stockptr; title : string;
                 VAR loc : stockptr);

VAR

    cur, prev : stockptr;

BEGIN

    (* locate where the title should go *)
    prev := NIL;
    cur := inventory;
    WHILE ((cur # NIL) AND
           (CompareStr(title, cur^.item.title) > 0)) DO
       prev := cur;
       cur := cur^.next;
    END;

    (* insert a new stock item if not already present *)
    IF ((cur = NIL) OR
        (CompareStr(title, cur^.item.title) # 0)) THEN

       (* create a node *)
       NEW(loc);
       loc^.wait := NIL;
       loc^.last := NIL;
       loc^.item.title := title;
       loc^.item.have := 0;
       loc^.item.want := 0;

       (* insert the node *)
       IF (prev = NIL) THEN
          loc^.next := inventory;
          inventory := loc;
       ELSE
          loc^.next := cur;
          prev^.next := loc;
       END;

    (* stock item is already present *)
    ELSE
       loc := cur;
```

```
        END;

END Insert;


END InvDataStruct.

DEFINITION MODULE InvProcs;
(*
    INVENTORY COMMANDS
*)

(* inventory data structures *)
FROM InvDataStruct IMPORT

    stockptr;

EXPORT QUALIFIED

    Help, Inquire, List, AddModify, Delivery, Order, Return,
    Sell;


(* ------------------------------------------------------------
    Help:  List out a summary of the valid commands.
   ------------------------------------------------------------ *)
PROCEDURE Help;

(* ------------------------------------------------------------
    Inquire:  Print out inventory data for a specified title.
   ------------------------------------------------------------ *)
PROCEDURE Inquire(inventory : stockptr);

(* ------------------------------------------------------------
    List:  List the entire inventory.
   ------------------------------------------------------------ *)
PROCEDURE List(inventory : stockptr);

(* ------------------------------------------------------------
    AddModify:  Add a new title to the inventory, or modify
    the want value for a title that already exists in the
    inventory.
   ------------------------------------------------------------ *)
PROCEDURE AddModify(VAR inventory : stockptr);

(* ------------------------------------------------------------
    Delivery:  Process a delivery.  The delivery information
    consists of counts and titles.  The user is prompted
    for the name of the delivery file.
```

```
              ASSUMPTION:  The delivery file is complete and correct.
              ----------------------------------------------------------- *)
   PROCEDURE Delivery(VAR inventory : stockptr);


     (* -----------------------------------------------------------
        Order:  Automatically generate a purchase order by comparing
        the have and want values of each title in the inventory.
        The object is to bring the have value up to the want value.
        ----------------------------------------------------------- *)
   PROCEDURE Order(inventory : stockptr);


     (* -----------------------------------------------------------
        Return:  Automatically generate a return order by comparing
        the have and want values of each title in the inventory.
        The object is to get the have value down to the want value.
        ----------------------------------------------------------- *)
   PROCEDURE Return(inventory : stockptr);


     (* -----------------------------------------------------------
        Sell:  Sell one copy of a specified title.  If the title
        is currently sold out.  Get a name for the wait list
        corresponding to the title.
        ----------------------------------------------------------- *)
   PROCEDURE Sell(inventory : stockptr);


   END InvProcs;

   IMPLEMENTATION MODULE InvProcs;
   (*
       INVENTORY COMMANDS
   *)

   (* inventory data structures *)
   FROM InvDataStruct IMPORT

       prompts, string, waitptr, waitnode, stockinfo, stockptr,
       stocknode, Find, Insert;

   (* inventory I/O utilities *)
   FROM InvIO IMPORT

       Prompt, Waitnames;

   (* string I/O *)
   FROM StringIO IMPORT

       ReadString, IReadString;
```

```
(* memory management procedures NEW and DISPOSE *)
FROM Storage IMPORT

    ALLOCATE, DEALLOCATE;

(* standard I/O *)
FROM InOut IMPORT

    OpenInput, CloseInput, Done, ReadInt, Write, WriteString,
    WriteInt, WriteLn;



(* -----------------------------------------------------------
    Help:  List out a summary of the valid commands.
    ----------------------------------------------------------- *)
PROCEDURE Help;
BEGIN

    WriteLn;
    WriteString('-----------------------------------------------');
    WriteLn;
    WriteString('Information Commands:                          ');
    WriteLn;
    WriteString('   H            - summarize the available commands');
    WriteLn;
    WriteString('   I <title> - print information on a title     ');
    WriteLn;
    WriteString('   L            - list the current inventory     ');
    WriteLn;
    WriteLn;
    WriteString('Action Commands:                              ');
    WriteLn;
    WriteString('   A <title> - add a new title to the inventory');
    WriteLn;
    WriteString('   M <title> - modify data for a title          ');
    WriteLn;
    WriteString('   D            - take delivery of a shipment    .');
    WriteLn;
    WriteString('   O            - write a purchase order         ');
    WriteLn;
    WriteString('   R            - write a return order           ');
    WriteLn;
    WriteString('   S <title> - sell one copy of a title          ');
    WriteLn;
    WriteLn;
    WriteString('Command Q saves the inventory and exits.       ');
    WriteLn;
    WriteString('-----------------------------------------------');
    WriteLn;
```

```
END Help;

(* -----------------------------------------------------------
    Inquire:   Print out inventory data for a specified title.

    Calls:  Prompt, Find, Waitnames
    ----------------------------------------------------------- *)
PROCEDURE Inquire(inventory : stockptr);

VAR

    title : string;
    loc : stockptr;

BEGIN

    (* get the title argument *)
    Prompt(titleprompt);
    IReadString(title);

    (* find the title in the inventory *)
    loc := Find(inventory, title);

    (* write out the information *)
    IF (loc = NIL) THEN
        WriteString('   *** Title is not in current inventory: ');
        WriteString(title);
        WriteLn;
    ELSE
        WriteString('     Title       ');
        WriteString('   Have in Stock');
        WriteString('   Want in Stock');
        WriteLn;

        WriteString('----------------');
        WriteString('   -------------');
        WriteString('   ------------');
        WriteLn;

        WITH loc^.item DO
            WriteString(title);
            WriteString('          ');
            WriteInt(have, 3);
            WriteString('             ');
            WriteInt(want, 3);
            WriteLn;
        END;
        Waitnames(loc^.wait);
    END;
```

END Inquire;

```
(* -----------------------------------------------------------
   List:   List the entire inventory.

   Calls:  Waitnames
   -------------------------------------------------------- *)
PROCEDURE List(inventory : stockptr);

VAR

   trav : stockptr;

BEGIN

   WriteLn;
   WriteString('-----------------');
   WriteLn;
   WriteString('CURRENT INVENTORY');
   WriteLn;
   WriteString('-----------------');
   WriteLn;
   WriteLn;

   WriteString('      Title        ');
   WriteString('   Have in Stock');
   WriteString('   Want in Stock');
   WriteLn;

   WriteString('----------------');
   WriteString('   ------------');
   WriteString('   ------------');
   WriteLn;

   (* traverse the entire inventory *)
   trav := inventory;
   WHILE (trav # NIL) DO
      WITH trav^.item DO
         WriteString(title);
         WriteString('         ');
         WriteInt(have,3);
         WriteString('            ');
         WriteInt(want,3);
         WriteLn;
      END;
      Waitnames(trav^.wait);
      trav := trav^.next;
   END;
```

```
                        END List;

    (* ------------------------------------------------------------
        AddModify:   Add a new title to the inventory, or modify
        the want value for a title that already exists in the
        inventory.

        Calls:  Prompt, Insert
        ------------------------------------------------------------ *)
    PROCEDURE AddModify(VAR inventory : stockptr);

    VAR

        loc : stockptr;
        wantval : INTEGER;
        newtitle : string;

    BEGIN

        (* get the title argument *)
        Prompt(titleprompt);
        IReadString(newtitle);

        (* insert a new stock item if necessary *)
        Insert(inventory, newtitle, loc);

        (* update the want value for the stock item *)
        WriteString('Title: ');
        WriteString(newtitle);
        WriteLn;

        WriteLn;
        WriteString('The current want value is ');
        WriteInt(loc^.item.want, 1);
        WriteString('.  Enter the correct value: ');

        ReadInt(wantval);
        IF (wantval < 0) THEN
            WriteString('*** Negative want value is not allowed.');
            WriteString('*** The want value will be set to 0.');
            loc^.item.want := 0;
        ELSE
            loc^.item.want := wantval;
        END;

    END AddModify;
```

```
(* --------------------------------------------------------------
    Delivery:   Process a delivery.   The delivery information
    consists of counts and titles.   The user is prompted
    for the name of the delivery file.

    ASSUMPTION:   The delivery file is complete and correct.

    Calls:   Insert
    ------------------------------------------------------- *)
PROCEDURE Delivery(VAR inventory : stockptr);

VAR

    loc : stockptr;
    ptr : waitptr;
    newtitle : string;
    count : INTEGER;

BEGIN

    WriteString('Processing a delivery ...');
    WriteLn;

    WriteLn;
    WriteString('Enter the name of the delivery file: ');
    OpenInput('');

    (* process the delivery *)
    ReadInt(count);
    WHILE (Done) DO

        (* read the count and title *)
        ReadString(newtitle);

        WriteString('   Accepting ');
        WriteInt(count,1);
        WriteString(' copies of title: ');
        WriteString(newtitle);
        WriteLn;

        (* update the have value in the inventory
            - create a new item if necessary *)
        Insert(inventory, newtitle, loc);
        loc^.item.have := loc^.item.have + count;

        (* process back orders if necessary *)
```

```
                WHILE  ((loc^.wait # NIL)  AND  (count > 0))  DO
                    ptr := loc^.wait;
                    WriteString('        ---> Hold one copy for ');
                    WriteString(ptr^.who);
                    WriteLn;
                    DEC(count);
                    loc^.wait := ptr^.next;
                    DISPOSE(ptr);
                END;

                IF (loc^.wait = NIL) THEN
                    loc^.last := NIL;
                END;

                ReadInt(count);

            END;  (* while Done *)

            CloseInput;

        END Delivery;

        (* ------------------------------------------------------------
            Order:  Automatically generate a purchase order by comparing
            the have and want values of each title in the inventory.
            The object is to bring the have value up to the want value.
            ------------------------------------------------------- *)
        PROCEDURE Order(inventory : stockptr);

        VAR

            trav : stockptr;
            size : INTEGER;

        BEGIN

            WriteLn;
            WriteString('--------------');
            WriteLn;
            WriteString('PURCHASE ORDER');
            WriteLn;
            WriteString('--------------');
            WriteLn;
            WriteLn;
            WriteString('     Title     ');
            WriteString('Number to Order');
            WriteLn;
            WriteString('--------------');
```

```
        WriteString('----------------');
        WriteLn;
        WriteLn;

      (* traverse the entire inventory *)
      trav := inventory;
      WHILE (trav # NIL) DO
          size := VAL(INTEGER, trav^.item.want) - trav^.item.have;
          IF (size > 0) THEN
              WriteString(trav^.item.title);
              WriteString('              ');
              WriteInt(size,3);
              WriteLn;
          END;
          trav := trav^.next;
      END;

END Order;

(* ------------------------------------------------------------
   Return:  Automatically generate a return order by comparing
   the have and want values of each title in the inventory.
   The object is to get the have value down to the want value.
   ------------------------------------------------------------ *)
PROCEDURE Return(inventory : stockptr);

VAR

    trav : stockptr;
    size : INTEGER;

BEGIN

    WriteLn;
    WriteString('------------');
    WriteLn;
    WriteString('RETURN ORDER');
    WriteLn;
    WriteString('------------');
    WriteLn;
    WriteLn;
    WriteString('     Title      ');
    WriteString('Number to Return');
    WriteLn;
    WriteString('----------------');
    WriteString('----------------');
    WriteLn;
    WriteLn;
```

```
        (* traverse the entire inventory *)
      trav := inventory;
      WHILE (trav # NIL) DO
          size := trav^.item.have - VAL(INTEGER, trav^.item.want);
          IF (size > 0) THEN
              WriteString(trav^.item.title);
              WriteString('           ');
              WriteInt(size,3);
              WriteLn;
              trav^.item.have := trav^.item.want;
          END;
          trav := trav^.next;
      END;

END Return;


(* -------------------------------------------------------------
    Sell:   Sell one copy of a specified title.  If the title
    is currently sold out.  Get a name for the wait list
    corresponding to the title.

    Calls:  Prompt, Find
    ------------------------------------------------------------- *)
PROCEDURE Sell(inventory : stockptr);

VAR

    title, who : string;
    ptr : waitptr;
    loc : stockptr;

BEGIN

    (* get the title argument *)
    Prompt(titleprompt);
    IReadString(title);

    (* find the title in the inventory *)
    loc := Find(inventory, title);

    (* decrease the have value by 1 if possible *)
    IF (loc = NIL) THEN
        WriteString('   *** Title is not in current inventory: ');
        WriteString(title);
        WriteLn;
    ELSE
        IF (loc^.item.have < 1) THEN
            WriteString('   *** Sorry, title is');
```

```
            WriteString(' out of stock: ');
            WriteString(title);
            WriteLn;

            (* get a name for the wait list *)
            Prompt(nameprompt);
            IReadString(who);

            (* add the name to end of the list *)
            NEW(ptr);
            ptr^.who := who;
            ptr^.next := NIL;
            IF (loc^.last = NIL) THEN
                loc^.wait := ptr;
            ELSE
                loc^.last^.next := ptr;
            END;
            loc^.last := ptr;

        END;

        DEC(loc^.item.have);
    END;

END Sell;


END InvProcs.

DEFINITION  MODULE InvIO;
(*
    INVENTORY INPUT AND OUTPUT UTILITIES
*)

(* inventory data structures *)
FROM InvDataStruct IMPORT

    string, prompts, waitptr, stockinfo, stockptr, stocknode;

(* external file operations *)
FROM FileIO IMPORT

    FixedFile;

EXPORT QUALIFIED

    Getwait, Getinv, Putwait, Putinv, Prompt, Getcmnd, Waitnames;
```

```
(* ------------------------------------------------------------
   Getwait:  Restore from waitfile the wait list for stockitem.
   ------------------------------------------------------------ *)
PROCEDURE Getwait(VAR stockitem : stocknode;
                  VAR waitfile : FixedFile);


(* ------------------------------------------------------------
   Getinv:  Restore inventory from external files.

   Read into the inventory structure from invfile.  Restore
   the corresponding wait lists from waitfile.
   ------------------------------------------------------------ *)
PROCEDURE Getinv(VAR inventory : stockptr;
                 VAR invfile : FixedFile;
                 VAR waitfile : FixedFile);


(* ------------------------------------------------------------
   Putwait:  Save in waitfile the wait list for stockitem.
   ------------------------------------------------------------ *)
PROCEDURE Putwait(VAR stockitem : stocknode;
                  VAR waitfile : FixedFile);


(* ------------------------------------------------------------
   Putinv:  Save inventory in external files.

   Write the current inventory list to invfile.  Write the
   associated wait lists to waitfile.  Items that have zero
   have and want values and empty wait lists are eliminated.
   ------------------------------------------------------------ *)
PROCEDURE Putinv(inventory : stockptr;
                 VAR invfile : FixedFile;
                 VAR waitfile : FixedFile);


(* ------------------------------------------------------------
   Prompt:  Prompt for interactive input.  Prompttype
   determines the appropriate prompt.
   ------------------------------------------------------------ *)
PROCEDURE Prompt(prompttype : prompts);


(* ------------------------------------------------------------
   Getcmnd:  Read in the next nonblank character as a command.
   ------------------------------------------------------------ *)
PROCEDURE Getcmnd(VAR command : CHAR);


(* ------------------------------------------------------------
   Waitnames:  Write out the names on the wait list specified
   by waitptr.
   ------------------------------------------------------------ *)
```

```
PROCEDURE Waitnames(ptr : waitptr);
```

```
END InvIO.

IMPLEMENTATION MODULE InvIO;
(*
    INVENTORY INPUT AND OUTPUT UTILITIES
*)

(* inventory data structures *)
FROM InvDataStruct IMPORT

    prompts, string, waitptr, waitnode, stockinfo, stockptr,
    stocknode;

(* memory management procedure NEW *)
FROM Storage IMPORT

    ALLOCATE;

(* standard I/O *)
FROM InOut IMPORT

    EOL, Read, Write, WriteString, WriteInt, WriteLn;

(* external file operations *)
FROM FileIO IMPORT

    CreateFile, CloseFile, FixedFile, OpenRead, OpenWrite,
    ReadItem, WriteItem, EOF;


(* ----------------------------------------------------------
    Getwait:  Restore from waitfile the wait list for stockitem.

    The size of the list is the negative of the have value of
    the inventory item.
    --------------------------------------------------------- *)
PROCEDURE Getwait(VAR stockitem : stocknode;
                  VAR waitfile : FixedFile);

VAR

    toread : INTEGER;
    tempfirst, templast : waitptr;

BEGIN
```

```
                    (* initialize the wait list *)
                    stockitem.wait := NIL;
                    stockitem.last := NIL;

                    (* size of list to read in *)
                    toread := -stockitem.item.have;

                    (*  read in the list of names and
                         attach it to the stock node *)
                    IF ((toread > 0) AND (NOT EOF(waitfile))) THEN
                       (* get the first item of the list *)
                       NEW(tempfirst);
                       templast := tempfirst;
                       ReadItem(waitfile, templast^.who);
                       DEC(toread);

                       (* get the rest of the list *)
                       WHILE ((toread > 0) AND (NOT EOF(waitfile))) DO
                          NEW(templast^.next);
                          templast := templast^.next;
                          ReadItem(waitfile, templast^.who);
                          DEC(toread);
                       END;

                       (* end the list *)
                       templast^.next := NIL;

                       (* attach the list to the stock item *)
                       stockitem.wait := tempfirst;
                       stockitem.last := templast;

                    END;

                    (* check for incomplete wait file *)
                    IF ((toread > 0) AND (EOF(waitfile))) THEN
                       WriteString('*** Error:  Incomplete wait file.');
                       WriteLn;
                       WriteString('*** Have value will be adjusted for title ');
                       WriteString(stockitem.item.title);
                       WriteLn;
                       stockitem.item.have := stockitem.item.have + toread;
                    END;

                 END Getwait;

                 (* ------------------------------------------------------------
                    Getinv:  Restore inventory from external files.
```

Read into the inventory structure from invfile. Restore
the corresponding wait lists from waitfile.

    Calls: Getwait
    --- *)
PROCEDURE Getinv(VAR inventory : stockptr;
                 VAR invfile : FixedFile;
                 VAR waitfile : FixedFile);

VAR

    tail : stockptr;

BEGIN

    OpenRead(invfile);
    OpenRead(waitfile);

    (* read in the list *)
    IF (NOT EOF(invfile)) THEN
        (* get the first item for the inventory list *)
        NEW(inventory);
        tail := inventory;
        ReadItem(invfile, tail^.item);
        Getwait(tail^, waitfile);

        (* get the rest of the list *)
        WHILE (NOT EOF(invfile)) DO
            NEW(tail^.next);
            tail := tail^.next;
            ReadItem(invfile, tail^.item);
            Getwait(tail^, waitfile);
        END;

        (* finish off the list *)
        tail^.next := NIL;

      (* invfile was empty *)
      ELSE
        inventory := NIL;

    END;

    CloseFile(invfile);
    CloseFile(waitfile);

END Getinv;

```
(* ------------------------------------------------------------
      Putwait:   Save in waitfile the wait list for stockitem.

      The size of the list is the negative of the have value of
      the inventory item.

      Note:   The size of the wait list is checked against the
      have value.   If they do not match, then a program error is
      indicated.   The have value is adjusted in order to allow
      the program to continue.
   ------------------------------------------------------------- *)
PROCEDURE Putwait(VAR stockitem : stocknode;
                  VAR waitfile : FixedFile);

VAR

    ptrav : waitptr;
    size : INTEGER;

BEGIN

    (* save the wait list for the item - count its size *)
    size := 0;
    ptrav := stockitem.wait;
    WHILE (ptrav # NIL) DO
       INC(size);
       WriteItem(waitfile, ptrav^.who);
       ptrav := ptrav^.next;
    END;

    (* check the have value against the size of the wait list *)
    IF ((size > 0) OR (stockitem.item.have < 0)) THEN
       IF (size # -stockitem.item.have) THEN
          WriteString('*** Program Error:  The size of the');
          WriteString(' wait list does not agree');
          WriteLn;
          WriteString('*** with the have value for title: ');
          WriteString(stockitem.item.title);
          WriteLn;
          WriteString('*** The have value will be reset.');
          WriteString('size/have before');
          WriteInt(size,5);
          WriteInt(stockitem.item.have,5);
          stockitem.item.have := -size;
          WriteString('size/have after');
          WriteInt(size,5);
          WriteInt(stockitem.item.have,5);
       END;
    END;
```

```
END Putwait;

(* ------------------------------------------------------------
    Putinv:   Save inventory in external files.

    Write the current inventory list to invfile.   Write the
    associated wait lists to waitfile.   Items that have zero
    have and want values and empty wait lists are eliminated.

    Calls:   Putwait
    ----------------------------------------------------------- *)
PROCEDURE Putinv(inventory : stockptr;
                 VAR invfile : FixedFile;
                 VAR waitfile : FixedFile);
VAR

    trav : stockptr;

BEGIN

    OpenWrite(invfile);
    OpenWrite(waitfile);

    (* traverse the inventory structure *)
    trav := inventory;
    WHILE (trav # NIL) DO

        (* eliminate items with zero have and
           want values and empty wait lists *)
        IF  ((trav^.item.have # 0) OR (trav^.item.want # 0)
                              OR (trav^.wait # NIL)) THEN
            (* write out the wait list *)
            Putwait(trav^, waitfile);

            (* write out the stock item *)
            WriteItem(invfile, trav^.item);
        END;
        trav := trav^.next;
    END;

    CloseFile(invfile);
    CloseFile(waitfile);

END Putinv;

(* ------------------------------------------------------------
    Prompt:  Prompt for interactive input.   Prompttype
    determines the appropriate prompt.
    ------------------------------------------------------------ *)
```

```
PROCEDURE Prompt(prompttype : prompts);
BEGIN

    WriteLn;
    CASE prompttype OF

        titleprompt:
            WriteString('Enter a title name: ');

    |   nameprompt:
            WriteString('Enter name for back order: ');

    END;

END Prompt;

(* -----------------------------------------------------------
    Getcmnd:   Read in the next nonblank character as a command.
    --------------------------------------------------------- *)
PROCEDURE Getcmnd(VAR command : CHAR);
BEGIN

    WriteLn;
    WriteString('Enter command.  (H for help)');
    WriteLn;

    Read(command);
    WHILE ((command = ' ') OR (command = EOL)) DO
        Write(command);
        Read(command);
    END;

    (* translate to upper case *)
    IF (('a' <= command) AND (command <= 'z')) THEN
        command := CAP(command);
    END;

END Getcmnd;

(* -----------------------------------------------------------
    Waitnames:   Write out the names on the wait list specified
    by waitptr.
    --------------------------------------------------------- *)
PROCEDURE Waitnames(ptr : waitptr);
BEGIN

    WHILE (ptr # NIL) DO
        WriteString('   ---> Back Ordered by: ');
```

```
      WriteString(ptr^.who);
      WriteLn;
      ptr := ptr^.next;
   END;

END Waitnames;


END InvIO.
```

SUMMARY

1. The linked list is a highly versatile data structure that we encounter through-out the book. Algorithms for inserting data into and deleting data from a sorted linked list consist of two steps: traverse the list from the beginning until the appropriate position is reached; perform pointer changes to alter the structure of the list.

2. Dummy head nodes provide a method for eliminating the special cases for insertion into and deletion from the beginning of a linked list. The use of dummy head nodes is a matter of personal taste.

3. The contents and structure of a linked list can easily be saved in a file by writing the data portion of the nodes in the order in which they appear on the list. This makes it easy to restore the linked list directly from the file at a later time.

4. The case study demonstrated how a methodical top-down approach can be used to solve a large problem. Several problem-solving principles were illustrated, including the following:

   a. We should split the problem into modules that are successively refined. For the most part we perform the refinements in isolation, although we should keep the overall picture in mind.

   b. After the design of the initial solution has been completed, we have a tree of modules. As we begin implementation of the modules with Modula-2 subprograms, we must decide which modules to code first. If the development of a module M depends on the actions of its submodules, then a reasonable approach is to start at the bottom of the tree and work up. On the other hand, if the modules that M uses are peripheral, they can be implemented initially with dummy procedures (called stubs) that simply report that they have been called. This allows us to focus on the more central aspects of the problem.

   c. Before we consider the programming task complete, we should carefully perform a final set of refinements. These include making the input modules as flexible as possible, adding fail-safe features, and polishing up the documentation.

COMMON PITFALLS / DEBUGGING

1. Insertions into and deletions from the beginning of a linked list must be handled as special cases (or, alternatively, dummy head nodes can be used). Failure to do this can result in referencing a pointer when its value is **NIL**.

2. When traversing a linked list with the pointer variable *cur*, care must be taken not to reference *cur* after it has "passed" the last node on the list and been assigned the value **NIL**. For example, the loop

```
WHILE (X > cur^.data) DO
    cur := cur^.next;
END;
```

results in an error if X is greater than all the values on the list. The problem is solved by modifying the loop termination condition to

```
WHILE ((cur # NIL) AND (X > cur^.data)) DO
    cur := cur^.next;
END;
```

Notice that this is sufficient because the second operand of the **AND** operator is not evaluated if *cur* = **NIL**.

EXERCISES

1. Complete the Modula-2 implementation of the procedure *Delete* described in the text.

Exercises 2–14 all refer to the following definitions:

```
TYPE

    nodeptr = POINTER TO node;
    node = RECORD
                data : INTEGER;
                next : nodeptr;
           END;
```

2. Write a procedure that will delete the ith node from a linked list.

3. Write a function

```
PROCEDURE Find(head : nodeptr; target : INTEGER) : nodeptr;
```

to return a pointer to the first record on the list pointed to by *head* that contains the value specified by *target*. If there is no such record on the list, *Find* should return NIL.

4. Write a procedure that will delete from a linked list the node with the largest data value. Can you do this with a single traversal of the list?

5. Write a procedure that will delete all of the nodes on a linked list and return them to memory.

6. Write a procedure that will copy a linked list to a new linked list.

7. Write a procedure that will merge two linked lists that are sorted by data value. The result should be a linked list that is the sorted combination of the original lists.

8. A list is **circular** if the last node on the list points to the first node on the list.

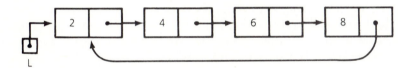

Figure 3–33
Circular list

Repeat Exercises 2–7 for a circular list.

9. Write a procedure that will determine if two circular lists are identical. The procedure is passed pointers indicating the "starting point" of each list.

   a. In the first version, you may assume that a data item will occur at most once on any list.

   b. In the second version, you must account for possible duplicates on a list.

10. Write a procedure *Linear* (VAR p : nodeptr) that is passed a pointer to some arbitrary node on a circular list. Your procedure should convert this circular list to a linear list that starts at the node containing the smallest integer on the list. On return, p should point to the head of the new list.

11. Write a procedure that will reverse the links of a circular linked list.

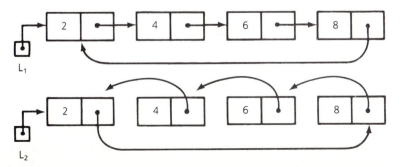

Figure 3–34
Two circular lists, one the reverse of the other

12. Write a program that will read a file of integers, insert each into a linked list so that the list is sorted by data value, and write out the final list. This **Insertion sort** is discussed in more detail in Chapter 13.

13. Write procedures for insertion into and deletion from a sorted linked list that has a dummy head node.

14. Describe a variant record type definition that will allow us to keep global information about a list in a dummy head node.

15. A character string can be implemented as a linked list of characters. Write subprograms for some typical string operations such as *concatenation* (append one string to another) and *length* computation. How can we implement the string so that the length can be obtained without traversing the list and counting?

PROJECTS

16. Write a complete string manipulation **package** (see Exercise 15), including more sophisticated string operations such as *index* (find the index of the leftmost occurrence of a character in a string) and *substring* (determine whether one string is a substring of another).

17. Modify and expand the inventory program. Here are a few suggestions:

    a. Add the ability to manipulate more than one inventory with the single program.

    b. Add the ability to keep various statistics about each of the inventory items (such as the average number sold per week for the last 10 weeks).

    c. Add the ability to modify the have value for an inventory item (for example, when a cassette is damaged or returned from a customer). Consider the implications for maintaining the relationship between a have value and the size of the corresponding wait list.

    d. Make the wait lists more sophisticated (for example, keep names and addresses and automatically mail letters when a cassette comes in).

    e. Make the ordering mechanism more sophisticated (for instance, don't order cassettes that have been ordered but not delivered).

PART II

RECURSION: THE MIRRORS

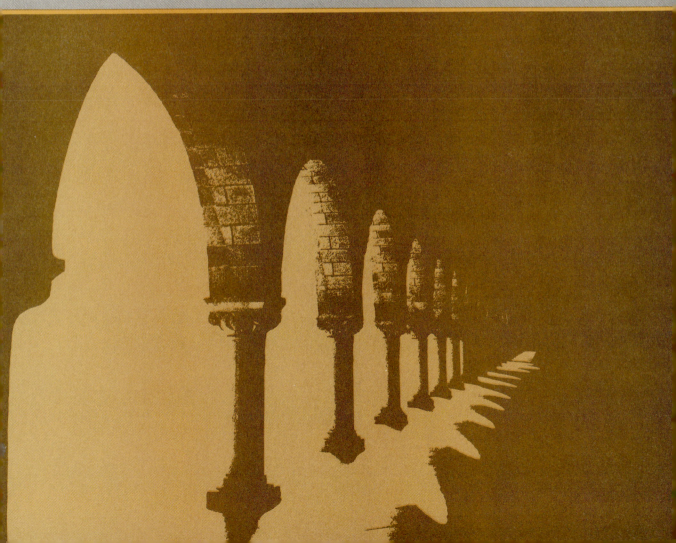

CHAPTER 4

INTRODUCTION TO RECURSION

PREVIEW The three chapters in Part I reinforced principles of program design and implementation. The primary concern of this and the following chapters is to develop a repertoire of problem-solving tools. The goal of this chapter is to help develop a basic understanding of recursion, one of the most powerful methods of solution available to the computer scientist. We study several relatively simple problems and follow the thought processes that lead to recursive solutions. In addition to studying recursion from a conceptual viewpoint, we discuss methods to help you to understand the mechanics of recursion. These methods are particularly useful for tracing and debugging recursive subprograms. We shall try to build an understanding of recursion by presenting several diverse examples. In this chapter and the next, we shall present examples of the following types of problems: computing things, counting things, searching for data, performing general tasks (for example, sorting data), defining things, and using mathematical induction to study properties of algorithms.

RECURSIVE SOLUTIONS

Recursive algorithms often provide elegantly simple solutions to problems of great complexity. Such solutions are, in general, very well structured and modular. In fact, the manner in which the modules of a recursive solution interact is precisely what makes recursion such a powerful and unique problem-solving tool.

Recursion will play a major role in many of the solutions that we construct throughout the remainder of the book. In this chapter and the next, we present several important applications of recursion, including recursive **search algorithms,** recursive **sorting algorithms,** and recursive **grammars** for defining the syntax of languages. Recursion will also be an integral part of many of the data structures studied in Parts III and IV of the book.

What exactly is recursion? It is a technique for performing a task T by performing another task T'. So far, this sounds like top-down design, where a large problem is solved by breaking it up into smaller problems. The difference is that, with recursion, the task T' is *exactly the same in nature* as the original task T. Thus, a recursive solution of task T might be described as:

Solution to T:

  solve task T', which is identical in nature to task T

It may seem strange that a task is solved by solving another task just like it. What have we gained? The crucial point is that, while T' is identical in nature to T, it is in some sense *smaller* than T.

We illustrate the elements of a recursive solution by considering the problem of looking up a word in a dictionary. A **binary search** of the dictionary can be formulated as follows:

```
Search the dictionary for a word:

   IF (the dictionary contains only one page) THEN

      scan the page for the word

   ELSE

      open the dictionary to a point near the middle

      determine which half of the dictionary contains the word

      IF (the word is in the first half of the dictionary) THEN
         search the first half of the dictionary for the word
      ELSE
         search the second half of the dictionary for the word
      END

   END
```

Parts of the solution are intentionally vague: How do we scan a single page? How do we find the middle of the dictionary? Once the middle is found, how do we determine which half contains the word? The answers to these questions are not difficult, but we do not obscure the solution strategy with these details at present.

Let us examine the strategy. We have accomplished the reduction of the problem of searching the dictionary for the word to a problem of searching half of the dictionary for the word.

Figure 4–1

Recursive solution

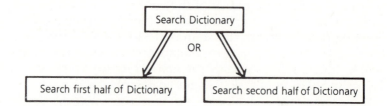

Notice two important points. First, once the dictionary is divided in half, it is already specified how the appropriate half will be searched. It will be searched using *exactly the same strategy* employed to search the original dictionary. Second, note that there is a *special case* that is handled differently than all the other cases; that is, once the dictionary has been divided so many times that it contains only a single page, the splitting ceases. At this point, the problem is sufficiently small that it can be solved directly by scanning the single page that remains. This special case is called the **degenerate case**.

We can view this strategy as one of **divide and conquer**—the problem of searching the dictionary is solved first by dividing the dictionary into two halves and then by conquering the appropriate half. The smaller problem is solved with the same divide-and-conquer strategy. The dividing continues until the degenerate case is reached. As we shall see, this strategy is inherent to many recursive solutions.

To further explore the nature of the solution to the dictionary problem, consider a slightly more rigorous formulation.

```
Search(dictionary, word)

    IF (dictionary is one page in size) THEN

        scan page for word

    ELSE

        open dictionary to a point near the middle

        determine which half of dictionary contains word

        IF (word is in the first half of dictionary) THEN
            Search( first half of dictionary, word )
        ELSE
            Search( second of half dictionary, word )
        END

    END
```

Writing the solution as a procedure allows us to make several important observations:

1. One of the actions of the procedure is to *call itself;* that is, the procedure *Search* is called from within the procedure *Search*. This action is what makes the solution recursive. The solution strategy is to split *dictionary* in half, determine which half contains *word*, and apply the same strategy to the appropriate half.

2. Each call to the procedure *Search* made from within the procedure *Search* passes a dictionary half the previous size; that is, at each successive call to *Search(dictionary, word)*, the size of *dictionary* is cut in half. The search problem is being solved by solving another search problem identical in nature *but smaller in size*.

3. There is one search problem that is handled differently than all of the others. When *dictionary* contains only a single page, it is solved by another method (here it is directly scanned). Searching a dictionary consisting of a single page is considered to be the degenerate case of the search problem. When the degenerate case is reached, the recursive calls stop, and the problem is solved directly. It is important to note that *the manner in which the problem size diminishes ensures that the degenerate case will eventually be reached*.

This is the general form of a recursive solution. Though not all recursive solutions fit the mold as nicely as this solution does, the similarities are far greater than the differences. In the examples to follow, we explicitly abstract these points from the solutions. As we attempt to construct a new recursive solution, three questions should be kept in mind.

> ### Three Questions for Constructing Recursive Solutions
> 1. How can we define the problem in terms of a smaller problem of the same type?
> 2. How is the size of the problem being diminished at each recursive call?
> 3. What instance of the problem can serve as the degenerate case, and does the manner in which the problem size is diminished ensure that this degenerate case will always be reached?

Before concluding this introductory section, we consider two relatively simple problems, computing the factorial of a number and writing a string backward. Their recursive solutions will further illustrate the points raised by the solution to the dictionary search problem.

Factorial

We begin by constructing a recursive solution to the problem of computing the factorial of a number. We choose to start with this problem because its recursive solution is easy to understand and neatly fits the mold given above. However, because there is a very simple nonrecursive solution to the problem, the recursive solution would probably not be used in practice.

To begin, consider the familiar iterative definition of Factorial(n) (more commonly written $n!$). For any integer $n > 0$, define

$$\text{Factorial}(n) = n * n - 1 * n - 2 * \ldots * 1$$

The value of 0! is defined as

$$\text{Factorial}(0) = 1$$

and the factorial of a negative integer is undefined. You should have no trouble writing an iterative factorial function based on this definition.

We can also construct a recursive definition of factorial. To define Factorial(n) in terms of the factorial of a smaller number, observe that the factorial of n is equal to the factorial of $(n - 1)$ multiplied by n; that is,

$$\text{Factorial}(n) = n * \text{Factorial}(n - 1)$$

This definition specifies that Factorial(n) is defined in terms of Factorial($n - 1$), and it also implies that Factorial($n - 1$) can be defined in terms of Factorial(n

− 2), and so forth. This is analogous to the dictionary search solution, where a dictionary is searched by searching a smaller dictionary, and that smaller dictionary is searched in exactly the same way.

The above definition lacks one key element, the degenerate case. As with the dictionary search example, one case must be defined differently than all the others, or else the recursion would never stop. The degenerate case for factorial is Factorial(0), which is simply defined to be 1. Since n, which is originally assumed to be greater than or equal to zero, is decremented by 1 at each call to factorial, the degenerate case will always be reached. Adding the degenerate case to the definition yields:

$$\text{Factorial}(n) = \begin{cases} 1 & \text{if } n = 0 \\ n * \text{Factorial}(n - 1) & \text{if } n > 0 \end{cases}$$

To be sure that you understand the recursive definition, we apply it to the computation of Factorial(4). The recursive definition states that, for $n > 0$, Factorial(n) = n * Factorial(n − 1). Thus,

Factorial(4) = 4 * Factorial(3)

By definition, Factorial(3) = 3 * Factorial(2)

By definition, Factorial(2) = 2 * Factorial(1)

By definition, Factorial(1) = 1 * Factorial(0)

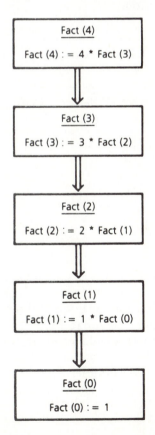

Figure 4–2
Factorial(4)

The degenerate case has been reached, and the definition directly states that Factorial(0) = 1

At this point the application of the recursive definition stops, and the information that has been gained can be used to answer the original question: What is Factorial(4)? To begin, since Factorial(0) = 1,

Factorial(1) = 1 * 1 = 1
Since Factorial(1) = 1, Factorial(2) = 2 * 1 = 2
Since Factorial(2) = 2, Factorial(3) = 3 * 2 = 6
Since Factorial(3) = 6, Factorial(4) = 4 * 6 = 24

Notice that the recursive definition of Factorial(4) yields the same value as the familiar definition, which gives 4 * 3 * 2 * 1 = 24. To prove that the two definitions of factorial are equivalent for all nonnegative integers, we would use **mathematical induction.** The close tie between recursion and mathematical induction is discussed in Chapter 5.

This recursive definition of factorial has illustrated two points: (1) *Intuitively,* Factorial(n) can be defined in terms of Factorial($n - 1$), and (2) *mechanically,* the definition can be applied to determine the value of a given factorial. Even in our simple example, the application of the recursive definition required quite a bit of work. That, of course, is where the computer comes in. Once we have a recursive definition of Factorial(n), it is easy to construct a Modula-2 function that implements the definition.

```
(* ---------------------------------------------------------------
   Factorial:  Compute the factorial of the nonnegative
   integer n.
   --------------------------------------------------------------- *)
PROCEDURE Factorial (n : CARDINAL) : CARDINAL;
BEGIN

   IF (n = 0) THEN
      RETURN (1);
   ELSE
      RETURN (n * Factorial (n-1));
   END;

END Factorial;
```

Declaring the parameter n to be of type *CARDINAL* rather than simply *INTEGER* guards against errors in the calling program's logic. If function *Factorial* is ever passed a negative value, the program will immediately abort because of a type clash. On the other hand, if n had been declared as an integer, passing a negative value to *Factorial* would result in an infinite sequence of recursive calls (terminated only by a system-defined limit), since the degenerate case would never be reached (for example, *Factorial (-4)* would call *Factorial (-5)*, which would call *Factorial (-6),...*).

This function fits the model of a recursive solution given in the previous section as follows:

1. One of the actions of the function *Factorial* is to *call itself*.
2. At each recursive call to *Factorial* the number whose factorial is to be computed is *diminished by 1*.
3. The factorial of 0 is handled differently than all the other factorials. This *degenerate case* does not generate a recursive call, and—as a result of (2) (and the fact that the argument is nonnegative)—we are assured that it is always reached.

At an intuitive level, it should be clear that this function implements the recursive definition of factorial. We shall now study the mechanics of executing this recursive function.

The *Factorial* function is straightforward except for the **RETURN** statement in the **ELSE** clause (**RETURN** (*n* *Factorial* (*n-1*))). This statement has the following effect:

1. The expression to be returned is evaluated.
2. Since the expression is a product, each operand is evaluated.
3. The second operand (*Factorial (n-1)*) is a call to the function *Factorial*. Although this is a recursive call (the function *Factorial* is called from within the function *Factorial*), there really is nothing special about it. Imagine substituting a call to another function (Modula-2's function *ABS*, for example) for the recursive call to *Factorial*. The principle is the same: Just evaluate the function.

Thus, in principle, the evaluation of a recursive function is no more difficult than that of a nonrecursive function. In practice, however, the bookkeeping can quickly get out of hand. We shall thus introduce the "box method," a systematic way to trace the actions of a recursive function or procedure. We emphasize, however, that such a mechanical device is no substitute for an intuitive understanding of recursion.

The Box Method. We illustrate the box method here for a recursive function. This method is somewhat simpler for a recursive procedure, as no value needs to be returned.

1. Label each recursive call in the body of the recursive subprogram (there may be several, and it will be important to distinguish among them). For example, mark the expression *Factorial (n − 1)* with the letter A:

```
(* ------------------------------------------------------------
   Factorial:  Compute the factorial of the nonnegative
   integer n.
   ------------------------------------------------------ *)
PROCEDURE Factorial(n : CARDINAL) : CARDINAL;
```

```
BEGIN

    IF (n = 0) THEN
        RETURN (1);
    ELSE                          A
        RETURN (n * Factorial(n-1));
    END;

END Factorial;
```

These labels help us to keep track of the correct place to which we must return after a function call has completed. In the *Factorial* function, we return to point A after each recursive call, plug in the value computed for *Factorial (n-1)*, and continue execution by evaluating the expression *n * Factorial (n-1)*.

2. Each call made to the subprogram in the course of the program's execution generates a new box, which is filled in with the subprogram's **local environment**. This consists of the variables and parameters that are created when a call initiates execution of the subprogram and that are destroyed when the call to the subprogram is terminated. More specifically, each box will contain:

   a. The value parameters of the formal parameter list
   b. The variables declared locally in the subprogram
   c. A placeholder for the value to be returned by each recursive call generated from the current box (marked to correspond to the labeling in Step 1)
   d. The value of the function itself

When the box is first created, only the values of the parameters will be known. The values of the other items are filled in as they are determined by the subprogram's execution. (We shall see in later examples that both variable parameters and global variables must be handled somewhat differently.) For example, when the call *Factorial (3)* is made, a box containing the following information is created.

Figure 4–3

A box

```
┌─────────────────────────────┐
│ n = 3                       │
│ A: Factorial (n−1)  = ?     │
│ Fact = ?                    │
└─────────────────────────────┘
```

This box is used during the execution of the corresponding call to *Factorial*.

3. When a new box is created due to a recursive call (see Step 2), an arrow is drawn from the box that the call was made from to the newly created box. If the call was made from outside of the recursive subprogram (for example, the call from the main program which initiates the recursive process), then the arrow is drawn from the statement containing the call to the new box. Each arrow must be marked to correspond to the label (from Step 1) of the recursive call, indicating *exactly* where to return after the call is completed.

   For example, Figure 4–4 shows the first two boxes generated by the statement *WriteInt (Factorial (3), 1)* in the main program.

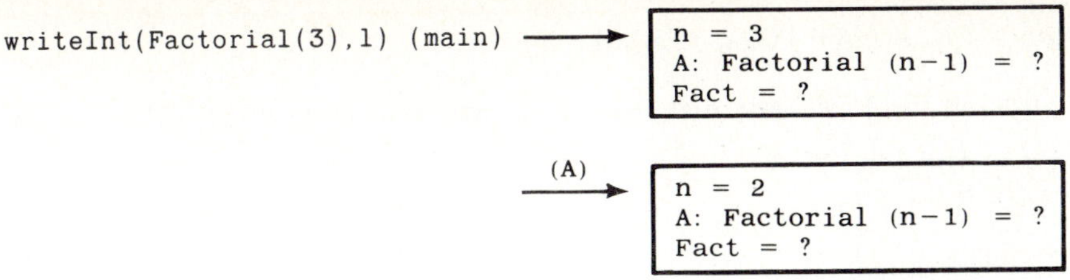

```
writeInt(Factorial(3),1) (main) ────────►   n = 3
                                             A: Factorial (n−1) = ?
                                             Fact = ?
```

```
                          (A)
                     ────────►   n = 2
                                 A: Factorial (n−1) = ?
                                 Fact = ?
```

Figure 4–4

Box method

4. After the new box and arrow have been set up as described in Steps 2 and 3, start executing the body of the subprogram. Each reference to an item in the subprogram's local environment references the corresponding value in the *current* box, regardless of how the current box was generated. In the sequence of diagrams in Figure 4–5, it is always clear which box is current—it is the deepest along the path of arrows.

5. Upon exiting the subprogram, cross off the current box and follow its arrow back to the box from which the subprogram call was made. This box now becomes the current box, and the label on the arrow specifies the exact location at which execution of the subprogram should continue. The value computed by the just-terminated function call is plugged into the appropriate item in the current box.

Figure 4–5 is a complete box trace for the call *Factorial (3)* made from the main program.

The box method is indicative of how recursion is implemented by many computer systems. Our boxes roughly correspond to what are known as **activation records,** which a system typically uses in its implementation of subprogram calls. We discuss this further in Chapter 7 as an application of **stacks.**

The box method also should give you a good indication of the special techniques that should be employed to *debug* a recursive subprogram. Write statements should be included to report the values of all parameters and local variables both at entry to and exit from the subprogram. Write statements should also report from what point in the program each recursive call was generated. We shall present an example of this at the end of this section.

Writing a String Backward

We now consider a problem slightly more difficult than computing the factorial of a number: Given a string of characters, we wish to print it out in *reverse* order (for example, the string 'cat' should be written as 'tac'). To construct a recursive solution, we should ask the three questions in the Key Concept box on page 144.

We shall construct a solution to the problem of writing a string of length n backward in terms of the problem of writing a string of length $n − 1$ backward. That is, at each recursive step of the solution, the length of the string to be written backward will be diminished by one. Since the strings will be getting smaller and smaller, this suggests that the problem of writing some "very small" string backward can serve as the degenerate case. One very small string is the

Figure 4–5

*Box trace of
Factorial(3)*

Example of the box method for call Fact(3):

The initial call is made and function Fact begins execution:

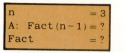

```
n             = 3
A: Fact(n-1) = ?
Fact          = ?
```

At point A, a recursive call is made and the new invocation of the function Fact begins execution:

```
n             = 3       n             = 2
A: Fact(n-1) = ?    A   A: Fact(n-1) = ?
Fact          = ?   →   Fact          = ?
```

At point A, a recursive call is made and the new invocation of the function Fact begins execution:

```
n             = 3       n             = 2       n             = 1
A: Fact(n-1) = ?    A   A: Fact(n-1) = ?    A   A: Fact(n-1) = ?
Fact          = ?   →   Fact          = ?   →   Fact          = ?
```

At point A, a recursive call is made and the new invocation of the function Fact begins execution:

```
n          = 3       n          = 2       n          = 1       n           = 0
A: Fact(n-1)=?   A   A: Fact(n-1)=?   A   A: Fact(n-1)=?   A   A: Fact(n-1)=?
Fact        = ?  →   Fact        = ?  →   Fact        = ?  →   Fact         = ?
```

This is the degenerate case, so this invocation of Fact completes.

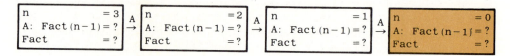

```
n          = 3       n          = 2       n          = 1       n           = 0
A: Fact(n-1)=?   A   A: Fact(n-1)=?   A   A: Fact(n-1)=?   A   A: Fact(n-1)=?
Fact        = ?  →   Fact        = ?  →   Fact        = ?  →   Fact         = 1
```

The function value is returned to the calling box which continues execution.

```
n          = 3       n          = 2       n          = 1       n           = 0
A: Fact(n-1)=?   A   A: Fact(n-1)=?   A   A: Fact(n-1)=1       A: Fact(n-1)=?
Fact        = ?  →   Fact        = ?  →   Fact        = ?      Fact         = 1
```

The current invocation of Fact completes.

```
n          = 3       n          = 2       n          = 1       n           = 0
A: Fact(n-1)=?   A   A: Fact(n-1)=?   A   A: Fact(n-1)=1       A: Fact(n-1)=?
Fact        = ?  →   Fact        = ?  →   Fact        = 1      Fact         = 1
```

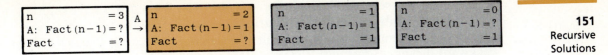

The current invocation of Fact completes.

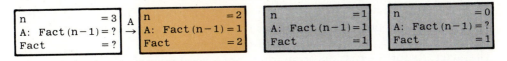

The function value is returned to the calling box which continues execution.

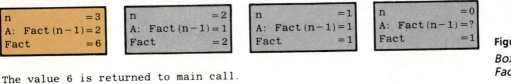

The current invocation of Fact completes.

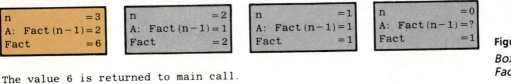

The value 6 is returned to main call.

Figure 4–5

Box trace of Factorial(3)

empty string, the string of length zero. We can thus choose for our degenerate case the problem

```
write the empty string backward
```

The solution to this problem is to do nothing at all—a very straightforward solution indeed! (Alternatively, consider defining the string of length one to be the degenerate case.)

We now must determine exactly how the solution to the problem of writing a string of length $n - 1$ backward can be used to solve the problem of writing a string of length n backward. This is analogous to the construction of the solution to the factorial problem, where we specified how Factorial($n - 1$) could be used in the computation of Factorial(n). Unlike the factorial problem, however, it is not immediately clear how this can be done for the string problem. Obviously, not just any string of length $n - 1$ will do. For example, there is no relation between writing 'apple' (a string of length 5) backward and writing 'pear' (a string of length 4) backward. We must choose the smaller problem carefully so that its solution can be used in the solution to the original problem.

The string of length $n - 1$ that we choose to solve must be a **substring** (part) of the original string. Suppose one character is stripped away from the original string, yielding a substring of length $n - 1$. In order for our recursive solution to be valid, the ability to write the substring backward, combined with the ability to perform some minor task, must result in the ability to write the original string backward. Compare this with the way in which factorial was recursively computed. The ability to compute Factorial($n-1$), combined with the ability to multiply this result by n, resulted in the ability to compute Factorial(n).

We need to decide which character should be stripped away and the minor task that must be performed. Consider the latter question first. Since characters are being printed, a likely candidate for the minor task is printing a single character. As for the first question, there are several possible alternatives for the character that should be stripped away from the string. Two of the more intuitive alternatives are:

```
strip away the last character

strip away the first character
```

Let us begin by selecting the first of these alternatives. For the solution to be valid, the first character printed must be the last character in the string. Therefore, the last character must be printed before the remainder of the string is written backward.

Figure 4–6

*Recursive
solution*

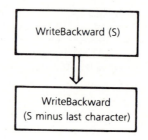

A high-level recursive solution is:

```
WriteBackward(S)

    IF (the string is empty) THEN
        don't do anything -- this is the degenerate case

    ELSE
        print the last character of S
        WriteBackward(S minus its last character)
    END
```

This is a conceptual solution to the problem. To obtain a Modula-2 program, a few implementation issues must be resolved. We assume that the procedure will be passed an array `str` containing the string to be written backward, and an integer `last` specifying the end of the string. To simplify matters, we assume that the string begins at position 0 and ends at position *last*; that is, all characters, including blanks, in that range are considered to be part of the string.

```
(* ------------------------------------------------------------
   WriteBackward:  Write string str[0..last] backward.
   --------------------------------------------------- *)
PROCEDURE WriteBackward(str : ARRAY OF CHAR; last : INTEGER);
BEGIN

   IF (last >= 0) THEN
      (* write the last character *)
      Write(str[last]);

      (* write the rest of the string backward *)
      WriteBackward(str, last-1);
   END;

   (* last < 0 is the degenerate
      case - no action is performed *)

END WriteBackward;
```

Notice that the recursive calls to *WriteBackward* are passed successively smaller values of *last*. This has the effect of stripping away the last character of the string and ensures that the degenerate case will be reached.

We can trace the execution of *WriteBackward* using the box method. As with the function *Factorial*, each box contains the local environment of the recursive call—in this case, the value parameters *str* and *last*. Because *WriteBackward* is a procedure rather than a function, there is no computed value to be returned. Figure 4–7 illustrates the action of the procedure *WriteBackward* when invoked from the main program with the string 'cat'.

Let us now consider a slightly different approach to the problem. Recall that, in our previous discussion, we mentioned two alternatives for the character to be stripped away from the string:

strip away the last character

strip away the first character

The solution just given is based on the first of these alternatives. It will now be interesting to construct a solution based on the second alternative.

To begin, consider the result of modifying the previous pseudocode solution so that the first character (rather than the last) is printed and then the remainder of the string is recursively written backward.

WriteBackward2(S)

```
   IF (the string is empty) THEN
      don't do anything -- this is the degenerate case
```

Figure 4–7

*Box trace of
WriteBack-
ward('cat')*

Box trace of call WriteBackward ('cat',3):

The initial call is made, and the procedure begins execution.

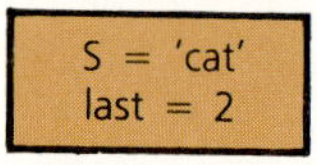

> S = 'cat'
> last = 2

Point A (WriteBackward (S,size-1)) is reached, and the recursive call
is made.

Output line just before call: t

The new invocation begins execution.

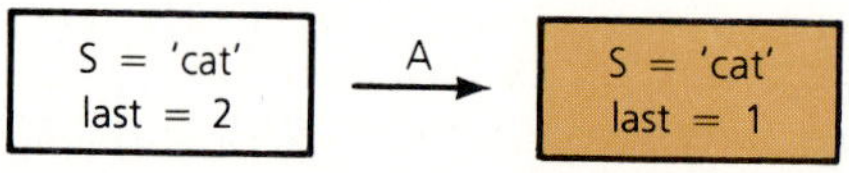

> S = 'cat'   A   S = 'cat'
> last = 2   →   last = 1

Point A is reached, and the recursive call is made.

Output line just before call: ta

The new invocation begins execution.

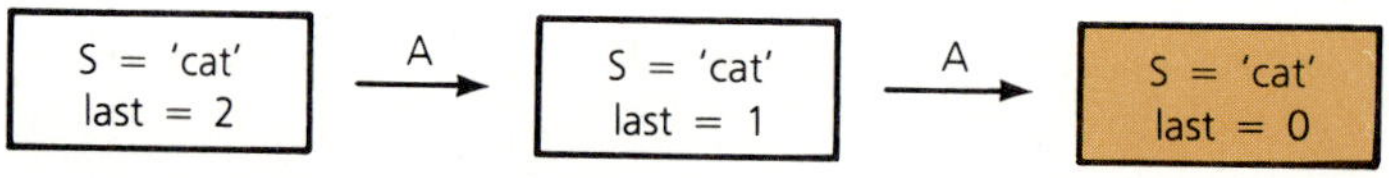

> S = 'cat'   A   S = 'cat'   A   S = 'cat'
> last = 2   →   last = 1   →   last = 0

Point A is reached, and the recursive call is made.

Output line just before call: tac

The new invocation begins execution.

> S = 'cat'   A   S = 'cat'   A   S = 'cat'   A   S = 'cat'
> last = 2 →   last = 1 →   last = 0 →   last = −1

This is the degenerate case, so this invocation completes.
Control returns to the calling box, which continues execution.

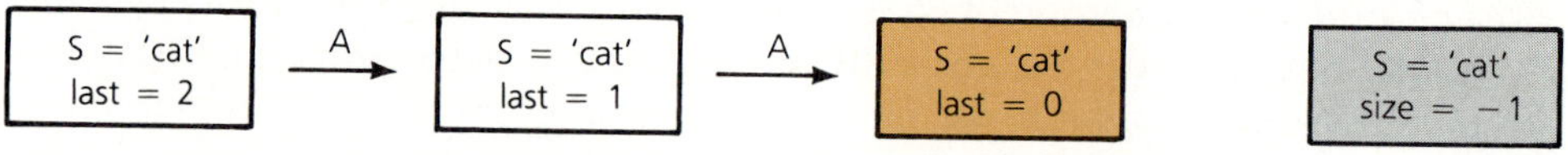

> S = 'cat'   A   S = 'cat'   A   S = 'cat'   S = 'cat'
> last = 2 →   last = 1 →   last = 0   size = −1

Output line just after return from last call: tac

This invocation completes. Control returns to the calling box, which
continues execution.

> S = 'cat'   A   S = 'cat'   S = 'cat'   S = 'cat'
> last = 2   →   last = 1   last = 0   last = −1

Output line just after return from last call: tac

This invocation completes. Control returns to the calling box, which
continues execution.

> S = 'cat'   S = 'cat'   S = 'cat'   S = 'cat'
> last = 2   last = 1   last = 0   last = −1

Output line just after return from last call: tac

This invocation completes. Control returns to the statement following the main call.

```
    ELSE
        print the first character of S
        WriteBackward2(S minus its first character)
    END
```

Does this solution do what we want it to? If you think about this procedure, you will realize that it prints the string in its normal, left-to-right direction rather than printing the string backward. What the procedure does is

```
print the first character of S
write the remainder of S
```

These steps result in simply printing the string S. Naming the procedure *WriteBackward* doesn't guarantee that it will actually write backward—recursion really isn't magic!

The correct solution can be obtained from the following recursive formulation. To write S backward:

```
write S minus its first character backward
print the first character of S
```

In other words, we write the first character of S *only after the rest of S has been written backward*. This leads to the following pseudocode procedure.

```
WriteBackward2(S)

    IF (the string is empty) THEN
        don't do anything -- this is the degenerate case

    ELSE
        WriteBackward2(S minus its first character)
        print the first character of S
    END
```

The translation of *WriteBackward2* into Modula-2 is similar to that for the original *WriteBackward* procedure and is left as an exercise.

It is instructive to trace carefully the actions of the two pseudocode procedures. First, let us alter each procedure so that output useful to the trace is provided.

```
WriteBackward(S)

    WriteString('Enter WriteBackward with string: ')
    WriteString(S)
    WriteLn

    IF (the string is empty) THEN
        don't do anything -- this is the degenerate case
```

```
      ELSE
          WriteString('About to write the last character of string: ')
          WriteString(S)
          WriteLn
          print the last character of S
          WriteBackward(S minus its last character)
      END

      WriteString('Leave WriteBackward with string: ')
      WriteString(S)
      WriteLn

WriteBackward2(S)

      WriteString('Enter WriteBackward2 with string: ')
      WriteString(S)
      WriteLn

      IF (the string is empty) THEN
          don't do anything -- this is the degenerate case

      ELSE
          WriteBackward2(S minus its first character)
          WriteString('About to write the first character of string: ')
          WriteString(S)
          WriteLn
          print the first character of S
      END

      WriteString('Leave WriteBackward2 with string: ')
      WriteString(S)
      WriteLn
```

The output of procedures *WriteBackward* and *WriteBackward2*, when initially called with the string 'cat', is shown in Figure 4–8.

You need to be comfortable with the differences between these two procedures. The recursive calls made by the two procedures generate a different sequence of values for the parameter S. Despite this fact, both procedures correctly write the string argument backward. The difference in the sequence of values for S is compensated for by which character of the string is printed and by when, in relation to the recursive calls, this character is printed. In terms of the diagrams of the box method in Figure 4–8, procedure *WriteBackward* prints a character just before a new box is generated (just before a new recursive call), whereas procedure *WriteBackward2* prints a character just after crossing off a box (just after returning from a recursive call). When these differences are put together, the result is two procedures that employ different strategies to accomplish the same task.

Box trace of WriteBackward ('cat') in pseudocode:

The output file is initially empty.

The initial call is made and the procedure begins execution.

Figure 4–8
*Box traces
of pseudocode
version*

S = 'cat'

Point A is reached, and the recursive call is made.

Output file just before call:

```
Enter WriteBackward with string: cat
About to print last character of string: cat
t
```

The new invocation begins execution.

S = 'cat' →A S = 'ca'

Point A is reached, and the recursive call is made.

Output file just before call:

```
Enter WriteBackward with string: cat
About to print last character of string: cat
t
Enter WriteBackward with string: ca
About to print last character of string: ca
a
```

The new invocation begins execution.

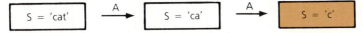

S = 'cat' →A S = 'ca' →A S = 'c'

Point A is reached, and the recursive call is made.

Output file just before call:

```
Enter WriteBackward with string: cat
About to print last character of string: cat
t
Enter WriteBackward with string: ca
About to print last character of string: ca
a
Enter WriteBackward with string: c
About to print last character of string: c
c
```

The new invocation begins execution.

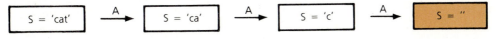

S = 'cat' →A S = 'ca' →A S = 'c' →A S = ''

This invocation completes execution and a return is made.

Output file just after return:

```
Enter WriteBackward with string: cat
About to print last character of string: cat
t
Enter WriteBackward with string: ca
About to print last character of string: ca
a
Enter WriteBackward with string: c
About to print last character of string: c
c
Enter WriteBackward with string:
Leave WriteBackward with string:
```

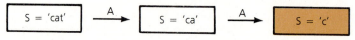

This invocation completes execution and a return is made.

Output file just after return:

```
Enter WriteBackward with string: cat
About to print last character of string: cat
t
Enter WriteBackward with string: ca
About to print last character of string: ca
a
Enter WriteBackward with string: c
About to print last character of string: c
c
Enter WriteBackward with string:
Leave WriteBackward with string:
Leave WriteBackward with string: c
```

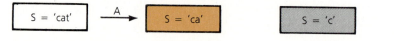

This invocation completes execution and a return is made.

Output file just after return:

```
Enter WriteBackward with string: cat
About to print last character of string: cat
t
Enter WriteBackward with string: ca
About to print last character of string: ca
a
Enter WriteBackward with string: c
About to print last character of string: c
c
Enter WriteBackward with string:
Leave WriteBackward with string:
Leave WriteBackward with string: c
Leave WriteBackward with string: ca
```

Figure 4–8

*Box traces
of pseudocode
version*

This invocation completes execution and a return is made.

Output file just after return:

```
Enter WriteBackward with string: cat
About to print last character of string: cat
t
Enter WriteBackward with string: ca
About to print last character of string: ca
a
Enter WriteBackward with string: c
About to print last character of string: c
c
Enter WriteBackward with string:
Leave WriteBackward with string:
Leave WriteBackward with string: c
Leave WriteBackward with string: ca
Leave WriteBackward with string: cat
```

Box trace of WriteBackward2('cat') in pseudocode:

The output file is initially empty.

The initial call is made and the procedure begins execution.

S = 'cat'

Point A is reached, and the recursive call is made.

Output file just before call:

```
Enter WriteBackward2 with string: cat
```

The new invocation begins execution.

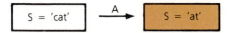

Point A is reached, and the recursive call is made.

Output file just before call:

```
Enter WriteBackward2 with string: cat
Enter WriteBackward2 with string: at
```

The new invocation begins execution.

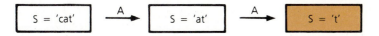

Point A is reached, and the recursive call is made.

Output file just before call:

```
Enter WriteBackward2 with string: cat
Enter WriteBackward2 with string: at
Enter WriteBackward2 with string: t
```

Figure 4–8

*Box traces
of pseudocode
version*

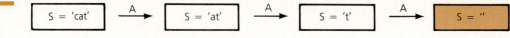

This invocation completes execution and a return is made.

Output file just after return:

```
Enter WriteBackward2 with string: cat
Enter WriteBackward2 with string: at
Enter WriteBackward2 with string: t
Enter WriteBackward2 with string:
Leave WriteBackward2 with string:
```

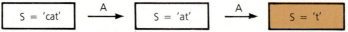

This invocation completes execution and a return is made.

Output file just after return:

```
Enter WriteBackward with string: cat
Enter WriteBackward with string: at
Enter WriteBackward with string: t
Enter WriteBackward with string:
Leave WriteBackward with string:
About to print first character of string: t
t
Leave WriteBackward2 with string: t
```

This invocation completes execution and a return is made.

Output file just after return:

```
Enter WriteBackward2 with string: cat
Enter WriteBackward2 with string: at
Enter WriteBackward2 with string: t
Enter WriteBackward2 with string:
Leave WriteBackward2 with string:
About to print first character of string: t
t
Leave WriteBackward2 with string: t
About to print first character of string: at
a
Leave WriteBackward2 with string: at
```

Figure 4–8

*Box traces
of pseudocode
version*

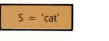

```
Enter WriteBackward2 with string: cat
Enter WriteBackward2 with string: at
Enter WriteBackward2 with string: t
Enter WriteBackward2 with string:
Leave WriteBackward2 with string:
About to print first character of string: t
t
Leave WriteBackward2 with string: t
About to print first character of string: at
a
Leave WriteBackward2 with string: at
About to print first character of string: cat
c
Leave WriteBackward2 with string: cat
```

Figure 4–8

*Box traces
of pseudocode
version*

This example also illustrates the value of the box method, combined with well-placed write statements, in debugging recursive subprograms. We placed write statements at the beginning, interior, and end of the recursive procedures to report the value of the parameter S. In general, when debugging a recursive subprogram, we would also report the values of local variables and the point in the subprogram from which each call is made.

```
Procedure R()

    (* this is point A *)
    WriteString('Procedure R is being called from point A.')
    R(...)

    (* this is point B *)
    WriteString('Procedure R is being called from point B.')
    R(...)

    (* this is point C *)
    WriteString('Procedure R is being called from point C.')
    R(...)
```

Before we leave this problem, let us consider a small modification. Suppose that the string to be written backward is stored in a linked list rather than in an array. That is, assume we have the following type definitions:

```
TYPE

    ptr = POINTER TO node;

    node = RECORD
                letter : CHAR;
                next   : ptr;
            END;
```

The variable *str* of type *ptr* points to the head of the list containing the string to be printed backward.

We have already developed two strategies for writing backward a string stored in an array. The strategy of procedure *WriteBackward* is

```
print the last character of S
write S minus its last character backward
```

The strategy of procedure *WriteBackward2* is

```
write S minus its first character backward
print the first character of S
```

We have seen that these two strategies work equally well when *S* is stored in an array. When *S* is stored in a linked list, however, the first strategy is very difficult to implement. If *str* points to the node containing the first character of the string, how do we get to the node containing the last character? Even if we had some way to get to the last node on the list quickly (such as by having a tail pointer as described in Chapter 3), it would be very difficult for us to move toward the front of the string at each recursive call; that is, it would be difficult for us to access the ends of the successively shorter strings generated by the recursive calls.

This discussion illustrates one of the primary disadvantages of linked lists— while an array provides direct access to any character in the string, a linked list does not. Fortunately, however, the strategy of procedure *WriteBackward2* requires that we have direct access only to the *first* character of the string. The linked list does indeed provide direct access to this character, as it is stored in the node pointed to by *str*. Furthermore, *S* minus its first character can easily be passed to the procedure *WriteBackward2*. If *str* points to the beginning of the string *S*, then *str^.next* points to *S* minus its first character.

The following is a Modula-2 procedure for implementing *WriteBackward2* when *S* is stored in a linked list.

```
(* -----------------------------------------------------------
   WriteBackward2:  Write a string (stored as a linked list)
   backward.
   ----------------------------------------------------------- *)
PROCEDURE WriteBackward2(str : ptr);
BEGIN

   IF (str # NIL) THEN
      (* write S minus its first character backward *)
      WriteBackward2(str^.next);

      (* print the first character of S *)
      Write(str^.letter);
   END;

END WriteBackward2;
```

We are now ready to use recursion to tackle some more challenging problems. The next two problems require us to compute some specified value.

Raising an Integer to a Power

Modula-2 has no exponentiation operator. That is, if we want to know the value of x^n, we have to write a function to compute it. In this section, we shall consider three functions for performing this task. To simplify matters, we shall concern ourselves only with raising integers to nonnegative integer powers.

The following iterative function performs the exponentiation.

```
(* ------------------------------------------------------------
   Pow1:  Compute x raised to the n-th power.
   ---------------------------------------------------- *)
PROCEDURE Pow1 (x : INTEGER; n : CARDINAL) : INTEGER;

VAR

   temp, i : INTEGER;

BEGIN

   temp := 1;
   FOR i := 1 TO n DO
      temp := x * temp;
   END;

   RETURN (temp);

END Pow1;
```

Let us now develop a recursive solution. How can we define raising x to the nth power in terms of raising x to a smaller power? The answer is found in the "rule of exponents":

$$x^n = x * x^{n-1}$$

That is, we can compute x^n by computing x^{n-1} and multiplying the result by x.

Our recursive solution lacks only a degenerate case. Recall that, by definition,

$$x^0 = 1$$

We thus have the following recursive formulation.

$$x^0 = 1$$

$$x^n = x * x^{n-1} \quad \text{if } n > 0$$

Since we are assuming n to be nonnegative, the degenerate case ($n = 0$) will always be reached.

This solution is directly implemented with the following Modula-2 function.

```
(* ------------------------------------------------------------
   Pow2:  Compute x raised to the n-th power.
   ------------------------------------------------------------ *)
PROCEDURE Pow2 (x :  INTEGER; n :  CARDINAL)  :  INTEGER;

BEGIN

   IF  (n = 0)  THEN
       RETURN  (1) ;
   ELSE
       RETURN  (x * Pow2 (x,  n-1)) ;
   END;

END Pow2;
```

To compute x^n, the function *Pow2* is called $n + 1$ times (once from the main program and n times recursively). We can greatly reduce the number of calls required by exploiting another rule of exponents:

$$x^n = (x^{n/m})^m$$

For example, taking m to be 2 gives

$$x^n = (x^{n/2})^2$$

We can use this rule to construct a more efficient recursive power function. The strategy of the following function is to halve the value of n at each recursive call rather than to simply decrement it by one. The result is that the degenerate case is reached with far fewer recursive calls.

```
(* ------------------------------------------------------------
   Pow3:  Compute x raised to the n-th power.

   Pow3 calls the locally defined function sqr.
   ------------------------------------------------------------ *)
PROCEDURE Pow3 (x :  INTEGER; n :  CARDINAL)  :  INTEGER;

   PROCEDURE sqr (x :  INTEGER)  :  INTEGER;
   BEGIN
```

```
        RETURN (x * x);

    END sqr;

BEGIN

    IF (n = 0) THEN
        RETURN (1);

    ELSIF (ODD(n)) THEN
        RETURN (x * sqr(Pow3(x, n DIV 2)));

    ELSE
        RETURN (sqr(Pow3(x, n DIV 2)));

    END;

END Pow3;
```

Observe that the function has a case for even n (when *ODD (n)* is false) and a different case for odd n (when *ODD (n)* is true). Consider first the case for even n. Here the value x^n is computed as

```
    sqr(Pow3(x, n DIV 2))
```

This computation is valid since

$$(x^{n\ div\ 2})^2 = (x^{n/2})^2 = x^n$$

when n is even.

Now consider the case when n is odd. Note that the value of $(n\ \boldsymbol{DIV}\ 2)$ is not the same as $n/2$ when n is odd. For example, the value of $(13\ \boldsymbol{DIV}\ 2)$ is 6 rather than 6.5, and consequently $(x^{(13\ div\ 2)})^2$ is equal to x^{12} rather than x^{13}. In general, when n is odd,

$$(x^{(n\ div\ 2)})^2 = x^{n-1}$$

To compensate for this fact in the function *Pow3*, when n is odd we multiply the result of

```
    sqr(Pow3(x, n DIV 2))
```

by x.

Figure 4–9 illustrates the dramatic reduction in the number of required calls to the power function achieved by halving n rather than decrementing it by one.

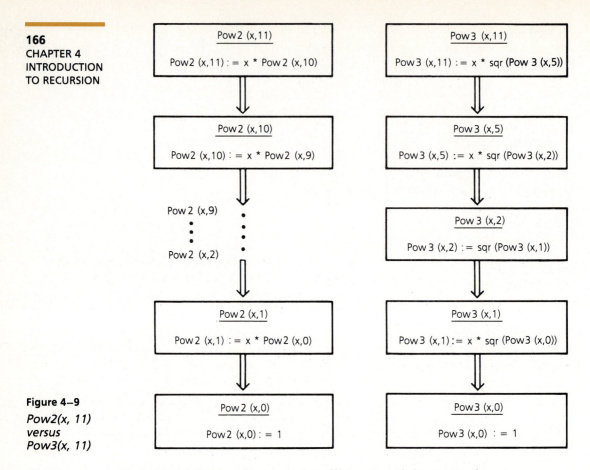

Figure 4–9

*Pow2(x, 11)
versus
Pow3(x, 11)*

Exercise 11 further discusses the efficiencies of the power functions.

Multiplying Rabbits

Rabbits are very prolific breeders. If rabbits did not die, their population would very quickly get out of hand. The following are some statistics obtained in a recent survey of randomly selected rabbits:

1. Rabbits never die.
2. A rabbit reaches sexual maturity exactly two months after birth (that is, at the beginning of its third month of life).
3. Rabbits are always born in male–female pairs. At the beginning of every month, each sexually mature male–female pair gives birth to exactly one male–female pair.

Suppose that we started with a single newborn male–female pair. How many pairs would there be in month 6, counting the births that took place at the beginning of month 6? Since 6 is relatively small, the solution can easily be obtained.

Month 1: 1 pair, the original.

Month 2: 1 pair still, since the pair is not yet sexually mature.

Month 3: 2 pairs; the original pair has reached sexual maturity and has given birth to a second pair.

Month 4: 3 pairs; the original pair has given birth again, but the pair born at the beginning of month 3 is not yet sexually mature.

Month 5: 5 pairs; all rabbits alive in month 3 (2 such pairs) are now sexually mature. Add their offspring to those pairs alive in month 4 (3 pairs) to yield 5 pairs.

Month 6: 8 pairs; (3 pairs sexually mature) plus (5 pairs alive in the previous month).

We now construct a recursive solution for computing Rabbit(n), the number of pairs alive in month n. Our first step is to determine how Rabbit($n-1$) can be used to compute Rabbit(n). If it were the case that all pairs of rabbits who were alive in month $n-1$ gave birth to a pair at the start of month n, we would simply have

$$\text{Rabbit}(n) = 2 * \text{Rabbit}(n - 1)$$

This is not correct, however, since not all of the rabbits who were alive in month $n-1$ are sexually mature at the start of month n. Only those who were alive in month $n-2$ are ready to reproduce at the start of month n. Hence, the correct relationship is

$$\text{Rabbit}(n) = \text{Rabbit}(n - 1) + \text{Rabbit}(n - 2)$$

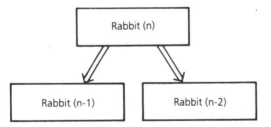

Figure 4–10

Recursive solution

This recursive relationship introduces a new point. In some cases, a problem is solved by solving *more than one* smaller problem of the same type. This does not add much conceptual difficulty, except that we must be very careful when selecting the degenerate case. The temptation is simply to say that Rabbit(1) should be the degenerate case, since it is given to be 1 in the problem's statement. But what about Rabbit(2)? Applying the recursive definition to Rabbit(2) would yield

$$\text{Rabbit}(2) = \text{Rabbit}(1) + \text{Rabbit}(0)$$

Thus, the recursive definition would need to specify the number of pairs alive in month 0. One possible solution is to define this number to be 0, but this seems very artificial. A slightly more attractive alternative is to treat Rabbit(2) itself as a special case with the value of 1. Thus, the recursive definition has two degenerate cases, Rabbit(2) and Rabbit(1). The recursive definition becomes

$$Rabbit\,(n) \;=\; \begin{cases} 1 & if\ n \leqslant 2 \\[2mm] Rabbit\,(n-1) + Rabbit\,(n-2) & if\ n > 2 \end{cases}$$

Incidentally, the series of numbers Rabbit(1), Rabbit(2), Rabbit(3), . . . is known as the **Fibonacci series,** which models many naturally occurring phenomena.

A pseudocode function computing Rabbit(*n*) is easy to write from the above definition.

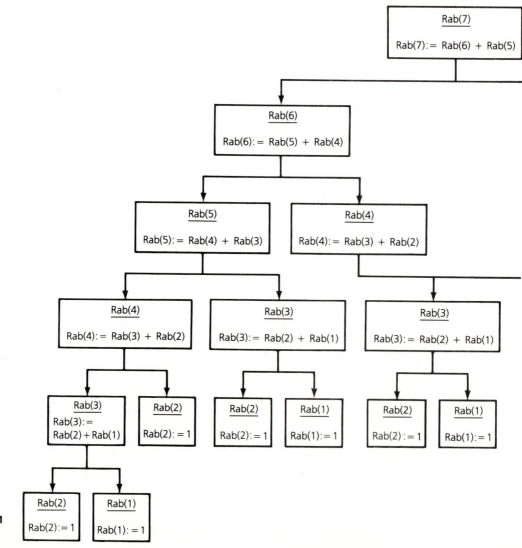

Figure 4–11
Rabbit(7)

```
PROCEDURE Rabbit(n) : returns a positive integer
(* n is assumed to be a positive integer *)

    IF  (n <= 2)  THEN
        RETURN (1)
    ELSE
        RETURN ( Rabbit(n-1) + Rabbit(n-2) )
    END
```

Should this function be implemented in Modula-2 and run? Figure 4–11 illustrates the recursive calls generated for *Rabbit (7)*. Think about how many recursive calls are generated for *Rabbit (10)*. For large values of *n*, it becomes infeasible to use the function *Rabbit*. This problem will be discussed in more detail at the end of the chapter, at which time we shall indicate some techniques for generating a more efficient solution from this same recursive relationship.

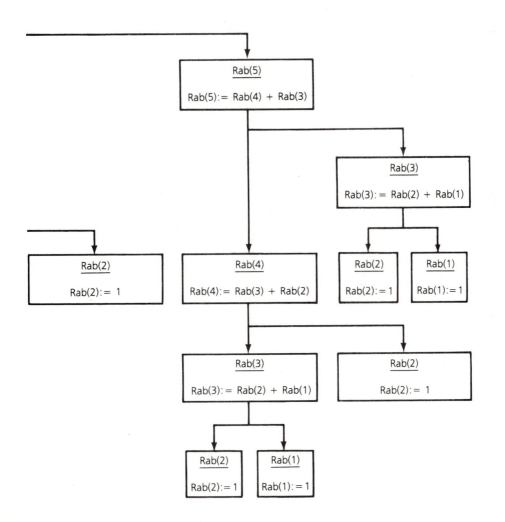

Figure 4–11
Rabbit(7)

Mr. Spock's Dilemma

The five-year mission of the U.S.S. *Enterprise* is to explore new worlds. The five years are almost up, but the *Enterprise* has just entered an unexplored solar system containing n planets. Unfortunately, time will allow only for k of them to be explored. Mr. Spock begins to ponder how many different ways he can choose k planets for exploration out of the n planets in the solar system.

Mr. Spock is especially fascinated by one particular planet. Scanners have indicated that this "Planet X" is unlike any previously encountered. It would be fascinating to visit Planet X, but then again, it might be very, very dangerous! Mr. Spock begins to think, in terms of Planet X, about how many ways there are to pick k planets out of the n. "There are two possibilities: Either we visit Planet X, or we do not visit Planet X. If we do visit Planet X, then I will have to choose $k-1$ other planets to visit from the $n-1$ remaining planets. On the other hand, if we do not visit Planet X, I will still have to choose k planets to visit from the remaining $n-1$ planets."

Logical. Impeccably logical. Mr. Spock is on his way to a recursive method of counting how many ways he can choose k planets from n. Let $C(n, k)$ be the number of ways of choosing k planets from n. Then, in terms of Planet X, Mr. Spock deduces

$C(n, k)$ = (the number of ways of choosing a group of k planets that includes Planet X)

+

(the number of ways of choosing a group of k planets that does *not* include Planet X)

But Mr. Spock has already reasoned that the number of ways to select a group that includes Planet X is $C(n-1, k-1)$, and the number of ways to select a group that does not include Planet X is $C(n-1, k)$. Mr. Spock has figured out a way to solve his counting problem in terms of two smaller counting problems of the same type:

$$C(n, k) = C(n-1, k-1) + C(n-1, k)$$

Mr. Spock now has to worry about the degenerate case(s). What selection problem does he immediately know the answer to? If the *Enterprise* had time to visit all the planets (that is, if $k = n$) then there would be no need for a decision; there is only one way to select all the planets. Thus,

$$C(n, n) = 1$$

Assuming that $k \leqslant n$ (otherwise the problem does not have much meaning), it is easy to see that $C(n-1, k)$ (the second term in the recursive definition) is "closer" to this degenerate case of the two arguments being the same than is $C(n, k)$. However, it is *not* the case that $C(n-1, k-1)$ (the first term) is closer to this degenerate case than is $C(n, k)$—they are the same "distance" apart. *When a problem is solved by solving two (or more) problems, each of the problems must be closer than the original to a degenerate case.*

After some highly logical thought, Mr. Spock realizes that there is another trivial selection problem that the first term does, in fact, approach. This problem is the counterpart of his first degenerate case $C(n, n)$. Just as there is only one way to select all the planets to visit ($C(n, n) = 1$), there is also only one way to select zero planets to visit. When there is no time to visit any of the planets ($k = 0$), the *Enterprise* must head home without any exploration—there is no decision to be made in this case either. We thus have the second degenerate case,

$$C(n, 0) = 1$$

This degenerate case does indeed have the property that $C(n-1, k-1)$ is closer to it than is $C(n, k)$. (Alternatively, we could define the second degenerate case to be $C(n, 1) = n$.)

Adopting the degenerate cases $C(n, n)$ and $C(n, 0)$ yields the following solution.

$$C(n, n) = 1$$
$$C(n, 0) = 1$$
$$C(n, k) = C(n-1, k-1) + C(n-1, k) \qquad \text{if } 0 < k < n$$

Mr. Spock adds one final part to his definition:

$$C(n, k) = 0 \qquad \text{if } k > n$$

Though k would not be greater than n in the context of this problem, the addition of this case makes Mr. Spock's definition more generally applicable.

We can easily derive the following pseudocode function from Mr. Spock's recursive definition:

```
PROCEDURE C(n, k) : CARDINAL
(* n and k are CARDINAL *)

   IF (k > n) THEN
       RETURN (0)
   ELSIF (n = k) THEN
       RETURN (1)
   ELSIF (k = 0) THEN
       RETURN (1)
   ELSE
       RETURN ( C(n-1, k-1) + C(n-1, k) )
   END
```

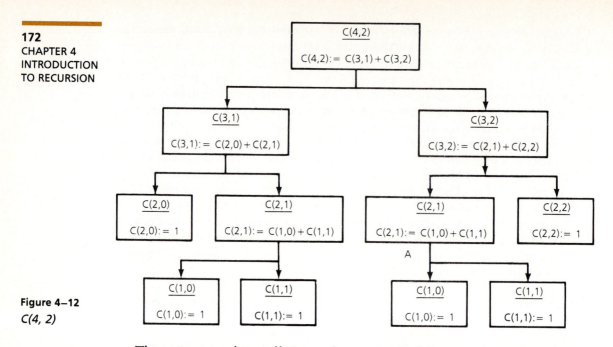

Figure 4–12
C(4, 2)

The comments about efficiency that we made following the rabbit problem apply here also.

Now that Mr. Spock has determined how many choices he has, he will have to rely on Captain Kirk's human intuition to determine which planets to visit.

The Mad Scientist Problem

The mad scientist wishes to make a chain out of plutonium and lead pieces. There is a problem however. If two pieces of plutonium are placed next to each other, BOOM! The question is, in how many ways can the scientist safely construct a chain of length n? (Assume that pieces of the same element are indistinguishable and that the scientist has at least n pieces of both plutonium and lead. Also note that the question asks for the number of ways to *construct* a chain. We will consider, for example, the chain constructed by first adding a lead piece and then a plutonium piece to be different from the chain constructed by first adding a plutonium piece and then adding a lead piece; that is, we will consider the chains lead–plutonium and plutonium–lead to be different.)

The scientist realizes that there are two classes of safe chains: safe chains that end with a lead piece and safe chains that end with a plutonium piece. By computing the number of chains of each type, the scientist would be able to obtain the answer to the question by adding together these two numbers. That is, let

$C(n)$ be the number of safe chains of length n.

$L(n)$ be the number of safe chains of length n ending with a piece of lead.

$P(n)$ be the number of safe chains of length n ending with a piece of plutonium.

Then,

$$C(n) = L(n) + P(n)$$

First the scientist considers $L(n)$. A safe chain of length n that ends with a lead piece can be obtained from *any* safe chain of length $n-1$ simply by tacking a lead piece onto its end. Hence, the number of safe chains of length n ending with a lead piece is precisely equal to the total number of safe chains of length $n-1$.

$$L(n) = C(n-1)$$

The scientist then considers $P(n)$. The only way a safe chain can end with a plutonium piece is if the piece just before the end is lead (if it is plutonium, then we can't add another plutonium piece). Thus, the only way to make a safe chain of length n that ends in plutonium is first to make a safe chain of length $n-1$ that ends in lead and then add a piece of plutonium to the end. Therefore, the number of safe chains of length n that end with a plutonium piece is precisely equal to the number of safe chains of length $n-1$ that end with a lead piece:

$$P(n) = L(n-1)$$

The scientist then uses the fact that $L(n) = C(n-1)$ (from above) to obtain

$$P(n) = C(n-2).$$

Thus, the scientist has solved $L(n)$ and $P(n)$ in terms of the smaller problems $C(n-1)$ and $C(n-2)$, respectively. The scientist then uses

$$C(n) = L(n) + P(n)$$

to obtain

$$C(n) = C(n-1) + C(n-2),$$

a familiar situation. This equation has a form identical to the solution to the multiplying rabbits problem (which generated the Fibonacci series). As we saw in the rabbit problem, since the recurrence defines a problem in terms of *two* smaller problems, two degenerate cases are needed. As we did for the rabbit problem, we will choose $n = 1$ and $n = 2$ for our degenerate cases.

Although both this problem and the rabbit problem use $n = 1$ and $n = 2$ as their degenerate cases, there is no reason to expect the values for these degenerate cases to be the same; that is, there is no reason to expect Rabbit(1) to be equal to C(1) and Rabbit(2) to be equal to C(2). A little thought reveals that for the chain problem,

$$C(1) = 2 \qquad \text{(A chain consisting of either a single piece of plutonium or a single piece of lead.)}$$

$C(2) = 3$ (The safe chains of length 2 are: lead–lead, plutonium–lead, lead–plutonium.)

The scientist puts it all together to obtain

$C(1) = 2$

$C(2) = 3$

$C(n) = C(n-1) + C(n-2)$ for $n > 2$

Moral of the Story: Sometimes a problem can be solved by breaking it up into cases (for example, chains which end in plutonium and chains which end in lead).

Another Moral of the Story: The values defined for the degenerate cases are extremely important. Although the recurrence for C and Rabbit differ only on their values for 1 and 2, they yield very different values for a given n. For example, Rabbit(20) = 6765, while $C(20) = 17,711$. The larger the value of n, the larger the discrepancy. You should think about why this is so.

SEARCHING FOR THINGS

Find the Largest Element of an Array

This section begins by outlining a solution to a simple problem. You should complete the solution before continuing.

Suppose we are given an array A of integers and that we wish to find its maximum element. An iterative solution could be constructed without too much difficulty, but instead consider a recursive formulation:

if A has only one element then
    MaxArray(A) = the element in A

if A has more than one element then
    MaxArray(A) = the maximum of { MaxArray(left half of A),
                                   MaxArray(right half of A) }

Notice that this strategy fits the divide-and-conquer model discussed earlier with regard to the high-level description of the binary search algorithm. That is, the algorithm proceeds by dividing the problem and conquering the subproblems. There is, however, a difference in the spirit of the two algorithms. While the binary search algorithm conquers only one of its subproblems at each step, *MaxArray* conquers both. In addition, after the subproblems have been conquered, *MaxArray* must reconcile the two solutions—that is, it must find the maximum of the two maximums.

We leave it to you to develop a recursive solution based on this formulation. In so doing, you may stumble upon several subtle programming issues. Virtually all these issues are discussed in the binary search problem that follows, but this

(a)

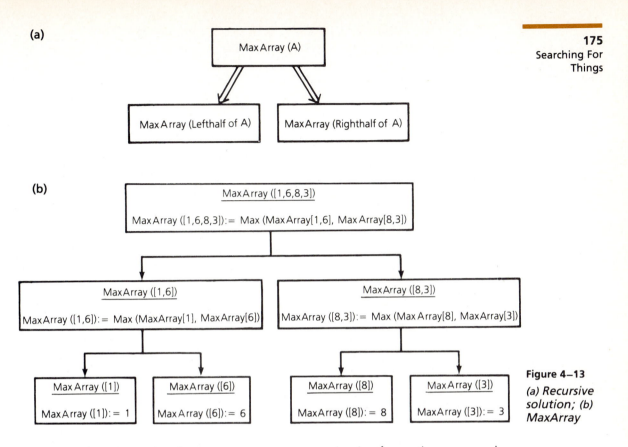

(b)

Figure 4–13
*(a) Recursive
solution; (b)
MaxArray*

is a good opportunity for you to get some practice implementing a recursive solution.

Binary Search

At the beginning of this chapter, we presented—at a high level—a recursive binary search algorithm for finding a word in a dictionary. This technique is now fully developed, illustrating some important programming issues. Recall the solution developed for the dictionary problem:

```
Search(dictionary, word)

    IF (dictionary is one page in size) THEN

        scan page for word

    ELSE

        open dictionary to a point near the middle

        determine which half of dictionary contains word
```

```
IF (word is in the first half of dictionary) THEN
    Search( first half of dictionary, word )
ELSE
    Search( second half of dictionary, word )
END

END
```

Let us now abstract the problem to searching an array *A* of integers for a given value *V*. The array must inherit from the dictionary the property that it is *sorted,* or else a binary search is not applicable. Hence, we assume that

$$A[1] \leq A[2] \leq A[3] \leq \ldots \leq A[n],$$

where *n* is the size of the array. A high-level binary search for the array problem is

```
BinSearch(A, V):

  IF (A is of size one) THEN

      determine if its element is equal to V

  ELSE
      find the midpoint of A

      determine which half of A contains V

      IF (V is in the first half of A) THEN
          BinSearch(first half of A, V)
      ELSE
          BinSearch(second half of A, V)
      END
  END
```

While the solution is conceptually sound, various considerations demand changes in its organization. Three of these considerations are the following:

1. **How are the recursive calls to BinSearch to be passed "half of" A?** An obvious solution is to pass *BinSearch* integers *first* and *last* that define the part of *A* that is currently under consideration. Thus, *BinSearch* would have two additional parameters

   BinSearch(A, V, first, last)

   The entire array *A* would always be passed, but *first* and *last* specify that conceptually the array *A[first..last]* is to be searched. Using this convention, the new midpoint can be established by

   mid := (first + last) DIV 2

   The first half of the array can be passed by

```
BinSearch(A, V, first, mid-1)
```

and the second half by

```
BinSearch(A, V, mid+1, last)
```

2. **How is it determined which half of the array contains V?** One implementation of

```
IF (V is in the first half of A) THEN
    BinSearch(A, V, first, mid-1)
ELSE
    BinSearch(A, V, mid+1, last)
END
```

is given by

```
IF (A[mid] > V) THEN
    BinSearch(A, V, first, mid-1)
ELSE
    BinSearch(A, V, mid+1, last)
END
```

The problem with this is that no test is made for equality between $A[mid]$ and V. This can cause V to be missed—after the split, $A[mid]$ is not in either of the halves of the array (in this case two halves don't make a whole!) and will not be inspected in the future. The interaction between the splitting criterion and the termination condition (the degenerate case) is subtle and is often misprogrammed. We need to re-think the degenerate case.

3. **What should the degenerate case(s) be?** As written, `BinSearch` terminates only when an array of size one is encountered—this is the only degenerate case. By changing the splitting procedure to address the problem discussed in the second point, it is possible to implement the binary search correctly so that it has only this single degenerate case. We believe, however, that it is clearer to have two distinct degenerate cases:

   a. The degenerate case $first > last$. This degenerate is always reached when the value V is not in the original array.

   b. The degenerate case $A[mid] = V$. This degenerate case is always reached when the value V is in the original array.

These degenerate cases are a bit different from any we have previously encountered. In a sense, the answer to the problem is determined by which degenerate case is reached. Many search problems have this flavor.

A sketch of this solution is:

```
PROCEDURE BinSearch(A, V, first, last) : returns an index in ARRAY A

   IF (first > last) THEN

        indicate that V is not present in the array
```

```
ELSE
    mid := (first + last) DIV 2
    IF (A[mid] = V) THEN
        indicate that V is found at mid
    ELSIF (A[mid] > V) THEN
        RETURN ( BinSearch(A, V, first, mid-1) )
    ELSE
        RETURN ( BinSearch(A, V, mid+1, last) )
    END
END
```

There is another implementation issue to be discussed, but since it deals specifically with Modula-2, the Modula-2 function is presented first.

Assume the type declaration

```
TYPE

    (* n is a constant declared to be the size of the array *)
    list = ARRAY [1..n] OF INTEGER;


(* -----------------------------------------------------------
    BinSearch:  Search array A[first..last] for the index of
    value V.  Return 0 if V is not found.

    Note:  The type list is ARRAY [1..n] OF INTEGER and thus
    first and last must be contained in the interval [1..n].
    ----------------------------------------------------------- *)
PROCEDURE BinSearch(A : list; V, first,
                    last : INTEGER) : INTEGER;


VAR

    mid : INTEGER;


BEGIN

    IF (first > last) THEN
        RETURN (0); (* V is not in the original array *)

    ELSE

        mid := (first + last) DIV 2;

        IF (A[mid] = V) THEN
            RETURN (mid); (* V found at A[mid] *)
        ELSIF (A[mid] > V) THEN
            RETURN (BinSearch(A, V, first, mid-1));
```

```
        ELSE
            RETURN (BinSearch(A, V, mid+1, last));
        END;

    END;

END BinSearch;
```

In this solution, *BinSearch* is passed *A* as a value parameter. This implies that each time *BinSearch* is called, a copy of *A* is made and placed in *BinSearch*'s local environment. If *A* is large, many calls may have to be made to *BinSearch,* with each call requiring a large array to be copied.

There are two obvious ways to avoid this problem, but neither way is satisfactory. The array *A* could be declared to be a global variable, or it could be passed to function *BinSearch* as a variable parameter. However, both of these solutions undermine modularity. Global variables should usually be avoided as they destroy the clean interface between a subprogram and the remainder of the program. Global variables also make the subprogram less general. In the case of the binary search function, a global declaration of the array *A* would allow only this specific array to be searched.

The second alternative of passing *A* as a variable parameter indicates that the function *BinSearch* needs to make a change to the parameter (recall our discussion on variable parameters in Chapter 1). This is not the case, however. Thus, to pass *A* as a variable parameter would convey misinformation about *BinSearch*'s interface with the rest of the program.

A third possibility is to build a nonrecursive "shell" around the search function, as follows.

Again, assume the type declaration

```
TYPE

    (* n is a constant declared to be the size of the array *)
    list = ARRAY [1..n] OF INTEGER;

(* ----------------------------------------------------------
    BinSearch:  Search for the index of value V in array A
    with a binary search.  Return 0 if V is not found.  The
    search is performed by the locally defined procedure
    dosearch.
    ---------------------------------------------------------- *)
PROCEDURE BinSearch(A : list ; V : INTEGER) : INTEGER;

    PROCEDURE dosearch(V, first, last : INTEGER) : INTEGER;

    VAR

        mid : INTEGER;
```

```
        BEGIN

    IF (first > last) THEN
        RETURN (0);
    ELSE
        mid := (first + last) DIV 2;
        IF (A[mid] = V) THEN
            RETURN (mid);
        ELSIF (A[mid] > V) THEN
            RETURN (dosearch(V, first, mid-1));
        ELSE
            RETURN (dosearch(V, mid+1, last));
        END;
    END;

END dosearch;


BEGIN   (* body of function BinSearch *)

    RETURN (dosearch(V, 1, n));

END BinSearch;
```

The only action of the function *BinSearch* is to call the function *dosearch*. Function *dosearch* is declared to be local to *BinSearch* and performs the actual binary search. The array *A* is passed as a value parameter to *BinSearch* and accessed as a nonlocal variable by *dosearch*. Since *BinSearch* is called only once (for each search problem), only a single copy of *A* is made. The objections to *dosearch* accessing a nonlocal variable are minimized because *dosearch* is local to *BinSearch* and thus can be invoked only from within *BinSearch*. Function *dosearch* can make no changes to *A* that will propagate to outside of *BinSearch*. The function is general, since *BinSearch* can be passed any array of the appropriate type. The solution is a good compromise between the concerns of programming style and efficiency.

There are, however, some situations where even one copy of *A* is too much, and in these situations it is necessary to pass the array *A* as a variable parameter. Being able to identify such a situation requires mathematical techniques for analyzing algorithms. In Chapter 13, we briefly introduce some of these techniques, but it will not be until a formal course on the analysis of algorithms that you will be exposed to them in earnest. Until then, we recommend that you use the nonrecursive shell approach as a reasonable compromise between efficiency and style.

The box trace of the recursive function *dosearch* contains a new development. The array *A* is neither a value parameter nor a local variable in the function *dosearch*. That is, *A* is not part of *dosearch*'s local environment and thus should *not* be included within each box.

The array *A* in Figure 4–14 is represented outside the boxes, with all references to *A* affecting this single representation.

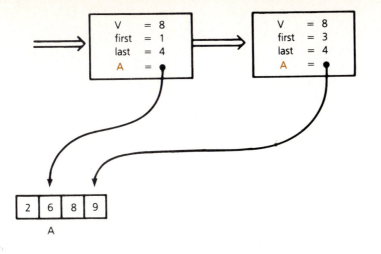

Figure 4–14

*Box method
with global
variable*

We make one final modification to our implementation of binary search. We employ open arrays in order to increase the generality of the procedure. Note that the returned value is computed with respect to the open array which starts at index 0.

```
(* ------------------------------------------------------------
   BinSearch:  Search for the value V in array A with a binary
   search.  Return the distance from the starting point of the
   array if V is found.  Return -1 if V is not found.  The
   search is performed by the locally defined procedure
   dosearch.

   Calls:  dosearch
   ------------------------------------------------------------ *)
PROCEDURE BinSearch(A : ARRAY OF INTEGER; V : INTEGER) : INTEGER;

   PROCEDURE dosearch(V, first, last : INTEGER) : INTEGER;

   VAR

      mid : INTEGER;

   BEGIN

      IF (first > last) THEN
         RETURN (-1);
      ELSE
         mid := (first + last) DIV 2;
         IF (A[mid] = V) THEN
            RETURN (mid);
         ELSIF (A[mid] > V) THEN
            RETURN (dosearch(V, first, mid-1));
```

```
              ELSE
                  RETURN (dosearch(V, mid+1, last));
              END;
          END;

     END dosearch;

BEGIN   (* body of function BinSearch *)

   RETURN ( dosearch(V, 0, HIGH(A)) );

END BinSearch;
```

Find the kth Smallest Element of an Array

The first two examples of this section presented recursive methods for finding the largest element in an arbitrary array and for finding an arbitrary element in a sorted array. We conclude the section on searching for things with a high-level description of a recursive solution for finding the kth smallest element in an arbitrary array A.

The problem could obviously be solved by sorting the array, as the kth smallest element will end up in $A[k]$. While this approach is a legitimate solution, it does more than the problem requires; a more efficient solution is possible. The solution outlined below finds the kth smallest element without completely sorting the array.

We have pointed out repeatedly that with recursive solutions, a problem is solved in terms of one or more smaller problems of the same type and that this notion of *smaller* ensures that a degenerate instance of the problem is always reached. The recursive solutions presented thus far share the property that the amount of the reduction in problem size between recursive calls is *predictable*. For example, the problem size is always decreased by one in the factorial problem and it is always halved in the exponentiation problem. In addition, the degenerate cases for all our problems (except binary search) have had a static, predefined size. We can thus determine, knowing only the size of the original problem, how many recursive calls will be made before the degenerate case is reached (again, binary search is an exception).

The solution we are about to present for finding the kth smallest element departs from these traditions. Although the problem is solved in terms of smaller problems, just how much smaller depends on the elements in the array and cannot be predicted in advance. Also, the size of the degenerate case, as with binary search, depends on the elements in the array (recall a degenerate case for binary search is reached when the middle element is the one sought).

This "unpredictable" type of solution is necessitated by the nature of the problem. The relationship between the rankings of the elements in any predetermined parts of the array and the ranking of the elements in the entire array is not strong enough to solve the kth smallest element problem. For example, suppose that A contains the elements shown in Figure 4–15.

Figure 4–15

Sample array

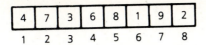

We find that $A[4] = 6$ is the third-smallest element in the first half of A and that $A[5] = 8$ is the third-smallest element in the second half of A. Can we conclude from this anything about the location of the third-smallest element in all of A? The answer is no; this relationship is not strong enough to allow us to draw any useful conclusions. You should experiment with other fixed splitting schemes as well.

Our recursive solution proceeds by:

1. Selecting a **pivot element** in the array
2. Cleverly arranging, or **partitioning,** the elements in the array about this pivot element
3. Recursively applying the strategy to *one* of the partitions

We now fill in the details of the recursive solution. Suppose that we wish to find the kth smallest element in the array segment $A[F..L]$. Let S be any element of the array segment (for now, we ignore how S is chosen, except that it must be some element in $A[F..L]$). We partition the elements of $A[F..L]$ into three regions: S_1, which contains those elements less than S; S_2, which contains those equal to S; and S_3, which contains those elements greater than S. Notice this implies that all the elements in S_1 are smaller than all the elements in S_2, which all are smaller than all the elements in S_3.

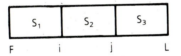

Figure 4–16

Partition about pivot

In terms of array subscripts, all elements in $A[F..i]$ are less than S, all elements in $A[(i + 1)..j]$ are equal to S, and all elements in $A[(j + 1)..L]$ are greater than S. Notice that i and j (and thus the sizes of the regions S_1, S_2, and S_3) depend on S and the other elements of $A[F..L]$.

This partition induces three "smaller problems," such that the solution to one of the problems will solve the original problem.

1. If there are k or more elements in S_1 (if $k \leqslant (i - F + 1)$), then the k smallest elements of the array segment $A[F..L]$ are contained in S_1. In this case, we must find the kth smallest element in S_1 (in $A[F..i]$).
2. If there are fewer than k elements in S_1 but k or more elements in S_1 combined with S_2 (if k lies in the range $(i - F + 2)$ to $(j - F + 1)$), then the kth smallest element of $A[F..L]$ must be contained in S_2. In this case, since all the elements in S_2 are equal to S, S must be the kth smallest element; this is the degenerate case.
3. If there are fewer than k elements in S_1 and S_2 combined (if $k > (j - F + 1)$), then the kth smallest element in $A[F..L]$ must be in S_3 (it must be in $A[j + 1..L]$). In this case, since there are $(j - F + 1)$ elements in

$A[F..j]$ (all of which are smaller than the elements in S_3), we want the $k - (j - F + 1)^{th}$ smallest element in S_3.

We can summarize this discussion with a recursive definition. Let

$Select(k, A, F, L) = k^{th}$ `smallest element in` $A[F..L]$

Then, after we have selected the pivot element S and partitioned $A[F..L]$ into S_1, S_2, and S_3 (using array indices i and j as described above), we have that

$$Select(k, A, F, L)$$
$$= \begin{cases} Select(k, A, F, i) & \text{if } k \leq i - F + 1 \\ S & \text{if } i - F + 1 < k \leq j - F + 1 \\ Select(k - (j - F + 1), A, j + 1, L) & \text{if } k > j - F + 1 \end{cases}$$

Notice that, since the middle region is never empty (it certainly contains S), the size of the array segment to be searched is decreased by at least one at each step, thus ensuring that the degenerate case (that the desired element is in region S_2 of the array segment) eventually will be reached. A high-level pseudocode solution is:

```
PROCEDURE Select(k, A, F, L) : returns a value from the array

    choose a pivot element S from A[F..L]

    partition the elements of A[F..L] about S

    IF (k <= i-F+1) THEN
        RETURN ( Select(k, A, F, i) )
    ELSIF (i-F+1 < k <= j-F+1) THEN
        RETURN (S)
    ELSE
        RETURN ( Select(k-(j-F+1), A, j+1, L) )
    END
```

This solution is not far from a Modula-2 function. The only questions that remain are how to choose S and how to partition the array about the chosen S. The choice of pivot element S is arbitrary. Any S in the array will work, although the sequence of choices will affect how soon the degenerate case is reached. A procedure for partitioning the elements about S is given in the next chapter, when we show how to turn function *Select* into a sorting algorithm.

RECURSION AND EFFICIENCY

Recursion is a powerful problem-solving tool that often produces very clean solutions to even the most complex problems. In this chapter, our overriding concern has been to give you a solid understanding of recursion so that you will be able to construct recursive solutions on your own. We should, however, briefly point out some of the drawbacks of recursion.

These drawbacks have to do with the issue of efficiency. It is often the case that a nonrecursive, iterative subprogram is more efficient than a recursive one. There are two factors contributing to this:

1. The overhead associated with subprogram calls
2. The inherent inefficiency of some recursive algorithms

The first of these factors does not pertain specifically to recursive subprograms but is true of subprograms in general. In most implementations of Modula-2 and other high-level programming languages, a subprogram call incurs a bookkeeping overhead. As we shall indicate in Chapter 7, the bookkeeping performed by a system is not unlike our own box method.

This overhead is magnified by a recursive subprogram, since a single initial call to the subprogram can generate a large number of recursive calls (for example, the call *Factorial (n)* generates *n* recursive calls). On the other hand, the use of recursion, like modularity in general, can greatly clarify complex programs. This clarification frequently more than compensates for the additional overhead. The use of recursion is thus often consistent with our view of the cost of a computer program.

We should not, however, use recursion just for the sake of using recursion. For example, the recursive *Factorial* function presented in the first section probably should not be used in practice. We can easily write an iterative *Factorial* function that is just about as clear as the recursive one. There is no reason to incur the overhead of recursion when its use does not gain anything for us. *The true value of recursion is as a tool for solving problems for which there is no simple nonrecursive solution.*

The second point about recursion and efficiency is that some recursive algorithms are inherently inefficient. This inefficiency is a very different issue than overhead. It has nothing to do with how a recursive subprogram happens to be implemented but rather is tied to the method of solution employed by the algorithm.

As an example, recall the solution for the multiplying rabbits problem presented earlier in this chapter.

```
PROCEDURE Rabbit(n) : returns a positive integer

   IF (n <= 2) THEN
      RETURN (1)
   ELSE
      RETURN ( Rabbit(n-1) + Rabbit(n-2) )
   END
```

We presented a diagram illustrating the actions of this function for *Rabbit (7)*. We also asked you to think about what the diagram would look like for *Rabbit (10)*. If you thought about this question, you may have come to the conclusion that such a diagram would fill up most of this chapter. The diagram for *Rabbit (100)* would fill up most of this universe!

The fundamental problem with this recursive function is that the same values are computed over and over again. For example, in our diagram for *Rabbit (7)*, we see that *Rabbit (3)* is computed five times. When *n* is moderately large, many of the values are recomputed literally trillions and trillions of times. Even if the computation of each of these values required only a trivial amount of work (for example, if we could perform a million of these computations per second), the enormity of the number of times that the values are computed would still make the solution completely infeasible.

This is not to say, however, that the recursive definition

$$\text{Rabbit}(n) = \begin{cases} 1 & \text{if } n \leq 2 \\ \text{Rabbit}(n-1) + \text{Rabbit}(n-2) & \text{if } n > 2 \end{cases}$$

is of no use. One way to solve the rabbit problem is to construct an iterative solution based on this same relationship. The iterative solution goes forward instead of backward and computes each value only once. This function can be used to compute *Rabbit (n)* for very large values of *n*.

```
(* ------------------------------------------------------------
   ItRabb:   Iterative solution to the rabbit problem.
   ------------------------------------------------------------ *)
PROCEDURE ItRabb(n : CARDINAL): CARDINAL;

VAR

   (* Just before the (i+1)-st iteration of the loop, R and R1
      contain Rabbit(i) and R2 contains Rabbit(i-1).  This way
      at the (i+1)-st iteration Rabbit(i+1) is computed as
      R1 + R2. *)

   R, R1, R2, i : CARDINAL;

BEGIN

   (* initialize as specified by the degenerate cases
      - R and R1 contain the value of Rabbit(2) and R2
      contains the value of Rabbit(1) *)
   R1 := 1;
   R2 := 1;
   R  := 1;

   FOR i := 3 TO n DO
       (* compute the value of Rabbit(i) *)
       R := R1 + R2;

       (* get the values ready for the next iteration *)
       R2 := R1;
       R1 := R;
   END;
```

1. A recursive solution must have a degenerate case that is solved directly, without making any recursive calls. Without such a case, an infinite sequence of calls will be generated.

2. A recursive solution must be in terms of one or more problems that are each closer to a degenerate case than is the original problem. When a recursive subprogram includes more than one recursive call, there often must be more than one degenerate case.

3. The box method, in conjunction with well-placed write statements, can be a good aid in debugging recursive subprograms. Write statements should be included to report the values of parameters and local variables both at entry to and exit from the subprogram. Write statements should also report from what point in the program each recursive call was generated.

```
RETURN (R);

END ItRabb;
```

Although our original recursive formulation of the `Rabbit` algorithm was inherently inefficient, there are recursive algorithms that are extremely efficient. For example, the recursive binary search algorithm is quite efficient. The ability to make the determination of whether or not a recursive algorithm is adequately efficient will be developed in more advanced courses concerned with analysis of algorithms. For now, we shall continue to present recursive algorithms without worrying too much about this issue.

SUMMARY

1. Recursion is a technique that solves a problem by solving a smaller problem of the same type.

2. When constructing a recursive solution, the following three questions should be kept in mind.

   a. How can we define the problem in terms of a smaller problem of the same type?

   b. How is the size of the problem being diminished at each recursive call?

   c. What instance of the problem can serve as the degenerate case, and does the manner in which the problem size is diminished ensure that this degenerate case will always be reached?

3. The box method can be used to trace the actions of a recursive subprogram. These boxes resemble activation records, which are used in many implemen-

tations of recursion (we talk more about this in Chapter 7). Although the box method is useful, it cannot replace an intuitive understanding of recursion.

EXERCISES

1. What output would be produced by the following program?

```
MODULE testfsqrt;

(* standard I/O *)
FROM InOut IMPORT

    Write, WriteString, WriteLn, WriteInt;

PROCEDURE sqr(value : INTEGER) : INTEGER;
BEGIN

    RETURN (value * value);

END sqr;

PROCEDURE fsqrt(value : INTEGER) : INTEGER;

    PROCEDURE dosearch(first, last : INTEGER) : INTEGER;

    VAR

        mid : INTEGER;

    BEGIN

        WriteString('Enter: first = ');
        WriteInt(first,2);
        WriteString('   last = ');
        WriteInt(last,2);
        WriteLn;

        mid := (first + last) DIV 2;

        IF ((sqr(mid) <= value) AND (value < sqr(mid+1))) THEN
            RETURN (mid);
        ELSIF (sqr(mid) > value) THEN
            RETURN (dosearch(first, mid-1));
        ELSE
            RETURN (dosearch(mid+1, last));
        END;

        WriteString('Leave: first = ');
```

```
        WriteInt(first,2);
        WriteString('   last = ');
        WriteInt(last,2);
        WriteLn;

    END dosearch;

BEGIN

    RETURN (dosearch(1, value));

END fsqrt;

BEGIN (* MAIN PROGRAM *)

    WriteInt(fsqrt(30),1);
    WriteLn;

END testfsqrt.
```

2. Consider the following function, which writes out a cardinal number in base 8:

```
PROCEDURE PrintOctal(n : CARDINAL);
BEGIN

    IF (n > 0) THEN
        IF (n DIV 8 > 0) THEN
            PrintOctal(n DIV 8);
        END;
        WriteCard(n MOD 8,1);
    ELSE
        WriteCard(0,1);
    END;

END PrintOctal;
```

Describe how the algorithm works. Hand-execute the function with $n = 100$.

3. Consider the following recursive definition:

$$Acker(m, n) = \begin{cases} n + 1 & \text{if } m = 0 \\ Acker(m - 1, 1) & \text{if } n = 0 \\ Acker(m - 1, Acker(m, n - 1)) & \text{otherwise} \end{cases}$$

This function, called **Ackermann's function**, is of interest because it grows quickly with respect to the sizes of m and n. What is $Acker(1, 2)$? Implement the function in Modula-2 and do a box trace of $Acker(1, 2)$.

4. Consider the following program:

```
MODULE demo;

(* standard I/O *)
FROM InOut IMPORT

    WriteString, WriteInt, WriteLn;

VAR

    temp : INTEGER;

PROCEDURE f (n : INTEGER) : INTEGER;

BEGIN

    WriteString ('function entered with n = ');
    WriteInt (n, 1);
    WriteLn;

    CASE n OF
        0: RETURN (1);
    |   1: RETURN (2);
    |   2: RETURN (3);
    ELSE
        RETURN (f (n-2) * f (n - 4));
    END;

END f;

BEGIN (* MAIN PROGRAM *)

    temp := f (8);    (* used because of write
                         statements in body of function *)
    WriteString ('The value of f (8) is ');
    WriteInt (temp, 1);
    WriteLn;

END demo.
```

Show the exact output of the program. Are there any values the function *f* could be called with that would cause the program to run forever? If so, describe all such values.

5. Consider the following procedure:

```
        PROCEDURE R (x, y : INTEGER);
```

```
    IF (y > 0) THEN
        INC(x);
        DEC(y);
        WriteInt(x,1);
        WriteString('    ');
        WriteInt(y,1);
        WriteLn;
        R(x, y);
        WriteInt(x,1);
        WriteString('    ');
        WriteInt(y,1);
        WriteLn;
    END;

END R;
```

Execute the procedure with $x = 5$ and $y = 3$. How is the output affected if x is a variable (**VAR**) parameter instead of a value parameter?

6. Implement *WriteBackward2* (discussed in this chapter) with a Modula-2 procedure.

7. Implement *MaxArray* (discussed in this chapter) with a Modula-2 function. What other recursive definitions of *MaxArray* can you describe?

8. Write a recursive function that will sum the elements in an array.

9. Write a recursive procedure that will merge two sorted linked lists into a single sorted list. The original lists need not be preserved. (See Exercise 3.7.)

10. Write a recursive procedure that will reverse a linked list. (See Exercise 3.11.)

11. Consider functions *Pow1*, *Pow2*, and *Pow3* discussed in this chapter. How many multiplications will be performed by each function (counting calls to function *sqr* as one multiplication) to compute 3^{32}? 3^{19}? How many recursive calls will be made by *Pow2* and *Pow3* to compute 3^{32}? 3^{19}?

12. Modify the recursive *Rabbit* function so that it is visually easy to follow the flow of execution. Instead of just adding "Enter" and "Leave" messages, have the trace messages be indented according to how "deep" the current recursive call is. For example, the call *Rabbit (4)* would produce the output:

```
      Enter Rabbit: n = 4

         Enter Rabbit:   n = 3

              Enter Rabbit:   n = 2
              Leave Rabbit:   n = 2   value = 1

              Enter Rabbit:   n = 1
              Leave Rabbit:   n = 1   value = 1
         Leave Rabbit:   n = 3   value = 2

            Enter Rabbit:   n = 2
            Leave Rabbit:   n = 2   value = 1
      Leave Rabbit: n = 4   value = 3
```

Note how this output corresponds to figures such as Figure 4–11.

*13. Consider the problem of finding the **greatest common divisor** (GCD) of two positive integers a and b. The algorithm we present is a variation of Euclid's algorithm, which is based on the following theorem:

THEOREM   If a and b are positive integers such that b is not a divisor of a, then GCD(a, b) = GCD(b, a mod b).

This relationship between GCD(a, b) and GCD(b, a mod b) is the heart of the recursive solution. It specifies how the problem of computing GCD (a, b) can be solved in terms of another problem of the same type. Also, if b does divide a, then b = GCD(a, b), so an appropriate choice for the degenerate case is (a mod b) = 0.

This leads to the following recursive definition:

$$GCD(a, b) = \begin{cases} b & \text{if } (a \bmod b) = 0 \\ GCD(b, a \bmod b) & \text{otherwise} \end{cases}$$

The following Modula-2 function implements the recursive algorithm.

```
(* -----------------------------------------------------------
   Return the greatest common divisor of a and b.

   ASSUMPTION: b is positive.
   ------------------------------------------------------- *)
PROCEDURE GCD (a, b : CARDINAL) : INTEGER;

BEGIN

   IF (a MOD b) = 0 THEN      (* degenerate case *)
      RETURN (b);
```

```
        ELSE
            RETURN (GCD(b, a MOD b));
        END;

    END GCD;
```

a. Prove the above theorem.

b. What happens if $b > a$?

c. What is the notion of smaller (that is, do we always approach a degenerate case)? Why is the degenerate case appropriate?

**14. Let $C(n)$ be the number of different ways to sum to n using the integers 1 through $n - 1$ (for example, $4 = 1 + 1 + 1 + 1 = 1 + 1 + 2 = 2 + 2 \cdots$). Write recursive definitions for $C(n)$ under the following variations:

a. Permutations are distinct versus permutations are not distinct (for example, $4 = 1 + 2 + 1$ and $4 = 1 + 1 + 2$).

b. We count n itself in the sum versus we do not count n (for example, $C(1) = 0$ versus $C(1) = 1$).

CHAPTER 5

RECURSION AS A PROBLEM-SOLVING TOOL

PREVIEW Most of the problems presented in this chapter are both difficult and important. For many of these problems, the recursive solutions are far more elegant and concise than the best of their nonrecursive counterparts. The classic Towers of Hanoi problem appears to be quite difficult, yet it has an extremely simple recursive solution. Two important recursive sorting algorithms, *Quicksort* and *Mergesort*, have elegant recursive formulations and are highly efficient. After the sorting algorithms, we introduce the basics of formal grammars and illustrate their usefulness by constructing grammars to define syntactically correct algebraic expressions. The chapter concludes with a discussion on the close relationship between recursion and mathematical induction.

Now that we have presented the basic concepts of recursion, we are ready to move on to some extremely useful and somewhat complex applications. Our examples in this chapter include two very efficient **sorting** algorithms and **grammars** for defining languages.

DOING THINGS

In this section we use recursion to "do things." Specifically, given some data organized in one way, we recursively transform it so that it is organized in another way. As we actually must effect some change (and not, for example, simply look for something), we use recursive procedures rather than functions. The first problem of the section is called the Towers of Hanoi. Unlike the other problems in this chapter, the Towers of Hanoi problem probably has no direct real-world application. We nevertheless begin with it because its solution so nicely illustrates doing things recursively. The second problem of the section is one that has many real-world applications: **sorting**. We present **Quicksort** and **Mergesort,** two highly efficient recursive sorting algorithms.

The Towers of Hanoi

Many, many years ago, in a distant part of the Orient (what is now the Vietnamese city of Hanoi), the Emperor's wiseperson passed on to meet his ancestors. The Emperor needed a replacement wiseperson. Being a rather wise person himself, the Emperor devised a puzzle, declaring that its solver could have the job of wiseperson.

The Emperor's puzzle consisted of N disks (he wasn't saying exactly how many) and three poles—A (the source), B (the destination), and C (the spare).

The disks were of different sizes and had holes in the middle so that they could fit on the poles. Because of their great weights, disks could be placed only on top of disks larger than themselves. Initially, all the disks were on pole A (see Figure 5–1a). The puzzle was to move the disks, one by one, from pole A to pole B. Pole C could also be used in the course of the transfer, but the rule that a disk could be placed on top of only a disk larger than itself would have to be obeyed for this pole as well.

Figure 5–1

(a) Initial state; (b) move N − 1 disks from A to C; (c) move one disk from A to B; (d) move N − 1 disks from C to B

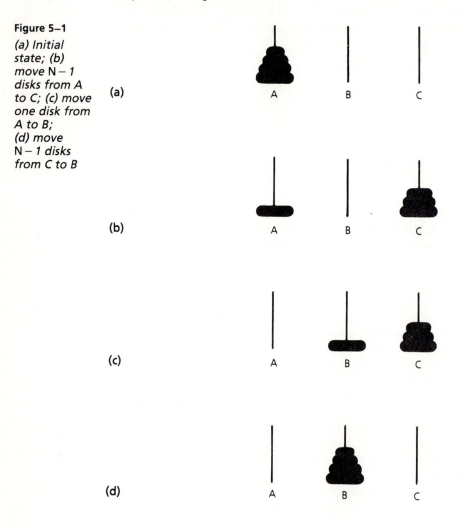

(a)

(b)

(c)

(d)

As the wiseperson position was generally known to be a soft job, there were many takers. Scholars and peasants alike brought the Emperor their solutions. Many solutions were thousands of steps long, and many contained goto's. "I can't understand these solutions," bellowed the Emperor. "There must be an easy way to solve this puzzle."

And indeed there was. A great Buddha came out of the mountains to see the Emperor. "My son, the puzzle is so easy, it almost solves itself." The Emperor's security chief wanted to throw this strange person out, but the Emperor let him continue.

"If there is only one disk (that is, $N = 1$), move it from pole A to pole B." So far, so good—but even the village idiot got this part right. "If there is more than one disk (that is, $N > 1$), simply:

1. Ignore the bottom disk and solve the problem for $N - 1$ disks—with the small modification that pole C is the destination and pole B is the spare (see Figure 5–1b).
2. After you've done this, $N - 1$ disks will be on pole C, and the largest disk will remain on pole A. So solve the problem for $N = 1$ (recall even the village idiot could do this) by moving the large disk from A to B (see Figure 5–1c).
3. Now all we have to do is move the $N - 1$ disks from pole C to pole B—that is, solve the problem with pole C being the source, pole B being the destination, and pole A being the spare." (See Figure 5–1d.)

There was silence for a few moments, and finally the Emperor said impatiently, "Well, are you going to tell us your solution or not?" The Buddha simply gave an all-knowing smile and vanished.

The Emperor was obviously not a recursive thinker, but you should realize that the solution given by the Buddha is perfectly correct. The key to the Buddha's solution is the observation that the Towers problem of N disks can be solved by solving three smaller (in the sense of number of disks) Towers problems. Let *Towers (count, source, dest, spare)* denote the problem of moving *count* disks from pole *source* to pole *dest*, using pole *spare* as a spare. Notice that this definition makes sense even if there are more than *count* disks on pole *source*; in this case, we concern ourselves with only the top *count* disks and ignore the others. Similarly, the poles *dest* and *spare* may have disks on them before we begin; these, too, are ignored (except that only smaller disks may be placed on top of them).

The problem posed by the Emperor can be stated as: Beginning with N disks on pole A and zero disks on poles B and C, solve *Towers (N, A, B, C)*. The Buddha's solution can be stated as follows.

Step 1. Starting in the *initial state* described above (all the disks on pole A),

    solve Towers (N-1, A, C, B)

That is, ignore the bottom (largest) disk and move the top $N - 1$ disks from pole A to pole C, using pole B as a spare. When this is done, the largest disk will remain on pole A, and all the other disks will be on pole C.

Step 2. Starting in the state produced by Step 1 (the largest disk on pole A and all others on pole C),

    solve Towers (1, A, B, C)

That is, move the largest disk from pole A to pole B. Since the disk to be moved is larger than the disks already on the spare (pole C), we really couldn't use the spare—fortunately, we obviously don't need to use the spare in this degenerate case. When this is done, the largest disk will be on pole B, and all other disks will remain on pole C.

Step 3. Starting in the state produced by Step 2 (the largest disk on pole B and all other disks on pole C),

```
solve Towers (N-1, C, B, A)
```

That is, move the $N - 1$ disks from pole C to pole B, using A as a spare. Notice that the destination, pole B, already has the largest disk, which is ignored. When this is done, the original problem will be solved—all the disks will be on pole B.

A concise description of the Buddha's solution is:

```
Towers (count, source, dest, spare)

  IF (count = 1) THEN
     move the disk directly
  ELSE
     solve Towers (count-1, source, spare, dest)
     solve Towers (1, source, dest, spare)
     solve Towers (count-1, spare, dest, source)
  END
```

This recursive solution follows the same basic pattern of the recursive solutions presented in the previous chapter:

1. A Towers problem is solved by solving other Towers problems.

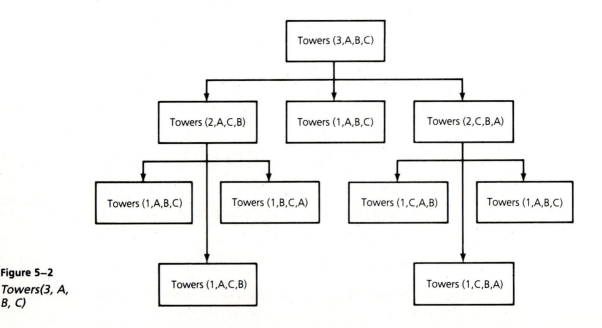

Figure 5–2

Towers(3, A, B, C)

2. These other Towers problems are smaller than the original (in the sense of fewer disks to be moved).

3. The notion of smaller ensures that a degenerate case (only one disk to be moved) is always reached. In addition, the degenerate case is easy to solve directly.

Notice that this recursive solution will call itself many, many times. Figure 5–2 illustrates the calls for $N = 3$ disks.

We next give a Modula-2 version of the Towers solution. Notice that since most computers do not have arms (at the time of this writing), moving a disk is accomplished by printing out a message instructing a human what to do. Following the program, we present the box trace for $N = 3$ (Figure 5–3). The points X, Y, and Z in the comments are used in the trace for reference.

```
PROCEDURE Towers(count, source, dest, spare : INTEGER);
BEGIN

    IF (count = 1) THEN
        WriteString('Move piece from pole ');
        WriteInt(source, 1);
        WriteString(' to pole ');
        WriteInt(dest, 1);
        Write('.');
        WriteLn;
    ELSE
        Towers(count-1, source, spare, dest);    (* point X *)
        Towers(1, source, dest, spare);          (* point Y *)
        Towers(count-1, spare, dest, source);    (* point Z *)
    END;

END Towers;
```

Sorting

Searching for data is one of the most common tasks performed by computers. When the amount of data to be searched is large, it is often necessary to employ an efficient method for searching. One such method is a binary search algorithm like the one presented in the previous chapter. For a binary search to be applicable, however, the data that is to be searched must be sorted. Good sorting algorithms are, therefore, very valuable. We present two highly efficient recursive sorting routines: *Quicksort* and *Mergesort*. The presentations are in the context of sorting arrays, but—as we shall see in Chapter 12—*Mergesort* generalizes to external files. In Chapter 13 we also present some other common sorting algorithms and develop techniques for comparing their efficiencies.

For concreteness, let us suppose that we wish to implement the following definition module (page 202).

Figure 5–3

*Box trace of
Towers(3, A,
B, C)*

Example of the box method for call Towers (3, A, B, C):

The initial call is made, and procedure Towers begins execution:

```
Count  = 3
Source = A
Dest   = B
Spare  = C
```

At point X, a recursive call is made, and the new invocation of the procedure begins execution:

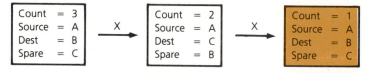

At point X, a recursive call is made, and the new invocation of the procedure begins execution:

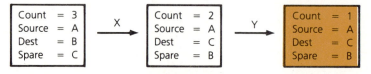

This is the degenerate case, so a disk is moved, the return is made, and the procedure continues execution.

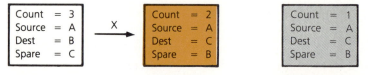

At point Y, a recursive call is made, and the new invocation of the procedure begins execution:

```
Count  = 3      X    Count  = 2      Y    Count  = 1
Source = A   ------> Source = A   ------> Source = A
Dest   = B           Dest   = C           Dest   = C
Spare  = C           Spare  = B           Spare  = B
```

This is the degenerate case, so a disk is moved, the return is made, and the procedure continues execution.

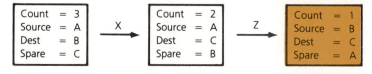

At point Z, a recursive call is made, and the new invocation of the procedure begins execution:

```
Count  = 3      X    Count  = 2      Z    Count  = 1
Source = A   ------> Source = A   ------> Source = B
Dest   = B           Dest   = C           Dest   = C
Spare  = C           Spare  = B           Spare  = A
```

This is the degenerate case, so a disk is moved, the return is made, and the procedure continues execution.

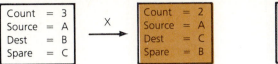

This invocation completes, the return is made, and the procedure continues execution.

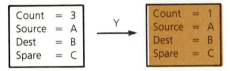

At point Y, a recursive call is made, and the new invocation of the procedure begins execution:

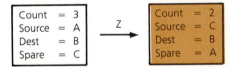

This is the degenerate case, so a disk is moved, the return is made, and the procedure continues execution.

At point Z, a recursive call is made, and the new invocation of the procedure begins execution:

At point X, a recursive call is made, and the new invocation of the procedure begins execution:

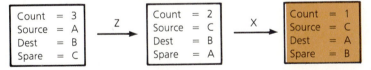

This is the degenerate case, so a disk is moved, the return is made, and the procedure continues execution.

At point Y, a recursive call is made, and the new invocation of the procedure begins execution:

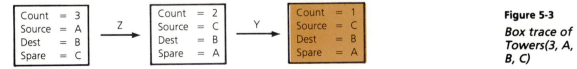

Figure 5-3

Box trace of Towers(3, A, B, C)

This is the degenerate case, so a disk is moved, the return is made, and the procedure continues execution.

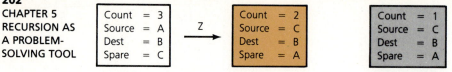

At point Z, a recursive call is made, and the new invocation of the procedure begins execution:

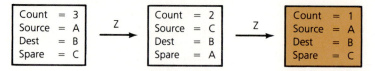

This is the degenerate case, so a disk is moved, the return is made, and the procedure continues execution.

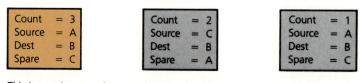

This invocation completes, the return is made, and the procedure continues execution.

Figure 5-3
Box trace of Towers(3, A, B, C)

This invocation completes, and a return is made to the main program.

```
DEFINITION MODULE SortProc;
(* *********************************************************
    Sort an array.
    ********************************************************* *)

(* user-defined sort item *)
FROM SortType IMPORT

    sortitem;

EXPORT QUALIFIED

    Sort;

(* -------------------------------------------------------
    Sort:  Sort array A of sortitem.
    ------------------------------------------------------- *)
PROCEDURE Sort(VAR A : ARRAY OF sortitem);

END SortProc.
```

Quicksort. Consider the first two steps of the problem of finding the kth smallest element from Chapter 4:

```
choose a pivot element S from A[F..L]
partition the elements of A[F..L] about S
```

Recall that the partition in Figure 5–4 has the property that all elements in $A[F..i]$ are less than S, all elements in $A[(i + 1)..j]$ are equal to S, and all elements in $A[(j + 1)..L]$ are greater than S. Though this property does not imply that the array is sorted, it does imply an extremely useful fact. The elements from F to i remain in positions F to i when the array is properly sorted (though their positions relative to one another may change). Similarly, the elements from $j + 1$ up to L will remain in positions $j + 1$ to L when the array is sorted (though their relative positions may change). Finally, the elements in positions $i + 1$ to j are already sorted (they're equal to one another, after all) and remain in their positions in the final, sorted array.

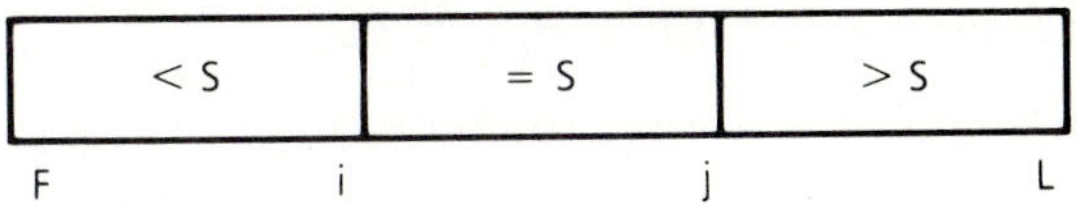

Figure 5–4

*Partition
about pivot*

These relationships between the array elements induced by the partition are the ingredients of a recursive solution. Arranging the array around the pivot element generates two smaller sorting problems—sort the left section of the array and sort the right section of the array. The relationships imply that once the left and right sorting problems are solved, the original sorting problem will have been solved. The middle section of the array does not generate a sorting problem because its elements are already sorted. Notice we are assured that the left and right sorting problems are each closer than the original sorting problem to the degenerate case (an array containing a single element), since the middle section of the array contains at least one element.

Quicksort can be stated as:

```
Quicksort(A, first, last)

    IF (first < last) THEN

        choose a pivot element S from A[first..last]

        partition the elements of A[first..last] about S

        Quicksort(A, first, i)

        Quicksort(A, j+1, last)

        (* if first >= last there is nothing to do *)

    END
```

It is worth contrasting this with the pseudocode function given for the kth smallest integer problem:

```
PROCEDURE Select(k, A, F, L) : returns a value from the array

    choose a pivot element S from A[F..L]

    partition the elements of A[F..L] about S

    IF (k ≤ i-F+1) THEN
        RETURN (Select(k, A, F, i))
    ELSIF (i-F+1 < k ≤ j-F+1) THEN
        RETURN (S)
    ELSE
        RETURN (Select(k-(j-F+1), A, j+1, L))
    END
```

There are two fundamental differences between Select and Quicksort:

1. *Select* is called recursively only on the section of the array that contains the desired element (and not called at all if the desired element is in the middle region), while *Quicksort* is called on both unsorted sections of the array (see Figure 5–5).

2. *Select* is a function that returns a value and does not alter the array it is passed (it is passed as a value parameter), while *Quicksort* is a procedure that does alter the array it is passed.

Figure 5–5

Quicksort ver-sus Select

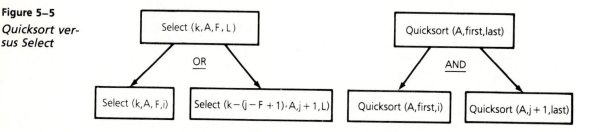

Using an Invariant to Develop a Partition Procedure. We now must consider the partition procedure required by both *Select* and *Quicksort*. Partitioning an array section about a pivot element is actually the most difficult part of the two problems. We'll develop a partitioning algorithm and then present a Modula-2 implementation of *Quicksort*.

The partition procedure is passed an array segment (which is determined by an array A and integers F and L to indicate the segment in question) and the value *pivot*, which is some element in the array. The procedure must arrange the elements of the array segment into three regions: S_1, the array of elements less than *pivot*; S_2, the array of elements equal to *pivot*; and S_3, the array of elements greater than *pivot*. The procedure arranges the array so that S_1 is in A[F..lastS1], S_2 is in A[lastS1 + 1..firstS3 - 1], and S_3 is in A[firstS3..L] (see Figure 5–6).

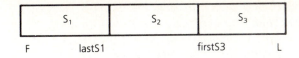

Figure 5–6
Array after partitioning

To accomplish its task, the partition procedure will impose a fourth region, called *unknown*, on the array. While the procedure is executing, the array should be viewed as shown in Figure 5–7.

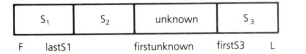

Figure 5–7
Invariant for partition algorithm

The array indices F, `lastS1`, `firstS3`, and L divide the array as described above, except that in the course of the procedure's execution, S_2 will be in `A[lastS1+1..firstunknown-1]`. We shall develop the partition procedure so that *throughout its entire execution*, the elements in the region S_1 are all less than `pivot`, those in S_2 are all equal to `pivot`, and those in S_3 are all greater than `pivot`. The relationship between the elements in the unknown region (which is in `A[firstunknown..firstS3-1]`) and `pivot` is, simply, unknown!

The condition stated above is known as an **invariant**—its validity is maintained throughout the course of the procedure's execution. Invariants play a central role in the design and analysis of algorithms. You will see the concept again in this book and certainly in formal courses on the analysis of algorithms.

For our invariant to be true at the procedure's start, the pointers must be initialized so that the unknown region spans the entire array segment to be partitioned. To perform such an initialization, we make the following assignments:

```
lastS1 := F-1
firstS3 := L+1
firstunknown := F
```

The initial status of the array is as shown in Figure 5–8.

Figure 5–8
Initial state of array

Each step of the partition procedure examines one element of the unknown region, determines in which of the three regions it belongs, and places it there. Thus, the size of the unknown region decreases by one at each step. As we shall see, this can be accomplished either by incrementing `firstunknown` or by decrementing `firstS3`. The procedure terminates when the size of the unknown region reaches zero—that is, when `firstunknown = firstS3`.

We can state the following high-level algorithm for partitioning.

```
(* initialize S1, S2, and S3 to empty, unknown to A[F..L] *)
lastS1 := F-1
firstS3 := L+1
firstunknown := F
```

```
(* process while the unknown region is not empty *)
WHILE (firstunknown < firstS3) DO
    (* consider the placement of the "leftmost"
       element in the unknown region *)
  IF (A[firstunknown] = pivot) THEN
     move A[firstunknown] into S2
  ELSIF (A[firstunknown] > pivot) THEN
     move A[firstunknown] into S3
  ELSE
     move A[firstunknown] into S1
  END
END
```

The algorithm is straightforward enough, but a naive implementation could be very inefficient. As the regions for S_1, S_2, and S_3 expand and the unknown region shrinks, we might expect that we would have to shift many array elements. However, extensive shifting of array elements is expensive, and we should avoid it if possible. It turns out that there is a very clever implementation of the above algorithm that swaps at most one pair of array elements at each iteration of the **WHILE** loop.

Consider the three possible actions that need to be taken at each iteration of the **WHILE** loop:

1. $A[firstunknown]$ is to be moved into S_2.
2. $A[firstunknown]$ is to be moved into S_3.
3. $A[firstunknown]$ is to be moved into S_1.

Let us examine how to perform each of these actions in a manner that keeps the shifting of array elements to a minimum.

1. **Move** A$[firstunknown]$ **into** S_2. This is the easiest of the three moves. Recall that the rightmost boundary of region S_2 is at position $firstunknown-1$; that is, regions S_2 and unknown are adjacent. Thus, it is very simple to move $A[firstunknown]$ into S_2—simply increment $firstunknown$ by 1. This way S_2 expands to the right.

   MOVE A$[firstunknown]$ INTO S_2:

   ```
   firstunknown := firstunknown + 1
   ```

   Note that this move preserves the invariant.

2. **Move** A $[firstunknown]$ **into** S_3. Recall that region S_3 is in $A[firstS3..L]$ and that the rightmost boundary of the unknown region is at position $firstS3-1$; that is, regions S_3 and unknown are adjacent. As we can't add $A[firstunknown]$ to the right end of region S_3 (this is the end of the array segment!), we'll add it to its left end. But is there room? Note that $A[firstS3-1]$ contains an element from the unknown region. What we'll do is simply swap the element in $A[firstS3-1]$ with $A[firstunknown]$. This way S_3 expands to the left.

MOVE A[$firstunknown$] INTO S$_3$:

```
firstS3 := firstS3 - 1
swap A[firstunknown] with A[firstS3]
```

Observe that we do not increment $firstunknown$—the array element it now points to belongs in the unknown region (remember where it came from!).

Note that this move preserves the invariant.

3. **Move A[$firstunknown$] into S$_1$.** This is the most difficult of the three moves. What makes it more difficult than the other two moves is that S$_1$ and the unknown region are, in general, not adjacent. S$_2$ is between the two regions. What we'll do here is swap A[$firstunknown$] with the leftmost element of S$_2$ (stored in A[$lastS1+1$]). After $lastS1$ is incremented by 1, the element that was in A[$firstunknown$] will be at the rightmost portion of S$_1$. Now, what about the element of S$_2$ that was moved to A[$firstunknown$]? If we increment $firstunknown$, then the element becomes the rightmost member of S$_2$.

MOVE A[$firstunknown$] INTO S$_1$:

```
lastS1 := lastS1 + 1
swap A[firstunknown] with A[lastS1]
firstunknown := firstunknown + 1
```

This strategy works even when S$_2$ is empty. In this case, after $lastS1$ is incremented, it will equal $firstunknown$, and thus the swap simply exchanges an element with itself.

Note that this move preserves the invariant.

We have concluded the development of the partition algorithm, but before using it in our implementation of $Quicksort$, let us briefly summarize and elaborate on the concept of an invariant. Invariants are typically used to develop and establish the correctness of iterative algorithms. In this context, they are referred to as **loop invariants**. The idea is that the invariant states a condition that is true before and after each execution of the algorithm's loop. For example, the loop invariant for the above partition procedure is as follows:

> All elements in S$_1$ (A[F..$lastS1$]) are less than the pivot, all elements in S$_2$ (A[$lastS1+1$..$firstunknown-1$]) are equal to the pivot, and all elements in S$_3$ (A[$firstS3$..L]) are greater than the pivot.

Using invariants to establish the correctness of an iterative algorithm is a four-step process:

1. The invariant must be shown to be *true initially*, that is, before the loop is entered for the first time. In the partition algorithm, before the loop that swaps array elements is entered, the unknown region is initialized to be all of A[F..L], and S$_1$, S$_2$, and S$_3$ are empty. The invariant is clearly true initially.

2. An execution of the loop must be shown to *preserve the invariant*. That is, it

must be shown that if the invariant is true before any given iteration of the loop, then it will necessarily be true after the iteration. In the partition algorithm, at each iteration of the loop a single element is moved from the unknown region into S_1, S_2, or S_3, depending on whether the element is less than, equal to, or greater than the pivot. Thus, if the invariant was true before the move, it will remain true after the move.

3. The invariant must be shown to *capture the correctness* of the algorithm. That is, it must be shown that if the invariant is true when the loop terminates (when the loop's termination condition becomes true), then the algorithm is correct. In the partition algorithm, the termination condition is that the unknown region is empty. But if the unknown region is empty, all the elements of $A[F..L]$ must be in S_1, S_2, or S_3—in which case, the invariant implies that the partition algorithm has done what it was supposed to do.

4. It must be shown that the loop is *guaranteed to terminate;* that is, it must be shown that the loop will terminate after a finite number of iterations. In the partition algorithm, the size of the unknown region is reduced by one at each iteration. Therefore, it will become empty after a finite number of iterations, and thus the termination condition for the loop will be met.

Notice the clear connection between mathematical induction and the use of loop invariants. Showing the invariant to be true initially establishes the base case (analogous to establishing that a property of the natural numbers is true for zero). Showing that the invariant is preserved by each iteration of the loop is the inductive step (analogous to showing that a property is true for an arbitrary natural number k implies that it is necessarily true for the natural number $k + 1$). Once these steps have been performed, we can conclude that the invariant is true after every iteration of the loop (just as mathematical induction allows us to conclude that a property is true for every natural number).

Now that we have developed a partition algorithm and established its correctness by using an invariant, there remains one final problem to be solved before we can implement *Quicksort*. How do we choose the pivot element? The choice of the pivot element directly affects the efficiency of the algorithm (although the algorithm will work with any choice from the array). Here we shall arbitrarily select the middle element of the array to be the pivot element. There are other more elaborate strategies, but their analyses are beyond the scope of this book.

We now present a Modula-2 implementation of *Quicksort*.

```
IMPLEMENTATION MODULE SortProc;
(* ********************************************************
    Sort an array with Quicksort.
    ******************************************************** *)


(* user-defined sort item *)
FROM SortType IMPORT

    sortitem;
```

```
(* ---------------------------------------------------------
    Swap:   Interchange items x and y.
    ------------------------------------------------------- *)
PROCEDURE Swap(VAR x, y : sortitem);

VAR

    temp : sortitem;

BEGIN

    temp := x;
    x := y;
    y := temp;

END Swap;

(* ---------------------------------------------------------
    Partition:  Partition A[f..l] such that:

        A[f..lasts1]            < pivot
        A[lasts1+1..firsts3-1]  = pivot
        A[firsts3..l]           > pivot

    The array is broken down into 4 regions:  S1, S2, unknown,
    and S3.  (The unknown region of the array is from
    firstunknown to firsts3-1.)  The algorithm consists of
    moving one element at a time from unknown into its proper
    region until unknown is empty.

    Calls:  Swap
    ------------------------------------------------------ *)
PROCEDURE Partition(VAR A : ARRAY OF sortitem; f, l : INTEGER;
                    pivot : sortitem;
                    VAR lasts1, firsts3: INTEGER);

VAR

    firstunknown : INTEGER;
    testval : sortitem;

BEGIN

    (* initially, everything is in unknown *)
    lasts1 := f-1;
    firsts3 := l+1;
    firstunknown := f;
```

```
            (* move one element at a time until unknown is empty *)
            WHILE (firstunknown < firsts3) DO
                (* choose element from unknown *)
                testval := A[firstunknown];

                (* put element into proper region *)

            (* testval belongs in S2 *)
            IF (testval = pivot) THEN

                INC(firstunknown);

            (* testval belongs in S1 *)
            ELSIF (testval < pivot) THEN

                INC(lasts1);
                Swap(A[firstunknown], A[lasts1]);
                INC(firstunknown);

            (* testval belongs in S3 *)
            ELSE
                DEC(firsts3);
                Swap(A[firstunknown], A[firsts3]);

            END;

    END;

END Partition;

(* ************************************************************
    Sort:   Sort the array A.

    This routine uses the locally defined procedure Quicksort.

    Calls:  Quicksort
    ************************************************************ *)
PROCEDURE Sort(VAR A : ARRAY OF sortitem);

(* ------------------------------------------------------------
    Quicksort:   Sort array A[f..l] with Quicksort.

    Quicksort is a recursive algorithm that sorts by:
        1.  choosing a pivot element S
        2.  partitioning the array into three regions S1, S2,
            and S3 such that:
                a.  each element in S1 is < S
                b.  each element in S2 is = S
                c.  each element in S3 is > S
```

```
    3.  sorting regions S1 and S3

    Calls:  Partition
    ------------------------------------------------------ *)
PROCEDURE Quicksort(VAR A : ARRAY OF sortitem; f, l : INTEGER);

VAR

    pivot, lasts1, firsts3 : INTEGER;

BEGIN

    IF (f < l) THEN

        (* pivot on the middle element of the array segment *)
        pivot := A[(f + l) DIV 2];

        (* create the partition *)
        Partition(A, f, l, pivot, lasts1, firsts3);

        (* sort regions S1 and S3 *)
        Quicksort(A, f, lasts1);
        Quicksort(A, firsts3, l);

    END;

END Quicksort;

(* main body of Sort *)
BEGIN

    Quicksort(A, 0, HIGH(A));

END Sort;

END SortProc.
```

Notice that since each call to procedure *Quicksort* must alter the array *A*, *A* must be passed as a variable parameter. Variable parameters must be represented differently than value parameters in our box method. A variable parameter, rather than being represented as part of the local environment of each recursive call, is viewed as external to the boxes (in much the same way as we represented a global variable for the binary search function in Chapter 4). Within each box corresponding to a call's local environment, we associate the name of the formal parameter with the actual parameter (Figure 5–9). References to the formal parameter from within different recursive calls to the subprogram lead to the *same* actual parameter.

How efficient is *Quicksort*? In Chapter 13 we compare it with other sorting algorithms, but at present we can say that, if the original arrangement of data

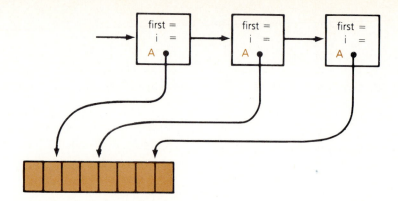

Figure 5–9

*Box trace
with variable
parameter*

in the array is "random," *Quicksort* performs at least as well as any known sorting algorithm. That is, unless one is very unlucky, *Quicksort* can't be beat. (*Quicksort* will perform worst if, at each recursive step, we happen to choose either the largest or smallest element of the array segment for the pivot element.) Unfortunately, luck is often against computer programs—or, more precisely, that which appears to be unlucky is often what a little thought would have warned us to expect. Even when luck is against *Quicksort*, its performance is acceptable for moderately large arrays.

Mergesort. *Mergesort* is a recursive sorting algorithm that always gives the same performance, regardless of luck. Its efficiency is somewhere between the possibilities for *Quicksort*: If luck is with *Quicksort*, *Mergesort* will not do quite as well as *Quicksort*; if luck is against *Quicksort*, *Mergesort* will do better than *Quicksort*.

Mergesort is similar to *Quicksort*, but while *Quicksort* does work before its recursive calls, *Mergesort* does work after its recursive calls. That is, while *Quicksort* has the form

```
Quicksort(A)

    IF (size = 1) THEN
        quit
    ELSE
        prepare array for recursive calls
        Quicksort(S1 region of A)
        Quicksort(S3 region of A)
    END
```

Mergesort has the general form

```
Mergesort(A)

    IF (size = 1) THEN
        quit
```

```
    ELSE
        Mergesort( Lefthalf(A) )
        Mergesort( Righthalf(A) )
        tidy up the array after the recursive calls
    END
```

The preparation in *Quicksort* is to partition the array into regions S_1, S_2, and S_3. Then S_1 and S_3 can be sorted independently, since every element in S_1 belongs to the left of every element in S_2 and every element in S_2 belongs to the left of every element in S_3. In *Mergesort*, on the other hand, no work is done before the recursive calls. Thus, each half of the array will be sorted with respect to itself, but the interaction between the elements of the two halves must still be dealt with. The action required after the recursive calls is to *merge* the two halves of the array into a single sorted array. This can be accomplished as follows.

```
(* merge sorted arrays B and C into
    array A by copying one item at a time *)
Merge(A, B, C)

    WHILE (both B have C more items to copy) DO
        compare the first uncopied item of B to the first
            uncopied item of C
        copy the smaller of the two into A
    END

    (* At this point exactly one of B and C
        will have more items to copy into A. *)
    copy the remaining items into A
```

The high-level description of *Mergesort* becomes

```
Mergesort(A)

    IF (size = 1) THEN
        quit
    ELSE
        Mergesort( Lefthalf(A) )
        Mergesort( Righthalf(A) )
        Merge( A, Lefthalf(A), Righthalf(A) )
    END
```

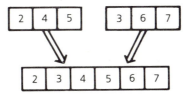

Figure 5–10

Mergesort with auxiliary array

A Modula-2 implementation follows. Notice that procedure *Merge* takes two array arguments, the array whose halves are to be merged and an array to contain the result. In the context of procedure *Mergesort* these two arrays are one and the same.

```
IMPLEMENTATION MODULE SortProc;
(* ***********************************************************
    Sort an array with Mergesort.
    ******************************************************** *)

(* user-defined sort item *)
FROM SortType IMPORT

    sortitem;

(* -----------------------------------------------------------
    Merge:  Merge A[first..mid] with A[mid+1..last] into array
    Result[first..last].

    Note that it is not possible, in general, to merge in
    place.  It is possible, however, to merge an array into
    itself with this procedure, since A is passed as a value
    parameter (and is thus copied).  This effect of Merge is
    accomplished with a call such as:

        Merge(A,A,first,mid,last)

    ASSUMPTIONS:

        1.  A[first..mid] and A[mid+1..last] are legal subarrays of
            A and are sorted in increasing order.

        2.  Result[first..last] is a legal subarray of Result.
    ----------------------------------------------------------- *)
PROCEDURE Merge(VAR Result : ARRAY OF sortitem;
                    A : ARRAY OF sortitem;
                    first, mid, last : INTEGER);

VAR

    first1, last1, first2, last2, index : INTEGER;

BEGIN

    (* initialize the local indices *)
    first1 := first;
    last1 := mid;
    first2 := mid+1;
    last2 := last;
```

```
    (* set the next available location in the Result array *)
    index := first1;

    (* while both subarrays are nonempty, copy the
       smaller element into the Result array *)
    WHILE ( (first1 <= last1) AND (first2 <= last2) ) DO
        IF (A[first1] < A[first2]) THEN
            Result[index] := A[first1];
            INC(first1);
            INC(index);
        ELSE
            Result[index] := A[first2];
            INC(first2);
            INC(index);
        END;
    END;

    (* finish off the nonempty subarray *)

    (* finish off the first subarray if necessary *)
    WHILE (first1 <= last1) DO
        Result[index] := A[first1];
        INC(first1);
        INC(index);
    END;

    (* finish off the second subarray if necessary *)
    WHILE (first2 <= last2) DO
        Result[index] := A[first2];
        INC(first2);
        INC(index);
    END;

END Merge;

(* ************************************************************
    Sort:  Sort the array A.

    This routine uses the locally defined procedure Mergesort.

    Calls:  Mergesort
    ********************************************************** *)
PROCEDURE Sort(VAR A : ARRAY OF sortitem);

(* ----------------------------------------------------------
    Mergesort:  Sort array A[first..last] with Mergesort.

    Mergesort is a recursive algorithm that sorts by:
        1.  sorting the first half of the array
```

2. sorting the second half of the array
3. merging the two sorted halves

Calls: Merge

-- *)

```
PROCEDURE Mergesort(VAR A : ARRAY OF sortitem;
                    first, last : INTEGER);

VAR

    mid : INTEGER;

BEGIN

    IF (first < last) THEN

        (* sort each half *)
        mid := (first + last) DIV 2;
        Mergesort(A, first, mid);
        Mergesort(A, mid+1, last);

        (* Merge the two halves.  Note that merge requires two
           arrays, the array whose halves are to be merged and an
           array to hold the result.  In the context of Mergesort
           we want these arrays to be one and the same. *)
        Merge(A, A, first, mid, last);

    END;

END Mergesort;

(* main body of Sort *)
BEGIN

    Mergesort(A,0,HIGH(A));

END Sort;

END SortProc.
```

DEFINING THINGS

In this section we demonstrate how recursion can be used to define **languages**. A language is nothing more than a set of strings of symbols. For example, consider the language comprised of all syntactically correct Modula-2 programs. If we view a program as one long string of characters, then we can define the set

Modula-2-Programs = {strings w | w is a syntactically correct Modula-2 program}

Notice that whereas all programs are strings, not all strings are programs. A Modula-2 compiler is a program that, among other things, determines if a given string is a member of the set Modula-2-Programs, that is, determines if the string is a syntactically correct Modula-2 program. Of course, the above definition of Modula-2-Programs is not descriptive enough to allow the construction of a compiler. The definition specifies a characteristic of the strings in the set Modula-2-Programs (they are all syntactically legal Modula-2 programs), but it does not give the rules for determining if a string is in the set or not (it does not specify what is meant by a syntactically correct Modula-2 program).

A **grammar** is one means of stating the rules of a language. As it is a complex task to present a grammar for the set Modula-2-Programs, we instead present grammars for some simpler languages. As we just said, a language is nothing more than a set of strings. Thus, when we say language, we do not necessarily mean a programming language or a communication language. For example, one type of language we shall study in this section is

Algebraic-Expressions = {strings w | w is an algebraic expression}

The language Algebraic-Expressions is the set of strings that meets certain rules of syntax (for example, matched parentheses, * has two operands). We will use grammars to state precisely the complete rules of syntax for several different common languages of algebraic expressions.

The Basics of Grammars

A grammar is a device for defining a language. One of the great benefits of using a grammar to define a language is that it is often straightforward to write a recursive algorithm, based on the grammar, for determining if a given string is a member of the language. Such an algorithm is called a **recognition algorithm** for the language.

A grammar uses several special symbols:

1. $x|y$ means x or y.
2. $x\ y$ means x *followed by* y. (When context requires clarification, we write $x \cdot y$.)
3. $<word>$ means that *word* is further **expanded** (defined) in the definition.

As an example, consider the language

Modula-2-Ids = {w | w is a legal Modula-2 identifier}

As you know, a legal Modula-2 identifier must begin with a letter and be followed by zero or more letters and digits (for simplicity, we'll assume that there is no restriction on the maximum length of an identifier). One way to represent this definition is with a syntax diagram, as shown in Figure 5–11.

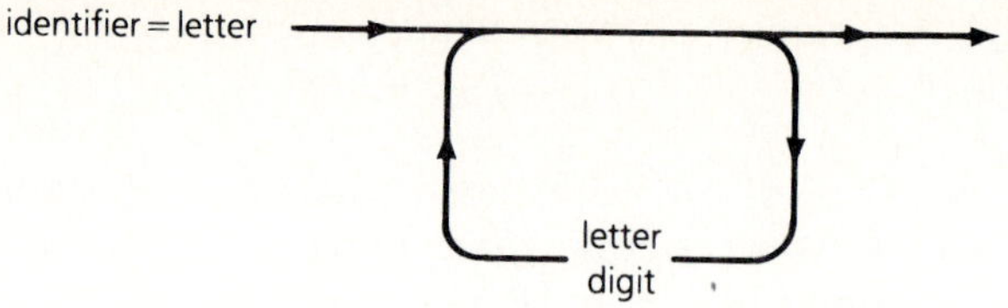

Figure 5–11

Syntax diagram for Modula-2 identifiers

identifier = letter

letter
digit

A syntax diagram is convenient for people to use, but a grammar is a better starting point for writing a program that will recognize an identifier. A grammar for the language Modula-2-Ids is

<Modula-2-id> = <letter> | <Modula-2-id><letter> | <Modula-2-id><digit>

<letter>   = A | B | ... | Z | a | b | ... | z

<digit>   = 0 | 1 | ... | 9

The definition is read as follows:

> *A Modula-2-id is a letter, or a Modula-2-id followed by a letter, or a Modula-2-id followed by a digit.*

The most striking aspect of the definition is that Modula-2-id, the object being defined, appears in its own definition. Grammars are often recursive.

Given a string w, we can determine if the string is in the language Modula-2-Ids by applying the definition given by the grammar: If w is of length one, then it is in the language if the character is a letter (this is the degenerate case, so to speak). If w is of length greater than one, then it is in the language if

(1) the last character of w is a letter, and w minus its last character is an identifier, or

(2) the last character of w is a digit, and w minus its last character is an identifier

The translation to a recursive function is direct.

```
PROCEDURE Id(w) : BOOLEAN
(* Determine if w is a legal Modula-2 identifier. *)

  IF (w is of length 1) THEN        (* degenerate case *)
      RETURN (w is a letter)

  ELSIF (the last character of w is a letter) THEN
      RETURN ( Id(w minus its last character) )

  ELSIF (the last character of w is a digit) THEN
      RETURN ( Id(w minus its last character) )
```

ELSE

      RETURN (FALSE)

END

Two Simple Languages

Palindromes.   A palindrome is a string that reads the same from left to right as it does from right to left. For example,

    radar and *deed*

are palindromes. We can define the language of palindromes as

    Palindromes $= \{w \mid w$ reads the same left to right as right to left$\}$

How can we use a grammar to define the language Palindromes? We need to devise a rule that allows us to determine if a given string w is a palindrome or not. In the spirit of recursive definitions, this rule should be stated in terms of determining if a *smaller string* is a palindrome. Our first instinct might be to choose w minus its last (or first) character for the smaller string. This does not work, however, as there is no relationship between the statements

    w is a palindrome

and

    w minus its last character is a palindrome

That is, w minus its last character might be a palindrome, although w is not (for example, w is *deeds*). Similarly, w might be a palindrome, although w minus its last character is not (for example, w is *deed*).

    A little thought reveals that characters must be considered in pairs. There is a relationship between the statements

    w is a palindrome

and

    w minus its first and last characters is a palindrome

Specifically, w is a palindrome if and only if

    the first and last characters of w are the same

and

    w minus its first and last characters is a palindrome

We need a degenerate case that will be reached after enough pairs of characters have been stripped away. If w is of even length, we will eventually be left with two characters, and then, after we strip away another pair, we will be left with zero characters. A string of length zero is called the **empty string** and is a palindrome. If w is of odd length, we will eventually be left with one character, after which we cannot strip away another pair. Hence, we must have a second degenerate case: A string of length one is a palindrome.

This leads to the following grammar for the language Palindromes:

$$<pal> = \text{empty string} \mid <ch> \mid a<pal>a \mid b<pal>b \mid ... \mid Z<pal>Z \, ...$$
$$<ch> = a \mid b \mid c ... z \mid A \mid ... Z \, ...$$

We can construct a recursive function, based on the grammar, for recognizing palindromes.

```
PROCEDURE Pal(w) :  BOOLEAN
(* Determine if w is a palindrome.  *)

   IF ((w is the empty string) OR (w is of length one)) THEN
      RETURN (TRUE)

   ELSIF (the first character of w is the same
          as the last character w) THEN
      RETURN ( Pal(w minus its first and last characters) )

   ELSE
      RETURN (FALSE)

   END
```

Strings of the Form $a^n b^n$.   The symbol $a^n b^n$ is standard notation for the string consisting of n consecutive a's, followed by n consecutive b's. Another simple language is

$$L = \{ \, w \mid w \text{ is of the form } a^n b^n \text{ for some } n \geq 0 \}$$

The grammar for this language is actually very similar to that for palindromes. We must strip away the first and last characters and check to see that the first is an a and the last is a b.

$$<legalword> = \text{empty string} \mid a<legalword>b$$

A recognition algorithm is

```
PROCEDURE Recognize(w) :  BOOLEAN
(* Determine if w is of the form aⁿbⁿ. *)
```

```
IF (the length of w is zero) THEN
    RETURN (TRUE)

ELSIF ((the first character of w is a) AND
        (the last character of w is b)) THEN

    RETURN (Recognize(w minus its first and last characters))

ELSE
    RETURN (FALSE)

END
```

Algebraic Expressions

One of the tasks a compiler must perform is to recognize and evaluate algebraic expressions. For example, consider the Modula-2 assignment statement

```
y := x + z * (w/k + z * (7 * 6))
```

A Modula-2 compiler must determine if the right side is a syntactically legal algebraic expression; if so, the compiler then must indicate how to compute its value.

There are several common definitions for a "syntactically legal" algebraic expression. Some definitions force an expression to be fully parenthesized, whereas others are more lenient. In general, the stricter a definition, the easier it is to recognize a syntactically legal expression. On the other hand, it is an inconvenience for the programmer to have to conform to overly strict rules of syntax. For example, if the syntax rule requires full parenthesization, then we would have to write ((x * y) * z) rather than x * y * z.

In the following sections we present five different languages for algebraic expressions. They are ordered from "easy to recognize and evaluate but inconvenient to use" to "difficult to recognize and evaluate but convenient to use." We present recursive recognition algorithms for two of the languages; in Chapter 7, we present a nonrecursive evaluation algorithm for another. To avoid unnecessary complications, we shall assume that we have only the binary operators +, −, *, and / (no unary operators or exponentiation). We also assume that all input operands are single-letter upper-case identifiers.

Infix, Prefix, and Postfix Expressions.   The type of algebraic expressions most of us learn about in grade school are called **infix expressions**. The term *infix* denotes the fact that every binary operator goes between its operands, for example, in the expression

$$a + b$$

the operand + goes between its operands *a* and *b*. This convention necessitates rules of associativity and precedence and the use of parentheses to avoid ambiguity. For example, the expression

$$a + b * c$$

is ambiguous. What is the second operand of the $+$? Is it b, or is it $(b * c)$? Similarly, the first operand of the $*$ could be either b or $(a + b)$. The rule that $*$ has higher precedence than $+$ removes the ambiguity by specifying that b is the first operand of the $*$ and that $(b * c)$ is the second operand of the $+$. If another interpretation is desired, parentheses must be used:

$$(a + b) * c$$

Even with precedence rules, there is ambiguity in an expression like

$$a / b * c$$

Since $/$ and $*$ are typically defined to have equal precedence, the expression could be interpreted either as $(a / b) * c$ or as $a / (b * c)$. The common practice is to *associate from left to right*, thus yielding the former interpretation.

Two alternatives to the traditional infix convention are **prefix** and **postfix**. Under these conventions, an operator appears before its operands and after its operands, respectively. Thus,

$$a + b$$

is written as

$$+ a b$$

in prefix and as

$$a b +$$

in postfix.

To further illustrate the conventions, consider the two interpretations of the infix expression

$$a + b * c$$

given at the beginning of this section. The expression $a + (b * c)$ is written as $+ a * b c$ in prefix. The $+$ appears before its operands a and $(* b c)$, and the $*$ appears before its operands b and c. The same expression is written as $a b c * +$ in postfix. The $*$ appears after its operands b and c, and the $+$ appears after its operands a and $(b c *)$.

Similarly, the expression $(a + b) * c$ is written as $* + a b c$ in prefix. The $*$ appears before its operands $(+ a b)$ and c, and the $+$ appears before its operands a and b. The same expression is written as $a b + c *$ in postfix. The $+$ appears after its operands a and b, and the $*$ appears after its operands $(a b +)$ and c.

The great advantage of prefix and postfix expressions is that precedence rules, association rules, and parentheses are never needed. This allows the grammars that define these types of expressions to be very simple. Of equal importance, the algorithms that recognize and evaluate these expressions are also relatively simple.

A grammar that defines the language of all prefix expressions is:

<pre-exp> = <letter> | <operator><pre-exp><pre-exp>

<operator> = + | − | * | /

<letter> = A | B |...| Z

We can construct a recursive recognition algorithm from this grammar as follows. Suppose the array $S[start..HIGH(S)]$ contains the string we wish to recognize. If the string $S[start..HIGH(S)]$ is of length one , then this is the degenerate case, and the string is a prefix expression if and only if $S[start]$ is an identifier (a single uppercase letter). If the length of $S[start..HIGH(S)]$ is greater than one, then in order for it to be a legal prefix expression, it must be of the form

operator·pre-exp·pre-exp

Thus, the algorithm must check to see that:

1. The first character $S[start]$ is an operator.
2. $S[start+1..HIGH(S)]$ consists of two consecutive prefix expressions.

The first task is trivial, but the second is a bit tricky. How can we determine if we are looking at two consecutive prefix expressions? A key observation is that if E is a prefix expression, then adding *any* string of characters to the end of E will destroy this property; that is, if E is a prefix expression and Y is any nonempty string, then E·Y *cannot* be a prefix expression. This is a subtle point, and we ask you to prove it in Exercise 5.5.

Given that the above observation is true, the rest of the algorithm falls into place. Once we have determined that the first character $S[start]$ is an operator, we can begin to determine if the remainder of the string ($S[start+1..HIGH(S)]$) consists of two consecutive prefix expressions by identifying a first prefix expression. If we can't find one, then the original string itself is not a prefix expression. If we do find one, we're interested in where it ends. Notice that the observation implies that there is only one possible end point for this first expression—given that $S[start+1..last1]$ is a prefix expression, there can be no other prefix expression that begins at $S[start+1]$; that is, it is not possible that $S[start+1..last2]$ is a prefix expression for any $last1 \neq last2$.

If we find that the first prefix expression ends at position $last$, we then attempt to find a second prefix expression beginning at position $last+1$ and ending at or before position $HIGH(S)$. If we find the second expression, we must make sure that there are no nonblank characters in S between the end of the expression and position *HIGH (S)* ; that is, we must check that we are at the end of the string in question.

We thus can construct, as follows, a function

```
Last (S, start)
```

that returns the position of the end of the prefix expression beginning at *S[start]* or signals (by returning the value -1) that there is no prefix expression beginning at *S[start]*.

```
PROCEDURE Last (S, start) : returns an index into array S
(* Return the index of the end of the prefix expression
   beginning at S[start].  Return the value -1 if there
   is no prefix expression beginning at S[start].       *)

   IF ((start < 0) OR (start > HIGH(S))) THEN
      RETURN (-1)

   ELSIF (S[start] is an identifier) THEN
      RETURN (start)

   ELSIF (S[start] is an operator) THEN

      (* find the end of the first prefix expression *)
      firstend := Last (S, start + 1)

      (*find the end of the second prefix expression
        if the end of the first one was found *)
      IF (firstend >= 0) THEN
         RETURN (Last (S, firstend + 1))
      ELSE
         RETURN (-1)
      END

   ELSE
      RETURN (-1)

   END
```

The function *Last* can be used to determine if *S[0..HIGH(S)]* is a prefix expression as follows:

```
PROCEDURE IsPre (S) : BOOLEAN
(* Determine if S[0..HIGH(S)] is a legal prefix expression. *)

   lastchar := Last (S, 0)
   RETURN ( (lastchar >= 0) AND
            (there are no nonblank characters
             in S[lastchar+1..HIGH(S)]) )
```

In the following Modula-2 implementation, the recursive function *Last* is nested within the function *IsPre*. The function *Last* will access *S* globally.

```
IMPLEMENTATION MODULE RecPre;
(*
    RECOGNIZE A PREFIX EXPRESSION

    INPUT:   A string of characters.

    OUTPUT:

        True if the string represents a legal prefix expression.
        False otherwise.

    The recognition is based on the recursive definition:

        prefix expression:

            <pre> = <identifier> | <operator><pre><pre>

        where an identifier is a single upper case letter

        and an operator is one of '+', '-', '*' and '/'
*)


(* ------------------------------------------------------------
    IsBlank:   Determine if the characters from position index
    of STR to the end of STR are all blanks.   STR is terminated
    by either the first NULL character or the upper bound of
    STR, i.e., HIGH(STR).
    ----------------------------------------------------------- *)
PROCEDURE IsBlank(STR : ARRAY OF CHAR; index : CARDINAL) : BOOLEAN;

CONST

    NULL = 0C;

VAR

    i : CARDINAL;

BEGIN

    i := index;
    WHILE ( (i <= HIGH(STR)) AND (STR[i] = ' ') ) DO
        INC(i);
    END;

    RETURN ( (i > HIGH(STR)) OR (STR[i] = NULL) )

END IsBlank;
```

```
(* **********************************************************
    IsPre:   Determine if PRE is a valid prefix expression.

    Calls: Last, IsBlank.
    ********************************************************** *)
PROCEDURE IsPre(PRE : ARRAY OF CHAR) : BOOLEAN;

VAR

    lastchar : INTEGER;

(* ----------------------------------------------------------
    Last:   Return the index of the end of the prefix expression
    beginning at PRE[start].   Return the value -1 if there is
    no prefix expression beginning at PRE[start].
    ---------------------------------------------------------- *)
PROCEDURE Last(start : CARDINAL) : INTEGER;

VAR

 firstend : INTEGER;

BEGIN

    (* test the bounds *)
    IF (start > HIGH(PRE)) THEN
        RETURN (-1);

    (* degenerate case - a single identifier *)
    ELSIF ((PRE[start] >= 'A') AND (PRE[start] <= 'Z')) THEN
        RETURN(start);

    (* general case - apply the recursive definition *)
    ELSIF ((PRE[start] = '+') OR
           (PRE[start] = '-') OR
           (PRE[start] = '*') OR
           (PRE[start] = '/')) THEN

    (* find the end of the first prefix expression *)
    firstend := Last(start+1);

    (* find the end of the second prefix expression *)
    IF (firstend >= 0)  THEN
        RETURN ( Last(firstend+1) );
    ELSE
        RETURN (-1);
    END;
```

```
    ELSE
        RETURN (-1);

    END;

END Last;

(* main body of IsPre *)
BEGIN

    (* the end of the legal expression beginning at index 0
       must be the last nonblank character of the input string *)
    lastchar := Last(0);
    RETURN ((lastchar >= 0) AND IsBlank(PRE, lastchar+1));

END IsPre;

END RecPre.
```

The following illustrates calls to *IsPre*.

PARAMETER PRE	FUNCTION VALUE
A	TRUE
+AB	TRUE
+/AB-CD	TRUE
A+B	FALSE
	FALSE
+A	FALSE
+ABC	FALSE
AB	FALSE
A B	FALSE
+AB C	FALSE

We now consider postfix expressions. A grammar that defines the language of all postfix expressions is

$$<\text{post-exp}> = <\text{letter}> \,|\, <\text{post-exp}><\text{post-exp}><\text{operator}>$$

$$<\text{operator}> = + \,|\, - \,|\, * \,|\, /$$

$$<\text{letter}> \quad = A \,|\, B \,|\, ... \,|\, Z$$

In Chapter 7 we present a nonrecursive algorithm for *evaluating* postfix expressions. Here we shall develop an algorithm for converting a prefix expression to a postfix expression. These two algorithms, combined with the above prefix recognition algorithm, give us a method for evaluating a prefix expression E.

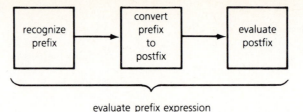

evaluate prefix expression

To simplify the conversion algorithm, we shall assume that the string to be converted has already been run through the prefix recognition algorithm; that is, we assume that the string is a syntactically correct prefix expression.

If we think recursively, the conversion algorithm is very straightforward. If the prefix expression E is a single letter, then

Convert(E) = E

Otherwise E must be of the form

operator·pre-exp1·pre-exp2

The postfix expression that E converts to must thus be

post-exp1·post-exp2·operator

where post-exp1 is the postfix expression that pre-exp1 converts to, post-exp2 is the postfix expression that pre-exp2 converts to, and the operator is the same. Therefore,

Convert(E) = Convert(pre-exp1)·Convert(pre-exp2)·operator

We can state the conversion algorithm as:

```
IF (E is a single letter) THEN
    RETURN (E)
ELSE
    RETURN (Convert(pre-exp1) · Convert(pre-exp2) · operator)
END
```

In the following Modula-2 implementation, procedure *Convert* is passed the array *PRE* containing the prefix expression and the array *POST*, in which the postfix expression will be constructed. The recursive procedure *doconvert* is nested within the nonrecursive *Convert* procedure and accesses the arrays *PRE* and *POST* globally. Notice that each recursive call to *doconvert* returns the pointer *preptr* pointing to the array location following the end of the prefix expression that it converted. This is the starting point of the prefix expression to be converted by the next recursive call to *dosearch*.

```
IMPLEMENTATION MODULE PrePost;
(*
    PREFIX TO POSTFIX CONVERSION

    INPUT:   An algebraic expression in prefix form.

    OUTPUT:   The equivalent expression in postfix form.

    ASSUMPTION:   The input string is syntactically correct.

    The conversion is based on the recursive definitions:

        prefix expression:

            <pre> = <identifier> | <operator><pre><pre>

        postfix expression:

            <post> = <identifier> | <post><post><operator>

        where an identifier is a single upper case letter

        and an operator is one of +, -, * and /
*)

(* ***********************************************************
    Convert:   Convert the prefix expression PRE to postfix
    form.   Put the result in POST.

    The conversion is done by the locally defined recursive
    procedure doconvert.   PRE and POST are global to doconvert.

    Calls: doconvert.
    *********************************************************** *)
PROCEDURE Convert(PRE : ARRAY OF CHAR; VAR POST : ARRAY OF CHAR);

VAR

    preptr, postptr : CARDINAL;

(* -----------------------------------------------------------
    Doconvert:   Convert the prefix expression beginning at
    location preptr of PRE and place the result in POST
    beginning at location postptr.

    Variables preptr and postptr are set to one past the ends
    of the respective substrings.
```

```
                    The conversion is done recursively.
          ------------------------------------------------------------- *)
PROCEDURE doconvert(VAR preptr, postptr : CARDINAL);

VAR

    ch : CHAR;

BEGIN

    (* check the first character of the prefix string *)
    ch := PRE[preptr];
    INC(preptr);

    IF ((ch >= 'A') AND (ch <= 'Z')) THEN

        (* degenerate case - single identifier *)
        POST[postptr] := ch;
        INC(postptr);

    ELSE

        (* do the conversion recursively *)

        (* first operand *)
        doconvert(preptr, postptr);

        (* second operand *)
        doconvert(preptr, postptr);

        (* operator *)
        POST[postptr] := ch;
        INC(postptr);

    END;

END doconvert;

(* main body of Convert *)
BEGIN

    (* initialize pointers to the beginning of the strings *)
    preptr := 0;
    postptr := 0;

    (* do the conversion *)
    doconvert(preptr, postptr);
```

```
END Convert;

END PrePost.
```

The following illustrates sample calls to *Convert*.

PARAMETER PRE	RESULT POST
A	A
+AB	AB+
+/AB-CD	AB/CD-+
+-AB*/CD-EF	AB-CD/EF-*+

Fully Parenthesized Expressions.   As most programmers would object to having to write their expressions in prefix or postfix notation, most programming languages use the infix convention. Programming languages that use infix notation must be able to deal with the potential for ambiguity by means of parenthesization, precedence rules, and rules for association. The simplest infix scheme (for recognition and evaluation) is to require all expressions to be *fully parenthesized*.

A grammar for the language of all fully parenthesized expressions is

<expression> = <letter> | (<expression><operator><expression>)

<operator>   = + | − | * | /

<letter>   = A | B | ... | Z

The definition requires that parentheses be placed around each pair of operands and their operator, so there is no possibility for ambiguity. Precedence and association rules are not needed, but the scheme is rather inconvenient for the programmer.

Most programming languages support a definition of algebraic expressions that includes precedence rules for the operators and rules of association. This frees the programmer from having to fully parenthesize every algebraic expression, but the grammars for defining such languages and algorithms for recognizing and evaluating their expressions are more difficult than those we have seen in this section. The optional section that follows discusses such languages.

* More Advanced Types of Algebraic Expressions

Algebraic Expressions with Precedence Rules.   It is standard practice to define * and / to have higher precedence than + and −. This rule of precedence is used to remove ambiguity if some parentheses are omitted. For example, the expression

$a + b * c$

is ambiguous without the precedence rules. The precedence rules specify that the * is to be applied before the +, and thus the expression is evaluated as

$$a + (b * c)$$

While precedence rules make life easier for the programmer, the task of recognition and evaluation is more difficult with these rules.

Notice that these precedence rules do not allow all parentheses to be omitted, since the rules do not remove ambiguity in all cases. For example, in the expression

$$a \mathbin{/} b * c$$

the precedence rules do not specify if the expression is to be evaluated as

$$(a \mathbin{/} b) * c \quad \text{or} \quad a \mathbin{/} (b * c)$$

Rules of association are needed to resolve this type of ambiguity. After presenting a grammar that includes rules of precedence, we present a grammar that also includes rules of association.

The following is a grammar that allows parentheses to be omitted when the precedence rules remove ambiguity but that requires parentheses when ambiguity would otherwise result. Notice that the definitions introduce **factors** and **terms.**

$$\langle\text{expression}\rangle = \langle\text{term}\rangle \mid \langle\text{term}\rangle + \langle\text{term}\rangle \mid \langle\text{term}\rangle - \langle\text{term}\rangle$$

$$\langle\text{term}\rangle \quad\quad = \langle\text{factor}\rangle \mid \langle\text{factor}\rangle * \langle\text{factor}\rangle \mid \langle\text{factor}\rangle / \langle\text{factor}\rangle$$

$$\langle\text{factor}\rangle \quad\quad = \langle\text{letter}\rangle \mid (\langle\text{expression}\rangle)$$

$$\langle\text{letter}\rangle \quad\quad = A \mid B \mid ... \mid Z$$

This grammar is such that the operators * and / can be applied only to an operand that is a factor; that is, the operand must be either a single letter or be enclosed in parentheses. The operators + and − can be applied to any operand that is a term; that is, the operand can be either a factor or the (possibly unparenthesized) product or quotient of a pair of factors.

Our recognition algorithm is based on a recursive chain of subtasks: *find an expression → find a term → find a factor.* What makes this a recursive chain is that *find an expression* uses *find a term,* which in turn uses *find a factor. Find a factor* either detects a degenerate case or uses *find an expression,* thus forming the recursive chain.

The algorithm can be described as follows.

FIND AN EXPRESSION

```
(* The grammar specifies that an expression is either a
   single term or a term followed by a '+' or '-', which
   then must be followed by a second term. *)
```

```
    find a term

    IF (the next symbol is a '+' or '-') THEN
       find a term
    END
```

FIND A TERM:

```
    (* The grammar specifies that a term is either a single
       factor or a factor followed by a '*' or '/', which
       then must be followed by a second factor *)

    find a factor

    IF (the next symbol is a '*' OR '/') THEN
       find a factor
    END
```

FIND A FACTOR:

```
    (* The grammar specifies that an expression is either a
       single letter (the degenerate case) or an expression
       enclosed in parentheses. *)

    IF (the next symbol is a letter) THEN
       done -- this is the degenerate case

    ELSIF (the next symbol is a '(') THEN
       find an expression
       check for ')'

    ELSE
       there is no factor

    END
```

The following Modula-2 implementation uses conventions similar to the programs previously presented.

```
IMPLEMENTATION MODULE RecExp;
(*
    RECOGNIZE ALGEBRAIC EXPRESSIONS

    INPUT:  A string of characters.

    OUTPUT:

       True if the string represents a legal algebraic
       expression.  False otherwise.
```

The recognition is based on the recursive definitions:

```
<expression> = <term> | <term>+<term> | <term>-<term>
<term> = <factor> | <factor>*<factor> | <factor>/<factor>
<factor> = <identifier> | (<expression>)
```

      where an identifier is a single upper case letter
*)

```
(* -----------------------------------------------------------
    IsBlank:  Determine if the characters from position index
    of STR to the end of STR are all blanks.  STR is terminated
    by either the first NULL character or the upper bound of
    STR, i.e., HIGH(STR).
    ----------------------------------------------------------- *)
PROCEDURE IsBlank(STR : ARRAY OF CHAR; index : CARDINAL) : BOOLEAN;

CONST

   NULL = 0C;

VAR

   i : CARDINAL;

BEGIN

   i := index;
   WHILE ( (i <= HIGH(STR)) AND (STR[i] = ' ') ) DO
     INC(i);
   END;

   RETURN ( (i > HIGH(STR)) OR (STR[i] = NULL) )

END IsBlank;

(* ***********************************************************
    IsExp:  Determine if EXP is a legal algebraic expression.

    This routine uses the locally defined recursive functions
    LastExp, LastTerm, and LastFact.  EXP is global to all of
    these functions.

    Calls:  IsBlank, LastExp, LastTerm, and LastFact.
    *********************************************************** *)
PROCEDURE IsExp(EXP : ARRAY OF CHAR) : BOOLEAN;

VAR
```

```
      lastchar, size : INTEGER;
```

```
(* ------------------------------------------------------------
    LastFact:  Find the end of a legal factor beginning at
    index, where

        <factor> = <letter> | (<expression>)

    Return -1 if none exists.
    ----------------------------------------------------- *)
PROCEDURE LastFact(index : INTEGER) : INTEGER;
VAR

  i, value : INTEGER;

BEGIN

    (* test the bounds *)
    IF ((index < 0) OR (index > size)) THEN
        RETURN (-1);

    (* <identifier> *)
    ELSIF ((EXP[index] >= 'A') AND (EXP[index] <= 'Z')) THEN
        RETURN (index);

    (* (<expression)> *)
    ELSE

    (* initialize *)
    value := -1;

    (* set the value *)
    IF EXP[index] = '(' THEN
        (* recognize an inner expression *)
        i := LastExp(index+1);

        (* verify a matching close parenthesis *)
    IF ((i > index) AND (i < size) AND
        (EXP[i+1] = ')')) THEN
        value := i+1;
    END;

    END;

    RETURN (value);

  END;

  END LastFact;
```

```
(* ------------------------------------------------------------
    LastTerm: Find the end of a legal term beginning at index,
    where

        <term> = <factor> | <factor>*<factor> | <factor>/<factor>

    Return -1 if none exists.

    Calls: LastFact.
   ------------------------------------------------------------ *)
PROCEDURE LastTerm(index : INTEGER) : INTEGER;

VAR

    i : INTEGER;

BEGIN

    (* find the first factor *)
    i := LastFact(index);

    (* verify *)
    IF (i = -1) THEN
        RETURN (-1);

    (* find the second factor if necessary *)
    ELSIF (i = size) THEN
        RETURN (size);

    ELSIF ((EXP[i+1] = '*') OR (EXP[i+1] = '/')) THEN
        RETURN (LastFact(i+2));

    ELSE
        RETURN (i);

    END;

END LastTerm;

(* ------------------------------------------------------------
    LastExp: Find the end of a legal expression beginning at
    index, where

        <expression> = <term> | <term>+<term> | <term>-<term>

    Return -1 if none exists.
   ------------------------------------------------------------ *)
PROCEDURE LastExp(index : INTEGER) : INTEGER;
```

```
VAR

    i : INTEGER;

BEGIN

    (* find the first term *)
    i := LastTerm(index);

    (* verify *)
    IF (i = -1) THEN
        RETURN (-1);

    (* find the second term if necessary *)
    ELSIF (i = size) THEN
        RETURN (size);

    ELSIF ((EXP[i+1] = '+') OR (EXP[i+1] = '-')) THEN
        RETURN (LastTerm(i+2));

    ELSE
        RETURN (i);

    END;

END LastExp;

(* main body of IsExp *)
BEGIN

    size := HIGH(EXP);

    (* the end of the legal expression beginning at index 0 must
       be the last nonblank character of the input string *)
    lastchar := LastExp(0);
    RETURN ((lastchar >= 0) AND IsBlank(EXP, lastchar+1));

END IsExp;

END RecExp.
```

The following illustrates calls to *IsExp*.

PARAMETER EXP	FUNCTION VALUE
A	TRUE
(A)	TRUE
((((A))))	TRUE
	FALSE
A + B	TRUE
A*B	TRUE
(A + B)	TRUE
((A) + (B))	TRUE
((A) + (B)	FALSE
A + B*C	TRUE
A*B + C	TRUE
A + B-C	FALSE
A/B/C	FALSE
A + (B-C)	TRUE
A B	FALSE
()	FALSE
A +	FALSE
A + B C	FALSE
A	FALSE

The last expression is not legal because it contains leading blanks.

Left-to-Right Association.   The expression

$a / b * c$

is not in the language defined by the previous grammar. In many programming languages (Modula-2 included), however, this is a legal expression. The rule used to resolve the ambiguity is **left-to-right association**—each operator applies to the leftmost possible (without violating precedence rules) operands. For example, the above expression would be interpreted as

$(a / b) * c$

A grammar for this language of all syntactically legal expressions (allowing precedence and association rules to resolve ambiguities) is straightforward.

<expression> = <letter> | <expression><operator><expression>
              | (<expression>)

<operator> = + | − | * | /

<letter>   = A | B | ... | Z

The grammar is very simple. It checks only that an expression has correctly placed operators. The task of applying the precedence and association rules to evaluate an expression, however, is actually quite difficult.

Most evaluation algorithms for expressions in this language are actually based on a more complex grammar. Although the grammars are equivalent in the sense that they define the same language, the more complex grammar is useful because it indicates how the parts of the expression should be grouped in the course of the evaluation (that is, how the expression should be **parsed**). We present that grammar here, and in Chapter 7 we present a nonrecursive algorithm for evaluating expressions in this language.

239
The Relation-
ship between
Recursion and
Mathematical
Induction

$$<expression> \ = \ <term> \ | \ <expression> + <term>$$
$$| \ <expression> - <term>$$

$$<term> \qquad = \ <factor> \ | \ <term> * <factor> \ | \ <term> / <factor>$$

$$<factor> \qquad = \ letter \ | \ (<expression>)$$

THE RELATIONSHIP BETWEEN RECURSION AND MATHEMATICAL INDUCTION

There is a very strong relationship between recursion and mathematical induction. Recursion solves a problem by specifying a solution to one or more degenerate cases and then demonstrating how the solution to a problem of an arbitrary size can be derived from the solutions to smaller problems of the same type. Similarly, mathematical induction proves a property about the natural numbers by proving the property about a base case (usually 0 or 1) and then proving that the property must be true for an arbitrary natural number N if it is true for the natural numbers smaller than N.

Given the similarities between recursion and mathematical induction, it should not be surprising that induction is often employed to prove properties about recursive algorithms. What types of properties would we like to prove about recursive algorithms? One obvious answer is that we would like to prove that an algorithm performs the task it is intended to perform. To illustrate this, we prove that the recursive *Factorial* algorithm of Chapter 4 does indeed compute the factorial of its argument. Another use of mathematical induction is to prove that a recursive algorithm performs a certain amount of work. To illustrate this, we will prove that the solution to the Towers of Hanoi problem makes exactly $2^N - 1$ moves when it starts with N disks.

Correctness of the Recursive Factorial Function

Recall the recursive *Factorial* function of Chapter 4.

```
Factorial(n)

    IF (n = 0)  THEN
        RETURN (1)
    ELSE
        RETURN (n * Factorial(n-1))
    END
```

We wish to prove that the function $Factorial$ returns the values

$$Factorial\ (0) = 0! = 1$$

$$Factorial\ (n) = n! = n * (n-1) * (n-2) * \ldots * 2 * 1 \text{ if } n > 0$$

The proof is by induction on n.

Basis. Show that the property is true for $n = 0$. That is, we must show that $Factorial\ (0)$ returns 1. But this is simply the degenerate case of the function, and $Factorial\ (0)$ returns 1 by its definition.

We now must establish that

property is true for an arbitrary $k \Rightarrow$ property is true for $k + 1$

Inductive Hypothesis. Assume that the property is true for $n = k$. That is, assume that $Factorial\ (k)$ returns the value

$$k * (k - 1) * (k - 2) * \cdots * 2 * 1$$

Inductive Conclusion. Show that the property is true for $n = k + 1$. That is, we must show that $Factorial\ (k+1)$ returns the value

$$(k + 1) * k * (k - 1) * (k - 2) * \cdots * 2 * 1$$

By definition of the function $Factorial$, $Factorial\ (k+1)$ returns the value

$$(k+1)\ *\ Factorial\ (k)$$

But by the inductive hypothesis, $Factorial\ (k)$ returns the value

$$k * (k - 1) * (k - 2) * \cdots * 2 * 1$$

Thus, $Factorial\ (k+1)$ returns the value

$$(k + 1) * k * (k - 1) * (k - 2) * \cdots * 2 * 1$$

which is what we needed to show to establish that

property is true for an arbitrary $k \Rightarrow$ property is true for $k + 1$

The inductive proof is thus complete.

Cost of Towers of Hanoi

At the beginning of this chapter, we presented the Buddha's solution to the Towers of Hanoi problem.

```
Towers (count, source, dest, spare)

    IF (count = 1) THEN
        move the disk directly
    ELSE
        solve Towers (count-1, source, dest, spare)
        solve Towers (1, source, dest, spare)
        solve Towers (count-1, spare, dest, source)
    END
```

241
The Relation-
ship between
Recursion and
Mathematical
Induction

We now pose the following question. If we begin with N disks, how many moves are made in the solution given by *Towers*?

Let Moves(N) be the number of moves made starting with N disks. When $N = 1$, the answer is easy,

$$\text{Moves}(1) = 1$$

When $N > 1$, the value of Moves(N) is not so apparent. An inspection of the *Towers* procedure, however, reveals a useful fact. If we knew how many moves are made starting with $N - 1$ disks, we could figure out how many moves are made starting with N disks; that is,

$$\text{Moves}(N) = \text{Moves}(N - 1) + \text{Moves}(1) + \text{Moves}(N - 1)$$

This simplifies to

$$\text{Moves}(N) = 2*\text{Moves}(N - 1) + 1$$

We have obtained a **recurrence relation** for the number of moves starting with N disks:

$$\text{Moves}(1) = 1$$

$$\text{Moves}(N) = 2*\text{Moves}(N - 1) + 1 \qquad \text{if } N > 1$$

For example, we can determine Moves(3) by applying the recurrence:

$$\text{Moves}(3) = 2 * \text{Moves}(2) + 1$$

$$= 2 * [2 * \text{Moves}(1) + 1] + 1$$

$$= 2 * [2 * 1 + 1] + 1$$

$$= 7$$

Although the recurrence gives us a means of computing Moves(N), this is not really a satisfactory answer to our question. We would like a **closed-form formula** (for example, an algebraic expression) into which we could substitute any given value for N and obtain the number of moves made. The recurrence relation is useful because there are techniques for solving recurrences to obtain such closed-form formulas. Unfortunately, these solution techniques are beyond the scope of this book. Therefore, we simply pull the solution out of the blue and use mathematical induction to prove that it is correct.

The solution to the above recurrence relation is

$$\text{Moves}(N) = 2^N - 1, \qquad \text{for all } N \geqslant 1$$

(For example, notice that $2^3 - 1$ agrees with the value that we computed for Moves(3)).

The proof is by induction on N.

Basis. Show that the property is true for $N = 1$. Here, $2^1 - 1 = 1$, which is consistent with the recurrence relation's specification that Moves(1) $= 1$.

We now must establish that

property is true for an arbitrary $k \Rightarrow$ property is true for $k + 1$

Inductive Hypothesis. Assume that the property is true for $N = k$. That is, assume

$$\text{Moves}(k) = 2^k - 1.$$

Inductive Conclusion. Show that the property is true for $N = k + 1$. That is, we must show that

$$
\begin{aligned}
\text{Moves}(k + 1) &= 2^{k+1} - 1 \\
\text{Moves}(k + 1) &= 2 * \text{Moves}(k) + 1 && \text{from definition in recurrence} \\
&= 2 * [2^k - 1] + 1 && \text{by inductive hypothesis} \\
&= 2^{k+1} - 1
\end{aligned}
$$

which is what we needed to show to establish that

property is true for an arbitrary $k \Rightarrow$ property is true for $k + 1$

The inductive proof is thus complete.

We do not wish to leave you with the false impression that proving properties of programs is an easy matter. These two proofs are about as easy as any will be. We do, however, wish to reiterate that well-structured programs are far more amenable to the techniques than are poorly structured programs. Earlier in this chapter we saw how mathematical induction also can be used to establish invariants for iterative algorithms. Recall that the concept of an invariant was used in developing the partition algorithm for Quicksort. The technique involves showing that the invariant holds at the beginning of a loop and then establishing that

1. When developing a recursive solution, we must be sure that the solutions to the smaller problems really do give us a solution to the original problem. For example, the `Quicksort` algorithm works only because the array segment is partitioned before making a recursive call. This ensures that when the smaller array segments are sorted, their elements will be in the proper relationship to the rest of the array.

2. We must be sure that all subproblems generated by a recursive solution are closer to a degenerate case than the original. Failure to do so could result in an algorithm that does not terminate. For example, the `Quicksort` algorithm is guaranteed to terminate because the middle region of the partition is always nonempty (it must contain the pivot). This ensures that the two sorting problems (S_1 and S_3) each must be smaller than the original.

3. Grammars, like recursive algorithms, must have carefully chosen degenerate cases. They must ensure that when a string is decomposed far enough it will always reach the form of one of the grammar's "base cases."

4. The subtleties of some of the algorithms encountered in this chapter indicate the need for mathematical techniques for proving their correctness. Two such techniques are the use of loop invariants and mathematical induction. The application of these techniques during the design of the various components of a solution can help to eliminate errors in logic before they appear in the program.

the invariant holds after iteration $k \Rightarrow$ the invariant holds after iteration $k + 1$

Imagine how difficult this would be for an algorithm with an unstructured flow of control!

SUMMARY

1. `Quicksort` and `Mergesort` are two very efficient recursive sorting algorithms. In the "average" case, `Quicksort` is among the fastest known sorting algorithms, though in certain cases it can be significantly slower. `Mergesort` is not quite as fast as `Quicksort` in the average case, although its performance is very good in all cases. Sorting algorithms are discussed further in Chapter 13.

2. A grammar is a device for defining a language—a set of strings of symbols. A benefit of using a grammar to define a language is that a recognition algorithm, based on the grammar, often can be constructed directly.

3. We illustrated the use of grammars by defining several different languages of algebraic expressions. These different languages have their relative advantages and disadvantages. Prefix and postfix expressions, while difficult for the programmer to use, eliminate problems of ambiguity. Infix expressions, on the other hand, require parentheses, precedence rules, and rules of association to eliminate ambiguity. The task of evaluating algebraic expressions is considered in Chapter 7.

4. A loop invariant is a property of an algorithm that is true before and after each iteration of a loop. Loop invariants are very useful in developing iterative algorithms and establishing their correctness.

5. There is a very close relationship between mathematical induction and recursion. Induction is often used to establish the correctness of a recursive algorithm and to prove properties about it (for example, the amount of work it requires).

EXERCISES

1. Consider palindromes over the alphabet consisting only of the lowercase letters (for example, level and deed, but not RadaR, ADA, or 101). Let $C(n)$ be the number of palindromes of length exactly equal to n. Give a recursive definition of $C(n)$.

2. Let L be the language

$$L = \{s \mid s \text{ is of the form } a^n b^{2n}, \text{ for some } n \geq 0\}$$

Thus, a string is in L if and only if it starts with a sequence of a's and is followed by a sequence of twice as many b's. For example

   aabbbb is in L

   abbb and *abbabb* are not in L

   a. Give a grammar for the language L.

   b. Write a recursive function

   ```
   PROCEDURE L(A : string; first, last : INTEGER) : BOOLEAN;
   ```

   which is passed a character array A and integers *first* and *last* and determines if the string in $A[first..last]$ is in L.

3. Consider the following recursive function:

   ```
   PROCEDURE p(x : INTEGER) : INTEGER;
   BEGIN

       IF (x < 3) THEN
           RETURN (x);
       ELSE
   ```

```
        RETURN (p(x-1) * p(x-3));
    END;

END;
```

Let $A(n)$ be the number of multiplication operations performed by the execution of function p when called with argument n. Write a recursive definition of $A(n)$.

4. The Mergesort algorithm was presented as:

```
Mergesort(A)

    IF (size > 1) THEN
        Mergesort(first half of A)
        Mergesort(second half of A)
        Merge(A, first half of A, second half of A)
    END
```

Suppose we removed the call to *Merge*, to obtain

```
Mergesort(A)

    IF (size > 1) THEN
        Mergesort(first half of A)
        Mergesort(second half of A)
    END
```

What would this new procedure do?

*5. Prove the following: If E is a prefix expression and Y is a nonempty string of characters, then E·Y cannot be a legal prefix expression (assuming single letter identifiers). (*Hint:* Prove by induction on the length of E.)

6. Consider the language defined by the following grammar:

$$<\text{word}> = \$ \mid a<\text{word}>a \mid b<\text{word}>b \mid ... \mid y<\text{word}>y \mid z<\text{word}>z$$

Equivalently,

$$L = \{w\$\text{reverse}(w) \mid w \text{ is a string of letters of length} \geqslant 0\}$$

Note that this is very similar to the language of palindromes (a special middle character has been added).

The algorithm that we gave for recognizing palindromes can easily be adapted to this language. The algorithm is recursive and processes from both ends of the string towards the middle:

a. A string with no characters (last < first) is not in the language.

b. A string with exactly one character (first = last) is in the language if the character is a $.

c. A longer string (first < last) is in the language if the ends are identical letters and the inner string (first + 1 to last − 1) is in the language.

Describe a recursive recognition algorithm that processes the string from left to right (reading one character at a time and not explicitly saving the string for future reference). Write a Modula-2 function that implements your algorithm.

7. In Chapter 4 we gave the following definition for $C(n, k)$, where n and k are assumed to be nonnegative integers:

$$C(n, n) = 1$$

$$C(n, 0) = 1$$

$$C(n, k) = C(n - 1, k - 1) + C(n - 1, k) \qquad \text{if } 0 < k < n$$

Prove by induction that the following is a closed form for $C(n, k)$:

$$C(n, k) = \frac{n!}{(n-k)!k!}$$

(*Hint:* Use induction on n.)

8. Recall that the partition procedure presented for `Quicksort` moves one item at a time from the unknown region into the appropriate region S_1, S_2, or S_3. Note that if the item to be moved belongs in region S_1, and S_2 is empty, then the procedure will swap an array element with itself. Modify the partition procedure to eliminate this unnecessary swapping.

9. How does the choice of the pivot element affect the behavior of `Quicksort`? For example, how many recursive calls will be made to sort an array of size N if we always choose the smallest element as the pivot? What if we always choose the median element?

10. We can describe another partitioning strategy for `Quicksort` as follows: Choose a pivot element and partition into two regions S_1 and S_2 such that all the elements in S_1 are less than or equal to the pivot and all the elements in S_2 are greater than or equal to the pivot.

a. Under this scheme we must take great care that neither of the two regions is empty. Why? How can we ensure that this won't happen?

b. Modify the partition procedure to implement this strategy.

c. We can describe another implementation of this partition strategy as follows. We have a pointer *low* that traverses the array segment that is to be partitioned from F to L, stopping when it encounters the first element that is greater than the pivot element. Similarly, we have a second pointer *high* that traverses from L to F, stopping when it encounters the first element that is smaller than the pivot element. We swap these two elements and continue (moving *low* up and *high* down) until the two pointers meet somewhere in the middle. Implement this version of `Quicksort` in Modula-2.

d. There are several variations of this partitioning strategy. What other strategies can you think of? How do they compare to the two that have been given?

11. What is an invariant? What are the four key steps to using an invariant to establish the correctness of an algorithm?

*12. Describe an iterative version of *Mergesort*. Define an appropriate invariant and show the correctness of your algorithm.

PART III

DATA ABSTRACTION AS A
PROBLEM-SOLVING TOOL:
THE WALLS

CHAPTER 6

DATA ABSTRACTION

PREVIEW   This chapter introduces data abstraction as a tool for increasing the modularity of a program—for building "walls" between a program and its data structures. As we refine the solution to a simple text-processing problem, we discover that we need to support several operations on the data. A collection of such operations defines an abstract data type, or ADT. Only after we have clearly defined the operations of an ADT do we consider data structures for implementing it. The collection of required operations for the text-processing problem defines a well-known ADT called a stack, for which we present both a sequential and a linked implementation.

INTRODUCTION

By now the advantages of top-down design should be quite clear. Throughout the first two parts of this book, we have espoused its virtues via argument and illustration. Programs can be developed by piecing together functions and procedures that have yet to be written. The trick is in knowing what *we would like* the subprograms to do and in proceeding under the assumption that they exist and work. In this way the subprograms can be written in relative isolation from one another, with the programmer knowing *what* each will do but not necessarily *how* each will eventually do it. This process yields **modular** programs; we discussed the advantages of these programs in Chapter 1. To summarize that discussion, modularity is a method that keeps the complexity of a large program under control by systematically controlling the interaction of its components.

A graphic way to view this is that modularity builds **walls** around the various tasks a program performs, thereby preventing the tasks from becoming entangled. The wall around each task T prevents the other tasks from "seeing how" T is performed (see Figure 6–1). One benefit of this is that if the method for performing task T should change, task Q will not be affected, since *the wall has prevented task Q's method of solution from depending on task T's method of solution.*

The isolation of the modules cannot, however, be total. While task Q is oblivious to *how* task T is performed, it may well have to know *what* task T is and how to initiate it. For example, suppose a program needs to operate on a sorted array of names. It may, for instance, need to search the array for a given name or print out the names in alphabetical order. The program thus needs a module S that sorts an array of names. While the rest of the program knows that module S will sort an array, it should not care how S accomplishes its task.

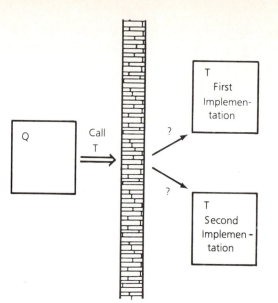

Figure 6–1

*Walls isolat-
ing imple-
mentations*

When the designer of the program realizes that there is a need to sort the names, he or she writes up the specifications for what the sort routine must do. For example:

> The routine is to be passed an array of no more than *maxname* names. Each name is of length no more than *maxlen*. The routine is to return the array with the names in ascending alphabetical order.

These specifications can be viewed as the terms of a **contract** stating that the program can rely on S to sort the array. If one programmer writes the entire program, this contract helps systematically decompose the problem into smaller tasks. If the program is a team project, the contract helps to delineate responsibilities.

Whoever writes the sort routine has this contract to live up to. After the sort routine has been written and tested, it will be relied upon by the rest of the program. The contract tells the other modules how to use the routine (for example, how to call the routine properly) and the result of doing so (for example, the routine will return the array sorted).

We thus see that there is a tiny slit in each wall. Things can be passed through the slit into and out of the module; for example, the array can be passed into the routine and the sorted array can be passed out. What goes in and comes out is governed by the terms of the module's contract: *If you use me in this way, this is exactly what I'll do for you.* It is very important to notice, however, that a module's contract does not commit the module to a particular method of performing its task. If another part of the program assumes anything about the method, it does so at its own risk. Thus, for example, if at some later date a different sort routine is used, the rest of the program should not need to change at all. The slit in the wall is not large enough to allow the outside world to see the inner workings of the module. As long as the new module honors the terms

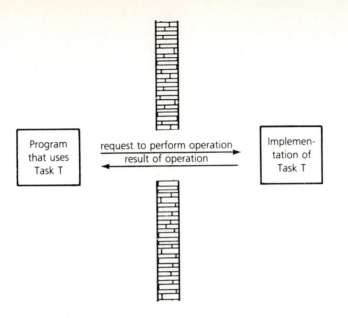

Figure 6–2

A slit in the wall

of the original contract, the rest of the program should be oblivious to the change.

This discussion should not be news to you. The concepts of **wall** and **contract** permeate the first two parts of the book. We've given you this synopsis now because we are about to introduce the less publicized half of modular program development. The half you are familiar with advocates partitioning a program into independent *algorithms,* which perform small, isolated tasks. Programs, however, are constructed out of *data structures* as well as algorithms. Just as modularity leads us to think in terms of *what an algorithm does* independently of *how it does it,* modularity should also lead us to think in terms of *what can be done to a data structure* independently of *what "it" is* that we are doing it to.

For example, you have all used a Modula-2 array, but have you ever stopped to think about what an array actually is? You can see many *pictures* of arrays throughout this book. Our artist's conception of an array may resemble the way a Modula-2 array is implemented on a computer, and then again it may not. The point is that we are able to use an array without knowing what it "looks like," that is, how it is implemented. Although Modula-2 arrays may be implemented differently by different systems, the differences are transparent to the programmer. For instance, regardless of how the array *A* is implemented, you can always store the value *x* in location *i* of *A* with the statement

```
A[i] := x
```

and later write out that value with the statement

```
write(A[i])
```

In other words, there is a *wall between the implementation of an array and a program that uses an array*. As in the example of the sort routine, this wall contains a tiny slit. In the case of the array, the slit allows the program to send the implementation a request that it perform an operation, and it allows the implementation to send back to the program the results of the operation. The array's contract specifies what these operations are but not how they are performed.

The specifications for two array operations might look something like the following.

> **ArrayStore.** "Associate" the value of expression x with index i of A, written as

```
A[i] := x;
```

> **ArrayRetrieve.** Return the value associated with index i of A, written as

```
A[i]
```

Note that the terms of the contract are *what* and not *how*. Modula-2's only commitment is that the *array operations* be supported.

The technique of thinking in terms of what can be done to data independently of how it is to be done is known as **data abstraction.** When a program must perform operations on its data that are not directly supported by the language, we ourselves must construct the data structures. This should be done first by carefully writing the specifications for what the operations are to do (the contract) and *then* (and only then) by implementing the operations with a data structure. If the implementation is done properly, the rest of the program will be able to depend on the fact that the operations perform as specified—that is, that the terms of the contract are honored. The program must not, however, depend on a particular method for supporting the operations.

To summarize, data abstraction results in walls between a program and its data structures. A slit in each wall allows requests that operations be performed to be passed through to the data structure and the results of these operations to be passed back (see Figure 6–3). The data structure's specifications govern what those operations are and what they do: *This is the exact result of each of my operations.* This approach allows the program to be oblivious to any change in the implementations of its data structures.

The data-abstraction approach just described is used throughout much of the remainder of the book. The next section describes how an **abstract data type** can be used to realize data abstraction's goal of defining a data structure by its operations. We then present an example designed to illustrate the usefulness of the approach in the parallel development of a solution's algorithms and data structures. The chapter also discusses the process of implementing an ADT once its operations have been clearly defined. This process is very similar to that of successive refinement as it is practiced in the top-down design of algorithms. We shall see that an ADT can be gradually transformed from a set of operations into a programming language realization.

We conclude this introduction to data abstraction with a general overview of the material in Parts III and IV. Part I reviewed aspects of problem solving that are closely related to programming issues. Part II introduced recursion, a problem-solving tool useful in the construction of algorithms. The primary con-

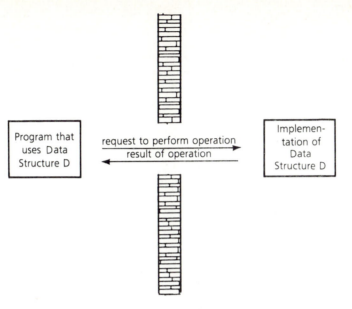

Figure 6–3

*Walls isolat-
ing data
structures*

cerns of Parts III and IV are the aspects of problem solving that involve the *management of data.*

The solution to a problem typically requires the performance of operations that can be broadly described in one of three ways:

put data into a data structure

take data out of a data structure

ask questions about the data in a data structure

The details of the operations, of course, vary from application to application, but the overall theme is the management of data. The eight chapters of Parts III and IV are concerned with the identification and implementation of some of the more common data management operations.

We have divided Part III into two units. The first unit (Chapters 7 and 8) deals with data organized by *position.* The second unit (Chapters 9 and 10) deals with data organized by *value.* In general, these organizations are appropriate for applications of rather different natures. For example, if an application needs to ask a question about the *first* person on line, then the data should be organized by position. On the other hand, if an application needs to ask a question about the employee *named Smith,* then the data should be organized by value. Part IV considers a few advanced techniques for organizing data by value, including techniques for organizing data stored in an external file and a comparison of sorting algorithms.

Our study of data management has three aspects. The first is the identification of useful sets of operations—that is, the identification of abstract data types. The second aspect is the presentation of applications that utilize these abstract data types. The third aspect is the development of implementations for the abstract data types—that is, the development of data structures. As we shall discover, the nature of the operations of an abstract data type, along with the application in which it is to be used, greatly influence the choice of its implementation.

ABSTRACT DATA TYPES

An **abstract data type** (**ADT**) is *a set of operations*. In general, these operations may be thought of as operating on *a collection of stored data*. The definition of the operations must be rigorous enough to specify completely the effect that they have on the data, yet it must not specify how the data is to be stored nor how the operations are to be carried out. This sounds like a formidable task, and indeed it is. An ADT is both a mathematical concept and a problem-solving tool. The formal mathematical study of ADT's utilizes systems of **axioms** to specify the behavior of the operations. In this book our goal is to give you a sense of the value of ADT's as a problem-solving tool rather than to develop mathematically rigorous definitions. Our approach, therefore, will be to rely primarily on informal, intuitive definitions. From time to time, however, we shall present a few axiomatic definitions for illustrative purposes.

To introduce the notion of an abstract data type, consider the following five operations, which define an ADT known as the **ordered list.**

```
Create(L)
(* Create an empty ordered list L. *)


Length(L)
(* Return the number of items that are in ordered list L. *)


Insert(L, i, e)
(* Insert item e at position i of ordered list L.  The value of
   i must be within the range 1 to Length(L)+1.  The item at
   position i becomes the item at position i+1, the item at
   position i+1 becomes the item at position i+2, ..., the
   item at position Length(L) becomes the item at position
   Length(L)+1. *)


Delete(L, i)
(* Delete the item at position i of ordered list L.  The value
   of i must be within the range 1 to Length(L).  The item at
   position i+1 becomes the item at position i, the item at
   position i+2 becomes the item at position i+1, ..., the
   item at position Length(L) becomes the item at position
   Length(L)-1. *)


Retrieve(L, i)
(* Retrieve the item at position i of ordered list L.  The
   value of i must be within the range 1 to Length(L).  The
   list is left unchanged by this operation. *)
```

The specifications of these five operations are the terms of the contract for the ADT ordered list. Notice that the specifications of the operations contain no mention of how the ordered list is to be stored or of how the operations are to be performed. The ADT definition tells us only what can be done to an ordered list. It is of fundamental importance that the definition of an ADT not include implementation issues. This restriction on the definition of an ordered list is what allows us to build a wall between an implementation of an ordered list and a program that uses it. The ADT operations are the sole terms of the contract between an implementation and a program: *If you request that these operations be performed, this is what will happen.* The *behavior* of the operations is the only thing on which a program should depend.

What does the definition of the ADT ordered list tell us about its behavior? It is apparent that the ordered list operations fall into the three broad categories presented in the chapter's introduction:

The operation *Insert* **puts data into** a data structure.

The operation *Delete* **takes data out of** a data structure.

The operations *Retrieve* and *Length* **ask questions about the data** in a data structure.

These are only general descriptions of the operations, but the definition of an ordered list does specify exactly what they do. To get a more precise idea of how the operations work, consider a type of list with which we are all familiar, a grocery list:

L = (apples, eggs, butter, pancake mix, corn flakes, chicken)

To begin, let us see how we can construct this list with the ordered list operations. One way we can do this is first to create an empty list and then use a series of *Insert* operations to successively append the items to the list.

```
Create(L)
Insert(L, 1, apples)
Insert(L, 2, eggs)
Insert(L, 3, butter)
Insert(L, 4, pancake mix)
Insert(L, 5, corn flakes)
Insert(L, 6, chicken)
```

Notice that the ordered list's *Insert* operation can be used to insert new items into any position of the list, not just its end. The definition specifies that if a new item is inserted into position *i*, then the position of each item which was at a position of *i* or greater is increased by one. Thus, for example, if starting with our grocery list

L = (apples, eggs, butter, pancake mix, corn flakes, chicken)

we perform the operation

Insert(L, 4, nuts)

the list

L = (apples, eggs, butter, nuts, pancake mix, corn flakes, chicken) would result. The position numbers of all items that were at position numbers greater than or equal to 4 were incremented after the insertion.

Similarly, the *Delete* operation specifies that if an item is deleted from position *i*, then the position of each item that was at a position greater than *i* is decremented by one. Thus, for example, if *L* is the list

L = (apples, eggs, butter, nuts, pancake mix, corn flakes, chicken)

and we perform the operation

Delete (L, 5)

the list

L = (apples, eggs, butter, nuts, corn flakes, chicken)

would result. The position numbers of all items that were at position numbers greater than 5 have had their position numbers decremented.

These examples illustrate that the definition of an ADT can specify the effects of its operations without having to indicate how the data is to be stored. However, we have stated the terms of an ordered list's contract (the specifications of its operations) rather informally. For instance, we are relying on your intuition to know what is meant when we say that an item is "at position *i*" in the ordered list. This is a simple notion, and most people will understand its intentions. Some abstract data types, however, are much more complex and less intuitive than an ordered list. For such data types it is necessary to use a more rigorous method of defining the behavior of their operations. This is accomplished by supplying a set of **axioms.** For example, the axiom

Retrieve(Insert(L, i, X), i) = X

specifies that *Retrieve* retrieves from position i the item that *Insert* has put there.*

Once the behavior of an ADT has been satisfactorily specified, we can write routines that access and manipulate its data *solely in terms of its operations.* As a very simple example, suppose that we wish to write a procedure that prints

---

* You may have noticed that there is a bit of an inconsistency in the way we have used the operations. In order for the above axiom to be syntactically correct,

    Insert (L, i, X)

must be an ordered list. This is compatible with *Insert* being a (Modula-2-like) function that returns as its value the ordered list resulting from applying *Insert* to L. On the other hand, our earlier definition implies that *Insert* changes the value of its argument L and does not return a value. The inconsistency results from our desire to define the operations on an intuitive level. As long as you are aware of the issue, it should not cause any difficulties.

out the items on an ordered list. Even though we have no idea how the ordered list is stored (the wall between the implementation of the ADT ordered list and the rest of the program will prevent us from knowing this), we can write the procedure *PrintList* in terms of the operations that define the ADT ordered list.

```
PrintList(L)
(* Print the items on the ordered list L (in order). *)

    FOR position := 1 TO Length(L) DO
        item := Retrieve(L, position)
        print item
    END
```

Notice that as long as the ADT ordered list is correctly implemented, our *PrintList* procedure will perform its task—it does not depend on *how* the ordered list is implemented.

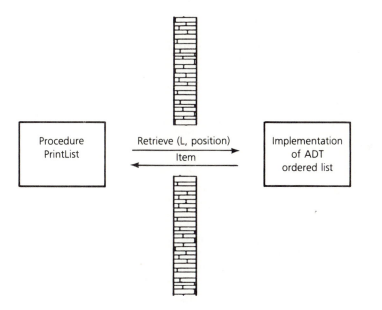

Figure 6–4

Wall between PrintList and the implementation of ADT ordered list

To summarize, we can specify the behavior of an ADT independently of its implementation, either with informal definitions or more formal axioms. Given such a specification, and without any knowledge of how the ADT is to be implemented, we can write routines that utilize the ADT's operations to access its data.

The question of how the ADT is implemented (how the data is stored and the operations carried out) is in the realm of **data structures.** In other words, we view data structures as *implementing* ADT's.

IMPLEMENTING ADT's

Let us examine the question of what it means to **implement** an ADT. Your first reaction might be that an implementation is a set of Modula-2 type definitions, functions, and procedures. While this point of view is not incorrect, hopefully you have learned not to jump right into code. An ADT, like an algorithm, should be successively refined through levels of abstraction. We can view each of the successively more concrete descriptions of the data structure as implementing its more abstract predecessors. As we shall see, there are decisions that should be made carefully at each level of the implementation. In a formal course on data structures, you will learn how to weigh quantitatively the trade-offs involved. For now, however, we will content ourselves with analyses at the intuitive level.

The refinement process stops when we reach an implementation at a level of abstraction supported by our programming language. If the implementation uses constructs such as records and pointers, we can stop if our language is Modula-2, since Modula-2 supports records and pointers. If, on the other hand, our language is FORTRAN, we must devise a way to implement records and pointers using the constructs which FORTRAN supplies. The more primitive our language, the more levels of implementation will be required.

We can illustrate the implementation of an ADT with our ordered list example. Recall that we defined the ADT ordered list by the following five operations:

$Create(L)$

$Length(L)$

$Insert(L, i, e)$

$Delete(L, i)$

$Retrieve(L, i)$

The first implementation to come to mind is an array that stores the items. The item at position i of the list is stored in $Items[i]$. As soon as we begin to explore this implementation, however, we discover a problem. An array has a fixed size (at least in most commonly used programming languages), but our ADT ordered list is permitted to be of an arbitrary length. Thus, in the strict sense, we cannot use an array to implement an ordered list, since it is certainly possible for the number of items that must be stored to exceed the fixed size of the array. When developing implementations for ADT's, we are often confronted with this **fixed-size** problem. In many contexts, an implementation with a fixed size must be rejected in favor of an implementation that can grow **dynamically**.

Let us thus consider how we can develop a dynamic implementation. Modula-2 supports the dynamic allocation of storage through its predefined procedure *NEW*. Recall that the procedure call *NEW(p)* returns p pointing to a newly allocated node of storage. We can use the techniques developed in Chapters 2 and 3 to link together these nodes, thereby representing the ADT ordered list with a linked list. As the length of the ordered list increases, we need only use procedure *NEW* to allocate nodes for the additional items. Unlike the situation under the array implementation, there is no need to impose a fixed maximum length on the list (except, of course, as imposed by the storage limits of the system).

The linked list thus provides an implementation for the ADT ordered list that essentially overcomes the fixed-size problem inherent to the sequential implementation. As we shall see, the decision between a sequential and linked implementation of an ADT is one that must be made time and time again. The need for dynamic storage is one factor that would lead us to choose a linked implementation. There are also other, more subtle factors that would push us in this direction. Some of these factors will come to light in Chapter 9 when we compare implementations of the ADT **table.**

It is important to point out that there are many contexts in which the fixed-size limitation of a sequential implementation is not a problem. For example, it would not be a problem if, from the context of the application, we knew that the length of an ordered list would never be greater than 100. In such an application, a sequential implementation might be more desirable than a linked implementation. To see why this is so, we briefly review the discussion from the end of Chapter 2 on the natures of sequential and linked data structures.

Recall from Chapter 2 that the primary difference between sequential and linked data structures is that a linked data structure orders its items by means of an explicit next while a sequential data structure orders its items by means of an implicit next. An important benefit of a data structure utilizing an explicit next is that the data structure can grow dynamically. An important benefit of a data structure utilizing an implicit next is that the data structure provides direct access, i.e., the ith item on a list is stored in *Items[i]*. The trade-off between dynamic size and direct access will be an issue affecting our selection of an implementation for many of the ADT's in the remainder of the book.

Let us return now to our development of an implementation for the ADT ordered list. It is clear from the above discussion that when selecting an implementation for an ADT, one of the first questions to ask is whether, in the context of the particular application, the fixed-size restriction of a sequential implementation is a problem. If it is a problem, then a linked implementation must be selected. To begin, we will suppose that we are confronted with a situation in which it suffices to implement an ordered list that never has length larger than the constant *maxlen*. In such a context, a sequential implementation might be desirable.

In the sequential implementation, we will define *L* to be a record with two fields:

> *Items*: an array that stores the items in the list
>
> *Len*: an integer that stores the length of the list

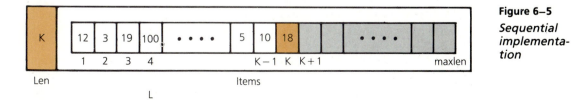

Figure 6–5

Sequential implementation

The five ordered list operations can then be written as follows:

```
Create (L)

    L. Len := 0

Length (L)

    return the value L. Len


Insert (L, i, newitem)

    IF ((i < 1) OR (i > Length (L)+1) OR
                    (Length (L) = maxlen)) THEN
        indicate an error
    ELSE
       (* shift all items at positions i or greater *)
       FOR j := Length (L) TO i BY -1 DO
          L. Items [j+1] := L. Items [j]
       END
       L. Items [i] := newitem
       L. Len := L. Len + 1
    END


Delete (L, i)

    IF ((i < 1) OR (i > Length (L))) THEN
       indicate an error
    ELSE
       (* shift all items at positions greater than i *)
       FOR j := i+1 TO Length (L) DO
          L. Items [j-1] := L. Items [j]
       END
       L. Len := L. Len - 1
    END


Retrieve (L, i)

    IF ((i < 1) OR (i > Length (L))) THEN
       indicate an error
    ELSE
       return the item L. Items [i]
    END
```

The above solution is very close to a Modula-2 implementation of the ADT ordered list. There are, however, a few details to be worked out, such as how

Retrieve can return an item and what to do in the event of an error. Issues similar to these are discussed later in this chapter in the section on implementing the ADT **stack**.

We can also devise a linked implementation of an ordered list (if, for example, the fixed maximum length is not acceptable). Here we will use a record *L* with fields:

> *Head*: a pointer to the item in the first position of the list
>
> *Len*: an integer that stores the length of the list

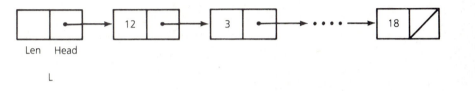

Figure 6–6

*Linked imple-
mentation*

The *Create* and *Length* operations are straightforward.

```
Create(L)

    L.Len  := 0
    L.Head := NIL

Length(L)

    return the value L.Len
```

For the implementation of the operations *Retrieve*, *Insert*, and *Delete*, it is convenient to define the function *Setptr*, which returns a pointer to the node at a specified position on the list. Since a linked list does not provide direct access to a specified position, *Setptr* must traverse the list from its beginning until the specified point is reached. As we shall see, this task is common to the linked list's implementation of the operations *Retrieve*, *Insert*, and *Delete*.

```
Setptr(L, pos)
(* Returns a pointer to the node at position pos in ordered
   list L.  If pos < 1 or pos > Length(L), Setptr returns the
   value NIL.  *)

    IF ( (pos < 1) OR (pos > Length(L)) ) THEN
       RETURN (NIL)

    ELSE
       (* count from the beginning of the list *)
       trav := L.Head
       FOR i := 1 TO pos-1 DO
          trav := trav^.next
       END
       RETURN (trav)
    END
```

The *Retrieve* operation can be implemented as

```
Retrieve(L, i)

    IF ((i < 1) OR (i > Length(L))) THEN
        indicate an error
    ELSE
        p := Setptr(L, i)
        return the item p^.item
    END
```

Notice that this linked implementation of *Retrieve* is quite a bit less efficient than the sequential implementation. In the sequential implementation the ith item can be accessed directly, since it is stored in *Items[i]*. In the linked implementation, however, the list must be traversed until the ith item is encountered.

The linked implementations of *Insert* and *Delete* utilize the general linked list processing techniques developed in Chapter 3. To insert an item at position i (for $i > 1$) of a list, we must obtain a pointer to the node at position $i - 1$. Insertion into the first position of a list is handled as a special case.

```
Insert(L, i, item)

    IF ((i < 1) OR (i > Length(L)+1)) THEN
        indicate an error
        L.Len := L.Len + 1
    ELSIF (i = 1) THEN
        insert at the beginning of the list
        L.Len := L.Len + 1
    ELSE
        p := Setptr(L, i-1)
        insert after the node pointed to by p
    END
```

The *Delete* operation is analogous to *Insert*. To delete an item from position i (for $i > 1$) of a list, we must obtain a pointer to the node at position $i - 1$. Deletion from the first position of a list is handled as a special case.

```
Delete(L, i)

    IF ((i < 1 ) OR (i > Length(L))) THEN
        indicate an error
    ELSIF (i = 1) THEN
        delete the first node from the list
        L.Len := L.Len - 1
    ELSE
        p := Setptr(L, i-1)
        delete the node following the node pointed to by p
        L.Len := L.Len - 1
    END
```

We leave the refinement of this implementation as an exercise.

This concludes our introduction to what an ADT is and what it means to implement one. In the next section we illustrate the usefulness of ADT's in program development and define an important ADT known as a **stack**. Following this we shall develop a sequential and linked implementation for a stack. In this context the issue of fixed versus dynamic size will again be the primary consideration for making the choice between implementations.

AN EXAMPLE OF ADT's IN PROGRAM DEVELOPMENT

In this section we present a short scenario illustrating how the ADT approach can be used in program development. The problem is as follows. An input file contains a single line of text. We wish to read in the line and then print the text out in *reversed order*. Complicating the problem is that the terminal to be used to enter the data has no backspace key. If a data entry error is made, the '#' character must be entered, which says to erase the previous character entered (not counting the '#' character as a character to be erased). For instance, if the input line is

    abc defgh#2klmnopqr##wxyz

the "corrected input" would be

    abc defg2klmnopwxyz

By convention, the consecutive ## characters do not cancel out but are applied in sequence. Given that the above is the corrected input, the reversed output is

    zyxwponmlk2gfed cba

Let us follow the process of constructing a solution. One design decision that must eventually be made is how the input line should be stored. In accordance with the ADT approach, we postpone this decision until we have a better idea of what operations will need to be performed on the data. We begin by breaking the problem into two tasks:

```
input the line, correcting ''errors'' along the way
print the line in reversed order
```

The first of these tasks can be refined as:

```
WHILE (not at the end of the line) DO
   read a new character ch
   IF (ch is not a '#') THEN
      add ch to the data structure
```

```
    ELSE
        remove from the data structure the
            item that was most recently added
    END
END
```

This refinement calls to attention two of the operations that the ADT will have to include.

```
insert a new item into the data structure
remove from the data structure the item that was most
    recently added
```

Notice that there is a potential for trouble in that the person entering data might type a '#' when the data structure is empty—that is, when there are no characters in the data structure. If this situation should occur, we have two options: (1) have the program terminate and print an error message, or (2) have the program ignore the '#' and continue. Either option is reasonable, and we decide to adopt the second. Therefore, the algorithm becomes:

```
WHILE (not at the end of the line) DO
    read a new character ch
    IF (ch is not a '#') THEN
        add ch to the data structure
    ELSIF (the data structure is not empty) THEN
        remove from the data structure the
            item that was most recently added
    ELSE
        ignore the '#'
    END
END
```

From this pseudocode we identify a third operation required by the ADT:

```
determine if the data structure is empty
```

The above algorithm performs our first task,

```
input the line
```

so we now move on to the second task,

```
print the line in reversed order
```

It at first appears that this can be accomplished using the three ADT operations already identified:

```
WHILE (the data structure is not empty) DO
    remove from the data structure the item
        that was most recently added
    print .....Uh, Oh!
END
```

We have discovered that, once removed, the item is gone. What we should have done was

```
retrieve from the data structure the item that was most
    recently added
```

and only then removed it (recall that *retrieve* means look at but leave unchanged). The print backward algorithm therefore becomes

```
WHILE (the data structure is not empty) DO
    retrieve from the data structure the item
        that was most recently added and put it in ch

    print ch

    remove from the data structure the item
        that was most recently added
END
```

We have thus identified a fourth operation required by our ADT:

```
retrieve from the data structure the item
    that was most recently added
```

We now have a high-level solution to the problem. Although we have yet to think about what the data structure is, we have surmised that we must be able to do the following.

KEY CONCEPTS

Summary of Operations
1. Determine if the data structure is empty.
2. Insert a new item into the data structure.
3. Remove from the data structure the item that was most recently added.
4. Retrieve from the data structure the item that was most recently added.

These operations define the ADT we need. It turns out that this is a very well-known ADT, which is usually referred to as a **stack**. We name the operations to conform with convention:

```
IsEmpty(S)
(* Determine if stack S is empty. *)

Push(S, e)
(* Add item e to stack S. *)

Pop(S)
(* Remove from stack S the item that was most recently added. *)

StackTop(S)
(* Retrieve from stack S the item that was
   most recently added, leaving S unchanged. *)
```

There is a fifth operation, which seems so obvious that there might be a tendency to neglect it. This is the operation that *creates* a new stack. In terms of a Modula-2 implementation, this corresponds roughly to declaring a variable of the appropriate type and initializing the variable so that it represents an empty stack. The `Create` operation is also important from a more theoretical point of view, as it allows us to state precisely the results of performing a sequence of one or more operations beginning with an empty stack. We thus include the operation

```
Create(S)
(* Create an empty stack S. *)
```

As we mentioned at the beginning of this chapter, intuitive definitions such as these are not really sufficient to define an ADT formally. For example, to capture formally the intuitive notion that the last item inserted into the stack is the first item to be removed, we would write an axiom such as

```
Pop(Push(S, e)) = S
```

We are now ready to put together our solution to the line reversal problem. We can write a nearly complete pseudocode program using the stack operations defined above. Notice that not only are these operations as yet unwritten but also that no thought has been given as to what a stack looks like. Because the ADT approach builds a wall around the implementation of the stack, the rest of the program can be written independently of this implementation. So long as the rest of the program honors the contract and correctly uses the ADT operations, it will work regardless of how the ADT is implemented.

```
MODULE LineReverse

(* Import the following stack operations. *)

Create(S)
```

```
IsEmpty (S)

Push (S,  e)

Pop (S)

StackTop (S)


ReadAndCorrect (S)
(* Read the input line.  For each character read, either
     enter it into stack S,  or correct the contents of S. *)

BEGIN

    WHILE (not at the end of the line) DO

        read (newchar)

        IF (newchar # '#')  THEN
            Push (S,  newchar)
        ELSIF (NOT IsEmpty (S))  THEN
            Pop (S)
        END

    END

END ReadAndCorrect


WriteBackward (S)
(* Print the reversed line by printing
    the contents of stack S.  *)

BEGIN

    WHILE ( NOT IsEmpty (S) ) DO

        newchar := StackTop (S)
        write (newchar)
        Pop (S)

    END

END WriteBackward
```

```
BEGIN  (* MAIN PROGRAM *)

    Create(S)

    ReadAndCorrect(S)

    WriteBackward(S)

END LineReverse
```

IMPLEMENTING ADT'S IN MODULA-2

Much of the discussion of this section addresses the issue of how Modula-2's support of independent program modules can best be utilized to achieve the principles of data abstraction. We begin with a general discussion of the structure of a Modula-2 program containing abstract data types. We also include some brief comments on ways in which Modula-2 fails to support fully the principles of data abstraction. Following these general discussions we develop sequential and linked Modula-2 implementations for the ADT stack.

The Structure of Modula-2 Programs with ADT's

One of the goals of Modula-2 is to provide a programming environment that supports abstract data types. Despite some shortcomings Modula-2 accomplishes this goal rather well.

The use of ADT's in program development can be viewed from several perspectives. One perspective is that there exists in our programming environment a library of implementations of common ADT's. When a programmer constructs a solution to a new application, often she can select from the library appropriate implementations for many of the ADT's that her program requires. A second perspective is that one or more programmers are constructing a solution from scratch. First the required data operations are identified and then a contract is drawn up defining the necessary ADT's. At this point implementations for the ADT's are developed as part of the programming task.

Since the identification and implementation of ADT's are both major topics of the book, we adopt the second perspective. In the following discussion we shall assume that there is a programmer who develops and implements the main algorithms and, in so doing, defines the required ADT's. An ADT implementor is then responsible for developing implementations for these ADT's. In reality, of course, there may be only one person, or there may be many people, involved in the programming task.

The Contract in Modula-2. In the context of Modula-2, the contract between the programmer and the ADT implementor takes the form of a definition module and an auxiliary set of application-dependent comments. For example, consider the following skeleton definition module for the ADT stack.

```
DEFINITION MODULE Stacks;
(* *******************************************************
    ADT STACK (basic form of definition module)

    The following hidden type is declared:

        Stack

    The following operations are supported:

        Create, IsEmpty, Push, Pop, StackTop
    ******************************************************* *)

(* Stack item *)
FROM ADTitem IMPORT

    itemtype;

EXPORT QUALIFIED

    Stack, Create, IsEmpty, Push, Pop, StackTop;

TYPE

    Stack;

(* procedure definitions go here *)

END Stacks.
```

This definition module illustrates three key aspects of the interface between the
"ADT portion" of a Modula-2 program and the "user portion" of a Modula-2
program.

1. Operation Definitions: The subprogram definitions (including comments)
   comprise the primary component of the contract. This component names the
   ADT operations, specifies the number and type of arguments of each operation, and gives a complete description of the effect of performing each operation. The contract contains no details of how the operations are implemented.

2. Hidden Type Definition for the ADT: The contract specifies that variables to
   be used as stacks must be declared to be of the hidden type *Stack*. Utilizing
   a hidden type definition in this manner hides from the user's portion of the
   program all information about the object used in the ADT's implementation.

3. Import Statement for *itemtype*: *itemtype* is the type of object that is to
   be stored in the ADT. The contract specifies that the user will supply a module
   called *ADTitem* containing the definition of *itemtype*. This convention
   allows some degree of generality in the ADT implementation, since the implementation can be written so as to be applicable to many different definitions

of *itemtype* that the user might supply. (However, as we shall see, there are limits to this generality.)

In addition to the definition module, the contract contains an auxiliary set of application-dependent comments. These comments allow the user to communicate to the ADT implementor important characteristics of how the application in question will utilize the ADT. The comments can appear either in the user module(s) that utilize the ADT or in a separate "documentation file" for the ADT contract. For example, the following is a sample auxiliary comment for an application that utilizes the ADT stack.

```
(* CONTRACT NOTES:  The ADT Stack is to be used in an
   application environment in which there is no good estimate
   on the maximum number of items that the stack can contain
   at any one time.  Of all the Stack operations, it is most
   important that StackTop be highly efficient. *)
```

Notice that because the contract notes are separated from the ADT's definition module, a single definition module suffices for all applications. As we shall see throughout the remainder of the book, information such as that contained in the above contract notes is crucial to the selection of an ADT implementation that is appropriate for the application in question.

The Implementor's Side of the Wall.   Consider the following skeleton implementation module for the ADT stack that, conceptually, resides on the ADT implementor's side of the wall.

```
IMPLEMENTATION MODULE Stacks;
(* ******************************************************
   ADT STACK (basic form of implementation module)

   The following operations are supported:

      Create, IsEmpty, Push, Pop, StackTop
   ****************************************************** *)


(* Stack item *)
FROM ADTitem IMPORT

   itemtype;

TYPE

   Stack   = POINTER TO "ADT Object"

(* Implementations of the stack procedures go here. *)

END Stacks.
```

As with other implementation modules we have seen throughout the book, the above implementation module contains the bodies of the subprograms declared in the corresponding definition module. In the context of implementation modules for ADT's, the subprograms implement the ADT operations. The operation names, arguments, and descriptions that appear in the definition module act as slits, allowing the operations to be invoked from the user's side of the wall and for data to be passed from one side of the wall to the other. Notice, however, that these slits are not large enough to allow the user's program to "see" how the operations are implemented. That is, the people involved in the development of the user's portion of the program need not (and in fact *should not*) ever see this implementation module.

Consider now the definition of *Stack* in the implementation module. *Stack* is defined to be a pointer type. It generally is necessary to define the ADT object to be a pointer type because most implementations of Modula-2 do not allow structured types to be hidden. Therefore, despite the fact that it often is more natural to define the ADT object to be an array or a record, the limitations of the language force us into the convention that the ADT object must be defined to be a pointer type, where the pointer points to the "real" ADT object.

While the indirection that results from defining the ADT object to be a pointer to the "real object" may at first be confusing, the convention is justified by the advantages of **data hiding**. A hidden type such as *Stack* provides a slit in the wall that allows the user's program only limited access to variables of the ADT type. In particular, the user's program can use ADT variables only as arguments to the ADT operations. Notice that since the user's program cannot manipulate variables of a hidden type*, the user's program is prevented from penetrating the wall in violation of the spirit of data abstraction. Therefore, declaring the ADT object to be of a hidden type provides the data hiding that the theory of data abstraction advocates.*

The User's Side of the Wall.   Consider now the type *itemtype*. The **IMPORT** statements in the stack's definition and implementation modules imply that it is the user's responsibility to supply a module called *ADTitem* that defines the type of items to be stored in the ADT. For example, if the user wishes to store integers in the stack, she would write the definition module *ADTitem* as follows.

```
DEFINITION MODULE ADTitem;
(* Define the ADT item type *)


EXPORT QUALIFIED


 itemtype;
```

---

*Most implementations of Modula-2 allow variables of a hidden type to be assigned to one another. Notice, however, that if the hidden type were defined to be a pointer, the assignment S2 := S1 would not create a new copy of S1 in the ADT variable S2, but rather would leave S1 and S2 referencing the same ADT structure. Presumably, this is not the effect the user intended. As a consequence, we avoid assigning one ADT variable to another, and instead define an ADT Assign operation when appropriate.

```
TYPE

    itemtype = INTEGER;

END ADTitem.
```

In this manner, the same stack implementation can be used for many different types of items, so long as the user supplies the appropriate definition of *itemtype* in the module *ADTitem*. (Unfortunately, the convention does not attain as full a degree of flexibility as we would like. This is one of the shortcomings of Modula-2 discussed at the end of the section.) Finally, any modules of the user's portion of the program that utilizes the ADT stack must import the definitions developed above. For example, if the implementation module *UseStack* declares and utilizes the ADT stack variable S, the module would have the following form.

```
IMPLEMENTATION MODULE UseStack;

(* Stack type and stack operations *)
FROM Stacks IMPORT

    Stack, Create, Push, Pop, IsEmpty, StackTop;

(* item type *)
FROM ADTitem IMPORT

    itemtype;

VAR

    S    : Stack;
    item : itemtype;

BEGIN
    .
    .
    .

    (* Sample Call *)
    Push(S, item);
```

Structure of a Modula-2 Program with ADT's
Contract: ADT definition module and auxiliary comments.
Implementor's Side of Wall: ADT implementation module.
User's Side of the Wall: Definition module for *itemtype* and any modules that use the ADT.

Program Modifiability. One of the major advantages of the ADT approach to program development is that the programs it produces are highly modifiable. In order to illustrate this point we consider two common types of modifications and discuss the impact of each on a Modula-2 program structured using the conventions described above.

Modifications to the ADT Implementation: If the ADT's implementation must be modified (for example, for reasons of efficiency) all program changes are isolated to the ADT's implementation module. In particular, the ADT's definition module does not change, even if the modification requires a change to the ADT's type definition (which is a hidden type). This in turn implies that no program modules that import the ADT need to be recompiled.

Modifications to the User's Portion of the Program: Most modifications to the user's portion of the program in no way affect the ADT's implementation module, and the implementation module thus does not need to be recompiled. The one exception to this rule occurs when the user redefines the type of items to be stored in the ADT. In this case, we must recompile the ADT's modules because they import the definition of *itemtype* from the module *ADTitem*. Note that in many cases no changes need be made to the ADT's modules before the recompilation is performed. However, there are some cases that do require that changes be made to the ADT's implementation module. For example, if the item type is a record and the ADT's implementation depends on the structure of the record (if, for example, the implementation module references a field in the record), the implementation module clearly must be modified if the record type should change.

The Library Perspective. We have seen that Modula-2's support of independent program modules allows us to realize many of the basic principles of data abstraction. However, Modula-2 comes up a bit short with regard to its support of some other aspects of data abstraction. A prime example of this is Modula-2's less than ideal support for the concept of a "library" of ADT implementations.

Suppose that we wish to maintain a programming environment that provides our programmers with a library of ADT implementations. For example, our library might contain one or more implementations of the ADT stack. Whenever a programmer requires the use of the ADT stack, she needs only choose an appropriate stack implementation module and "connect" her program modules to it. Modula-2's difficulty with this programming environment is rooted in the manner in which these module connections are made. The difficulties can materialize when a program must utilize simultaneously two or more different instances of the same ADT.

For example, suppose that a program must utilize simultaneously a stack of integers and a stack of characters. We would expect to be able to use the same stack implementation by specifying different definitions for *itemtype* (one *itemtype* is defined to be an integer and the other a character). We have seen, however, that the type of item to be stored in the ADT is specified in a user-created module *ADTitem*, and this type definition is imported into the ADT's implementation and definition modules. How can the *same* implementation and definition modules simultaneously import both the integer and character definitions of *itemtype?* The answer is that the same implementation and definition modules cannot simultaneously import both definitions of *itemtype.* Consequently, the programmer must make two copies of the library's stack modules and connect each copy to the *ADTitem* module containing the appropriate type definition. Continuing with our stack example, the user would have to create the two versions of the module *ADTitem*, defining *itemtype* to be an integer in one version and a character in the other version. The user then has to give distinct names to the two copies of the stack implementation modules (for example, *StacksI* and *StacksC*) and connect each stack module to the appropriate *ADTitem* module. Notice that, to avoid ambiguity, all calls to the ADT operations must be qualified with the name of the appropriate ADT stack module (for example, *StacksI.Pop* and *StacksC.Pop) *.

We observe that the Modula-2 type **WORD** provides us with an alternative to the above process. However, the use of the type **WORD** forces ADT's to be implemented with procedures written at a very low level of detail (utilizing address arithmetic, for example). We therefore feel that the use of the type **WORD** in this context is not appropriate since we wish to focus our attention on algorithmic concepts arising in the implementation of ADT's.

Modula-2's support of the library perspective thus is somewhat inadequate. How could the library perspective be better realized? One approach is to generalize the way that Modula-2 makes connections between the user's modules and the ADT's implementation module. For example, the programming language Ada includes a facility that allows an ADT implementation to be defined with respect to a generic item type. This facility of Ada allows the *exact same* implementation module to be connected simultaneously to one or more item types and thus the same implementation module can implement simultaneously ADT's containing different types of items. This is not to say, however, that Ada is a better language than Modula-2. Anyone who has studied Ada knows that it is a far more complex language than Modula-2—a great deal of apparatus is needed to provide the support of generic ADT's. This added complexity is a high price to pay for the resulting increase in flexibility. In a programming environment in which a library of ADT implementations is relied on heavily, Ada might be an appropriate choice. In many environments, however, Modula-2 is a good compromise in that it is a relatively simple language that supports many of the important principles of data abstraction.

Sequential and Linked Stack Implementations

In this section we develop Modula-2 implementations of the ADT stack. As was the case for the ADT ordered list, the primary decision is whether to choose a sequential or linked implementation. If we were to choose a sequential imple-

---

*Observe that analogous steps are required when a program must utilize simultaneously two stacks that require different implementations, even when the two stacks contain the same type of item.

mentation, we would have to place a restriction on the *Push* operation so that it would not attempt to add an item to the stack if its size limit (as imposed by the size of the array used in the implementation) has been reached. If this restriction is not acceptable, a linked implementation must be used (see Figure 6–7).

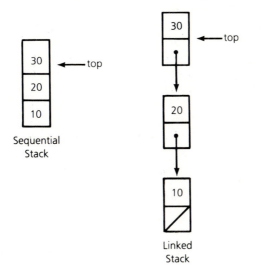

Figure 6–7

Sequential and linked implementations of ADT stack

As a first step, we present a Modula-2 definition module that formalizes and refines the contract.

```
DEFINITION MODULE Stacks;
(* *********************************************************
    ADT STACK

    The following hidden type is declared:

        Stack

    The following operations are supported:

        Create, IsEmpty, Push, Pop, StackTop
    ********************************************************* *)

(* Stack item *)
FROM ADTitem IMPORT

    itemtype;

EXPORT QUALIFIED

    Stack, Create, IsEmpty, Push, Pop, StackTop;
```

```
TYPE

   Stack;

(* ----------------------------------------------------------
   Create:   Create an empty stack S.
   ---------------------------------------------------------- *)
PROCEDURE Create(VAR S : Stack);

(* ----------------------------------------------------------
   IsEmpty:   Determine if stack S is empty.

   ASSUMPTION:   Stack S has been created.
   ---------------------------------------------------------- *)
PROCEDURE IsEmpty(S : Stack) : BOOLEAN;

(* ----------------------------------------------------------
   Push:   Add newitem to stack S.   The Boolean flag success
   is returned TRUE if the Push was successful, and FALSE
   otherwise (e.g., because of memory limitations).   In
   the event of an unsuccessful Push, the stack is unchanged.

   ASSUMPTION:   Stack S has been created.
   ---------------------------------------------------------- *)
PROCEDURE Push(VAR S : Stack; newitem : itemtype;
               VAR success : BOOLEAN);

(* ----------------------------------------------------------
   Pop:   Remove from stack S the item which was most
   recently added.   The operation fails if the stack is
   empty.   The Boolean flag success indicates whether the
   operation succeeded.   In the event of an unsuccessful
   Pop, the stack is unchanged.

   ASSUMPTION:   Stack S has been created.
   ---------------------------------------------------------- *)
PROCEDURE Pop(VAR S : Stack; VAR success : BOOLEAN);

(* ----------------------------------------------------------
   StackTop:   Retrieve into getitem the item from stack S
   which was most recently added, leaving S unchanged.   The
   operation fails if the stack is empty.   The Boolean flag
   success indicates whether the operation succeeded.

   ASSUMPTION:   Stack S has been created.
   ---------------------------------------------------------- *)
PROCEDURE StackTop(S : Stack; VAR getitem : itemtype;
                   VAR success : BOOLEAN);

END Stacks.
```

We need to note a few things about the contract as defined in the above definition module:

1. *StackTop* will be implemented as a procedure rather than as a function. The primary reason for this is to allow full generality of what *itemtype* may be—that is, what type of items may be placed on the stack. Since Modula-2 allows functions to return only simple values, a function *StackTop* could not be used if *itemtype* were, for instance, a record or an array. The limitations of Modula-2 have forced a refinement of the original definition of a stack for the sake of generality.

2. *StackTop* and *Pop* return Boolean success flags. This is to account for the possibility that these operations will be called with an empty stack as an argument. The calling program can take appropriate action based on the value of the flag.

3. *Push* returns a Boolean success flag. This is to account for the possibility that there is insufficient memory to add a new item to the stack argument. This could easily happen in the context of a sequential implementation. For the linked implementation there are two motivations for inclusion of the success flag. First, the inclusion of the success flag allows the linked and sequential implementations to share the same definition module, making it easier to switch between implementations. Second, it is conceivable that the operation could fail in a linked implementation because some memory limit has been reached, e.g., the memory limit of the system.

In practice, when choosing between a sequential and linked implementation of a stack (or another ADT), we must ask the question, does the fixed-size restriction of a sequential implementation present a problem *in the context of a particular application*? The answer to this question depends on two factors. The obvious factor is whether or not, for a given application, we can predict in advance the maximum number of items in the stack at any one time. If we cannot, then the sequential solution is not adequate; it is quite possible that the *Push* operation—and hence the entire program—will fail because the implementation does not completely meet the specifications of a stack *in the context of the application*.

If, on the other hand, we can predict in advance the maximum number of items in the stack at any one time for a given application, we must explore a more subtle factor. This factor is whether or not it would be wasteful of storage to use an array declared to be large enough to accommodate this maximum number of items. Consider a case where the maximum number of items is large, but we suspect that this number will rarely be achieved. For example, suppose that there *could* be as many as 10,000 items in the stack, but the number of items in the stack rarely exceeds 10. The array would have to be declared large enough to hold 10,000 items, but for the majority of the program's execution, at least 9990 array locations would be wasted. If we used a linked implementation, we could use procedure *DISPOSE* to recycle nodes when they are no longer needed for the stack.

We thus see that there are many types of applications for which the fixed-size restriction of a sequential implementation of a stack is unacceptable. These situations necessitate a linked implementation. For our particular line-reverse problem, however, it is conceivable that the fixed-size restriction does not present a problem (for example, the terminal allows a line length of only 80 characters). If that were the case, we could use the sequential implementation that follows.

A Sequential Implementation of the ADT Stack. Consider the sequential implementation of the ADT stack in Figure 6−8. This figure suggests that we represent a stack with a record containing the array *Items* and an index *Top* to a position in *Items*. In Modula-2, this would be realized with the following type definitions:

```
CONST

    maxstack = maximum size of stack

TYPE

    itemtype = desired type of stack item
    stack    = RECORD
                  Items : ARRAY [1..maxstack] OF itemtype
                  Top   : [0..maxstack]
               END
```

Figure 6−8

*Sequential
implementation*

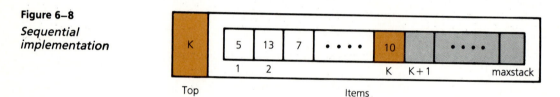

Top   Items

```
IMPLEMENTATION MODULE Stacks;
(* ********************************************************
   ADT STACK - Sequential Implementation

   The following Stack operations are supported:

      Create, IsEmpty, Push, Pop, StackTop

   Type Stack is a pointer to a record that is created
   dynamically with a call to procedure NEW.  This
   indirection allows type Stack to be a hidden type.
   ******************************************************** *)

(* memory management procedure NEW *)
FROM Storage IMPORT
```

```
    ALLOCATE;

(* Stack item *)
FROM ADTitem IMPORT

    itemtype;

(* fixed maximum size inferred from User's Documentation File *)
CONST

    maxstack = 80;

(* Stack structure *)
TYPE

    body   = RECORD
                Items: ARRAY [1..maxstack] OF itemtype;
                Top : [0..maxstack];
            END;

    Stack = POINTER TO body;

(* -----------------------------------------------------------
    Create:   Create an empty stack S.
    ------------------------------------------------------- *)
PROCEDURE Create(VAR S : Stack);

BEGIN

    NEW(S);
    S^.Top := 0;

END Create;

(* -----------------------------------------------------------
    IsEmpty:   Determine if stack S is empty.

    ASSUMPTION:   Stack S has been created.
    ------------------------------------------------------- *)
PROCEDURE IsEmpty(S : Stack) : BOOLEAN;

BEGIN

    RETURN (S^.Top < 1);

END IsEmpty;
```

```
(* ------------------------------------------------------------
    Push:   Add newitem to stack S.   The Boolean flag success
    is returned TRUE if the Push was successful, and FALSE
    otherwise (e.g., because of memory limitations).   In
    the event of an unsuccessful Push, the stack is unchanged.

    ASSUMPTION:   Stack S has been created.
    ------------------------------------------------------- *)
PROCEDURE Push(VAR S : Stack; newitem : itemtype ;
                  VAR success : BOOLEAN);

BEGIN

    IF (S^.Top = maxstack) THEN
        success := FALSE;
    ELSE
        INC(S^.Top);
        S^.Items[S^.Top] := newitem;
        success := TRUE;
    END;

END Push;
```

```
(* ------------------------------------------------------------
    Pop:   Remove from stack S the item which was most
    recently added.   The operation fails if the stack is
    empty.   The Boolean flag success indicates whether the
    operation succeeded.   In the event of an unsuccessful
    Pop, the stack is unchanged.

    ASSUMPTION:   Stack S has been created.

    CALLS:   IsEmpty
    ------------------------------------------------------- *)
PROCEDURE Pop(VAR S : Stack; VAR success : BOOLEAN);

BEGIN

    IF (IsEmpty(S)) THEN
        success := FALSE
    ELSE
        DEC(S^.Top);
        success := TRUE;
    END;

END Pop;
```

```
(* ---------------------------------------------------------------
   StackTop:  Retrieve into getitem the item from stack S
   which was most recently added, leaving S unchanged.   The
   operation fails if the stack is empty.   The Boolean flag
   success indicates whether the operation succeeded.


   ASSUMPTION:   Stack S has been created.


   CALLS:   IsEmpty
   --------------------------------------------------------- *)
PROCEDURE StackTop(S : Stack; VAR getitem : itemtype;
                   VAR success : BOOLEAN);


BEGIN

   IF (IsEmpty(S)) THEN
      success := FALSE
   ELSE
      getitem := S^.Items[S^.Top];
      success := TRUE;
   END;


END StackTop;


END Stacks.
```

A Linked Implementation of the ADT Stack. Many applications require a linked implementation of a stack so that it can grow and shrink dynamically.

In Figure 6–9, S is a pointer to the head of a linked list of items. In Modula-2, this would be realized as follows:

```
TYPE

   itemtype = desired type of stack item
   nodeptr  = POINTER TO node
   node     = RECORD
                  item : itemtype
                  next : nodeptr
              END
   stack    = nodeptr

VAR

   S : stack



IMPLEMENTATION MODULE Stacks;
```

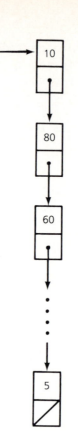

Figure 6–9

*Linked imple-
mentation*

```
(* *********************************************************
    ADT STACK - Linked Implementation

    The following operations are supported:

        Create, IsEmpty, Push, Pop, StackTop
    ********************************************************* *)

(* memory management procedures NEW and DISPOSE *)
FROM Storage IMPORT

    ALLOCATE, DEALLOCATE;

(* Stack item *)
FROM ADTitem IMPORT

    itemtype;
```

```
    (* Stack structure *)
    nodeptr = POINTER TO node;
    node    = RECORD
                  item : itemtype;
                  next : nodeptr;
              END;
    Stack   = nodeptr;


(* -----------------------------------------------------------
   Create:   Create an empty stack S.
   --------------------------------------------------------- *)
PROCEDURE Create(VAR S : Stack);

BEGIN

    S := NIL;

END Create;

(* -----------------------------------------------------------
   IsEmpty:   Determine if stack S is empty.

   ASSUMPTION:   Stack S has been created.
   --------------------------------------------------------- *)
PROCEDURE IsEmpty(S : Stack) : BOOLEAN;

BEGIN

    RETURN (S = NIL);

END IsEmpty;

(* -----------------------------------------------------------
   Push:   Add newitem to stack S.   The Boolean flag success
   is returned TRUE if the Push was successful, and FALSE
   otherwise (e.g., because of memory limitations).   In
   the event of an unsuccessful Push, the stack is unchanged.

   NOTE:   In most implementations of Modula-2 there is no way
   for a call to NEW to fail gracefully.   Therefore, the
   program will terminate abnormally if it exceeds memory
   limitations.

   ASSUMPTION:   Stack S has been created.
   --------------------------------------------------------- *)
```

```
PROCEDURE Push(VAR S : Stack; newitem : itemtype;
                    VAR success : BOOLEAN);

VAR

    p : nodeptr;

BEGIN

    (* create a new node *)
    NEW(p);
    p^.item := newitem;

    (* insert the new node *)
    p^.next := S;
    S := p;

    success := TRUE;

END Push;

(* -------------------------------------------------------------
   Pop:   Remove from stack S the item which was most
   recently added.   The operation fails if the stack is
   empty.   The Boolean flag success indicates whether the
   operation succeeded.   In the event of an unsuccessful
   Pop, the stack is unchanged.

   ASSUMPTION:   Stack S has been created.

   CALLS:   IsEmpty
   ------------------------------------------------------------- *)
PROCEDURE Pop(VAR S : Stack; VAR success : BOOLEAN);

VAR

    delptr : nodeptr;

BEGIN

    IF (IsEmpty(S)) THEN
        success := FALSE;
    ELSE
        delptr := S;
        S := S^.next;
        DISPOSE(delptr);
        success := TRUE;
    END;
```

```
END Pop;

(*  ----------------------------------------------------
    StackTop:  Retrieve into getitem the item from stack S
    which was most recently added, leaving S unchanged.  The
    operation fails if the stack is empty.  The Boolean flag
    success indicates whether the operation succeeded.

    ASSUMPTION:  Stack S has been created.

    CALLS:  IsEmpty
    ---------------------------------------------------- *)
PROCEDURE StackTop(S : Stack; VAR getitem : itemtype;
                   VAR success : BOOLEAN);

BEGIN

    IF (IsEmpty(S)) THEN
        success := FALSE;
    ELSE
        getitem := S^.item;
        success := TRUE;
    END;

END StackTop;

END Stacks.
```

SUMMARY

1. Data abstraction is a technique for controlling the interaction between a program and its data structures. It builds walls around a program's data structures, just as other aspects of modularity build walls around a program's algorithms. Such walls make programs easier to design, implement, read, and modify.

2. The specifications of a set of such data-management operations define an abstract data type (ADT).

3. Only after an ADT has been fully defined should we think about how to implement it with a data structure. Even after an implementation has been selected, the remainder of the program should not depend on the particular choice.

4. The proper choice of a data structure depends both on the details of the operations and on the context in which the operations are to be used.

COMMON PITFALLS / DEBUGGING

1. A program should not depend on how its ADT's are implemented.

2. If a sequential implementation is chosen for an ADT, there will be a maximum number of items that can be stored. Thus, the implementation will have to check if there is room in the data structure before inserting a new item, and the calling program will have to take appropriate action if there is no room.

3. Operations such as *Stacktop* and *Pop* must take reasonable action if they are called on an empty data structure. One possibility is to return a success flag with the value *false* in this event.

4. Modula-2 does not allow functions to return complex structures such as arrays and records. Therefore, an ADT's retrieval operations should generally be written as procedures, with a variable parameter used to return the item. This allows us to define the ADT's items to be of any type.

5. A sequential implementation is one that utilizes an implicit ordering scheme—for example, the item that follows $A[i]$ is stored in $A[i+1]$. A linked implementation is one that utilizes an explicit ordering scheme—for example, the item that follows the one in node N is found by following node N's pointer.

6. We often must choose between a sequential and linked implementation. One important criterion on which to base this choice is whether or not, in the context of a particular problem, the fixed-size limitations of a sequential implementation are acceptable. If not, the dynamic storage allocation provided by a linked implementation is required. On the other hand, an array provides direct access to its ith item, while a linked list does not. In the chapters that follow, we shall encounter applications with a wide range of data-management requirements. The process of selecting data structures for these applications will illustrate some of the other important criteria on which to base the choice of a data structure.

EXERCISES

1. What is the significance of *wall* and *contract*? Why do these notions help us to become better problem solvers?

2. Develop a sequential implementation of ADT ordered list. Don't forget to consider the issue of error checking and handling.

3. Develop a linked implementation of ADT ordered list.

4. Compare the sequential and linked implementations of the *Delete* (L, i) operation for an ordered list. Describe the work required for various values of i under each implementation. What are the implications for

efficiency if the cost of shifting data is large compared to the cost of following a pointer? When would this situation occur? What if the costs are approximately the same?

5. Write a procedure *Swap (L, i, j)* that will interchange the ith and j^{th} items of list *L*. The new procedure should be defined in terms of the ADT ordered list operations.

6. Consider the following recurrence relation:

$$f(1) = 1$$

$$f(2) = 1$$

$$f(3) = 1$$

$$f(4) = 3$$

$$f(5) = 5$$

$$f(n) = f(n - 1) + 3*f(n - 5) \qquad \text{for all } n > 5$$

a. Compute $f(n)$ for the following values of *n*: 6, 7, 12, 15

b. If you were careful, rather than computing $f(15)$ from scratch (the way a recursive Modula-2 subprogram would compute it), you would have computed $f(6)$, then $f(7)$, then $f(8)$, and so on up to $f(15)$, recording the values as you computed them. This would have saved you the effort of ever computing the same value more than once. (Recall the nonrecursive version of the *Rabbit* program discussed at the end of Chapter 4.)

   When doing this, note that you never really needed to remember all the previously computed values—only the last 5. Taking advantage of these observations, write a Modula-2 function that uses a variation of ADT ordered list to compute $f(n)$ for arbitrary values of *n*.

7. What do the stacks S and T "look like" after the following sequence of operations:

```
Create (S)
Push (S,  1)
Push (S,  2)
Create (T)
Push (T,  3)
Push (T,  4)
Pop (S)
Push (S,  StackTop (T))
Push (S,  5)
Pop (T)
Push (T,  6)
```

8. Code up the line reversal problem described in the chapter. Under what conditions would you choose a sequential implementation for the stack? Under what conditions would you choose a linked implementation?

9. Let's say that we want to redefine the *Pop* operation for a stack as follows:

```
Pop (S,  n)
(* Remove from stack S the n items that were most recently
   added.   It is an error if there are less than n elements
   on S.  *)
```

Modify the linked and sequential implementations to reflect this change. Could we define the new operation in terms of the old operations? Which implementation of the new operation would be more efficient?

*10. In this chapter, ADT operations have been defined in an intuitive way that reflects a programming perspective. As we pointed out, operations can also be defined in a more mathematically formal way with axioms. For example, we can formally define the ADT stack with the following axioms:

> Let S be an arbitrary stack and e an arbitrary stack item.
> Note that Create is treated as a constant that represents a "newly created empty stack."
>
> IsEmpty(Create) = true (a newly created stack is empty)
> IsEmpty(Push(S,e)) = false
>
> Pop(Create) = Create (this could be defined to be an error)
> Pop(Push(S,e)) = S
>
> StackTop(Create) = error
> StackTop(Push(S,e)) = e

The axioms can be used, for example, to prove that the stack defined by the sequence of operations

> Pop(Push(Push(Pop(Push(Push(Push(Create,5),7),3)),9),4))

> (that is, Create an empty stack,
>   Push a 5,
>   Push a 7,
>   Push a 3,
>   Pop (the 3),
>   Push a 9,
>   Push a 4,
>   Pop (the 4)   )

is exactly the same as the stack defined by the sequence:

> Push(Push(Push(Create,5),7),9)

> (that is, Create an empty stack,
>   Push a 5,
>   Push a 7,
>   Push a 9   )

Similarly, the axioms can be used to show

$$IsEmpty(Pop(Pop(Push(Pop(Push(Push(Create,1),2)),3)))) = true$$

a. The representation of a stack as a sequence Push(Push(...Push(Create,...) without any Pop operations is called a **canonical form.** Prove that any stack is equal to a stack that is in canonical form.

b. Prove that the canonical form is unique. That is, a stack is equal to exactly one stack that is in canonical form.

c. Use the axioms to formally show the following:

$$StackTop(Pop(Push(Push(Pop(Push(Push(Pop(Pop(Push \\ (Create,6))),9),2)),3),1))) = 3$$

PROJECT

11. Consider the ADT **polynomial**—polynomials in a single variable x. This ADT can be defined by the following operations:

```
Create (P)
(* Initialize P to be the zero polynomial.  *)

Degree (P)
(* Return the degree of the polynomial P.   This is defined to
    be the highest power of a term with a nonzero coefficient.  *)

Set (P, i, value)
(* Set the coefficient of the degree i  (xⁱ) term to value.  *)

Retrieve (P, i)
(* Return the coefficient of the degree i  (xⁱ) term.  *)
```

For this problem we will restrict ourselves to polynomials whose exponents are nonnegative integers. For example, consider the following polynomial:

$$P = 4x^5 + 7x^3 - x^2 + 9$$

Degree$(P) = 5$ (the highest power of a term with a nonzero coefficient)
Retrieve$(P, 3) = 7$ (the coefficient of the degree 3 (x^3) term)
Retrieve$(P, 2) = -1$ (the coefficient of the degree 2 (x^2) term)
Retrieve$(P, 4) = 0$ (the coefficient of a missing term is implicitly 0)
Retrieve$(P, 6) = 0$ (the coefficient of a missing term is implicitly 0)
Set$(P, 7, -3)$ produces the polynomial

$$P = -3x^7 + 4x^5 + 7x^3 - x^2 + 9$$

a. How can we define the ADT polynomial operations in terms of the ADT ordered list operations?

b. We would like to develop a **sparse** implementation of ADT polynomial. That is, we would like to implement the ADT in such a way that only the terms with nonzero coefficients are explicitly stored. For example, the polynomial P above can be represented as shown in Figure 6–10. Complete the sparse implementation.

Figure 6–10

Sparse polynomial

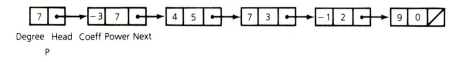

Degree Head Coeff Power Next

P

c. Write a procedure *Add* that will add two polynomials. The new procedure should be written in terms of the ADT polynomial operations.

d. Define a **traverse** operation for ADT polynomial that will allow us to add two sparse polynomials without having explicitly to consider terms with zero coefficients.

CHAPTER 7

STACKS

PREVIEW   The previous chapter used the ADT stack as a way of demonstrating the general concept of data abstraction. In this chapter we discuss how its operations give the stack its last-in, first-out behavior. Two of the several important applications we consider are evaluating algebraic expressions and searching for a path through a graph. We also discuss the important relationship between stacks and recursion, and we introduce a variation, the traversable stack.

MORE ON THE NATURE OF THE ABSTRACT DATA TYPE STACK

The term **stack** is intended to conjure up visions of objects encountered in daily life, such as a stack of dishes in your school's cafeteria, a stack of books on your desk, or a stack of assignments waiting for you to work on. In common English usage, *stack of* and *pile of* are synonymous. To computer scientists, however, a *stack* is not just any old *pile*. A *stack* of objects has the property that the last object placed on the stack will be the first object removed. This property is commonly referred to as **last in, first out,** or simply **LIFO.**

A stack of dishes in a cafeteria makes a very good analogy with the abstract data type stack (see Figure 7–1). As new dishes are added, the old dishes drop farther into the well beneath the surface. At any particular time, only the dish last placed on the stack is above the surface and visible. This is the dish that must be removed next. In general, the dishes are removed in exactly the opposite order from which they were added.

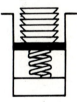

Figure 7–1
Stack of cafeteria dishes

The LIFO property of stacks seems inherently unfair. Think of the poor person who finally gets the last dish on the cafeteria's stack, a dish which may have been placed there six years ago. Or, how would you like to be the first person to arrive on the stack for a movie (as opposed to the line for a movie). You would be the last person allowed in! This is the reason that stacks are not especially prevalent in everyday life. The property that is usually desired in our daily lives is **first in, first out,** or **FIFO.** A **queue** is the abstract data type with this property. Most people would much prefer to wait in a movie *queue* (as it is commonly called in Britain) than in a movie *stack*. The ADT queue will be presented in the next chapter.

While the LIFO property of stacks is not appropriate for very many day-to-day situations, it is precisely what is needed for a large number of problems that arise in computer science. Recall the five operations that define the ADT stack:

```
Create(S)
(* Create an empty stack S. *)


IsEmpty(S)
(* Determine if stack S is empty. *)


Push(S, e)
(* Add item e to stack S. *)


Pop(S)
(* Remove from stack S the item which was
   most recently added. *)


StackTop(S)
(* Retrieve from stack S the item which was
   most recently added, leaving S unchanged. *)
```

Notice how well the analogy holds between the abstract data type stack and the stack of cafeteria dishes. The above five operations are the only operations of the ADT stack, and they correspond to the only things that can be done to a stack of dishes. We can determine if the stack of dishes is empty (but not how many dishes are on the stack), we can inspect the top dish (but no other dish), we can place a dish on top of the stack (but at no other position), and we can remove a dish from the top of the stack (but from no other position). If we were permitted to perform any other operations (or not all of the above), the data type would not be a stack.

We should point out, however, that there are some common variations of our definition. For example, you sometimes see a stack defined to have *Pop (S, e)* remove the top item and return its value in *e*, and not have the operation *StackTop (S)*.

If we were to adopt this definition of a stack, how could we inspect the top item of a stack without removing it? If this were necessary, the user could write an auxiliary function that utilizes *Pop* and *Push*.

```
PROCEDURE AuxStackTop(S) : returns a value from the stack

   Pop(S, e)
   Push(S, e)
   RETURN (e)
```

This is a bit awkward, but on the other hand it is very common to have to inspect and remove the top item of a stack simultaneously. Whereas our definition of a stack requires the sequence

```
e := StackTop(S)
Pop(S)
```

the task is accomplished by the single operation

```
Pop(S, e)
```

under the alternative definition. Both definitions of a stack are reasonable, each having its relative advantage. For the remainder of the book, we shall use the first definition presented.

In the sections to follow we present several applications for which the LIFO property of stacks is appropriate. The first two examples are rather simple; the others are more substantial. Keep in mind throughout that we are using the *ADT* stack to solve the problems. This means that we may use the five stack operations, but we may not assume any implementation. We would choose an implementation only as a last step.

TWO SIMPLE APPLICATIONS OF THE ADT STACK

One application of a stack is to verify that a given input string contains *balanced parentheses*. For example, the string

abc(defg(ijk)(l(mn))op)qr

is balanced, while the string

abc(def))(ghij(kl)m

is not balanced. We can check if a string is balanced by traversing it from left to right. As we move from left to right, we match each successive close parenthesis ')' with the rightmost unmatched open parenthesis, '(', which has already been encountered—that is, the '(' must be to the left of the current ')'. The string is balanced if

(1) each time we encounter a ')' the required matching '(' is found

(2) when we reach the end of the string, each '(' has been matched

The solution requires that we keep track of each unmatched '(' and discard one each time a ')' is encountered. One way to perform this task is to push each encountered '(' onto a stack and pop one off each time a ')' is encountered.

```
WHILE (not at the end of the string) DO
   IF (the next character is a '(') THEN
      Push(S, '(')
   ELSIF (the character is a ')') THEN
      Pop(S)
   END
END
```

Missing from this solution are the checks that conditions (1) and (2) are met. To verify condition (1), when a ')' is encountered we must check to see if the stack is empty before popping from it. If it is empty, we terminate the loop and report that the string is not balanced. To verify condition (2), we check that the stack is empty when the end of the string is reached.

The solution thus becomes

```
Create(S)
stillokay := TRUE
read(ch)
WHILE (stillokay AND (ch is not the EOL character)) DO

    (* push an open parenthesis *)
    IF (ch = '(') THEN
        Push(S, '(')

    ELSIF (ch = ')') THEN

        (* pop a matching open parenthesis *)
        IF (NOT IsEmpty(S)) THEN
          Pop(S)

        (* there is no matching open parenthesis *)
        ELSE
            stillokay := FALSE
        END

    (* else ignore all other characters *)

    END

    read(ch)

END (* while *)

(* note that the input line is necessarily
   finished if stillokay is true *)

IF (stillokay AND IsEmpty(S)) THEN
    is balanced
ELSE
    not balanced
END
```

It may have occurred to you that a simpler solution to this problem is possible. We need only keep count of the current number of unmatched '('. Each time a '(' is encountered, the count is incremented; each time a ')' is encountered, the count is decremented. If this count ever falls below zero or if it is greater than zero when the end of the string is reached, then the string is unbalanced. The '('s need not actually be stored on a stack.

This stack-based solution is conceptually useful, however, as it previews more legitimate uses of stacks. For example, consider the problem of recognizing the language

$$L = \{w\$w' \mid w \text{ is string of characters, } w' = \text{reverse}(w)\}$$

Strings w and w' are assumed not to contain the special symbol '$'. (This language was introduced in Exercise 5.6.)

A stack is very useful in determining if a given string is in L. We traverse the first half of the string, pushing each character onto a stack. When we reach the '$' we undo the process—for each character in the second half of the string, we pop a character off the stack. In order that the second half of the string be the reverse of the first half, each character popped must match the character at the current position of the string. To ensure that the two "halves" are of equal length, we must check that the stack is empty when (and only when) the end of the string is reached.

The following algorithm implements this strategy. To avoid unnecessary complications, we assume that the input string contains exactly one '$'.

```
Create(S)
read(ch)
(* push w *)
WHILE (ch # '$') DO
    Push(S, ch)
    read(ch)
END

(* skip the $ *)
read(ch)

(* match the reverse of w *)
stillokay := TRUE
WHILE (stillokay and (ch is not the EOL character)) DO

    (* first half is shorter than second half *)
    IF (IsEmpty(S)) THEN
        stillokay := FALSE

    (* characters do not match *)
    ELSIF (ch # StackTop(S)) THEN
        stillokay := FALSE

    (* characters match *)
    ELSE
        Pop(S)
        read(ch)

    END

END (* while *)
```

```
(* note that the input line is necessarily
   finished if stillokay is true *)

IF (stillokay AND IsEmpty(S)) THEN
   in language
ELSE
   not in language
END
```

Notice that the two algorithms we have presented in this section depend only on the the fact that the stack operations will be supported and not on how the stack is implemented. The primary consideration in choosing a sequential or linked implementation for the stack is whether or not there is a reasonable limit on the size of the string. If, for example, the string to be recognized is stored in an array, a sequential stack implementation with a maximum size corresponding to the size of the array holding the string can be used. On the other hand, if the string is stored in a linked list or in a file, a linked stack implementation might be required.

MORE COMPLEX APPLICATIONS OF STACKS

This section contains several problems that are very neatly solved using the ADT stack. Many problems of a similar nature were encountered in Chapter 5, when we studied recursive grammars as a way to specify the syntax of algebraic expressions. In a later section of this chapter we shall explicitly discuss the relationship between stacks and recursion. At that time you will see that the ADT stack has a hidden presence in the concept of recursion and, in fact, that stacks have an active role in most computer implementations of recursion.

Algebraic Expressions

In Chapter 5 we presented grammars for several types of algebraic expressions. Recall that we introduced prefix and postfix expressions as a way to avoid the ambiguity inherent in the evaluation of infix expressions. We then discussed how parentheses, precedence rules, and left-to-right association can be used to remove this ambiguity. We now present stack-based solutions to the problems of evaluating infix and postfix expressions. To avoid distracting programming issues, we allow only the binary operators $*$, $/$, $+$, and $-$ (no unary operators or exponentiation). The strategy we shall adopt is first to develop an algorithm for evaluating postfix expressions and then to develop an algorithm for transforming an infix expression into an equivalent postfix expression. This eliminates the need for an algorithm that directly evaluates infix expressions, a more difficult problem. We begin with an example illustrating how a postfix expression can be evaluated.

Many hand-held calculators use postfix convention. To compute the value of

$$(2 * (3 + 4))$$

one would enter the sequence

2
3
4
+
*

which corresponds to the postfix expression

2 3 4 + *

The calculator pushes each operand onto a stack as the operand is entered. When an operator is entered, it is applied to the top two operands on the stack, the operands are popped from the stack, and the result of the operation is pushed onto the stack. Thus, the action of the calculator for the above sequence is

KEY ENTERED	CALCULATOR ACTION
2	Push(S, 2)
3	Push(S, 3)
4	Push(S, 4)
+	op2 ← StackTop(S)
	Pop(S)
	op1 ← StackTop(S)
	Pop(S)
	result ← op1 + op2
	Push(S, result)
*	op2 ← StackTop(S)
	Pop(S)
	op1 ← StackTop(S)
	Pop(S)
	result ← op1 * op2
	Push(S, result)

The final result is on the top of the stack.

We thus see that the required operations are provided by the ADT stack. An algorithm that evaluates a postfix expression (assumed entered as a string of characters) is as follows. For simplicity (to avoid issues that cloud the algorithm with programming details), we will assume that the string is a syntactically correct postfix expression

there are no unary operations

there is no exponentiation operation

operands are single uppercase letters

```
FOR each character ch in the string DO
    IF (ch is an operator called op) THEN
        (* evaluate and push the result *)
        op2 := StackTop(S)
        Pop(S)
        op1 := StackTop(S)
        Pop(S)
        result := op1 op op2
        Push(S, result)

    ELSE
        Push(S, ch)

    END

END
```

Upon termination of the algorithm, the value of the expression will be on the top of the stack.

A Modula-2 implementation follows. For illustrative purposes, in the program we have assigned values to the operands as follows: $A := 5$, $B := 7$, $C := -1$, $D := 11$, and $E := 25$. Any other operand that is encountered will be assumed to have the value zero.

```
IMPLEMENTATION MODULE posteval;
(*

    EVALUATE POSTFIX EXPRESSIONS

    INPUT:  A legal postfix expression.

    OUTPUT:  The value of the postfix expression.

    ASSUMPTIONS:

        1.  The input string is a legal postfix expression.

        2.  The operators are the binary operators +, -, * and /

        3.  Every other character is an operand.  The values of
            the operands are given by function Operand.

    The evaluation uses a stack.
*)
```

```
(* Stack type and stack operatons *)
FROM Stacks IMPORT

    Stack, Create, Push, Pop, StackTop;


(* -----------------------------------------------------------
    Operand:  Convert a character operand to an integer value.

    The values have been chosen arbitrarily for illustration.
    ----------------------------------------------------- *)
PROCEDURE Operand(name : CHAR) : INTEGER;

BEGIN

    CASE name OF
        'A' : RETURN (5);
    |   'B' : RETURN (7);
    |   'C' : RETURN (-1);
    |   'D' : RETURN (11);
    |   'E' : RETURN (25);
    ELSE
        RETURN (0);
    END;

END Operand;

(* -----------------------------------------------------------
    PostEval:  Evaluate a postfix expression.

    An expression is an array of characters in postfix form:

        operators:  +, -, * or /
        operands :  a character with value defined by function
                    Operand

    ASSUMPTION:  E[0..last] is a legal postfix expression

    Calls:  Operand, Create, StackTop, Push, Pop
    ----------------------------------------------------- *)
PROCEDURE PostEval(E : ARRAY OF CHAR; last : INTEGER) : INTEGER;

VAR

    S : Stack;
    success : BOOLEAN;
    i, oper1, oper2, ans : INTEGER;
    ch : CHAR;

BEGIN
```

```
                    (* create a stack *)
                    Create (S);

                    (* process each character in the expression *)
                    FOR i := 0 TO last DO
                        ch := E[i];

                        (* ch is an operator - perform the operation on
                           the top two stack elements and push the result *)
                        IF ((ch = '*') OR (ch = '/') OR (ch = '-') OR (ch = '+')) THEN
                            StackTop (S, oper2, success);
                            Pop (S, success);
                            StackTop (S, oper1, success);
                            Pop (S, success);
                            CASE ch OF
                             '+' : ans := oper1 + oper2;
                           | '-' : ans := oper1 - oper2;
                           | '*' : ans := oper1 * oper2;
                           | '/' : ans := oper1 DIV oper2;
                            END;
                            Push (S, ans, success);

                        (* ch is an operand - push onto the stack *)
                        ELSE
                            Push (S, Operand(ch), success);

                        END;

                    END; (* for *)

                    (* the top of the stack is the answer *)
                    StackTop (S, ans, success);
                    RETURN (ans);

            END PostEval;

            END posteval.
```

The following illustrates calls to *PostEval*:

PARAMETER E	FUNCTION VALUE
A	5
B	7
C	-1
D	11
E	25
AB-	-2
ABC+-	-1
AB+C-	13

Our next problem is to convert an infix expression to a postfix expression. If you manually convert a few infix expressions to postfix form you will discover three important facts:

1. The operands always stay in the same order with respect to each other.
2. An operator will move only "to the right" with respect to the operands; that is, if, in the infix expression, operand X precedes operator op, it is also true that in the postfix expression operand X precedes operator op.
3. All parentheses are removed.

As a consequence of these three facts, we can view the determination of where to place each operator as the primary task of the conversion algorithm.

A very high-level solution for writing the desired postfix expression to the string PE is:

```
FOR each character ch in the expression DO
   CASE ch OF
      ch is an operand  :  append ch to PE
      ch is an operator :  store ch until it can be  determined
                              where to place it
      ch is '(' or ')' :  discard ch
   END (* case *)
```

You may have guessed that we do not really want simply to discard the parentheses, since they play an important role in determining the placement of the operators. Since in any infix expression a set of matching parentheses defines an *isolated unit* consisting of an operator and its two operands, the unit must be evaluated independently of the rest of the expression. Regardless of what the rest of the expression looks like, the operator within the unit belongs with the operands in that unit. The parentheses tell the rest of the expression:

> *You can have the value of this unit after it's evaluated, but don't concern yourself with the operators or operands inside.*

Parentheses are thus one of the factors that determine the placement of the operators. The other factors are precedence and left-to-right association.

If the infix expression were always fully parenthesized, the conversion would be conceptually straightforward. Since each operator would correspond to a pair of parentheses, we would simply move the operator to the position marked by the ')'—this position follows the operands of the operator. All parentheses would then be removed. For example, consider the infix expression

$$((A + B) * C)$$

First we move each operator to the position marked by its corresponding ')',

$$((A B) C)$$
$$\quad _+ \ _*$$

and then we remove the parentheses:

Since we are allowing for precedence and left-to-right association, however, the problem is more difficult, and a more complex algorithm is needed. The following is a high-level description of what must be done for each character encountered as we read the infix string from left to right.

1. Append an operand to the output string PE when it is encountered. *Justification:* The order of the operands in the postfix expression agrees with the order in the infix expression, and the operands that appear to the left of an operator in the infix expression also appear to its left in the postfix expression.

2. Push an '(' onto the stack.

3. When we encounter a ')', we pop operators off the stack, appending them to PE until we hit the matching '('. *Justification:* Within a '(' ')' grouping, precedence and left-to-right association determine the order of the operators, and step 4 (below) has already ordered the operators in accordance with these rules.

4. When we encounter an operator, we pop from the stack operators of greater or equal precedence, appending them to PE. We stop when we hit an '(' or an operator of lower precedence (or when the stack becomes empty). We then push the new operator onto the stack. This has the effect of ordering operators by precedence and in accordance with left-to-right association. Notice that we continue popping from the stack until we hit an operator of *strictly* lower precedence than the current operator. We do not stop on equality because the left-to-right association rule says that in case of a tie in precedence, the leftmost operator is to be applied first—and this is the operator that is already on the stack.

5. When we reach the end of the string, we append the remaining contents of the stack to PE.

For example, let's follow the action of the algorithm on the infix expression $A - B + C$:

Stack S and string PE are initially empty.

ch	S	PE	
A		A	
−	−	A	
B	−	AB	
+	+	AB −	{ pop operators of $\geq$ precedence }
C	+	AB − C	
		AB − C +	{ remove remaining stack to PE }

PE now contains the resulting postfix expression $AB - C +$.

We can use these rules to develop a fairly concise pseudocode solution. We use a stack S, which is initially empty. The postfix expression is constructed in *PE*, which is also initially empty. The symbol · means concatenate (append), so *PE* · *x* means concatenate the string currently in *PE* with an *x*.

```
FOR each character ch in the string DO
    CASE ch OF

        operand :

                PE := PE · ch

    |   '(' : Push(S, ch)

    |   ')' : (* pop down to the matching open parenthesis *)
            WHILE (StackTop # '(') DO
                PE := PE · StackTop(S)
                Pop(S)
            END
            Pop(S)   (* remove the open parenthesis *)


    |   operator :

            WHILE ( (NOT IsEmpty(S)) AND
                    (StackTop(S) # '(') AND
                    (precedence(StackTop(S)) >=
                                precedence(ch)) ) DO
                PE := PE · StackTop(S)
                Pop(S)
            END
            Push(S, ch)


    END  (* case *)

(* append to PE the operators remaining on the stack *)
WHILE (NOT IsEmpty(S)) DO
    PE := PE · StackTop(S)
    Pop(S)
END
```

A Modula-2 solution follows.

```
IMPLEMENTATION MODULE postconv;
(*
    INFIX TO POSTFIX CONVERSION

    INPUT:  A legal infix expression.

    OUTPUT:  The equivalent postfix expression.

    ASSUMPTIONS:

        1.  The input string is a legal infix expression
            (including possible parentheses).
```

2.   The operators are the binary operators +, -, * and /.

3.   Every character that is not an operator or a parenthesis is a legal operand.

The conversion is done with a stack.
*)

```
(* Stack type and stack operations *)
FROM Stacks IMPORT

    Stack, Create, IsEmpty, Push, Pop, StackTop;

TYPE

    (* classes of characters *)
    chartypes = (operand, operator, open, close);

(* ------------------------------------------------------------
   Prec:   Compute the precedence of an operator.
   ------------------------------------------------------ *)
PROCEDURE Prec(op : CHAR) : INTEGER;

BEGIN

    CASE op OF
        '+', '-' : RETURN (1);
    |   '*', '/' : RETURN (2);
    ELSE
        RETURN (0);
    END;

END Prec;

(* ------------------------------------------------------------
   CharType:   Compute the type of a character.
   ------------------------------------------------------ *)
PROCEDURE CharType(ch : CHAR) : chartypes;

BEGIN

    CASE ch OF
        '+', '-', '*', '/'  :   RETURN (operator);
    |   '('                 :   RETURN (open);
    |   ')'                 :   RETURN (close);
    ELSE
        RETURN (operand);
    END;
```

END CharType;

```
(* ------------------------------------------------------------
    PostConv:  Convert an infix expression to postfix.

    The input expression Ein[0..lastin] is an array of
    characters representing an infix expression:

        operators:  +, -, *, or /
        open paren:  (
        close paren:  )
        operands :  any other character

    On output, Eout[0..lastout] will be the corresponding
    postfix expression.

    ASSUMPTION:  Ein[0..lastin] is a legal infix expression

    Calls:  CharType, Prec, Create, IsEmpty, Push, Pop, StackTop
   --------------------------------------------------------- *)
PROCEDURE PostConv(Ein : ARRAY OF CHAR; lastin : INTEGER;
                   VAR Eout : ARRAY OF CHAR;
                   VAR lastout : INTEGER);

VAR

    S : Stack;
    success : BOOLEAN;
    ch, checktop : CHAR;
    i : INTEGER;

BEGIN

    (* create a stack *)
    Create(S);

    (* initialize the output string *)
    lastout := -1;

    (* process each character in the expression *)
    FOR i := 0 TO lastin DO

        ch := Ein[i];

        CASE CharType(ch) OF

            (* operand - concatenate to the output string *)
            operand:
```

```
            INC(lastout);
            Eout[lastout] := ch;

        (* open paren - push onto the stack *)
        | open: Push(S, ch, success);

        (* close paren - pop operators until a
           matching open paren is found *)
        | close:
              StackTop(S, checktop, success);
              WHILE ( checktop # '(' ) DO
                Pop(S, success);
                INC(lastout);
                Eout[lastout] := checktop;
                StackTop(S, checktop, success);
              END;
              Pop(S, success);

        (* operator - pop operators of >= precedence *)
        | operator:
              (* StackTop can be called on an empty stack *)
              StackTop(S, checktop, success);
              WHILE ( (success) AND (checktop # '(' )
                        AND (Prec(checktop) >= Prec(ch)) ) DO

                INC(lastout);
                Eout[lastout] := checktop;
                Pop(S, success);
                StackTop(S, checktop, success);

              END;
              Push(S, ch, success);

          END; (* case *)

    END; (* for *)

    (* move the rest of the stack to the output string *)
    WHILE (NOT IsEmpty(S)) DO
        StackTop(S, checktop, success);
        Pop(S, success);
        INC(lastout);
        Eout[lastout] := checktop;
    END;

END PostConv;

END postconv.
```

The following illustrates calls to *PostConv*.

PARAMETER Ein	RESULT Eout
A	A
(A)	A
A + B	AB +
(A + B)	AB +
A + B*C	ABC* +
A*B + C	AB*C +
A*(B + C)	ABC + *
(A + B)*C	AB + C*
A-B + C	AB-C +
A-(B + C)	ABC + -

≠ A + BC (handwritten)

A Graph Search Problem

Our final application of stacks is designed to give you the flavor of a general type of problem for which stacks are very useful. This type of problem, known as a **search problem**, requires that we find a way to perform a given task, such as getting from some point of origin to some destination point. In the next section we shall again consider this type of problem, but there we shall construct a recursive solution. This will bring to light the very close relationship between stacks and recursion.

The particular problem that we shall consider here is to write a program that will act as a simple travel agent for the High Planes Airline Company (HPair). Given all of the flight information for HPair, the program will process customer requests to fly from some origin city to some destination city. To be able to focus on the issue at hand—the use of stacks as a problem-solving tool—the program will be required to produce only a yes or no answer for each customer request. That is, the program will indicate whether or not there exists a sequence of HPair flights from the origin city to the destination city. The more realistic problem of actually producing an itinerary (a sequence of flights) will be discussed at the end of the chapter.

INPUT

There are three input files. All the numbers are integers. All the names are character strings.

cityfile   each line is the name of a city serviced by HPair

              The names are assumed to be in alphabetical order, one per line

flightfile   each line is a pair of city names representing the origin and destination of one of HPair's flights

requestfile   each line is a pair of city names representing a request to fly from some origin to some destination

OUTPUT

For each customer request, a message indicates whether or not the request can be satisfied by a sequence of HPair flights.

ASSUMPTIONS

1. City names are up to 12 characters in length.
2. There are at most 20 cities serviced by HPair.
3. The input data is correct.

EXAMPLE

`cityfile`	Albuquerque	
	Chicago	
	San Diego	
`flightfile`	Chicago	San Diego
	Chicago	Albuquerque
	Albuquerque	Chicago
`requestfile`	Albuquerque	San Diego
	Albuquerque	Paris
	San Diego	Chicago

CORRESPONDING OUTPUT

```
Request is to fly from Albuquerque to San Diego.
HPair has service from Albuquerque to San Diego.

Request is to fly from Albuquerque to Paris.
Sorry.  HPair does not service Paris.

Request is to fly from San Diego to Chicago
Sorry.  HPair does not have service from San Diego to Chicago.
```

Graphs and Data Structures for Implementing Them. A **graph** is a very natural representation for a problem of this type. We can represent an airline's cities-serviced map as shown in Figure 7–2. The graph consists of a set of **vertices**, which represent the cities serviced by the airline, and a set of **directed edges**, which represent flights between pairs of cities. We will draw a directed edge from city C_1 to city C_2 if there is a flight from city C_1 to city C_2. In this case we say that C_2 is **adjacent to** C_1 (notice that C_2 is adjacent to C_1 does *not* imply that C_1 is adjacent to C_2). For example, in Figure 7–2, city X is adjacent to city R,

Figure 7–2

*Graph repre-
senting flight
information*

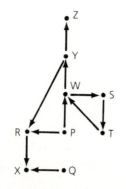

indicating that there is a flight from R to X (but R is *not* adjacent to X, indicating that there is no flight from X to R).

In order to process a customer's request to fly from some origin city to some destination city, we must determine if our flight map contains a **directed path** from the origin to the destination—that is, a route from the origin to the destination that travels edges only in the proper direction. With respect to the above graph, a customer could, for example, fly from city P to city Z, since $P \rightarrow W$, $W \rightarrow Y$, $Y \rightarrow Z$ is a directed path from P to Z.

Before developing our algorithm for determining if there is a directed path between a pair of cities, let us consider two data structures for implementing a graph. The two most common implementations of a graph are the **adjacency matrix** and the **adjacency list**. An adjacency matrix for a graph with vertices numbered $1, 2, \ldots, N$ is an $N \times N$ Boolean array such that $A[i, j]$ = true if and only if there is an edge from vertex i to vertex j. The adjacency matrix for the graph in Figure 7–2 is shown in Figure 7–3(a).

An adjacency list for a graph with vertices numbered $1, 2, \ldots, N$ consists of N linked lists. There is a node for vertex j on list i if and only if there is an edge from vertex i to vertex j. The adjacency list for the graph in Figure 7–2 is shown in Figure 7–3(b).

Which of these two implementations of a graph is better? The answer depends on how the particular application is to use the graph. For example, the two most commonly performed graph operations are:

> given two vertices i and j, determine if there is an edge from i to j
>
> find all vertices adjacent to a given vertex i

The adjacency matrix supports the first operation somewhat more efficiently than does the adjacency list. For the adjacency matrix, we need only examine the value of $A[i, j]$. For the adjacency list, we must traverse the ith linked list to determine if a node corresponding to vertex j is present. On the other hand, the second operation is supported more efficiently by the adjacency list. For the adjacency matrix we must traverse the ith row of the array, while for the adjacency list we must traverse the ith linked list. The ith row of the adjacency matrix always has N entries, whereas the ith linked list has only as many nodes as there are vertices adjacent to vertex i, a number typically far less than N.

Consider now the space requirements of the two implementations. On the surface it might appear that the matrix implementation requires less space than does the list implementation, since each entry in the matrix is smaller than each entry in the lists (a single Boolean value versus an integer and a pointer). Notice, however, that the adjacency matrix always has N^2 entries (N is the number of nodes in the graph), whereas the number of entries in an adjacency list is equal to the number of edges in the graph. Since the number of edges is often much smaller than N^2, an adjacency list often requires less space than an adjacency matrix.

Thus, when choosing a graph implementation for a particular application, we must consider such factors as what operations will be performed most frequently on the graph and the number of edges that the graph is likely to contain. In the next section, we shall discuss these issues in the context of the HPair problem.

	P	Q	R	S	T	W	X	Y	Z
P	F	F	T	F	F	T	F	F	F
Q	F	F	F	F	F	F	T	F	F
R	F	F	F	F	F	F	T	F	F
S	F	F	F	F	T	F	F	F	F
T	F	F	F	F	F	T	F	F	F
W	F	F	F	T	F	F	F	T	F
X	F	F	F	F	F	F	F	F	F
Y	F	F	T	F	F	F	F	F	T
Z	F	F	F	F	F	F	F	F	F

(a)

(b)

Figure 7–3

(a) Adjacency matrix for graph in Figure 7–2; (b) adjacency list for graph in Figure 7–2

Searching a Graph with a Stack.   Now that we have seen how to use a graph to represent HPair's flight information, we must develop an algorithm that searches the graph for a directed path (recall such a path represents a sequence of flights) from the origin city to the destination city. The solution we shall develop performs an **exhaustive search**. That is, beginning at the origin city, our solution will try every possible sequence of flights until either it finds a sequence that gets to the destination city or until it determines that no such sequence exists.

It will turn out that the ADT stack is very useful in helping the solution to organize this search.

Let us begin by considering how we might perform the search "by hand." One approach is to start at the origin city and select an arbitrary edge to travel— that is, select an arbitrary flight departing from the origin city. This will lead us to a new city, C_1. If city C_1 happens to be the destination city, then we're done; otherwise, we must attempt to get from C_1 to the destination city. To do this, we select an edge to travel out of C_1. This will lead us to a city C_2. If C_2 is the destination, we're done; otherwise, we must attempt to get from C_2 to the destination city, and so forth.

Consider the possible outcomes of applying the above strategy.

1. We eventually reach the destination city and can conclude that it is possible to fly from the origin to the destination.

2. We reach a city C from which there are no departing flights.

3. We go around in circles. For example, from C_1 we go to C_2, from C_2 we go to C_3, and from C_3 we go back to C_1. We might continue this tour of the three cities forever; that is, the algorithm is in an infinite loop.

If we always obtained the first outcome, everyone would be happy. However, since HPair does not fly between all pairs of cities, we certainly cannot expect that the algorithm will always produce this outcome. For example, if city P in Figure 7–2 is the origin city and city Q is the destination city, the algorithm could not possibly produce the first outcome—there is no way to get from city P to city $Q!$

Even if there were a way to get from the origin to the destination, it would take a bit of luck for the above strategy to discover it—the algorithm would have to select a "correct" flight at each step. In other words, the strategy described above could result in outcome 2 or 3 *even if there were a sequence of flights from the origin to the destination.* For example, even though there is a way to get from city P to city Z in Figure 7–2, the algorithm might not find it. Suppose that from city P the algorithm chose to go to city R. From city R the algorithm would have to go to city X, from which there are no flights out (outcome 2). On the other hand, suppose that the algorithm chose to go to city W from city P. From city W the algorithm might choose to go to city S. It would then have to go to city T and then back to W. From W it might once again choose to go to city S and continue to go around in circles (outcome 3).

We thus need to make our algorithm more sophisticated so that it always finds a path from the origin to the destination if such a path exists and otherwise terminates with the conclusion that there is no such path. Let's suppose that the strategy described above results in outcome 2—we reach a city C from which there are no departing flights. This certainly does not imply that there is no way to get from the origin to the destination. It implies only that there is no way to get from city C to the destination. In other words, it was a mistake to go to city C. After discovering such a mistake, our algorithm can retrace its steps, or **backtrack,** to the city C' that was visited just before city C was visited. Once back at city C', our algorithm can select a flight to some city other than C. Notice that it is possible that there are no other flights out of city C'. If this were the case, it would mean that it was a mistake to visit city C', and thus we want to backtrack again, this time to the city that was visited just before city C'.

For example, we saw that in trying to get from city P to city Z (Figure 7–2), our algorithm might first choose to go from city P to city R. From city R it would then go to city X. Since city X is a city with no departing flights, our algorithm must backtrack to city R, the city visited before city X. Once back at city R, the algorithm would attempt to go to some city other than city X but would discover that this is not possible. The algorithm would thus backtrack once more, this time to city P, which was visited just before city R. From city P the algorithm would choose to go to city W, which is a step in the right direction!

For our algorithm to implement the above strategy, it must maintain information about the order in which the cities have been visited. First notice that when the algorithm backtracks from a city C it must go to the city that was visited *most recently* before C. This suggests that we maintain the sequence of visited cities in a stack. That is, each time we decide to visit a city, we push it onto the stack. The next city to visit is selected from those adjacent to the city on the top of the stack. When we need to backtrack from the city C at the top of the stack (for example, because there are no flights out of the city) we simply pop from the stack. After the pop, the city on the top of the stack is the city that was visited most recently before C (on the current path).

We can describe as follows the algorithm as it has been developed so far.

```
(* push the origin city onto the stack *)
Push(S, origin)


WHILE (we have not yet determined if there is a sequence of
        flights from the origin to the destination) DO

   IF (we need to backtrack from the
        city on the top of the stack) THEN
      Pop(S)

   ELSE
      select a city C adjacent to the city on the top
        of the stack
      Push(S, C)

   END

END
```

Notice that at any point in the algorithm, the contents of the stack correspond to the sequence of flights currently being explored. The city on the top of the stack is the city we are currently visiting, directly "below" it is the city visited previously, and so forth down to the bottom city, which is the first city visited in the sequence (which is always the origin city). In other words, an *invariant* of the **WHILE** loop is that the stack contains a directed path from the origin city (which is at the bottom of the stack) to the city at the top of the stack. We can, therefore, always retrace our steps as far back through the sequence as needed.

We now need to consider the question of when to

backtrack from the city on the top of the stack

We have already identified one case when backtracking is necessary. We must backtrack from the city on the top of the stack when there are no flights out of that city. Another time when we need to backtrack is related to the problem of going around in circles described above as the third possible outcome of the original strategy.

A key observation that will answer the question, when should we backtrack? is: *We never want to visit a city that the search has already visited.* As a consequence, we must backtrack from a city whenever there remain no unvisited cities adjacent to it. To see why we never want to visit a city a second time, we consider two cases:

1. If a city C has been visited and it is still somewhere in the stack (it is part of the sequence of cities that we are currently exploring), we don't want to visit C again. This is true because a sequence that goes from C through C_1, C_2, ..., C_k, back to C, and then to C' might just as well skip the intermediate cities and go from C directly to C'.

   For example, suppose that the algorithm starting at P in Figure 7–2 visits W, S, and T. There is now no reason for the algorithm to consider the flight from T to W because W is already on the stack. Anywhere we could fly to by going from W to S, from S to T, and then back to W (that is, Y), we could fly to directly from W without first going through S and T. Given that we do not allow the algorithm to visit W a second time, it will backtrack from S and T to W (notice that backtracking to W is very different than visiting W for a second time) and then go from W directly to Y (see Figure 7–4).

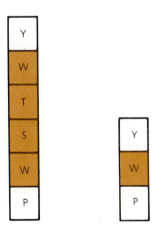

Figure 7–4

Revisiting a city.

2. If a city C has been visited and it is no longer on the stack (that is, we have backtracked from a city C and thus popped it from the stack), we don't want to visit C again. This is a subtle point; we will break it into two cases, which depend on why we backtracked from the city.

   If we backtracked from C because there were no flights out of it, then we certainly don't ever want to try going through C again. For example, if—

starting at *P*—the algorithm goes to *R* and then to *X*, it will backtrack from *X* to *R*. At this point *X* has already been visited (although it is no longer on the stack) and we certainly don't want to visit *X* again (since we know there are no flights out of it).

Now suppose that we backtracked from *C* because all cities adjacent to it had been visited. This implies that from *C* we have already tried all possible flights and have failed to find a way to get to the destination city. There is thus no reason to go to *C* again. For example, suppose that starting from *P* the algorithm executes the following sequence: Visit *R*, visit *X*, backtrack to *R* (because there are no flights out of *X*), backtrack to *P* (because there are no more unvisited cities adjacent to *R*), visit *W*, visit *Y*. At this point the stack contains *P-W-Y* (with *Y* on top), and we need to choose a flight out of *Y*. City *R* is adjacent to *Y*, but *R* has already been visited (though it is no longer on the stack). We don't want to fly from *Y* to *R* since we have already tried all possible flights out of *R*.

In both cases, visiting a city a second time doesn't gain us anything, and in fact it may cause us to go around in circles.

To implement this rule of not visiting a city more than once, we simply mark a city when it is visited. When choosing the next city to visit, we restrict consideration to unmarked cities adjacent to the city on the top of the stack. Our algorithm thus becomes

```
(* push the origin city onto the stack *)
Push(S, origin)
mark the origin visited

(* an invariant of the while loop is that S contains a
   directed path from the origin to the city on the top of S *)
WHILE (we have not yet determined if there is a sequence of
        flights from the origin to the destination) DO

   IF (there are no unvisited cities adjacent
        to the city on the top of the stack) THEN

      (* backtrack *)
      Pop (S)

   ELSE
      select an unvisited city C adjacent to the city
        on the top of the stack
      Push (S, C)
      mark C visited

   END

END
```

One last refinement needs to be made. This involves how the algorithm makes its final determination of whether there exists a path from the origin to the destination. The invariant that the stack contains a directed path from the origin city to the city on the top of the stack implies that the algorithm can reach an affirmative conclusion if *the city at the top of the stack is the destination city.* On the other hand, the algorithm can reach a negative conclusion only after all possibilities have been exhausted. This occurs after the algorithm has back-tracked to the origin and there remain no unvisited cities adjacent to it. At this point, the *origin city will be popped from the stack and the stack will become empty.*

With this refinement, the final version of the algorithm can be written as follows.

```
SearchS(origin, destination)

    (* push the origin city onto the stack *)
    Push(S, origin)
    mark the origin visited

    (* an invariant of the while loop is that S contains
       a directed path from the origin to the city on the
       top of S *)
    WHILE ( (NOT IsEmpty(S)) AND (StackTop(S) # destination) ) DO

        IF (there are no unvisited cities adjacent
                to the city on the top of the stack) THEN

            (* backtrack *)
            Pop(S)

        ELSE
            select an unvisited city C adjacent to the city
                on the top of the stack

            Push(S, C)
            mark C visited

        END

    END
```

We can trace the action of this algorithm against the graph of Figure 7-2. Notice that the statement of the algorithm does not specify the order of selection for the unvisited cities adjacent to the city on the top of the stack. It really does not matter what selection criteria the algorithm uses, since the choice will not affect the final outcome. (There is either a sequence of flights or there isn't.) The choice, however, will affect our trace of the algorithm's action. (It will affect which cities are visited and when they are visited.) For the sake of the example, let us suppose that the algorithm always chooses the alphabetically earliest unvisited city that is adjacent to the city on the top of the stack.

The following is a trace of the algorithm's action, assuming that P is the departure city and Z is the destination city.

ACTION	REASON	CONTENTS OF STACK
Push P	initialize	S: P
Push R	next unvisited adjacent city	S: PR
Push X	next unvisited adjacent city	S: PRX
Pop X	no unvisited adjacent city	S: PR
Pop R	no unvisited adjacent city	S: P
Push W	next unvisited adjacent city	S: PW
Push S	next unvisited adjacent city	S: PWS
Push T	next unvisited adjacent city	S: PWST
Pop T	no unvisited adjacent city	S: PWS
Pop S	no unvisited adjacent city	S: PW
Push Y	next unvisited adjacent city	S: PWY
Push Z	next unvisited adjacent city	S: PWYZ

The algorithm terminates with success.

Before turning to the Modula-2 implementation of this algorithm, let us make one final point. Algorithm *SearchS* performs a variation of what is known as a **graph traversal**. The algorithm starts at a given vertex and visits other vertices by crossing the graph's edges. What distinguishes our algorithm from a standard graph traversal is that *SearchS* stops when the designated destination vertex is encountered. A graph-traversal algorithm, on the other hand, will not stop until it has visited all the vertices that it can reach. Our algorithm can easily be modified to a graph-traversal algorithm by removing from the **WHILE** loop the termination condition *(StackTop(S) # destination)*.

```
Traverse(v)

    (* push v onto the stack *)
    Push(S, v)
    mark v visited

    WHILE (NOT IsEmpty(S)) DO

        IF (there are no unvisited vertices adjacent
                to the vertex on the top of the stack) THEN

            (* backtrack *)
            Pop(S)
```

```
ELSE
    select an unvisited vertex w adjacent
        to the vertex on the top of the stack

    Push(S, w)
    mark w visited

END

END
```

With this modification, the algorithm will continue until it has visited all the vertices that can be reached from the starting vertex *v*; that is, it will visit *all* vertices *u* for which there is a directed path from *v* to *u*.

This particular graph traversal is called **depth first search(DFS)**, reflecting the fact that from a given vertex the algorithm goes as deep into the graph as it can before backtracking. A recursive version of DFS is also often used—its form will become apparent in the next section. There are several other traversal algorithms that traverse a graph in an order different from DFS (but—given that they start at the same vertex—they, of course, will visit the *same* set of vertices). Another important traversal order is called **breadth first search(BFS)**. This traversal uses a *queue* rather than a stack to organize its traversal. This is discussed in Exercise 8.6.

We now present a Modula-2 program to implement our solution to the HPair problem. One decision that we must make is whether to use an adjacency matrix or an adjacency list to represent the graph. The primary operation that the algorithm must perform on the graph is to determine which cities are adjacent to a given city. As we discussed in the previous section, this operation is, in general, supported more efficiently by an adjacency list. In addition, it is reasonable to expect the graph to contain far fewer than N^2 edges, where N is the number of cities. We thus can expect the adjacency list to be efficient with respect to storage as well, making it the clear choice for this application.

The program builds a table that associates each city name with an integer. As the program reads in the names of the cities serviced by HPair, it places them in the array `CityNames`. The ith city read is placed into `CityNames[i]` and is referred to as city *i* by the program (for example, integers rather than strings are placed on the stack). Since the cities are assumed to be in alphabetical order in the input file, the array `CityNames` is guaranteed to be sorted. This allows us to perform a binary search on the array to find which city number is associated with a given name (for example, to find the number of a given origin city).

Function `IsPath` implements the search algorithm described above. Since there are several ways to search for a solution, we chose to implement this function in a separate module with the following definition.

```
DEFINITION MODULE ispath;
(* search for a path *)


EXPORT QUALIFIED
```

```
    IsPath;

(* ------------------------------------------------------------
    IsPath:   Determine if there is a sequence of flights from
    city fromcity to city tocity.
    ------------------------------------------------------------ *)
PROCEDURE IsPath(fromcity, tocity : INTEGER) : BOOLEAN;

END ispath.
```

This separation allows easy modification of the search algorithm. An alternative algorithm is presented in the next section.

```
DEFINITION MODULE agenttypes;
(* global type definitions and data
    structures for the agent program *)

EXPORT QUALIFIED

    maxcities, namesize, CityName, namelist, adjptr, adjnode,
    CityNames, cities, Flights;

CONST

    maxcities  = 20;
    namesize   = 12;

TYPE

    CityName    = ARRAY [0..namesize-1] OF CHAR;

    namelist    = ARRAY [1..maxcities] OF CityName;

    (* nodes for the adjacency list *)
    adjptr = POINTER TO adjnode;
    adjnode = RECORD
                    data : INTEGER;
                    next : adjptr;
                END;

VAR

    (* cities serviced by HPair *)
    CityNames : namelist;

    (* adjacency lists for the flight information *)
    Flights  : ARRAY [1..maxcities] OF adjptr;
```

```
        (* number of cities serviced by HPair *)
        cities : INTEGER;

END agenttypes.


IMPLEMENTATION MODULE ispath;
(* implement stack-based graph search *)

(* global type definitions and data structures *)
FROM agenttypes IMPORT

    Flights, cities, maxcities, adjptr, adjnode;

(* stack type and stack opertions *)
FROM Stacks IMPORT

    Stack, IsEmpty, Push, Pop, StackTop, Create;

(* -----------------------------------------------------------
    IsPath:  Determine if there is a sequence of flights from
    city fromcity to city tocity.

    The data structure for the search consists of a stack (city
    numbers of a potential path) and a Boolean array to keep
    track of cities that have been visited by the search.

    CALLS:  IsEmpty, Push, Pop, StackTop, Create.
    ----------------------------------------------------------- *)
PROCEDURE IsPath(fromcity, tocity : INTEGER) : BOOLEAN;

VAR

    S : Stack;

    visited : ARRAY [1..maxcities] OF BOOLEAN;

    checktop, topcity, nextcity, i : INTEGER;
    success : BOOLEAN;
    cityptr : adjptr;

BEGIN

    (* initialize for the search *)
    Create(S);
    FOR i := 1 TO cities DO
        visited[i] := FALSE;
    END;
```

```
                    (* search - stack version *)
                    Push(S, fromcity, success);
                    visited[fromcity] := TRUE;

                    StackTop(S, checktop, success);
                    WHILE ((NOT IsEmpty(S)) AND (checktop # tocity)) DO

                        (* find an unvisited city adjacent to the city
                           on the top of the stack - note that the search
                           starts at the beginning of the adjacency list
                           each time (see Exercise 7.11) *)
                        StackTop(S, topcity, success);
                        cityptr := Flights[topcity];
                        WHILE ((cityptr # NIL) AND (visited[cityptr^.data])) DO
                            cityptr := cityptr^.next;
                        END;

                        (* pop the stack at a dead end, or push
                           the next city and continue the search *)
                        IF (cityptr = NIL) THEN
                            Pop(S, success);

                        ELSE
                            nextcity := cityptr^.data;
                            Push(S, nextcity, success);
                            visited[nextcity] := TRUE;
                            StackTop(S, checktop, success);

                        END;

                    END; (* while *)

                    RETURN (NOT IsEmpty(S));

                END IsPath;

            END ispath.


            MODULE agent;
            (*
                HPAIR - TRAVEL AGENT

                Given data describing all of the flights operated by HPair,
                this program processes requests to fly from a city A to a
                city B.  The requests are processed by determining whether
                or not there is a sequence of flights from A to B.

                INPUT:  There are three input files.
```

```
cityfile     -   each line is the name of a city
                 serviced by HPair

                 The names are assumed to be in
                 alphabetical order, one per line.

flightfile   -   each line is a pair of city names
                 representing the origin and destination
                 of one of HPair's flights

requestfile  -   each line is a pair of city names
                 representing a request to fly from
                 some origin to some destination
```

All of the numbers are integers. All of the names are character strings.

OUTPUT:

For each customer request, a message indicating whether or not the request can be satisfied by a sequence of HPair flights.

ASSUMPTIONS:

1. City names are exactly namesize characters in length. (Names are padded on the right with blanks.)

2. There are between 1 and maxcities cities serviced by HPair.

3. The input data is correct.

DATA STRUCTURES:

1. CityNames - array of city names indexed by city
               number - the names are in alphabetical
               order

2. Flights - adjacency list representation of HPair's
               flights - Flights[i] is a pointer to the
               list of city numbers adjacent to city i
               (i.e., there is an HPair flight from i
               to each city on its list)

GLOBAL VARIABLES:

```
cities      - actual number of cities serviced by HPair
CityNames   - list of city names
Flights     - adjacency lists for the flight information
```

```
                    The actual search for a path between two cities is done by
                    Boolean valued function IsPath.
*)


(* standard I/O *)
FROM InOut IMPORT

    EOL, Done, OpenInput, Read, ReadInt,
    Write, WriteString, WriteInt, WriteLn;


(* special string I/O *)
FROM StringIO IMPORT

    ReadString, WriteName;


(* standard string package *)
FROM Strings IMPORT

    CompareStr;


(* memory management procedure NEW *)
FROM Storage IMPORT

    ALLOCATE;


(* global type definitions an data structures *)
FROM agenttypes IMPORT

    maxcities, namesize, CityName, namelist,
    adjptr, adjnode, Flights, CityNames, cities;


(* graph search procedure *)
FROM ispath IMPORT

    IsPath;


VAR

    newcity, fromname, toname : CityName;
    fromnum, tonum, i : INTEGER;
    cityptr : adjptr;


(* -----------------------------------------------------------
    FindIndex:  Find the index of city acity in the list of
    city names.

    Return 0 if the city is not found.

    The algorithm is an iterative binary search.
```

```
        NOTE:   The comments on implementations of binary search
        (Chapter 4) regarding whether to make the array parameter VAR
        apply to this function.
        ------------------------------------------------------------ *)
PROCEDURE FindIndex(CityNames : namelist;
                    acity : CityName) : INTEGER;

VAR

    first, last, mid : INTEGER;

BEGIN

    (* binary search *)
    first := 1;
    last := cities;
    WHILE (first < last) DO
        mid := (first + last) DIV 2;
        IF (CompareStr(CityNames[mid],acity) < 0) THEN
            first := mid + 1;
        ELSE
            last := mid;
        END;
    END;

    (* test termination conditions *)
    IF (CompareStr(CityNames[first],acity) = 0) THEN
        RETURN (first);
    ELSE
        RETURN (0);
    END;

END FindIndex;

(* ------------------------------------------------------------
    ReadData:  Read and echo the data from cityfile and
    flightfile.  The global data structures cities, CityNames,
    and Flights are initialized from this data.

    CALLS:  FindIndex
    ------------------------------------------------------------ *)
PROCEDURE ReadData;

BEGIN

    (* read in and count the city names *)
    cities := 0;

    WriteLn;
```

```
WriteString('Enter the name of the file of city names:  ');
OpenInput('in');
ReadString(newcity);
WHILE (Done AND (cities < maxcities)) DO
    INC(cities);
    CityNames[cities] := newcity;
    ReadString(newcity);
END;

(* write out the city names *)
WriteString('*********************************************');
WriteLn;
WriteString('*********  HPair FLIGHT INFORMATION  *********');
WriteLn;
WriteString('*********************************************');
WriteLn;
WriteLn;
WriteString('Cities serviced by HPair:');
WriteLn;
WriteLn;
FOR i := 1 TO cities DO
    WriteString('    ');
    WriteString(CityNames[i]);
    WriteLn;
END;

(* initialize the adjacency lists *)
FOR i := 1 TO maxcities DO
    Flights[i] := NIL;
END;

(* read in all of the flight information *)
WriteLn;
WriteString('Enter the name of the file of flight information:  ');
OpenInput('in');
ReadString(fromname);
WHILE (Done) DO
    (* read destination city of flight *)
    ReadString(toname);
    fromnum := FindIndex(CityNames, fromname);
    tonum := FindIndex(CityNames, toname);

    (* add tonum to fromnum's adjacency list *)
    IF ((tonum = 0) OR (fromnum = 0)) THEN
        WriteString('Warning.  Bad input data.');
        WriteLn;
    ELSE
```

```
            NEW(cityptr);
            cityptr^.data := tonum;
            cityptr^.next := Flights[fromnum];
            Flights[fromnum] := cityptr;
        END;


        (* read origin city of next flight *)
        ReadString(fromname);
    END;


    (* write out all of the flight information *)
    WriteLn;
    WriteString('Flights operated by HPair:');
    WriteLn;
    WriteLn;
    FOR i := 1 TO cities DO
        cityptr := Flights[i];
        WHILE (cityptr # NIL) DO
            WriteString('  From ');
            WriteString(CityNames[i]);
            WriteString(' to ');
            WriteString(CityNames[cityptr^.data]);
            WriteLn;
            cityptr := cityptr^.next;
        END;
    END;

END ReadData;


(* ------------------------------------------------------------
   ProcessReqs:  Process the requests in requestfile.

   CALLS:  FindIndex, IsPath
   ------------------------------------------------------------ *)
PROCEDURE ProcessReqs;

BEGIN

    (* process each request until end of file *)
    WriteLn;
    WriteString('*******************************************');
    WriteLn;
    WriteString('********  SAMPLE ITINERARY REQUESTS  ********');
    WriteLn;
    WriteString('*******************************************');
    WriteLn;
    WriteLn;
```

```
WriteLn;
WriteString('Enter the name of the file of sample requests:   ');
OpenInput('in');
ReadString(fromname);
WHILE (Done) DO
    (* read rest of request *)
    ReadString(toname);

    (* write the request *)
    WriteString('Request is to fly from ');
    WriteName(fromname);
    WriteString(' to ');
    WriteName(toname);
    Write('.');
    WriteLn;

    (* process the request *)
    fromnum := FindIndex(CityNames, fromname);
    tonum := FindIndex(CityNames, toname);

    (* test for legal to and from cities *)
    IF ((fromnum # 0) AND (tonum # 0)
                    AND (fromnum # tonum)) THEN

        (* search for a solution *)
        IF (IsPath(fromnum, tonum)) THEN
            WriteString('HPair has service from ');
        ELSE
            WriteString('Sorry.  HPair does not have service from ');
        END;

        WriteName(CityNames[fromnum]);
        WriteString(' to ');
        WriteName(CityNames[tonum]);
        Write('.');
        WriteLn;

    ELSE

        (* write appropriate messages
           for an illegal request *)

        (* unknown city of origin *)
        IF (fromnum = 0) THEN
            WriteString('Sorry.  HPair does not service ');
            WriteName(fromname);
            Write('.');
            WriteLn;
        END;
```

```
                (* unknown destination city *)
                IF (tonum = 0) THEN
                    WriteString('HPair does not service ');
                    WriteName(toname);
                    Write('.');
                    WriteLn;
                END;

                (* origin equals destination *)
                IF (fromnum = tonum) THEN
                    WriteString('Walk!!!');
                    WriteLn;
                END;

            END;

            WriteLn;

            (* read first part of next request *)
            ReadString(fromname);

        END; (* while *)

    END ProcessReqs;


    BEGIN  (* MAIN PROGRAM *)

        ReadData;
        ProcessReqs;

    END agent.
```

THE RELATIONSHIP BETWEEN STACKS AND RECURSION

The ADT stack proved to be very useful in the solution to the HPair problem of the previous section. Our goal in this section is to relate the way the stack organizes the search for a sequence of flights to the way a recursive algorithm organizes the search. This will help to illustrate the general relationship between stacks and recursion.

Recall from the previous section our initial attempt at a solution to the HPair problem of searching for a sequence of flights from some origin city to some destination city. Let us consider how we might perform the search "by hand." One approach is to start at the origin city and select an arbitrary edge to travel (an arbitrary flight departing from the origin city). This will lead us to a new city C_1. If city C_1 happens to be the destination city, then we're done; otherwise, we must attempt to get from C_1 to the destination city. To do this, we select an edge to travel out of C_1. This will lead us to a city C_2. If C_2 is the destination, we're done; otherwise, we must attempt to get from C_2 to the destination city, and so forth.

There is a very distinct recursive flavor to this search strategy. We can restate the strategy as follows:

```
To fly from the origin to the destination:

    select a city C adjacent to the origin
    fly from the origin to city C
    IF (C is the destination city) THEN
        we are done
    ELSE
        fly from city C to the destination
    END
```

This statement of the search strategy makes its recursive nature very apparent. The first step in flying from the origin city to the destination city is to fly from the origin city to city C. Once at city C, we are confronted with another problem of the same type—we now must fly from city C to the destination.

This recursive formulation is nothing more than a restatement of the initial (incomplete) strategy developed in the previous section. As such it has the same three possible outcomes:

1. We eventually reach the destination city and can conclude that it is possible to fly from the origin to the destination.
2. We reach a city C from which there are no departing flights.
3. We go around in circles.

The first of these outcomes corresponds to a degenerate case of the above algorithm. If we ever reach the destination city, no additional problems of the form "fly from city C to the destination" are generated, and the algorithm terminates. However, as we observed in the previous section, there is no guarantee that the algorithm will produce this outcome, that is, that this degenerate case will be reached. The algorithm might reach a city C from which there are no departing flights (notice that the algorithm does not specify what to do if we reach a city C from which there are no departing flights—in this sense the algorithm is incomplete), or it might repeatedly cycle through the same sequence of cities and thus never terminate.

We can resolve these problems by mirroring what we did in the previous section. Consider the following refinement in which we mark visited cities and never fly to a city once it has been visited.

```
SearchR(fromcity, destination)
(* Search for a sequence of flights from
   city fromcity to the destination city. *)

    mark fromcity visited
```

```
IF (fromcity is the destination city) THEN
     terminate -- we have reached the destination

ELSE
     FOR each unvisited city C adjacent to fromcity DO
        SearchR(C, destination)
     END

END
```

Let us consider what happens when the algorithm reaches a city that has no unvisited city adjacent to it. For example, consider the piece of a graph in Figure 7–5.

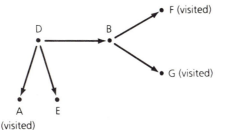

Figure 7–5

Piece of a graph

When *SearchR* reaches city *B* (that is, it is called with parameter *fromcity* having the value *B*), the **FOR** loop will not be entered, since there are no unvisited cities adjacent to *B*. This causes a return to be made from the procedure *SearchR*. This return has the effect of *backtracking* to city *D*, from where the flight to *B* was made. In terms of the above pseudocode, the return is made to the point from which the call *SearchR(B, destination)* was issued. This point is within the **FOR** loop where we are iterating through the unvisited cities adjacent to *D* (that is, parameter *fromcity* has the value *D*).

After backtracking from *B* to *D*, the **FOR** loop will continue execution; this time the loop chooses city *E*, resulting in the recursive call *SearchR (E,destination)*. From this point, the algorithm will eventually either reach the destination city and terminate, or it will backtrack once again to city *D*. In the latter case, since there are no more unvisited cities adjacent to *D*, the **FOR** loop will terminate and a return from *SearchR* will be made. The effect is to backtrack to the city from which the flight to *D* was made. If the algorithm ever backtracks to the origin city and there remain no unvisited cities adjacent to it, the algorithm will terminate, and we can conclude that there is no sequence of flights from the origin to the destination. Notice that the algorithm will always terminate in one way or another, since it will either reach the destination city or run out of unvisited cities to try.

We can transform the program that implements the stack-based search to one that implements this recursive search by simply replacing the implementation module *ispath* with the following:

```
IMPLEMENTATION MODULE ispath;
(* recursive graph search algorithm *)
```

```
(* type and constant definitions *)
FROM agenttypes IMPORT

    maxcities, Flights, cities, adjptr, adjnode;

(* ------------------------------------------------------------
    IsPath:   Indicate whether there is a sequence of flights
    from city fromcity to city tocity.

    The search is done by the locally defined recursive
    function try.   A visited array is used to prevent the search
    from looping (i.e., having the same cities searched
    repeatedly).

    Calls:   try
    ------------------------------------------------------------ *)
PROCEDURE IsPath(fromcity, tocity : INTEGER) : BOOLEAN;

VAR

    visited : ARRAY [1..maxcities] OF BOOLEAN;
    solved :  BOOLEAN;
    i : CARDINAL;

(* ------------------------------------------------------------
    Try:   Do the recursive search.   For each city that has a
    flight from fromcity, try and find a sequence of flights
    to tocity.
    ------------------------------------------------------------ *)
PROCEDURE try(fromcity : INTEGER) : BOOLEAN;

VAR

    nextcity : INTEGER;
    cityptr : adjptr;

BEGIN

    (* mark the current city visited *)
    visited[fromcity] := TRUE;

    (* degenerate case - we have reached the destination *)
    IF fromcity = tocity THEN
        solved := TRUE;

    ELSE
        cityptr := Flights[fromcity];
```

```
    (* try a flight to each unvisited city *)
    WHILE ((cityptr # NIL) AND (NOT solved)) DO

        (* find an unvisited city adjacent to fromcity *)
        WHILE ((cityptr # NIL) AND (visited[cityptr^.data])) DO
            cityptr := cityptr^.next;
        END;

        (* visit the next city *)
        IF (cityptr # NIL) THEN
            nextcity := cityptr^.data;
            solved := try(nextcity);
        END;

    END;

    END;

    RETURN (solved);

END try;

BEGIN

    (* initialize for search *)
    solved := FALSE;
    FOR i := 1 TO cities DO
        visited[i] := FALSE;
    END;

    RETURN (try(fromcity));

END IsPath;

END ispath.
```

You have probably noticed a very close parallel between this recursive algorithm and the stack-based algorithm of the previous section.

```
SearchS(origin, destination)

    (* push the origin onto the stack *)
    Push(S, origin)
    mark the origin visited
```

```
(* an invariant of the while loop is that S contains
    a directed path from the origin to the city on the
    top of S *)
WHILE ( (NOT IsEmpty(S)) AND (StackTop(S) # destination) ) DO

    IF (there are no unvisited cities adjacent
            to the city on the top of the stack) THEN

        (* backtrack *)
        Pop(S)

    ELSE
        select an unvisited city C adjacent to
            the city on the top of the stack

        Push(S, C)
        mark C visited

    END

END
```

In fact, the two algorithms simply employ different mechanisms to implement the *identical search strategy*. Let us look at how the two algorithms implement three key aspects of their common strategy.

1. Visiting a new city. The recursive algorithm *SearchR* visits a new city C by making the call *SearchR(C, destination)*. The algorithm *SearchS* visits city C by pushing C onto the stack. Notice that if we were to use the box method to trace the execution of *SearchR*, the call *SearchR (C, destination)* would generate a box in which the city C is associated with the formal parameter *fromcity* of *SearchR*.

For example, Figure 7–6 shows the state of the box trace for *SearchR* and the stack for *SearchS* at corresponding points of their search for a path from city P to city Z in Figure 7–2.

Figure 7–6

Box trace versus stack

Search has visited city P then R then X.

Boxes:

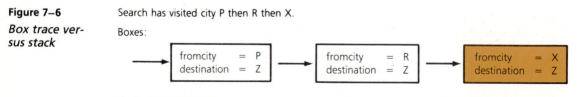

Stack: PRX (X is top)

2. Backtracking. Both algorithms attempt to visit an unvisited city adjacent to the current city. Notice that this current city is the value associated with formal parameter *fromcity* in the deepest box of *SearchR*'s box trace. Similarly, the current city is on the top of *SearchS*'s stack. In the example of Figure 7–6, this is city X. If there are no unvisited cities adjacent to the current city, the algorithms must backtrack to the previous city. The algorithm $SearchR$ backtracks by returning from the current recursive call. We visualize this in the box method by crossing off the deepest box. The algorithm $SearchS$ backtracks by explicitly popping from its stack.

For example, from the state depicted in Figure 7–6, both algorithms backtrack to city R and then to city P.

Search backtracks from X then R back to P

Boxes:

| fromcity = P | fromcity = R | fromcity = X |
| destination = Z | destination = Z | destination = Z |

Stack: originally PRX, then PR, then P

Figure 7–7

Box trace versus stack

3. Termination. The algorithms terminate either when the destination city has been reached or when all possibilities have been exhausted. The latter case occurs when we have backtracked to the origin city and there remain no unvisited cities adjacent to it. For $SearchR$ this means that all boxes have been crossed off in the trace and a return is made to the point of the original call (for example, in the main program). For $SearchS$ this means that the stack has become empty.

The two algorithms thus really do perform the identical action. In fact, provided that they use the same rule to select an unvisited city (for example, traverse the current city's list of adjacent cities), they will always visit the identical cities in the identical order. The similarities between the algorithms is far more than coincidence. In fact, it is always possible to capture the actions of a recursive subprogram with a stack.

An important context in which the close tie between stacks and recursion is explicitly utilized is a computer system's implementation of a recursive subprogram. It is common for a system to use a stack to implement a recursive subprogram in a manner that greatly resembles our own box method. When a recursive call to a subprogram is made, the system must remember certain information. This information consists essentially of the same local environment that we place in our boxes—that is, values of parameters, local variables, and a reference to the point from which the recursive call was made.

The system must manage these boxes of information, or **activation records,** just as we must manage them on paper. As our HPair example has indicated, the operations needed to manage the activation records are those provided by a stack. When a recursive call is made, a new activation record is created and pushed onto a stack. This corresponds to the creation of a new box at the deepest point in the sequence. When a return is made from a recursive call, the stack is popped, bringing the activation record containing the appropriate local environment to the top of the stack. This corresponds to crossing off the deepest box and following the arrow back to the preceding box. Though we have greatly simplified the process, most implementations of recursion are based on stacks of activation records.

A similar strategy is used by a programmer when coding a nonrecursive version of a recursive algorithm. There are several reasons why this might be necessary, the most obvious of which is that there are languages (such as FOR-TRAN 77) that do not support recursion. The above discussion should give you a taste of the basic techniques for removing recursion from a program. You will encounter recursion removal as a formal topic in more advanced courses, such as compiler construction.

A VARIATION OF THE ADT STACK: THE TRAVERSABLE STACK

We begin by considering a slight modification to the HPair problem. The problem, as described earlier, requires that we determine if there is a sequence of flights from an origin city to a destination city. Let us now add the (very realistic) requirement that our program, upon finding a sequence of flights from the origin city to the destination city, not only report that the sequence exists but also report what the sequence is (that is, origin city, city C_1, city C_2, . . . , destination city).

Recall that when our program finds a sequence of flights from the origin city to the destination city, its stack contains the corresponding path of cities. The stumbling block to reporting this path is that the cities appear on the stack in *reverse order,* that is, the destination city is at the top of the stack and the origin city is at the bottom. For example, if we use the program to find a path from city P to city Z in Figure 7–2, the final contents of the stack will be P-W-Y-Z(with Z on top). Since we wish to print the path in the correct order (origin city first—destination city last), this creates something of a problem.

If we restrict ourselves to the stack operations, the only way that we can print the path in its correct order is to reverse the stack by popping it onto a temporary stack and then print the cities as we pop them off the temporary stack. Note that this solution requires each city on the path to be processed twice.

Another possible solution is to exploit the fact that our HPair program implements the stack with an array. We can simply print the array elements from 1 to *Top*. This solution is far from satisfactory, however, as it violates the wall between an ADT and its implementation—the solution would not work if the linked implementation of a stack were used.

The problems we are encountering are indicative of the fact that a stack is not the appropriate ADT for the problem of printing the path of cities in the correct order. The appropriate ADT is a **traversable stack**. A traversable stack is intuitively simple. In addition to the five standard stack operations, *Create*, *IsEmpty*, *Push*, *Pop*, and *StackTop*, we have an operation *Traverse*. *Traverse* begins at one end of the stack and visits each item in the stack until the other end of the stack is reached. In the HPair problem, we would want *Traverse* to begin at the bottom of the stack and move toward the top. In other applications, we might want the traversal to go in the opposite direction.

The notion of traversing an ADT is very important and is actually more difficult than we might imagine. Intuitively, it means to visit each item in the

ADT. This is a difficult notion because there is the question of what we wish to do to each item when we are visiting it. In the HPair problem, we simply wish to print each item. But there are many other things that we might wish to do to an item when we visit it. For example, we might wish to assign its value to a variable or even place a copy of it into another data structure.

The details of *Traverse* are thus very application dependent. This makes it difficult to define the operation within the ADT framework. We certainly don't want to have a different *Traverse* operation for each thing that we might want to do to an item when it is visited. The solution that we adopt is for the *Traverse* operation to utilize a *user-defined* procedure. The name of the procedure that *Traverse* is to call is passed as an argument. Thus, the form of a *Traverse* operation that visits items of a stack from bottom to top is

```
Traverse(S, Visit)
(* Traverse stack S from bottom to top,
   calling procedure Visit for each item. *)
```

(Note that Modula-2 allows the name of a subprogram to be passed as an argument.)

In the HPair problem, where we wish to print each item as it is visited, *Traverse* would be invoked with the call

```
Traverse(S, PrintItem)
```

where *PrintItem* is the name of a procedure that the user has written to print out the value of a variable of type *itemtype*.

Notice that the sanctity of the wall between the program and the implementation of the ADT has not been violated despite the fact that the ADT operation *Traverse* calls a user-supplied procedure. Since *Visit* is on the user's side of the wall, it can access the data structure only through the ADT operations. This eliminates the objection to the solution that exploits the fact that the stack is implemented with an array. Further, since *Visit* can access the data structure only through the ADT operations, *Traverse* cannot do anything "unstack-like," such as delete an item from the middle of the stack as it is visited.

Let us use the following definition module as our contract for the ADT.

```
DEFINITION MODULE Tstacks;
(* ***********************************************************
   ADT TRAVERSABLE STACK

   The following hidden type is declared:

       Tstack

   The following operations are supported:

       Create, IsEmpty, Push, Pop, StackTop, Traverse
   *********************************************************** *)
```

```
                      (* Traversable stack item *)
                      FROM ADTitem IMPORT

                          itemtype;

                      EXPORT QUALIFIED

                          Tstack, Create, IsEmpty, Push, Pop, StackTop, Traverse;

                      TYPE

                          Tstack;

                          (* required for procedure Traverse *)
                          ProcType = PROCEDURE(itemtype);


                      (* --------------------------------------------------------
                          Create:   Create an empty traversable stack S.
                         --------------------------------------------------- *)
                      PROCEDURE Create(VAR S : Tstack);

                      (* --------------------------------------------------------
                          IsEmpty:   Determine if traversable stack S is empty.

                          ASSUMPTION:   Traversable stack S has been created.
                         --------------------------------------------------- *)
                      PROCEDURE IsEmpty(S : Tstack) : BOOLEAN;


                      (* --------------------------------------------------------
                          Push:   Add newitem to traversable stack S.   The Boolean
                          flag success is returned TRUE if the Push was successful,
                          and FALSE otherwise (e.g., because of memory limitations).
                          In the event of an unsuccessful Push, the stack is unchanged.

                          ASSUMPTION:   Traversable stack S has been created.
                         --------------------------------------------------- *)
                      PROCEDURE Push(VAR S : Tstack; newitem : itemtype;
                                     VAR success : BOOLEAN);

                      (* --------------------------------------------------------
                          Pop:   Remove from traversable stack S the item which was
                          most recently added.   The operation fails if the stack is
                          empty.   The Boolean flag success indicates whether the
                          operation succeeded.   In the event of an unsuccessful
                          Pop, the stack is unchanged.

                          ASSUMPTION:   Traversable stack S has been created.
                         --------------------------------------------------- *)
```

```
PROCEDURE Pop (VAR S : Tstack; VAR success : BOOLEAN);
```

```
(* ------------------------------------------------------------
   StackTop:  Retrieve into getitem the item from traversable
   stack S which was most recently added, leaving S unchanged.
   The operation fails if the stack is empty.  The Boolean
   flag success indicates whether the operation succeeded.

   ASSUMPTION:  Traversable stack S has been created.
   ------------------------------------------------------- *)
PROCEDURE StackTop (S : Tstack; VAR getitem : itemtype;
                    VAR success : BOOLEAN);


(* ------------------------------------------------------------
   Traverse:  Traverse traversable stack S from bottom to top,
   calling procedure Visit for each item.

   Procedure Visit exists outside of the ADT implementation.

   ASSUMPTION:  Traversable stack S has been created.
   ------------------------------------------------------- *)
PROCEDURE Traverse (S : Tstack ; Visit : ProcType);

END Tstacks.
```

We now consider implementations for the ADT traversable stack. Since this ADT is not very different from an ordinary stack, it makes sense to attempt to modify the two stack implementations presented in Chapter 6.

Sequential Implementation. Recall that the sequential stack implementation uses a record with fields *Top* and *Items*. To transform this into an implementation of a traversable stack, we need only write the procedure *Traverse*. Assuming that, as is the case for the HPair problem, we wish to traverse the stack from bottom to top, the procedure is

```
Traverse (S, Visit)

   FOR i := 1 TO S.Top DO
      Visit (S.Items [i])
   END
```

Linked Implementation. As we shall see, the modifications required for the linked implementation are far more substantial than those for the sequential implementation. The sequential implementation of a traversable stack, because of its simplicity, is far more desirable than the linked. An application for which we do not have a good estimate of the maximum number of items in the stack, however, mandates that we choose the linked implementation because only it can utilize dynamic storage allocation.

Recall that the linked implementation of a stack is based on a linked list of nodes containing the stack items. *S* points to the item on the top of the stack, thus making operations *Push*, *Pop*, and *StackTop* easy to perform. However, it is very difficult to *traverse* this linked list from bottom to top. The links are in the wrong direction.

A first attempt at a solution might be to link the nodes in the opposite direction—that is, link the nodes from the bottom towards the top (see Figure 7–8). *S. Bottom* points to the bottom of the stack and *S. Top* points to its top. The traverse operation can now be performed by starting at the node pointed to by *S. Bottom* and following the links towards the top.

Figure 7–8

(a) Stack linked in usual direction; (b) stack with links reversed

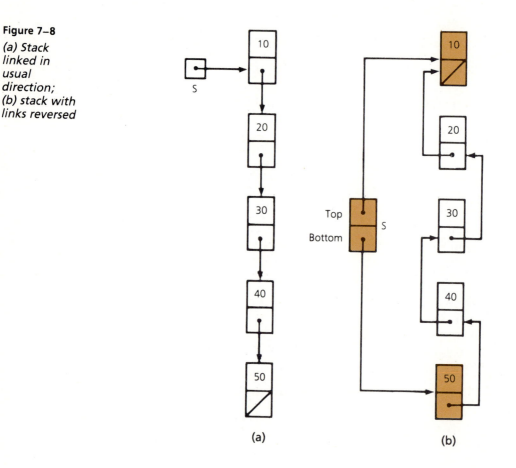

(a)   (b)

The operations *StackTop* and *Push* remain relatively simple under this scheme. *S. Top* points to the node that the operation *StackTop* needs to inspect, and the operation *Push* adds a new node so that it follows the node pointed to by *S. Top*.

The problem with the scheme is that the *Pop* operation is now very difficult. *S. Top* points to the node N that is to be deleted, but to perform the deletion we need a pointer to the node that precedes N on the list. Since the links now go in the opposite direction, there is no easy way to get there.

An Implementation Using a Doubly Linked List

We see that *Traverse* (from bottom to top) is very difficult to perform if the links go from top to bottom, while *Pop* is very difficult to perform if the links go from bottom to top. A solution is to have links *going in both directions*, as shown in Figure 7–9. Each node now has two pointer fields. The pointer field *ToBottom* points to the next node on the way to the *bottom* of the stack and the pointer field *ToTop* points to the next node on the way to the *top* of the stack. This is an instance of a data structure known as a **doubly linked list**.

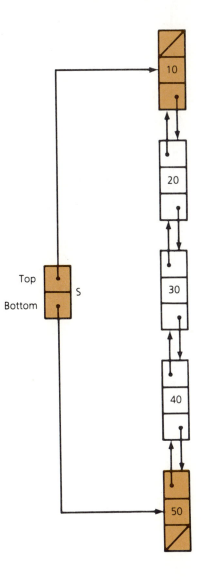

Figure 7–9
Doubly linked list

The *Traverse* operation can be performed by following the *ToTop* links

```
Traverse(S, Visit)

    p := S.Bottom
    WHILE (p # NIL) DO
        Visit(p^.Item)
        p := p^.ToTop
    END
```

The *Pop* and *Push* operations are slightly more difficult than for an ordinary stack (see Figure 7–10).

Figure 7–10

(a) Push onto nonempty stack; (b) pop from nonempty stack

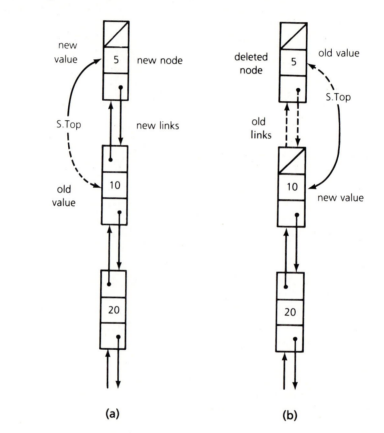

(a)   (b)

```
Push(S, newitem)

    (* create a new node *)
    NEW(p)
    p^.item := newitem

    IF (S is empty) THEN
        (* special case -- push onto an empty stack *)
```

```
            p^.ToTop := NIL
            p^.ToBottom := NIL
            S.Top := p
            S.Bottom := p

        ELSE
            (* general case -- push onto a non-empty stack *)
            p^.ToTop := NIL
            set p^.ToBottom to point to the old top of the stack
            set the ToTop pointer field of the old top of stack to
                point to the new node
            S.Top := p

    END


Pop(S, success)

    IF (S is empty) THEN
        success := FALSE

    ELSIF (the stack has only one item) THEN
        set S.Top and S.Bottom to NIL

    ELSE
        (* stack has more than one item *)
        set S.Top to point to the new top of the stack -- this
            is the node pointed to by the ToBottom pointer of
            the old top

        set the ToTop field of the new top to NIL

    END
```

A Modula-2 implementation follows.

```
IMPLEMENTATION MODULE Tstacks;
(* ************************************************************
    ADT TRAVERSABLE STACK - Linked Implementation

    The following traversable stack operations are supported:

        Create, IsEmpty, Push, Pop, StackTop, Traverse

    The traversable stack is implemented as a doubly linked list.
    ************************************************************ *)

(* memory management procedures NEW and DISPOSE *)
FROM Storage IMPORT
```

```
                    ALLOCATE, DEALLOCATE;

        (* Traversable stack item *)
        FROM ADTitem IMPORT

            itemtype;

        TYPE

            (* Traversable stack structure *)
            nodeptr  = POINTER TO node;
            node     = RECORD
                           item : itemtype;
                           ToBottom, ToTop : nodeptr;
                       END;


            Tbody    =   RECORD
                             Top, Bottom : nodeptr;
                         END;


            Tstack   = POINTER TO Tbody;

        (* -------------------------------------------------------------
           Create:   Create an empty traversable stack S.
           ------------------------------------------------------------- *)
        PROCEDURE Create(VAR S : Tstack);

        BEGIN

            NEW(S);
            S^.Top := NIL;
            S^.Bottom := NIL;

        END Create;

        (* -------------------------------------------------------------
           IsEmpty:   Determine if traversable stack S is empty.

           ASSUMPTION:   Traversable stack S has been created.
           ------------------------------------------------------------- *)
        PROCEDURE IsEmpty(S : Tstack) : BOOLEAN;

        BEGIN

            RETURN (S^.Top = NIL);

        END IsEmpty;
```

```
(* -------------------------------------------------------------
   Push:   Add newitem to traversable stack S.   The Boolean
   flag success is returned TRUE if the Push was successful,
   and FALSE otherwise (e.g., because of memory limitations).
   In the event of an unsuccessful Push, the stack is unchanged.

   NOTE:   In most implementations of Modula-2 there is no way
   for a call to NEW to fail gracefully.   Therefore, the
   program will terminate abnormally if it exceeds memory
   limitations.

   ASSUMPTION:   Traversable stack S has been created.
   ------------------------------------------------------------ *)
PROCEDURE Push(VAR S : Tstack; newitem : itemtype;
               VAR success : BOOLEAN);

VAR

   p : nodeptr;

BEGIN

   (* create a new node *)
   NEW(p);
   p^.item := newitem;
   p^.ToTop := NIL;

   (* insert the new node *)
   p^.ToBottom := S^.Top;
   IF (S^.Top = NIL) THEN
      S^.Bottom := p;
   ELSE
      S^.Top^.ToTop := p;
   END;
   S^.Top := p;
   success := TRUE;

END Push;

(* -------------------------------------------------------------
   Pop:   Remove from traversable stack S the item which was
   most recently added.   The operation fails if the stack is
   empty.   The Boolean flag success indicates whether the
   operation succeeded.   In the event of an unsuccessful
   Pop, the stack is unchanged.

   ASSUMPTION:   Traversable stack S has been created.
```

```
        Calls:  IsEmpty
    ------------------------------------------------------------ *)
PROCEDURE Pop (VAR S : Tstack; VAR success : BOOLEAN);

VAR

    delptr : nodeptr;

BEGIN

    IF (IsEmpty(S)) THEN
        success := FALSE;

    ELSE
        delptr := S^.Top;
        S^.Top := S^.Top^.ToBottom;
        DISPOSE(delptr);
        IF (S^.Top = NIL) THEN
            S^.Bottom := NIL;
        ELSE
            S^.Top^.ToTop := NIL;
        END;
        success := TRUE;

    END;

END Pop;

(* ------------------------------------------------------------
    StackTop:  Retrieve into getitem the item from traversable
    stack S which was most recently added, leaving S unchanged.
    The operation fails if the stack is empty.  The Boolean
    flag success indicates whether the operation succeeded.

    ASSUMPTION:  Traversable stack S has been created.

    Calls:  IsEmpty
    ------------------------------------------------------------ *)
PROCEDURE StackTop (S : Tstack; VAR getitem : itemtype;
                    VAR success : BOOLEAN);

BEGIN

    IF (IsEmpty(S)) THEN
        success := FALSE;
    ELSE
        getitem := S^.Top^.item;
        success := TRUE;
    END;
```

```
END StackTop;

(* -----------------------------------------------------------
     Traverse:   Traverse traversable stack S from bottom to top,
     calling procedure Visit for each item.

     Procedure Visit exists outside of the ADT implementation.

     ASSUMPTION:   Traversable stack S has been created.
     ---------------------------------------------------------- *)
PROCEDURE Traverse (S : Tstack ; Visit : ProcType) ;

VAR

     trav : nodeptr;

BEGIN

     trav := S^.Bottom;
     WHILE (trav # NIL) DO
        Visit (trav^.item) ;
        trav := trav^.ToTop;
     END;

END Traverse;

END Tstacks.
```

   To summarize, this implementation of a traversable stack utilizes a doubly
linked list. Each node on a doubly linked list has one pointer to the *next* node
on the list and another pointer to the *previous* node on the list. The *Push* and
Pop procedures demonstrate how a node is inserted into and deleted from an
end of a doubly linked list. In Chapter 10 we shall use doubly linked lists in the
implemention of another ADT. For that implementation, we shall need general
insertion and deletion procedures that are not limited to an end of a doubly
linked list but rather can operate on a list's interior.

SUMMARY

1. The definition of the stack operations give this ADT last-in, first-out (LIFO)
   behavior.

2. Algorithms that operate on algebraic expressions are an important application
   of stacks. The LIFO nature of stacks is exactly what is needed to organize the
   operands for our algorithm that evaluates postfix expressions. Similarly, our
   algorithm that transforms infix expressions to postfix uses a stack to organize
   the operators in accordance with precedence rules and left-to-right association.

COMMON PITFALLS / DEBUGGING

1. When evaluating or transforming an infix expression, a sophisticated algorithm must be employed. Because we wish to account for precedence and left-to-right association (in order that parentheses can be omitted), we must determine to which operands a given operator should be applied.

2. When searching a graph, we must take into account the possibility that the algorithm will take wrong turns. For example, we must eliminate the possibility of the algorithm cycling, and the algorithm must be able to backtrack when it hits a dead end.

3. If we need to traverse an ADT, we should not write a procedure that depends on the implementation of the ADT. This would violate the wall between the implementation and the traverse procedure, and we want our traversal to work if the implementation of the ADT should change. This was one of our motivations for including a *Traverse* operation in the ADT definition.

---

3. Graph searching is another important application of stacks. A stack organizes the search by keeping track of the sequence of visited vertices. Depth first search is a graph traversal algorithm that uses a stack.

4. The two most common implementations of a graph are the adjacency matrix and the adjacency list. Each has its relative advantages and disadvantages. The choice should depend on the needs of the given application.

5. There is a very strong relationship between recursion and stacks. Most implementations of recursion maintain a stack of activation records in a manner that resembles our box method.

6. Traversing an ADT is an important concept. Intuitively, traversing means to visit every item in the ADT. Because the meaning of *visit* is application dependent, we defined a *Traverse* operation so that it is passed a user-defined *Visit* procedure.

EXERCISES

1. Consider a popular variation of the ADT stack. Instead of having *Pop* and *StackTop* operations, we shall define *Pop* to both retrieve and remove the top element from a stack. Modify the linked and sequential implementations of ADT stack accordingly.

   How does this definition of the ADT stack affect the infix to postfix conversion and postfix evaluation programs? How does it affect the HPair program?

2. The diagram of a railroad switching system in Figure 7–11 is commonly used to illustrate the notion of a stack. Identify the three stacks and how they

Figure 7–11

Railroad switching system

relate to each other. How can this system be used to construct any possible permutation of railroad cars?

3. Two stacks can be implemented in one array by having them grow towards each other from the opposite ends of the array, as shown in Figure 7–12. What are the advantages of having one array rather than two separate arrays of half the size? Work out the details of an implementation. How are the limiting conditions (empty and full) recognized? (Note that it is important that the two stacks don't run into each other.)

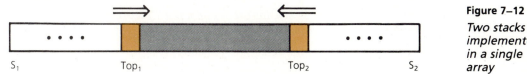

Figure 7–12

Two stacks implemented in a single array

4. Evaluate the following postfix expressions. Assume the following values for the identifiers: $A = 7$; $B = 3$; $C = -2$; $D = -5$; $E = 1$.

   a. ABC + −

   b. AB − C +

   c. ABC − D * +

   d. AB + C − DE * +

5. Convert the following infix expressions to postfix. Don't forget to account for the precedence rules and left-to-right association.

   a. A/B * C

   b. A/(B * C)

   c. A − (B/C * D)

   d. A/B/C − (D + E) * F

6. Repeat Exercises 4 and 5 using the algorithms described in this chapter. Show the status of the stack after each step.

7. Explain the significance of the precedence tests in the infix to postfix conversion algorithm. Why is the test a $\geq$ test rather than a $>$ test?

8. Let's say that we have a stack S and an empty auxiliary stack T. Show how we can do each of the following.

   a. Print the contents of S in reverse order.

   b. Count the number of items in S, leaving S unchanged.

   c. Delete every occurrence of a specified item from S, leaving the order of the remaining items unchanged.

9. Consider the directed graph in Figure 7–13. Give the adjacency matrix and adjacency list representations of the graph.

Figure 7–13

Sample graph

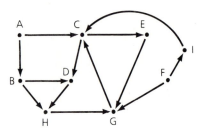

10. Execute the HPair algorithm for the graph in Figure 7–13 for the following requests. Show the state of the stack after each step.

    a. Fly from *A* to *G*

    b. Fly from *A* to *D*

    c. Fly from *F* to *H*

    d. Fly from *E* to *I*

    e. Fly from *A* to *B*

    f. Fly from *C* to *C*

    g. Fly from *I* to *G*

11. In our implementation of the HPair program, the search for the next unvisited city adjacent to a city *i* always begins at the beginning of the ith adjacency list. This is actually a bit inefficient, since a city can never become unvisited after it has already been visited by the search. Modify the program so that the search for the next city begins where the last search left off. That is, maintain an array of *trynext* pointers into the adjacency list.

PROJECT

12. Consider an expanded statement of the HPair problem. In addition to the *from* and *to* cities, each line of input contains a flight number (an integer) and the cost of the flight (an integer). Modify the HPair program so that it

will produce a complete itinerary for each request, including the flight number of each flight, the cost of each flight, and the total cost of the trip.

EXAMPLE

```
cityfile:        Albuquerque
                 Chicago
                 San Diego

flightfile:      703   Chicago      San Diego    125
                 111   Chicago      Albuquerque  450
                 178   Albuquerque  Chicago      450

requestfile:     Albuquerque       San Diego
                 Albuquerque       Paris
                 San Diego         Chicago
```

CORRESPONDING OUTPUT

```
Request to fly from Albuquerque to San Diego.
Flight #178  from  Albuquerque  to  Chicago      Cost:  450
Flight #703  from  Chicago      to  San Diego    Cost:  125
Total Cost . . . . . . . . . . . .   $575


Request to fly from Albuquerque to Paris.
Sorry.   HPair does not service Paris.


Request to fly from San Diego to Chicago.
Sorry.   HPair does not have service from San Diego to Chicago.
```

What modifications would be required to find a least-cost trip for each request? How could we incorporate time considerations into the problem?

CHAPTER 8

QUEUES

PREVIEW   The operations that define a queue give this ADT a behavior opposite from that of a stack. While a stack's behavior is characterized as last in, first out, a queue's behavior is characterized as first in, first out. We define the operations that give a queue this behavior and discuss strategies for implementing the ADT. As an application of a queue, we consider an event-driven simulation, an important technique for analyzing the behavior of complex systems. The problem considered here is the simulation of people waiting in line at a bank. The first-in, first-out behavior of a queue makes the ADT an appropriate model of the behavior of the people in the line.

THE ABSTRACT DATA TYPE QUEUE

A stack can be thought of as having only *one end*, since all operations are performed at the *top* of the stack. This is what gives it its last-in, first-out behavior. A **queue**, on the other hand, is viewed as having *two ends*: a *rear*, where new items are inserted, and a *front*, from which items are deleted. This gives a queue its first-in, first-out (FIFO) behavior, which makes it appropriate for modeling real-world structures such as a line of customers.

The abstract data type queue is defined by five operations:

```
Create(Q)
(* Create an empty queue Q. *)


IsEmpty(Q)
(* Determine if queue Q is empty. *)


Add(Q, e)
(* Add item e to queue Q. *)


Remove(Q)
(* Remove from queue Q the item which was added earliest. *)


QueueFront(Q)
(* Retrieve from queue Q the item which was
   added earliest, leaving Q unchanged. *)
```

Consider how we might formalize the FIFO property of a queue. For example, we need an axiom that indicates that after a series of *Add* operations, *QueueFront* returns the item added the longest time ago. Intuitively, we want the axiom to say

$$\text{QueueFront}(\text{Add}(...\text{Add}(\text{Add}(\textit{empty queue},e_1),e_2),...,e_n)) = e_1$$

This is not completely rigorous, however, since the meaning of the dots, ... , is not well defined. See Exercise 8.8 for a discussion of the formal axioms that define the ADT queue.

We will use the following definition module as our contract for the ADT queue.

```
DEFINITION MODULE Queues;
(* **********************************************************
    ADT QUEUE

    The following hidden type is declared:

        Queue

    The following operations are supported:

        Create, IsEmpty, Add, Remove, QueueFront
    ********************************************************** *)

(* Queue item *)
FROM ADTitem IMPORT

    itemtype;

EXPORT QUALIFIED

    Queue, Create, IsEmpty, Add, Remove, QueueFront;

TYPE

    Queue;

(* ------------------------------------------------------------
    Create:  Create an empty queue Q.
   ------------------------------------------------------------ *)
PROCEDURE Create(VAR Q : Queue);

(* ------------------------------------------------------------
    IsEmpty:  Determine if queue Q is empty.
```

ASSUMPTION: Queue Q has been created.
-- *)
PROCEDURE IsEmpty(Q : Queue) : BOOLEAN;

(* --
    Add: Add newitem to queue Q. The Boolean flag success
    is returned TRUE if the Add was successful, and FALSE
    otherwise (e.g., because of memory limitations).   In
    the event of an unsuccessful Add, the queue is unchanged.

    ASSUMPTION: Queue Q has been created.
-- *)
PROCEDURE Add(VAR Q : Queue; newitem : itemtype;
              VAR success : BOOLEAN);

(* --
    Remove: Remove from queue Q the item that was added
    earliest.   The operation fails if the queue is empty.
    The Boolean flag success indicates whether the operation
    succeeded.   In the event of an unsuccessful Remove, the
    queue is unchanged.

    ASSUMPTION: Queue Q has been created.
-- *)
PROCEDURE Remove(VAR Q : Queue; VAR success : BOOLEAN);

(* --
    QueueFront: Retrieve into getitem the item from queue
    Q that was added earliest, leaving Q unchanged.   The
    operation fails if the queue is empty.   The Boolean
    flag success indicates whether the operation succeeded.

    ASSUMPTION: Queue Q has been created.
-- *)
PROCEDURE QueueFront(Q : Queue; VAR getitem : itemtype;
                     VAR success : BOOLEAN);

END Queues.

IMPLEMENTATIONS OF THE ADT QUEUE

As with stacks, there are sequential and linked implementations of queues. The choice between the two implementations once again boils down to the question of whether or not the fixed-size restriction of a sequential implementation is a problem.

For queues, the linked implementation is a bit more straightforward than the sequential, so we start with it.

A Linked Implementation of the ADT Queue

We might expect a linked implementation to utilize two external pointers, one to the front and one to the rear.

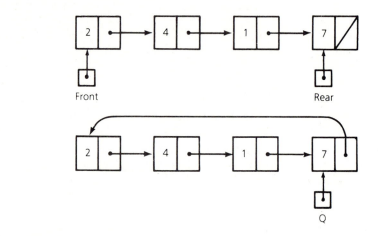

(a)   Front   Rear

(b)   Q

Figure 8–1   *(a) Linked implementation with two external pointers; (b) circular linked implementation*

We actually can get by with a single external pointer (to the rear) if we make the queue *circular*.

Here the node at the rear of the queue points to the node at the front. Thus, the node at the rear of the queue can be referenced by

         Q^

and the node at the front can be referenced by

         Q^.next;

Insertion at the rear and deletion from the front are straightforward. A Modula-2 implementation follows.

```
IMPLEMENTATION MODULE Queues;
(* *****************************************************************
    ADT QUEUE - Linked Implementation

  The following Queue operations are supported:

     Create, IsEmpty, Add, Remove, QueueFront
```

```
    The Queue is implemented as a circular linked list.   The
    single external pointer points to the rear of the Queue.
    ************************************************************ *)

(* memory management procedures NEW and DISPOSE *)
FROM Storage IMPORT

    ALLOCATE, DEALLOCATE;

(* Queue item *)
FROM ADTitem IMPORT

    itemtype;

TYPE

    (* queue structure *)
    nodeptr = POINTER TO node;
    node    = RECORD
                  item : itemtype;
                  next : nodeptr;
              END;

    Queue   = nodeptr;

(* ------------------------------------------------------------
   Create:   Create an empty queue Q.
   ---------------------------------------------------------- *)
PROCEDURE Create(VAR Q : Queue);

BEGIN

    Q := NIL;

END Create;

(* ------------------------------------------------------------
   IsEmpty:   Determine if queue Q is empty.

   ASSUMPTION:   Queue Q has been created.
   ---------------------------------------------------------- *)
PROCEDURE IsEmpty(Q : Queue) : BOOLEAN;

BEGIN

    RETURN (Q = NIL);

END IsEmpty;
```

```
(* -----------------------------------------------------------
   Add:   Add newitem to queue Q.  The Boolean flag success
   is returned TRUE if the Add was successful, and FALSE
   otherwise (e.g., because of memory limitations).   In
   the event of an unsuccessful Add, the queue is unchanged.

   NOTE:   In most implementations of Modula-2 there is no way
   for a call to NEW to fail gracefully.   Therefore, the
   program will terminate abnormally if it exceeds memory
   limitations.

   ASSUMPTION:   Queue Q has been created.
   ----------------------------------------------------------- *)
PROCEDURE Add(VAR Q : Queue; newitem : itemtype;
             VAR success : BOOLEAN);

VAR

    p : nodeptr;

BEGIN

    (* create a NEW node *)
    NEW(p);
    p^.item := newitem;

    (* insert the new node *)
    IF (Q = NIL) THEN
        p^.next := p;
    ELSE
        p^.next := Q^.next;
        Q^.next := p;
    END;
    Q := p;
    success := TRUE;

END Add;


(* -----------------------------------------------------------
   Remove:   Remove from queue Q the item that was added
   earliest.   The operation fails if the queue is empty.
   The Boolean flag success indicates whether the operation
   succeeded.   In the event of an unsuccessful Remove, the
   queue is unchanged.

   ASSUMPTION:   Queue Q has been created.

   CALLS:   IsEmpty
   ----------------------------------------------------------- *)
```

```
PROCEDURE Remove(VAR Q : Queue; VAR success : BOOLEAN);

VAR

    front :  nodeptr;

BEGIN

    IF (IsEmpty(Q)) THEN
       success := FALSE;
    ELSE
       front := Q^.next;
       IF (front = Q) THEN
          Q := NIL;
       ELSE
          Q^.next := front^.next;
       END;
       DISPOSE(front);
       success := TRUE;
    END;

END Remove;

(* ------------------------------------------------------------
   QueueFront:  Retrieve into getitem the item from queue
   Q that was added earliest, leaving Q unchanged.  The
   operation fails if the queue is empty.  The Boolean
   flag success indicates whether the operation succeeded.

   ASSUMPTION:  Queue Q has been created.

   CALLS:  IsEmpty
   ------------------------------------------------------------ *)
PROCEDURE QueueFront(Q : Queue; VAR getitem : itemtype;
                     VAR success : BOOLEAN);

BEGIN

    IF (IsEmpty(Q)) THEN
       success := FALSE;
    ELSE
       getitem := Q^.next^.item;
       success := TRUE;
    END;

END QueueFront;

END Queues.
```

A Sequential Implementation of the ADT Queue

A sequential implementation can be used for applications in which a fixed-sized queue does not present a problem.

A naive sequential implementation might define a queue as

```
CONST

    maxqueue = maximum size of queue

TYPE

    itemtype = desired type of queue item
    queue = RECORD
                Items : ARRAY [1..maxqueue] OF itemtype
                Front : [1..maxqueue]
                Rear  : [0..maxqueue]
            END
```

Figure 8–2

(a) Sequential implementation; (b) problem of drifting

(a)

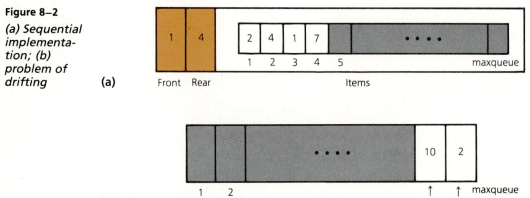

Front   Rear   Items

(b)

The queue is initialized with *Front* = *1* and *Rear* = *0*. When a new item is to be added, *Rear* is incremented and the item is placed in the position it now references. When an item is to be deleted, *Front* is incremented. The queue is empty whenever *Rear* < *Front*. The queue is full when *Rear* = *maxqueue*.

The problem with this strategy is that after a sequence of additions and removals, the items in the queue will drift down to the high end of the array and *Rear* could equal *maxqueue* even when there are only a few items currently in the queue. One possible solution to this problem is to shift array elements to the left, either after each deletion or whenever *Rear* = *maxqueue*. This would guarantee that the queue can always contain up to *maxqueue* items. The solution is not really satisfactory, however, as the shifting would dominate the cost of the implementation.

A much more elegant solution is obtained by viewing the array as circular (see Figure 8–3). We advance the queue pointers *Front* (to remove an item) and *Rear* (to add an item) by moving them clockwise around the array. When *Front* or *Rear* is advanced past location *maxqueue*, it wraps around to location

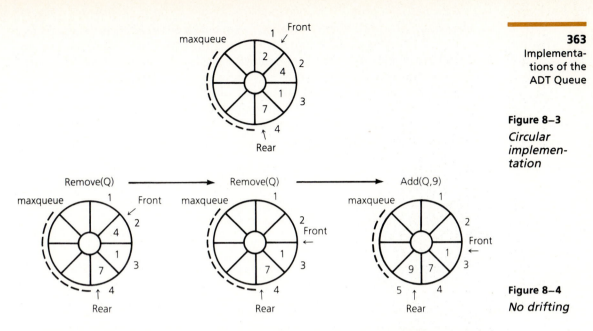

Figure 8–3
*Circular
implemen-
tation*

Figure 8–4
No drifting

1. This eliminates the problem encountered in the previous implementation of items drifting to the high end of the array. (There is no end!) See Figure 8–4.

The only difficulty with this scheme is the detection of the queue-empty and queue-full conditions. It seems reasonable to select as the queue-empty condition

> Front is one slot ahead of Rear

since this seems to indicate that *Front* has "passed" *Rear* in the course of the queue becoming empty (see Figure 8–5). However, it is also possible that this

Figure 8–5
(a) **Front
passes Rear;**
(b) **Rear
catches up to
Front**

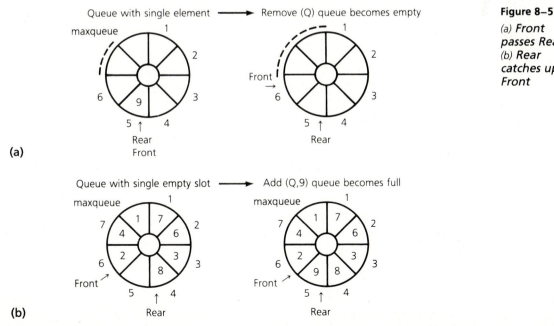

condition signals a full queue. Because the queue is circular, *Rear* might in fact "catch up" with *Front* as the queue becomes full. We obviously need a means of distinguishing between the two conditions.

One solution to this problem is to keep a count of the number of items in the queue. Before adding to the queue, we check to see if the count is equal to *maxqueue*—this would signal a full queue. Before removing from the queue, we check to see if the count is equal to zero—this would signal an empty queue.

To implement this scheme, we use definitions of the following form.

```
CONST

    maxqueue = maximum size of queue

TYPE

    itemtype = desired type of queue item
    queue    = RECORD
                  Items : ARRAY [1..maxqueue] OF itemtype
                  Front, Rear : [1..maxqueue]
                  Count : [0..maxqueue]
               END
```

The queue is initialized with *Front* = 1, *Rear* = *maxqueue*, and *Count* = 0. We obtain the wrap-around effect of a circular queue by using modulo arithmetic (that is, Modula-2's **MOD** operator) when incrementing *Front* and *Rear*. We can add *newitem* to the queue with the statements

```
    Q.Rear := (Q.Rear MOD maxqueue) + 1;
    Q.Items[Q.Rear] := newitem;
    INC(Q.Count);
```

Notice that if *Rear* had been pointing to location *maxqueue* before the insertion of *newitem*, the statement *Q.Rear := (Q.Rear **MOD** maxqueue) + 1* would have the effect of wrapping *Rear* around to location 1.

Similarly, we remove from the queue with the statements

```
    Q.Front := (Q.Front MOD maxqueue) + 1;
    DEC(Q.Count);
```

The Modula-2 routines follow. Note that in keeping with our convention, *Queue* is defined to be a hidden pointer type.

```
IMPLEMENTATION MODULE Queues;
(* ********************************************************
   ADT QUEUE - Sequential Implementation

   The following Queue operations are supported:

      Create, IsEmpty, Add, Remove, QueueFront
```

This is a circular implementation of a queue. Front and
Rear point respectively to the front and rear of the queue.
Count indicates the number of items currently in the queue.

Type queue is a pointer to a record that is created
dynamically with a call to procedure NEW. This
indirection allows type Queue to be a hidden type.
*** *)

```
(* memory management procedure NEW *)
FROM Storage IMPORT

    ALLOCATE;

(* Queue item *)
FROM ADTitem IMPORT

    itemtype;

(* fixed maximum size inferred from User's Documentation File *)
CONST

    maxqueue = 20;

TYPE

    (* queue structure *)
    Qbody    = RECORD
                   Items : ARRAY [1..maxqueue] OF itemtype;
                   Front, Rear : [1..maxqueue];
                   Count : [0..maxqueue];
                END;

    Queue    = POINTER TO Qbody;


(* ------------------------------------------------------------
   Create:  Create an empty queue Q.
   ------------------------------------------------------ *)
PROCEDURE Create(VAR Q : Queue);

BEGIN

    NEW(Q);
    Q^.Front := 1;
    Q^.Rear := maxqueue;
    Q^.Count := 0;

END Create;
```

```
(* ------------------------------------------------------------
    Isempty:   Determine if queue Q is empty.

    ASSUMPTION:   Queue Q has been created.
   ------------------------------------------------------------ *)
PROCEDURE IsEmpty(Q : Queue) : BOOLEAN;

BEGIN

    RETURN (Q^.Count = 0);

END IsEmpty;

(* ------------------------------------------------------------
    Add:   Add newitem to queue Q.   The Boolean flag success
    is returned TRUE if the Add was successful, and FALSE
    otherwise (e.g., because of memory limitations).   In
    the event of an unsuccessful Add, the queue is unchanged.

    ASSUMPTION:   Queue Q has been created.
   ------------------------------------------------------------ *)
PROCEDURE Add(VAR Q : Queue; newitem : itemtype;
              VAR success : BOOLEAN);

BEGIN

    IF (Q^.Count = maxqueue) THEN
        success := FALSE;
    ELSE
        Q^.Rear := (Q^.Rear MOD maxqueue) + 1;
        Q^.Items[Q^.Rear] := newitem;
        INC(Q^.Count);
        success := TRUE;
    END;

END Add;

(* ------------------------------------------------------------
    Remove:   Remove from queue Q the item that was added
    earliest.   The operation fails if the queue is empty.
    The Boolean flag success indicates whether the operation
    succeeded.   In the event of an unsuccessful Remove, the
    queue is unchanged.

    ASSUMPTION:   Queue Q has been created.

    CALLS:   IsEmpty
   ------------------------------------------------------------ *)
PROCEDURE Remove(VAR Q : Queue; VAR success : BOOLEAN);

BEGIN
```

```
  IF (IsEmpty(Q)) THEN
    success := FALSE;
  ELSE
    Q^.Front := (Q^.Front MOD maxqueue) + 1;
    DEC(Q^.Count);
    success := TRUE;
  END;

END Remove;


(* ------------------------------------------------------------

  QueueFront:  Retrieve into getitem the item from queue
  Q that was added earliest, leaving Q unchanged.  The
  operation fails if the queue is empty.  The Boolean
  flag success indicates whether the operation succeeded.

  ASSUMPTION:  Queue Q has been created.

  CALLS:  IsEmpty
  ------------------------------------------------------------ *)
PROCEDURE QueueFront(Q : Queue; VAR getitem : itemtype;
                     VAR success : BOOLEAN);

BEGIN

  IF (IsEmpty(Q)) THEN
    success := FALSE;
  ELSE
    getitem := Q^.Items[Q^.Front];
    success := TRUE;
  END;

END QueueFront;

END Queues.
```

There are several commonly used variations of this scheme that do not require keeping a count of the number of items in the queue. In our opinion, however, these implementations are not quite as clean as the one presented above. Exercises 8.1 and 8.2 consider two of the alternate schemes.

AN APPLICATION OF THE ADT QUEUE

Simulation is a major application area for computers. It is a technique for modeling the behavior of both natural and man-made systems. Generally, the goal of a simulation is to generate statistics that summarize the performance of an existing system or to predict the performance of a proposed system. In this section we present a very simple example illustrating one important type of simulation, **event-driven simulation.** The exercises at the end of the chapter elaborate on the problem presented here.

Consider the following problem. Ms. Drysdale, president of the First City Bank of Shiprock, is considering hiring a second teller. Drysdale is considering this expansion because she has heard her customers complain about how long they have to wait for service. As a result, many are considering switching their accounts to another bank.

Ms. Drysdale would like to get an approximation of how long, on the average, a customer has to wait for service from First City's only teller. How can Ms. Drysdale obtain this information? She could stand with a stopwatch in the bank's lobby all day, but she does not find this prospect particularly exciting. Besides, she would like to use a method that would also allow her to predict how much improvement she could expect if the bank hired a given number of additional tellers. She certainly doesn't want to hire the tellers on trial bases and monitor the bank's performance before making a final decision.

Ms. Drysdale concludes that the best way to obtain the information she wants is to **simulate** the behavior of her bank. The first step in simulating a system such as the bank is to construct a mathematical model that captures the relevant information about the system, such as how many tellers the bank has or how often customers arrive. If the information specified in the model accurately describes the real-world system, a simulation can be used to derive accurate predictions about the system's overall performance. For example, a simulation could predict the average amount of time a customer has to wait before receiving service. The simulation can also be used to evaluate proposed changes to the real-world system, such as an increase in the number of tellers in the bank. To do this we would simply modify the corresponding information in the model (for example, the number of tellers) and use the simulation to predict the behavior of this hypothetical system. A large decrease in the amount of time predicted for the average wait of a customer might justify the cost of hiring additional tellers.

Central to a simulation is the concept of **simulated time.** Envision a stopwatch measuring elapsed time as our simulation mimics the behavior of the system under study. For example, suppose that our model of the bank specifies that there is one teller. At Time = 0 (at the start of the banking day) the simulated system might be in the state depicted in Figure 8-6(a).

As the simulation runs, the stopwatch ticks away units of time (for example, minutes), and certain **events** occur. At Time = 45 the bank's first customer arrives. Since there is no line, the customer goes directly to the teller and begins her transaction. At Time = 123 a second customer arrives. Since the first customer has not yet completed her transaction, the second customer must wait in line. At Time = 235, the first customer completes her transaction and the second customer can begin hers.

In order to gather the information we need, we would let this simulation continue to run for a certain amount of time, for example, until a month of banking has been simulated. In the course of the run we would keep track of certain statistics, such as the average amount of time a customer has to wait for service. Notice that in the small example of Figure 8-6, the first customer had to wait 0 minutes for service, and the second customer had to wait 112 minutes for service—an average of 56 minutes.

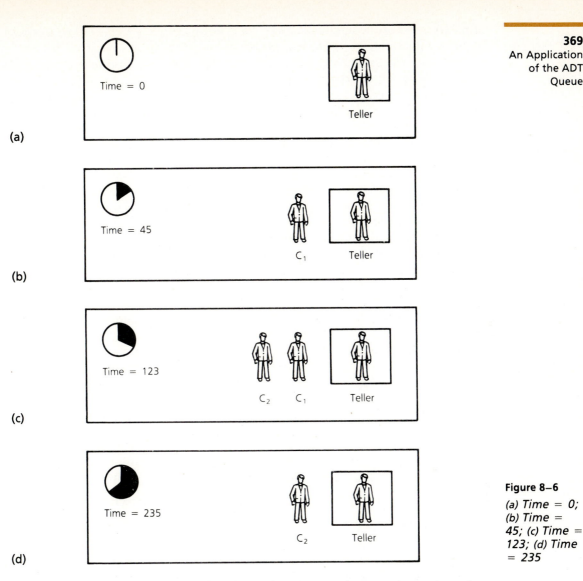

(a)

(b)

(c)

(d)

Figure 8–6

(a) Time = 0; (b) Time = 45; (c) Time = 123; (d) Time = 235

One point not addressed in the above discussion is how to determine when certain events occur. For example, why did we say that the first customer arrived at Time = 45 and the second at Time = 123? From studying real-world systems such as our bank, mathematicians have learned to model events such as the arrival of people using techniques from probability theory. This statistical information has been incorporated into the mathematical model of the system and is used to generate events in a way that reflects the real world. Note that the goal is to reflect long-term average behavior of the system rather than to predict occurrences of specific events. This is sufficient for the needs of the simulation.

While the techniques for generating events to reflect the real world are interesting and important, they require a good deal of mathematical sophistication. What we shall do here is assume that these techniques have already been applied and that the results are now available for our use. In particular, for our bank problem, we shall assume that a file contains data indicating the time (elapsed time into the simulation) of each customer's arrival and the amount of time that the customer's transaction will take (from the time the customer reaches the teller and begins service). For example, the data

20   3

22   9

30   6

indicates that the first customer arrives 20 minutes into the simulation, and the transaction (once begun) requires 3 minutes; the second customer arrives 22 minutes into the simulation, and the transaction requires 9 minutes; and the third customer arrives 30 minutes into the simulation, and the transaction requires 6 minutes. We will assume that the input file is ordered by arrival time.

Notice that there are no departure events in the data: it is not specified when a customer will complete the transaction and leave. It is the job of the simulation to determine when these events occur. By using the time specified for each customer's arrival and the specified transaction length, the simulation can determine the time at which each customer departs. To see how this works, let us conduct a simulation by hand using the above data.

TIME	EVENT
20	customer 1 enters bank and begins transaction
22	customer 2 enters bank and stands at end of line
23	customer 1 departs; customer 2 begins transaction
30	customer 3 enters bank and stands at end of line
32	customer 2 departs; customer 3 begins transaction
38	customer 3 departs

Notice that the amount of time that elapses between a customer's arrival in the bank and the time that the customer reaches the front of the line and begins service is the amount of time the customer has to wait. It is the average of this wait time over all the customers that we are interested in obtaining.

To summarize, our simulation is concerned with two types of events:

1. **Arrival events (A).** These events indicate the arrival at the bank of a new customer. The times at which these events occur is specified in the input file. As such, they are called **external events.** When a customer arrives at the bank, one of two things happens. If the teller is idle when the customer arrives, the customer begins the transaction immediately. If the teller is busy, the new customer must stand at the end of the line and wait for service.

2. **Departure events (D).** These events indicate the departure from the bank of a customer who has completed a transaction. The times at which these events occur is determined in the course of the simulation. As such, they are called **internal events.** When a customer completes the transaction, he or she departs and the next person in line (if there is one) begins a transaction.

We now must develop an algorithm to perform the simulation. The main task of the algorithm is to determine the times at which the events occur and to process the events when they do occur. We can state the algorithm at a high level as follows:

```
(* initialize *)
Time := 0
initialize the line to "no customers"

WHILE (Time <= time of the final event) DO

   IF (an arrival event occurs at time Time) THEN
      process the arrival event
   END

   IF (a departure event occurs at time Time) THEN
      process the departure event
   END

   (* notice that if an arrival event and departure event
      occur at the same time, we arbitrarily choose to
      process the arrival event first *)

   Time := Time + 1
END
```

We now make a key observation. We are interested only in those time steps (minutes) at which events occur. That is, since no action is required at the time steps between the occurrences of events, we can always advance *Time* from the time of one event directly to the time of the next. In this sense the simulation is **event driven**—time is advanced by the occurrence of events rather than by the ticking of a clock.

To be able to implement an event-driven simulation, we must be able to determine the time steps at which the events occur. If we could accomplish this, the simulation could be performed as:

```
(* initialize *)
initialize the line to "no customers"

WHILE (there remain events to be processed) DO
   Time := time of next event

   IF (it is an arrival event) THEN
      process the arrival event
   ELSE
      process the departure event (* the other possibility *)
   END
END
```

We must now solve the problem of determining the time of the next event so that we can implement the statement

Time := time of next event

The solution entails the maintenance of an **event list.** An event list consists of events that will occur but *have not yet occurred.* The event list is ordered by the times of the events (in ascending order), and thus the next event to be processed is always at the head of the list. Our algorithm simply gets the event from the head of the list, advances to the time specified, and processes the event. The difficulty lies in successfully managing such an event list.

For this problem we can manage the event list so that it always contains at most one event of each kind. Recall that the arrival events are specified in the input file and that they appear in ascending time order. We thus never need to worry about an arrival event until all the arrival events that precede it in the file have been processed. We simply keep the earliest unprocessed arrival event on the event list, and when this event eventually is processed (that is, when it is time for this customer to arrive), we replace it on the event list by the next unprocessed arrival event (which is the next item in the input file).

Similarly, we need to keep on the event list only the next departure event to occur. But how are the times for the departure events to be determined? Observe that "the next" departure event always corresponds to the customer currently receiving service from the teller—that is, the next customer to depart is this customer. As soon as a customer begins service, we can determine the time of his or her departure. This time is simply

$$\text{time of next departure} = \text{time service begins} + \text{length of customer's transaction}$$

Recall that the length of the customer's transaction is specified in the input file along with the arrival time. Thus, as soon as a customer begins service, we place a departure event corresponding to this customer on the event list.

Let us now consider how we process an event when it is time for the event to occur. There are two general types of actions that must be performed:

Update the line. Customers may be added or removed.

Update the event list. New events may be added or removed.

Notice that when a customer arrives, he or she is added to the rear of the line. The customer at the front of the line is currently receiving service, and it is this customer that is next removed from the system. It is thus natural to use a queue to manage the customers in the system. For this problem, the only information that we store in the queue about each customer is the time of arrival and the length of the transaction.

We can now specify the details of processing an event.

TO PROCESS AN ARRIVAL EVENT FOR CUSTOMER C

Update the line:

```
          add the new customer C to the queue

Update the event list:

remove the arrival event for Customer C from the event list
IF (not at the end of the input file) THEN
    add a new arrival event
        (time of event = time specified in file)
END

IF (the new customer C began service immediately, (i.e.,
        the queue was empty, so customer C went directly
        to the teller)) THEN
    add to the event list a departure event corresponding
        to customer C (time = current time + transaction length)
END


TO PROCESS A DEPARTURE EVENT

Update the line:

remove the first customer from the queue
(* if the queue does not become empty then
    the new first customer begins service *)

Update the event list:

remove the departure event from the event list
IF (the queue has not become empty) THEN
    add to the event list the departure event corresponding
        to the person now at the front of the queue
        (time = current time + transaction length)
END
```

Let us make a few observations about the structure of the event list that should help explain the workings of the above algorithm. In the general case, the event list contains exactly two events, one arrival event A and one departure event D.

> Event List: $D \rightarrow A$ (general case—next event is a departure), or

> Event List: $A \rightarrow D$ (general case—next event is an arrival)

If, starting from the first case, the departure event leaves the queue empty, a new departure event does not replace the just-processed event (there is no one currently being served). Thus, after a departure leaves the queue empty, the event list has the form

> Event List: A   (a departure leaves the queue empty)

This is also the initial state of the event list—that is, after the first arrival event has been read in from the input file but before it has been processed.

There is also a case in which the event list contains only a departure event. This case occurs after all the arrival events in the input file have been processed. Thus, the fourth form that the event list can take on is

> Event List: D   (the input has been exhausted)

A final observation is that new events may be inserted either at the beginning of the event list or at the end, depending on the relative times of the new event and the event currently on the list. For example, starting in the state

> Event List: D → A

we process the departure event and the event list becomes

> Event List: A

At this point we generate a departure event corresponding to the customer who is now at the front of the queue beginning a transaction. If the customer's departure time is before the time of the arrival event currently on the list, then the departure event must be inserted before the A event. However, if the departure time is after the time of the arrival event, the departure event must be inserted after the arrival event. In the case of a tie, we shall need a rule to determine which event should take precedence. In our solution we have arbitrarily chosen to place the departure event after the arrival event.

We are now ready to combine and refine the pieces of our solution into an algorithm for performing the simulation. The following algorithm uses the ADT queue operations to manage the bank line. Notice that in the procedure *ProcessA*, we update the event list *before* updating the line. This allows us to use function *IsEmpty* to determine if the new arrival begins service immediately. If this is the case, then we must add a departure event for this person to the event list. Also, before calling procedures *ProcessA* and *ProcessD*, the main program removes from the event list the event that is about to be processed—this task is thus not performed by procedures *ProcessA* and *ProcessD*. The other refinements to the algorithm should be self-explanatory.

```
ProcessA (event)
(* Procedure to process an arrival event. *)

   (* update the event list *)

   IF (IsEmpty(Q)) THEN

      (* customer goes directly to the teller *)
      add to the event list a departure event corresponding
         to the new customer with (Time = Time + transaction
         length)
```

```
        END

        IF (not at the end of the input file) THEN

            get the next arrival event from the input file and add
                it to the event list, with (time of event = time
                specified in file)

        END

        (* update the line by adding the new customer to the queue *)

        item := information about the new customer
        Add(Q, item)


ProcessD(event)
(* Procedure to process a departure event. *)

        (* update the line by removing the first customer *)

        Remove(Q, success)

        (* update the event list *)

        IF (NOT IsEmpty(Q)) THEN
            add to the event list a departure event corresponding
                to the customer now at the front of the queue, with
                (Time = Time + transaction length)
        END


(* MAIN PROGRAM *)

(* initialize the event list *)
get the first arrival event from the input file
    and place it on the event list

(* initialize the bank line *)
Create(Q)

WHILE (the event list is not empty) DO

        (* get the next event from the beginning of the event list *)
        let newevent be the first event on the event list
        remove the first event from the event list

        Time := time specified by newevent
```

```
     IF (newevent is an arrival event)  THEN
          ProcessA (newevent)
     ELSE
          ProcessD (newevent)
     END
END
```

A Modula-2 implementation of the simulation follows. It is natural to implement the event list with the modules that follow.

```
DEFINITION MODULE EventList;
(* ************************************************************
   Event list operations.

   The following hidden type is declared:

        EList

   The following operations are supported:

        EListCreate, EListEmpty, EListInsert, NextEvent
   ************************************************************ *)


(* event information record *)
FROM ADTitem IMPORT

    eventinfo;

EXPORT QUALIFIED

    EList, EListCreate, EListEmpty, EListInsert, NextEvent;

TYPE

    EList;



(* ------------------------------------------------------------
   EListCreate:  Create an empty event list.
   ------------------------------------------------------ *)
PROCEDURE EListCreate(VAR E : EList);

(* ------------------------------------------------------------
   EListEmpty:  Determine if the event list is empty.

   ASSUMPTION:  The event list E has been created.
   ------------------------------------------------------ *)
PROCEDURE EListEmpty(E : EList) : BOOLEAN;
```

```
(* --------------------------------------------------------------
    EListInsert:  Insert into the event list E an event node
    containing the information in record Event.

    ASSUMPTION:  The event list E has been created.
    ------------------------------------------------------------ *)
PROCEDURE EListInsert(VAR E : EList; Event : eventinfo);


(* --------------------------------------------------------------
    NextEvent:  Return into Event the first event on the event
    list E.  If E is empty, return success FALSE; return succcess
    TRUE otherwise and remove the first event from the list.

    ASSUMPTION:  The event list E has been created.
    ------------------------------------------------------------ *)
PROCEDURE NextEvent(VAR E : EList; VAR Event : eventinfo;
                    VAR success : BOOLEAN);

END EventList.



IMPLEMENTATION MODULE EventList;
(* **************************************************************
    Data structure and operations for the event list.  The
    event list is implemented as a linked list sorted by time.
    The following operations are used to manage the event list.

        EListCreate, EListEmpty, EListInsert, NextEvent
    ************************************************************** *)

(* memory management procedures NEW and DISPOSE *)
FROM Storage IMPORT

    ALLOCATE, DEALLOCATE;

(* event information record *)
FROM ADTitem IMPORT

    events, eventinfo;

TYPE

    (* event list *)
    enodeptr = POINTER TO enode;
    enode    = RECORD
                    info : eventinfo; (* event information record *)
                    next : enodeptr; (* next event              *)
               END;
```

```
    EList    = enodeptr;

(* --------------------------------------------------------------
    EListCreate:  Create an empty event list.
   ------------------------------------------------------------ *)
PROCEDURE EListCreate(VAR E : EList);

BEGIN

    E := NIL;

END EListCreate;

(* --------------------------------------------------------------
    EListEmpty:  Determine if the event list is empty.

    ASSUMPTION:  The event list E has been created.
   ------------------------------------------------------------ *)
PROCEDURE EListEmpty(E : EList) : BOOLEAN;

BEGIN

    RETURN(E = NIL);

END EListEmpty;

(* --------------------------------------------------------------
    EListInsert:  Insert into the event list E an event node
    containing the information in record Event.  The event list
    is maintained ordered by time.

    In case of ties, arrival events are preferred over
    departure events.

    ASSUMPTION:  The event list E has been created.
   ------------------------------------------------------------ *)
PROCEDURE EListInsert(VAR E : EList; Event : eventinfo);

VAR

    cur, prev, newnode : enodeptr;

BEGIN

    cur := E;
    prev := NIL;
```

```
WHILE ( (cur # NIL) AND

            (* new event goes later in the list *)
            ( (Event.time > cur^.info.time) OR
              ((Event.time = cur^.info.time) AND
               (Event.etype = D)) ) ) DO


      prev := cur;
      cur := cur^.next;

   END;   (* while *)

   (* insert the new node *)
   NEW(newnode);
   newnode^.info := Event;
   IF (prev = NIL) THEN
       (* insert at the beginning of the list *)
       newnode^.next := E;
       E := newnode;

   ELSE
       (* insert between the nodes
          pointed to by prev and cur *)
       newnode^.next := cur;
       prev^.next := newnode;

   END;

END EListInsert;


(* ------------------------------------------------------------
   NextEvent:  Return into Event the first event on the event
   list E.  If E is empty, return success FALSE; return succccess
   TRUE otherwise and remove the first event from the list.

   ASSUMPTION:  The event list E has been created.

   CALLS:  EListEmpty
   ------------------------------------------------------------ *)
PROCEDURE NextEvent(VAR E : EList; VAR Event : eventinfo;
                    VAR success : BOOLEAN);
VAR

   delptr : enodeptr;

BEGIN
```

```
       IF (NOT EListEmpty(E)) THEN
          Event := E^.info;
          delptr := E;
          E := E^.next;
          DISPOSE(delptr);
          success := TRUE;

       ELSE
          success := FALSE;

       END;

   END NextEvent;


   END EventList.
```

The implementation of the simulation follows. Note that we have added global variables to count customers and to keep track of their cumulative waiting time. This is sufficient to compute the average waiting time after the last event has been processed.

```
MODULE Simulation;
(* ***********************************************************
    SAMPLE EVENT DRIVEN SIMULATION

    Simulation of a single line.

    There are two kinds of events:

        A : arrival - enter the line
        D : departure - complete transaction and leave the line

    INPUT

        One line of input for each person, including the arrival
        time and required transaction time.

    ASSUMPTION

        The input file is correct.
        The arrival times are ordered by increasing time.

    OUTPUT

        A trace of the events executed.

        Summary statistics (total number of arrivals, average
        time spent waiting in line).
```

The event list E will be managed by a separate module.
There are two kinds of events:

arrival   - consisting of an arrival time and a
                transaction time

departure - consisting of a departure time

The line of people will be modeled by a queue.

GLOBAL VARIABLES

Q   - queue (models line of people)
totnum   - total number of arrivals
totwait   - accumulated time spent waiting in line
** *)

```
(* standard I/O *)
FROM InOut IMPORT

    Done, Write, WriteString, WriteInt, WriteLn,
    Read, ReadInt, ReadString, OpenInput;


(* standard I/O *)
FROM RealInOut IMPORT

    WriteReal;


(* memory management procedure NEW *)
FROM Storage IMPORT

    ALLOCATE;


(* queue item and event information record *)
FROM ADTitem IMPORT

    itemtype, events, eventinfo;


(* Queue type and queue operations *)
FROM Queues IMPORT

    Queue, Create, Add, Remove, QueueFront, IsEmpty;


(* Event list type and event list operations *)
FROM EventList IMPORT

    EList, EListCreate, EListEmpty, EListInsert, NextEvent;
```

```
VAR

    Q : Queue;
    E : EList;

    doevent : eventinfo;   (* local copy of current
                                event information *)

    totnum, totwait : INTEGER;   (* global statistics *)
    succ : BOOLEAN;

(* -----------------------------------------------------------
   GetA:  Read in information for the next arrival event,
   and insert the new arrival event in the event list.

   CALLS:  EListInsert
   ----------------------------------------------------------- *)
PROCEDURE getA(VAR E : EList);

VAR

    newevent : eventinfo;

BEGIN

    IF (Done) THEN
       (* get new event information *)
       newevent.etype := A;
       ReadInt(newevent.time);
       IF (Done) THEN
          ReadInt(newevent.trans);

          (* insert the event into the event list *)
          EListInsert(E, newevent);
       END;
    END;

END getA;

(* -----------------------------------------------------------
   ProcessA:  Execute the arrival event specified by event
   doevent.

   CALLS:  IsEmpty, EListInsert, Add, getA
   ----------------------------------------------------------- *)
PROCEDURE ProcessA(doevent : eventinfo);

VAR
```

```
            current : INTEGER;
            info : itemtype;
            newevent : eventinfo;
            succ : BOOLEAN;

    BEGIN

            (* update the global statistics *)
            INC(totnum);

            current := doevent.time;
            WriteString('Processing an arrival event at time:  ');
            WriteInt(current,1);
            WriteLn;

            (* update the event list *)

            (* if the line is empty, then the
               person starts a transaction *)
            IF (IsEmpty(Q)) THEN
               (* create a departure event *)
               newevent.etype := D;
               newevent.time := current + doevent.trans;

               (* insert the event into the event list *)
               EListInsert(E, newevent);
            END;

            (* get the next arrival event from input *)
            getA(E);

            (* update the line (person arrives) *)
            info.trans := doevent.trans;
            info.arrive := current;
            Add(Q, info, succ);

    END ProcessA;

    (* ------------------------------------------------------------
       ProcessD:  Execute the departure event specified by doevent.

       CALLS:  IsEmpty, Remove, QueueFront, EListInsert
       ----------------------------------------------------------- *)
    PROCEDURE ProcessD(doevent : eventinfo);

    VAR

            current: INTEGER;
```

```
       info : itemtype;
       newevent : eventinfo;
       flag : BOOLEAN;

BEGIN

    current := doevent.time;
    WriteString('Processing a departure event at time: ');
    WriteInt(current,1);
    WriteLn;

    (* update the line (person departs) *)
    Remove(Q, flag);

    (* update the event list *)

    (* if the line is not empty, then the
       next person starts a transaction *)
    IF (NOT IsEmpty(Q)) THEN
       (* create a departure event *)
       QueueFront(Q, info, flag);
       newevent.etype := D;
       newevent.time := current + info.trans;

       (* insert the event into the event list *)
       EListInsert(E, newevent);

       (* update the global statistics *)
       totwait := totwait + (current - info.arrive);
    END;

END ProcessD;

BEGIN  (* MAIN PROGRAM *)

    (* open the input file *)
    WriteString('Enter name of file containing list of events.');
    WriteLn;
    OpenInput('');
    WriteLn;

    (* initialize *)
    Create(Q);
    EListCreate(E);
    totnum := 0;
    totwait := 0;

    WriteString('Simulation Begins');
    WriteLn;
```

```
      (* get the first arrival event *)
      Done := TRUE;
      getA(E);

      (* process events until the event list is empty *)
      WHILE (NOT EListEmpty(E)) DO
         NextEvent(E, doevent, succ);
         IF (doevent.etype = A) THEN
            ProcessA(doevent);
         ELSE
            ProcessD(doevent);
         END;
      END;

      WriteString('Simulation Ends');
      WriteLn;

      (* write out the final statistics *)
      WriteLn;
      WriteString('Final Statistics:');
      WriteLn;
      WriteString('  Total number of people processed: ');
      WriteInt(totnum,1);
      WriteLn;
      WriteString('  Average amount of time spent on line: ');
      IF (totnum = 0) THEN
         WriteReal(0.0,1);
      ELSE
         WriteReal(FLOAT(totwait)/FLOAT(totnum),1);
      END;
      WriteLn;

END Simulation.


DEFINITION MODULE ADTitem;
(* ********************************************************
   This module contains the user-defined data types that
   are specific to the simulation.

   These types include the item type for ADT queue and the
   information record for managing events.
   ******************************************************** *)

EXPORT QUALIFIED

   itemtype, events, eventinfo;

TYPE
```

```
(* Queue item *)
itemtype  = RECORD
                trans: INTEGER;   (* transaction time *)
                arrive: INTEGER;  (* time of arrival *)
            END;


(* Event information *)
events    = (A, D);   (* arrival and departure *)
eventinfo = RECORD
                time : INTEGER;            (* time of event    *)
                CASE etype : events OF   (* type of event    *)
                    A : trans : INTEGER; (* transaction time *)
                  | D : (* no fields in this variant *)
                END;
            END;

END ADTitem.
```

If this program were run on the input file shown at the left, it would produce
the output shown at the right:

INPUT		OUTPUT
1	5	Simulation Begins
2	5	Processing an arrival event at time: 1
4	5	Processing an arrival event at time: 2
20	5	Processing an arrival event at time: 4
22	5	Processing a departure event at time: 6
24	5	Processing a departure event at time: 11
26	5	Processing a departure event at time: 16
28	5	Processing an arrival event at time: 20
30	5	Processing an arrival event at time: 22
88	3	Processing an arrival event at time: 24
		Processing a departure event at time: 25
		Processing an arrival event at time: 26
		Processing an arrival event at time: 28
		Processing an arrival event at time: 30
		Processing a departure event at time: 30
		Processing a departure event at time: 35
		Processing a departure event at time: 40
		Processing a departure event at time: 45
		Processing a departure event at time: 50
		Processing an arrival event at time: 88
		Processing a departure event at time: 91
		Simulation Ends

```
Final Statistics:
 Total number of people processed: 10
 Average amount of time spent on line:  5.60E + 000
```

A SUMMARY OF POSITION-ORIENTED ADT's

We have now reached the end of the unit on data organized by *position*. It therefore seems appropriate to summarize and compare the ADT's that have been introduced.

In Chapters 6 through 8 we have introduced four abstract data types: the ordered list, the stack, the traversable stack, and the queue. The thread that ties these ADT's together is that all their operations are defined in terms of the positions of their data items. Stacks and queues greatly restrict the positions that their operations can affect—they can affect only the end positions of their structures. The traversable stack and the ordered list have successively fewer restrictions.

There is really a great deal of similarity between stacks and queues. This similarity can be made apparent if we pair off their operations (we have changed the names of the operations where necessary to avoid ambiguity).

> **CreateStack(S) and CreateQueue(Q).** These operations create an empty structure of the appropriate type.
>
> **StackEmpty(S) and QueueEmpty(Q).** These operations tell if there are any items in the structure. Notice that in both cases the operations do not look past the ends of their structures to see *how many* items are present. Rather, the operations tell only if there is an item present at one of the ends.
>
> **Push(S, e) and Add(Q, e).** These operations insert a new item into the last position (top and rear) of their structures.
>
> **Pop(S) and Remove(Q).** *Pop* deletes the item from the last position (top) of the stack, and *Remove* deletes the item from the first position (front) of the queue.
>
> **StackTop(S) and QueueFront(Q).** *StackTop* retrieves the item at the last position (top) of the stack, and *QueueFront* retrieves the item at the first position (front) of the queue.

The traversable stack removes some of the restrictiveness of a stack by including the *Traverse* operation, which allows us to look past the top of the stack to see the items at every position of the structure. The restriction that items can be inserted into and deleted from only the top position of the structure is, however, not removed.

The ordered list was the first ADT that we studied (it was introduced in Chapter 6). This ADT allows us to insert into, delete from, and inspect the item at *any position* of the structure. It is thus defined by the most flexible version of position-oriented operations.

The ordered list operations *Length*, *Insert*, *Delete*, and *Retrieve* can be viewed as generalizing the stack and queue operations to the logical extreme.

> **Length(L).** When we remove the restriction that *StackEmpty* and *QueueEmpty* can see only if an item is present at the ends of their structures, we obtain an operation that can count the number of items which are present.

Insert(L, i, e). When we remove the restriction that *Push* and *Add* can insert new items only into the last position, we obtain a general `Insert` operation that can insert a new item into any position *i* of the list.

Delete(L, i): When we remove the restriction that *Pop* and *Remove* can delete items only from the last and first positions, we obtain a general `Delete` operation that can delete an item from any position *i* of the list.

Retrieve(L, i). When we remove the restriction that `StackTop` and `QueueFront` can retrieve items only from the last and first positions, we obtain a general `Retrieve` operation that can retrieve the item from any position *i* of the list.

Since each of these four ADT's defines its operations in terms of an item's position in the structure, we have constructed implementations for them that can provide easy access to specified positions. For example, both our stack implementations allow the first position (top) to be accessed quickly, while both our queue implementations allow the first position (front) and the last position (rear) to be accessed quickly.

In the remainder of the book, we shall study ADT's that organize their data by *value*. That is, rather than asking for the ith item on a list, the operations of these ADT's will, for example, ask for the item with name *John Smith*. To support these types of operations efficiently, we will need to devise new and more complex data structures.

SUMMARY

1. The definition of the queue operations gives this ADT first-in, first-out (FIFO) behavior.

2. As is the case for the other ADT's that we have studied, the primary criterion for choosing between a sequential and linked implementation is the issue of fixed versus dynamic size.

3. Queues are often used in the modeling of real-world systems. We presented an event-driven simulation, where a queue was used to model a line of customers.

4. Central to a simulation is the notion of simulated time. In an event-driven simulation, simulated time is advanced to the time of the next event (rather than by a single time unit). To implement this strategy, we maintain an event list containing events that have not yet occurred. The list is ordered by the time of the events so that the next event to occur is always at the head of the list.

EXERCISES

1. Consider the sequential implementation of a queue described in the text. Instead of counting the number of items in the queue, we could maintain a Boolean flag `IsFull` to distinguish between the full and empty conditions. Redo the sequential implementation using the `IsFull` flag.

1. The linked queue implementation is straightforward, but the sequential implementation has to overcome the problem of right-ward drift of the elements in the array. This problem can lead to a queue-full condition even though there are only a few items present.

2. We can solve the problem of rightward drift by viewing the array as circular. When this is done, care must be taken that the queue-full and queue-empty conditions are distinguishable. One way to do this is to maintain a count of the number of items in the queue.

3. The management of an event list in an event-driven simulation is typically more difficult than it was in the example presented in this chapter. For example, if there were more than one line in the bank, the structure of the event list would be much more complex as would the processing of events.

2. Another popular implementation of a queue (see Exercise 8.1) uses no special data field (such as *count* or *IsFull*). In this implementation, we will declare the array *Items* to be *[0..maxqueue]* instead of *[1..maxqueue]* and will sacrifice one of the array locations as follows. By convention, *Front* will always point to the array location preceding the location holding the item that is at the front of the queue; that is, the front item of the queue is always at the location one past the location pointed to by *Front*. (Note that location 0 follows location *maxqueue*.) Before adding to the queue we check to see if incrementing *Rear* would result in *Rear* becoming equal to *Front*. If this is the case, we disallow the insertion because it would violate our rule that at least one array location be empty. How does this allow us to distinguish between the full and empty conditions? Redo the sequential implementation using this convention.

3. What do the queues Q and T "look like" after the following sequence of operations?

```
Create(Q)
Add(Q, 1)
Add(Q, 2)
Create(T)
Add(T, 3)
Add(T, 4)
Remove(Q)
Add(Q, QueueFront(T))
Add(Q, 5)
Remove(T)
Add(T, 6)
```

Compare these results with Exercise 6.7.

4. Consider a slight variation of the ADT queue. In this variation, new items can be added to and deleted from either end. This ADT is commonly called a **doubly ended queue**, or **deque**. Construct sequential and linked implementations.

5. Hand execute the simulation described in the text on the following sample data. Show the state of the queue and the event list at each step.

```
5  9
7  5
14 5
30 5
32 5
34 5
```

Note that there is a tie between the execution of an arrival event and a departure event at time = 14.

6. Consider the stack-based depth first search (DFS) of a directed graph described in Chapter 7 (for example, for HPair). If we replace the stack used by the search with a queue, we get a **breadth first search (BFS)** of the graph. That is, replace every call to *Push* with a call to *Add*, every call to *Pop* with a call to *Remove* and every call to *StackTop* with a call to *QueueFront*. Execute BFS on the graph in Figure 7–2.

*7. The stack-based DFS (see Exercise 8.6) has a recursive counterpart, but the queue-based BFS does not. Why is this so?

*8. Consider the following axioms for ADT queue (see Exercise 6.10).

> Let Q be an arbitrary queue and e an arbitrary queue item.
> IsEmpty(Create) = true (a newly created queue is empty)
> IsEmpty(Add(Q, e)) = false
>
> Remove(Create) = error
> Remove(Add(Create, e)) = Create
> IsEmpty(Q) = false ⇒ Remove(Add(Q, e)) = Add(Remove(Q), e)
>
> QueueFront(Create) = error
> QueueFront(Add(Create, e)) = e
> IsEmpty(Q) = false ⇒ QueueFront(Add(Q, e)) = QueueFront(Q)

a. Note the recursive nature of the definition of operation QueueFront. What is the degenerate case? What is the recursive step? What is the significance of the IsEmpty test? Why is this recursive in nature while operation StackTop for ADT stack is not?

b. The representation of a stack as a sequence Push(Push(...Push(Create,...)) without any Pop operations was called a **canonical form**. Is there a canonical form for ADT queue that just uses Add operations? That is, is every

queue equal to a queue that can be written with just Adds? Prove your
answer.

PROJECTS

9. Modify and expand the event-driven simulation program described in this
chapter. Here are a few suggestions:

   a. Add some statistics to the simulation (for example: maximum wait in line,
   average length of line, maximum length of line).

   b. Modify the simulation so that it accounts for three tellers, each with a
   distinct line. You should keep in mind that there should be:

      three queues, one for each teller

      a rule for choosing a line when processing an arrival event (for
      example, enter the shortest line)

      three distinct departure events, one for each line

      rules for breaking ties on the event list

   Run both simulations on several sets of input data. How do the statistics
   compare?

   c. The bank is considering the following change: Instead of having three
   distinct lines (one for each teller), there will be a single line for the three
   tellers. The person at the front of the line will go to the first available
   teller. Modify the simulation of part (b) to account for this variation. Run
   both simulations on several sets of input data. How do the various statistics
   compare (averages and maximums)? What can you conclude about having
   a single line as opposed to having distinct lines?

10. The people that run the Motor Vehicle Department have a problem. They
are concerned that people don't spend enough time waiting in lines to appreciate the privilege of owning and driving an automobile. The current arrangement is as follows:

      When someone walks in the door, they must wait in a line to sign in.

      Once they have signed in, they are told either to stand in line for
      registration renewal or to wait until they are called for license renewal.

      Once they have completed their desired transaction, they must go and
      wait in line for the cashier.

      Many people expect to pay by check. When a person finally gets to
      the front of the cashier's line, if she expects to pay by check, she is
      told that all checks must get approved. To do this, it is necessary to
      go over to the check-approver's table and then reenter the cashier's
      line at the end.

The object of this problem is to write an event-driven simulation to help the Motor Vehicle Department gather statistics.

INPUT

Each line of input will contain:

An arrival time (integer).

A name (8 characters). To simplify reading in the data, you can assume that every name will contain exactly 8 characters (possibly ending in blanks).

A desired transaction (char—'L' for license renewal, 'R' for registration renewal).

Method of payment (char—'$' for cash, 'C' for check).

OUTPUT

Write out the details of each event (when, who, what, ...).

FINAL STATISTICS

Licenses—total number and average time spent in MVD (arrival until completion of payment)

Registrations—total number and average time spent in MVD (arrival until completion of payment)

DETAILS OF THE SIMULATION

a. Define the following events: arrive, sign in, renew license, renew registration, and cope with the cashier (make a payment or find out about check approval).

b. In case of ties, let the order be determined by the order of the events just given (arrivals have the highest priority).

c. The amount of time taken for the various transactions can be summarized as follows:

sign in	10 seconds
renew license	90 seconds
registration	60 seconds
cashier (payment)	30 seconds
cashier (check not approved)	10 seconds

d. As ridiculous as it may seem, the people waiting for license renewal are called in alphabetical order. Note, however, that people are not pushed back once their transactions have started.

e. For the sake of this simulation, we can assume that checks get approved instantly. Therefore, the rule for arriving at the front of the cashier's line with a check that has not been approved is to go to the rear of the cashier's line with a check that has been approved.

CHAPTER 9

THE ADT TABLE: LINEAR AND NONLINEAR IMPLEMENTATIONS

PREVIEW   This is the first of four chapters in which we study the ADT table. The ADT's presented in Chapters 6, 7, and 8 are appropriate for problems that must manage data by position; the ADT table is appropriate for problems that must manage data by value. To make an intelligent choice among the various possible table implementations, we must be able to analyze the efficiency with which each of the implementations supports the table operations. We analyze the efficiencies of sequential and linked-list-based table implementations and conclude that, in many applications, they do not support the operations as efficiently as we would like. This motivates the need for a more sophisticated table implementation, the binary search tree.

Let us begin by considering three categories of operations:

> operations that insert data into a data structure
>
> operations that delete data from a data structure
>
> operations that ask questions about the data in a data structure

In a broad sense, these operations are what the management of data is all about. The operations of the ADT's presented in the previous chapters each fit into at least one of these categories, as do the operations of the ADT table. To see how the operations of a table differ from those of the previously presented ADT's, we need to consider the *orientation* of the operations.

The ADT's stack, queue, traversable stack, and ordered list are all *position oriented*. The operations of these ADT's take the form:

> insert a data item into the ith position of a data structure
>
> delete a data item from the ith position of a data structure
>
> ask a question about the data item in the ith position of a data structure

As we have seen, the ADT ordered list places no restriction on the value of i, while the other ADT's do impose some restrictions. For example, the operations of the ADT stack are restricted to insert into, delete from, and ask a question about the *last position* of the data structure (the top of the stack). Thus, although they differ with respect to the flexibility of their operations, all the ADT's that we have considered until now manage an association between data items and positions.

The ADT table operations, on the other hand, are of the form

> insert a data item containing the *value x* into a data structure
>
> delete a data item containing the *value x* from a data structure
>
> ask a question about a data item containing the *value x*

396

CHAPTER 9
THE ADT
TABLE:
LINEAR AND
NONLINEAR
IMPLEMEN-
TATIONS

In this chapter we shall encounter applications that require such *value-oriented* operations. As you might imagine, such applications are extremely prevalent, for example,

find the phone number of *John Smith*

delete all the information about the employee with ID number *12908*.

In this and the chapters to follow we shall see that the ADT table supplies operations appropriate for the performance of these types of tasks. We shall study several implementations of a table and analyze the advantages and disadvantages of each. These implementations range from familiar data structures based on arrays and linked lists to new and very important data structures based on trees and address calculators. We shall present several applications that require the ADT table or a variant of a table, and for each application we shall illustrate the process of selecting an appropriate implementation. In a case study in Chapter 10, we shall expand the video-cassette inventory problem of Chapter 3 and formulate the solution in terms of the ADT table and the ADT **priority queue**, a variant of a table.

THE ADT TABLE

The name *table*, like the names of other ADT's, is intended to conjure up images of familiar objects that possess properties resembling those of the ADT. For example, the name *stack* might remind you of a stack of dishes. What does the name *table* bring to mind? If we had asked the question before you read this chapter's Preview, you might have answered, "my favorite mahogany coffee table."

We hope, however, that your answer now will be something more like "a table of the major cities of the world."

Name	Country	Population
Athens	Greece	2,100,000
Barcelona	Spain	2,000,000
Cairo	Egypt	5,100,000
London	Britain	7,000,000
Rome	Italy	2,900,000
Toronto	Canada	3,000,000
Turin	Italy	1,200,000

A property this table of cities shares with the ADT table is that it is designed to allow us to *look up* information easily. Given the name of a city, we can find it in the table and discover the country in which it is located and the city's population. The ADT table, as we shall see, provides an operation for performing this type of *information lookup*.

The above table contains several pieces of information about each city. This is also often the case for the ADT table—that is, the items of a table are often records. Recall that we have always allowed the items of our ADT's to be records.

In our implementations of stacks, queues, and ordered lists, the user could define *itemtype* to be a record, and the operations would still make sense without modification. Because the ADT table is *value oriented,* there is a greater significance attached to its items being records. We can illustrate this point by more closely examining how we might use the table of cities.

Suppose that we wish to know the population of Toronto. We could scan the column of city names, starting at the top, until we come to Toronto. However, since the cities are listed in alphabetical order, we can mimic a binary search. We could begin the search near the middle of the table, determine in which half Toronto lies, and recursively apply the binary search to the appropriate half. This is far more efficient than scanning the entire table from the beginning.

Now suppose that we wish to find which of the major cities are in Italy. To answer this question, we have no choice but to scan the entire table. The fact that the city names are in alphabetical order does not help us for this problem at all. The table has been arranged to facilitate the search for a given city, but other types of questions require a complete scan of the table.

This point is highly relevant to the ADT table since its items are very often records. One of the fields of the records is designated as the **search key,** indicating that we will want to retrieve items based on a specified value for this field. In our table of cities, for example, we would designate Name to be the search key if we often needed to perform an operation such as *retrieve the information about Toronto.* We shall devise implementations of a table that allow the rapid retrieval of the item(s) with a search key that matches some specified value. If, however, we need to retrieve the item(s) with a non–search key field that matches some specified value, the entire table will have to be inspected. Therefore, when the problem solver designates a given field to be a search key, he or she is sending the ADT implementor the message:

> *Arrange the data in a way that facilitates the search for an item with a specified value in its search key.*

We now present a set of four basic operations that define the ADT table. It should be emphasized that these are only one possible set of table operations. The problem solver should tailor the operations selected to fit the application at hand. The problem solver may require only a subset of these operations, or she may require other operations that are not here. It may be convenient to modify our definitions of some of the operations. For example, our definitions assume that no two table items have the same values in their search keys. In many applications it is quite reasonable to expect duplicate search-key values. If this is the case, several of the operations must be redefined to eliminate the ambiguity that would arise from duplicate search-key values; for example, which item should be returned by *Retrieve* if several items have the specified value in their search keys? (The problem of duplicate search-key values is the subject of Exercises 1 through 3 at the end of the chapter.) The point is that *your* definition of the ADT table should be tailored to the problem you are solving.

```
Create(T)
(* Create an empty table T. *)
```

398
CHAPTER 9
THE ADT
TABLE:
LINEAR AND
NONLINEAR
IMPLEMEN-
TATIONS

```
Insert(T, e)
(* Insert item e into table T.  Note that if the table items
   are records, e must specify a value for each field.  It is
   assumed that there is no item in the table with the same
   search key as e.  *)

Delete(T, X, success)
(* Delete from table T the item with search key X.  The
   operation fails if there is no such item.  The flag
   success indicates whether the operation succeeded.  *)

Retrieve(T, X, success)
(* Retrieve from table T the item with search key X.  The
   operation fails if there is no such item.  The flag
   success indicates whether the operation succeeded.  *)
```

Although this set of operations is sufficient for some applications, several important things cannot be done without additional operations. For instance, we can *Retrieve* a data item only if we know the value of its search key. One consequence of this is that we cannot perform many seemingly critical tasks, such as

```
print out all the items that are in the table
```

This is one example of an entire class of tasks that require that we be able to *traverse* the table.

The *Traverse* operation for a table is defined very similarly to the way that it was defined in Chapter 7 for a stack. *Traverse* will be passed the name of a user-defined *Visit* procedure, which it will call for each item in the table. The user, in defining the *Traverse* operation, must specify the order in which *Traverse* should visit the items. One common order is **sorted by search key**. It is also possible that the user does not care in what order the items are visited. If this is the case, the user should say so in her definition of the operation *Traverse*. As we shall see, the way the user defines *Traverse* (if it is requested at all) may affect the way that the table is implemented.

Because the user can define the *Visit* procedure to do any number of things—including access the table via the ADT operations—*Traverse* is a very versatile operation. We illustrate this with three brief examples. Suppose that the table of major cities given above is represented as an ADT table. The items of the table are records of the form

```
TYPE

    tableitem = RECORD
                    Name   ...
                    Country ...
                    Pop ...
                END
```

The *Name* field is designated as the search key.

Suppose that three of the things we wish to do to this table are:

> Print, in alphabetical order, the name of each city and its population.
>
> Print the name of each city whose population is greater than 1,000,000.
>
> Increase the population of each city by 10%.

Notice that while the first of the tasks requires that *Traverse* visit the items in alphabetical order, the visitation order is immaterial for the other two tasks.

To perform the first task, we would pass to *Traverse* the name of the procedure *PrintInfo* defined by

```
PrintInfo(CityRec)

  Print(CityRec.Name, CityRec.Pop)
```

To perform the second task, we would pass to *Traverse* the name of the procedure *PrintLarge* defined by

```
PrintLarge(CityRec)

  IF (CityRec.Pop > 1,000,000) THEN
     print(CityRec.Name)
  END
```

To perform the third task, we would pass to *Traverse* the name of the procedure *UpdatePop*, which we might consider defining as

```
UpdatePop(T, CityRec)

  CityRec.Pop := CityRec.Pop + (10% of CityRec.Pop)
  Delete(T, CityRec.Name, success)
  Insert(T, CityRec)
```

Observe that this procedure updates the population of a city by deleting the appropriate table item and then inserting a new item with the updated field. In general, if an application frequently requires such a *replace* operation, it might be wise to include *Replace* as one of the ADT table operations. As we shall see, due to implementation considerations for the operation *Traverse*, it might in fact be *necessary* to include a *Replace* operation in the ADT definition.

A major goal of the material on tables is to indicate how the requirements of a particular application influence the selection of an implementation. The four operations given above, along with *Traverse*, make table a powerful ADT. Some applications will require all the operations; others, only a subset of them. It is very important that, before requesting a set of table operations to be implemented, the problem solver carefully analyze which operations are really needed for the application at hand. It is tempting always to request that all the operations be supported. This, however, is a bad strategy. In the sections to follow,

400
CHAPTER 9
THE ADT
TABLE:
LINEAR AND
NONLINEAR
IMPLEMEN-
TATIONS

we shall discuss the *trade-offs* between various implementations of a table. We shall see it is often the case that one implementation supports some of the operations more efficiently than another implementation but that the converse is true for other operations. Therefore, if you request an operation that is never to be used, the implementor of the ADT might select an implementation that is not best suited for what you are really doing.

In addition to knowing what operations must be supported for a given application, it is often important that the ADT implementor know approximately *how frequently* the application will perform each of the operations. For example, if we were to maintain a table of major cities such as the one given at the beginning of this section, we would expect far more retrieve operations to be performed than insertions or deletions. Other applications may require many more insertions and deletions than retrieves. Still others may require a large number of each of these operations. The *mix of operations* is one of the factors that influences which implementation of table should be selected for a particular application.

Later in the chapter we shall study several different application scenarios. Each of these scenarios involves an application that requires us to devise some particular mix of the table operations.

The scenarios will present successively more challenging problems. We shall start with scenarios for which adequate implementations can be derived from arrays and linked lists. We shall then present scenarios that require a new type of data structure, the **binary search tree**. As we shall see, binary search trees combine the best features of arrays and linked lists to provide an excellent implementation for the ADT table.

If you reflect upon the last few paragraphs, you will detect a new emphasis on *efficiency*. In the past we have asked you to worry first and foremost about style and readability. In the sections that follow, however, we are going to contrast different implementations of the ADT table and use efficiency as one of the criteria in the selection process. Notice that we did say *one* of the criteria. We wouldn't want you to think that we have changed our minds about what is important. In fact, to help you to maintain the proper point of view, we are going to precede our discussion on implementations with a brief section on *keeping your perspective*.

KEEPING YOUR PERSPECTIVE

In Chapter 1 we discussed the cost of a computer program. We viewed this cost as being composed of several components. Some of these components involve the cost of human time—the time of the humans who develop, maintain, and use the program. The other components involve the expenses incurred when the program is executed on the computer. These costs in computer resources are referred to as the program's *efficiency*.

We have, up to this point, emphasized the human cost components. Our primary concern has been the development of good problem-solving skills and programming style. We have and shall continue to concentrate our efforts in that direction. Even so, we have for the most part presented solutions that incur relatively low computing costs. The solutions in this book, in addition to illustrating what we feel to be a good programming style, are frequently based on algorithms that are relatively efficient.

The **analysis of algorithms** is the area of computer science that provides tools for contrasting the efficiencies of *methods of solution*. Notice that we said *methods of solution* rather than *programs* because we want to emphasize that the analysis primarily concerns itself only with significant differences in efficiency—differences that usually can be obtained only through superior methods of solution and rarely through clever tricks in coding. Reductions in computing costs that are accomplished through clever coding tricks tend to be more than offset by the increases in human costs that are associated with reduced readability. An analysis should focus on gross differences in the efficiencies of algorithms that are likely to dominate the overall cost of a solution.

Our analysis of various implementations of the ADT table will provide an introduction to some of the basic concerns of the analysis of algorithms. Given an application, we will illustrate how to select an implementation that supports, in a reasonably efficient manner, the required mix of table operations. Since we shall be contrasting the efficiencies of various implementations, we had better first make explicit what we mean when we speak of the *efficiency* of an algorithm or data structure.

We generally are interested in the amounts of computer **time** and computer memory, or **space,** that are required to run a program. Very often we have to weigh *trade-offs* carefully. We are rarely able to make a statement as strong as, "Method A is the best method of performing the task." A solution that requires a relatively small amount of time often also requires a relatively large amount of space. It may not even be possible to say that one solution requires less time than another. Solution A may perform some components of the task faster than Solution B, while Solution B performs other components of the task faster than Solution A. Often we must analyze the solutions in the light of a particular application. For example, the determination, for a given application, of the *most appropriate* implementation of the ADT table very much depends on the frequencies with which the application is to perform the operations.

Throughout the course of the analysis, we should always keep in mind that *we are interested in only significant differences in efficiency*. To get a better idea of what we mean by *significant differences,* let us consider an example. Recall that in Chapter 6 we introduced the ADT ordered list and presented two implementations. The sequential implementation stored the items in an array (see Figure 6–5), whereas the linked implementation stored the items in a linked list (see Figure 6–6). One ordered list operation is `Retrieve (L, i)`, which retrieves the value of the item at the ith position in the list L. There is a potentially significant difference in the efficiency with which the two implementations support this operation. The sequential implementation can *directly access* the ith item since it is stored in

```
L.Items[i];
```

However, the linked implementation must traverse the list from its beginning until the ith node is reached.

What makes this a significant difference? Notice that as the size of the list

402

CHAPTER 9
THE ADT
TABLE:
LINEAR AND
NONLINEAR
IMPLEMEN-
TATIONS

grows, the linked implementation requires potentially *more and more time,* since the desired position can be farther and farther away from the beginning of the list. In contrast, regardless of how large the list is, the sequential implementation always requires the same **constant** amount of time. Thus, no matter what one's notion of a *significant difference in the amount of time required* is, this difference can be realized if the list is large enough.

In the above example, observe that there is only the *potential* for the two implementations to be significantly different. If the ordered list never has more than ten elements, for example, then the difference in the implementation is not significant at all. In general, if the maximum size for a given problem is small, then the time requirements of any two solutions for that problem are not likely to be significantly different. If you know that your problem size is always going to be small, *don't overanalyze*. In this case you should go for simplicity: Select the algorithm that is easier to code and understand.

In summary, the type of analysis that we are about to perform on the various implementations of the ADT table is consistent with our philosophy of what you should be concerned with. It focuses only on gross differences in efficiency and does not reward coding tricks that save milliseconds. This type of analysis is compatible with the discussion of a program's cost we presented in Chapter 1. If a method of solution is found to be significantly better than others, it should be selected—unless the maximum problem size is known to be quite small. Any finer differences in efficiency are likely to interact with coding issues, which we feel should not interfere with the development of your programming style. In Chapter 13 we will introduce mathematical methods for quantifying what is meant by "significant" differences in the efficiencies of algorithms.

LINEAR STRUCTURES: IMPLEMENTING THE ADT TABLE WITH LISTS OF ITEMS

Linear implementation is a generic term that covers both sequential and linked list-based implementations. This type of implementation resembles in structure the table of cities illustrated in the first section of the chapter. A linear implementation represents the items one after another in the data structure and thus mirrors the flat, list-like appearance of our table of cities.

Linear implementations are less sophisticated than the **tree implementations** presented later in this chapter, but nevertheless they are appropriate for many applications. Because linear implementations are easier to understand conceptually, they are appropriate for tables that will contain only a small number of items. In this case efficiency is not as great a concern as simplicity and clarity.

Even when a table is large, a linear implementation may still be appropriate. Whether or not this is the case depends upon the mix of operations required by the given application. As a first step in the examination of this issue, we shall propose four different linear implementations. Following this we shall study several application scenarios; for each, we shall analyze the effectiveness of the linear implementations. The analysis of the last two scenarios will lead us to the development of a nonlinear implementation—the **binary search tree**.

The linear implementations fall into four categories:

Unsorted–sequential

Unsorted–linked

Sorted–sequential (sorted by search key)

Sorted–linked (sorted by search key)

403

Linear Struc-
tures: Imple-
menting the
ADT Table with
Lists of Items

Whether sorted or unsorted, the sequential and linked implementations have the basic structures shown in Figure 9–1.

(a)

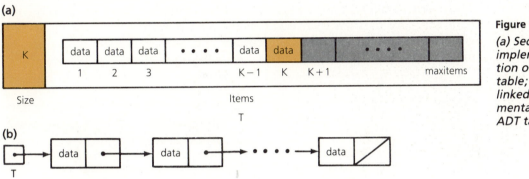

Size   Items

T

(b)

T

Figure 9–1

*(a) Sequential
implementa-
tion of ADT
table; (b)
linked imple-
mentation of
ADT table*

Sequential Implementation: A table *T* is a record with fields

> *Size*: an integer indicating the number of items currently in the table

> *Items*: an array *[1..maxitems]* of *itemtype* holding the items of the table

Linked Implementation: A table *T* is a pointer to the first node on a linked list. (Note that each node on the list contains data fields and a pointer to the next node.)

The unsorted implementations store the items in no particular order—a new item can be inserted into any convenient location. The sorted implementations must insert a new item into its proper position as determined by the value of its search key. You should review the techniques for inserting into and deleting from a sorted linked list, which were first presented in Chapter 3. As we shall see, the unsorted and sorted implementations have their relative advantages and disadvantages.

Scenario A: Insert and Traverse in No Particular Order

Consider an application where the predominant tasks are to insert a new item into a table and print out a report of the items currently present. We do not care how that report of items is organized; for example, we do not care if it is sorted.

404

CHAPTER 9
THE ADT
TABLE:
LINEAR AND
NONLINEAR
IMPLEMEN-
TATIONS

If the application needs to perform any of the operations *Retrieve*, *Delete*, or *Traverse* in sorted order, it does so infrequently enough that these operations should not influence our choice of an implementation.

For this application there is no advantage to be gained from maintaining the items in a sorted order. In fact, by not bothering to maintain a sorted order, the *Insert* operation can be performed very efficiently. Under either the sequential or linked unsorted implementation, a new item may be inserted into any convenient location. Under the sequential implementation, it is convenient to insert a new item at the end of the used portion of the array—that is, at location *Items[Size + 1]*. Under the linked implementation, it is convenient to insert a new item at the beginning of the linked list—that is, have *T* point to the new item and have the new item point to the item previously pointed to by *T*. In either case, the *Insert* operation requires only a **constant** amount of time—no matter how big the table gets, a new item can be inserted very quickly.

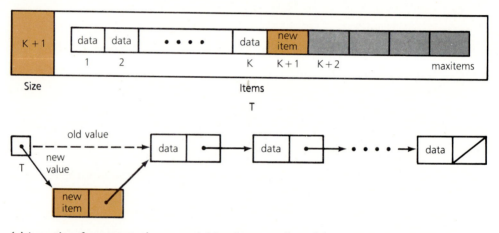

Figure 9–2 *(a) Insertion for unsorted-sequential implementation; (b) insertion for unsorted-linked implementation*

As for whether the sequential or linked implementation should be chosen, there's really only one significant issue given this particular mix of operations. As we have seen with the other ADT's, the dynamic nature of linked lists makes it appropriate if we do not have a good estimate of the maximum possible size of the table. In other situations, the choice is mostly a matter of style. The space requirements of the sequential implementation are slightly less than for the linked implementation (because there is no explicit pointer stored), but in most situations the difference is unlikely to be significant.

Scenario B: Traverse in Sorted Order

It is perhaps most common for an application to have to traverse a table in order sorted by the items' search keys. Let us begin with an application where such a traversal is the predominant operation, and *Insert* and *Delete* operations are performed only infrequently. The following simple library catalogue system is such an application. A program is to be written to keep a computerized catalogue of the books currently in a library's collection. The most frequently required task is, by far, the printing for a patron of the current catalogue. In order for the catalogue to be of greatest use to the patron, it should be printed in order sorted by the books' titles. By comparison to this sorted *Traverse* operation, updates to the catalogue (for example, *Insert* and *Delete* operations) are required very infrequently.

This application obviously requires that we maintain the table sorted by title (the search key). The question thus becomes, should we use a sorted-sequential or sorted-linked implementation? This question arises quite frequently. In general, there are three issues to consider:

1. Do we require the dynamic nature of linked lists?
2. How quickly can we locate an item with a given value in its search key?
3. How quickly can we insert and delete a given item?

For the library problem under consideration, since insertions and deletions are rare (and there is no mention of a *Retrieve* operation), the second and third issues are not of great importance. If we do not have a good idea of the maximum number of books that can be in the library, then the linked implementation is necessitated.

What if we do know the maximum number of books that can be in the library? For this mix of operations (many sorted traversals, very few insertions and deletions), the two implementations do not differ significantly in their efficiencies, since the amount of time required to traverse the table under the two implementations is roughly the same.

Even though the *Insert* and *Delete* operations are performed infrequently in this scenario, it is instructive to analyze briefly how efficiently the two implementations support these operations. As we shall see, the amount of time required to insert or delete under the sorted-sequential and sorted-linked implementations is also roughly the same. In fact, neither implementation supports these operations as well as we might wish.

Let us then consider how to perform the *Insert* and *Delete* operations under the two sorted implementations. To insert into the table an item with value X in its search key, we must first find the location in the sorted order at which this item belongs. Similarly, to delete from the table an item with value X in its search key, we must first locate the item. This first step of both the *Insert* and *Delete* operations is accomplished far more efficiently under the sequential implementation than it is under the linked. Under the sequential implementation, we can—in the case of insertion—use a binary search to determine where the new item X belongs and—in the case of deletion—where the item to be deleted is located. On the other hand, under a linked implementation, we must traverse the list from its beginning until the appropriate location on the list is encountered. (Question: Why couldn't we use the binary search on the linked implementation? This is an important question that we shall address shortly.) The binary search performs this step in *significantly* less time than the time required under the linked implementation to traverse the list. (Question: How much less time?)

406

CHAPTER 9
THE ADT
TABLE:
LINEAR AND
NONLINEAR
IMPLEMEN-
TATIONS

Thus, because of its ability to perform a binary search, the sequential implementation is superior with respect to the first step of *Insert* and *Delete*. However, as you may have guessed, the linked implementation is going to be better for the second step. Once the appropriate position is located, the *Insert* operation must insert the new item into this position, and the *Delete* operation must remove the item from this position. Under the sequential implementation, *Insert* must shift array items to make room for the new item, while *Delete* must shift array items to fill in the gap created when the item is removed. In the worst case, this would require that every array item be shifted (see Figure 9–3). On the other hand, under the linked implementation, this second step can always be accomplished by changing a couple of pointers.

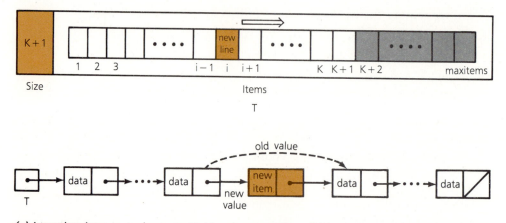

Figure 9–3 *(a) Insertion into sorted-sequential implementation; (b) insertion into sorted-linked implementation*

Taking the two steps of *Insert* and *Delete* together, we shall say that the two implementations require roughly the same amount of time. In fact, it is possible to do quite a bit better than either of these implementations. If the *Insert* and *Delete* operations had to be performed more often than they do in the application under study and, if the table were large, we would not be satisfied with either the sequential or linked implementation. What would we do? This situation is one of the motivations for a binary search tree, which is developed in the following sections.

To summarize, we have discovered that the sequential and linked implementations are of roughly the same efficiency for the mix of operations conjectured in this scenario (predominant operation is *Traverse* in sorted order). The choice is thus mostly one of personal taste, unless the lack of a good estimate of the maximum size of the table mandates that a linked implementation be selected because of its dynamic nature.

Scenario C: Traverse in Sorted Order and Retrieve

The librarian from the previous scenario has realized that very frequently a patron wants information about a particular title rather than the entire catalogue. Therefore, to the environment of Scenario B (frequent sorted *Traverse* operations, rare *Insert* and *Delete* operations), we add frequent *Retrieve* operations. The addition of the *Retrieve* operation causes us to seek a table implementation that allows us to search efficiently for an item with a specified value in its search key.

Let us begin this discussion by examining two questions that were posed in the previous discussion:

1. Why can't we perform a binary search under a linear linked implementation?
2. How much more efficient is a binary search than the *traverse from the beginning* solution forced by the linear linked solution?

Why can't we perform a binary search under a linked implementation? Consider the very first step of the binary search algorithm:

```
look at the "middle" item in the table
```

If the items are in an array *Items[1..N]*, then this middle item is at location *N* **DIV** *2* and can be directly accessed. On the other hand, if the items are in a linked list, how can we possibly get to the middle item on the list? The only way that comes to mind (for now) is to traverse the list from the beginning until we have visited *N* **DIV** *2* items. But, as we shall see shortly when we answer the second question, the time required to do just this *first step* will often be more than the time required to perform the *entire* binary search algorithm on an array. Further, we would have the same problem of finding the "middle" element at each recursive step.

It is thus not feasible to perform a binary search under the linked implementation. This is an extremely significant observation. A binary search requires *considerably* less time than an algorithm that may have to inspect every item in the table.

To fully appreciate the significance of a binary search, we must be more precise about what *considerably* less time means, which brings us to the second question. As we have indicated, without the ability to perform a binary search, every item in the table may have to be inspected in order to locate an item with a particular value in its search key (or to determine that such an item is not present). In other words, if a table has size N, then up to N items will have to be inspected. How much better can we do with a binary search? We can informally derive the fact that the algorithm, at worst, must inspect approximately $\log_2 N$ items (recall that $\log_2 N$ is the logarithm, base 2, of N). Now $\log_2 N$ may at first sound like a very strange quantity, but as you shall see, it arises quite often in the analysis of algorithms.

Think about how binary search looks for the value X. It repeatedly splits the table in half, determines which half the value X must be in (if it is indeed present), and discards the other half. Thus, we can view the binary search algorithm as searching tables of successively smaller sizes—the size of a table is approximately one-half the size of the table previously searched.

Step 1: Inspect the middle item of a table of size N.

Step 2: Inspect the middle item of a table of size $\dfrac{N}{2}$.

408

CHAPTER 9
THE ADT
TABLE:
LINEAR AND
NONLINEAR
IMPLEMEN-
TATIONS

Step 3: Inspect the middle item of a table of size $\dfrac{N}{2^2}$.

$$\vdots$$

Step i: Inspect the middle item of a table of size $\dfrac{N}{2^{i-1}}$.

How many items are inspected by the binary search algorithm? Well, in the worst case, the search will terminate on a table of size 1. It will thus terminate by Step k, where k is large enough so that

$$\frac{N}{2^{k-1}} = 1$$

But this says that

$$2^{k-1} = N$$

which, by the definition of logarithms, is true when

$$k - 1 = \log_2 N$$

Thus, in the worst case, the binary search requires that about $\log_2 N$ items be inspected to search a table of size N. How much better is $\log_2 N$ than N? It's a lot better! For example, $\log_2 1024 = 10$ and $\log_2 1{,}048{,}576 = 20$. For large tables, the binary search has an enormous advantage.

What impact will the above discussion have on our implementation decisions for Scenario C? Since `Retrieve` is one of the predominant operations, unless we know that the library's catalogue will be quite small, we shall insist on an implementation under which a binary search can be performed. As we have just seen, this eliminates the linear-linked implementation and leaves us with only the sorted-sequential. This is fine if we have a good estimate on the maximum size of the table. Unfortunately we often do not have a good estimate, and thus we shall require the dynamic nature of the linked implementation.

We therefore find ourselves in what seems to be an irreconcilable position. Our requirement that binary search be used mandates a sequential implementation, yet we suspect that most applications will require the dynamic storage allocation available only to the linked implementation. A satisfactory solution requires that we develop a new type of implementation. We shall for this problem reject the linear implementations and, in the following sections, introduce the binary search tree. This nonlinear implementation is the solution to our dilemma. It is a linked implementation on which we can perform a binary search-like algorithm. Before presenting this important structure, however, we have one more scenario to discuss. This scenario, which conjectures frequent `Insert` and `Delete` operations, will be further motivation for the binary search tree, as it too will find the linear implementations to be unsatisfactory.

Scenario D: Traverse in Sorted Order, Insert, and Delete

Scenario B introduced the library catalogue problem. In that scenario the predominant operation was *Traverse* in sorted order, with occasional *Insert* and *Delete* operations. The linear implementations were found to be satisfactory for this mix of operations. We obtained Scenario C by adding frequent *Retrieve* operations and discovered that the linear implementations were no longer adequate. If, instead of adding to Scenario B the *Retrieve* operation, we conjecture that insertions and deletions must be performed frequently, we will reach the same conclusion.

Recall that in Scenario B we broke down the *Insert* and *Delete* operations into two steps:

Step 1: Find the appropriate position in the table.

Step 2: Insert into (or delete from) this position.

If the table is implemented sequentially, a binary search can perform the first step for both operations. The discussion of binary search in Scenario C implies that, with respect to Step 1 of *Insert* or *Delete*, the sequential implementation is vastly superior to the linked implementation. On the other hand, the discussion in Scenario B of Step 2 resulted in the opposite conclusion. Under the sequential implementation, all the items in the table may have to be shifted to make room for the new item or to fill the gap created by the removed item. Under the linked implementation, Step 2 requires only that the values of at most two pointers be changed.

Once again we find ourselves in what seems to be an irreconcilable position. If the table is large, we very much desire the speed of a binary search in performing Step 1 and thus require the sequential implementation. On the other hand, we just as strongly desire to avoid the necessity of shifting the array elements in Step 2 and thus require the linked implementation. Once again, what we really need is a linked structure on which we can perform a binary search.

We have presented scenarios in which the linear table implementations are adequate and scenarios in which they are not. Those latter situations give us the motivation to develop a different type of implementation for a table, one that combines the best features of the linear implementations. The binary search tree is such an implementation, and its development is the topic of much of the remainder of this chapter.

For purposes of illustration we use the following definition module to specify the ADT operations.

```
DEFINITION MODULE Tables;
(* ************************************************************

   ADT TABLE

   The following hidden type is declared:

     Table
```

410

CHAPTER 9
THE ADT
TABLE:
LINEAR AND
NONLINEAR
IMPLEMEN-
TATIONS

The following operations are supported:

```
        Create, Insert, Delete, Retrieve, Traverse (sorted)
        ********************************************************* *)

(* Table item and key types -- it is assumed that the
    item type contains a field named key of type keytype *)
FROM ADTitem IMPORT

    itemtype, keytype;

EXPORT QUALIFIED

    Table, Create, Insert, Delete, Retrieve, Traverse;

TYPE

    Table;

    (* required for procedure Traverse *)
    ProcType = PROCEDURE (Table, itemtype);

(* ------------------------------------------------------------
    Create:  Create an empty table T.
    ------------------------------------------------------------ *)
PROCEDURE Create(VAR T : Table);

(* ------------------------------------------------------------
    Insert:  Insert newitem into table T.  The Boolean flag
    success is returned TRUE if the Insert was successful, and
    FALSE otherwise (e.g., because of memory limitations).  In
    the event of an unsuccessful Insert, the table is unchanged.

    ASSUMPTION:  Table T has been created.
    ------------------------------------------------------------ *)
PROCEDURE Insert(VAR T : Table; newitem : itemtype;
                VAR success : BOOLEAN);

(* ------------------------------------------------------------
    Delete:  Delete from table T the item with search key
    keyval.  The operation fails if there is no such item.  The
    Boolean flag success indicates whether the operation succeeded.
    In the event of an unsuccessful Delete, the table is unchanged.

    ASSUMPTION:  Table T has been created.
    ------------------------------------------------------------ *)
PROCEDURE Delete(VAR T : Table; keyval : keytype;
                VAR success : BOOLEAN);
```

```
(* ------------------------------------------------------------
    Retrieve:  Retrieve into getitem the item from table T
    with search key keyval.  The operation fails if there is
    no such item.  The flag success indicates whether the
    operation succeeded.

    ASSUMPTION:  Table T has been created.
    ---------------------------------------------------------- *)
PROCEDURE Retrieve(T : Table; keyval : keytype;
                   VAR getitem: itemtype;
                   VAR success : BOOLEAN);


(* ------------------------------------------------------------
    Traverse:  Traverse table T in sorted order, calling
    procedure Visit for each item.

    Procedure Visit exists outside of the ADT implementation.

    WARNING: Visit may call only "read only" ADT operations
    on table T (e.g., Retrieve).

    ASSUMPTION:  Table T has been created.
    ---------------------------------------------------------- *)
PROCEDURE Traverse(T : Table; Visit : ProcType);

END Tables.
```

Note that the user's specification for the operation *Traverse* must be chosen to reflect its actual requirements, since this specification can impact the implementation of *Traverse* and other ADT operations. In particular, the implementor should know which, if any, table operations *Visit* can call on the table being traversed. Consider the following cases:

Case 1: *Visit* may call no table operations. In this case the table being traversed need not be a parameter to *Visit*, and no additional implementation considerations arise (other than the usual issue of in what order *Traverse* must visit the table items).

Case 2: *Visit* may call only "read only" table operations (for example, *Retrieve*). In this case, the table being traversed must be a parameter to *Visit*, but no additional implementation considerations arise.

Case 3: *Visit* may call *value-modifying* table operations (for example, *Replace*). In this case, the table being traversed must be a parameter to *Visit*, and further, the value-modifying operation or operations must be implemented in a way that ensures that they do not alter the *structure* of the ADT implementation. (See Case 4.) Note that this restriction rules out implementing *Replace* in terms of the *Delete* and *Insert* operations.

Case 4: *Visit* may call *structure-modifying* table operations (for example, *Insert* and *Delete*). Since such operations can have serious consequences for the correctness of the *Traverse* procedure (for example, delete the node that is cur-

412

CHAPTER 9
THE ADT
TABLE:
LINEAR AND
NONLINEAR
IMPLEMEN-
TATIONS

rently being visited), we dissallow such calls. If the user requires general structure-modifying capabilities, these should be defined outside of the context of a general *Traverse* operation as special ADT operations. (Note that one possible implementation of such an ADT operation would be to make a copy of the entire implementation structure and perform the traversal on the copy, while making any modifications to the original.)

The above definition module reflects Case 2.

We now present a Modula-2 version of the sorted-sequential implementation. The other linear implementations are left as an exercise (Exercise 9.4).

```
IMPLEMENTATION MODULE Tables;
(* ************************************************************
    ADT TABLE - Sorted Sequential Implementation

    The following table operations are supported:

        Create, Insert, Delete, Retrieve, Traverse (sorted)

    ASSUMPTION:  At any time a table contains at most one item
    with a given search key.  See Exercise 9.1.

    This is a sorted sequential implementation of a table.
    Function Locate is defined to use a binary search to
    determine where in the sorted list a search key belongs.

    Type Table is a pointer to a record that is created
    dynamically with a call to procedure NEW.  This
    indirection allows type Table to be a hidden type.
    ************************************************************ *)

(* memory management procedure NEW *)
FROM Storage IMPORT

    ALLOCATE;

(* Table item and key types -- it is assumed that the
    item type contains a field named key of type keytype *)
FROM ADTitem IMPORT

    itemtype, keytype;

(* fixed maximum size inferred from User's Documentation File *)
CONST

    maxtable = 20;

TYPE
```

413
Linear Struc-
tures: Imple-
menting the
ADT Table with
Lists of Items

```
        (* Table structure *)
     Tbody = RECORD
                Items : ARRAY [1..maxtable] OF itemtype;
                Last : [0..maxtable];
             END;


     Table = POINTER TO Tbody;

  (* ---------------------------------------------------------
     Locate:  Find where in the sorted list T search key
     keyval belongs.

     This is a recursive binary search.
     --------------------------------------------------------- *)
  PROCEDURE Locate(T : Table ; keyval : keytype) : INTEGER;

     (* do the recursive binary search *)
     PROCEDURE dosearch(first, last : INTEGER) : INTEGER;

     VAR

        mid : INTEGER;

     BEGIN

        IF (first > last) THEN
           RETURN(first);

        ELSE
           mid := (first + last) DIV 2;
           IF (T^.Items[mid].key = keyval) THEN
              RETURN(mid);
           ELSIF (T^.Items[mid].key > keyval) THEN
              RETURN(dosearch(first, mid-1));
           ELSE
              RETURN(dosearch(mid+1, last));
           END;

        END;

     END dosearch;

  BEGIN  (* body of function Locate *)

     RETURN (dosearch(1, T^.Last));

  END Locate;
```

414
CHAPTER 9
THE ADT
TABLE:
LINEAR AND
NONLINEAR
IMPLEMEN-
TATIONS

```
(* -------------------------------------------------------------
    Create:  Create an empty table T.
   ------------------------------------------------------------- *)
PROCEDURE Create(VAR T : Table);

BEGIN

    NEW(T);
    T^.Last := 0;

END Create;


(* -------------------------------------------------------------
    Insert:  Insert newitem into table T.  The Boolean flag
    success is returned TRUE if the Insert was successful, and
    FALSE otherwise (e.g., because of memory limitations).  In
    the event of an unsuccessful Insert, the table is unchanged.

    ASSUMPTION:  Table T has been created.

    CALLS:  Locate
   ------------------------------------------------------------- *)
PROCEDURE Insert(VAR T : Table; newitem : itemtype;
                 VAR success : BOOLEAN);

VAR

    i, loc : CARDINAL;

BEGIN

    IF (T^.Last = maxtable) THEN
        success := FALSE;
    ELSE
        (* locate the position where keyval belongs *)
        loc := Locate(T, newitem.key);

        (* shift up to make room for the new item *)
        FOR i := T^.Last TO loc BY -1 DO
            T^.Items[i+1] := T^.Items[i];
        END;

        T^.Items[loc] := newitem;
        INC(T^.Last);
        success := TRUE;
    END;

END Insert;
```

```
(* ------------------------------------------------------------
   Delete:   Delete from table T the item with search key
   keyval.   The operation fails if there is no such item.
   The Boolean flag success indicates whether the operation
   succeeded. In the event of an unsuccessful Delete, the
   table is unchanged.

   ASSUMPTION:   Table T has been created.

   CALLS:   Locate
   ------------------------------------------------------------ *)
PROCEDURE Delete(VAR T : Table; keyval : keytype;
                 VAR success : BOOLEAN);

VAR

    i, loc : CARDINAL;

BEGIN

    (* locate the position where keyval belongs *)
    loc := Locate(T, keyval);

    (* delete if present *)
    IF (loc > T^.Last) THEN
       success := FALSE;

    ELSIF (T^.Items[loc].key # keyval) THEN
       success := FALSE

    ELSE

       (* delete the item *)

       (* shift down to fill the gap *)
       FOR i := loc TO T^.Last-1 DO
          T^.Items[i] := T^.Items[i+1];
       END;

       DEC(T^.Last);
       success := TRUE;
    END;

END Delete;

(* ------------------------------------------------------------
   Retrieve:   Retrieve into getitem the item from table T
   with search key keyval.   The operation fails if there is
```

416
CHAPTER 9
THE ADT
TABLE:
LINEAR AND
NONLINEAR
IMPLEMEN-
TATIONS

no such item.   The flag success indicates whether the
operation succeeded.

ASSUMPTION: Table T has been created.

CALLS: Locate
-- *)
PROCEDURE Retrieve(T : Table; keyval : keytype;
                        VAR getitem: itemtype;
                        VAR success : BOOLEAN);

VAR

    loc : CARDINAL;

BEGIN

    (* locate the item *)
    loc := Locate(T, keyval);

    (* retrieve if present *)
    IF (loc > T^.Last) THEN
        success := FALSE;
    ELSIF (keyval # T^.Items[loc].key) THEN
        success := FALSE;
    ELSE
        getitem := T^.Items[loc];
        success := TRUE;
    END;

END Retrieve;

(* --
    Traverse: Traverse table T in sorted order, calling
    procedure Visit for each item.

    Procedure Visit exists outside of the ADT implementation.

    WARNING: Visit may call only "read only" ADT operations
    on table T (e.g., Retrieve).

    ASSUMPTION: Table T has been created.
    -- *)
PROCEDURE Traverse(T : Table; Visit : ProcType);

VAR

    i : CARDINAL;

```
BEGIN

    FOR i := 1 TO T^.Last DO
        Visit(T, T^.Items[i]);
    END;

END Traverse;

END Tables.
```

BINARY TREES

The binary search tree supports all the table operations in a very efficient manner. It is a data structure that provides the best features of the sequential and linked table implementations presented in the previous section. Because it is a linked data structure, the binary search tree can take advantage of dynamic storage allocation. In addition, the insertion and deletion of data items can be accomplished through pointer changes and thus do not require the shifting of data. Data items can be located with a binary search-like algorithm, a technique we have previously been able to apply only to a sequential implementation.

Before developing the binary search tree implementation, we must briefly discuss the more general concept of binary trees. Trees are used to represent relationships between objects. In previous chapters we have informally used tree diagrams to represent the relationships between the calls of a recursive algorithm. Recall, for example, the tree used in Chapter 4 for the *Rabbit* algorithm (see Figure 4–11). Each call to *Rabbit* is represented by a **node** in the tree. The **directed edges** in the tree represent information about which subproblems make which recursive calls. For example, the directed edges from *Rabbit(7)* to *Rabbit(6)* and *Rabbit(5)* indicate that subproblem *Rabbit(7)* makes calls to *Rabbit(6)* and *Rabbit(5)*.

All trees are **hierarchical** in nature. Intuitively, this means that there is a "parent–child" relationship between the nodes in the tree (see Figure 9–4). If there is an edge from node N to node M, we say that N is the **parent** of M and that M is a **child** of N. In the tree in Figure 9–4, nodes B and C are children of node A. Children of the same parent (for example, B and C) are called **siblings.** Each node in a tree has at most one parent, and there is exactly one node, called the **root** of the tree, which has no parent (node A is the root of the tree in Figure 9–4). A node that has no children is called a **leaf** of the tree. The leaves of the tree in Figure 9–4 are C, D, E, and F.

We generalize the parent–child relationship between the nodes to the relationships **ancestor of** and **descendant of**. In Figure 9–4, A is an ancestor of D (and thus D is a descendant of A). Notice that not all nodes are related by the ancestor (or descendant) relationship—C and B, for instance, are not so related. The root of any tree, however, is an ancestor of every node in that tree.

One kind of application for which trees are useful is the representation of information which itself is hierarchical in nature. Examples of this include orga-

418

CHAPTER 9
THE ADT
TABLE:
LINEAR AND
NONLINEAR
IMPLEMEN-
TATIONS

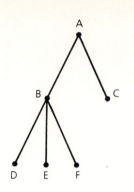

Figure 9–4

A tree

nization charts and family trees (see Figure 9–5). It may be disconcerting that the nodes in the family tree that represent person X's *parents* are the *children* of the node which represents person X! Similarly, the nodes in the family tree that represent X's *ancestors* are the *descendants* of X's node. It's no wonder that computer scientists often seem to be confused by reality.

Figure 9–5

*(a) An organi-
zation chart;
(b) a family
tree*

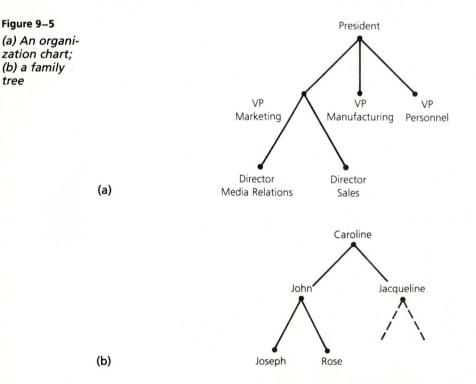

For the remainder of this chapter we shall be interested in **binary trees.** A binary tree is a tree in which each node has *no more than two children.* Thus, the trees in Figures 4–11 and 9–5(b) are binary; the trees in Figures 9–4 and 9–5(a) are not. Trees that are not binary trees are called **general trees** and will be discussed briefly in Exercise 9.18. A formal, recursive definition of a binary tree follows:

A set T of elements (called nodes) is a **binary tree** if either:

(1) T is empty, or

(2) T is partitioned into three disjoint sets:

    (a) a single element R, called the **root**

    (b) two sets that are binary trees, called left and right **subtrees** of R

In our presentation it will be useful to have the following intuitive restatement of the definition. You should convince yourself that the formal definition agrees with the intuitive one.

T is a **binary tree** if either:

    (1) T has no nodes, or

    (2) T is of the form

$$n$$

$$T_L \quad T_R$$

where n is a node and T_L and T_R are both binary trees.

If T is the binary tree

$$n$$

$$T_L \quad T_R$$

we say that n is the **root** of T, that binary tree T_L is the **left subtree** of T, and that binary tree T_R is the **right subtree** of T (we also say that T_L is the left subtree of node n and that T_R is the right subtree of node n). If T_L is not empty, its root is the **left child** of n, and if T_R is not empty, its root is the **right child** of n. Notice that if both subtrees of a node are empty, then that node is a **leaf**. (All this terminology is summarized in a Key Concepts box on page 430.)

Implementations

We now discuss how a binary tree can be implemented using the constructs of Modula-2. For example, suppose that we have the binary tree of names in Figure 9–6.

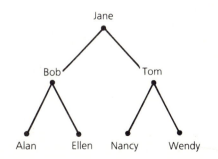

Figure 9–6

A binary tree of names

420

CHAPTER 9
THE ADT
TABLE:
LINEAR AND
NONLINEAR
IMPLEMEN-
TATIONS

Notice that each node in the tree contains a name and is linked to at most two other nodes. We can thus represent each node in Modula-2 with the following definitions.

```
TYPE

    string = ARRAY [0..maxsize-1] OF CHAR;


    ptr = POINTER TO node;
    node = RECORD
               name : string;
               Lchild,            (* pointer to the left child *)
               Rchild : ptr;  (* pointer to the right child *)
           END;
```

Figure 9–7

*(a) One node;
(b) tree
structure
with external
pointer*

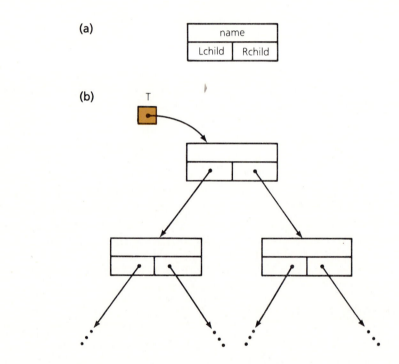

Just as a linked list must have an external pointer to its head, a tree must have an external pointer to its root. If the tree is empty, this external pointer will have the value **NIL**.

Recall from the recursive definition of a binary tree that every nonempty binary tree consists of a left subtree and a right subtree, each of which is a binary tree. Under our representation, if T points to the root R of a binary tree, then $T^\wedge.Lchild$ points to the root of the left subtree of R (which itself is a binary tree), and $T^\wedge.Rchild$ points to the root of the right subtree of R (which itself is a binary tree). Many of our recursive Modula-2 procedures will be based on this observation.

Traversals

The definitions of a binary tree make apparent its recursive nature. This recursive nature will be reflected in many of our algorithms and future definitions. As an illustration, let us now construct algorithms for traversing a binary tree. Such an algorithm is useful in many contexts, including that of the binary search tree implementation of the ADT table.

Suppose that we wish to traverse the binary tree T—that is, visit each node in T. For simplicity, we assume here that to visit a node means to print out its data. With the recursive definition of a binary tree in mind, we shall construct a recursive solution as follows. According to the definition, the tree T is either empty or is of the form

$$n$$
$$T_L \quad T_R$$

If T is empty, then the traversal algorithm takes no action—this is the degenerate case. If T is not empty, then the traversal algorithm must perform three tasks: It must print the data in the root n, and it must traverse the subtrees T_L and T_R, each of which is a binary tree smaller than T.

The general form of the recursive traversal algorithm is thus:

```
Traverse (T)
(* Traverse the binary tree T. *)

   IF (T is not empty) THEN
      Traverse (left subtree of T)
      Traverse (right subtree of T)
   END
```

This algorithm is not quite complete, however. What's missing is the instruction to print out the data in the nodes. When traversing any subtree T of the form

$$n$$
$$T_L \quad T_R$$

the algorithm has three choices of when to process the node n. It can process n before it traverses either of T's subtrees, it can process n after it has traversed T's left subtree, T_L, but before it traverses its right subtree T_R, or it can process n after it has traversed both of T's subtrees. These traversals are called **preorder**, **inorder**, and **postorder**, respectively.

The three tree traversals are presented below, and we show what they would do to the tree of integers in Figure 9–8.

422
CHAPTER 9
THE ADT
TABLE:
LINEAR AND
NONLINEAR
IMPLEMEN-
TATIONS

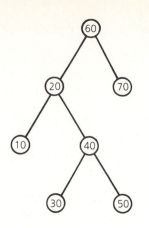

Figure 9–8

Binary tree of integers

```
Preorder(T)
(* Traverse the binary tree T in preorder.
   Visit a node means print out its data. *)

   IF (T is not empty) THEN
      print the data in the root of T
      Preorder(left subtree of T)
      Preorder(right subtree of T)
   END
```

The result of the preorder traversal on the tree in Figure 9–8 is: 60, 20, 10, 40, 30, 50, 70.

```
Inorder(T)
(* Traverse the binary tree T in inorder.
   Visit a node means print out its data. *)

   IF (T is not empty) THEN
      Inorder(left subtree of T)
      print the data in the root of T
      Inorder(right subtree of T)
   END
```

The result of the inorder traversal on the tree in Figure 9–8 is: 10, 20, 30, 40, 50, 60, 70.

```
Postorder(T)
(* Traverse the binary tree T in postorder.
   Visit a node means print out its data. *)

   IF (T is not empty) THEN
      Postorder(left subtree of T)
      Postorder(right subtree of T)
      print the data in the root of T
   END
```

The result of the postorder traversal on the tree in Figure 9–8 is: 10, 30, 50, 40, 20, 70, 60.

Each of these traversals can be directly implemented as a recursive Modula-2 procedure. For example, if a binary tree is represented by the linked implementation described in the previous section, the inorder traversal can be written in Modula-2 as follows.

```
PROCEDURE Inorder(T : ptr);
(* Traverse the binary tree T in inorder.
   Visit a node means print out its data. *)

BEGIN

   IF (T # NIL) THEN
      Inorder(T^.Lchild);
      WriteString(T^.name);
      Inorder(T^.Rchild);
   END;

END Inorder;
```

We shall encounter several additional recursive tree algorithms when we develop the binary search tree implementation of the ADT table in the following sections. Before leaving the topic of traversals, however, it will be useful to develop a *nonrecursive* traversal algorithm. One motivation for doing this is that, as we have pointed out, several popular programming languages (for example, FORTRAN 77) do not support recursion, and it will thus be desirable to see how a traversal of a binary tree can be performed in a nonrecursive environment. A second motivation is that our development of a nonrecursive traversal will help to illustrate further the relationship between stacks and recursion that was first discussed in Chapter 7.

To illustrate nonrecursive traversal techniques, we shall develop a nonrecursive inorder traversal for the linked implementation of a binary tree. The conceptually difficult part of the nonrecursive traversal is determining where to go next after a particular node has been visited. We can gain some insight into this problem by studying how the recursive inorder traversal works. In the *Inorder* algorithm below, we have marked the two points from which a recursive call is made.

```
Inorder(T)
(* Traverse the binary tree T in inorder.
   Visit a node means print out its data. *)

   IF (T # NIL) THEN
      Inorder(T^.Lchild)    (* Point A *)
      write(T^.name)
      Inorder(T^.Rchild)    (* Point B *)
   END
```

424

CHAPTER 9
THE ADT
TABLE:
LINEAR AND
NONLINEAR
IMPLEMEN-
TATIONS

In the course of the traversal's execution, the current value of the pointer *T* can be thought of as marking our position in the tree. Each time *Inorder* makes a recursive call (from either point A or B), the effect is to descend the tree. In terms of the implicit recursive stack, a call to *Inorder* causes a pointer to the new current node (that is, the new value of *T*) to be pushed onto the stack. At any point in time the stack contains pointers to the nodes along the path from the tree's root to the current node N, with the pointer to N at the top of the stack and the pointer to the root at the bottom (see Figure 9–9).

Figure 9–9

Traversal using a stack

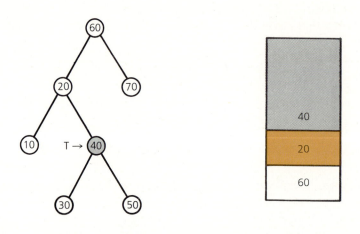

Let us now consider what happens when we return from a recursive call. The effect of the return is to backtrack up the tree from a node M (which is possibly "empty," that is, is indicated by a **NIL** value for *T* at the top of the stack) to its parent N, from which the recursive call to M was made. A pointer to N comes to the top of the stack when, as the return is made from the recursive call, the pointer to M is popped from the stack. What happens next depends on which subtree of N has just been traversed (see Figure 9–10).

Figure 9–10

Traversing left and right subtrees

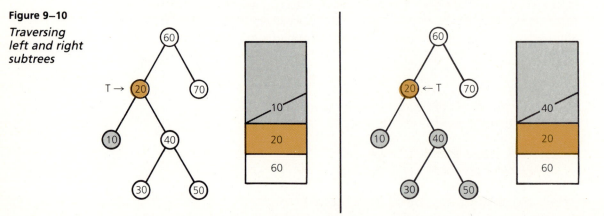

If we have just finished traversing N's left subtree (that is, M is the left child of N and thus the return is made to point A in the *Inorder* procedure), then control is returned to the statement that prints out the data in node N. After the data in N has been printed, a recursive call is made from point B and the right subtree of N is traversed. If, however, we have just traversed N's right subtree (that is , M is the right child of N and thus the return is made to point B), then control is returned to the end of the procedure. As a consequence, another return is made, the pointer to N is popped off the stack, and we backtrack up the tree to N's parent, from where the recursive call to N was made. Notice that in this latter case, the data in N is not printed—it was printed *before* the recursive call to M was made from point B.

We thus see that in the recursive version of the *Inorder* procedure, when a return is made from a recursive call:

1. The implicit recursive stack of pointers is used to find the node N to which the traversal must backtrack.

2. Once the traversal backtracks to node N, it either visits N (for example, prints out its data) or backtracks further up the tree. It visits N if N's left subtree has just been traversed and backtracks if its right subtree has just been traversed. The appropriate action is taken simply as a consequence of the point, A or B, to which control is returned.

We could directly mimic this action with an iterative procedure and an explicit stack, as long as some bookkeeping device keeps track of which subtree of a node has just been traversed. We can, however, use the following observation both to eliminate the need for the bookkeeping device and to speed up the traversal somewhat. Consider the subtree in Figure 9–11. After we have finished

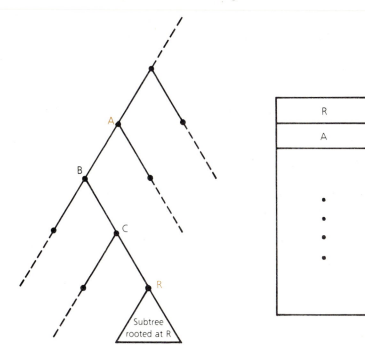

Figure 9–11

Subtree with stack

426

CHAPTER 9
THE ADT
TABLE:
LINEAR AND
NONLINEAR
IMPLEMEN-
TATIONS

traversing the subtree rooted at node R, there is no need for us to return to nodes B and C because the right subtrees of these nodes have already been traversed. We can instead return directly to node A, which is *the nearest ancestor of R whose right subtree has not yet been traversed.*

It is a simple matter to implement this strategy of not returning to a node after its right subtree has been traversed. All that is required is that we place a pointer to node N on the stack only before its *left* subtree is traversed and *not* before its *right* subtree is traversed. Thus, in Figure 9–11, when we are at node R the contents of the stack is A-R (with R on top). Nodes B and C are not on the stack because we are currently traversing their *right* subtrees, while, on the other hand, A is on the stack because we are currently traversing its *left* subtree. When we return from node R, nodes B and C are thus bypassed (we've finished with their right subtrees and do not need to return to these nodes), and we go directly to node A (whose *left* subtree has just been traversed). We then visit A, pop its pointer from the stack, and traverse A's right subtree.

This nonrecursive traversal strategy is captured by the following algorithm.

```
(* initialize *)
p := root
Push (S, p)
done := FALSE

WHILE (NOT done) DO

   IF (p # NIL) THEN

      (* traverse the left subtree *)
      p := p^.Lchild
      Push (S, p)

   (* backtrack from the empty subtree *)
   ELSE

      (* pop the NIL pointer *)
      Pop (S)

      (* visit the node at the top of the stack
         - if the stack is empty then we are done *)
      IF (NOT IsEmpty (S)) THEN
         p := StackTop (S)
         Visit (p)

         (* traverse the right subtree
            of the node just visited *)
         Pop (S)
         p := p^.Rchild
         Push (S, p)
```

```
        ELSE
            done := TRUE
        END
    END

END (* while *)
```

Full and Complete Trees

Binary trees come in many shapes. For example, although the trees in Figure
9–12 all contain the same nodes, their structures are quite different.

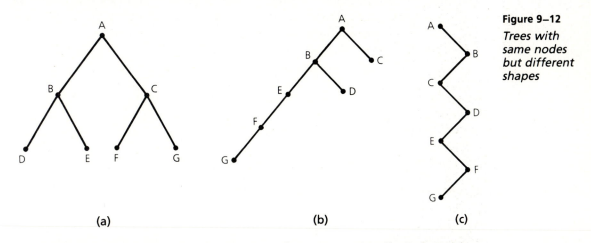

Figure 9–12

Trees with same nodes but different shapes

(a)   (b)   (c)

Although each of these trees has seven nodes, some are "taller" than others.
In the following sections we shall see that, in the context of binary search trees,
a tree's **height** is an extremely important characteristic. Intuitively, the height of
a tree is the distance from its root to its farthest leaf. To formalize this, we first
define the **level** of a node in a tree T as follows:

(1) If n is the root of T, then it is at level 1.
(2) If n is not the root of T, then its level is one greater than the level of
    its parent.

For example, in Figure 9–12(a), node A is at level 1, node C is at level 2, and
node D is at level 3.

The **height** of a tree T can now be defined in terms of the levels of its nodes:

(1) If T is empty, then its height is 0.
(2) If T is not empty, then its height is equal to the maximum level of its
    nodes.

For example, the trees in Figure 9–12(a), (b), and (c) have respective heights
of 3, 5, and 7. We acknowledge that many people's intuitive notion of height
would lead them to say that these trees have heights 2, 4, and 6. Indeed, many

428

CHAPTER 9
THE ADT
TABLE:
LINEAR AND
NONLINEAR
IMPLEMEN-
TATIONS

authors define height to agree with this intuition. We have found, however, that the first definition of height leads to a cleaner statement of many algorithms and properties of trees.

Rather than using the above definition of height based on the levels of a tree's nodes, it will often be convenient to use the following equivalent recursive definition.

(1) If T is empty, its height is 0.

(2) If T is not empty, then it is of the form

$$n$$

$$T_L \quad T_R$$

In this case the height of T is defined to be one greater than the height of its higher subtree; that is,

$$\text{height}(T) = 1 + \max\{\text{height}(T_L), \text{height}(T_R)\}$$

A type of question that we will want to ask when we study binary search trees in the next sections is, given that a binary tree has N nodes, what are the maximum and minimum heights that the tree can have? The answer to the first question is easy. We can maximize the height of a tree with N nodes by giving each internal node (nonleaf) exactly one child (see Figure 9–13). This will result in a tree of height N. Notice that an N-node tree with height N very much resembles a *linear* list.

Figure 9–13

A linear tree

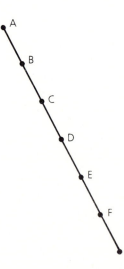

The answer to the second question, concerning the minimum height of a binary tree with N nodes, is a bit more difficult. To answer this question, it is useful to consider the number of nodes that trees with a given height h can have. For example, if $h = 3$, we see that the possible trees include those in Figure 9–14. We thus see that binary trees of height 3 can have between 3 and 7 nodes.

It should also be clear from these diagrams that 3 is the minimum height for a tree with 4, 5, 6, or 7 nodes. Similarly, trees with more than 7 nodes require a height greater than 3.

Figure 9–14
*Trees of
height 3*

To obtain a general answer to our question, we must establish a relationship between the height h of a tree and the maximum number of nodes which that tree can contain. Intuitively, if a tree of a given height h is to have the maximum possible number of nodes, all its leaves should be at level h, and nodes at a level less than h should each have two children.

Such a tree is called a **full** binary tree of height h. When proving properties about full trees (such as how many nodes they have), it will be convenient to use the following recursive definition, which closely reflects the recursive nature of a binary tree. A binary tree T is **full** if:

(1) T is empty, in which case it is a full tree of height 0, or

(2) T is of height h ($h > 0$), and its subtrees are both full trees of height $h - 1$.

Figure 9–15
*Full tree of
height 3*

It should be intuitively clear that a full binary tree of height h contains the maximum possible number of nodes for a binary tree of height h, but we still need to know exactly how many nodes this is. The following theorem and its proof answer this question.

A full binary tree of height h ($h \geq 0$) has $2^h - 1$ nodes.

**THEOREM
9–1**

The proof is by induction on h.

PROOF

Basis: $h = 0$. Then the full binary tree is empty, and it contains $0 = 2^0 - 1$ nodes.

430

CHAPTER 9
THE ADT
TABLE:
LINEAR AND
NONLINEAR
IMPLEMEN-
TATIONS

Inductive Hypothesis: Assume *true* for all k, $0 \leq k < h$. That is, assume for all k ($0 \leq k < h$) that a full binary tree of height k has $2^k - 1$ nodes.

Inductive Conclusion: We must show the statement is true for h ($h > 0$). That is, we must show that a full binary tree of height h has $2^h - 1$ nodes.

If T is a full binary tree of height h (with $h > 0$), then it is of the form

$$n$$

$$T_L \quad T_R$$

where T_L and T_R are full binary trees of height $h - 1$ (from the definition of a full tree). The number of nodes in T is thus

(number of nodes in T_L) + (number of nodes in T_R) + (1 for the root n)

By the inductive hypothesis, T_L and T_R each have $2^{h-1} - 1$ nodes since each is a full binary tree of height $h - 1$. Thus, the number of nodes in T is

$$(2^{h-1} - 1) + (2^{h-1} - 1) + 1 = 2 * (2^{h-1} - 1) + 1$$

$$= 2^h - 1$$

which is what we needed to show.

We have thus established that a full binary tree of height h contains $2^h - 1$ nodes. Although it seems obvious that no binary tree of height h can have more nodes than a full binary tree of height h, this fact should be formally established. We state the fact as a theorem and leave the proof, which closely parallels that of Theorem 9–1, as an exercise.

THEOREM 9–2 The maximum number of nodes that a binary tree of height h can have is $2^h - 1$.

We can now use Theorems 9–1 and 9–2 to answer the question, what is the minimum height of a binary tree that contains some given number N of nodes? The problem is to find the smallest integer h such that $N \leq 2^h - 1$. We claim that this is the minimum height of a binary tree with N nodes. To establish this claim, we make two observations:

1. **No binary tree of height less than h can have N nodes.** By the way h was selected, $N > 2^{(h-1)} - 1$; otherwise $k = (h - 1)$ would be such that $N \leq 2^k - 1$, and thus h would not be the smallest integer with this property. Therefore, Theorem 9–2 implies that there is no tree of height less than h that has N nodes; that is, the full tree of height $h - 1$ does not have enough nodes.

2. **There is a binary tree of height h that has exactly N nodes.** Start with a full tree of height $h - 1$ and add nodes to level h until we have N nodes. Since Theorem 9–1 implies that the full tree of height h has at least N nodes (recall

that h was selected so that $N \leqslant 2^h - 1$), we are assured that N nodes will be reached by the time level h is filled up.

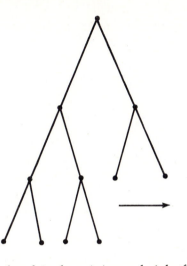

Figure 9–16

Filling in the last level of a tree

We have thus established that h is the minimum height for a tree with N nodes.

Now, how can we express, as a function of N, *the smallest integer h such that $N \leqslant 2^h - 1$*? To approach this question, consider the equivalent problem of finding the smallest integer h such that $(N + 1) \leqslant 2^h$.

If we set $h = \log_2(N + 1)$, it follows from the definition of logarithms that $2^h = (N + 1)$. This h is clearly the smallest *number* such that $(N + 1) \leqslant 2^h$. The only problem is that if $(N + 1)$ is not a power of 2, then $\log_2(N + 1)$ is not an integer. Recall that since h is to be the height of a tree, we want it to be the smallest *integer* such that $(N + 1) \leqslant 2^h$.

If we choose an h smaller than $\log_2(N + 1)$, then clearly $2^h < (N + 1)$; therefore, we cannot round $\log_2(N + 1)$ down to an integer. Thus, if we let h be the next integer larger than $\log_2(N + 1)$ (or $\log_2(N + 1)$ itself if it happens to be an integer), we will have found the smallest integer h such that $(N + 1) \leqslant 2^h$.

To summarize, the smallest integer h such that $(N + 1) \leqslant 2^h$ is $\log_2(N + 1)$ *rounded up*. The standard way of writing X rounded up is $\lceil X \rceil$, which is read the **ceiling of X** (for example, $\lceil 6 \rceil = 6$, $\lceil 6.1 \rceil = 7$, $\lceil 6.8 \rceil = 7$).

Thus, $h = \lceil \log_2(N + 1) \rceil$ is the smallest integer such that $(N + 1) \leqslant 2^h$, or equivalently, it is the smallest integer such that $N \leqslant 2^h - 1$. From our earlier remarks, it follows that this h is the minimum height of a binary tree with N nodes. We have thus established the following theorem.

The minimum height of a binary tree with N nodes is $\lceil \log_2(N + 1) \rceil$.

As we shall see in Chapter 10, the type of tree obtained in Figure 9–16 by filling in level h until we ran out of nodes is important in its own right. This tree is called a **complete tree**. We can informally define a complete tree of height h to be a tree that is full down to level $h - 1$ with level h filled in from left to right. More formally, a binary tree T is a **complete** tree of height h if:

432

CHAPTER 9
THE ADT
TABLE:
LINEAR AND
NONLINEAR
IMPLEMEN-
TATIONS

(1) T is empty, or

(2) the left subtree of T is a full tree of height $h - 1$ and the right subtree of T is a complete tree of height $h - 1$, or

(3) the left subtree of T is a full tree of height $h - 1$ and the right subtree of T is a full tree of height $h - 2$, or

(4) the left subtree of T is a complete tree of height $h - 1$ and the right subtree of T is a full tree of height $h - 2$.

Notice that if a tree is full, it is necessarily complete.

When we discuss binary search trees in the next section, we shall see the desirability of having trees with small heights. Full trees and complete trees with N nodes have heights of $\lceil \log_2(N + 1) \rceil$, which, as we have proved, is the theoretical minimum. The term **balanced tree** is generally applied to any N-node binary tree with height approximately equal to $\log_2 N$. Full and complete trees are balanced in the strictest sense, but there are other types of trees that are also balanced. In general, we will be content with any balanced binary search tree—its height being close to the theoretical minimum for the number of nodes it contains.

KEY CONCEPTS

> *Summary of Binary Tree Terminology*
>
> 1. **Parent of N**   the node directly above node N in the tree
> 2. **Child of N**   a node directly below node N in the tree. We distinguish between N's **left child** and its **right child.**
> 3. **Root**   the only node in the tree with no parent
> 4. **Leaf**   a node with no children
> 5. **Sibling**   two nodes with a common parent
> 6. **Ancestor of N**   a node on the path from the root to N
> 7. **Descendant of N**   a node on a path from N to a leaf
> 8. **Empty tree**   a tree with no nodes
> 9. **Subtree of N**   the left child of N plus its descendants form the **left subtree;** the right child of N plus its descendants form the **right subtree.** If a left or right child is not present, the corresponding subtree is the empty tree.
> 10. **Height**   number of nodes on the longest path from the root to a leaf

NONLINEAR STRUCTURES: IMPLEMENTING THE ADT TABLE WITH A BINARY SEARCH TREE

We are now just about ready to develop the binary search tree implementation for the ADT table. Recall that, according to our claims, this data structure provides the best features of the sequential and linked table implementations.

Given that this is indeed true, you might be tempted to wonder why we bothered to study the linear implementations at all. This is a valid point that we feel should be addressed before we begin to develop the binary search tree implementations.

There are three main reasons why it was appropriate to discuss the linear table implementations before introducing binary search trees. The first and foremost reason has to do with *perspective*. Earlier in this chapter, we spoke of the dangers of overanalyzing a problem. If the size of the problem is small, then it is unlikely that there will be a significant difference between the efficiencies of the possible solutions. In particular, if the size of the table is going to be small, then a linear implementation should be selected on the grounds that it is simple to code and read.

The second reason is that we actually did discover scenarios for which a linear implementation is very efficient. Recall that the linear implementations were deemed adequate for Scenario A (predominant operations are `Insert` and `Traverse` in no particular order), Scenario B (predominant operation is `Traverse` in sorted order) and, given that the maximum number of items is known, for Scenario C (predominant operations are `Traverse` in sorted order and `Retrieve`). This fact, coupled with the concern for simplicity, dictates that a linear implementation and not a binary search tree be used in such situations, even for large tables.

The third reason is that in order to appreciate binary search trees fully, we first had to discover scenarios for which the linear implementations were not adequate. Having set up situations in which there seem to be irreconcilably conflicting needs, we can now view the binary search tree as reconciling the irreconcilable. Let us briefly review what those conflicting needs are. We wish to be able to use a binary search to locate a table item, in both the `Retrieve` operation and the first steps of the `Insert` and `Delete` operations. This pushes us in the direction of a sequential implementation. On the other hand, the need for dynamic storage allocation and the desire not to have to shift items in the second steps of the `Insert` and `Delete` operations pushes us, with equal force, in the direction of a linked implementation. *If only there were a linked structure on which we could perform a binary search.*

The binary search tree is exactly such a data structure. The binary tree of names in Figure 9–6 happens to be a binary search tree. In addition to satisfying the definition of a binary tree, the tree is in a sense "sorted." By this we mean that

> *for any node N, N.name is greater than all the names in N's left subtree and less than all the names in N's right subtree.*

This organization of data values in a tree is the defining property of a **binary search tree.** The sorted property of a binary search tree allows us to perform the table operations `Retrieve`, `Insert`, `Delete`, and `Traverse` (in sorted order) very efficiently. Algorithms for these operations can be based on the following recursive definition of a binary search tree (assuming no duplicate values):

> Given a set of nodes (with one data field designated as the search key), T is a **binary search tree** if it is a binary tree such that:

434

CHAPTER 9
THE ADT
TABLE:
LINEAR AND
NONLINEAR
IMPLEMEN-
TATIONS

(1) T is the empty tree, or

(2) T is of the form

$$n$$

$$T_L \quad T_R$$

and

(a) n's search key is greater than all of the search keys in T_L.

(b) n's search key is smaller than all of the search keys in T_R.

(c) Both T_L and T_R are binary search trees.

Let us illustrate how this recursive definition can be used to search a binary search tree for a given name. Suppose that we wish to locate the name Ellen in the binary search tree of Figure 9–6. We notice that Jane is at the root of the tree. Since (search key) Ellen is less than (search key) Jane, if the name Ellen is present in the tree, it would have to be in Jane's left subtree (since, by definition of a binary search tree, all the names in Jane's right subtree are greater than Jane). Now, from the recursive definition, we know that Jane's left subtree is also a binary search tree, so we use *exactly the same strategy* to search this subtree for Ellen. The name Bob is in the root of this binary search tree, and since Ellen is greater than Bob, it would have to be in Bob's right subtree. Bob's right subtree is also a binary search tree, and it happens that Ellen is in the root node of this tree—the search has located the name.

We can implement the above search strategy as follows.

```
Find(T, X)
(* Search the binary search tree
   pointed to by T for the name X. *)

   (* searching an empty tree *)
   IF (T = NIL) THEN
      write 'X is not present'

   (* find the name *)
   ELSIF (X = T^.name) THEN
      write 'X is present'

   (* search the left subtree *)
   ELSIF (X < T^.name) THEN
      Find(T^.Lchild, X)

   (* search the right subtree *)
   ELSE
      Find(T^.Rchild, X)

END
```

The table operations `Retrieve`, `Insert`, and `Delete` will be based on this `Find` algorithm. Before turning to these operations, however, we shall further study the structure of binary search trees and the `Find` algorithm.

To begin, it is very important to note that there are many different binary search trees containing the names Alan, Bob, Ellen, Jane, Nancy, Tom, and Wendy. For example, each tree in Figure 9–17 is a valid binary search tree for these names. Although these trees are of different shapes, the `Find` algorithm can still be used. The shape of the tree in *no way* affects the validity of the algorithm. That a tree is a binary search tree is the only property that `Find` needs to know about.

435

Nonlinear
Structures:
Implementing
the ADT Table
with a Binary
Search Tree

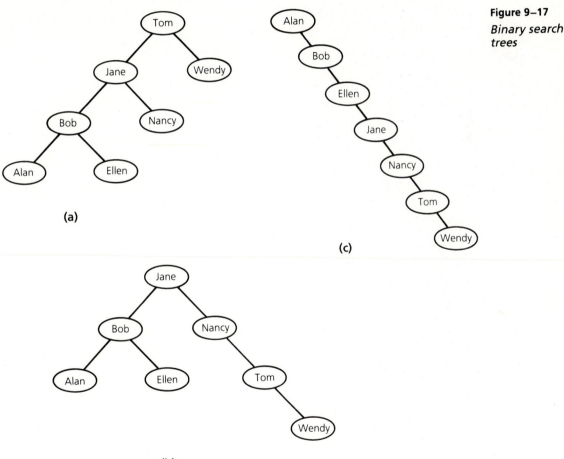

Figure 9–17

*Binary search
trees*

While the `Find` algorithm will work on any of the above binary search trees, we should note that it will work more efficiently on some of the trees than on others. For example, on the tree in Figure 9–17(c), the `Find` algorithm would inspect every node before locating Wendy. In fact, this binary tree really has the same structure as a sorted linear linked list. On the other hand, on the balanced tree of Figure 9–6 (which is a full tree), the `Find` algorithm needs to inspect

436

CHAPTER 9
THE ADT
TABLE:
LINEAR AND
NONLINEAR
IMPLEMEN-
TATIONS

only the nodes containing Jane, Tom, and Wendy. Notice that these are exactly the same names that would be inspected by a binary search of the array in Figure 9–18. Later in this chapter we shall further discuss the effect of a binary search tree's shape on efficiency, and we shall see how the `Insert` and `Delete` operations affect this shape.

Alan	Bob	Ellen	Jane	Nancy	Tom	Wendy
1	2	3	4	5	6	7

Figure 9–18

Array of names

What are the implications of using a binary search tree for the ADT table operation *Traverse* in sorted order? This operation can easily be implemented using the inorder traversal presented in the previous section.

```
Inorder (T)
(* Traverse the binary tree T in inorder. *)

   IF (T is not empty) THEN
      Inorder (left subtree of T)
      visit the root of T
      Inorder (right subtree of T)
   END
```

THEOREM 9–4

The inorder traversal of a binary search tree T will visit its names in sorted order.

PROOF:

The proof is by induction on h, the height of T.

> *Basis:* $h = 0$. Then T is empty, and the algorithm does not visit any names. This is the proper sorted order for the 0 names that are in the tree!
>
> *Inductive Hypothesis:* Assume true for all k, $0 \leq k < h$. That is, assume for all k ($0 \leq k < h$) that the inorder traversal visits the names in sorted order.
>
> *Inductive Conclusion:* We must show the statement is true for h, $h > 0$. That is, we must show that *Inorder* visits the names in the tree T

$$
\begin{array}{c}
n \\
T_L \quad T_R
\end{array}
$$

of height h in sorted order.

Since T is a binary search tree, all the names in subtree T_L are less than the name in n and all the names in T_R are greater than the name in n. The *Inorder* algorithm will visit all the names in T_L, then visit n, and then visit all the names in T_R. Thus, the only concern is that *Inorder* visit the names within each of the subtrees T_L and T_R in the correct sorted order. But since T is a binary search tree of height h, each subtree is a binary search tree of height less than h. Therefore, by the inductive hypothesis, *Inorder* visits the names in each subtree T_L and T_R in the correct sorted order. This completes the proof.

437
Insert and
Delete Opera-
tions for a
Binary Search
Tree

As a result of the theorem, we are assured that the inorder traversal correctly implements the table's *Traverse* in sorted order operation. It can thus be used when an application needs to visit the items of a table in sorted-by-search-key order.

Let us now see where we stand in our quest for a table implementation that provides the best features of the sequential and linked implementations. We have seen that the structure of a binary search tree allows it to be traversed in sorted order and for a binary search-like algorithm to be performed. The closer the shape of the tree is to balanced (and the further it is from a linear structure) the closer will be the behavior of the *Find* algorithm to a binary search (and the further it will be from the behavior of a linear search). A logical question to ask is, given that *balanced* binary search trees are the most desirable, why should we ever accept anything else? The answer is found in the implementations of the *Insert* and *Delete* operations.

While it is relatively simple to insert into and delete from a binary search tree in a manner that preserves the tree's binary search tree property, it is rather difficult to do so in a manner that preserves its balance as well. Therefore, since the *Find* algorithm requires only that a tree be a binary search tree and not that it be balanced, we initially shall develop *Insert* and *Delete* algorithms without concern for the balance of the tree. After we have developed these basic algorithms, we shall raise the balance issue once again.

INSERT AND DELETE OPERATIONS FOR A BINARY SEARCH TREE

Suppose that we wish to insert the name Frank into the binary search tree of Figure 9–6. As a first step, let us pretend that we are trying to find the item with search key Frank rather than to insert it. The *Find* algorithm first searches the tree rooted at Jane, then the tree rooted at Bob, and then the tree rooted at Ellen. It then searches the tree rooted at the right child of Ellen. Since this tree is empty, the *Find* algorithm has reached a degenerate case and will terminate with the report that Frank is not present (see Figure 9–19). Now what does it mean to us that *Find* looked for Frank in the right subtree of Ellen? For one thing, it means that if Frank *were* the right child of Ellen, *Find* *would* have found Frank there.

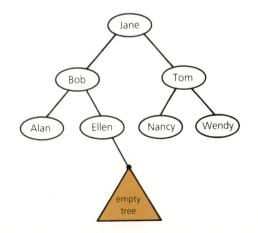

Figure 9–19

Empty subtree where Find terminates

438

CHAPTER 9
THE ADT
TABLE:
LINEAR AND
NONLINEAR
IMPLEMEN-
TATIONS

This observation indicates that a good place for Frank to be inserted is as the right child of Ellen. Since Ellen has no right child, the insertion would be very simple, requiring only that Ellen's *Rchild* pointer field be set to point to Frank. More importantly, Frank *belongs* in this location—*Find* will look for Frank here. Specifically, inserting Frank as the right child of Ellen will *preserve the tree's binary search tree property*. Since *Find*, when searching for Frank, would follow a path that leads to the right child of Ellen, we are assured that Frank is in the proper relation to the names above it in the tree. Notice that this strategy of using *Find* to determine where in the tree the new name should be inserted always leads to an easy insertion. No matter what name it is that we are inserting into the tree, *Find* will always terminate at an empty subtree, and thus it will always indicate that the name should be inserted as a new *leaf*. Since adding a leaf requires only the setting of the appropriate pointer field in the parent, the work required for an insertion is virtually the same as that for the corresponding find.

The above process can be described, at a very high level, as follows:

```
Insert(T, newitem)
(* Insert newitem into table T. It is assumed that there
   is no item in T with the same search key as newitem. *)

   (* X is the search key of newitem *)
   let N be the parent of the empty subtree
      at which Find(T, X) terminates

   IF (the empty subtree is the left subtree of N) THEN
      set Lchild of N to point to newitem
   ELSE
      set Rchild of N to point to newitem
   END
```

This algorithm is refined later in this chapter.

The *Delete* operation is a bit more involved. We first use the *Find* algorithm to attempt to locate the node with the specified name, and if it is found, we then must remove the node from the tree. We can begin to write the procedure as follows:

```
Delete(T, X, success)
(* Delete from table T the item with search key X.   The
   operation fails if there is no such item.   The flag
   success indicates whether the operation succeeded. *)

   use Find(T, X) to locate node N with value X

   IF (X is found) THEN
      remove node N from the tree
      success := TRUE
   ELSE
      success := FALSE
   END
```

The problem we need to solve is how to

remove node N from the tree

We break the problem into three cases:

    (1) N is a leaf.

    (2) N has only one child.

    (3) N has two children.

439
Insert and
Delete Opera-
tions for a
Binary Search
Tree

The removal of a leaf is the easiest of the cases. We need only set the pointer field of its parent to **NIL**. The second case is a bit more difficult. There are really two subcases:

    (a) N has only a left child.

    (b) N has only a right child.

The two cases are completely symmetric, and we shall illustrate the solution in the case of a left child. In the following diagram, L is the left child of N and P is the parent of N. Notice that N can be either the left or right child of P. If N is deleted from the tree, L would be without a parent, and P would be without one of its children. We can try to make these nodes happy by letting L take the place of N as one of P's children (see Figure 9–20).

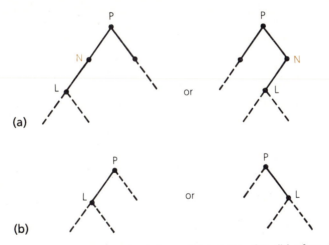

(a) N with only left child—N can be the left or right child of P; (b) after deleting node N

Figure 9–20

We need to convince ourselves that this adoption preserves the binary search tree property. If N is the *left child* of P, then all the search keys in the subtree rooted at N must be less than the search key in P. But this certainly implies that all the search keys in the subtree rooted at L are less than the search key in P. Therefore, after N is removed and L is adopted by P, all the search keys in P's left subtree are still less than the search key in P. This deletion strategy thus preserves the binary search tree property. A parallel argument holds if N is a *right child* of P, and therefore we are assured that the binary search tree property is preserved in either case.

440

CHAPTER 9
THE ADT
TABLE:
LINEAR AND
NONLINEAR
IMPLEMEN-
TATIONS

The most difficult of the three cases occurs when the node N to be deleted has two children, as in Figure 9–21.

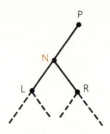

Figure 9–21

N with two children

The strategy for deleting N when it has only one child was to move up this child by having it replace N as a child of N's parent. But when N has two children, these children cannot both move up—N's parent has room for only one of N's children as a replacement for N.

We need a different strategy for deleting N when it has two children. We are, in fact, not going to delete the node N at all. We are going to find another node that is easier to delete and delete it instead of N. Now that sounds like cheating, doesn't it? After all, the programmer who requests

```
Delete(T, X, success)
```

expects that the item with value X in its search key will be deleted from the table. The point is that the programmer expects the *item* will be deleted and has no right, because of the wall between the program and the ADT implementation, to expect a particular *node* in the tree to be deleted. In fact, because of the wall, the programmer has no right to even expect that there is a tree at all!

Let us then rephrase our strategy. To delete from a binary search tree an item residing in a node N that has two children, we shall:

1. Locate some other item residing in a node M that is easier to remove from the tree than is the node N.

2. Copy the item from M to N, thus effectively deleting from the table the item originally in N.

3. Remove the node M from the tree.

Consider the first of these steps. What kind of node M is easier to remove than the node N? Since we have already solved the problems of deleting a node that has zero or one children, we will be satisfied if M is such a node. We have to be careful though. Can we choose just *any* node and copy its value into N? No, because we must be sure to preserve the binary search tree property of the tree. For example, if in the tree of Figure 9–22, we copied the value from M to N, the result would no longer be a binary search tree.

We need to think about what value, when copied into the node N, will preserve the binary search tree property. If X is the value of the search key presently in the node N, we know that all the search keys in the left subtree of N are less than X and all the search keys in the right subtree are greater than X. The value of the search key Y that is copied into N must have this same property. There are two possibilities for the value Y: Y can come immediately

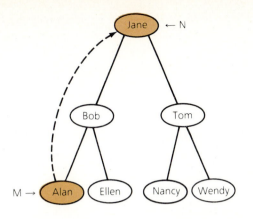

441
Insert and
Delete Opera-
tions for a
Binary Search
Tree

Figure 9–22

*Not just any
node will do*

before or immediately after X in the sorted order of search keys. If Y comes immediately after X, then clearly all search keys in the left subtree of N are smaller than Y, since they are all smaller than X. Further, since Y is the smallest search key greater than X, no search key Z in the right subtree of N could be smaller than Y—otherwise Y could not be the smallest search key greater than X, since Z would be both smaller than Y and greater than X (since it's in N's right subtree). Thus, Y is smaller than all the search keys in the right subtree of N. A similar argument illustrates that if Y comes immediately before X in the sorted order, then it is greater than all search keys in the left subtree of N and smaller than all search keys in the right subtree of N.

We have thus identified two items that can be copied into N. The next question is how can we locate one of these items. The choice of which of the items to locate is arbitrary, and we shall discuss how to locate the search key Y that comes immediately after X. Recall that the inorder traversal will visit the search keys of a binary search tree in proper sorted order. Therefore, search key Y is contained in the node that the inorder traversal visits immediately after node N. This node is called N's **inorder successor.** Given that N has two children, its inorder successor is the leftmost node of N's right subtree. That is, to find the node containing Y, we follow N's *Rchild* pointer to its right child R, which must be present since N has two children. We then descend the tree rooted at R by taking left branches at each node until we encounter a node M with no left

Figure 9–23

*Copying
inorder
successor to N*

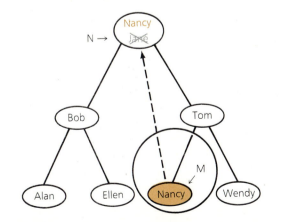

442

CHAPTER 9
THE ADT
TABLE:
LINEAR AND
NONLINEAR
IMPLEMEN-
TATIONS

child. The value of the item in this node M is copied into node N, and—since M has no left child—it can be removed from the tree as one of the two easy cases (see Figure 9–23).

A high-level description of the *Delete* algorithm is as follows.

```
Delete(T, X, success)
(* Delete from table T the item with search key X.  The
   operation fails if there is no such item.  The flag
   success indicates whether the operation succeeded. *)

   use Find(T, X) to locate node N with value X

   IF (X is found) THEN
      Delitem(N)   (* Delitem is defined below *)
      success := TRUE
   ELSE
      success := FALSE
   END
```

```
Delitem(N)
(* Delete the item in node N of a binary search tree. *)

   IF (N is a leaf) THEN
      remove N from the tree

   ELSIF (N has only one child C) THEN

      IF (N was a left child of its parent P) THEN
         make C the left child of P
      ELSE
         make C the right child of P
      END

   ELSE (* N has two children *)

      find N's inorder successor M
      copy the item from M into N

      remove M from the tree using the above technique
         for a leaf or a node with one child

   END
```

This procedure is refined later in this chapter.

Let us now analyze this high-level binary search tree implementation for the ADT table to see if it succeeds where the linear implementations failed.

THE EFFICIENCY OF THE BINARY SEARCH TREE ALGORITHMS

443
The Efficiency
of the Binary
Search Tree
Algorithms

We have seen that binary search trees come in shapes ranging from balanced to linear (see Figures 9–6 and 9–17c). Let us take a closer look at the relationship between the height of a binary search tree and the efficiency of the operations `Retrieve`, `Insert`, and `Delete`.

Each of these operations compares the specified value X to the search keys in the nodes along a **path** through the tree. This path always starts at the root of the tree and, at each node N, chooses the left or right branch depending on the comparison of X to the search key in N. The path terminates at the node containing X or, in the case that X is not present, at an empty subtree. The number of comparisons that are made by the operations is thus equal to the number of nodes along this path.

The number of comparisons required by `Retrieve`, `Insert`, and `Delete` therefore depends on the location in the tree of the node (or empty subtree) at which that path terminates. This in turn depends on the value X and on the values in the tree. Let us ask what is the *maximum* number of comparisons that the operations can require. This is equal to the number of nodes on the *longest* path through the tree. In other words, the maximum number of comparisons that these operations can require is equal to the *height* of the binary search tree.

We have proved that the minimum possible height for a binary tree with N nodes is approximately $\log_2 N$. The more balanced a tree is, the closer is its height to this theoretical minimum. Notice that this minimum height agrees with the maximum number of comparisons a binary search must make to search an array with N elements. Therefore, if a binary search tree is balanced, the time it takes to search it for a value is about the same as is required by a binary search of an array. On the other hand, as we go from balanced trees toward trees with a linear structure, the height approaches the number of nodes N. This number agrees with the maximum number of comparisons that must be made when searching a linked list with N nodes.

Given that the height of an N-node binary search tree can vary from a maximum of N to a minimum of approximately $\log_2 N$, what height should we use for the purpose of comparison with the linear implementations? We shall begin by assuming that the height of our binary search tree is very close to the theoretical minimum of $\log_2 N$. While this may seem overly optimistic, we shall shortly present arguments that the optimism is quite justified.

If we accept the fact that the height of our binary search tree is approximately $\log_2 N$, the binary search tree implementation of a table certainly succeeds where the linear implementations failed. Using a binary search tree we can, with efficiency comparable to that of binary search, locate a table item in both the `Retrieve` operation and the first steps of the `Insert` and `Delete` operations. In addition the binary search tree is a linked structure; thus, like a linked list, it can have its nodes dynamically allocated and can easily handle a table of an unknown maximum size. Also, the binary search tree, again like the linked list, very efficiently performs the second step of the `Insert` and `Delete` operations. The actual insertion and removal of a node is accomplished via a few pointer changes (plus a short traversal to the inorder successor if the node to be removed

444

CHAPTER 9
THE ADT
TABLE:
LINEAR AND
NONLINEAR
IMPLEMEN-
TATIONS

has two children) rather than, as the sequential implementations require, via the shifting of possibly *all* the table items. The binary search tree, therefore, is a table implementation that combines the best aspects of the two linear implementations.

This is all very nice, but the outstanding efficiency of the binary search tree implementation hinges on the assumption that the height of the tree is approximately $\log_2 N$. What can we really *expect* the height of our binary search tree to be? The factor that determines the height of a binary search tree is the order in which the `Insert` and `Delete` operations are performed on the tree. For example, if starting with an empty tree, we insert names in the order Alan, Bob, Ellen, Jane, Nancy, Tom, Wendy, we would obtain a binary search tree of maximum height (see Figure 9–17c). On the other hand, if we insert in the order Jane, Bob, Tom, Alan, Ellen, Nancy, Wendy, we would obtain a binary search tree of minimum height (see Figure 9–6).

Which of these situations should we expect to encounter in the course of a real application? It can be proven mathematically that if the `Insert` and `Delete` operations come in a *random* order, then the height of the binary search tree can be expected to be very close to $\log_2 N$. Thus, in this sense, the above analysis was not unduly optimistic.

In a real-world application, is it realistic to expect the `Insert` and `Delete` operations to come in random order? In many applications, the answer is yes. There are applications, however, where the assumption would be dubious. For example, the person preparing the above sequence of `Insert` operations might well decide to "help us out" by arranging the names to be inserted into sorted order. This arrangement, as we have seen, would lead to a tree of maximum height. Thus, while in many applications we can expect the behavior of a binary search tree to be excellent, we should be wary of the possibility that some characteristic of a given application may lead to poor performance.

Is there anything we can do if we suspect that the operations might not be performed in a random order? Similarly, is there anything we can do if we have a table of an enormous size and need to *ensure* that the height of the tree be very close to $\log_2 N$? In Chapter 11, we shall look at a variation of the basic binary search tree, called a **2–3 tree**, which is *guaranteed* always to remain balanced. The fact that we can, if need be, always keep the height of a search tree near $\log_2 N$ justifies the claim that a search tree provides the best aspects of the two linear implementations.

The following table summarizes the approximate maximum amount of work (comparisons and assignments) required by each of the implementations for the table operations `Retrieve`, `Insert`, and `Delete`.

	RETRIEVE	INSERT	DELETE
Sorted-sequential	$\log N$ comps	$\log N$ comps $+$ N item shifts	$\log N$ comps $+$ N item shifts
Sorted-linked	N comps	N comps	N comps
BST	$\log N$ comps	$\log N$ comps	$\log N$ comps

DETAILS OF THE BINARY SEARCH TREE IMPLEMENTATION

445
Details of the
Binary Search
Tree
Implementation

In this section we shall develop the details of the binary search tree implementation of the ADT table. A full Modula-2 implementation appears at the end of this section.

We begin by viewing from a new perspective the insertion of a node into a sorted linked list. The binary search tree algorithms are recursive and it will be good preparation to develop a recursive *Insert* algorithm for a sorted linked list. Interestingly enough, the recursive *Insert* eliminates the need for both a trailing pointer and a special case for inserting into the beginning of the list.

Consider the following recursive view of a sorted linked list: A linked list is sorted if the first item is less than the second item and the list that begins with the second item is sorted. This definition can be stated more formally as follows.

The list pointed to by L is a sorted linked list if

L is **NIL** (the empty list is a sorted linked list), or

L^.next is **NIL** (a list with a single node is a sorted linked list), or

L^.search-key < L^.next^.search-key, and

L^.next points to a sorted linked list.

We can base a recursive *Insert* procedure on this definition. Notice that in the following algorithm, the insertion of the node is performed at the degenerate case—either when the list is empty or when *X* is smaller than all the search keys in the list. Both cases call for the new item to be inserted at the beginning of the list.

```
Insert(L, newitem)
(* Insert newitem in the sorted linked list pointed to by
   by L.  It is assumed that there are no duplicate search
   key values. *)

   let X be the value of the search key of the new item

   IF ((L = NIL) OR (X < L^.search-key)) THEN

      (* degenerate case *)
      insert the new node at the beginning of the
         list pointed to by L

   ELSE

      Insert(L^.next, newitem)

   END
```

How, when the degenerate case is reached, can the insertion of the new node be accomplished? After all, we did not maintain a trailing pointer. As a consequence

446

CHAPTER 9
THE ADT
TABLE:
LINEAR AND
NONLINEAR
IMPLEMEN-
TATIONS

of the recursive statement of the algorithm, the insertion of the new node can easily be accomplished as follows.

```
Insert (L, newitem)

   let X be the value of the search key of the new item

   IF ((L = NIL) OR (X < L^.search-key)) THEN

      (* degenerate case *)
      NEW(s)
      s^.item := newitem
      s^.next := L
      L := s

   ELSE

      Insert (L^.next, newitem)

   END
```

The conceptually difficult part of this procedure is the statement

```
L := s
```

This assignment is all that is necessary to set the pointer field of the appropriate node to point to the new node. Note that *L* is pointing to the beginning of a sorted list. Recall that to insert the node pointed to by *s* at the beginning of this list, we need to set *L* to point to the node pointed to by *s*. But does this really change the pointer field of the node that precedes the new node on the original list (on the list pointed to by the external pointer *Listhead*)? Yes it does, assuming that *L* is passed as a *variable parameter*.

Let us first consider the case when the new item is to be inserted at the beginning of the original list—that is, at the beginning of the list pointed to by the external pointer *Listhead*. In this case, no recursive calls are made, and thus when the degenerate case is reached ($X < L^.search-key$), *Listhead* is the actual parameter corresponding to *L* (see Figure 9–24).

Hence, the assignment

```
L := s
```

sets the value of *Listhead* to *s*, that is, *Listhead* now points to the new node (we are assuming that *L* is a variable parameter).

The general case, in which the new item is to be inserted into the interior of the list pointed to by *Listhead*, is very similar. When the degenerate case is reached, what is the actual parameter corresponding to *L*? It is the *next* field of the node that should precede the new node; that is, it is the *next* field of the last node with a search key value less than *X*. Therefore, since *L* is a variable

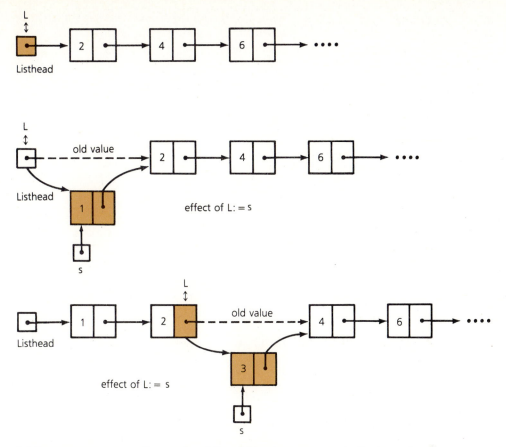

(a) Degenerate case—first node of list; (b) assignment made for insertion at beginning of list; (c) search stopping in middle of list.

Figure 9–24

parameter, the assignment

```
L := s
```

sets the *next* field of the appropriate node to point to the new node.

   Though a case could be made that the operations on a sorted linked list should be done recursively (after all, it does eliminate special cases and the need for a trailing pointer!), our primary purpose in presenting the recursive *Insert* is to prepare you for the binary search tree algorithms. A binary search tree is recursive by nature, and it is thus natural to formulate the algorithms recursively. As you study the binary search tree algorithms, keep in mind the point from the above discussion that the actual parameters of the recursive calls to *Insert* are pointer fields of nodes on the list. An analogous situation will arise in our implementations of *Insert* and *Delete* for a binary search tree. This will allow us easily to set the pointer fields in the parent of a given node in the tree.

   With the lessons of the sorted linked list's recursive *Insert* operation in

448
CHAPTER 9
THE ADT
TABLE:
LINEAR AND
NONLINEAR
IMPLEMEN-
TATIONS

mind, we shall now tackle the refinements to the binary search tree algorithms. Let us begin by refining the *Find* algorithm into an implementation of the table's *Retrieve* operation. Recall that the *Find* algorithm is as follows.

```
Find(T, X)
(* Search the binary search tree
   pointed to by T for the name X. *)

   (* searching an empty tree *)
   IF (T = NIL) THEN
     write 'X is NOT present'

   (* find the name *)
   ELSIF (X = T^.name) THEN
      write 'X is present'

   (* search the left subtree *)
   ELSIF (X < T^.name) THEN
     Find(T^.Lchild, X)

   (* search the right subtree *)
   ELSE
     Find(T^.Rchild, X)

END
```

There are only two minor issues with which we must deal. First, recall that the items of a table are, in general, records with one of the fields designated as the search key. Therefore, the nodes of the tree may contain, in addition to the two pointer fields, several data fields, one of which is named *key*. We must implement the *Retrieve* operation to reflect this fact. The second issue is that *Retrieve* must return the item with the desired search key if it exists, and otherwise it must return the Boolean flag *success* with the value *false*. These actions replace the *write* statements in the *Find* algorithm.

We thus write the *Retrieve* procedure as follows.

```
Retrieve(T, X, getitem, success)
(* Retrieve into getitem the item from table T with search
   key X.  The operation fails if there is no such item.  The
   flag success indicates whether the operation succeeded.  *)

   IF (T = NIL) THEN
     success := FALSE

   ELSIF (X = T^.key) THEN
      getitem := data fields of the record pointed to by T
      success := TRUE
```

```
    (* search the left subtree *)
ELSIF  (X < T^.key)  THEN
    Retrieve(T^.Lchild, X)

    (* search the right subtree *)
ELSE
    Retrieve(T^.Rchild, X)

END
```

Now let us consider the mechanics of the *Insert* procedure. Recall our high-level description of *Insert*.

```
Insert(T, newitem)
(* Insert newitem into table T. It is assumed that there
   is no item in T with the same search key as newitem. *)

    (* X is the search key of newitem *)
    let N be the parent of the empty subtree
       at which Find(T, X) terminates

    IF (the empty subtree is the left subtree of N) THEN
       set Lchild of N to point to newitem
    ELSE
       set Rchild of N to point to newitem
    END
```

The trick is to set the appropriate pointer of node N to point to the new node. The recursive nature of the algorithm provides an elegant means to do this, provided that *T* is passed as a variable parameter.

```
Insert(T, newitem)
(* Insert newitem into table T. It is assumed that there
   is no item in T with the same search key as newitem. *)

    IF (T = NIL) THEN
       (* create a new record with T pointing to it *)
       NEW(T)
       set the data fields of the new record
          to the values in newitem
       set the pointer fields of the new record to NIL

    ELSIF (newitem.key < T^.key) THEN
       Insert(T^.Lchild, newitem)

    ELSE
       Insert(T^.Rchild, newitem)

END
```

450

CHAPTER 9
THE ADT
TABLE:
LINEAR AND
NONLINEAR
IMPLEMEN-
TATIONS

Let us convince ourselves that this procedure really does set the appropriate pointer variable to point to the new node. The situation is very similar to the recursive *Insert* procedure for the sorted linked list. If before the insertion the tree were empty, then the external pointer to the root of the tree would be **NIL**,

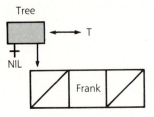

effect of NEW (T)

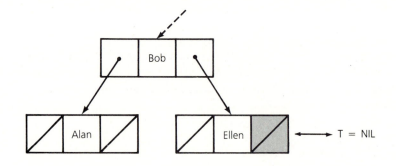

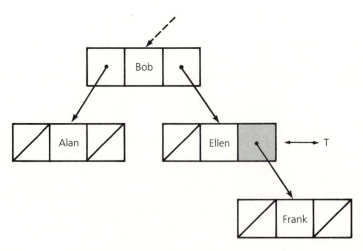

effect of NEW (T)

Figure 9–25   *(a) Insertion into empty tree; (b) search terminates at a leaf; (c) insertion at a leaf*

and the procedure would not make a recursive call. In this case, the actual parameter is therefore the external pointer to the root of the tree. Since T is a variable parameter, when it is set to point to the new record, the effect is to set the external pointer to point to the new record (see Figure 9–25).

The general case of *Insert* is similar. When the formal parameter T becomes **NIL**, the corresponding actual parameter is the *Lchild* or *Rchild* pointer field of the parent of the empty subtree; that is, this pointer field has the value **NIL**. This pointer field was passed to the *Insert* procedure by one of the recursive calls

```
Insert(T^.Lchild, newitem) or
Insert(T^.Rchild, newitem)
```

Thus, when T is set to point to the new record, the effect is to set the actual parameter (which is the appropriate pointer field of the parent) to point to the new record.

The refinement of the *Delete* algorithm follows similar lines. Recall that we defined *Delete* to call the procedure *Delitem*.

```
Delete(T, X, success)
(* Delete from table T the item with search key X.   The
   operation fails if there is no such node.   The flag
   success indicates whether the operation succeeded.   *)

   use Find(T, X) to locate node N with value X

   IF (X is found) THEN
      Delitem(N)   (* Delitem is defined below *)
      success := TRUE

   ELSE
      success := FALSE

   END

Delitem(N)
(* Delete the item in the node N of a binary search tree. *)

   IF (N is a leaf) THEN
      remove N from the tree

   ELSIF (N has only one child C) THEN
      (* remove N from the tree *)
      IF (N was a left child of its parent P) THEN
         make C the left child of P
      ELSE
         make C the right child of P
      END
```

452

CHAPTER 9
THE ADT
TABLE:
LINEAR AND
NONLINEAR
IMPLEMEN-
TATIONS

```
    ELSE  (* N has two children *)
        find N's inorder successor M
        copy value from M into N

        remove M from the tree using the above technique
            for a leaf or a node with one child
END
```

In the following refinement, the procedure *Delitem* uses the procedure *Leftmost* to find the node containing the inorder successor of the item in N. *Leftmost* deletes this node from the tree and returns the inorder successor. This item then replaces in node N the item to be deleted from the table.

```
Delete(T, X, success)
(* Delete from table T the item with search key X.   The
   operation fails if there is no such item.   The flag
   success indicates whether the operation succeeded.  *)

    IF  (T = NIL)  THEN
        success := FALSE

    ELSIF  (X = T^.key)  THEN
        (* remove the item in the node pointed to by T *)
        Delitem(T)

        success := TRUE

    (* search the left subtree *)
    ELSIF  (X < T^.key)  THEN
        Delete(T^.Lchild, X, success)

    (* search the right subtree *)
    ELSE
        Delete(T^.Rchild, X, success)

    END


Delitem(delptr)
(* Remove the item in the node N pointed to by delptr.  *)

    IF  (N is a leaf)  THEN
        (* remove from the tree *)
        DISPOSE(delptr)
        delptr := NIL

    ELSIF  (N has only one child C)  THEN
        (* C replaces N as its parent's child *)
```

```
        p := delptr
        IF (C is the left child of N) THEN
            delptr := delptr^.left
        ELSE
            delptr := delptr^.right
        END
        DISPOSE(p)

    (* N has two children *)
    ELSE
        (* find the inorder successor of value in N - it is in
           the leftmost node of the subtree rooted at N's right
           child *)

        Leftmost(delptr^.Rchild, ReplacementItem)

        put ReplacementItem in N

    END


Leftmost(p, getitem)
(* Retrieve into getitem the item in the leftmost descendant
   of the node pointed to by p.  Delete the node which contains
   this item. *)

    IF (p^.Lchild = NIL) THEN
        (* this is the node we want - it has no left
           child but it might have a right subtree *)
        getitem := p^.item
        temp := p

        (* notice that the actual parameter corresponding to p
           is a child pointer field of p's parent - the following
           thus correctly "moves up" p's right subtree *)
        p := p^.Rchild

        DISPOSE(temp)

    ELSE
        Leftmost(p^.Lchild, getitem)

    END
```

Observe that, as in the case of the *Insert* procedure, the actual parameter corresponding to *T* is one of the pointer fields of the parent of N (or is the external pointer to the root in the case that N is the root of the original tree) (see Figure 9–26). Thus, any change we should make to *T* (which points to node

454

CHAPTER 9
THE ADT
TABLE:
LINEAR AND
NONLINEAR
IMPLEMEN-
TATIONS

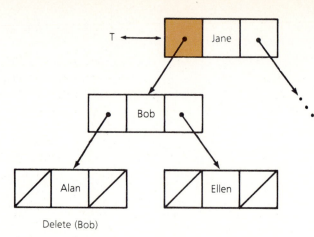

Figure 9–26

*Recursive
deletion*

Delete (Bob)

Any change to T changes Lchild of Jane

N) by calling the procedure *Delitem* with actual parameter *T* has the effect of changing the pointer field of the parent of N. The recursive procedure *Leftmost*, which is called by *Delitem* if N has two children, also uses this strategy to remove the node containing the inorder successor of the item to be deleted.

We now present the Modula-2 implementation.

```
IMPLEMENTATION MODULE Tables;
(* **********************************************************
   ADT TABLE - Binary Search Tree Implementation

   The following table operations are supported:

      Create, Insert, Delete, Retrieve, Traverse (sorted)

   ASSUMPTION:  At any time a table contains at most one item
   with a given search key.  See Exercise 9.1.

   The table is implemented as a binary search tree.
   Two procedures, Delitem and Leftmost, are written to delete
   nodes from a binary search tree.
   ********************************************************** *)

(* memory management procedures NEW and DISPOSE *)
FROM Storage IMPORT

     ALLOCATE, DEALLOCATE;

(* Table item and key types—it is assumed that the
   item type contains a field named key of type keytype *)
FROM ADTitem IMPORT

     itemtype, keytype;
```

```
TYPE

    (* Table structure *)
    Table  = POINTER TO node;
    node   = RECORD
                 item : itemtype;
                 Lchild, Rchild : Table;
             END;


(* ------------------------------------------------------------
   Leftmost:  Retrieve into getitem the item in the leftmost
   descendant of the node pointed to by p.  Delete the node
   which contains this item.
   ------------------------------------------------------------ *)
PROCEDURE Leftmost(VAR p : Table;
                   VAR getitem : itemtype);

VAR

    delnode : Table;

BEGIN

    IF (p # NIL) THEN
       IF (p^.Lchild = NIL) THEN
          getitem := p^.item;
          delnode := p;
          p := p^.Rchild;
          DISPOSE(delnode);
       ELSE
          Leftmost(p^.Lchild, getitem);
       END;
    END;

END Leftmost;

(* ------------------------------------------------------------
   Delitem:  Delete the item in the root of the tree pointed
   to by delptr.

   There are four cases to consider:
        1.   the root is a leaf
        2.   the root has no left child
        3.   the root has no right child
        4.   the root has two children

   CALLS:  Leftmost
   ------------------------------------------------------------ *)
```

456
CHAPTER 9
THE ADT
TABLE:
LINEAR AND
NONLINEAR
IMPLEMEN-
TATIONS

```
PROCEDURE Delitem(VAR delptr : Table);

VAR

   p : Table;
   replitem : itemtype;

BEGIN

   IF (delptr # NIL) THEN

      (* test for a leaf *)
      IF (delptr^.Lchild = NIL) AND
            (delptr^.Rchild = NIL) THEN
         DISPOSE(delptr);
         delptr := NIL;

      (* test for no left child *)
      ELSIF (delptr^.Lchild = NIL) THEN
         p := delptr;
         delptr := delptr^.Rchild;
         DISPOSE(p);

      (* test for no right child *)
      ELSIF (delptr^.Rchild = NIL) THEN
         p := delptr;
         delptr := delptr^.Lchild;
         DISPOSE(p);

      (* there are two children - delete and
         retrieve the inorder successor *)
      ELSE
         Leftmost(delptr^.Rchild, replitem);
         delptr^.item := replitem;

      END;

   END;

END Delitem;

(* ------------------------------------------------------------
   Create:  Create an empty table T.
   ------------------------------------------------------------ *)
PROCEDURE Create(VAR T : Table);

BEGIN
```

```
        T := NIL;

END Create;

(* ------------------------------------------------------------
    Insert:   Insert newitem into table T.  The Boolean flag
    success is returned TRUE if the Insert was successful, and
    FALSE otherwise (e.g., because of memory limitations).  In
    the event of an unsuccessful Insert, the table is unchanged.

    NOTE:   In most implementations of Modula-2 there is no way
    for a call to NEW to fail gracefully.  Therefore, the
    program will terminate abnormally if it exceeds memory
    limitations.

    ASSUMPTION:   Table T has been created.
    ------------------------------------------------------------ *)
PROCEDURE Insert(VAR T : Table; newitem : itemtype;
                 VAR success : BOOLEAN);

BEGIN

    (* the position has been found *)
    IF (T = NIL) THEN
        NEW(T);
        T^.item := newitem;
        T^.Lchild := NIL;
        T^.Rchild := NIL;

    (* search for the position *)
    ELSIF (newitem.key < T^.item.key) THEN
        Insert(T^.Lchild, newitem, success);

    ELSE
        Insert(T^.Rchild, newitem, success);

    END;

    success := TRUE;

END Insert;

(* ------------------------------------------------------------
    Delete:   Delete from table T the item with search key
    keyval.  The operation fails if there is no such item.  The
    Boolean flag success indicates whether the operation succeeded.
    In the event of an unsuccessful Delete, the table is unchanged.
```

458
CHAPTER 9
THE ADT
TABLE:
LINEAR AND
NONLINEAR
IMPLEMEN-
TATIONS

```
    ASSUMPTION:   Table T has been created.
    --------------------------------------------------------- *)
PROCEDURE Delete(VAR T : Table; keyval : keytype;
                    VAR success : BOOLEAN);

BEGIN

    IF (T = NIL) THEN
        success := FALSE;

    (* the item has been found - the
       node is the root of some subtree *)
    ELSIF (keyval = T^.item.key) THEN
        Delitem(T);
        success := TRUE;

    (* search for the item *)
    ELSIF (keyval < T^.item.key) THEN
        Delete(T^.Lchild, keyval, success);

    ELSE
        Delete(T^.Rchild, keyval, success);

    END;

END Delete;

(* ---------------------------------------------------------
    Retrieve:  Retrieve into getitem the item from table T
    with search key keyval.  The operation fails if there is
    no such item.  The flag success indicates whether the
    operation succeeded.

    ASSUMPTION:   Table T has been created.
    --------------------------------------------------------- *)
PROCEDURE Retrieve(T : Table; keyval : keytype;
                    VAR getitem : itemtype;
                    VAR success : BOOLEAN);

BEGIN

    IF (T = NIL) THEN
        success := FALSE;

    (* the item has been found *)
    ELSIF (keyval = T^.item.key) THEN
        getitem := T^.item;
        success := TRUE;
```

```
   (* search for the item *)
   ELSIF (keyval < T^.item.key) THEN
       Retrieve(T^.Lchild, keyval, getitem, success);


   ELSE
       Retrieve(T^.Rchild, keyval, getitem, success);


   END;


END Retrieve;


(* ----------------------------------------------------------
   Traverse:  Traverse table T in sorted order, calling
   procedure Visit for each item.

   Procedure Visit exists outside of the ADT implementation.

   WARNING: Visit may call only "read only" ADT operations
   on table T (e.g., Retrieve).

   ASSUMPTION:  Table T has been created.
   ------------------------------------------------------- *)
PROCEDURE Traverse(T : Table; Visit : ProcType);


BEGIN


   (* inorder traversal *)
   IF (T # NIL) THEN
       Traverse(T^.Lchild, Visit);
       Visit(T, T^.item);
       Traverse(T^.Rchild, Visit);
   END;


END Traverse;


END Tables.
```

SUMMARY

1. The ADT table supports value-oriented operations, such as *retrieve all the information about John Smith.*

2. The linear implementations (sequential and linked) of a table are adequate only in limited situations; for example, the table is small or an easy mix of operations is required. The fundamental problem with the linear implementations is that a binary search to locate a specified value (or the location for an insertion) can be performed only under a sequential implementation and

460

CHAPTER 9
THE ADT
TABLE:
LINEAR AND
NONLINEAR
IMPLEMEN-
TATIONS

the shifting of items (for insertions and deletions) can be avoided only under a linked implementation.

3. The binary search tree provides the best aspects of the two linear implementations. Because a binary search tree is a linked structure, it has the advantages of being able to grow dynamically and of allowing the insertion and deletion of data to be carried out through pointer changes. In addition, the linking strategy of a binary search tree allows a binary search-like algorithm to be used when searching for an item with a specified value. These characteristics make a binary search tree, in many applications, far superior to the linear table implementations.

4. Binary search trees come in many shapes. The height of a binary search tree with N nodes can range from a minimum of about $\log_2 N$ to a maximum of N. The shape of a binary search tree determines how efficiently it is able to support the table operations.

EXERCISES

Exercises 9.1 through 9.3 discuss the problem of having duplication in an ADT or data structure. By duplication we can mean either items that are identical in all fields or, more subtly, items that have identical search keys but differ in other fields.

1. In our implementations of the ADT table, we have made the following assumption: At any time, a table contains at most one item with a given search key. Although the ADT definition required for a specific application may not allow duplicates, it is probably wise to test for them rather than just to assume that they won't occur. Why? What are the implications of a user inserting duplicate items? What are the implications of a user inserting items that have the same search key but that have other data fields that differ? Specifically, what would our implementations of *Insert*, *Delete* and *Retrieve* do?

   Modify our table implementations so that they test for (and disallow) any duplicates. What table operations are affected? What are the implications for the unsorted-linear implementations?

2. Although disallowing duplicates (see Exercise 9.1) is reasonable for some applications, it is just as reasonable to have an application that will allow duplicates. What are the implications for the definitions of the ADT operations? In particular, how can the *Retrieve* and *Delete* operations be defined?

*3. If duplicates are allowed in a binary search tree, it is important to have a convention that determines the relationship between the duplicates in the data structure. Items that duplicate the root of a tree should either all be in the left subtree or all be in the right subtree (and of course, this property must hold for every subtree). Why is the convention critical to the effective use of the binary search tree?

1. When defining an ADT to solve a particular problem, don't request operations you don't need. The proper choice of an implementation depends on the mix of requested operations, and if you request an operation that you do not need, you might get an implementation that does not best support what you are really doing.

2. When comparing the efficiencies of various solutions, look only at significant differences. This rule is consistent with our multidimensional view of the cost of a computer program.

3. If the problem to be solved is small, don't overanalyze. In such a situation the primary concern should be simplicity.

4. A linked list, despite the fact that it eliminates the need to shift data, does not support the *Insert* and *Delete* operations any more efficiently than does a sequential implementation. This is because a binary search cannot be performed on a linked list.

5. While a binary search tree can be expected to support the table operations very efficiently, in the worst case (the tree approaches a linear shape), its performance is comparable to that of a linear linked list. If such a situation must be avoided for a given application, the balancing methods presented in Chapter 11 should be used.

In the text, it was stated that an item could be deleted from a binary search tree by replacing it with either its inorder predecessor or its inorder successor. If duplicates are to be allowed, however, the choice (inorder predecessor versus inorder successor) is no longer arbitrary. How does the convention of putting duplicates in either the left or right subtree affect this choice?

4. Complete the sorted-linked, unsorted-sequential, and unsorted-linked implementations of ADT table described in the chapter.

5. Many applications call for a *Replace* operation to be included in the definition of ADT table. Although this operation can be simulated with a call to *Retrieve*, followed by a call to *Delete*, followed by a call to *Insert* (to insert the modified item), it is more efficient to implement the operation directly. Write implementations of *Replace* for the five implementations (four linear and the binary search tree) of ADT table described in this chapter.

6. Consider a nonempty binary tree with two types of nodes, **min** nodes and **max** nodes. Each node has an integer value initially associated with it. We can define the **value** of such a tree as follows:

462

CHAPTER 9
THE ADT
TABLE:
LINEAR AND
NONLINEAR
IMPLEMEN-
TATIONS

(1) If the root is a min node, then the value of the tree is equal to the *minimum* of:

    (a) the integer stored in the root

    (b) the value of the left subtree (considered only if nonempty)

    (c) the value of the right subtree (considered only if nonempty)

(2) If the root is a max node, then the value of the tree is equal to the *maximum* of the above three values.

Compute the value of the tree in Figure 9–27. Each node is labeled with its initial value.

Figure 9–27

Minimax tree

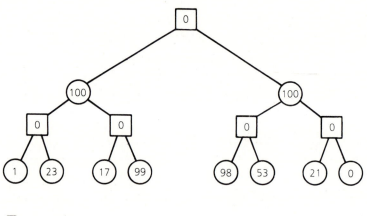

☐ - max nodes
○ - min nodes

Write a general solution for representing and evaluating these trees in Modula-2.

7. Write out the preorder, inorder, and postorder traversals of the tree in Figure 9–27.

8. Does the sequence of operations, *Remove (T, X)* followed by *Insert (T, X)*, ever change the shape of the binary search tree T?

*9. Recall that a binary search tree with a given set of data items can have several different structures that preserve the binary search tree property. Suppose that we are given a list of data items and told that it represents the preorder traversal of a binary search tree. Is there always at least one binary search tree that has the given preorder traversal? Is there ever more than one binary search tree that has the given preorder traversal?

*10. How many different (in shape) binary trees are there of size N? How many different binary search trees are there of size N? (Write recursive definitions.)

11. Prove Theorem 9–2 by induction.

12. What is the maximum number of nodes that can exist at level N of a binary tree? Prove your answer by induction. Use this fact to do the following:

   a. Rewrite the formal definition of a complete tree of height h.

   b. Derive a closed form for the formula

$$\sum_{i=1}^{h} 2^{i-1}$$

   What is the significance of this sum?

13. Prove by induction that a binary tree with N nodes has exactly $N + 1$ empty subtrees (or in Modula-2 terms, $N + 1$ **NIL** pointers).

14. A binary tree is **strictly binary** if every nonleaf node has exactly two children. Prove by induction on the number of leaves that a strictly binary tree with N leaves has exactly $2N - 1$ nodes.

15. We can define a routine for constructing a binary tree from two binary trees and a data item for the root as follows:

```
TYPE

    nodeptr  =  POINTER TO treenode;

    treenode = RECORD
                   data : INTEGER;
                   Lchild, Rchild : nodeptr;
               END;

VAR

    p, q, r, s, t : nodeptr;

PROCEDURE Maketree(VAR p : nodeptr; value : INTEGER;
                   l, r : nodeptr);
BEGIN

    NEW(p);
    WITH p^ DO
       data := value;
       Lchild := l;
       Rchild := r;
    END;

END Maketree;
```

464

CHAPTER 9
THE ADT
TABLE:
LINEAR AND
NONLINEAR
IMPLEMEN-
TATIONS

What tree(s) would be produced by the following sequence of statements?

```
Maketree(t, 1, NIL, NIL);
Maketree(t^.Lchild, 2, NIL, NIL);
Maketree(t^.Rchild, 3, NIL, NIL);
Maketree(t^.Lchild^.Rchild, 4, NIL, NIL);
Maketree(t^.Lchild, 5, NIL, NIL);   (* subtree is "lost" *)
Maketree(p, 6, NIL, NIL);
Maketree(q, 7, NIL, NIL);
Maketree(r, 8, p, q);
Maketree(r, 9, NIL, r);   (* second r is a value parameter *)
NEW(r^.Lchild);
s := r^.Lchild;
s^.data := 10;
s^.Lchild := t;
s^.Rchild: = NIL;
```

16. Many algorithms on binary trees reflect the recursive nature of the tree. A good strategy for writing a Modula-2 subprogram that operates on a binary tree is often to first write a recursive definition of the task. For example, let's say that the task is to count the number of nodes in a binary tree. An appropriate definition for the number of nodes $C(T)$ of binary tree T is:

$$C(T) = \begin{cases} 0 & \text{if } T \text{ is the empty tree.} \\ C(\text{left subtree of } T) \\ \quad + \; C(\text{right subtree of } T) \\ \quad + \; 1 \text{ for the root} & \text{otherwise} \end{cases}$$

Given a recursive definition, a Modula-2 implementation is often very straightforward. Write recursive definitions that perform the following tasks on arbitrary binary trees. Implement the definitions in Modula-2. For simplicity, assume that a tree data item is a single integer and that there are no duplicates.

a. Compute the height of a tree.

b. Find the maximum element.

c. Find the sum of the elements.

*d. Find the average of the elements.

e. Find a specific item.

f. Determine whether one item is an ancestor of another (that is, whether one item is in the subtree rooted at the other item).

g. Determine the highest level that is full (that is, has the maximum number of nodes for that level (see Exercise 9.12)).

*h. *Dispose* all of the nodes.

17. We will describe two algorithms for traversing a binary tree. Both are non-recursive algorithms that use an extra list for bookkeeping. Both algorithms have the following basic form:

```
initialize the list with the root of the tree
WHILE (the list is not empty) DO
    remove a node from the list and call it N
    visit N
    put the left child of N on the list (if it exists)
    put the right child of N on the list (if it exists)
END
```

The difference between the two algorithms is the method for choosing a node N to remove from the list.

Algorithm X: Remove the newest node (most recently added to the list).

Algorithm Y: Remove the oldest node (earliest added to the list).

a. In what order would each algorithm visit the nodes of the tree in Figure 9–27?

b. For each algorithm, describe an ADT that is appropriate for maintaining the bookkeeping list. What should the list item be? Note that we don't want to use an unnecessary amount of extra memory for the bookkeeping list. Also, note that the traversal of a tree should not alter the tree in any way.

*18. A node in a **general tree** (such as the one pictured in Figure 9–4) can have an arbitrary number of children. How can we implement a general tree in Modula-2?

a. Describe an implementation in which every node contains an array of child pointers. What are the advantages and disadvantages of this implementation?

b. What happens if we replace the array of children with a linked list of children? Observe that every node will have two pointers, a pointer to its **oldest child** (the first node on its linked list of children) and a pointer to its **next sibling** (which follows this node on its parent's list of children). Consider a tree T in which every node has at most two children. Compare the oldest-child/next-sibling representation of T to the left-child/right-child representation described in this chapter. Are the two representations ever the same?

19. Consider the table of cities described at the beginning of this chapter. Suppose we wish to perform the task of deleting from the table all cities with a population less than 1,000,000. Would this be an appropriate application of operation Traverse? How would this task be best defined and implemented as a new ADT table operation?

CHAPTER 10

VARIATIONS OF THE ADT TABLE

PREVIEW   This chapter introduces an important variation of the ADT table, the priority queue. This ADT supports operations that allow the item containing the largest value to be easily retrieved and deleted. Although a priority queue can be implemented with a binary search tree, we develop a simpler tree structure, known as a heap, which is often more appropriate for this purpose. We also consider methods for maintaining data simultaneously organized in different ways. One of our implementations utilizes doubly linked lists. The case study in this chapter incorporates modifications to the solutions we developed in the case study in Chapter 3.

The table is one of the most useful abstract data types that we have studied. In addition to the basic table presented in the previous chapter, there are several classical variations of the ADT table. In this chapter, we study one of these variants, the ADT **priority queue.**

The chapter is divided into three sections. The first section defines a priority queue and develops implementations for it. We then present a case study that illustrates modifications to the video-cassette inventory system originally developed in Chapter 3. One of the modifications to the system serves to illustrate an application of the ADT priority queue. The third section considers the problem of organizing data to simultaneously support diverse kinds of operations.

THE ADT PRIORITY QUEUE

The **priority queue** is an abstract data type whose operations make it useful in the solution to many problems. For example, one of the desired enhancements to the video-cassette inventory system developed in Chapter 3 is that it be able to manage the repair of cassettes. If a cassette in the inventory is found to be in need of repair, it is placed on a *repair queue*. When a worker becomes available to fix a cassette, a cassette is selected from the repair queue (see Figure 10–1).

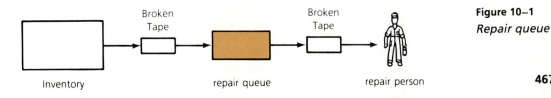

Figure 10–1
Repair queue

467

A concern of the video-cassette dealer is that the tapes that are most important to the inventory be repaired as quickly as possible. That is, we do not necessarily want the *first in, first out* rule of a standard queue to govern the behavior of the repair queue. Rather, we would like to assign some measure of importance, or **priority**, to the tapes awaiting repair and to select for repair the tape with the *highest priority*.

When a cassette first enters the repair queue it is assigned a **priority value,** *P*, which reflects the urgency with which the tape should be repaired. What quantity should our video-cassette dealer use for this priority value? There are many reasonable possibilities, including possibilities that take into account the title's popularity, its selling price, and the number of other tapes of the title currently in the inventory. For our problem, we shall select the ratio

$$P = \frac{\text{want value of tape}}{\text{have value of tape}}$$

for a tape's priority value. Recall from the case study in Chapter 3 that the inventory system maintains a *have value* and a *want value* for each tape. The have value of a tape is the number of copies of the tape currently in stock. The want value of a tape is used to determine how many new copies should be ordered—enough are ordered so that the have value is brought up to the want value. The want value presumably reflects the popularity of a title.

To summarize, when a tape is found to be defective, it is assigned a priority value and placed on the repair queue. When a worker becomes available, the tape with the highest priority value is selected from the repair queue. This management of the repair queue describes an ADT known as a **priority queue**. More formally, a priority queue is an abstract data type that supports the following operations.

```
Create (PQ)
(* Create an empty priority queue PQ. *)

IsEmpty (PQ)
(* Determine if priority queue PQ is empty. *)

Insert (PQ, e)
(* Add item e to priority queue PQ. *)

Remove (PQ)
(* Remove and retrieve from priority queue PQ
   the item with the highest priority value. *)
```

These operations resemble a subset of the table operations. The significant difference is the *Remove* operation. While the sequence `Retrieve-Delete` of table operations allows us to retrieve and delete an item with a *specified* value in its search key, *Remove* allows us to retrieve and delete the item with the *highest* priority value. Notice that *Remove*, unlike `Retrieve` and `Delete`, is not told the value in question. Since, in general, we shall not know what the highest priority value is, *Retrieve* and *Delete* could not easily perform this task. On the other hand, *Remove* could not be used to retrieve and delete an item with some specified value.

The ADT priority queue is thus both similar to and dissimilar from the ADT table, a fact that is reflected in their implementations. The binary search tree is a good implementation of both a table and a priority queue. On the other hand, we shall develop an implementation that, for many applications, is the most appropriate implementation of a priority queue but that is not at all appropriate as an implementation of a table.

Let us begin by considering some of the table implementations as implementations for a priority queue. The sorted linear implementations are appropriate if the number of items in the priority queue is small. The sequential implementation would maintain the items sorted in *ascending* order of priority value, so that the item with the highest priority value is at the end of the array (see Figure 10–2). This way *Remove* simply returns the item in *PQ[last]* and decrements *last*. However, the *Insert* operation, after using binary search to find the correct position for the insertion, must shift the array elements to make room for the new item.

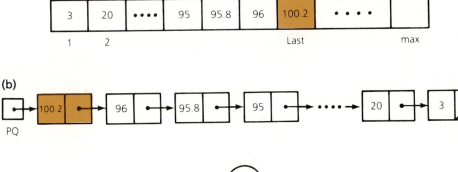

(a) Sequential implementation of ADT priority queue; (b) linked implementation; (c)   **Figure 10–2**
binary search tree implementation

The linked implementation maintains the items sorted in *descending* order of priority value, so that the item with the highest priority value is at the beginning of the list. This way *Remove* simply returns the item pointed to by *PQ* and changes *PQ* to point to the next item. The *Insert* operation, however, must traverse the list to find the correct position for the insertion.

We thus see that the linear implementations suffer from the same problems when they are used for priority queues as when they are used for tables. This leads us to consider a binary search tree as an implementation for a priority queue. The *Insert* operation is performed exactly as it is in the case of a table, but the *Remove* operation has no direct analog among the table operations. *Remove* must locate the item with the highest priority value, without knowing what this value is. The task is not difficult, however, since this item is always in the rightmost node of the tree. (Why?) We thus need only follow *Rchild* links until a node with a **NIL** *Rchild* link is encountered (a procedure analogous to the binary search tree's *Leftmost* can accomplish this task). The removal of this node from the tree is particularly easy since it has at most one child.

The binary search tree is thus a very good implementation of a priority queue. For some applications, however, we can do even better. A **heap** is an important array-based implementation of a priority queue. Since it is array-based, it is appropriate only for applications in which a fixed-size data structure is not a problem.

A Sequential Representation of Complete Trees

In Chapter 9, we developed a linked representation of a binary tree. There is also an array-based representation of a binary tree that is very useful, provided that the tree is of a certain form. As we shall see, a heap is a binary tree that happens to be of this form.

In Chapter 9 we defined a **complete** binary tree. Recall that definition:

A binary tree T is a **complete** tree of height *h* if:

(1) T is empty, or

(2) the left subtree of T is a full tree of height *h* - 1 and the right subtree of T is a complete tree of height *h* - 1, or

(3) the left subtree of T is a full tree of height *h* - 1 and the right subtree of T is a full tree of height *h* - 2, or

(4) the left subtree of T is a complete tree of height *h* - 1 and the right subtree of T is a full tree of height *h* - 2.

Figure 10–3 shows a complete tree with 9 nodes. The nodes have been numbered according to a standard **level-by-level** numbering scheme. The root is numbered 1, then the children of the root (the next level of the tree) are numbered, left to right, 2 and 3. The nodes at the next level are numbered, left to right, 4, 5, 6, and 7, and so forth. It is convenient to use this level-by-level numbering scheme for a complete tree because it will allow us to develop a simple sequential implementation.

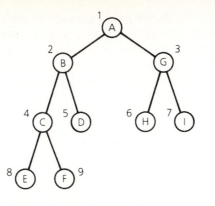

Figure 10–3

*Level-by-level
numbering of
complete
binary tree*

There is a very elegant array-based representation of a complete binary tree. Node 1 (the root) is stored in *Tree[1]*, node 2 is stored in *Tree[2]*, and so forth (see Figure 10–4). The key observation is that, given any node, we can easily locate both of its children and its parent. If you study the tree in the above diagram, you will observe that for any node i, its left child (if it exists) is node $2*i$, and its right child (if it exists) is node $(2*i)+1$. Further, the parent of node i (assuming the node is not the root) is node (i **DIV** 2). Since the array representation stores node i in *Tree[i]*, it is very simple to go from any node to either of its children or to its parent.

1	A
2	B
3	G
4	C
5	D
6	H
7	I
8	E
9	F

Figure 10–4

*Array repre-
sentation*

For this sequential representation to be appropriate for a binary tree, two conditions must be satisfied. First, the tree must be complete. If there were nodes missing from the middle of the tree, the numbering scheme would be thrown off, and there would be ambiguity as to who was the child of whom. In addition, since the representation is array-based, the maximum number of nodes must be known.

Heaps

A **heap** is a data structure similar to a binary search tree, although it does differ from a binary search tree in two significant ways. First, while a binary search tree can be viewed as being sorted, a heap is ordered in a much weaker sense.

As we shall see, however, the manner in which a heap is ordered is sufficient for the efficient performance of the priority queue operations (*Create*, *IsEmpty*, *Insert*, and *Remove*). The second significant difference is that while binary search trees come in many different shapes, heaps are always *complete* binary trees. As a consequence, if we know the maximum size of a heap, the sequential binary tree representation can be used.

A **heap** is a *complete* binary tree such that

(1) it is empty, or

(2a) the (priority) value in the root is *greater than or equal to* the priority value in either of its children, and

(2b) both subtrees are themselves heaps.

For example, Figure 10–5 shows a heap along with its array representation. Notice that, unlike a binary search tree, the value of each node is greater than the value of *both* of its children and that there is no relationship between the values of the children—that is, we don't know which child contains the larger value.

Figure 10–5

Heap with array representation

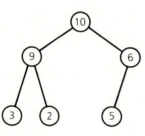

1	10
2	9
3	6
4	3
5	2
6	5

A Heap as an Implementation of a Priority Queue

We now need to show how a heap can be used to implement the priority-queue operations *Remove* and *Insert*. Let *PQ* be a record with two fields:

   Last: an integer indicating the number of items in the priority queue

   Items: an array of priority-queue items

The array *Items* corresponds to the sequential representation of a tree as described above. (To simplify the following examples, we shall assume that the priority-queue items are simply integers.)

   Let us begin with the *Remove* operation. What can we say about the location of the largest value in the heap? Since the value of every node is greater than that of either of its children, the largest value must be in the root of the tree. Thus, the first step of the *Remove* operation is

```
(* return the item in the root *)
return the item in PQ.Items[1]
```

That was easy, but we're not quite done. Once we remove the largest value, we are left with two disjoint heaps, as in Figure 10−6.

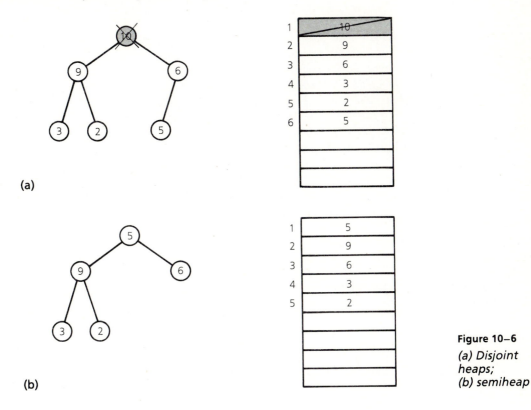

(a)

(b)

Therefore, we need a method of transforming back into a heap the nodes that remain after the root is removed. The first step is to take the item in the *last* node of the tree and place it in the root. This is easily accomplished by

```
(* copy the item from the last node into the root *)
PQ.Items[1] := PQ.Items[last]

(* remove the last node *)
last := last - 1
```

As the above diagram suggests, the result of this is *not* necessarily a heap. It is, however, a complete binary tree whose left and right subtrees are both heaps. The only problem is that the item in the root may be out of place. Such a structure is called a **semiheap**. We thus need a way to transform a semiheap into a heap. Our strategy will be to allow the value in the root to *trickle down* the tree until it reaches a node in which it will not be out of place; that is, the value will come to rest in the first node where it would be greater than (or equal to) the value of each of its children. To accomplish this, we shall first compare the value in the root of the semiheap to the values of its children. If the value is smaller than either of its children, we shall swap the item in the root with the larger of the two children. Once the values in the root and the larger child C have been swapped, C becomes the root of a semiheap. This suggests the following recursive procedure.

```
Adjust(PQ, root)
(* Convert the semiheap PQ rooted at position root into a heap.
   Recursively trickle the item at position root down to its
   proper position by swapping it with its larger child (if
   the child is larger than the item).  If (2 * root) > PQ.Last
   then the item is at a leaf and nothing needs to be done. *)

   IF ((root is a leaf (i.e., 2*root > PQ.Last)) OR (the value
        in node root (stored in PQ.Items[root]) is greater than
        or equal to the value of its children (stored in
        PQ.Items[2*root] and PQ.Items[2*root + 1]))) THEN

      the value is in the correct place and we are done

   ELSE
      let node j be the larger of the two children

      (* swap the value in node j with the value in node root *)
      Swap(PQ.Items[root], PQ.Items[j])

      (* recursively call Adjust on the
         semiheap rooted at node j *)
      Adjust(PQ, j)
   END
```

Figure 10–7

Calls to procedure Adjust

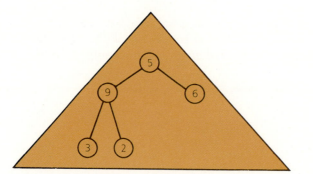

semiheap Adjust first called on

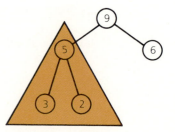

semiheap Adjust next called on

We can now write the entire *Remove* operation as follows.

```
Remove(PQ)

   (* return the item in the root *)
   return the item in PQ.Items[1]
```

```
(* copy the item from the last node into the root *)
PQ.Items[1] := PQ.Items[PQ.Last]

(* remove the last node *)
PQ.Last := PQ.Last - 1

(* transform the semi-heap back into a heap *)
Adjust(PQ, 1)
```

Before developing the *Insert* algorithm, let us briefly analyze the efficiency of *Remove*. It may have concerned you that, since the tree is stored in an array, the removal of a node requires us to swap array elements rather than simply to change a few pointers. While this is true, it is not necessarily an indication that the algorithm is inefficient. We must ask, *what is the largest number of array elements that may have to be swapped?* The algorithm first copies the item in the last node of the tree into the root. *Adjust* then trickles this item down the tree until its appropriate place is found. The key observation is that this item travels down a *single path* from the root to, at worst, a leaf. Therefore, the number of array items that *Adjust* must swap is no greater than the height of the tree. Since the height of a complete binary tree with N nodes is always approximately $\log_2 N$, *Remove* is in fact quite efficient.

The strategy for the *Insert* algorithm is the opposite of that for *Remove*. A new item will be inserted at the *bottom* of the tree and it will *trickle up* to its proper place. It is easy to trickle up a node, since the parent of node i (unless i is the root) is always stored in *PQ.Items[(i **DIV** 2)]*.

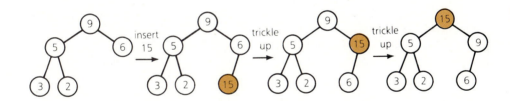

Figure 10–8
Insertion into heap

```
Insert(PQ, newitem)

    (* insert the new item into the last position of the tree *)
    PQ.Last := PQ.Last + 1
    PQ.Items[PQ.Last] := newitem

    (* trickle up the item to the appropriate spot in the tree *)
    place := PQ.Last
    parent := place DIV 2
    WHILE ((place > 1) AND
            (PQ.Items[place] > PQ.Items[parent])) DO
        Swap(PQ.Items[place], PQ.Items[parent])
        place := parent
        parent := place DIV 2
    END
```

The analysis of the efficiency of *Insert* is very similar to that for *Remove*. *Insert*, at worst, has to swap array elements on a path from a leaf to the root. The number of swaps, therefore, cannot exceed the height of the tree. Since the height of the tree (recall that it is complete) is always approximately $\log_2 N$, *Insert* is also very efficient.

We thus see that a heap is a very efficient implementation of a priority queue. How does a heap stack up to a binary search tree as an implementation of a priority queue? As we stated, because a heap is an array-based implementation, it is only appropriate if we know the maximum number of items that the priority queue can contain. If this is the case, a heap has several advantages over a binary search tree. For one thing, since a heap does not store explicit pointers, it requires slightly less space than a binary search tree. In most settings, however, this is not a major issue.

The real advantage of a heap is that it is always guaranteed to be balanced. (Recall that complete is a stronger condition than balanced.) As we have discussed, the height of a binary search tree can greatly exceed $\log_2 N$. Since the heap operations are far simpler than those needed to keep a binary search tree balanced, a heap is much more desirable in this respect. But don't think that a heap can replace a binary search tree as a table implementation, for, as we have said, a heap is not appropriate in this role. If this is not apparent, try to perform the table operation

```
Retrieve(T, X)
```

on a heap, or try to traverse a heap in sorted order.

Here is a definition module for the ADT priority queue.

```
DEFINITION MODULE PQueues;
(* ****************************************************************
    ADT PRIORITY QUEUE

    The following hidden type is declared:

        PQueue

    The following operations are supported:

        Create, IsEmpty, Insert, and Remove
    *************************************************************** *)

(* Priority queue item and key types—it is assumed that
the item type contains a field named key of type keytype *)
FROM ADTitem IMPORT

    itemtype, keytype;

EXPORT QUALIFIED
```

```
      PQueue, Create, IsEmpty, Insert, Remove;

TYPE

    PQueue;

(* ----------------------------------------------------------
    Create:  Create an empty priority queue PQ.
    ---------------------------------------------------------- *)
PROCEDURE Create(VAR PQ : PQueue);

(* ----------------------------------------------------------
    IsEmpty:  Determine if priority queue PQ is empty.

    ASSUMPTION:  Priority queue PQ has been created.
    ---------------------------------------------------------- *)
PROCEDURE IsEmpty(PQ : PQueue) : BOOLEAN;

(* ----------------------------------------------------------
    Insert:  Add newitem to priority queue PQ.  The Boolean flag
    success is returned TRUE if the Insert was successful, and
    FALSE otherwise (e.g., because of memory limitations).  In
    the event of an unsuccessful Insert, the priority queue is
    unchanged.

    ASSUMPTION:  Priority queue PQ has been created.
    ---------------------------------------------------------- *)
PROCEDURE Insert(VAR PQ : PQueue; newitem : itemtype;
                 VAR success : BOOLEAN);

(* ----------------------------------------------------------
    Remove:  Delete and retrieve from priority queue PQ the
    item with the largest priority value.  The operation fails
    if the priority queue is empty.  The Boolean flag success
    indicates whether the operation succeeded.  In the event of
    an unsuccessful Remove, the priority queue is unchanged.

    ASSUMPTION:  Priority queue PQ has been created.
    ---------------------------------------------------------- *)
PROCEDURE Remove(VAR PQ : PQueue; VAR getitem : itemtype;
                 VAR success : BOOLEAN);

END PQueues.


IMPLEMENTATION MODULE PQueues;
(* ***********************************************************
    ADT PRIORITY QUEUE - Heap Implementation
```

The following operations are supported:

    Create, IsEmpty, Insert, Remove

The priority queue is implemented as a heap.
Procedure Adjust is defined to help maintain a heap.
Type PQueue is a pointer to a record that is created
dynamically with a call to procedure NEW. This
indirection allowed type PQueue to be a hidden type.
*** *)

(* memory management procedure NEW *)
FROM Storage IMPORT

    ALLOCATE;

(* Priority queue item and key types—it is assumed that
the item type contains a field named key of type keytype *)
FROM ADTitem IMPORT

    itemtype, keytype;

(* fixed maximum size inferred from User's Documentation File *)
CONST

    maxqueue = 20;

TYPE

    (* priority queue structure *)
    pqbody = RECORD
                Items : ARRAY [1..maxqueue] OF itemtype;
                Last : [0..maxqueue];
             END;

    PQueue = POINTER TO pqbody;

(* --
   Adjust: Convert the semiheap H rooted at position root
   into a heap.

   Recursively trickle the item at position root down to its
   proper position by swapping it with its larger child (if
   the child is larger than the item).

   If (2 * root) > H^.Last then the item is at a leaf and
   nothing needs to be done.
   -- *)

```
PROCEDURE Adjust(VAR H : PQueue; root : CARDINAL);

VAR

    child : CARDINAL;
    temp : itemtype;

BEGIN

    (* stop if the root is a leaf *)
    IF ((2 * root) <= H^.Last) THEN
        (* child is the index of the left child of root *)
        child := 2 * root;

        (* child is the index of the larger child of root *)
        IF ((child + 1 <= H^.Last) AND
                (H^.Items[child+1].key > H^.Items[child].key)) THEN
            INC(child);
        END;

        (* swap if the item at position root
           is smaller than the larger child *)
        IF (H^.Items[child].key > H^.Items[root].key) THEN
            temp := H^.Items[root];
            H^.Items[root] := H^.Items[child];
            H^.Items[child] := temp;

            (* adjust the new subtree *)
            Adjust(H, child);
        END;
    END;

END Adjust;

(* -----------------------------------------------------------
   Create:  Create an empty priority queue PQ.
   ----------------------------------------------------------- *)
PROCEDURE Create(VAR PQ : PQueue);

BEGIN

    NEW(PQ);
    PQ^.Last := 0;

END Create;

(* -----------------------------------------------------------
   IsEmpty:  Determine if priority queue PQ is empty.
```

```
                ASSUMPTION:   Priority queue PQ has been created.
                ------------------------------------------------------------ *)
PROCEDURE IsEmpty(PQ : PQueue) : BOOLEAN;

BEGIN

    RETURN (PQ^.Last = 0);

END IsEmpty;

    (* ---------------------------------------------------------------
    Insert:   Add newitem to priority queue PQ.   The Boolean flag
    success is returned TRUE if the Insert was successful, and
    FALSE otherwise (e.g., because of memory limitations).   In
    the event of an unsuccessful Insert, the priority queue is
    unchanged.

    ASSUMPTION:   Priority queue PQ has been created.

    Method:   Insert the new item after the last item in the
    heap and trickle it up to its proper position.
    ------------------------------------------------------------ *)
PROCEDURE Insert(VAR PQ : PQueue; newitem : itemtype;
                      VAR success : BOOLEAN);

VAR

    parent, place : INTEGER;
    temp : itemtype;

BEGIN

    IF (PQ^.Last = maxqueue) THEN
        success := FALSE;
    ELSE
        (* place the new item at the end of the heap *)
        INC(PQ^.Last);
        PQ^.Items[PQ^.Last] := newitem;

        (* trickle it up to its proper position *)
        place := PQ^.Last;
        parent := place DIV 2;
        WHILE ((parent > 0) AND
                    (PQ^.Items[parent].key < PQ^.Items[place].key)) DO
            temp := PQ^.Items[parent];
            PQ^.Items[parent] := PQ^.Items[place];
            PQ^.Items[place] := temp;
            place := parent;
            parent := place DIV 2;
        END
```

```
        success := TRUE;
    END;

END Insert;
```

481
A Case Study:
Enhancements
to the Video-
Cassette Inven-
tory System

```
(* -----------------------------------------------------------
   Remove:  Delete and retrieve from priority queue PQ the
   item with the largest priority value.  The operation fails
   if the priority queue is empty.  The Boolean flag success
   indicates whether the operation succeeded.  In the event of
   an unsuccessful Remove, the priority queue is unchanged.

   ASSUMPTION:  Priority queue PQ has been created.

   Method:  Swap the last item in the heap to the root and
   trickle it down to its proper position.

   CALLS:  Adjust, IsEmpty
   ----------------------------------------------------------- *)
PROCEDURE Remove(VAR PQ : PQueue; VAR getitem : itemtype;
                 VAR success : BOOLEAN);

BEGIN

    IF (IsEmpty(PQ)) THEN
        success := FALSE;
    ELSE
        getitem := PQ^.Items[1]
        PQ^.Items[1] := PQ^.Items[PQ^.Last];
        DEC(PQ^.Last);
        Adjust(PQ, 1);
        success := TRUE;
    END;

END Remove;

END PQueues.
```

A CASE STUDY: ENHANCEMENTS TO THE VIDEO-CASSETTE INVENTORY SYSTEM

We next present a case study to help illustrate the use of ADT's in the problem-solving process. Rather than develop a new program, we shall modify and enhance the inventory program that was presented in Chapter 3.

Although a program might meet the needs of its users at the time of the original design, those needs can change as the environment of the users changes (for example, as a company grows). Ideally, we would like to see the program evolve along with the needs. There are at least two types of changes to a program that could be called for:

1. The program specifications might change. For example, the program could be required to do more (perform more functions) than was previously needed or desired.

2. The requirements for performance might change. When the program was originally written, the demands on computer resources may have been minimal. As the usage of the program or the size of the problem increases (for instance, the size of an inventory grows), a simple implementation that was satisfactory before may become unsatisfactory.

One of the things that we have tried to stress throughout this book is that a program that has been properly modularized with respect to both its processes and the management of its data will be much more amenable to modification. Imagine that the video-cassette dealership discussed in Chapter 3 has grown considerably since we first designed the inventory program and that our program is no longer completely addressing its current needs. The object of this case study is to bring the implementation up to date with these needs (and the material that we have been studying!). The new requirements can be classified as follows:

1. *Performance*. At the time of the original program design, the dealership was quite small and efficient management of data was not a major concern. (Also, of course, we had not yet considered the issue of efficiency.) We would now like to review our original implementation in the context of the material that we have been studying. As a consequence of this review, we shall consider alternate implementations for the parts of the program that are concerned with the management of data.

2. *Features*. The dealer would like the program to help keep track of the cassettes that need to be repaired. Because the store repairperson can fix only one cassette at a time, it is important that at any time the most needed cassette be repaired first.

In particular, the program should be able to execute the following three new commands associated with the repair of cassettes:

B<title>	(broken cassette)	Move the specified cassette from the stock shelves to the repair area (so the corresponding have value in the inventory decreases by 1). If the number of cassettes waiting to be repaired is at some prespecified maximum (that is, the backlog is too great), then send the new cassette out to be repaired somewhere else.

When the B command is executed, a priority value is assigned to the cassette, which determines how soon the cassette should be repaired. This value is defined to be the cassette's want value divided by its have value. The idea is that the more popular the cassette is (based on the want value), the sooner we need it, and the more we have on hand (based on the have value), the less urgent the repair becomes.

F	(start repairing the most needed cassette)	The most needed cassette in the repair area is identified (the one with the highest priority value) and the repairperson starts working on it.
P<title>	(put a cassette back into the inventory)	Add one copy of the specified title to the inventory. This command would be executed when a repair is completed.

As when designing a solution from scratch, the best approach to making changes to an existing program is to make a few related modifications at a time. The program should be fully tested and debugged with each new set of modifications before proceeding to the next set. Ideally, this strategy will ensure that we shall be making changes only to a few isolated modules at a time. In this spirit, the modification of the inventory program will occur in two stages that correspond to the two classes of requirements (performance and features) described above.

Modification of the Previous Implementation

If we go over the original implementation of the inventory program with our discussions of ADT's in mind, we can identify the key data-management operations that are performed on the inventory items. Since the operations are essentially value-oriented rather than position-oriented, the ADT resembles a variation of the ADT table.

BASIC TABLE OPERATIONS FOR THE INVENTORY

```
Insert
(* Insert an item into a table if it is not already present.
   (Called by AddModify and Delivery.) *)


Retrieve
(* Retrieve an item from a table.
   (Called by Inquire, AddModify, Delivery, and Sell.) *)


Replace
(* Replace an item in a table.
   (Called by AddModify, Delivery, Return, and Sell.) *)


Traverse
(* Traverse a table in sorted order, calling a user supplied
   procedure Visit on each item.
   (Called by List, Order, and Return.) *)
```

OPERATIONS THAT ARE PARTICULAR TO THE WAIT LIST ASSOCIATED WITH EACH INVENTORY ITEM

```
Waitnames
(* Write out the names on the wait list associated with
   an inventory item.
   (Called by List and Inquire.) *)


Addwait
(* Add a new name to the wait list associated with an
   inventory item.
   (Called by Sell.) *)


Delwait
(* Delete and retrieve the first name from the wait list
   associated with an inventory item.
   (Called by Delivery.) *)
```

OPERATIONS PARTICULAR TO SAVING AND RESTORING THE INVENTORY EACH DAY

```
Putinv
(* Save a table in specified files for use by the restore
   operation.
   (Called by the main program.) *)


Getinv
(* Restore a table from specified files created by the
   save operation.
   (Called by the main program) *)
```

Note that there are no *Create* or *Delete* operations. There is no *Create* operation because the intention is that the inventory is being restored (the table already exists). There is no *Delete* operation because the only time an item is deleted is when the inventory is written to the file. The deletion of an unwanted item is therefore handled by the *Putinv* operation.

We can rewrite the original program (described in Chapter 3) in terms of these ADT operations. The result is a program with a much clearer wall between the implementation of the data-management operations and the rest of the program.

The transformation to the ADT version of the program is straightforward. The ADT operations have already been implemented in the original program, and all that is needed is for them to be isolated into separate modules and subprograms. Here, for example, is the new version of one of the procedures (*AddModify*) that uses the ADT operations. The rest of the transformation is left as an exercise.

```
(* ------------------------------------------------------------
   AddModify:  Add a new title to the inventory, or modify
   the want value for a title that already exists in the
   inventory.
```

485
A Case Study:
Enhancements
to the Video-
Cassette Inven-
tory System

```
    Calls:  Prompt, Insert, Retrieve, Replace
    ------------------------------------------------------------ *)
PROCEDURE AddModify(VAR inventory : invtype);

VAR

    oneitem : stockinfo;
    wantval : INTEGER;
    newtitle : string;
    success : BOOLEAN;

BEGIN

    (* get the title argument *)
    Prompt(titleprompt);
    IReadString(newtitle);

    (* insert a new stock item if necessary *)
    Insert(inventory, newtitle);
    Retrieve(inventory, newtitle, oneitem, success);

    (* update the want value for the stock item *)
    WriteString('Title: ');
    WriteString(newtitle);
    WriteLn;
    WriteString('The current want value is ');
    WriteInt(oneitem.want,1);
    WriteString('.  Enter correct value: ');
    ReadInt(wantval);
    WriteLn;

    IF (wantval < 0) THEN
        WriteString('*** Negative want value is not allowed.');
        WriteLn;
        WriteString('*** The want value will be set to 0.');
        WriteLn;
        oneitem.want := 0;
    ELSE
        oneitem.want := wantval;
    END;

    (* replace the item in the inventory *)
    Replace(inventory, oneitem, success);

END AddModify;
```

We shall perform the remaining modifications to the ADT version of the program.
    Before continuing with the modification of the program, it will be useful to

make a few comments about the ADT version just described. In the original program, the data structure is very much integrated with the rest of the program. For example, the *Insert* routine returns a pointer to the inserted item; the pointer can then be used to make direct changes (without using ADT operations) to that item in the data structure. Note how this violates the spirit of the wall.

What is the consequence of rewriting the program in terms of the above ADT operations? Consider, for example, the old and new versions of procedure *AddModify* (add or modify an inventory item). In the original version, a call to *Insert* is made to locate or insert an item, and the have value of the item is directly modified by referencing the pointer returned by procedure *Insert*. In the new version a call to *Insert* is made, followed by a call to *Retrieve*, followed by a call to *Replace*. Unless we have a clever implementation or redefine the ADT operations (see Exercise 9), we are going to have to search the data structure three times instead of the one time required by the original insert-modify sequence.

On the surface it seems that we are paying a large price for the sake of clarity and the wall. Recall, however, the comments in Chapter 9 about keeping our perspective. In this spirit, a good argument can be made that this extra cost is of no real consequence. We shall formalize this notion in Chapter 13.

In contrast to procedure *AddModify*, let's consider the old and new versions of procedure *Delivery* (process a delivery). In particular, let's focus on the modification of the wait list associated with a newly delivered cassette. In the original version, a call to *Insert* is made to locate and/or insert an item, and the wait list is directly modified by referencing the pointer returned by procedure *Insert*. In the new version, however, *Insert* does not return a pointer. Otherwise, the wall around the ADT implementation would be violated. Instead, a call to the ADT operation *Delwait* must be made for each name that is to be removed from the wait list. Note that *Delwait* must search for the item each time it is called. As a consequence, if we receive several copies of a single title, we could be searching for the same inventory item repeatedly.

It is important to appreciate how significant the difference between the old and new versions of *Delivery* is. In *AddModify*, we replaced one search of the inventory with exactly three searches (calls to *Insert*, *Retrieve*, and *Replace*). On the other hand, in *Delivery* we are replacing one search (for each delivered title) with a number of searches that depends on the size of the shipment (the quantity of each title delivered). This number can easily be large enough to make the cost of the extra searches of the inventory prohibitive. We need to rethink our operations.

We can eliminate the redundant searching in *Delivery* by modifying the definition of the operation *Delwait*. Instead of deleting and retrieving one name at a time from a specified wait list, we shall pass an extra argument that allows us to delete several items at once. A consequence of this modification is that the message that must be written out for each name removed from the wait list will now be defined as part of the ADT operation.

```
Delwait(inventory, title, count)
(* Delete count names from the wait list associated with the
   specified inventory item.  Write a message for each name.  *)
```

With this digression out of the way, we now take a closer look at the implementation of the ADT operations. We are assuming that the inventory has grown quite large and that we are now concerned with the efficiency of the data management operations. It should not be difficult to see that the original implementation of the inventory corresponds to the sorted-linear implementation of the ADT table discussed in Chapter 9. Given that the inventory has grown quite large and that it may continue to grow, the binary search tree implementation should immediately come to mind.

The conversion to the binary search tree implementation of the ADT operations is straightforward, and we will present most of the routines without special comment. The only routines that require some special attention are the *Getinv* and *Putinv* operations for saving and restoring the inventory structure.

How can we save the data in a binary search tree so that the tree can later be restored? We'll present two different algorithms for saving and restoring a tree. The first will restore a tree to its original shape. The second will restore a tree to a shape that is *balanced*.

487
A Case Study:
Enhancements
to the Video-
Cassette Inven-
tory System

SAVE

Save the tree in preorder (that is, write out the data items in the order of the tree's preorder traversal).

RESTORE

Insert each item (as it is read back in) with the usual binary search tree *Insert* operation.

ALGORITHM 1

You should convince yourself that the restored tree will have exactly the same shape as the original. For example, consider the tree in Figure 10–9.

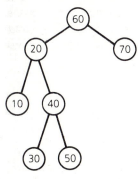

Figure 10–9

*A binary
search tree*

If we save the tree in preorder, we get the sequence 60, 20, 10, 40, 30, 50, 70. The claim is that the following sequence of *Insert* operations will yield the original tree.

```
Insert (T, 60)
Insert (T, 20)
Insert (T, 10)
Insert (T, 40)
Insert (T, 30)
Insert (T, 50)
Insert (T, 70)
```

Algorithm 1 restores a tree to exactly the same shape that it had before it was saved. Can we do better than this? That is, do we necessarily want the restored tree to have its original shape? Recall that a given set of data items can be organized into many different binary search trees (that is, trees with different shapes). All that is required for the inventory program to work correctly is that the restored tree have the binary search tree property. That is, the search key in any node must be greater than all the search keys in its left subtree and less than all of the search keys in its right subtree (assuming no duplicate search keys).

Although the shape of a binary search tree has no affect whatsoever on the correctness of the program, it will affect the *efficiency* of the tree operations, and we *are* concerned about efficiency. After all, this is why we are considering a binary search tree implementation in the first place! What we would really like to have is an algorithm that will restore a tree to a shape that is *balanced*.

It turns out that this is a surprisingly simple thing to do. In fact, we can even guarantee that the restored tree will be of minimum height (a condition stronger than balanced). To see how we can do this, first recall that the whole purpose of a balanced binary search tree is to give us a linked structure on which we can perform a binary search. That is, each node of the tree represents the middle item of a subproblem that the binary search algorithm could encounter. This tells us exactly how to build a balanced binary search tree from a fixed set of data—let the middle item be the root of the tree, and make the left and right subtrees into balanced binary search trees.

Consider, for example, a full tree with exactly $N = 2^h - 1$ nodes for some height h (see Figure 10–10). Note that, as a consequence of the definition of a full tree, the root contains the exact middle of the data items and the left and right subtrees are full trees of size $2^{h-1} - 1$ (that is, half of $N - 1$, or, equivalently, N **DIV** 2 since N is odd). Thus, the following recursive algorithm can be used to restore a full tree T with N nodes, provided that it has been saved in sorted order (with an inorder traversal). It may be surprising that the tree can be constructed directly by reading the sorted data from left to right.

Figure 10–10

Building full tree from a file

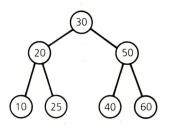

10	20	25	30	40	50	60

file contents

```
Readfull(T, N)

    (* construct the left subtree *)
    Readfull(left subtree of T, N DIV 2)

    (* get the root *)
    read(item for the root of T)

    (* construct the right subtree *)
    Readfull(right subtree of T, N DIV 2)
```

We have a simple solution for restoring a full tree, but what can we do if the tree to be restored is not full (that is, if it does not have $N = 2^h - 1$ nodes for some h)? The first thing that comes to mind is that the restored tree should be complete (full up to the last level with the last level filled in from left to right). Actually, since all we care about is minimizing the height of the restored tree, it is sufficient that the tree be full up to the last level. That is, we really don't care where the nodes on the last level go (see Figure 10–11).

Figure 10–11

Tree of minimum height (not complete)

Procedure *Readfull* is essentially correct even if the tree is not full. We do, however, have to be a bit careful when computing the sizes of the left and right subtrees. If N is odd, then both subtrees are of size N **DIV** 2 as before (the root is automatically accounted for). If N is even, however, then we have to take care to account for the root and the fact that one subtree will have one more node than the other. In this case, we arbitrarily choose to put the extra node in the left subtree.

```
Readtree (T, N)

    (* construct the left subtree *)
    Readtree (left subtree of T, N DIV 2)

    (* get the root *)
    read (item for the root of T)

    (* construct the right subtree *)
    Readtree (right subtree of T, (N - 1) DIV 2)
```

To summarize, we can easily restore a tree as a balanced binary search tree if the data is sorted (that is, produced from the inorder traversal) and we know the size of the tree. The size of the tree is necessary to be able to determine the middle item and, in turn, the sizes of the left and right subtrees. Knowing the size is a simple matter of counting as the tree is traversed and then saving the size in a file that can be read by the restore operation.

SAVE   ALGORITHM 2

(1) Save the data items in inorder (with an inorder traversal), counting the number of nodes in the tree.

(2) Save the size of the tree.

RESTORE

(1) Read the size of the tree.

(2) Execute the recursive *Readtree* procedure.

Modula-2 procedures for the ADT operations follow. We include only the procedures that are relevant to the implementation of the binary search tree. Note that the restore operation is part of procedure *Getinv* and that the save operation is part of procedure *Putinv*.

```
(* ------------------------------------------------------------
    Find:  Return a pointer to the item in inventory that
    contains title.  Return NIL if title is not present.
    ------------------------------------------------------- *)
PROCEDURE Find(inventory : invtype; title : string) : invtype;

VAR

    value : invtype;

BEGIN

    (* empty tree - title is not found *)
    IF (inventory = NIL)  THEN
        value : = NIL;

    (* the title has been found *)
    ELSIF (CompareStr(title,inventory^.item.title) = 0)  THEN
        value : = inventory;

    (* search the left subtree *)
    ELSIF (CompareStr(title,inventory^.item.title) < 0)  THEN
        value : = Find(inventory^.left, title);

    (* search the right subtree *)
    ELSE
        value : = Find(inventory^.right, title);

    END;

    RETURN (value);

END Find;

(* ------------------------------------------------------------
    Insert:  Insert title in inventory if it is not already
    present.
    ------------------------------------------------------- *)
```

491
A Case Study:
Enhancements
to the Video-
Cassette Inven-
tory System

```
PROCEDURE Insert(VAR inventory : invtype; title : string);
BEGIN

    (* insert the new item in the empty tree *)
    IF (inventory = NIL) THEN

        NEW(inventory);
        inventory^.left := NIL;
        inventory^.right := NIL;
        inventory^.wait := NIL;
        inventory^.item.title := title;
        inventory^.item.have := 0;
        inventory^.item.want := 0;

    (* search the left subtree *)
    ELSIF (CompareStr(title,inventory^.item.title) < 0) THEN
        Insert(inventory^.left, title);

    (* search the right subtree *)
    ELSIF (CompareStr(title,inventory^.item.title) > 0) THEN
        Insert(inventory^.right, title);

    (* do nothing if it is already present *)

    END;

END Insert;


(* -----------------------------------------------------------
   Retrieve:  Retrieve into getitem the inventory item with
   the specified title.  The operation fails if the item
   is not present.  The flag success indicates whether the
   operation succeeded.

   Calls:  Find
   ----------------------------------------------------------- *)
PROCEDURE Retrieve(inventory : invtype; title : string;
                   VAR getitem : stockinfo;
                   VAR success : BOOLEAN);

VAR

    loc : invtype;

BEGIN

    (* search for the title *)
    loc := Find(inventory, title);
```

```
        IF (loc = NIL) THEN
            success := FALSE;
        ELSE
            getitem := loc^.item;
            success := TRUE;
        END;

    END Retrieve;

    (* ------------------------------------------------------------
        Replace:  Replace the inventory item specified by replitem.
        The operation fails if there is no such item.  The flag
        success indicates whether the operation succeeded.

        Calls:  Find
        ------------------------------------------------------------ *)
    PROCEDURE Replace(inventory : invtype; replitem : stockinfo;
                        VAR success : BOOLEAN);

    VAR

        loc : invtype;

    BEGIN

        (* search for the title *)
        loc := Find(inventory, replitem.title);

        IF (loc = NIL) THEN
            success := FALSE;
        ELSE
            loc^.item := replitem;
            success := TRUE;
        END;

    END Replace;

    (* ------------------------------------------------------------
        Traverse:  Traverse inventory inventory in sorted order,
        calling procedure Visit for each item.
        ------------------------------------------------------------ *)
    PROCEDURE Traverse(inventory : invtype; Visit : ProcType);
    BEGIN

        IF (inventory # NIL) THEN

            (* traverse the left subtree *)
            Traverse(inventory^.left, Visit);
```

493

A Case Study:
Enhancements
to the Video-
Cassette Inven-
tory System

```
        (* visit the root *)
        Visit(inventory, inventory^.item);

        (* traverse the right subtree *)
        Traverse(inventory^.right, Visit);
    END;

END Traverse;

(* ------------------------------------------------------------
    Addwait:  Add a name to the wait list associated with the
    specified title.  The operation fails if the title is not
    present in the inventory.

    Calls:  Find
    ------------------------------------------------------------ *)
PROCEDURE Addwait(VAR inventory : invtype;
                      title, who : string;
                      VAR success : BOOLEAN);

VAR

    loc : invtype;
    ptr : waitptr;

BEGIN

    (* search for the title *)
    loc := Find(inventory, title);

    IF (loc = NIL) THEN
        success := FALSE;
    ELSE
        NEW(ptr);
        ptr^.who := who;
        ptr^.next := NIL;
        IF (loc^.last = NIL) THEN
            loc^.wait := ptr;
        ELSE
            loc^.last^.next := ptr;
        END;
        loc^.last := ptr;
        success := TRUE;
    END;

END Addwait;
```

```
(* ----------------------------------------------------------------
    Delwait:  Delete and retrieve up to count names from the
    wait list associated with the title.  Write out a message
    for each name.

    Calls:  Find
    ---------------------------------------------------------------- *)
PROCEDURE Delwait(VAR inventory : invtype; title : string;
                       count : INTEGER);

VAR

    loc : invtype;
    ptr : waitptr;

BEGIN

    (* search for the title *)
    loc := Find(inventory, title);

    IF (loc # NIL) THEN

        (* remove names from the wait list *)
        WHILE ((loc^.wait # NIL) AND (count > 0)) DO
            ptr := loc^.wait;
            WriteString('      ---> Hold one copy for ');
            WriteString(ptr^.who);
            WriteLn;
            count := count - 1;
            loc^.wait := loc^.wait^.next;
            DISPOSE(ptr);
        END;

        (* set empty wait list if necessary *)
        IF (loc^.wait = NIL) THEN
            loc^.last := NIL;
        END;

    END;

END Delwait;

(* ----------------------------------------------------------------
    Getwait:  Restore from waitfile the wait list for stockitem.

    The size of the list is the negative of the have value of
    the inventory item.
    ---------------------------------------------------------------- *)
```

495
A Case Study:
Enhancements
to the Video-
Cassette Inven-
tory System

```
PROCEDURE Getwait(VAR stockitem : stocknode;
                  VAR waitfile : FixedFile);

VAR

    toread : INTEGER;
    tempfirst, templast : waitptr;

BEGIN

    (* initialize the wait list *)
    stockitem.wait := NIL;
    stockitem.last := NIL;

    (* size of list to read in *)
    toread := -stockitem.item.have;

    (*  read in the list of names and
        attach it to the stock node *)
    IF ((toread > 0) AND (NOT EOF(waitfile))) THEN
        (* get the first item of the list *)
        NEW(tempfirst);
        templast := tempfirst;
        ReadItem(waitfile, templast^.who);
        DEC(toread);

        (* get the rest of the list *)
        WHILE ((toread > 0) AND (NOT EOF(waitfile))) DO
            NEW(templast^.next);
            templast := templast^.next;
            ReadItem(waitfile, templast^.who);
            DEC(toread);
        END;

        (* end the list *)
        templast^.next := NIL;

        (* attach the list to the stock item *)
        stockitem.wait := tempfirst;
        stockitem.last := templast;

    END;

    (* check for incomplete wait file *)
    IF ((toread > 0) AND (EOF(waitfile))) THEN
        WriteString('*** Error:  Incomplete wait file.');
        WriteLn;
        WriteString('*** The have value will be adjusted for title');
```

```
            WriteString(stockitem.item.title);
            WriteLn;
            stockitem.item.have := stockitem.item.have + toread;
      END;

END Getwait;


(* -----------------------------------------------------------
   Getinv:   Restore inventory from a sorted file into a
   binary search tree.   Restore the corresponding wait lists.
   The restored tree will be of minimum height.

   Files:   invfile  - the main inventory structure
            sizefile - the size of the inventory
            waitfile - the associated wait lists

   The structure is read by the locally defined procedure
   doread.

   Calls:   Getwait
   ------------------------------------------------------------- *)
PROCEDURE Getinv(VAR inventory : invtype;
                 VAR invfile : FixedFile;
                 VAR sizefile : FixedFile;
                 VAR waitfile : FixedFile);

VAR

   size : INTEGER;

   PROCEDURE doread(VAR inventory : invtype; size : INTEGER);
   BEGIN

      IF ((size = 0) OR ( EOF(invfile) )) THEN
         inventory := NIL;
      ELSE
         NEW(inventory);

         (* read into the left subtree *)
         doread(inventory^.left, size DIV 2);

         (* read into the root *)
         ReadItem(invfile, inventory^.item);
         Getwait(inventory^, waitfile);

         (* read into the right subtree *)
         doread(inventory^.right, (size - 1) DIV 2);
      END;
```

497

A Case Study:
Enhancements
to the Video-
Cassette Inven-
tory System

```
    END doread;

(* main body of Getinv *)
BEGIN

    (* initialize *)
    OpenRead(invfile);
    OpenRead(waitfile);
    OpenRead(sizefile);
    IF (EOF(sizefile)) THEN
        size := 0;
    ELSE
        ReadItem(sizefile,size);
    END;

    (* restore the inventory *)
    doread(inventory, size)

END Getinv;

(* -----------------------------------------------------------
    Putwait:   Save in waitfile the wait list for stockitem.

    The size of the list is the negative of the have value of
    the inventory item.

    Note:  The size of the wait list is checked against the
    have value.  If they do not match, then a program error is
    indicated.  The have value is adjusted in order to allow
    the program to continue.
    ----------------------------------------------------------- *)
PROCEDURE Putwait(VAR stockitem : stocknode;
                  VAR waitfile : FixedFile);

VAR

    ptrav : waitptr;
    size : INTEGER;

BEGIN

    (* save the wait list for the item - count its size *)
    size := 0;
    ptrav := stockitem.wait;
    WHILE (ptrav # NIL) DO
        INC(size);
        WriteItem(waitfile, ptrav^.who);
        ptrav := ptrav^.next;
    END;
```

```
                 (* check the have value against the size of the wait list *)
            IF ((size > 0) OR (stockitem.item.have < 0)) THEN
                IF (size # -stockitem.item.have) THEN
                    WriteString('*** Program Error:  The size of the');
                    WriteString(' wait list does not agree');
                    WriteLn;
                    WriteString('*** with the have value for title: ');
                    WriteString(stockitem.item.title);
                    WriteLn;
                    WriteString('*** The have value will be reset.');
                    WriteString('size/have before');
                    WriteInt(size,5);
                    WriteInt(stockitem.item.have,5);
                    stockitem.item.have := -size;
                    WriteString('size/have after');
                    WriteInt(size,5);
                    WriteInt(stockitem.item.have,5);
                END;
            END;


END Putwait;


(* ------------------------------------------------------------
    Putinv:  Save inventory in external files.

    The size of the inventory structure, the structure itself,
    and the associated wait lists are saved in separate files.
    Items that have zero have and want values and empty wait
    lists are eliminated.

    Files:   invfile  - the main inventory structure
             sizefile - the size of the inventory
             waitfile - the associated wait lists

    The structure is written out by the locally defined
    procedure doput.

    Calls:  Putwait
    ------------------------------------------------------------ *)
PROCEDURE Putinv(inventory : invtype;
                 VAR invfile : FixedFile;
                 VAR sizefile : FixedFile;
                 VAR waitfile : FixedFile);

VAR

    size : INTEGER;
```

499
A Case Study:
Enhancements
to the Video-
Cassette Inven-
tory System

```
(* recursively write the inventory structure to a file,
    counting the number of items that have been written *)
PROCEDURE doput(invptr : invtype);
BEGIN

    IF (invptr # NIL) THEN

        (* save the left subtree *)
        doput(invptr^.left);

        (* save the root item - eliminate items with
           zero have and want values and empty wait lists *)
        IF ((invptr^.item.have # 0)
                OR (invptr^.item.want # 0)
                OR (invptr^.wait # NIL)) THEN
            Putwait(invptr^, waitfile);
            WriteItem(invfile, invptr^.item);
            size := size + 1;
        END;

        (* save the right subtree *)
        doput(invptr^.right);
    END;

END doput;

(* main body of Putinv *)
BEGIN

    (* initialize *)
    OpenWrite(invfile);
    OpenWrite(sizefile);
    OpenWrite(waitfile);
    size := 0;

    (* save the inventory *)
    doput(inventory);
    WriteItem(sizefile, size);

END Putinv;

(* -----------------------------------------------------------
   Waitnames:  Write out the names on the wait list specified
   by waitptr.

   Calls:  Find
   ----------------------------------------------------- *)
PROCEDURE Waitnames(inventory : invtype; title : string);
```

```
VAR

   ptr : waitptr;
   loc : invtype;

BEGIN

   (* search for the title *)
   loc := Find(inventory, title);

   (* write out the names *)
   ptr := loc^.wait;
   WHILE (ptr <> NIL) DO
      WriteString('   ---> Back Ordered by: ');
      WriteString(ptr^.who);
      WriteLn;
      ptr := ptr^.next;
   END;

END Waitnames;
```

Once again, we have a complete working program that solves the original problem. The primary differences from the original program are as follows:

1. The program has been converted to a version that is based on the identified ADT operations. This further modularizes the program by separating the implementation of the data-management operations from the rest of the program. The implication is that if the underlying data structure changes, we need modify only the implementations of the ADT operations—behind the wall.

2. The data structure that supports the inventory has been converted from a sorted linked list to a binary search tree. The intention is that the binary search tree will support the data management operations more efficiently.

The second major task in bringing the program up to date with the users' current needs is to add the repair queue as described above.

Adding New Features to the Program

The video-cassette dealer has requested that the program help keep track of cassettes that need to be repaired (see the description of the B, F, and P commands earlier). The addition of these new features can be broken down into the following seven subtasks:

      I. Process command B (*Break*).

     II. Process command F (*Fix*).

   III. Process command P (*PutBack*).

   IV. Identify the ADT operations needed to support the repair queue.

V. Choose an implementation for the defined ADT.

VI. Modify the main program to accommodate the B, F, and P commands and the repair queue.

VII. Modify the H command (*Help*) to list the B, F, and P commands.

501
A Case Study:
Enhancements
to the Video-
Cassette Inven-
tory System

Subproblem I. Process command B. Move a specified cassette from the inventory to the repair queue.

FIRST PASS

```
Break(inventory, repair)

    read in a title argument
    retrieve the inventory item

    (* add the title to the repair queue *)
    compute the priority value for the cassette
    add the title to the repair queue

    (* update the inventory item *)
    decrement the have value by 1
    replace the inventory item
```

Because we are working from an existing program, many of the implementation details have already been worked out. Therefore, the second refinement can be fairly complete.

SECOND PASS

```
Break(inventory, repair)

    Prompt(titleprompt)
    IReadString(title)
    Retrieve(inventory, title, oneitem, success)
    IF ((NOT success) OR (oneitem.have < 1)) THEN
        write a message
    ELSE
        (* add the title to the repair queue *)
        priority := oneitem.want/oneitem.have
        add the title to the repair queue
        IF (the add is not successful
                 (i.e., repair area is full)) THEN
            write a message (send cassette out to be repaired)
        END

        (* update the inventory item *)
        oneitem.have := oneitem.have - 1
```

```
      Replace(inventory, oneitem, success)
END
```

Subproblem II.   Process command F. Identify the most needed cassette and start repairing it.

```
Fix(inventory, repair)

    IF (the repair queue is empty) THEN
        write a message
    ELSE
        remove from the repair queue the cassette
            with the highest priority value
    END
```

Subproblem III.   Process command P. Put a cassette into the inventory.

FIRST PASS

```
PutBack(inventory)

    read in a title argument
    insert a new item if necessary
    retrieve the item
    add 1 to the have value (call Delwait if necessary)
    replace the modified item
```

SECOND PASS

```
PutBack(inventory)

    Prompt(titleprompt)
    IReadString(title)
    Insert(inventory, title)
    Retrieve(inventory, title, oneitem, success)
    IF (oneitem.have < 0) THEN
        Delwait(inventory, title, 1)
    END
    oneitem.have := oneitem.have + 1
    Replace(inventory, oneitem, success)
```

Subproblem IV.   Identify the ADT operations needed to support the repair queue.
   So far, we have identified the following operations:

```
Insert
(* Add a title to the repair queue. *)
```

503
A Case Study:
Enhancements
to the Video-
Cassette Inven-
tory System

Remove
(Remove the title with highest priority value. *)*

IsEmpty
(Determine if the repair queue is empty. *)*

In addition to these operations, we will need *Save* and *Restore* operations so that the repair queue can be saved along with the rest of the inventory at the end of the day. Note that this defines a variation of the classic priority queue with the added operations of *Save* and *Restore*. As with the table for the inventory structure, we do not include a *Create* operation as the priority queue will be restored from a file.

Subproblem V. Choose an implementation for the repair queue.
   The fixed maximum size of the repair queue suggests a heap implementation of the priority queue.

```
CONST

    maxqueue =  desired size of repair queue

TYPE

    keytype   = REAL

    itemtype = RECORD
                  key : keytype
                  title : string
               END

    pqueue    = RECORD
                  Items : ARRAY [1..maxqueue] OF itemtype
                  Last : [0..maxqueue]
               END

VAR

    repair : pqueue
```

This implementation, in turn, suggests a simple implementation for the *Save* and *Restore* operations, since we can use the module *FileIO* (introduced in Chapter 3 and defined in the appendix) to define a file that contains items of type *pqueue*.
   We can create the priority queue file with a call to *CreateFile*. We can save the priority queue with:

Save (PQ, PQfile)

```
open PQfile for writing
write PQ as a single item to PQfile
close PQfile
```

We can restore the priority queue with:

```
Restore(PQ, PQfile)
```

```
open PQfile for reading
read PQ as a single item from PQfile
close PQfile
```

Subproblem VI. Modify the main program to accommodate the B, F, and P commands and the repair queue.

We simply have to add the following:

> Add B, F and P to the list of recognized command characters.
>
> Add calls to *Break*, *Fix*, and *PutBack* in the case statement.
>
> Add calls to *Save* and *Restore* along with *Putinv* and *Getinv*.

Subproblem VII. Modify the H command (*Help*) to list the B, F, and P commands.

The modification to *Help* is simply a matter of listing the three new commands in the help listing.

> ### Summary of Modifications and Enhancements to the Video-Cassette Inventory Problem
>
> 1. When making changes to a program, it is best to make a few at a time. By maintaining a modular design, we can reduce a fairly large modification to a set of small and fairly simple modifications to isolated parts of the program.
>
> 2. New features can be added to a program by applying the same techniques that we use in an original design. These include the use of top-down design and data abstraction.
>
> 3. If a program is properly modularized, it is a simple matter to replace implementations of specific algorithms or data structures with new implementations.

Here are the Modula-2 implementations of *Break*, *Fix*, *PutBack*, *Save*, and *Restore*. Note that we also include a procedure *CreatePQfile*, which creates the priority queue file.

```
(* ---------------------------------------------------------------
   Break:   Move a broken cassette to the repair queue.

   Calls:   Prompt, Retrieve, Add, Replace
   --------------------------------------------------------------- *)
```

505
A Case Study:
Enhancements
to the Video-
Cassette Inven-
tory System

```
PROCEDURE Break(inventory : invtype; VAR repair : pqueue);

VAR

    title : string;
    repairitem : itemtype;
    oneitem : stockinfo;
    success : BOOLEAN;

BEGIN

    (* get the title argument *)
    Prompt(titleprompt);
    IReadString(title);

    (* retrieve the title from the inventory *)
    Retrieve(inventory, title, oneitem, success);

    (* add a cassette to the repair
       queue and update the inventory *)
    IF (NOT success) THEN
        WriteString('    *** Title is not in current inventory: ');
        WriteString(title);
        WriteLn;
    ELSIF (oneitem.have < 1) THEN
        WriteString('    *** Title is currently out of stock: ');
        WriteString(title);
        WriteLn;
    ELSE
        (* add a cassette to the repair queue *)
        repairitem.key := FLOAT(oneitem.want)/FLOAT(oneitem.have);
        repairitem.title := title;
        Add(repair, repairitem, success);
        IF (success) THEN
            WriteString('Cassette moved to repair queue.');
            WriteLn;
        ELSE
            WriteString('There is no room on the repair queue.');
            WriteLn;
            WriteString('The item has been sent out.');
            WriteLn;
        END;

        (* update the inventory *)
        oneitem.have := oneitem.have - 1;
        Replace(inventory, oneitem, success);
    END;
END Break;
```

```
(* ------------------------------------------------------------
    Fix:   Fix a cassette and put it back in the inventory.

    Calls:  IsEmpty, Remove
   ------------------------------------------------------------ *)
PROCEDURE Fix(VAR repair : pqueue);

VAR

    repairitem : itemtype;
    success : BOOLEAN;

BEGIN

    (* get the repaired cassette from the repair queue *)
    IF (IsEmpty(repair)) THEN
        WriteString('There are no cassettes waiting to be repaired.');
        WriteLn;
    ELSE
        Remove(repair, repairitem, success);
        WriteString('Cassette is being repaired: ');
        WriteString(repairitem.title);
        WriteLn;
    END;

END Fix;

(* ------------------------------------------------------------
    PutBack:  Put a repaired cassette back into the inventory.

    Calls:  Prompt, Insert, Retrieve, Delwait, Replace
   ------------------------------------------------------------ *)
PROCEDURE PutBack(VAR inventory : invtype);

VAR

    title : string;
    oneitem : stockinfo;
    success : BOOLEAN;

BEGIN

    (* get the title argument *)
    Prompt(titleprompt);
    IReadString(title);

    (* insert a new stock item if necessary *)
    Insert(inventory, title);
    Retrieve(inventory, title, oneitem, success);
```

507

A Case Study:
Enhancements
to the Video-
Cassette Inven-
tory System

```
    (* process at most one back order *)
    IF  (oneitem.have < 0)  THEN
        Delwait(inventory, title, 1);
    END;

    (* update the have value *)
    oneitem.have := oneitem.have + 1;
    Replace(inventory, oneitem, success);

END PutBack;

(* -----------------------------------------------------------
    CreatePQfile:   Create file PQfile for saving a priority
    queue.
    --------------------------------------------------------- *)
PROCEDURE CreatePQfile(VAR PQfile : FixedFile;
                           name : ARRAY OF CHAR);
BEGIN

    CreateFile(PQfile, name, TSIZE(pqbody));

END CreatePQfile;

(* -----------------------------------------------------------
    Save:   Save priority queue PQ in file PQfile.
    --------------------------------------------------------- *)
PROCEDURE Save(PQ : pqueue; VAR PQfile : FixedFile);
BEGIN

    OpenWrite(PQfile);
    WriteItem(PQfile, PQ^);
    CloseFile(PQfile);

END Save;

(* -----------------------------------------------------------
    Restore:   Restore priority queue PQ from file PQfile.
    --------------------------------------------------------- *)
PROCEDURE Restore(VAR PQ : pqueue; VAR PQfile : FixedFile);
BEGIN

    OpenRead(PQfile);
    IF  (EOF(PQfile))  THEN
        PQ^.Last := 0;
    ELSE
        ReadItem(PQfile, PQ^);
    END;
    CloseFile(PQfile);

END Restore;
```

The Concept

Many applications require us to organize data in a manner that simultaneously supports several different data-management tasks. As a very simple example, let us suppose that we must maintain a (FIFO) queue of customer records; for example, the customers are on some type of a waiting list. In other words, we must support the standard queue operations *Isempty*, *Add*, *Remove*, and *QueueFront*.

Let us suppose that in addition to requiring the basic queue operations, the application frequently requires a listing of the records of the customers in the queue. In order that this listing be of most use, the records should appear *sorted* by customer name. That is, we must be able to support the basic queue operations *plus* a *Traverse* operation that visits the customer records in sorted order.

This presents us with an interesting problem. If we simply store the customer records in a queue, they will not, in general, be sorted by name. If, on the other hand, we simply store the records in sorted order, we will not be able to perform the queue operations (for example, process the customers on a first-come, first-served basis). We seem to require that the data be organized in two different ways.

One solution is to maintain two independent structures, one organized to support the sorted traversal and the other organized to support the queue operations. Figure 10–12 depicts a sorted linked list of customer records and a linked implementation of the queue. We choose linked implementations because we have no good estimate of the maximum number of customer records that we will have to store.

Figure 10–12
Independent data structures

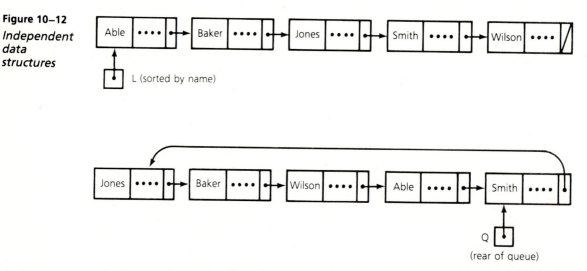

One obvious disadvantage of this scheme is the space that it requires to store two copies of each customer record. In addition, not all the required operations are supported as efficiently as we would like them to be. Before proposing a better scheme, let us consider how well this one supports the required operations.

The operations that require us only to *retrieve* data—sorted *Traverse* and *QueueFront*—are easy to perform. A sorted listing of customer records can be obtained by traversing the sorted linked list, and the *QueueFront* operation can be performed by inspecting the record at the front of the queue. The operations *Add* and *Remove* are, however, more difficult to perform because they must *modify* the data.

The *Add* operation now has two steps:

(1) Insert a copy of the new customer record at the rear of the queue. This step requires only a few pointer changes.

(2) Insert a copy of the new customer record into its proper position in the sorted linked list. This step requires that we traverse the sorted linked list.

Similarly, the *Remove* operation has two steps:

(1) Delete the customer at the front of the queue, remembering the name. This step requires only a few pointer changes.

(2) Scan the sorted linked list for the name just removed from the queue, and delete from the list the customer record containing this name. This step requires that we traverse the sorted linked list.

We thus see that while the scheme efficiently supports the *Traverse* and *Queuefront* operations, the operations *Add* and *Remove* require the sorted linked list to be traversed (whereas in a basic queue they can be performed with a small, *constant* number of steps). Is there any way to improve this scheme? One thing that comes to mind is to store the customer records in a binary search tree rather than a sorted linked list. This would allow the second steps of the *Add* and *Remove* operations to be performed much more efficiently. This is certainly an improvement over the original scheme, but the *Add* and *Remove* operations still require significantly more work than they would for a normal queue.

We can, in fact, devise a different kind of scheme, which supports the *Remove* operation almost as efficiently as if we were maintaining only a basic queue. The idea is to allow our data structures to *communicate* with each other. We shall introduce the concept with a sorted linked list and a queue, and later we shall indicate how this concept can be applied to more complex structures, such as a binary search tree.

In the scheme shown in Figure 10–13, the sorted linked list still contains customer records, but the queue now contains only *pointers* to customer records. That is, each entry of the queue points to the record (stored in the sorted linked list) of the customer at the given queue position. An obvious advantage of storing only pointers in the queue is that the storage requirements are reduced, since a pointer is likely to be much smaller than a customer record (which could contain a large number of fields). As we shall now see, this type of scheme also significantly improves the efficiency of the *Remove* operation.

The efficiencies of the *Traverse*, *QueueFront*, and *Add* operations do not differ significantly from the original scheme depicted in Figure 10–12. The

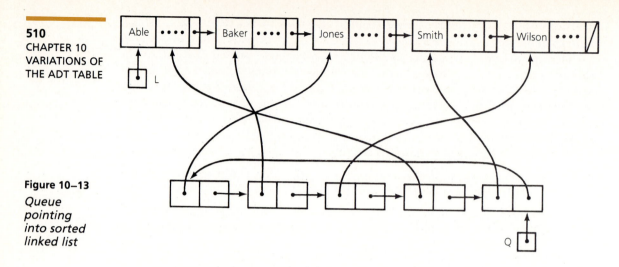

Figure 10–13

*Queue
pointing
into sorted
linked list*

Traverse operation is still performed by traversing the sorted linked list.
Queuefront and *Add* are now performed as follows:

QueueFront (Q)

```
let p be the pointer stored at the front of the queue

(* p points to the record in the sorted linked list
      corresponding to the customer at the front of the queue *)

return the record pointed to by p
```

Add (Q, newitem)

```
find the proper position for newitem
    in the sorted linked list

insert a record containing newitem into this position

add to the rear of the queue a pointer to the new record
```

The real benefit of the scheme is in the implementation of the *Remove* operation.

Remove (Q)

```
remove the item from the front of the queue and remember its
    value p

(* p points to the customer record which is to be deleted *)

delete from the sorted linked list the customer record R pointed
    to by p
```

Because the front of the queue contains a pointer to the customer record to be deleted, there is no need to search the sorted linked list. We have a pointer to the appropriate record and all we need to do is delete it. However, there is one big problem. Since we were able to go directly to the record R to be deleted (that is, without traversing the list from its beginning), we have no trailing pointer to the record that precedes R on the linked list! As you recall, we must have a trailing pointer in order to delete the record.

As our scheme now stands, the only way to obtain the trailing pointer is to traverse the linked list from its beginning—but this would negate the advantage gained by having the queue point into the linked list. What we have discovered is the classic motivation for a different kind of linked list, the **doubly linked list**.

Doubly Linked Lists

The problem we have just encountered is one that commonly arises when we have a method for directly accessing a node that we wish to delete from a linked list. If we have been able to locate the node without a traversal, we will not have established a trailing pointer to the node that precedes it on the list. A **doubly linked list** is a data structure that overcomes this problem by giving us a way to back up from the node we wish to delete to the node that precedes it.

We have seen doubly linked lists before. At the end of Chapter 7, we introduced a doubly linked list as an implemention of a traversable stack. In that setting, the list was used in a very restricted manner. Insertions and deletions were performed only at the top of the stack, that is, only at one of the ends of the list. For our purposes here, however, we must be able to insert into and delete from an arbitrary position of a doubly linked list.

We will structure our sorted list of customers so that each node contains (in addition to its data fields) two pointer fields, *prev* and *next*. As usual, the *next* field of node N points to the node that follows N on the list. The *prev* field points to the node that precedes N on the list. Thus, the form of our sorted linked list of customers is as shown in Figure 10–14.

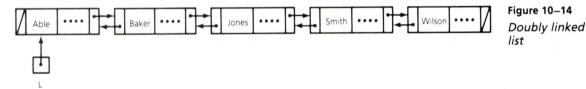

Figure 10–14
*Doubly linked
list*

Notice that if *p* points to a node N that we wish to delete (for example, this is the pointer stored at the front of the queue), a pointer to the node that precedes N on the list can be obtained with the assignment

previous : = *p*ˆ. *prev*

A doubly linked list thus allows us to delete a node without traversing the list to establish a trailing pointer.

We now must consider the mechanics (that is, how to set the pointers on the list) of inserting into and deleting from a doubly linked list. Because there are more pointers to set, the details are a bit more involved than for a singly linked list. In addition, the special cases (inserting into and deleting from either the beginning or the end of the list) are more complicated.

It is common to eliminate the special cases by structuring a doubly linked list to contain a **dummy head node**. In Chapter 3 we briefly discussed the use of dummy head nodes for singly linked lists. While we personally do not find them worthwhile for singly linked lists, the more complicated special cases for doubly linked lists make head nodes very attractive.

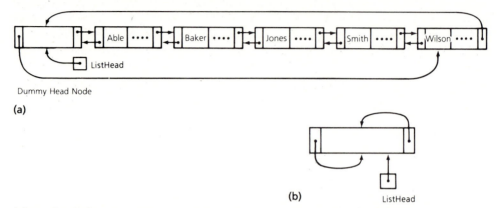

Dummy Head Node

(a)

(b)   ListHead

Figure 10–15   *(a) Doubly linked list with dummy head node; (b) empty list with head node*

As pictured in Figure 10–15, the external pointer *ListHead* always points to the dummy head node. Note that the head node is of the same type as the other nodes on the list (and thus it also contains *prev* and *next* pointer fields). We link the list so that it becomes **circular**. The *next* field of the head node points to the first "real node" (for example, the first customer) on the list, and the *prev* field of the first real node points back to the head node. Similarly, the *prev* field of the head node points to the last node on the list, and the *next* field of the last node points to the head node. Note that the head node is present even when the list is empty. In this case we set both pointer fields of the head node to point to the head node itself.

Using this structure, insertions and deletions can be performed without special cases—inserting into and deleting from the first or last position is the same as for any other position. Let us begin by considering how to delete the node N pointed to by *p*. We need to:

(1) change the *next* field of the node that precedes N so that it points to the node that follows N.

(2) change the *prev* field of the node that follows N so that it points to the node that precedes N.

Figure 10–16

Pointer changes for deletion

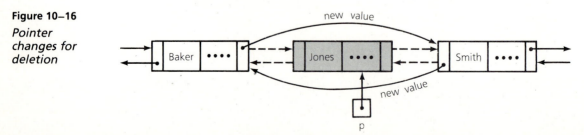

These steps can be accomplished with two assignment statements

```
p^. prev^. next  := p^. next
p^. next^. prev  := p^. prev
```

You should convince yourself that this works even when the node to be deleted is the first, last, or only data (nonhead) node on the list.

Let us now consider the problem of inserting into a doubly linked list. In general, the fact that the list is doubly linked does not save us from having to traverse the list to find the proper place for the new item. For example, if we insert a new customer into the queue (for example, we perform the *Add* operation considered earlier), we must find the proper place in the sorted linked list for the new record. The following traversal sets *cur* to point to the node which should follow the new node in the list.

```
cur  := ListHead^. next
WHILE ((cur # ListHead) AND (newname > cur^. name)) DO
  cur  := cur^. next
END
```

Notice that if the new record is to be inserted at the end of the list (or into an empty list), the loop will set *cur* to point to the dummy head node.

Once the loop has set *cur* to point to the node that is to follow the new node, we need to:

(1) set the *next* field of the new node to point to the node that is to follow it.

(2) set the *prev* field of the new node to point to the node that is to precede it.

(3) set the *prev* field of the node that is to follow the new node so that it points to the new node.

(4) set the *next* field of the node that is to precede the new node so that it points to the new node.

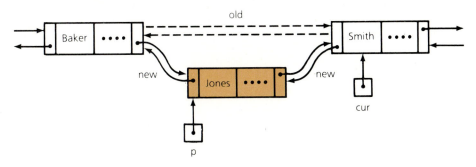

Figure 10–17
Pointer changes for insertion

This is accomplished with the following assignment statements:

```
(* insert the node pointed to by p
   before the node pointed to by cur *)
p^. next := cur
```

$p^\wedge.prev := cur^\wedge.prev$
$p^\wedge.next^\wedge.prev := p$
$p^\wedge.prev^\wedge.next := p$

You should convince yourself that this works even when inserting into the beginning or end of a list (in the latter case, *cur* will point to the head node), or into an empty list (in which case *cur* also will point to the head node).

To summarize, we have developed a fairly good scheme for supporting the queue operations plus a sorted traversal. Let us now consider ways to improve the efficiency of the *Add* operation. Recall that to perform the *Add* operation, we still must traverse the linked list to find the proper place to insert a new customer record.

Our choice to store the customer records in a *linear* linked list was made to simplify the discussion. We can also devise a more efficient scheme where the queue points into a binary search tree rather than a linked list (see Figure 10–18). This would allow the *Add* operation to be performed in logarithmic time (assuming the tree remains balanced). Notice, however, that we would need the analogue of a doubly linked tree to be able to efficiently support the *Remove* operation. That is, we would need each node in the tree to point to its parent. This is required if we are easily to delete the node pointed to by the front of the queue. This implementation is further discussed in Exercise 10.12.

Figure 10–18

Queue pointing into a binary search tree

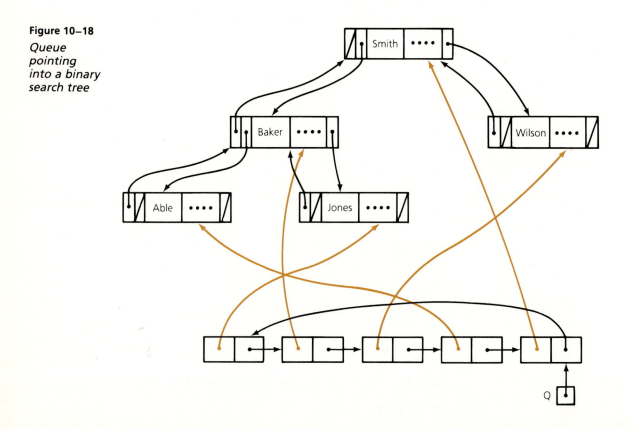

In general, it is possible to impose several independent organizations simultaneously on a set of data items. This concept will be discussed further in Chapter 12 in the context of indexing external storage.

SUMMARY

1. A priority queue is a variation of the ADT table. Its operations allow us to retrieve and remove the item in the queue with the largest priority value.

2. A heap is a very good implementation of a priority queue when we know the maximum number of items that will be stored at any one time. A heap utilizes a sequential representation of a complete binary tree.

3. An important principle raised by our discussion in the last section of the chapter is that it is possible to impose several independent organizations on a given set of data. We illustrated the technique by storing records sorted in a doubly linked list, with a FIFO order imposed by a queue of pointers into the list.

4. The case study illustrated that a modular program is easy to modify and expand. It is a simple matter to replace implementations of algorithms and data structures with new ones. New features should be added to the program in accordance with principles of top-down design and data abstraction.

5. The case study developed a simple algorithm for saving an arbitrary binary search tree in a file and restoring it to a binary search tree which is of the minimum possible height.

EXERCISES

1. Prove that the root of a heap is the largest element in the tree.

2. The heap that we described in the text is called a **maxheap** because the largest element is at the root (see Exercise 10.1). This is appropriate because the *Remove* operation for the priority queue that it is implementing is defined to delete the element with highest priority value. Suppose that we redefine the *Remove* operation to delete the element with lowest priority value instead. We would then want to implement a **minheap**. Convert the maxheap implementation to a minheap implementation.

3. How does the order in which two items with the same priority value are inserted into a heap affect the order in which they will be deleted? What can we do if we need elements with equal priority value to be served on a first-come, first-served basis?

4. Let's say that we would like to maintain the index of the item with smallest priority value in a maxheap. That is, in addition to a *Removemax* operation, we might want to support a *Retrievemin* operation. How hard will this index be to maintain under *Insert* and *Removemax* operations?

COMMON PITFALLS / DEBUGGING

1. A heap is a very good implementation of a priority queue, but it is not appropriate for a table. Specifically, the *Retrieve* and *Traverse* sorted operations are not supported efficiently.

2. The sequential representation of a binary tree is appropriate only when the tree is complete and the maximum number of nodes is known.

3. A doubly linked list is a construct that programmers tend to over-use. One situation where they are appropriate is when we have a way to access directly (that is, without a traversal from the beginning of the list) a node that must be deleted. Doubly linking the list gives an easy way to get to the node that precedes the node to be deleted.

4. The mechanics of inserting into and deleting from a doubly linked list are a bit involved. Special cases for the beginning and end of the list are complicated and can be eliminated by using a dummy head node.

5. We want to implement a priority queue under the assumption that there are only 10 distinct priority values. How does this assumption affect our choice of an implementation? How can we ensure that items with equal priority will be served on a first-come, first-served basis?

6. Rewrite the original inventory program from Chapter 3 in terms of the ADT operations described in this chapter.

7. Suppose that we want to count the total number of copies of each title in the inventory that are sold. Which routines in the inventory program have to be modified? How might we use this sales information to determine a priority value for the repair queue?

8. If we modify the inventory structure for an existing inventory (for example, if we add a new data field to a stock item), the restore operation that executes at the very beginning of the program will not be valid. (Why?) Write a program that will convert all the files associated with a saved inventory to a new format. Try and keep your conversion program as general as possible to account for future modifications to the inventory program.

9. Suppose that we know in advance that table items tend to be accessed in streaks. That is, we tend to access a given item several times in a row before accessing a different item. We would like to take advantage of this knowledge to avoid having to search for the same item repeatedly.

In the case study, we were faced with this problem to a small extent when we had to perform *Insert-Retrieve-Replace* sequences for a given title. More significantly, we faced the problem with the *Delwait* operation when we had to delete several names at a time from a wait list associated with an inventory item. Recall that we resolved this problem by redefining the *Delwait* operation to include an integer argument that specified the number of names to delete. Unfortunately, it won't always be easy to address this problem by redefining a simple ADT operation.

Another way to address this problem is to add an extra bookkeeping pointer to our implementation. That is, we can maintain a last-accessed pointer that will always reference the last item that was accessed in the table (by any operation). Whenever an operation is performed that references the location of a specific table item, the last-accessed item can be checked before starting the search.

For example, if we use this scheme with a binary search implementation, *table* becomes a record of type:

```
    TYPE

table = RECORD
            root,
            lastaccessed : nodeptr;
        END;
```

Complete the implementation of the basic ADT table operations under this scheme. Note the problem that is caused with the operations that are currently implemented recursively. The initial call is passed a record (of type *table*) as an argument, but the recursive calls are passed a pointer (of type *nodeptr*). We can resolve this problem by adding a nonrecursive shell around our recursive procedures (as we did for binary search in Chapter 4).

10. Suppose that we want to support deletion operations for two different search keys (for example, *DeleteN* (delete by name) and *DeleteS* (delete by social security number)). Describe an efficient implementation.

11. Implement *Delete*, *Retrieve*, *Traverse*, and *Replace* operations for a doubly linked list with a dummy head node. Assume that the items on the list are sorted by search key.

12. Recall that the motivation for a doubly linked list is the need to delete a node on a list that is located without traversing the list. The analogy for binary search trees is to maintain parent pointers. That is, every node (except the root) will have a pointer to its parent in the tree. Write *Insert* and *Delete* operations for this structure.

13. Redo Exercise 10.10, organizing one of the search keys with a binary search tree and the other with a sorted linked list.

*14. Recall the use of the repair queue in the inventory program. Imagine that we would like to adjust the priority of an item in the queue after each sale (for example, if we sell out of a title that is on the repair queue, then it becomes important to repair it more quickly).

a. How can we adjust a heap if a single priority value changes?

b. How can we link the two main structures (the inventory and the repair queue) together to make updates easy?

PROJECT

15. Write an interactive program that will monitor the flow of patients in a large hospital. The program should account for patients checking in and out of the hospital and should allow access to information about a given patient. In addition, the program should manage the scheduling of three operating rooms. Doctors make a request that includes a patient's name and a priority value between 1 and 10 that reflects the urgency of the operation. Patients are chosen for the operating room by priority value, and patients with the same priority should be served on a first-come, first-served basis. The basic control of the program should be with external commands (as in the inventory case studies). Although this problem is very similar in spirit to the inventory case study that we have developed, the object of this exercise is to design a program from scratch by incorporating the techniques of data abstraction into your problem-solving process. That is, as you design your solution, try and identify the essential operations (excuse the pun) that will be performed on the data and only then choose an appropriate data structure for implementation. This will allow you to maintain the wall between the main part of the program and the implementations. An interesting exercise would be to do a variation of this problem as an event-driven simulation.

PART IV

ADVANCED TECHNIQUES
FOR THE MANAGEMENT OF DATA

CHAPTER 11

ADVANCED IMPLEMENTATIONS OF THE ADT TABLE

PREVIEW   The final part of the book introduces several advanced topics in data management. The first topic discussed is balanced search trees. In Chapter 9 we saw that the efficiency of the binary search tree implementation of a table depends on the tree being relatively balanced. In this chapter we discuss modifications to the basic binary search tree algorithms that guarantee that the search tree will always remain balanced. We then consider a completely different implementation of the ADT table called hashing, which attempts to provide direct access to the data item with a given key value. In principle, we tell the hashing algorithm the key value that we are interested in, and it calculates where to look for the data with that key value rather than searching for it.

In this final part of the book we shall look at several fundamentally important techniques for managing data. These techniques can all be characterized as advanced methods for implementing the ADT table and its variants. Some of the techniques provide improvements to the table implementations that we have already studied, while others adopt approaches to implementing a table that are completely different from anything we have seen so far. We shall also consider methods for implementing a table that, because of its great size, must reside on an external storage device such as a disk. Sorting, which impinges upon many aspects of data management, will be further studied in Chapter 13.

Let us begin with a thumbnail description of the topics that we shall encounter in these last three chapters.

1. **Balanced search trees.** The high degree of efficiency with which a binary search tree can implement a table depends on the tree being balanced. We shall study a slightly different type of search tree, which *remains balanced in all situations* and thus always can be searched with efficiency comparable to a binary search.

2. **Hashing.** Hashing is a technique that, for many types of applications, can provide a table implementation that is even more efficient than a search tree. Hashing locates a data item by *calculating* the location where it should be stored rather than by searching for it.

3. **External methods.** All the table implementations discussed so far assume that the table will reside in the computer's internal memory at the time the operations are to be performed. In many real-world applications, however, the size of a table greatly exceeds the amount of available internal memory. In such situations we must be able to operate on the table while it resides on an external device. In Chapter 12 we shall briefly examine the nature of external storage and describe methods for implementing a table which must be stored externally.

522

CHAPTER 11
ADVANCED
IMPLEMENTA-
TIONS OF THE
ADT TABLE

4. **Sorting.** Sorting is a task that frequently must be performed for the management of data. We have already seen three different sorting algorithms (*Insertion sort*, *Quicksort*, and *Mergesort*) and, in Chapter 13, we shall introduce a fourth, *Heapsort*. We shall also study the basic mathematical techniques necessary for comparing the sorting algorithms. This will give us a basis for making a selection in a given situation.

Most computer scientists would agree that these are fairly advanced topics. Indeed, aspects of this material are often encountered in graduate courses and even in research articles. Interestingly enough, however, while the details and mathematical analyses of these techniques are quite difficult, their underlying concepts are at a level compatible with this book. We therefore feel that, by focusing on only the basic concepts, we can present a useful introduction to this material, which is so central to the efficient management of data.

BALANCED SEARCH TREES

Recall from our presentation of binary search trees in Chapter 9 how a tree's performance is tied to its height. To perform the table operations *Retrieve*, *Insert*, and *Delete*, a path must be followed from the root of the tree down to the node that contains the desired item (or, in the case of the *Insert* operation, to the node that is to become the parent of the new item). At each node along the path, the search value is compared to the value in the node in order to determine which branch to follow next. Since the maximum number of nodes that can be on such a path is equal to the height of the tree, the maximum number of comparisons that can be required by the table operations is equal to this height.

We have seen that a binary search tree that contains N items can have a height ranging from a maximum of N to a minimum of $\lceil \log_2(N + 1) \rceil$. As a consequence, the number of comparisons that could be required to locate a particular item can be anywhere between that required by a sequential search of a linked list and that required by a binary search of an array. Since our motivation for developing the binary search tree implementation was to obtain a linked structure that could be searched with speed comparable to a binary search, it is certainly critical that the most optimistic behavior of a binary search tree be realized.

Let us consider the factors that determine the height that a binary search tree will have. The algorithms developed in Chapter 9 for maintaining a binary search tree make the height of the tree very sensitive to the order in which items are inserted and deleted. For example, consider a binary search tree containing the items 10, 20, 30, 40, 50, 60, and 70 (for simplicity we are assuming that each item consists solely of a search key that is an integer). If the items were inserted into the tree in the order 40, 20, 60, 10, 30, 50, 70, we would obtain a binary search tree of minimum height. If, on the other hand, the items were inserted in the order 10, 20, 30, 40, 50, 60, 70, we would obtain a binary search tree of maximum height (see Figure 11–1).

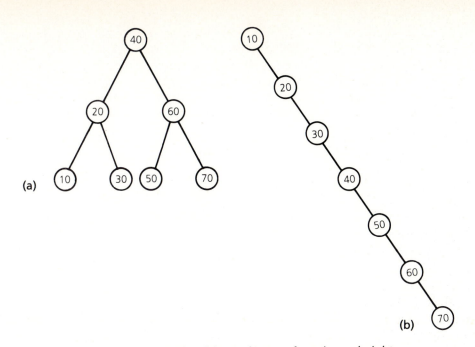

(a)

(b)

(a) Search tree of minimum height; (b) search tree of maximum height

Figure 11–1

We thus see that if our algorithms are used to maintain a binary search tree, there is always the possibility that the tree will approach a linear shape, and, as a consequence, its behavior would be no better than that of a linked list. For this reason, it is desirable in many applications to use one of several variations of the basic binary search tree algorithms that can prevent the shape of the tree from degenerating. Two of the better-known variations are the **AVL tree** (named for its inventors Adel'son–Vel'skii and Landis) and the **2–3 tree**.

AVL TREES

We shall concentrate primarily on the 2–3 tree, but let us first briefly illustrate how an AVL tree works. The basic strategy of the AVL method is to monitor the shape of the search tree. If an insertion or deletion ever causes the tree to stray too far from a balanced shape, corrective measures are taken. For example, suppose that the search tree in Figure 11–2 is the result of a sequence of insertions and deletions. The performance of this tree can be improved if we rearrange its nodes to make the tree more balanced. We can, for instance, rotate the tree so that the node <20> becomes the root with left child <10> and right child <30>. Notice that we cannot arbitrarily rearrange the tree's nodes, but rather we must take care not to destroy the search tree's ordering property in the course of the rebalancing.

It is, in fact, possible to rearrange any binary search tree to obtain a binary search tree with the minimum possible height—that is, $\lceil \log_2(N + 1) \rceil$ for a tree with N nodes. Recall, for example, the algorithm developed in the case study of

524

CHAPTER 11
ADVANCED
IMPLEMENTA-
TIONS OF THE
ADT TABLE

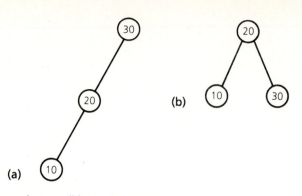

Figure 11–2   *(a) Small linear search tree; (b) rotated tree*

Chapter 10. The algorithm starts with an arbitrary binary search tree, saves its values in a file, and then constructs a new binary search tree of minimum height containing these same values. Although this approach was appropriate in the context of the inventory system (since the rebuilding was performed only once a day), it requires too much work to be performed every time an insertion or deletion leaves our tree unbalanced. The cost of repeatedly rebuilding the tree could very well outweigh the benefit of searching a tree of minimum height.

The AVL method is a compromise. It maintains a binary search tree with a height *close* to the minimum, but it is able to do so with far less work than would be required to keep the height of the tree *exactly* equal to the minimum. The details of how this is accomplished are rather involved, but the concept is simple. If, after an insertion or deletion, there is any node N in the tree such that the heights of the left and right subtrees of N differ by more than one, a rebalancing rotation such as the one depicted in Figure 11–2 is performed. As we have already observed, this rotation must be such that the search tree property is preserved.

We can illustrate the actions of the AVL tree algorithm on the following sequence of insertions.

```
Insert (T, 10)
Insert (T, 20)
Insert (T, 30)
Insert (T, 40)
Insert (T, 50)
Insert (T, 60)
Insert (T, 70)
```

In this example, notice how the rotations have kept the height of the tree at the minimum. It can, in fact, be proved that the height of an AVL tree with N nodes will always be very close to the theoretical minimum of $\lceil \log_2(N + 1) \rceil$. The AVL tree is, therefore, one method for guaranteeing binary search-like efficiency in the search tree implementation of a table.

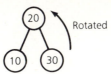

Insert(T,10)   Insert(T,20)   Insert(T,30)

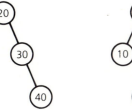

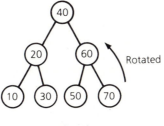

Insert(T,40)   Insert(T,50)   Insert(T,60)

Insert(T,70)

Figure 11–3

Insertions into an AVL tree

2–3 TREES

We shall study 2–3 trees in somewhat greater detail. One reason for concentrating on the 2–3 tree rather than on the AVL tree is that the 2–3 tree generalizes to a structure that can be used to implement a table stored in external memory (for example, on a disk). This structure, known as a **B-tree**, is discussed in the next chapter.

As is the case for an AVL tree, a 2–3 tree can be searched with efficiency very close to that of a minimum height binary search tree, yet it is far easier to maintain than a minimum height binary search tree. The strategy of a 2–3 tree is to permit the number of children of an internal node to vary between two and three. As we shall see, this allows insertions and deletions to be absorbed without a deterioration of the tree's shape.

526
CHAPTER 11
ADVANCED
IMPLEMENTA-
TIONS OF THE
ADT TABLE

A **2–3 tree** is a tree such that each internal node (nonleaf) has either two or three children, and all leaves are at the same level. A recursive definition is:

T is a **2–3 tree** of height h if:

(1) T is empty (this is a 2–3 tree of height 0). Or,

(2) T is of the form

       n

  T_L T_R

where n is a node, and T_L and T_R are 2–3 trees, each of height $h - 1$. In this case, T_L is called the **left subtree**, and T_R is called the **right subtree**. Or,

(3) T is of the form

       n

  T_L T_M T_R

where n is a node, and T_L, T_M, and T_R are 2–3 trees, each of height $h - 1$. In this case, T_L is called the **left subtree**, T_M is called the **middle subtree**, and T_R is called the **right subtree**.

For example, Figure 11–4 shows a 2–3 tree of height 3.

Figure 11–4

*2–3 tree of
height 3*

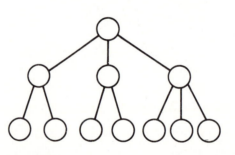

The most striking thing about a 2–3 tree is that it is *not* necessarily a binary tree since a node can have three children. A 2–3 tree does, nevertheless, very much resemble a full binary tree. If a 2–3 tree contains no node that has three children (this is certainly permitted by the definition), then it *is* in fact a full binary tree, since all internal nodes would have two children and all leaves would be at the same level. If, on the other hand, some of the internal nodes of a 2–3 tree do have three children, then the tree will contain more nodes than a full binary tree of the same height. Therefore, a 2–3 tree of height h always has at least as many nodes as a full binary tree of height h; that is, it always has at least $2^h - 1$ nodes. To put this another way, a 2–3 tree with N nodes never has height greater than $\lceil \log_2(N + 1) \rceil$, the minimum height of a binary tree with N nodes.

The above observations should lead us to suspect that a 2–3 tree is a type of balanced tree that might be very useful in the implementation of the ADT table, and this is indeed the case. We will use a **2–3 search tree**, defined as follows, to implement a table of data items.

The 2–3 tree T is a **2–3 search tree** if:

(1) T is empty. Or,

(2) T is of the form

$$n$$

$$T_L \qquad T_R$$

and node n contains one data item. In this case, the value of the search key in n must be greater than the value of each search key in the left subtree T_L and smaller than the value of each search key in the right subtree T_R. Also, T_L and T_R must each be a 2–3 search tree. Or,

(3) T is of the form

$$n$$

$$T_L \quad T_M \quad T_R$$

and node n contains two data items. In this case, the value of the smaller search key in n (denoted by S) must be greater than the value of each search key in the left subtree T_L and smaller than the value of each search key in the middle subtree T_M. The value of the larger search key in n (denoted L) must be greater than the value of each search key in the middle subtree T_M and smaller than the value of each search key in the right subtree T_R. In addition, T_L, T_M, and T_R must each be a 2–3 search tree.

This definition sets several rules for how data items may be placed in the nodes of a 2–3 search tree.

KEY CONCEPTS

Rules for Placing Data Items in the Nodes of a 2–3 Search Tree

1. If n has two children, then it must contain a single data item.

2. If n has three children, then it must contain two data items.

3. If n is a leaf, then it may contain either one or two data items.

In addition to these three structural rules, the definition of a 2–3 search tree implies that its values must be ordered in a manner analogous to the way the values in a binary search tree are ordered. As we shall see, this allows us to search a 2–3 tree efficiently for the item with a given search key.

To illustrate a 2–3 search tree, let us assume that each data item consists of a single integer value. The tree in Figure 11–5 satisfies the definition. (Notice that if the data items were records, then nodes with three children would each have to accommodate two records.)

528

CHAPTER 11
ADVANCED
IMPLEMENTA-
TIONS OF THE
ADT TABLE

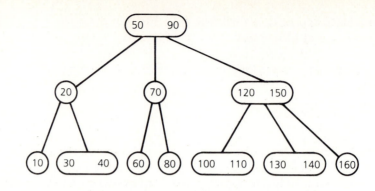

Figure 11–5

*2–3 search
tree*

Because a 2–3 search tree has an ordering property analogous to the ordering property of a binary search tree, the `Retrieve` operation of a 2–3 search tree is very similar to that of a binary search tree.

```
Retrieve(T, X, getitem, success)
(* Retrieve into getitem the item from table T with search
   key X.   The operation fails if there is no such item.   The
   flag success indicates whether the operation succeeded. *)

   let R be the root node of T

   (* the item has been found *)
   IF (X is in R) THEN
      getitem := the appropriate item from R
      success := TRUE

   (* failure *)
   ELSIF (R is a leaf) THEN
      success := FALSE

   (* search the appropriate subtree *)

   (* R has two data items *)
   ELSIF (R has two data items) THEN

      IF (X < the smaller search key of R) THEN
         Retrieve(left subtree, X, getitem, success)
      ELSIF (X < the larger search key of R) THEN
         Retrieve(middle subtree, X, getitem, success)
      ELSE
         Retrieve(right subtree, X, getitem, success)
      END

   (* R has one data item *)
   ELSE
```

```
    IF  (X < search key)  THEN
        Retrieve(left subtree, X, getitem, success)
    ELSE
        Retrieve(right subtree, X, getitem, success)
    END

END
```

For the 2–3 tree algorithms, it is convenient to define the degenerate case to be a leaf rather than an empty subtree. As a result, our algorithms must assume that they are not passed an empty tree as an argument. This will allow us to avoid distracting implementation details.

The ordering of a 2–3 search tree also allows it to be traversed in sorted order by performing the analogue of an inorder traversal.

```
Inorder(T)

    let R be the root node of T

    IF  (R is a leaf)  THEN
        print the data item(s)

    (* R has two data items *)
    ELSIF  (R has two data items)  THEN
        Inorder(left subtree)
        print the first data item
        Inorder(middle subtree)
        print the second data item
        Inorder(right subtree)

    (* R has one data item *)
    ELSE
        Inorder(left subtree)
        print the data item
        Inorder(right subtree)
    END
```

Let us now see what we have gained by using a 2–3 tree rather than a binary search tree (from now on we shall, as most authors do, use the term 2–3 tree to mean 2–3 search tree). Earlier we observed that a 2–3 tree with N nodes can have height no greater than $\lceil \log_2(N + 1) \rceil$. Thus, a 2–3 tree representing a given table of items always has height less than or equal to that of the *best possible* binary search tree for that same table. This fact, plus the fact that no node in a 2–3 tree has more than two items, can be shown to imply that a table represented by a 2–3 tree can be searched with approximately the same efficiency as if the table were represented by a binary tree that is *as balanced as possible*.

530

CHAPTER 11
ADVANCED
IMPLEMENTA-
TIONS OF THE
ADT TABLE

It may have surprised you that we said that the 2–3 tree can be searched with *approximately* the same efficiency as, rather than with *greater* efficiency than, the binary search tree. After all, the 2–3 tree might very well be even shorter than the balanced binary search tree. It is a common misconception that the advantage gained by a 2–3 tree allowing its nodes to have three children is that it can be shorter than even a balanced binary tree. This is *not correct*. Though the height of a 2–3 tree might indeed be less than that of a balanced binary tree, this advantage is canceled out by the fact that, when searching a 2–3 tree for a given value X, at some nodes X must be compared to two search key values instead of just one. In other words, though we might visit fewer nodes when searching a 2–3 tree, we might have to make more comparisons at each node. As a consequence, we can say only that the number of comparisons required to search a 2–3 tree for a given value is *approximately equal* to the number of comparisons required to search a binary search tree that is as balanced as possible (and this number is approximately $\log_2 N$, where N is the number of items in the table).

If a 2–3 tree and a balanced binary search tree can be searched with approximately the same efficiency, why then should we use a 2–3 tree? The answer is that, although it is difficult to maintain the balance of a binary search tree in the face of `Insert` and `Delete` operations, *it is relatively simple to maintain the shape of a 2–3 tree*. For example, consider the two trees in Figures 11–6(a) and (b), which contain the same data items.

The binary search tree is as balanced as possible, and thus it and the 2–3 tree can be searched for a value with approximately the same efficiency. However, if we perform a sequence of insertions on the binary search tree (using the `Insert` algorithm of Chapter 9), it can quickly lose its balance. As we shall now see, the fact that the nodes of a 2–3 tree are permitted to have either two or three children (and contain one or two values) will allow the same sequence of insertions to be performed without a degradation in the tree's shape—it will retain its 2–3 tree structure.

Insertion into a 2–3 Tree

We shall first informally describe the effect of the above sequence of insertions on the 2–3 tree shown in Figure 11–6(b), and then we shall present the general insertion algorithm.

Insert(39). As with a binary search tree, the first step is to locate the node at which the search for 39 would terminate. To do this, we use the search strategy of the above `Retrieve` algorithm, and thus an unsuccessful search will always terminate at a leaf. In this case, the search for 39 terminates at the leaf <40>. Since this node contains only one item, we can simply insert the new item into this node. The result is the 2–3 tree in Figure 11–7.

Insert(38). We determine that the search for 38 would terminate at the node containing <39 40>. As a conceptual first step, we place 38 in this node (see Figure 11–8a).

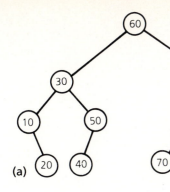

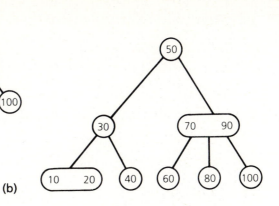

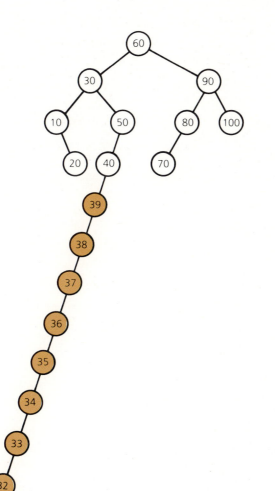

(a) Balanced binary search tree; (b) 2–3 tree with same elements; (c) binary search tree after sequence of insertions

Figure 11–6

532
CHAPTER 11
ADVANCED
IMPLEMENTA-
TIONS OF THE
ADT TABLE

Figure 11–7
Insert 39

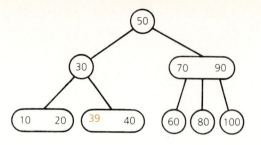

Figure 11–8
Insert 38

(a)

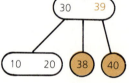

(b)

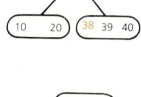

(c)

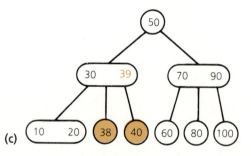

The problem with this placement is that a node is not permitted to contain three values. What we shall do is divide these three values into the smallest (38), the middle (39), and the largest (40) values. We send up the middle value (39) to the parent P and attach to P (as children) a node containing the smallest value (38) and a node containing the largest value (40). Notice that since we chose to send up the middle value of <38 39 40>, the parent correctly separates the values of its children; that is, 38 < 39 < 40. The result of the insertion is the 2–3 tree of Figure 11–8(c).

Insert(37). This is an easy insertion, since 37 belongs in a leaf that currently contains only one value. The result of this insertion is the 2–3 tree in Figure 11–9.

Figure 11–9
Insert 37

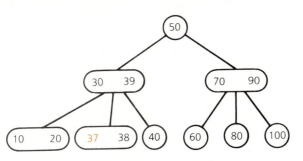

Insert(36). We determine that 36 belongs in the node containing <37 38> and conceptually place it there (see Figure 11–10).

Figure 11–10
Insert 36

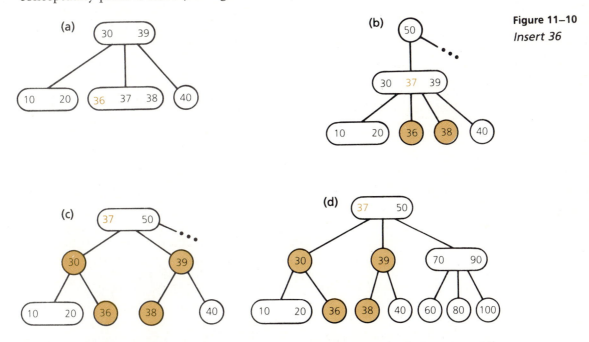

Since this node now contains three values, we divide it into smallest (36), middle (37), and largest (38). We send the middle value (37) up to the parent P and attach to P (as children) nodes containing the smallest (36) and largest (38) values. But we're not finished. We now have a node <30 37 39> that contains three values and has four children. What should we do next? (*Hint:* Think recursively.) We find ourselves in a familiar position, with the slight difference that the overcrowded node is not a leaf but rather has four children. As before, we divide the values into smallest (30), middle (37), and largest (39), sending the middle value up. Since we are splitting an internal node, we now must account for its four children (that is, what happens to nodes <10 20>, <36>,

534

CHAPTER 11
ADVANCED
IMPLEMENTA-
TIONS OF THE
ADT TABLE

<38>, and <40>, which were the children of node <30 37 39>?). The solution is to attach the left pair of children (nodes <10 20> and <36>) to the smallest value (30) and attach the right pair of children (nodes <38> and <40>) to the largest value (39). The final result of this insertion is the 2–3 tree in Figure 11–10(d).

Insert(35–34–33). Each of these insertions is along the lines of what we have done previously. The tree that results after the three insertions is shown in Figure 11–11.

Figure 11–11

Tree after insertion of 35, 34, and 33

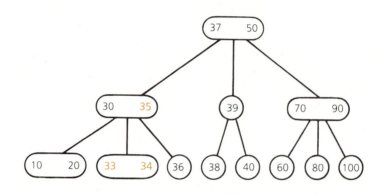

Before performing the final insertion of the value 32, let us summarize the 2–3 tree's insertion strategy. To insert the value *X* into a 2–3 tree, we first locate the leaf L at which the search for *X* would terminate. We insert the new value *X* into L, and if L now contains only two values, we're done. If L contains three values, we must split it into two nodes, L_1 and L_2. L_1 gets the smallest of the three values in L, L_2 gets the largest of the values, and the middle value is sent up to L's parent P. Nodes L_1 and L_2 then become children of P (see Figure 11–12).

If P now has only three children (and two values), we are finished. If, on the other hand, P now has four children (and three values), we must split P. The internal node P is split completely analogously to the way the leaf L was just split, the only difference being that we must take care of P's four children. We split P into P_1 and P_2, give P_1 the smallest value in P and P's two leftmost children, we send the middle value of P up to its parent and give P_2 the largest value in P and P's two rightmost children.

After this, the process of splitting a node and sending up a value to the parent continues recursively until a node is reached that had only one value before the insertion and thus has only two values after it takes on a new value. Notice in the above sequence of insertions that the tree's height never increased from its original value of 3. In general, an insertion *will not result in an increase in the height of the tree* as long as the path from the root to the leaf into which the new value is inserted includes at least one node that contains only one value. The insertion strategy of a 2–3 tree has thus postponed the growth of the tree's height much better than did the strategy of a basic binary search tree.

When the height of a 2–3 tree does grow, it does so from the top. An increase in the height of a 2–3 tree will occur if every node on the path from the root of the tree to the leaf into which the new value is inserted contains two values. In

(a)

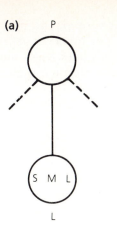
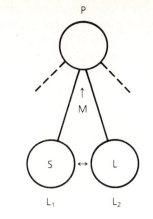

(b)

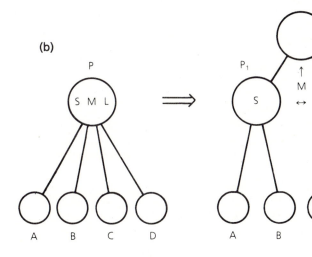

(c)

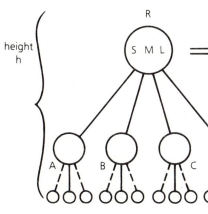

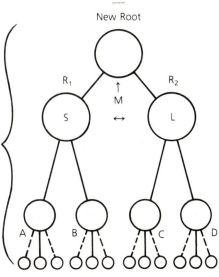

height
h

height
h + 1

New Root

Figure 11–12

*(a) Split a leaf;
(b) split an
internal node;
(c) split the root*

536

CHAPTER 11
ADVANCED
IMPLEMENTA-
TIONS OF THE
ADT TABLE

this case, the recursive process of splitting a node and sending up a value to the parent will eventually reach the root R, so R must now be split into R_1 and R_2 exactly like any other internal node; in this case, however, a new node must be created to contain the middle value of R and to become the parent of R_1 and R_2 and thus the new root of the tree (see Figure 11–12c).

We can summarize the entire insertion strategy with the following algorithm.

```
Insert(T, newitem)
(* Insert newitem into table T implemented as a 2-3 tree. *)

    let X be the search key of newitem

    locate the leaf L in which X belongs

    add newitem to L

    IF (L now has three items) THEN
        Split(L)
    END
```

```
Split(N)
(* Split node N which contains 3 items.   Note
   that if N is internal then it has 4 children. *)

    let P be the parent of N
        (if N is the root, then create a new node P)

    replace node N by two nodes, N₁ and N₂

    give N₁ the item in N with the smallest search key value
    give N₂ the item in N with the largest search key value

    IF (N is an internal node) THEN
        N₁ becomes the parent of N's two leftmost children
        N₂ becomes the parent of N's two rightmost children
    END

    send up to P the item in N with the middle search key value

    IF (P now has three items) THEN
        Split(P)
    END
```

To be sure that you fully understand the insertion algorithm, go through the steps of inserting the value 32 into the 2–3 tree in Figure 11–11. The tree you end up with should be the one shown in Figure 11–13.

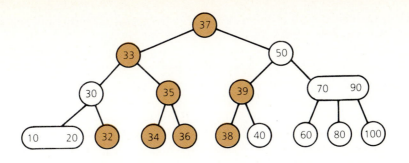

Figure 11–13
*Tree after
insert of 32*

A comparison of the 2–3 tree in Figure 11–13 with the binary search tree in Figure 11–6(c) will help to dramatize the advantage of the 2–3 tree's insertion strategy. Notice how in the binary search tree the new values (32 through 39) have all been inserted along a *single path*. This has resulted in an increase in height of 8 from the original binary search tree in Figure 11–6(a). On the other hand, in the above 2–3 tree, we see that the new values have been *spread throughout the tree*. As a consequence, the height of the resulting tree is only one greater than that of the original 2–3 tree in Figure 11–6(b).

Deletion from a 2–3 Tree

The deletion strategy for a 2–3 tree is the mirror image of its insertion strategy. Just as a 2–3 tree spreads insertions throughout the tree by splitting nodes when they become too full, it spreads deletions throughout the tree by *merging* nodes when they become empty. Before illustrating how this spread-out deletion strategy works, let us motivate its advantage by performing a few deletions on the balanced binary search tree in Figure 11–6(a).

After performing the deletions

Delete(70)
Delete(100)
Delete(80)

on the binary search tree in Figure 11–6(a), we are left with the tree in Figure 11–14. Notice how the deletions affected only one part of the tree, causing it to lose its balance. The left subtree has not been affected at all, and thus the overall height of the tree has not been diminished.

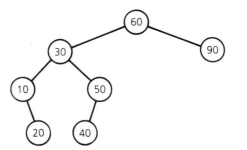

Figure 11–14
*Binary search
tree after
deletions*

538
CHAPTER 11
ADVANCED
IMPLEMENTA-
TIONS OF THE
ADT TABLE

We now illustrate the 2–3 tree's strategy by performing the same three deletions, beginning on the tree in Figure 11–6(b).

Delete(70).   We search the tree and discover that the value 70 is in the node <70 90>. Since we always wish to begin the deletion process at a leaf, the first step is to swap the value 70 with its inorder successor—the value that follows it in the sorted order (see Figure 11–15). Since 70 is the smaller of the two values in the node, its inorder successor (80) is the smallest value in the node's middle subtree. (The inorder successor of an item in an internal node will always be in a leaf.) After the swap, the value 80 is in a legal position of the search tree, since it is larger than all the values in its node's left subtree and smaller than all the values in its node's right subtree. The value 70, however, is not in a legal position,

Figure 11–15

Delete 70

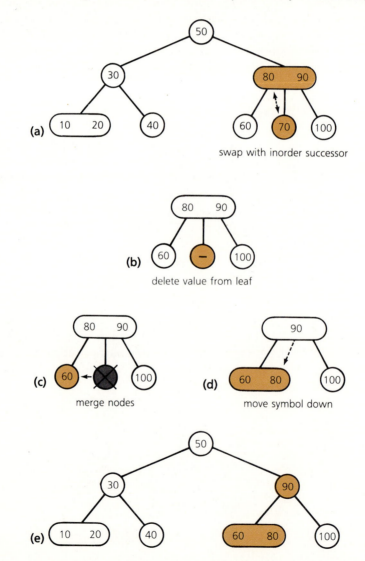

but this is of no concern, since the next step is to delete this value from the leaf.

In general, after a value is deleted from a leaf, it may be the case that there remains another value in the leaf (that is, the leaf contained two values before the deletion). If this is the case, we're done, since a leaf of a 2–3 tree is permitted to contain a single value. In our example, however, once 70 is deleted from the leaf, it is left without a value, and we delete the node by merging it with one of its siblings.

At this point we see that the parent of the deleted node contains two values (80 and 90) but has only two children (<60> and <100>). Since this is not allowed in a 2–3 tree, we must somehow remedy the situation. We do this by moving down the smaller value (80) from the parent into the left child. The 2–3 tree which results from this deletion is shown in Figure 11–15(e).

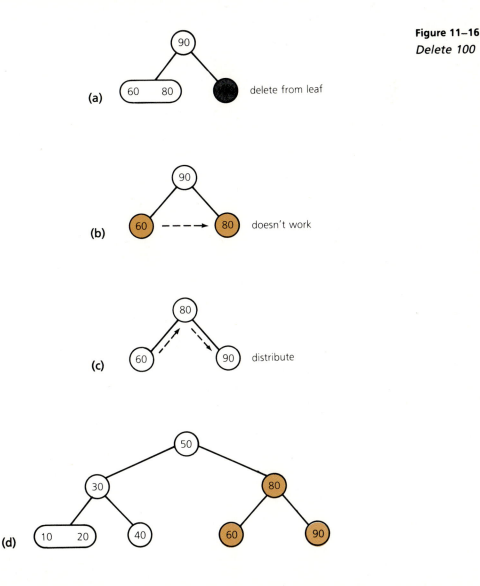

Figure 11–16

Delete 100

540

CHAPTER 11
ADVANCED
IMPLEMENTA-
TIONS OF THE
ADT TABLE

Delete(100).   We discover that 100 is in the leaf <100>. When we delete the value from this leaf, the node becomes empty (see Figure 11–16). In this case, however, no merging of nodes is required, since the sibling <60 80> can spare a value. That is, the sibling has two values, whereas a 2–3 tree requires only that it have at least one value. If we simply move the value 80 into the empty node, however, we find that the search tree order is destroyed—the value in <90>'s right child is 80 (whereas it should be larger than 90). The solution to this problem is to redistribute the values between the empty node, its sibling, and its parent. Here we have moved the larger value (80) from the sibling into the parent and have moved the value 90 down from the parent into the node that had been empty. Notice that this distribution preserves the search tree order, and we have thus completed the deletion. The resulting 2–3 tree is shown in Figure 11–16(d).

Figure 11–17

Delete 80

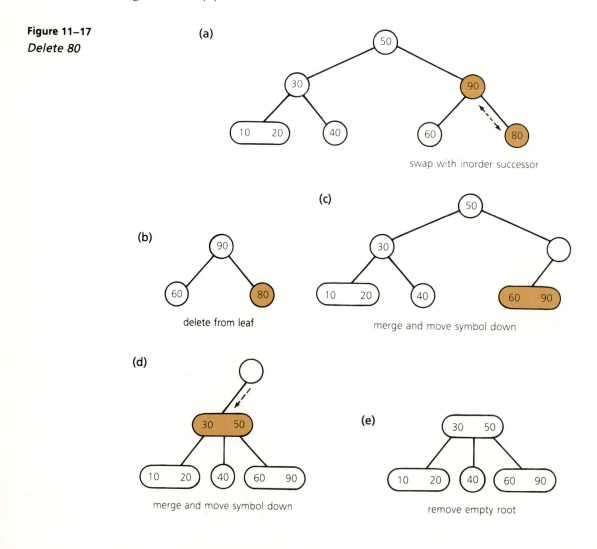

Delete(80).   We find that 80 is in an internal node, and thus we swap the value with its inorder successor (90) (see Figure 11–17). When we delete 80 from the leaf, the node becomes empty. Since the sibling of the empty node has only one value, we cannot redistribute as we did in the deletion of 100. Instead we must merge the nodes, bringing the value 90 down from the parent.

We are not yet finished, however, since the parent now contains no values and has only one child. We must recursively apply the deletion strategy to this internal node. We first check to see if its sibling can spare a value. Since it contains only the single value 30, we cannot redistribute—we must merge the nodes. The merging of two internal nodes is identical to the merging of leaves, except that the child of the empty node (<60 90>) must be adopted. Since we have already determined that the sibling contains only one value (and hence has only two children), it can become the parent of <60 90>. Note that this operation preserves the search property of the tree.

After we bring the value 50 down from the parent of the merged nodes, we find that the parent is now left with no values and only a single child. In general we would simply apply the recursive deletion strategy to this node, but this is a special case because the node is the root. Since the root is empty and has only one child, we can simply delete it, allowing <30 50> to become the root of the tree. This deletion has thus caused the height of the tree to shrink by one.

Let us now summarize the deletion procedure. To delete X from a 2–3 tree we first locate the node N that contains it. If N is an internal node, we find X's inorder successor and swap it with X. As a result of the swap, the deletion always begins at a leaf L. If L contains a value in addition to X, we simply delete X from L and we are done. On the other hand, if L contains only X, then deleting it would leave L without a value. In this case we must perform some additional work to complete the deletion.

We first check the siblings of the now-empty leaf L. If a sibling has two values, we redistribute the values among L, L's sibling, and L's parent (see Figure 11–18a). If no sibling of L has two values, we merge L with an adjacent sibling and bring down a value from L's parent (the sibling had only one value before, so it has room for another). This is shown in Figure 11–18(b).

The merging of L may have caused its parent P to be left without a value and with only one child. If so, we recursively apply the deletion procedure to P. If P has a sibling with two values (and three children), we redistribute the values among P, the sibling, and P's parent. We also give P one of its sibling's children (see Figure 11–18c).

If P has no sibling with two values, we merge P with a sibling (Figure 11–18d). A value is brought down from the parent and P's one child is adopted by the sibling. (At this point we know that the sibling previously had only one value and two children.) If the merge caused P's parent to be without a value, we recursively apply the deletion process to it.

If the merging continues so that the root of the tree is without a value (and with only one child), we simply delete the root. When this step occurs, the height of the tree is reduced by one (Figure 11–18e).

The following (page 543) is a high-level statement of the algorithm for deleting from a 2–3 tree.

542

CHAPTER 11
ADVANCED
IMPLEMENTA-
TIONS OF THE
ADT TABLE

(a)

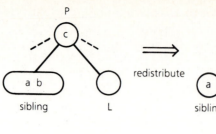 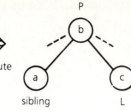 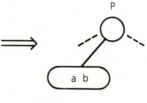

redistribute

(b)

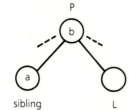

merge and bring down symbol

(c)

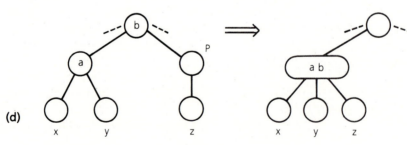

redistribute between P, its parent, and its sibling

(d)

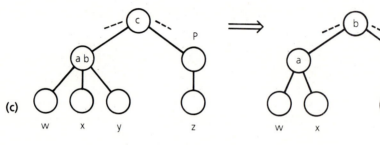

merge and bring symbol down

Figure 11–18

*(a) Redistribute values;
(b) merge a leaf;
(c) redistribute values
and children;
(d) merge internal node;
(e) delete root*

(e)

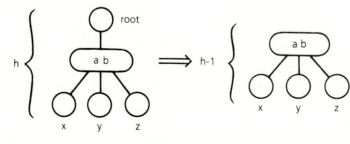

remove empty root

```
Delete(T, X, success)
(* Delete from table T the item with search key X.   The
   tree is implemented with a 2-3 tree.   The operation
   fails if there is no such item.   The flag success
   indicates whether the operation succeeded. *)

   attempt to locate item I with search key X

   IF (I is present) THEN

       swap item I into leaf L which contains
          the inorder successor of I

       (* the deletion always begins at a leaf *)

       delete item I from leaf L

       IF (L now has no items) THEN
          Fix(L)
       END

       success := TRUE

   ELSE
       success := FALSE

   END


Fix(N)
(* N is a node with no item.   Note that
   if N is internal, then it has one child. *)

   let P be the parent of N -- if N is the root, delete it and Return

   IF (some sibling of N has two items) THEN

       appropriately distribute items among N, the sibling, and P

       IF (N is internal) THEN
          move the appropriate child from the sibling to N
       END

   ELSE (* must merge the node *)

       choose an adjacent sibling S of N

       bring the appropriate item down from P into S
```

544

CHAPTER 11
ADVANCED
IMPLEMENTA-
TIONS OF THE
ADT TABLE

```
IF (N is internal) THEN
   move N's child to S
END


delete node N

IF (P is now without an item) THEN
   Fix(P)
END


END
```

The details of converting this deletion algorithm and the insertion algorithm presented earlier into a Modula-2 implementation are rather involved. We leave this task as a challenging programming project.

We have thus developed algorithms for inserting into and deleting from a 2–3 tree. Since a 2–3 tree is always balanced, we have achieved our goal of a linked tree structure that can, *in all situations*, be searched with the logarithmic efficiency of a binary search.

It might have concerned you that the insertion and deletion algorithms incur some overhead in the course of maintaining the 2–3 structure of the tree. That is, after the item (or the position for the new item) has been located, the *Insert* and *Delete* algorithms sometimes have to perform extra work (for example, splitting and merging of nodes). This, however, is not a real concern. A rigorous mathematical analysis would show that the extra work required to maintain the structure of a 2–3 tree after an insertion or deletion is *not significant*. In other words, when analyzing the efficiency of the *Insert* and *Delete* algorithms, it is sufficient to consider only the time required to locate the item (or the position for the insertion). As we have already indicated, this step is highly efficient in all situations. We thus really do have an implementation that is guaranteed to support all the table operations in logarithmic time.

Before we leave the topic of 2–3 trees, let us consider one final question: If a 2–3 tree is so good, are trees whose nodes can have more than 3 children even better? We actually came close to this question at the beginning of the section. Recall that the advantage of a 2–3 tree is that it is a balanced structure that is easy to maintain, not that it might be shorter than a balanced binary tree. The reduction in height is offset by the fact that at each node the search algorithm may require more comparisons to determine which branch to take.

Similarly, though a tree whose nodes can have 100 children would be shorter than a 2–3 tree, more comparisons would be required at each node in order to determine the appropriate subtree to search. It can be shown, in fact, that a binary tree that is as balanced as possible minimizes the amount of work required to support the ADT table operations. The problem with a binary tree is, of course, that its balance is difficult to maintain. A 2–3 tree is a compromise—although it may not be quite as good as a binary tree of minimum height, it is relatively simple to maintain. Allowing the nodes of a tree to have more than three children would be counterproductive because searches would require more comparisons.

Although searching a tree whose nodes have more than three children requires more comparisons than does searching a 2–3 tree, there are contexts in which they should be used. In the next chapter, for example, we shall see that when a search tree is implemented in *external storage,* it is desirable to reduce its height, even at the expense of additional comparisons. The justification is that when a search tree is implemented externally, it is far more expensive to go from node to node than it is to perform comparisons with the data values in a node. As a consequence, we will want a search tree with the minimum possible height even if it means that we will have to perform several comparisons at each node. In Chapter 12 we shall discuss this point further and introduce an external search tree known as a **B-tree.**

HASHING

The binary search tree and its balanced variants, such as 2–3 and AVL trees, provide excellent implementations of the ADT table. They allow us to perform all the table operations with a very high degree of efficiency. If, for example, a table contains 10,000 items, then the operations `Retrieve`, `Insert`, and `Delete` each require approximately $\log_2 10{,}000 \approx 13$ steps. Though it may be difficult from the types of applications that we have studied to imagine situations in which the search tree implementations are not adequate, let us nevertheless ask the question, can we devise an even better implementation of a table? One reason for asking this question is that, in the context of searching external storage (to be discussed in Chapter 12), even a small number of steps can actually require a good deal of time.

If we are going to be able to locate an item with fewer than the $\log_2 N$ comparisons required by a search tree, we are going to have to come up with a radically different strategy. Let us begin by using our imagination to try to devise a method that would allow us to locate (and insert and delete) an item virtually instantaneously.

Suppose that we have an array $T[1..N]$, with each array slot capable of holding a single table item. We also have a seemingly magical box called an *address calculator.* We won't yet specify how the address calculator works, but we will assume that it is capable of performing the following extremely useful task. Whenever we have a new item that we wish to insert into the table, we can consult the address calculator. We will tell it that we have an item with search

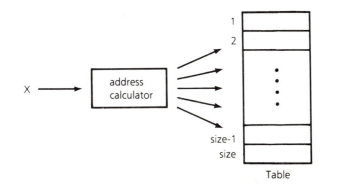

Figure 11–19
Address calculator

546

CHAPTER 11
ADVANCED
IMPLEMENTA-
TIONS OF THE
ADT TABLE

key X, and the address calculator will tell us *into which array location we should place the new item* (see Figure 11–19). We thus can easily perform an insertion into the table as follows:

```
Insert(T, newitem)

    tell the address calculator the search key of newitem

    let i be the location where the address calculator
       tells us to put the new item

    T[i] := newitem
```

An insertion is performed virtually instantaneously.

We also use the address calculator for the *Retrieve* and *Delete* operations. If we wish to retrieve the item with search key X, we ask the address calculator where it would tell us to insert such an item. Since the item would have been inserted using the *Insert* algorithm just given, if it is present in the table, the desired item would be in the array location specified by the address calculator. The *Retrieve* operation can thus be written as:

```
Retrieve(T, X, getitem, success)

    let i be the location where the address calculator
       would put an item with search key X

    IF (X = T[i].key) THEN
       getitem := T[i]
       success := TRUE

    (* the item is not in the table *)
    ELSE
       success := FALSE

    END
```

Similarly, the *Delete* operation is

```
Delete(T, X, success)

    let i be the location where the address calculator
       would put an item with search key X

    IF (X = T[i].key) THEN
       delete the item from T[i]
       success := TRUE
```

```
            (* the item is not in the table *)
ELSE
    success := FALSE
```

```
END
```

It thus appears that the operations `Retrieve`, `Insert`, and `Delete` can be performed virtually instantaneously. We never have to search for an item; instead, we simply let the address calculator *calculate* where the item should be. The amount of time required to carry out the operations depends only on how quickly the address calculator can perform this calculation.

The scheme just described is an idealized description of a method known as **hashing**. If we are to implement such a scheme we must, of course, be able to construct an address calculator that can, with very little work, tell us where a given item should be. Address calculators are actually not as mysterious as they seem and, in fact, there are many well-known address calculators that can approximate the idealized behavior described above. Such an address calculator is usually referred to as a **hash function**.

To illustrate how a hash function works, let us suppose that our array T has locations 0..100. Suppose also that the search keys of the table items are positive integers (for example, employee ID numbers). Then a hash function h must take an arbitrary positive integer x and map it into an integer in the range 0..100; that is, h is a function such that for any positive integer x,

$$h(x) = n, \quad \text{where } n \text{ is an integer in the range } 0..100$$

There are many ways to convert an arbitrary positive integer x into an integer in the range 0..100. One very good way (good in the sense that we shall discuss shortly) is to take x modulo 101. That is,

$$h(x) = x \bmod 101$$

If we use this hash function, then the ID number 234661234, for example, would map into array location 56 (234661234 mod 101). (A search key that is not an integer does not present any real problem. If, for example, the search key is a character string (such as a name), we would, as a first step, convert it into an integer. This could be done in any one of several ways, the simplest of which is to assign each character in the string an integer value (for example, A = 1, B = 2, . . .) and sum the values of the characters in the string. This result would then be taken mod 101. For example, the name Jones would be converted into the integer $10 + 15 + 14 + 5 + 19 = 63$, which taken mod 101 is still 63.)

Once we have selected a hash function such as h, the table operations are easy to write. The `Retrieve` operation, for instance, is written as

```
Retrieve(T, X, getitem, success)

    i := h(X)
```

548

CHAPTER 11
ADVANCED
IMPLEMENTA-
TIONS OF THE
ADT TABLE

```
IF (X = T[i].key)  THEN
    getitem := T[i]
    success := TRUE

(* item not in table *)
ELSE
    success := FALSE
```

```
END
```

Since the computation of h requires only a single division, the table operations would seem to be virtually instantaneous. But is hashing really as good as it sounds? If it really were this good, there would have been little reason for developing all those other table implementations. Hashing would beat them hands down!

Let us investigate why the scheme is not quite as simple as it seems. We might first notice that since the hashing scheme stores the items in an array, it would appear to suffer from the familiar problems associated with a fixed-size implementation. This, however, is not the crux of the implementation's difficulty, for—as we shall see when we explore the details—there are ways to allow the table to grow dynamically.

There is, however, a major pitfall in the implementation even under the assumption that the number of items in the table will never exceed 101. Let us examine the hash function

$$h(x) = x \bmod 101$$

a bit more closely. The function maps every positive integer into an integer in the range 0..100. Since a person presumably can have any positive integer as an ID number, h will necessarily map many *different ID numbers into the same integer n*. Thus, even if there are fewer than 101 table items present, h could very well tell us to place more than one item into the same array location. For example, since

$$h(123445678) = h(123445779) = 44,$$

if there are items in the table with search keys 123445678 and 123445779, h will tell us to place the two items into the same array location, $T[44]$. In hashing terminology, the search keys 123445678 and 123445779 have **collided**.

The only way to avoid the problem of collisions completely is to have one array location for each possible ID number. If, for example, Social Security numbers were used for ID numbers, we would need an array location for each integer in the range 000000000 through 999999999. This would certainly require a good deal of storage! In general, even if the number of items that can be in the table at any one time is small, the only way to avoid collisions completely is for the array to be large enough so that each possible search key value can have its own location. Since this is usually not practical, we need a way to deal with, or **resolve**, collisions when they occur.

Consider the problems caused by a collision. Suppose that we wish to insert

an item with ID number 123445678 into the table. We apply the hash function
h to 123445678 and determine that the new item should be placed in *T[44]*. We
discover, however, that *T[44]* already contains an item with ID number
123445779 (see Figure 11–20). The question is, what do we do with the new
item? We certainly don't want to disallow the insertion on the grounds that the
table is full—we could have a collision even when inserting into a table containing only a single item!

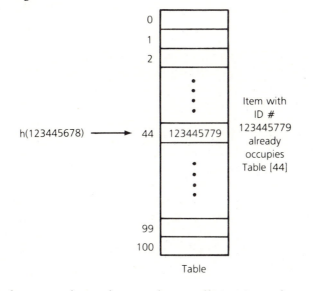

Figure 11–20

Collision

One method commonly used to resolve a collision is to change the structure
of the array *T* so that it can accommodate more than one item in the same
location. We could, for example, change *T* so that each location *T[i]* is itself
an array capable of holding *N* items. The problem with this, of course, is knowing how big *N* should be. If *N* is too small, we will have only postponed the
problem of collisions until *N* + 1 items map into some array location. If we
attempt to make *N* large enough so that each array location can accommodate
the largest number of items which might map into it, we are likely to waste a
good deal of storage.

A better solution is to allow a linked list of items to form from each array
location. In this collision resolution method, known as **chaining**, each entry
T[i] is a pointer to the item at the beginning of the list of items that the hash
function has mapped into location *i* (see Figure 11–21). When a new item is to
be inserted into the table, we simply place it at the beginning of the list indicated
by the hash function.

```
Insert(T, newitem)

    let X be the search key of newitem
    i := h(X)
    NEW(p)
    p^.item := newitem
    p^.next := T[i]
    T[i] := p
```

550

CHAPTER 11
ADVANCED
IMPLEMENTA-
TIONS OF THE
ADT TABLE

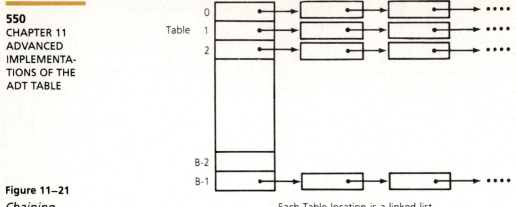

Figure 11–21

Chaining

Each Table location is a linked list

When we wish to retrieve an item, we search the list indicated by the hash function.

```
Retrieve(T, X, getitem, success)

    i := h(X)
    p := T[i]

    WHILE ((p # NIL) AND (X # p^.key)) DO
        p := p^.next
    END

    IF (p # NIL) THEN
        getitem := p^.item
        success := TRUE
    ELSE
        success := FALSE
    END
```

The *Delete* algorithm is very similar to *Retrieve*.

Chaining is thus a successful method of resolving collisions. Notice also that the total size of the table is now dynamic, since each list can be as long as needed. This observation that each list can be as long as needed brings us to the next question: How efficient are the table operations under this scheme? While the *Insert* operation is still instantaneous, the *Retrieve* and *Delete* operations are not. They require us to search a linked list of items.

To analyze the efficiencies of the *Retrieve* and *Delete* operations, we must get an estimate on the length of the lists that need to be searched. If our array *T* has *B* entries (that is, it is an array *T[0..B-1]*) and there are *N* items in the table, then the average length of a list is *N/B*. In choosing the size of the array *T*, we should attempt to estimate how large *N* can be and select an array size *B* so that the average list length *N/B* is small (for example, select *B* to be near the expected maximum number of items in the table). If we are successful at this, then it is *likely* that the lists that *Retrieve* and *Delete* must search will be quite small.

Even if it is likely that the lists that must be searched will be quite small, we still should ask: *In the worst case*, how long can a list be? If we seriously underestimated the maximum size of the table or if we are extremely unlucky and most of the table items happen to hash into the same location (we shall shortly discuss circumstances that might make us appear to be unlucky), then the number of items on a list could be quite large. In fact, in the worst case, all N items in the table could be on the same list!

We thus see that the time required to perform a `Retrieve` or `Delete` operation can range between almost nothing (if the list to be searched has only one or two items on it) to the time required to search a linked list containing all the items in the table (if all the items hashed into the same location). Therefore, though the hashing implementation might often be faster than a search tree implementation, in the worst case it can be much slower. That is, it can be much slower unless we are more clever.

We can greatly improve the worst-case behavior of hashing by more carefully organizing the items associated with each location $T[i]$. Rather than simply storing the items as a linked list, let us apply the data-management techniques that we have been studying. For example, we can organize the items associated with each location $T[i]$ into a binary search tree or even a 2–3 tree.

In the scheme shown in Figure 11–22, we have B independent binary search trees, each coming from one of the entries $T[i]$. In most cases the tree associated with $T[i]$ will be quite small, containing no more than one or two items. In the worst case, if all the table items hash into the same location, a single tree will contain all N table items. However, since this is a search tree (which could be kept balanced), the time required to retrieve, insert, or delete is only $\log_2 N$. Therefore, with this modification, the time to perform the operations on a table with N items ranges from almost nothing to a maximum of only $\log_2 N$. In other words, in the very worst case, this hybrid hashing–search tree scheme is as good as the balanced binary search tree scheme, and in the more likely cases it is even faster!

For many applications, the hashing and hashing–search tree hybrid schemes provide the most efficient implementation of the ADT table. There is, however, one important table operation not yet considered that the hashing schemes do

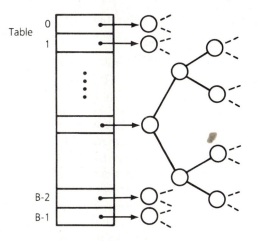

Figure 11–22

Collision resolution with search trees

Table

Each Table location is a binary search tree

552

CHAPTER 11
ADVANCED
IMPLEMENTA-
TIONS OF THE
ADT TABLE

not support well at all, the operation of traversing the table in *sorted order*. A hash function scatters the items randomly throughout the array so that there is no ordering relationship between the search keys that hash into $T[i]$ and those that hash into $T[i+1]$ (in fact, we will indicate shortly that a good hash function *necessarily* scatters the search keys as randomly as possible). As a consequence, if we are required to traverse the table in sorted order (for example, to print it out) we would first have to perform a sort on the items. If this operation were required frequently, hashing would be a far less attractive implementation than a search tree.

Traversing a table in sorted order is really just an example of a whole class of operations that are not supported well by the hashing implementations. There are many similar operations that we often wish to perform on a table that require the items to be ordered. For example, consider an operation that must find the table item with the smallest or largest value in its search key. If a search tree implementation is used, then these items are in the leftmost and rightmost nodes of the tree, respectively. If a hashing implementation is used, however, there is no way of knowing where these items are—the entire table would have to be searched. A similar type of operation is a **range query**, which requires that we retrieve all items with a search key that falls into a given range of values. For example, we might want to retrieve all of the items with an ID number in the range 129 to 755. This is relatively easy to perform using a search tree (see Exercise 11.1), but if hashing is used, there is no efficient way to answer the range query.

In general, if an application requires any of these ordered operations, then a search tree should probably be used. Though hashing does support the *Retrieve*, *Insert*, and *Delete* operations somewhat more efficiently than does a balanced search tree, the balanced search tree supports these operations so efficiently itself that, in most contexts, the difference in speed for these operations is negligible (whereas the advantage of the search tree over hashing for the ordered operations is significant). In the context of external storage, however, the story is different. For data that is stored externally, the difference in speed between hashing's implementation of *Retrieve* and a search tree's implementation may well be significant. As we shall indicate in Chapter 12, in an external setting it is not uncommon to see a hashing implementation used to support the *Retrieve* operation and a simultaneous search tree implementation used to support the ordered operations.

WHAT CONSTITUTES A GOOD HASH FUNCTION?

Before concluding our introduction to hashing, let us briefly examine the issue of choosing a hash function to perform the address calculations for a given application. There has been a great deal written on this subject, most of which is beyond the mathematical level of this book. We can, however, present a brief summary of the major concerns.

(1) **A hash function should be easy to compute.** If a hashing scheme is to provide almost instantaneous performance of the table operations, we certainly must be able to calculate the hash function extremely quickly. Most of the

common hash functions require only a single division (like our modulo function), a single multiplication, or some kind of "bit level" operation on the internal representation of the search key. In all these cases, the requirement that the hash function be easy to compute is satisfied.

(2) **A hash function should uniformly scatter the data throughout the array.** No matter what hash function we use, there is, in general, no way to completely avoid collisions. To achieve the best performance from our hashing scheme, each entry $T[i]$ should contain approximately the same number of items on its chain; that is, each chain should contain approximately N/B items (and thus no chain should contain significantly more items than this). To accomplish this, our hash function should scatter the search keys *uniformly* throughout the array.

There are two issues to consider with regard to how uniformly a hash function scatters the search keys.

(a) **How well does the hash function scatter random data?** If every search key value is equally likely, will the hash function scatter the search keys uniformly? For example, consider the following scheme for hashing ID numbers.

T is an array [0..39] and the hash function is

$h(x) = $ (first two digits of x) mod 40

The question is: Given the assumption that all employee ID numbers are equally likely, does a given ID number x have equal probability of hashing into any one of the 40 array locations? For this hash function, the answer is no. Notice that there are three different ID prefixes (that is, the first two digits of an ID number) that map into each array location 0..19, while there are only two different prefixes that map into each array location 20..39. For example, ID numbers that start with 19, 59, and 99 map into $T[19]$, while only ID numbers that start with 20 and 60 map into $T[20]$. Given that all ID numbers are equally likely (and thus that all prefixes 00 through 99 are equally likely), a given ID number is 50 percent more likely to hash into one of the locations 0..19 than it is to hash into one of the locations 20..39. As a result, each array location 0..19 would contain, on average, 50 percent more items than each location 20..39.

We thus conclude that the hash function

$h(x) = $ (first two digits of x) mod 40

does not scatter random data uniformly throughout the array $T[0..39]$.

On the other hand, it can be shown that our hash function

$h(x) = x$ mod 101

does, in fact, scatter random data uniformly throughout the array $T[0..100]$.

(b) **How well does the hash function scatter nonrandom data?** Even if a hash function scatters random data uniformly, it may have trouble with nonrandom data. In general, no matter what hash function we select, it is always possible that the data will have some unlucky pattern that will result in nonuniform scattering. Though there is no way to guarantee that all data will be scattered uniformly, there are hashing techniques that can greatly increase the likelihood of uniformity.

554

CHAPTER 11
ADVANCED
IMPLEMENTA-
TIONS OF THE
ADT TABLE

As an example, consider the following scheme:

T is an array $[0..99]$ and h is the hash function

$h(x) = $ first two digits of x

If every ID number is equally likely, then it is apparent that h will scatter the search keys uniformly throughout the array. But what if every ID number is not equally likely? For example, suppose that a company assigns employee ID's according to department. For instance, suppose that ID numbers are assigned according to the following convention:

10xxxxx—Sales

20xxxxx—Customer relations

:

:

90xxxxx—Data processing

If this were the case, only 9 out of the 100 array locations would contain any items at all. Further, those locations corresponding to the largest departments (for example, $T[10]$, corresponding to Sales) would contain more items than those locations corresponding to the smallest departments. This scheme certainly does not scatter the data uniformly. There is a large body of theoretical results describing types of hash functions that should be used to guard against various types of patterns in the data. These results are really in the province of more advanced courses, but two general principles are:

1. The calculation of the hash function should involve the entire search key. Thus, for example, computing a modulo of the entire ID number is much safer than using only its first two digits.

2. If a hash function uses modulo arithmetic, the base should be prime; that is, if h is of the form

$$h(x) = x \bmod n$$

then n should be a prime number. This is a safeguard against many subtle kinds of patterns in the data (for example, search keys whose digits are likely to be permutations of one another). Although each application can have its own particular kind of patterns and thus should be analyzed on an individual basis, choosing n to be prime is an easy way to safeguard against some common types of patterns in the data.

To summarize, hashing is a table implementation, which in many cases can support the operations `Retrieve`, `Insert`, and `Delete` even faster than a balanced search tree. Though hashing does not efficiently support operations that require the table items to be ordered (for example, traverse the table in sorted order), it is nevertheless the most efficient table implementation for many types of applications. We shall return to hashing in the next chapter when we discuss external searching techniques.

1. Even though search trees that allow their nodes to have more than two children are shorter than binary search trees, they are not necessarily easier to search. This is because more comparisons are needed at each node to determine which subtree should be searched next.

2. A hashing scheme in general must provide a means of resolving collisions. A hash function should be chosen so that the number of collisions is kept at a minimum. We should be careful to avoid a hash function that will map more items into one location than another.

3. Hashing is not a good table implementation if we need to perform operations such as a sorted traversal or finding the item with the largest search-key value.

SUMMARY

1. An AVL tree is a binary search tree that is guaranteed to remain balanced. The insertion and deletion algorithms perform rotations in the event that the tree starts to stray from a balanced shape.

2. A 2–3 tree is a variant of a binary search tree. The internal nodes of a 2–3 tree are permitted to have either two or three children. The motivation for this structure is that by allowing the number of children to vary, the insertion and deletion algorithms can easily maintain the balance of the tree.

3. Hashing is a table implementation that allows for very efficient retrievals, insertions, and deletions. Rather than searching for a data item, hashing calculates where it should be.

4. The hash function should be very easy to compute (it should require only a few operations), and it should scatter the search keys uniformly throughout the array.

5. A collision occurs when two different search keys hash into the same array location. A way to resolve collisions is through chaining. We can reduce the worst-case behavior of hashing by structuring each chain as a search tree.

EXERCISES

1. Write a procedure to implement a **range query** for a binary search tree. That is, write a procedure that will visit all items that have a search key in a given range of values (such as all values between 100 and 1000).

2. Implement a range query for a 2–3 tree (in pseudocode). (See Exercise 11.1.)

556

CHAPTER 11
ADVANCED
IMPLEMENTA-
TIONS OF THE
ADT TABLE

3. What are the advantages of implementing the ADT table with a 2–3 tree instead of a binary search tree? Why don't we, in general, maintain a completely balanced binary search tree?

4. Execute the following sequence of operations on an empty binary search tree and on an empty 2–3 tree. Note that insertion into an empty 2–3 tree will create a single node containing the inserted item.

```
Insert(10)
Insert(100)
Insert(30)
Insert(80)
Insert(50)
Delete(10)
Insert(60)
Insert(70)
Insert(40)
Delete(80)
Insert(90)
Insert(20)
Delete(30)
Delete(70)
```

5. We have described hash table implementations of the ADT table, where the search key was assumed to be an integer. There are several simple schemes for defining hash functions for search keys that are not integers. Typically they involve a convention for mapping a search key into an integer hash key (which is then hashed on in the usual way). For example, if we define the correspondence A = 1, B = 2, . . . , Z = 26, we can map strings of letters to integers either by summing the values for the letters (for example, 'THE' would map to 20 + 8 + 5 = 33 because T = 20, H = 8, and E = 5) or by replacing each character with its value and using the resulting integer (for example, 'THE' would map to 2085).

   a. Write a program that will implement a hash table for English words using the following scheme: Let A = 1, B = 2, . . ., Z = 26 and hash on the first character of the search key (for example, 'THE' maps to 20). Resolve collisions by chaining with unsorted linked lists.

   b. How appropriate is this choice of hash function if we are entering random strings into a table? What if the words come from English text?

   c. Experiment with other hashing schemes. Experiment with other implementations of chaining (for example, binary search trees, 2–3 trees, and other hash functions).

6. The success of a hash table implementation of ADT table is related to the choice of a good hash function. A good hash function is one that is easy to compute and will uniformly distribute the possible data. Comment on the appropriateness of the following hash functions. What patterns would hash to the same location?

a. The hash table has size 2048. The keys are identifier names in Modula-2. The hash function is

$$h(key) = (\text{position of first letter of key in alphabet}) \bmod 2048$$

b. The hash table is 10,000 entries long. The keys to be hashed are integers in the range 0..9999. The hash function is

$$h(key) = \text{truncate}(key * random)$$

where random is a sophisticated random-number generator that returns a real value between 0 and 1.

c. The keys are integers in the range 0..9999. The hash function is

```
    TYPE

    hashrange = [0..tablesize-1];

PROCEDURE hash(x : INTEGER) : hashrange;

VAR

    i : INTEGER;

BEGIN

    FOR i := 1 TO 10000 DO
        x := (x * x) MOD tablesize;
    END;
    RETURN (x);

END hash;
```

d. The keys are English words. The hash function is

$$h(key) = (\text{sum of positions of letters of key in alphabet}) \bmod tablesize$$

7. Modify the hashing algorithms to check for duplicates on insertion. That is, an item should be added to a table only if its search key is not already present. What are the implications for the time that is required to perform an insertion?

8. We have discussed chaining as one method for resolving collisions. Other commonly used methods are based on the notion of **open addressing**. The basic idea is that when we are trying to insert a new item into a table and it hashes to a location that is already occupied, we "probe" for some other empty location in which to place the item. The concern, of course, is that we must be able to find a table item efficiently after we have inserted it. That is, the insertion-probe sequence must be reproducible by the delete and retrieve operations.

558

CHAPTER 11
ADVANCED
IMPLEMENTA-
TIONS OF THE
ADT TABLE

The difference between the various open addressing schemes is the method used to probe for an empty location. One common scheme is called **linear probing.** In this scheme we search the hash table sequentially, starting from the original hash location. More specifically, if $Table[h(key)]$ is occupied, then we check $Table[h(key)+1]$, $Table[h(key)+2]$, ... and so on until we find an available location. (Note that we would wrap around from the last table location to the first table location if necessary.)

In the absence of deletions, it is straightforward to implement the $Retrieve$ operation under this scheme. We need only follow the same probe sequence used by the $Insert$ operation until we either find the item we are searching for, reach an empty location (which indicates that the item is not present), or visit every table location.

The presence of deletions, however, adds a slight complication. The $Delete$ operation itself is no problem. We merely find the desired item, as in the $Retrieve$ operation, and delete the item (marking the location empty). But what happens to the $Retrieve$ operation? The creation of new empty locations along a probe sequence (due to deletions) could cause the $Retrieve$ operation to incorrectly stop with failure. We can resolve this problem by allowing a table location to be in one of three states: full (currently being used), empty (has not been used), or deleted (was full once, but is now available). The $Retrieve$ operation is then modified to continue probing when it encounters a location in state deleted. Similarly, the $Insert$ operation is modified to insert in either empty or deleted locations.

Redo Exercise 11.5 using linear probing as the collision-resolution scheme.

9. One of the problems with the linear-probing scheme described in Exercise 11.8 is that table items tend to cluster together in the hash table. That is, one part of the table might be quite dense, even though another part has relatively few items. It can be shown that this form of clustering is detrimental to the overall efficiency of hashing (because it causes long probe searches).

A second open-addressing scheme that is intended to lessen the amount of clustering is called **double hashing.** Note that the probe sequences defined for linear probing are *key independent.* That is, the probe sequence is the same (inspect the table locations sequentially) no matter what the hash key is. Double hashing is used to define *key-dependent* probe sequences. In this scheme the probe sequence still searches the table in a linear order, but the size of the steps taken will be determined by a second hash function. For example, let h_1 and h_2 be the primary and secondary hash functions defined as follows:

$$h_1(key) = key \bmod 11$$

$$h_2(key) = key \bmod 7$$

If key = 25, then h_1 indicates that the key hashes to table location 3, and h_2 indicates that the probe sequence should take steps of size 4. In other words, the probe sequence will be 3, 7, 0 (wraps around), 4, 8, 1 (wraps around), 5, 9, 2, 6, 10, 3. On the other hand, if key = 9, then h_1 indicates that the key hashes to table location 9, and h_2 indicates that the probe sequence should take steps of size 2 (and so the probe sequence would be 9, 0, 2, 4, 6, 8, 10, 1, 3, 5, 7, 9). (You should determine the probe sequences for several different keys.)

Note that all the table locations are visited by each of these probe sequences. This will always be true if the size of the table and size of the step taken are relatively prime (their greatest common divisor is 1). Because the size of a hash table is commonly chosen to be a prime number, it will be relatively prime to all step sizes and this won't be a concern.

Redo Exercise 11.5 using double hashing as the collision-resolution scheme.

PROJECT

*10. Implement the ADT table with a 2–3 tree. Include the operations `Insert`, `Delete`, and `Retrieve`.

CHAPTER 12

EXTERNAL METHODS

PREVIEW In this chapter we consider the problem of managing a table that is so large that it must be stored in an external file. We begin by introducing the general concept of a direct-access file. Using this as our model of external storage, we show how Mergesort can be modified to sort data that resides in a file. We then show how data in an external file can be indexed using generalizations of the hashing and search tree schemes developed in the previous chapter.

A LOOK AT EXTERNAL STORAGE

In this chapter we shall consider the problem of data management in a different type of environment. Whereas we have previously been assuming that our table of data items is stored in the internal memory of the computer, we are now going to assume that the table resides on an external storage device, such as a disk.

So far, we have had only limited interaction with files. For example, recall the video-cassette-inventory system developed in the case studies of Chapters 3 and 10. At the end of each business day, our system saves the current inventory in a Modula-2 file so that at the beginning of the next day, the inventory can be restored by reading the file. This scenario illustrates one of the advantages of external storage: It is *permanent* rather than being limited to the execution period of a program.

Another advantage of external storage is that, in general, it is available in a far greater quantity than is internal memory. If we have a table of 1,000,000 data items, each of which is a record of moderate size, it is not likely that we will be able to store the entire table in internal memory at one time. On the other hand, this much data can easily reside on an external disk. As a consequence, when dealing with tables of this magnitude, we cannot simply read the table in when we want to operate on it, and write it out when we are finished. Instead, we must devise ways to operate on data (for example, sort it and search it) while it resides externally.

The files we have considered to this point have been *sequential files*. In order to access the data stored at a given position of a sequential file, we must first read past all the data that precede it. In this sense, a sequential file resembles a linked list. In order to access a particular node in the list, the list must be traversed from its beginning until the desired node is reached. In contrast, many types of files allow the data at a given position to be accessed directly. These **direct-access** files resemble arrays in that the element at $A[i]$ can be accessed without first accessing $A[1]$, $A[2]$, ..., $A[i-1]$. (This standard terminology is unfortunately somewhat confusing. We have used the term *sequential* when referring to an array as opposed to a *linked* structure. In the context of files, however, the term *sequential* is used in opposition to the term *direct access*. In this context, a *sequential file* has characteristics resembling a linked list, whereas a *direct-access* file has characteristics resembling an array.)

Without direct-access files it would be impossible to support efficiently the table operations in an external environment. We shall therefore make the assumption that we are dealing with direct-access files. Many programming languages, including most implementations of Modula-2, support direct-access files. In order to keep our discussion language independent, however, we shall construct a general model of direct access files. Our model will be a simplification of reality but will include the features necessary for our discussion.

We view the memory of a computer as being divided into two parts: *internal* memory and *external* memory (see Figure 12–1). An executing program, along with its nonfile data, can be thought of as residing in the computer's internal memory. The permanent files of a computer system reside in the external memory. We shall assume that the external storage devices have the characteristics of a **disk** (though some systems use other devices, such as tapes).

Figure 12–1

Internal memory and disk

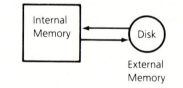

A file consists of **data records**. A data record can be anything from a simple value (such as an integer) to a multifield Modula-2-like record (such as an employee record). For simplicity we shall assume that the data records in any one file are all of the same type.

The records of a file are partitioned into one or more **blocks**, with each block typically containing many data records (see Figure 12–2). The size of a block (the number of bits of data it can contain) is determined by the hardware con-

Figure 12–2

File partitioned into blocks of records

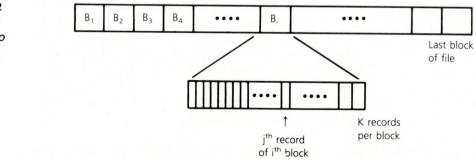

figuration and system software of the computer—an individual program, in general, has no control over this. Therefore, the number of records that can fit per block is a function of the size of the records in the file. For example, a file of integer records will have more records per block than a file of employee records.

We can view the blocks of a file as being linearly numbered, very much like an array. With a direct-access file, a program can read a given block from the file by specifying its block number, and, similarly, it can write data out to a particular block. In this regard a direct-access file very much resembles an array of arrays, with each block of the file analogous to a single array entry, which is itself an array containing several records.

You will notice that in our model *all input and output is at the block level rather than at the record level.* That is, we can read and write a block of records, but we cannot read or write an individual record. It is interesting to note that there are several programming languages, including several implementations of Modula-2, with commands that make it appear that records can be accessed one at a time. In general, however, the system is actually performing I/O (input and output) at the block level, although this might be invisible to the program. For example, if a programming language includes the command

```
ReadRecord(f, i, R)
(* Read the i^th record of file f into variable R. *)
```

the system is probably accessing the entire block that contains the ith record. Our model of I/O therefore approximates reality reasonably well.

In the algorithms presented in this chapter, we shall assume that our language has two commands for performing block I/O. The statement

```
ReadBlock(f, i, B)
```

will read the ith block of file f and place it in program variable B. Notice that variable B must be able to accommodate the many records that each block of file f contains. For example, if each block contains 100 employee records, then program variable B must be an array $B[1..100]$ of employee records.

Once a block has been read into B, its records can be processed (for example, inspected or modified) by the program. It is very important to note that *data can be processed only after it has been brought from the file into the internal memory of the computer.* Also, since the records in the program variable B are only *copies* of the records in the file f, if a program does make modifications to the records in B, B must be written back out to f in order for the modifications to be reflected in the file. This can be accomplished with our statement

```
WriteBlock(f, i, B)
```

which writes the contents of B to the ith block of file f. If f contains n blocks, then the statement

```
WriteBlock(f, n+1, B)
```

can be used to append a new block to *f*, and thus our files can grow dynamically just like Modula-2 files.

We emphasize that our I/O commands allow only entire blocks to be read and written. As a consequence, even if we need to operate only on a single record of the file we must access an entire block. For example, suppose that we wish to give employee Smith a $1000 raise. If Smith's record is in block i (how we can discover this is discussed later in the chapter), then we would perform the following steps:

```
(* read block i from file f into array B *)
ReadBlock(f, i, B)


find the entry B[j] which contains
    the record with Name = "Smith"


(* increment the Salary field of Smith's record *)
B[j].Salary := B[j].Salary + 1000


(* write the block back to file f
    so that the change is reflected *)
WriteBlock(f, i, B)
```

We have one final issue to consider in our introduction to external storage. This has to do with the amount of time required to read or write a block of data. The amount of time required for a **block access** (a read or write) is typically very large when compared with the time required to operate on the block's data once it is in the computer's internal memory. For example, it is reasonable to assume that the time required to inspect every record in a block is less than the time required to read or write that block. Thus, in most external data management applications, the time required for block accesses typically dominates all other factors. As a consequence, in the next two sections, when we devise schemes to sort and search data that is stored externally, *our goal will be to reduce the number of required block accesses.* We will pay little attention to the time required to operate on a block of data once it has been read into internal memory.

SORTING DATA IN AN EXTERNAL FILE

In this section we shall consider the problem of sorting data that resides in an external file.

An external file contains 1600 employee records. We wish to sort these records by the Social Security number field.

Each block contains 100 records, and thus the file contains 16 blocks of records, $B_1, B_2, \ldots, B_{16}$. A program can be allocated enough internal memory to manipulate only about 300 records (three blocks' worth) at one time.

Sorting the file might not sound like a difficult problem, since we have already developed three sorting algorithms—*Insertion sort* (in Chapter 3), *Quick-sort*, and *Mergesort* (in Chapter 5). There is, however, a fundamental difference here in that the file is far too large to fit into internal memory all at once. This creates somewhat of a problem since the sorting algorithms previously presented assume that all the data to be sorted is available at one time (for example, it is all in an array). Fortunately, however, *Mergesort* can be modified so that this assumption is not necessary.

The basis of the *Mergesort* algorithm is that two sorted segments (such as arrays) of data records can easily be merged into a third sorted segment, which is the combination of the two. What makes *Mergesort* appropriate for the problem of sorting external files is that the merge step needs to look at only the leading edge of each of the segments. For example, if S_1 and S_2 are sorted segments of records, the first step of the merge is to compare the first record of each segment and select the record with the smaller search key. If the record from S_1 was selected, then the next step would be to compare the second record of S_1 to the first record of S_2. This is continued until all the records are exhausted. The key observation is that, at any step, the merge never needs to look past the leading edge of either segment.

Let us now look at the details of modifying *Mergesort* so that it can be used for external files. Suppose that the 1600 records to be sorted are in the file F_1 and that we are not permitted to alter this file. We have two work files, F_2 and F_3. One of these files will contain the sorted records when the algorithm terminates. The algorithm has two phases. Phase I sorts each block of records, and Phase II performs a series of merges.

Phase I. The 16 blocks are read, one at a time, from F_1 into internal memory and sorted using an internal sort. After a block has been sorted, it is written out to F_2 before the next block is read in. The result of Phase I is that F_2 contains 16 **sorted runs** $R_1, R_2, \ldots, R_{16}$, that is, 16 groups of records, with the records within each group sorted among themselves (see Figure 12–3a).

Phase II. Phase II consists of a sequence of merge steps. At each merge step, pairs of sorted runs are merged to form larger sorted runs. Each merge step doubles the number of blocks in each sorted run and thus halves the total number of sorted runs. The first merge step merges 8 pairs of sorted runs from F_2 (R_1 with R_2, R_3 with R_4, $\ldots$, R_{15} with R_{16}) to form 8 sorted runs, each 2 blocks long, which are written to F_3. The next merge step merges 4 pairs of sorted runs from F_3 (R_1 with R_2, R_3 with R_4, $\ldots$, R_7 with R_8) to form 4 sorted runs, each 4 blocks long, which are written to F_2. The next step merges the 2 pairs of sorted runs from F_2 to form 2 sorted runs which are written to F_3. The final step merges the 2 sorted runs into 1, which is written to F_2. At this point, F_2 will contain all of the records of the original file in sorted order.

This is the strategy of the algorithm. It still remains to be determined how, at each step of Phase II, the sorted runs can be merged. The statement of our problem specifies that internal memory can manipulate at most 300 records at once. Since the later steps of Phase II require that we merge runs containing more than 300 records, we must be able to merge the runs a piece at a time. To accomplish this, our program will divide its internal memory into three arrays *In1*, *In2*, and *Out*, each capable of holding 100 records (the block size). Block-

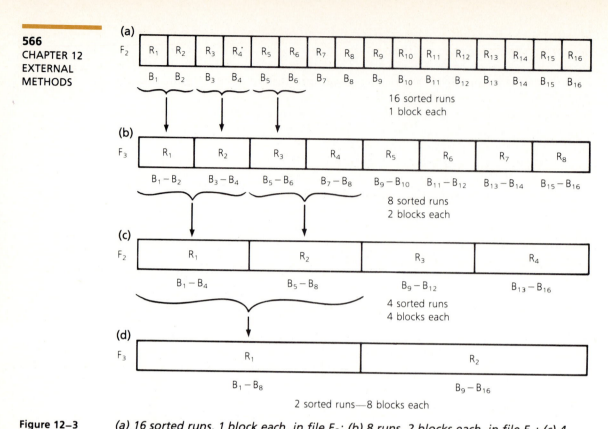

(a)

F_2 | R_1 | R_2 | R_3 | R_4 | R_5 | R_6 | R_7 | R_8 | R_9 | R_{10} | R_{11} | R_{12} | R_{13} | R_{14} | R_{15} | R_{16}

B_1 B_2 B_3 B_4 B_5 B_6 B_7 B_8 B_9 B_{10} B_{11} B_{12} B_{13} B_{14} B_{15} B_{16}

16 sorted runs
1 block each

(b)

F_3 | R_1 | R_2 | R_3 | R_4 | R_5 | R_6 | R_7 | R_8

$B_1 - B_2$ $B_3 - B_4$ $B_5 - B_6$ $B_7 - B_8$ $B_9 - B_{10}$ $B_{11} - B_{12}$ $B_{13} - B_{14}$ $B_{15} - B_{16}$

8 sorted runs
2 blocks each

(c)

F_2 | R_1 | R_2 | R_3 | R_4

$B_1 - B_4$ $B_5 - B_8$ $B_9 - B_{12}$ $B_{13} - B_{16}$

4 sorted runs
4 blocks each

(d)

F_3 | R_1 | R_2

$B_1 - B_8$ $B_9 - B_{16}$

2 sorted runs—8 blocks each

Figure 12–3   *(a) 16 sorted runs, 1 block each, in file F_2; (b) 8 runs, 2 blocks each, in file F_3; (c) 4 runs, 4 blocks each, in file F_2; (d) 2 runs, 8 blocks each, in file F_3*

sized pieces of the runs will be read into the *In* arrays and merged into the *Out* array. Whenever an *In* array is exhausted, the next piece of the run will be read in, and whenever the *Out* array becomes full, this completed piece of the new sorted run will be written to one of the files.

Let us begin by seeing how the first merge step can be performed. We start this merge step with the pair of runs R_1 (which is in the first block of file F_2) and R_2 (which is in the second block of F_2). Since at this first merge step, each run is only one block in size, an entire run can fit into one of the *In* arrays. We can thus read R_1 and R_2 into the arrays *In1* and *In2*, and then merge *In1* and *In2* into *Out*. The only difficulty is that the result of merging *In1* and *In2* is a sorted run 2 blocks long (200 records), and *Out* can hold only 1 block (100 records). The solution is that when in the course of the merge *Out* becomes full, its contents will be written out to the first block of F_3 (see Figure 12–4). The merging of *In1* and *In2* into *Out* then resumes. The array *Out* will become full for a second time only after the records in *In1* and *In2* have been exhausted. At this time, the contents of *Out* are written to the second block of F_3. The remaining 7 pairs from F_1 are merged in the same manner, with the resulting runs appended to F_3.

This first merge step is conceptually a bit easier than the others because the runs to be merged are only one block in size, and thus each can fit in its entirety

(a)

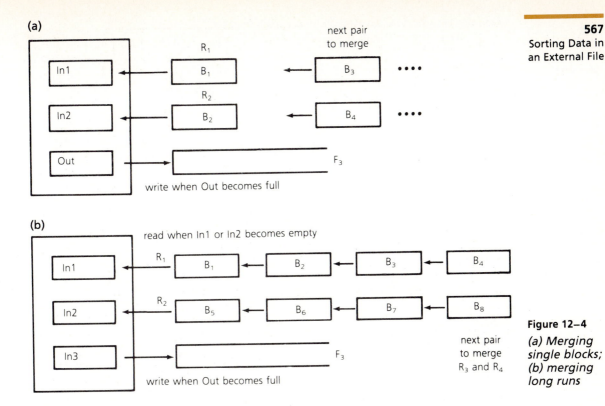

(b)

Figure 12–4

*(a) Merging
single blocks;
(b) merging
long runs*

into one of the *In* arrays. What do we do in the later steps when the runs to be merged are larger than a single block? Let us consider, for example, the merge step in which runs of size 4 blocks each are to be merged to form runs of size 8 blocks each. The first pair of these runs to be merged is in blocks 1–4 and 5–8 of F_2.

The algorithm will read the first block of R_1 (which is the first block of the file, denoted by B_1) into *In1* and the first block of R_2 (which is B_5) into *In2*. Then, as earlier, the algorithm merges *In1* and *In2* into *Out*. The complication here is that as soon as *In1* or *In2* exhausts its records, the next block from the corresponding run must be read in. For example, if *In2* exhausts its records first, the next block of R_2 (which is B_6) must be read into *In2* before the merge can continue. The algorithm thus must detect when the *In* arrays become exhausted as well as when the *Out* array becomes full.

A high-level description of the algorithm for merging arbitrary-sized sorted runs R_i and R_j from F_2 into F_3 is as follows:

```
read the first block of R_i into In1
read the first block of R_j into In2

WHILE (either In1 or In2 is not exhausted) DO

    select the smaller "leading" record of In1 and In2
        and place it into the next position of Out
```

```
                    (if one of the arrays is exhausted, select the
                    leading record from the other)

            IF (Out is full) THEN
                write its contents to the next block of F₃
            END


            IF ((In1 is exhausted) AND (more blocks remain in Rᵢ)) THEN
                read the next block into In1
            END


            IF ((In2 is exhausted) AND (more blocks remain in Rⱼ)) THEN
                read the next block into In2
            END


        END
```

A pseudocode version of the external sorting program follows. Notice that it uses the statements *ReadBlock* and *WriteBlock* introduced in the previous section. In order not to make the solution overly complicated, we assume that the number of blocks in the file is a power of two. This allows the program to assume that, at each step of the merge phase, the sorted runs can always be paired off. Also note that the program uses two scratch files and copies the final sorted scratch file to the designated output file.

```
MODULE ExtMerge
(*
    EXTERNAL MERGE SORT

    Sort file infile putting the result in outfile.

    Note that this assumes the existence of procedures ReadBlock
    and WriteBlock for performing direct access input and output.

    SIMPLIFYING ASSUMPTION:

        The size of the file (in blocks) is an exact power of 2.

        The removal of this assumption involves special end of
        file testing that would obscure the algorithm that we
        are trying to illustrate.
*)


Blocksort(infile, outfile, numblocks)
(* Sort each block of infile and put the result into outfile.
   Set numblocks to the number of blocks processed. *)
```

```
BEGIN
    OpenRead(infile)
    OpenWrite(outfile)

    numblocks := 0
    WHILE (NOT EOF(infile)) DO
        numblocks := numblocks + 1
        ReadBlock(infile, numblocks, buffer)

        (* sort with some internal sort *)
        Sort(buffer)

        WriteBlock(outfile, numblocks, buffer)
    END
END Blocksort

Merge(fromfile, tofile, start, size)
(*
    Merge two consecutive sorted runs from fromfile to tofile.

    Run 1:  block start to block start + size - 1
    Run 2:  block start + size to start + (2 * size) - 1
*)
BEGIN

    (* initialize the input buffer for Run 1
       with the first block of the run *)
    ReadBlock(fromfile, first block of Run 1, In1)

    (* initialize the input buffer for Run 2
       with the first block of the run *)
    ReadBlock(fromfile, first block of Run 2, In2)

    (* Merge until one of the runs is finished.  Whenever an
       input buffer is exhausted, the next block is read in.
       Whenever the output buffer is full, it is written out. *)

    WHILE (neither run is finished) DO

        select the smaller "leading edge" of In1 and In2
            and place it in the next position of Out

        IF (Out is full) THEN
            WriteBlock(tofile, next block of tofile, Out)
        END

        IF ((In1 is exhausted) AND
            (more blocks remain in Run 1)) THEN
```

```
                    ReadBlock(fromfile, next block of Run 1, In1)
             END

             IF ((In2 is exhausted) AND
                 (more blocks remain in Run 2)) THEN
                    ReadBlock(fromfile, next block of Run 2, In2)
             END

       END

       (*
          At this point, exactly one of the runs is complete.
          The remainder of the incomplete run must be appended
          to the output file.  We must:

             1.  Append the remainder of the unfinished input
                 buffer to the output buffer and write it out.

             2.  Append the remaining complete blocks.
       *)

       (* finish off the remaining input buffer and write out the
          output buffer - only one of these loops will execute *)

       WHILE (In1 is not exhausted) DO
          place the next item of In1 into the next position of Out
       END

       WHILE (In2 is not exhausted) DO
          place the next item of In2 into the next position of Out
       END

       WriteBlock(tofile, next block of tofile, Out)

       (* finish off the remaining complete blocks
          - only one of these loops will execute *)

       WHILE (there remain blocks in Run 1) DO
          ReadBlock(fromfile, next block of Run 1, In1)
          WriteBlock(tofile, next block of tofile, In1)
       END

       WHILE (there remain blocks in Run 2) DO
          ReadBlock(fromfile, next block of Run 2, In2)
          WriteBlock(tofile, next block of tofile, In2)
       END

   END Merge
```

```
Mergefile(infile, outfile, runsize, numblocks)
(* Merge numblocks blocks from infile
    to outfile in runs of size = runsize. *)

BEGIN

    OpenRead(infile)
    OpenWrite(outfile)

    next := 1
    WHILE (next <= numblocks) DO
        Merge(infile, outfile, next, runsize)
        next := next + (2 * runsize)
    END
END Mergefile

(* MAIN PROGRAM *)
BEGIN

    (* Phase I:  sort the file block by block
        and count how many blocks there are *)
    Blocksort(infile, tempfile1, numblocks)

    (* Phase II:  merge runs of size 1, 2, 4,...numblocks
        - two temporary files are used - a toggle is used to
        keep track of the from file and the to file for each
        merge step *)
    size := 1
    toggle := 1
    WHILE (size < numblocks) DO
        IF (toggle = 1) THEN
            Mergefile(tempfile1, tempfile2, size, numblocks)
        ELSE
            Mergefile(tempfile2, tempfile1, size, numblocks)
        END
        size := 2 * size
        toggle := -toggle
    END

    (* copy the current temporary file to outfile *)
    IF (toggle = 1) THEN
        copyfile(tempfile1, outfile)
    ELSE
        copyfile(tempfile2, outfile)
    END

END
```

SEARCHING EXTERNAL TABLES

In this section we shall discuss techniques for organizing records in external storage so that table operations such as *Retrieve*, *Insert*, *Delete*, and *Traverse* can be efficiently performed. Although we shall only scratch the surface of this topic, we do have the advantage of a head start. Two of the most important external table implementations are variations of the 2–3 tree and hashing, methods introduced in Chapter 11.

Let us suppose that we have a file of records, each of which is to be a table item. The file is partitioned into blocks, as described earlier in the chapter. One of the simplest table implementations stores the records sorted by their search key, perhaps accomplishing this using the external sorting algorithm developed in the previous section. Once sorted, the file can easily be traversed in sorted order.

```
Traverse(F, Visit)
(* Traverse in sorted order the sorted file F,
   calling procedure Visit for each item. *)

   (* read each block of file F into internal array B *)
   FOR i := 1 TO NumberOfBlocks DO

      ReadBlock(F, i, B)

      (* visit each record in the block *)
      FOR j := 1 TO RecordsPerBlock DO
         Visit(B[j])
   END
END
```

To perform the *Retrieve* operation on the sorted file, we can use a binary search algorithm.

```
Retrieve(F, X, getitem, success)
(* Retrieve into getitem the record of file F with search
   key X.  The operation fails if there is no such item.  The
   flag success indicates whether the operation succeeded. *)

   (* read the middle block of file F into internal array B *)
   mid := number of middle block of file F
   ReadBlock(F, mid, B)

   (* the desired block has been found *)
   IF ((X >= B[1].key) AND (X <= B[RecordsPerBlock].key)) THEN

      search array B for record B[j] with search key X
```

```
IF (found) THEN
    getitem := B[j]
    success := TRUE
ELSE
    success := FALSE
END

(* there are no more blocks in the file to search *)
ELSIF (F is one block in size) THEN
    success := FALSE

(* the desired block is in the first half of the file *)
ELSIF (X < B[1].key) THEN
    Retrieve(first half of file F, X, getitem, success)

(* the desired block is in the second half of the file *)
ELSE
    Retrieve(second half of file F, X, getitem, success)

END
```

In the above algorithm, we recursively split the file in half, reading the middle block into the internal array B. Note that splitting a file segment requires that we know the numbers of the first and last blocks of the segment. These values would be passed as parameters along with the file name.

Once we have read the middle block of the file segment into B, we determine if a record with search key X could be in this block. This is accomplished by comparing X to the smallest search key in B (which is in $B[1]$) and to the largest search key in B (which is in $B[RecordsPerBlock]$). If X does not lie between the values of the smallest and largest search keys in B, we must recursively search one of the halves of the file (which half to search depends on whether X is less than or greater than the search keys in the block just examined). If, on the other hand, X does lie between the values of the smallest and largest search keys of the block in B, we must search B for the record. Notice that since the records within the block B are sorted, we could use a binary search on the records within this block. However, the number of records in the block B is typically small, and thus the time to scan the block sequentially is insignificant compared to the time to access the block. It is therefore common to simply scan the block sequentially.

This external implementation of the table is not very different from the internal sorted-sequential implementation. As such, it has many of the same advantages and disadvantages. Its main advantage is that, because the records are sequentially sorted, a binary search can be used to locate the block containing a given search key. The main disadvantage of the implementation is that, as with a sequential implementation, table items must be shifted by the *Insert* and *Delete* operations. Shifting records in an external file is, in general, far more costly than shifting array items. A file may contain an enormous number of large records, which are spread over several thousands of blocks. As a consequence, the shifting could require a prohibitively large number of block accesses. Consider, for example, Figure 12–5.

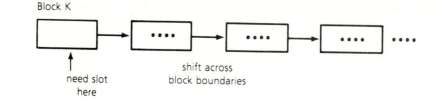

Block K

need slot
here

shift across
block boundaries

Figure 12–5

*Shifting
across block
boundaries*

If the new record is inserted into block k, then every block with a number k or greater must be read into internal memory so that its records can be shifted with an assignment such as

```
B[i+1] := B[i]
```

After the records of a block are shifted, the block must be written out again so that the change is reflected in the file. This large number of block accesses makes the external sorted-sequential implementation practical only for tables where insertions and deletions are rare. See Exercise 12.1.

Indexing an External File

Two of the best external table implementations are variations of the internal hashing and search tree schemes. The biggest difference between the internal and external versions of these implementations is that, in the external versions, it is often advantageous to organize an **index** to the data file rather than to organize the data file itself. An index to a data file is conceptually similar to other indices with which you are familiar. For example, consider a card catalogue in a library. Rather than looking all over the library for a particular title, we can simply search the card catalogue. The catalogue is typically organized alphabetically by title (as well as by author), so it is a simple matter to locate the appropriate entry. The entry for each book contains a pointer (for example, a Dewey decimal number), which indicates where on the shelves the book can be found.

Using a card catalogue to index the books in a library has at least three benefits:

1. The books can be placed on the shelves in any way we wish, without regard to how easy it will be for a patron to scan the shelves for a particular book. When a patron wishes to locate a particular book, he or she will search the card catalogue for the appropriate entry.

2. Because each catalogue entry is small (for example, a 3-inch by 5-inch index card) the entire catalogue for a large library can fit into a small area. A patron can thus locate a particular book without running all over the library.

3. We can have different types of catalogues to facilitate different types of searches. For example, we can have one catalogue organized by title and another organized by author.

We shall now describe how an index to a data file can be used to much the same advantage as the card catalogue (see Figure 12–6). We shall leave the data file in a disorganized state and maintain an index to it. When we need to locate a particular record in the data file, we search the index for the corresponding entry, which will tell us where in the data file the desired record is located.

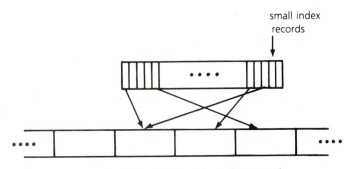

small index records

unorganized data—blocks of large data records

Figure 12–6
Small data file with index

An index to the data file is a file that contains an **index record** for each record in the data file, just as a card catalogue contains an entry for each book in the library. An index record has two fields, a **key field** and a **pointer field**. The key field of an index record contains the same value as the search key of its corresponding record in the data file, and its pointer field shows the number of the block in the data file that contains this data record. We can thus determine which block of the data file contains the record with the value X in its search key by searching the index file for the index record with key value X. (This type of index is often called a **dense index** to distinguish it from other types of indices.)

The approach of maintaining an index to the data file yields benefits analogous to those provided by the library's card catalogue:

1. Since the data file does not need to be maintained in any particular order, new records can be inserted in any convenient location, for example, at the end of the file. As we shall see, this eliminates the need for shifting the data records during insertions and deletions.

2. In general, an index record will be much smaller than a data record. While the data record may contain many fields, an index record contains only one of the fields of the data record (the search key) and a single integer pointer (a block number). Thus, just as the library's card catalogue occupies only a small fraction of the space occupied by the books it indexes, an index file is only a fraction of the size of the data file. As we shall see, this often allows us to manipulate the index file with fewer block accesses than would be required to manipulate the data file.

3. We can maintain several indices simultaneously. Just as a library can have one card catalogue organized by title and another organized by author, we

can have one file indexing the data file by one search key (for example, an index file that consists of <Name, pointer> records), and a second file indexing the data file by another search key (for example, an index file that consists of <SocSec, pointer> records). We shall briefly discuss multiple indexing at the end of this chapter.

Although we do not organize the data file, we must organize the index file so that it can be rapidly searched and updated. Before we describe how an index file can be organized with hashing and search tree schemes, let us first illustrate the concepts of indexing with a less complex organization that simply stores the index records sequentially sorted by their key fields (see Figure 12–7).

Figure 12–7

Small data file with sorted index file

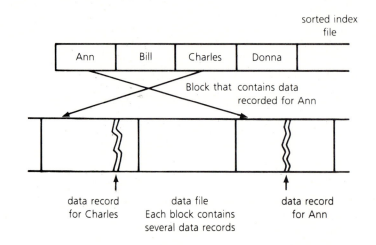

Since the index records are far smaller than the data records, the index file is spread over far fewer blocks than is the data file. For example, if the index records are one-tenth the size of the data records and the data file is spread over one thousand blocks, then the index file will be spread over only about 100 blocks. As a result, the operations `Retrieve`, `Insert`, and `Delete` can be performed with fewer block accesses. For example, to perform the `Retrieve` operation, we can now use a binary search on the index file.

```
Retrieve(Tindex, Tdata, X, getitem, success)
(* Retrieve into getitem the record with search key X, where
    Tindex is the index file and Tdata is the data file.  The
    operation fails if there is no such record.  The flag
    success indicates whether the operation succeeded.  *)

    (* read the middle block of the
        index file into internal array B *)
    mid := middle block of index file Tindex
    ReadBlock(Tindex, mid, B)

    (* the desired block of the index file has been found *)
    IF  (X >= B[1].key)  AND
        (X <= B[IndexRecordsPerBlock].key)  THEN
```

```
        (* determine the desired block number of the data file *)
        search array B for index record B[j] with key value X

    IF (found) THEN
        blocknum := block number of
                        the data file pointed to by B[j]

        (* read the block from the
            data file into internal array D *)
        ReadBlock(Tdata, blocknum, D)

        (* search for the table item *)
        find data record D[k] with search key X
        getitem := D[k]

        success := TRUE

    ELSE
        success := FALSE

    END

    (* there are no more blocks in the file to search *)
    ELSIF (Tindex is one block in size) THEN
        success := FALSE

    (* the desired block is in the
        first half of the index file *)
    ELSIF (X < B[1].key) THEN
        Retrieve(first half of Tindex, Tdata, X, getitem, success)

    (* the desired block is in the
        second half of the index file *)
    ELSE
        Retrieve(second half of Tindex, Tdata, X, getitem, success)

    END
```

This cuts the number of block accesses down from about $\log_2 1000 = 10$ to about $\log_2 100 + 1 = 8$ (the one additional block access is for going into the data file once the appropriate index record has been located).

The reduction in block accesses is far more dramatic for the *Insert* and *Delete* operations. In the original implementation, an insertion or a deletion can possibly cause every data record to be shifted, requiring that all 1000 blocks of the data file be accessed. This would occur if the record is inserted into or deleted from the first block.

When we perform an insertion or a deletion using the index scheme, however, only index records will ever have to be shifted. When using the index scheme, the data file is not kept in any particular order, so we can insert a new data record anywhere in the data file we wish. This means that we can simply insert a new data record at the end of the file or at a position left vacant by a previous deletion (see below). As a result, no data records ever need to be shifted. The only shifting required is in the index file to create an opening so that the corresponding index entry can be inserted into its proper sorted position. Since there are only 100 blocks of the index file, the maximum number of block accesses that can be required is greatly reduced. A secondary benefit of shifting index records rather than data records is that, since the records themselves are smaller, the amount of time required for a single shift is less; that is, time required for the assignment $B[i+1] := B[i]$ is reduced.

Deletions under the index scheme reap similar benefits. Once the data record to be deleted is located (by searching the index), we can simply leave its location vacant and thus need not shift any data records. We keep track of the vacant locations in the data file (see Exercise 12.2), and new data records can be inserted into the vacancies as described above. The only shifting required is in the index file to fill the gap created when the index record corresponding to the deleted data record is removed.

Even though this scheme is an improvement over maintaining a sorted data file, in many applications it is far from satisfactory. The 100 block accesses that could be required to insert or delete an index record would often be prohibitive. Far better implementations are obtained when the index file is organized into hashing or search trees schemes.

External Hashing

The external hashing scheme is very similar to the internal scheme described in Chapter 11. Recall in the internal hashing scheme each entry of the array $T[0..B-1]$ contains a pointer to the beginning of the list (or tree) of items

Figure 12–8

Hashed index file

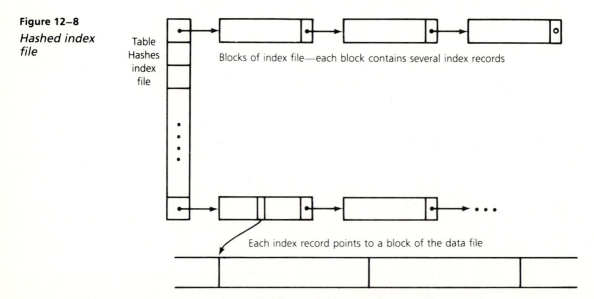

Table
Hashes
index
file

Blocks of index file—each block contains several index records

Each index record points to a block of the data file

data file—each block contains several data records

which hash into that location. In the external hashing scheme each entry of T still contains a pointer to the beginning of a list, but here each list consists of *blocks of index records*. In other words, we are going to hash an index file rather than the data file (see Figure 12–8). (In many applications the array T is itself so large that it must be kept in external storage, for example, in the first K blocks of the index file. To avoid this extra detail, we shall assume that the array T is an internal array.)

In Figure 12–8, we see that associated with each entry $T[i]$ is a linked list of blocks of the index file. Each block of $T[i]$'s list contains index records whose keys (and thus whose corresponding data-records' search keys) hash into location i. To form the linked lists, we must reserve space in each block for a block pointer—the integer block number of the next block in the chain. By convention, the value zero is placed in the last block on the chain (this is analogous to setting a Modula-2 pointer to **NIL**) (see Figure 12–9).

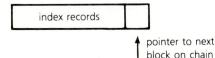

Figure 12–9

*Single block
with pointer*

The following is a high-level description of the *Retrieve* algorithm:

```
Retrieve(Tindex, Tdata, X, getitem, success)
(* Retrieve into getitem the item with search key X, where
   Tindex is the index file which is hashed, and Tdata is
   the data file.  The operation fails if there is no such
   record.  The flag success indicates whether the operation
   succeeded. *)

   (* apply the hash function to search key X *)
   i : = h(X)

   (* find the first block on the chain of index blocks
      containing index records which hash into location i *)
   p := T[i]

   (* if p = 0 then no values have hashed into location i *)
   IF (p # 0) THEN
       ReadBlock(Tindex, p, B)
   END

   (* search for the block with the desired index record *)
   WHILE ((p # 0) AND
           (B does not contain an index
            record with key value X)) DO
      p := block number of next block on chain

      (* if p = 0 then we are at the last block in the chain *)
      IF (p # 0) THEN
```

```
            ReadBlock (Tindex,  p,  B)
      END
   END


   (* retrieve the data item if present *)
   IF  (p # 0)  THEN

      (* B[j] is the index record with key value X *)

      blocknum := block number of data file pointed to by B[j]

      (* read the block from the data
         file into internal array D *)
      ReadBlock (Tdata,  blocknum,  D)

      (* search for the table item *)
      find data record D[k] with search key X
      getitem := D[k]

      success := TRUE

   ELSE
      success := FALSE

   END
```

The `Insert` and `Delete` algorithms are also similar to those for internal hashing. The major difference is that, in the external environment, both a data record and a corresponding index record must be inserted or deleted. We first consider the steps of the insertion algorithm.

INSERT A NEW DATA RECORD WITH SEARCH KEY X

1. **Insert the data record into the data file.** Since the data file is not ordered, the new record can go anywhere we wish. If a previous deletion has left a free slot in the middle of the data file, we can insert it there (see Exercise 12.2).

   If there are no free slots, we insert the new data record at the end of the last block, or, if necessary, we append a new block to the end of the data file and store the record there. In either case, let p denote the number of the block that contains this new data record.

2. **Insert a corresponding index record into the index file.** We need to insert into the index file an index record with key value X and pointer value p (recall that p is the number of the block in the data file into which the new data record has been inserted). Since the index file is hashed, we first apply the hash function to search key X, letting

   $i := h(X)$

We then insert the index record $<X, p>$ into the chain of blocks pointed to by the entry $T[i]$. We can insert this record into any block on the chain that contains a free slot, or, if necessary, we can allocate a new block and link it to the beginning of the chain.

The steps for a deletion are as follows.

DELETE A DATA RECORD WITH SEARCH KEY X

1. **Search the index file for the corresponding index record.** We apply the hash function to the search key X, letting

   $i \; : = \; h\,(X)$

   We then search the chain of index blocks pointed to by entry $T[i]$ for an index record with key value X. If no such record is found, we can conclude that there is no record in the data file with search key X. If we find an index record $<X, p>$, we delete it from the index file after noting the block number p, which indicates where in the data file we can find the data record to be deleted.

2. **Delete the data record from the data file.** We know that the data record is in block p of the data file. We simply access this block, search the block for the record, delete the record, and write the block back to the file.

   Observe that for each of the operations `Retrieve`, `Insert`, and `Delete`, the number of block accesses is very low. We never have to access more than one block of the data file, and, at worst, we have to access all of the blocks along a *single* hash chain of the index file. As with internal hashing, we can take measures to keep the length of each of the chains quite short (for example, one or two blocks long). The size of the array T should be chosen to be large enough so that the average length of a chain is near one block, and the hash function should scatter the keys uniformly. If necessary, we can even structure each chain as an external search tree, using the techniques described below.

   The hashing implementation is the one to choose when we need to perform the operations `Retrieve`, `Insert`, and `Delete` on a large external table. As with internal hashing, however, there are operations that this implementation does not support well. These are operations such as sorted traversal, retrieval of the smallest or largest item, and range queries that require the data to be ordered. When these types of operations are added to the basic table operations `Retrieve`, `Insert`, and `Delete`, a search tree implementation may be more appropriate than hashing.

B-Trees

The external search tree implementation we develop here is a generalization of the 2–3 tree of Chapter 11. As with the external hashing implementation, we shall impose the organization on an index file rather than on the data file.

   Let us begin by observing that the blocks of an external file can be organized into a tree structure by using block numbers for child pointers. In Figure 12–10, for example, the blocks have been organized into a 2–3 tree. Each block of the file is a node in the tree and contains three child pointers, each of which is the integer block number of the child. A child pointer value of zero plays the role of a nil pointer, and thus, for example, a leaf will contain three child pointers with the value zero.

If we organized the index file into a 2–3 tree, each node (block of the index file) would contain either one or two index records, each of the form <Key, Pointer>, along with three child pointers. It is important to remember that the pointer field of the record <X, p> indicates the block of the data file which contains the data record with search key X and has nothing to do with the tree structure of the index file. To help avoid confusion, we shall use the term **child pointers** when referring to the pointers that are used to maintain the tree structure of the index file.

The index records must be organized in the tree so that their keys obey the same search tree ordering property as an internal 2–3 tree. This allows the data record with a given value in its search key to be retrieved as follows:

Figure 12–10

(a) Blocks organized into a 2–3 tree; (b) single node of 2–3 tree

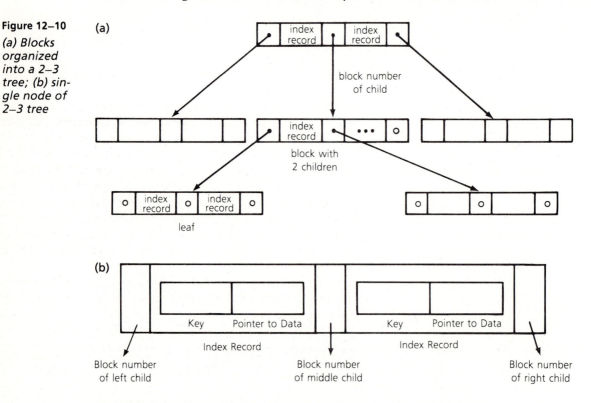

```
Retrieve(Tindex, Tdata, rootnum, X, getitem, success)
(* Retrieve into getitem the record with search key X.
   Tindex is the index file which is organized into a
   2-3 tree.  Rootnum is the block number of the index
   file which contains the root of the tree.  Tdata is
   the data file.  The operation fails if there is no
   such item.  The flag success indicates whether the
   operation succeeded.  *)

(* read into internal array B the block of the
```

```
                index file containing the root of the 2-3 tree *)
        ReadBlock(Tindex, rootnum, B)

        (* search for the index record with key value X *)
        IF (X is in the root) THEN
            blocknum := block number of the data file specified
                            by the index record

            (* read the block from the data
                file into internal array D *)
            ReadBlock(Tdata, blocknum, D)

            (* search for the table item *)
            find data record D[k] with search key X
            getitem := D[k]

            success := TRUE

        ELSE
            (* search the appropriate subtree *)
            IF (the root is a leaf) THEN
                success := FALSE
            ELSE
                child := block number of the
                            root of the appropriate subtree
                Retrieve(Tindex, Tdata, child, X, getitem, success)
            END

        END
```

Insertions and deletions can also be performed in a manner similar to the internal version, with the addition that records must be inserted into and deleted from both the index file and the data file (as was the case in the external hashing scheme described earlier). In the course of insertions into and deletions from the index file, nodes of the tree will be split and merged just as they are in the internal version. Insertions into and deletions from the data file (which, recall, is not ordered in any way) are performed exactly as described for the external hashing implementation.

We can thus support the table operations fairly well with an external version of the 2–3 tree. We can, however, generalize the 2–3 tree to a structure that is even more suitable for an external environment. Recall our discussion in Chapter 11 about search trees that allow their nodes to have more than 3 children. We argued that any reduction in the search tree's height obtained by allowing its nodes to have more than 3 children is offset by the fact that, in the course of searching for a value, more comparisons would have to be made at each node visited. In an external environment, however, the advantage of keeping a search tree short far outweighs the disadvantage of having to perform extra work at each node.

```
child := block number of the root of Sᵢ
    Retrieve(Tindex, Tdata, child, X, getitem, success)
END
```

END

We can now return to the question of how many children the nodes of our search tree can have—that is, how big can m be? If we wish to organize the index file into a search tree, then the items that are stored in each node will be records of the form <Key, Pointer>. Thus if each node in the tree (which, recall, is a block of the index file) is to have m children, it must be large enough to accommodate m child pointers and $m - 1$ records of the form <Key, Pointer>. We shall choose m to be the largest integer such that m child pointers (which, recall, are integers) and $m - 1$ <Key, Pointer> records can fit into a single block of the file. (Actually, the algorithms are somewhat simplified if m is always chosen to be odd; that is, we shall choose m to be the largest odd integer such that m child pointers and $m - 1$ index records can fit into a single block.)

Ideally, then, our external search tree should be structured so that every internal node has m children (where m is chosen as just described) and, as is the case with full trees and 2–3 trees, all leaves are at the same level (see Figure 12–12). Although this structure would give us the search tree with the minimum possible height, it is too difficult to maintain in the face of insertions and deletions. As a consequence, we must make a compromise. We shall still insist that all the leaves of the search tree be at the same level (that the tree be balanced), but we shall allow the number of children that an internal node has to fluctuate between m and $(m \text{ div } 2) + 1$.

Figure 12–12

Full tree of order 5

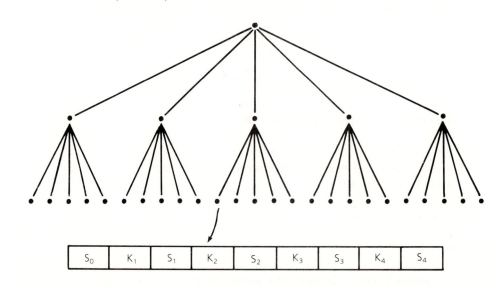

This type of search tree is known as a **B-tree**. A **B-tree of degree m** is a search tree such that:

1. All leaves are at the same level.

In general, if a node N in a search tree is to have m children, then it must contain $m - 1$ key values to separate the values in its subtrees correctly. Let us denote the subtrees of N as $S_0, S_1, S_2, \ldots, S_{m-1}$ and denote the key values in N as $K_1, K_2, \ldots, K_{m-1}$ (with $K_1 < K_2 < \ldots < K_{m-1}$). The key values in N must separate the values in its subtrees as follows:

1. All the values in subtree S_0 must be less than the key value K_1.
2. For all i, $1 \leq i \leq m - 2$, all the values in subtree S_i must lie between the key values K_i and K_{i+1}.
3. All the values in subtree S_{m-1} must be greater than the key value K_{m-1}

If every node in the tree obeys this property, then the tree can be searched with a generalized version of a search tree's retrieve algorithm.

```
Retrieve(Tindex, Tdata, rootnum, X, getitem, success)
(* Retrieve into getitem the record with search key X.  Tindex
    is the index file which is organized into a search tree.
    Rootnum is the block number of the index file which contains
    the root of the tree.  Tdata is the data file.  The operation
    fails if there is no such item.  The flag success indicates
    whether the operation succeeded. *)

    (* read into internal array B the block of the
        index file containing the root of the tree *)
    ReadBlock(Tindex, rootnum, B)

    (* search for the index record with key value X *)
    IF (X is in the root (is one of the K_i)) THEN
        blocknum := block number of the data file specified
                        by the index record

        (* read the block from the data
            file into internal array D *)
        ReadBlock(Tdata, blocknum, D)

        (* search for the table item *)
        find the data record D[k] with search key X
        getitem := D[k]

        success := TRUE

    ELSE

        (* search the appropriate subtree *)
        IF (root is a leaf) THEN
            success := FALSE
        ELSE
            determine which subtree S_i to search
```

```
            child := block number of the root of S_i
            Retrieve(Tindex, Tdata, child, X, getitem, success)
      END

   END
```

We can now return to the question of how many children the nodes of our search tree can have—that is, how big can m be? If we wish to organize the index file into a search tree, then the items that are stored in each node will be records of the form <Key, Pointer>. Thus if each node in the tree (which, recall, is a block of the index file) is to have m children, it must be large enough to accommodate m child pointers and $m - 1$ records of the form <Key, Pointer>. We shall choose m to be the largest integer such that m child pointers (which, recall, are integers) and $m - 1$ <Key, Pointer> records can fit into a single block of the file. (Actually, the algorithms are somewhat simplified if m is always chosen to be odd; that is, we shall choose m to be the largest odd integer such that m child pointers and $m - 1$ index records can fit into a single block.)

Ideally, then, our external search tree should be structured so that every internal node has m children (where m is chosen as just described) and, as is the case with full trees and 2–3 trees, all leaves are at the same level (see Figure 12–12). Although this structure would give us the search tree with the minimum possible height, it is too difficult to maintain in the face of insertions and deletions. As a consequence, we must make a compromise. We shall still insist that all the leaves of the search tree be at the same level (that the tree be balanced), but we shall allow the number of children that an internal node has to fluctuate between m and $(m \text{ div } 2) + 1$.

Figure 12–12

Full tree of order 5

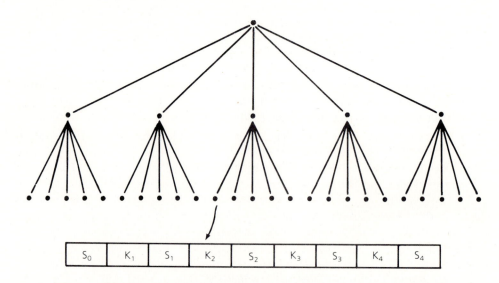

This type of search tree is known as a **B-tree**. A **B-tree of degree** m is a search tree such that:

1. All leaves are at the same level.

```
           index file containing the root of the 2-3 tree *)
    ReadBlock(Tindex, rootnum, B)

       (* search for the index record with key value X *)
       IF (X is in the root) THEN
          blocknum := block number of the data file specified
                         by the index record

          (* read the block from the data
             file into internal array D *)
          ReadBlock(Tdata, blocknum, D)

          (* search for the table item *)
          find data record D[k] with search key X
          getitem := D[k]

          success := TRUE

       ELSE
          (* search the appropriate subtree *)
          IF (the root is a leaf) THEN
             success := FALSE
          ELSE
             child := block number of the
                         root of the appropriate subtree
             Retrieve(Tindex, Tdata, child, X, getitem, success)
          END

    END
```

Insertions and deletions can also be performed in a manner similar to the internal version, with the addition that records must be inserted into and deleted from both the index file and the data file (as was the case in the external hashing scheme described earlier). In the course of insertions into and deletions from the index file, nodes of the tree will be split and merged just as they are in the internal version. Insertions into and deletions from the data file (which, recall, is not ordered in any way) are performed exactly as described for the external hashing implementation.

We can thus support the table operations fairly well with an external version of the 2–3 tree. We can, however, generalize the 2–3 tree to a structure that is even more suitable for an external environment. Recall our discussion in Chapter 11 about search trees that allow their nodes to have more than 3 children. We argued that any reduction in the search tree's height obtained by allowing its nodes to have more than 3 children is offset by the fact that, in the course of searching for a value, more comparisons would have to be made at each node visited. In an external environment, however, the advantage of keeping a search tree short far outweighs the disadvantage of having to perform extra work at each node.

In an external environment, as we traverse the search tree we must perform a block access for each node visited. Since the time required to access a block of an external file is, in general, far greater than the time required to operate on that block once it has been read in (for example, the time required to inspect its data), the overriding concern is to reduce the number of block accesses required. This implies that we should attempt to reduce the height of the tree, even at the expense of requiring more comparisons at each node. In an external search tree, we should thus allow each node to have as many children as possible, with the only limiting factor being the block size.

How many children can be accommodated by a block of some fixed size? If a node is to have m children, then clearly we must be able to fit m child pointers in the node. In addition to child pointers, however, the node must also contain index records.

Before we can answer the question of how many children a block can accommodate, we must first consider this related question: If a node N in a search tree has m children, how many key values (and thus how many index records) must it contain?

In a binary search tree, if N has two children, then it must contain one key value (see Figure 12–11). The key value in node N can be thought of as *separating* the values in N's two subtrees—all the values in N's left subtree are less than N's value, and all the values in N's right subtree are greater than N's value. When searching the tree for a given value, the value in N tells us which branch to take.

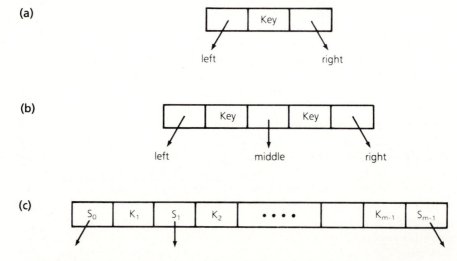

(a)

(b)

(c)

Figure 12–11   *(a) Node with two children; (b) node with three children; (c) node with m children*

Similarly, if a node N in a 2–3 tree has three children, then it must contain two key values. These two values separate the values in N's three subtrees—all the values in the left subtree are less than N's smaller value, all the values in N's middle subtree lie between N's two values, and all the values in N's right subtree are greater than N's larger value. As with a binary search tree, this allows a search algorithm to know which branch to take at any given node.

2. Each node contains between $m - 1$ and (m div 2) records, and each internal node has one more child than it has records. An exception to this rule is that the root of the tree is permitted to contain as few as one record and to have as few as two children. This exception is necessitated by the insertion and deletion algorithms described below.

Notice that a 2–3 tree is a B-tree of degree 3. Furthermore, the manner in which the B-tree insertion and deletion algorithms maintain the structure of the tree is a direct generalization of the 2–3 tree's strategy of splitting and merging nodes. We shall illustrate the B-tree's insertion and deletion algorithms by way of example.

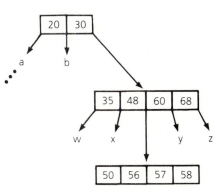

Figure 12–13

A B-tree.

Insertions into a B-tree. Suppose that our index file is organized into a B-tree of degree 5—that is, 5 is the maximum and 3 is the minimum number of children that an internal node in the tree (other than the root) can have. (Typically a B-tree will be of a higher degree, but the diagrams would get out of hand!) The steps of inserting a data record with search key 55 into the tree of Figure 12–13 are as follows:

1. **Insert the data record into the data file.** As with the external hashing implementation, we find a block p in the data file into which the new record can be inserted (that is, p is any block with a vacant slot or is a new block).

2. **Insert a corresponding index record into the index file.** The index record $<55, p>$ must now be inserted into the index file that is a B-tree of degree 5. The first step is to locate the leaf of the tree in which this index record belongs (by seeing where the search for 55 would terminate).

   Suppose that this is the leaf L shown in Figure 12–14. Conceptually, we insert the new index record into L, causing it to contain 5 records (Figure 12–14b). Since a node is permitted to contain only 4 records, we must split L into L_1 and L_2. Analogous to the splitting of a node in a 2–3 tree, L_1 gets the 2 records with the smallest key values, L_2 gets the 2 records with the largest key values, and the record with the middle key value is sent up to the parent P (Figure 12–14c).

   In this example, P now has 6 children and 5 records, so it must be split into P_1 and P_2. As with a 2–3 tree, when an internal node is split, its children must be distributed appropriately.

The insertion is complete since P's parent Q now contains only 3 records and has only 4 children (Figure 12–14d). In general, though, an insertion might cause splitting to propagate all the way up to the root (Figure 12–14e). Notice that, if the root must be split, the new root will contain only one record and have only two children (recall that the definition of a B-tree allows for this eventuality).

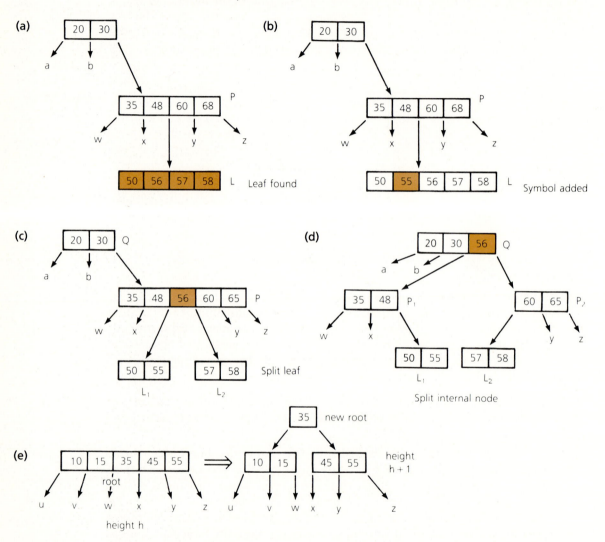

Figure 12–14

Insert 55

Deletions from a B-tree. We wish to delete the data record with search key 73.

1. **Locate the index record in the index file.** We use the search procedure to locate the index record with key value 73. If this record is not already in a leaf, we swap it with its inorder successor (see Exercise 5). Suppose that the leaf L shown in Figure 12–15 contains the index record with key value 73. After noting the value p of the pointer field of this index record (which indicates the block of the data file that contains the data record with search

key 73), we remove the record from L (Figure 12–15b). Since L now contains only one value (recall that two is the minimum number of values that a node is permitted to contain), and since L's siblings cannot spare a value, we merge L with one of the siblings, bringing down a record from the parent P (Figure 12–15c). Notice how this is analogous to the merge step for a 2–3 tree. But P now has only one value and 2 children, and, since its siblings cannot spare a record and child, we must merge P with sibling P_1. Since P is an internal node, its children must be adopted by P_1 (Figure 12–15d).

After this merge, P's parent Q is left with only 2 children and one record. In this case, however, Q's sibling Q_1 can spare a record and a child, so we redistribute children and records among Q_1, Q, and the parent T to complete the deletion (Figure 12–15e). Notice that if a deletion ever propagates all the way up to the root so that it has only two children and contains only one record, we simply let this situation stand. Recall that this eventuality is accounted for in the definition of a B-tree. If a future deletion causes the root to have a single child and no records, we remove the root and the tree's height decreases by one (Figure 12–15f). This completes the deletion of the index record, and we now must delete the data record.

2. **Delete the data record from the data file.** We know that the data record is in block P of the data file. We simply access this block, delete the record, and write the block back to the file.

The high-level pseudocode for the insertion and deletion algorithms parallels those of the 2–3 tree and are left as exercises.

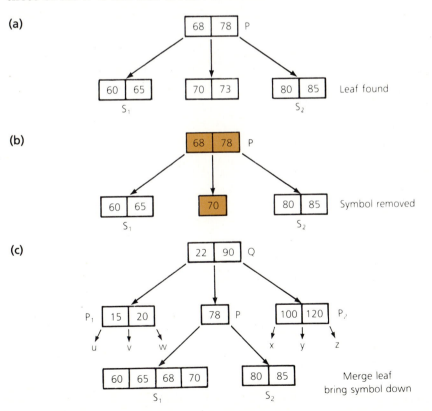

(a)

68 | 78 P

60 | 65 S_1 70 | 73   80 | 85 S_2 Leaf found

(b)

68 | 78 P

60 | 65 S_1 70   80 | 85 S_2 Symbol removed

(c)

22 | 90 Q

P_1 15 | 20   u v w   78 P   100 | 120 P_2 x y z

60 | 65 | 68 | 70 S_1 80 | 85 S_2 Merge leaf
bring symbol down

Figure 12–15
Delete 73

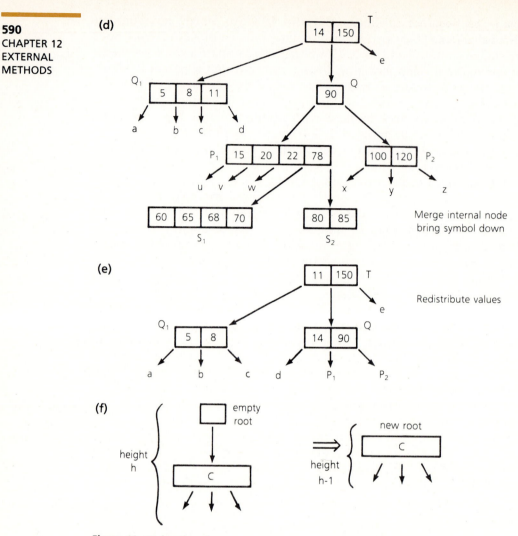

Figure 12–15 *(continued)*

Traversals

We now consider the operation *Traverse* in sorted order, which is one of the operations not supported at all efficiently by hashing. Often an application requires only that the traversal print the search keys of the records. If this is the case, then the B-tree implementation can efficiently support the operation. The search keys can be visited in sorted order with an inorder traversal of the B-tree, and we don't have to access the data file.

```
Traverse (blocknum)
(* Traverse in sorted order a file that is indexed with a
   B-tree. Blocknum is the block number of the root of the
   B-tree. *)
```

```
(* read the root into internal array B *)
ReadBlock(indexfile, blocknum, B)


(* traverse the children *)


(* traverse S₀ *)
let p be the block number of the "0ᵗʰ" child of B
Traverse(p)

FOR i := 1 TO m-1 DO
    write key Kᵢ of B

    (* traverse Sᵢ *)
    let p be block number of the iᵗʰ child of B
    Traverse(p)


    END
```

This traversal accomplishes the task with the minimum possible number of block accesses, since each block of the index file is read only once. Notice, however, that the above algorithm assumes that there is enough internal memory to accommodate a recursive stack containing h blocks, where h is the height of the tree. In many situations this is a reasonable assumption—for example, a 255-degree B-tree indexing a file containing 16 million data records has a height of no more than 3. When h blocks cannot be accommodated by internal memory, a different algorithm must be used (see Exercise 12.9).

If the traversal is required to print the entire data record (and not just the search key), then our B-tree implementation is less attractive. In this case, as we traverse the B-tree, the appropriate block of the data file must be accessed. The traversal would become:

```
Traverse(blocknum)
(* Traverse in sorted order a file that is indexed with a
    B-tree.  Blocknum is the block number of the root of the
    B-tree. *)

  IF (blocknum # 0) THEN

      (* read the root into internal array B *)
      ReadBlock(indexfile, blocknum, B)

      (* traverse S₀ *)
      let p be block number of the "0ᵗʰ" child of B
      Traverse(p)

      FOR i := 1 TO m-1 DO
          let pdata be the pointer in the iᵗʰ index record of B
          ReadBlock(datafile, pdata, D)
```

> *extract from D the data record with search key K_i*
> *print the data record*
>
> *(* traverse S_i *)*
> *let p be block number of the ith child of B*
> *Traverse (p)*
> > *END*
>
> > *END*

Notice that this traversal requires a block of the data file to be read before each data record is printed; that is, the number of data file block accesses is equal to the number of data records. In general, such a large number of block accesses would not be acceptable. If this type of traversal must be performed frequently, a modification to our B-tree scheme in which the data file itself is kept nearly sorted would probably be used.

Multiple Indexing

There is one final point to be made before we conclude our discussion of external implementations. This concerns the multiple indexing of a data file. Chapter 10 presented a problem where we had to support multiple organizations for data stored in internal memory. Such a problem is also common for data stored externally. For example, suppose that a data file contains a collection of employee records on which we need to perform two types of retrievals:

RetrieveN(name)
(* Retrieve the item with value name in the Name field. *)

RetrieveS(ss)
(* Retrieve the item with value ss in the SocSec field. *)

One solution to the problem is to maintain two independent index files to the data file. For example, we could have one index file with index records of the form <Name, Pointer> and a second index file with index records of the form <SocSec, Pointer>. These index files could both be hashed, could both be B-trees, or could be one of each. The choice would depend on the operations we wished to perform with each search key (see Figure 12–16). (Similarly, if an application requires extremely fast retrievals on SocSec and also requires operations such as traverse in sorted SocSec order and range queries on SocSec, it might be reasonable to have two SocSec index files—one hashed, the other a B-tree.)

Notice that while each *Retrieve* operation can be performed by using only one of the indices (that is, use the Name index for *RetrieveN* and the SocSec index for *RetrieveS*), insertion and deletion operations must update both indices. For example, the operation *DeleteN(Jones)* (delete by name) requires that we:

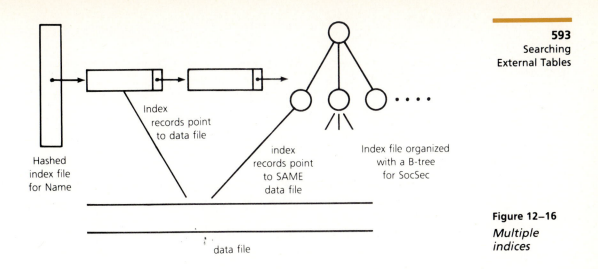

Figure 12–16

*Multiple
indices*

1. Search the Name index file for Jones and delete the index record.
2. Delete the appropriate data record from the data file, noting the SocSec value S of this record.
3. Search the SocSec index file for S and delete this index record.

In general, the price paid for multiple indexing is more storage space and an additional overhead for updating each index whenever the data file is modified.

We have presented at a very high level the basic principles of managing data in external storage. The details of implementing the algorithms are quite complex and depend heavily on the specific computing system. There are many possible variations of these methods (and completely different methods) that specific applications often mandate. In future courses and work experience, you will undoubtedly learn quite a bit more about these techniques.

SUMMARY

1. An external file is partitioned into blocks. Each block typically contains many data records, and a block is generally the smallest unit of transfer between internal and external memory; that is, to access a record, we must access the block that contains it.

2. The ith block of a direct-access file can be accessed without accessing the blocks that precede it. In this sense, direct-access files resemble arrays.

3. *Mergesort* can be modified so that it can sort a file of records without requiring all the records to be in internal memory at one time.

4. A dense index to a data file is a file that contains an index record for each record in the data file. An index record contains the key of the corresponding data record and a pointer to the block of the data file that contains that record.

5. We can organize the index file using hashing and B-trees. These schemes allow the basic table operations to be performed with only a few block accesses.

1. Before a record can be processed (for example, inspected or updated), it must be read from an external file into internal memory. Once a record is updated, it must be written back to the file.

2. Block accesses are typically quite slow when compared with other computer operations. Therefore, care must be taken to organize a file so that tasks can be performed with only a few block accesses. Otherwise, response time can be very poor.

3. If a record is inserted into or deleted from a data file, the corresponding change must be made to the index file. If a file is indexed by more than one index file, each index file must be updated. Thus, there is an overhead associated with multiple indexing.

4. While hashing generally supports retrievals, insertions, and deletions more quickly than does a B-tree, it does not support operations such as sorted traversals or range queries. This is one motivation for multiple indexing.

6. It is possible to have several files indexing the same data file. This allows different types of operations to be performed efficiently, such as, retrieve by name and retrieve by Social Security number.

EXERCISES

1. Assuming the existence of *ReadBlock* and *WriteBlock* procedures, write a pseudocode program for shifting data to make a gap at some specified location of a sorted file. Pay particular attention to the details of shifting the last item out of one block and into the first position of the next block. You can assume that the last record of the file is in record *LastRec* of block *LastBlock* and that *LastBlock* is not full. (Note that this permits shifting without allocating a new block to the file.)

2. The problem of managing the blocks of an external data file indexed by a B-tree or external hashing scheme is similar to that of managing memory for internal structures. When an external structure such as a data file needs more memory (for example, to insert a new record), it gets a new block from a "free list" that is managed by the system. That is, if the file contains N blocks, then the system can **allocate** to it an $(N + 1)^{st}$ block. When the file no longer needs a block, we can **deallocate** it and return it to the system.

   The complication in the management of external storage is that a block allocated to a file may have available space interspersed with data. For example, after deleting a record from the middle of a data file, the block that contained that record now has space available for at least one record, even though it may not be completely empty. Therefore, we must be able to keep track of blocks that have space available for one or more records as well as recognize when blocks are completely empty (so that they can be returned to the system).

Assuming the existence of *AllocateBlock* and *ReturnBlock* procedures that get empty blocks from and return empty blocks to the system, write pseudocode implementations of the following external memory management procedures:

```
GetSlot(F, blocknum, recnum)
(* Determine the block number (blocknum) and record number
   (recnum) of an available slot in file F.  A new block is
   allocated to the file from the system if necessary. *)

FreeSlot(F, blocknum, recnum)
(* Make record recnum in block blocknum of file F available.
   The block is returned to the system if it becomes empty. *)
```

What data structure is appropriate to support these operations? You may assume that slots of a block that do not contain a record can be distinguished from those that do. This can be done either by having a convention for nil values in the fields of a record or by adding an empty/full Boolean field.

3. Describe pseudocode algorithms for insertion into and deletion from a table implemented externally with a hashed index file.

4. Execute the following sequence of operations on an empty B-tree of order 5. Note that insertion into an empty B-tree will create a single node containing the inserted item.

```
Insert(10)
Insert(100)
Insert(30)
Insert(80)
Insert(50)
Delete(10)
Insert(60)
Insert(70)
Insert(40)
Delete(80)
Insert(90)
Insert(20)
Delete(30)
Delete(70)
```

5. Describe a pseudocode algorithm for finding an item's inorder successor in an external B-tree.

6. Describe pseudocode algorithms for insertion into and deletion from a table implemented with an index file organized as a B-tree.

7. Implement a range query for a B-tree in pseudocode (see Exercises 11.1 and 11.2). Assume that only the key values are needed (as opposed to the entire data record).

8. Integrate calls to the appropriate memory management procedures (see Exercise 12.2) into the pseudocode for *Insert* and *Delete* under both the B-tree and hashing schemes (see Exercises 12.3 and 12.6).

9. The B-tree traversal algorithm presented in this chapter assumes that internal memory is large enough to accommodate the recursive stack that contains up to h blocks, where h is the height of the B-tree. Suppose that we are in an environment where this assumption is not true. Modify the traversal algorithm so that the recursive stack contains block numbers rather than the actual blocks. How many block accesses does your algorithm have to perform?

10. a. Suppose that traversals and range queries need to access entire data records, not simply the search key. Write pseudocode implementations of such operations against a B-tree. How many block accesses do your procedures require?

    b. To reduce the number of block accesses required by these operations, various modifications of the basic B-tree structure are frequently used. The central idea behind such structures is to keep the data file itself sorted. First assume that the data file could be kept in sequential sorted order—that is, so that the records are sorted within each block and the records in B_{i-1} are less than the records in B_i for $i = 2, 3, \ldots$ number of blocks in file. Rewrite your implementations of the traversal and range query operations to take advantage of this fact. How many block accesses do these operations now require?

    c. Because it is too inefficient to maintain a sequentially sorted data file in the face of frequent insertions and deletions, a compromise scheme is often employed. One such possible compromise is as follows. If a data record belongs in block B and B is full, a new block is allocated and linked to B, allowing the new record to be inserted into its proper sorted location. The difficulty is that we must now view each index record in the B-tree as indicating the first of possibly several blocks on a chain of blocks that might contain the corresponding data record. Rewrite the *Insert*, *Delete*, *Retrieve*, *Traverse*, and *Range Query* operations in terms of this implementation. What is the effect on their efficiencies?

PROJECT

*11. Implement *Mergesort* using the direct-access file mechanisms that are supported by your implementation of Modula-2.

CHAPTER 13

A COMPARISON
OF SORTING ALGORITHMS

PREVIEW   In this chapter we introduce the basic mathematical techniques for analyzing the efficiencies of algorithms. These techniques, which are central to more advanced topics in computer science, give us a way to formalize the notion that one algorithm is significantly more efficient than another. We apply the techniques to the three sorting algorithms already presented—Insertion sort, Quicksort, and Mergesort—and develop a fourth sorting algorithm, Heapsort.

The need for sorting arises in many situations. One situation is when we wish to sort a collection of data before displaying it for human consumption. Sorting also must be performed as an initialization step for many algorithms. For example, in the case study of Chapter 10, we developed an algorithm for building a balanced binary search tree from a collection of *sorted* data items. If we wished to apply this algorithm to a collection of data items that is not already sorted, we would first have to perform a sort. This situation is quite common in problem solving.

Thus, there is ample motivation for a good sorting algorithm. The fact that we have already presented three sorting algorithms (*Insertion sort*, *Quicksort*, and *Mergesort*) might, however, lead you to question the need for an entire chapter on the subject. The primary purpose of this chapter is to introduce techniques that can be used to *choose* between the sorting algorithms. Such techniques are quite important since it often makes a great deal of difference which sorting algorithm is used for a given application.

The comparison or analysis of algorithms is a topic that is central to computer science. With this in mind, our treatment of the sorting algorithms should be viewed as addressing the more general question of *what it means to compare one algorithm with another*. In previous chapters we have informally compared different methods for performing a task. For example, we compared a sequential search of an array with a binary search and concluded that the binary search is *significantly more efficient*. Before we can compare the various sorting algorithms, we need to give a more rigorous meaning to the term *significantly more efficient*. The next section introduces **order-of-magnitude analysis** and illustrates how it can be used to formalize the intuitive notion that one algorithm is significantly more efficient than another.

HOW TO ANALYZE AN ALGORITHM

Suppose we have two algorithms for performing the same task (for example, sorting). What does it mean to compare the algorithms and conclude that one is better than the other? As we have discussed previously, it is important to compare the algorithms for both style and efficiency. The early chapters of this book emphasized style and pointed out that well-structured algorithms reduce human costs in implementing the algorithm with a program, in maintaining the program, and in modifying the program. In the later chapters, we also began to concern ourselves with the efficiency of algorithms—that is, with the amount of computer time and space that they require.

Because of the need to balance the concerns of style and efficiency when comparing two algorithms, we have continually emphasized that only *significant* differences between the efficiencies of algorithms should be considered. To do otherwise could very well result in selecting an algorithm that runs a small fraction of a second faster than another algorithm, yet requires many more hours of human time to implement and maintain. With this point in mind, we shall now introduce the basic techniques for determining if one algorithm is *significantly* more efficient than another.

Suppose we have two algorithms for solving the same problem, and we wish to see which one is more time efficient. One approach would be to code up the two algorithms and run the programs. There are at least three fundamental problems with this approach:

1. **How should the algorithms be coded?** If algorithm A_1 runs faster than A_2, it could be the result of a more efficient coding job. Thus, if we compare the running times of the programs, we are really comparing *implementations* of the algorithms rather than the algorithms themselves. We want to avoid this because the implementations are sensitive to factors, such as programming style, that tend to cloud the issue of which algorithm is inherently more efficient.

2. **What machine should the programs be run on?** The particular computer on which the programs are run also clouds the issue of which algorithm is inherently more efficient. It may be that, because of the types of operations required by the algorithms, A_1 runs faster than A_2 on one machine, while the opposite is true on another machine. We would like to compare the efficiencies of the algorithms independent of a particular computer.

3. **What data should the program be run on?** Perhaps the most important problem with this method of comparing the algorithms is selecting the data on which the programs should be run. There is always the danger that we will select instances of the problem on which one of the algorithms runs uncharacteristically fast. For example, if we are comparing a sequential and binary search, we might happen to ask the algorithms to find the smallest item in the array. In this case, the sequential search will find the item more quickly than the binary search (since it is the first item that the sequential search will examine). We would like to perform our analysis independent of specific data.

Order-of-Magnitude Analysis

To overcome these problems, computer scientists employ mathematical techniques to analyze algorithms independent of specific implementations, computers, or data. The mathematical approach is to consider the time requirement of an algorithm as a function of problem size. The way a problem's size is measured is application dependent—typical examples are the number of items in a table, the size of an array, the number of nodes in a tree, and the number of blocks in a file.

What specifically do we want to know about the time requirement of an algorithm? The most important thing to learn is how quickly the algorithm's *time requirement grows* as a function of the problem size. We typically characterize this growth rate as a proportion of the problem size. For example, we might conclude that an algorithm requires time proportional to $\log N$, N, N^2, or 2^N, where N is the size of the problem.*

Consider the statement

Algorithm A requires time proportional to N^2.

What can we conclude from this statement? One thing that we *cannot* conclude is *the exact amount of time* that A will require to solve a problem of size N. Notice that the statement

A requires time proportional to N^2

would be equally valid if, to solve a problem of size N, A required N^2 seconds, $5*N^2$ seconds, or $1/10*N^2$ seconds.

Such characterizations of an algorithm's efficiency might thus appear to be of little use. Recall, however, our discussion in the previous section. What would it mean if we said that

A requires $5*N^2$ seconds to solve a problem of size N?

On what computer does the algorithm require $5*N^2$ seconds? What implementation of the algorithm requires $5*N^2$ seconds? Is there another implementation of the algorithm that requires only $3*N^2$ seconds (but is perhaps less readable)? On the other hand, a statement like

A requires time proportional to N^2

is exactly the kind of statement that characterizes the inherent efficiency of an algorithm independent of such factors as particular computers and implementations.

The significance of an algorithm's proportional time requirement can be seen if we compare two algorithms for which the requirement differs. For example, suppose that we have a second algorithm B such that

---

* When speaking of proportional growth rates, we do not specify the base of the log. See Exercise 13.4.

B requires time proportional to N.

Although we cannot determine the exact amount of time required by either algorithm A or B, we can determine that for large problems, B will require significantly less time than A. This is a consequence of the fact that the amount of time required by B *increases at a slower rate* (as a function of problem size) than the amount of time required by A. Even if B actually requires $5*N$ seconds and A actually requires $1/10*N^2$ seconds, as the size of the problem increases, the amount of time required by B will become significantly less than the time required by A.

To further dramatize the significance of an algorithm's proportional growth rate, consider the given table. The values in this table are approximate.

N	10	100	1,000	10,000	100,000	1,000,000
$\log_2 N$	3	6	9	13	16	19
N	10	10^2	10^3	10^4	10^5	10^6
$N \log_2 N$	30	664	9,965	10^5	10^6	10^7
N^2	10^2	10^4	10^6	10^8	10^{10}	10^{12}
N^3	10^3	10^6	10^9	10^{12}	10^{15}	10^{18}
2^N	10^3	10^{30}	10^{301}	$10^{3,010}$	$10^{30,103}$	$10^{301,030}$

(using the fact that $2^{10} \approx 10^{3.0103}$)

The table gives, for various values of N, the values of six common growth-rate functions. The table demonstrates how much more quickly the value of a function grows than that of the functions preceding it in the table. If algorithm A requires time proportional to function f and algorithm B requires time proportional to a slower-growing function g, it is apparent that, for large enough problems, B will always be significantly more efficient than A. For large problem sizes, the proportional growth rate dominates all other factors in determining an algorithm's efficiency.

Big O Notation

Let us now formalize the concept of an algorithm's proportional growth rate. When we make the statement

Algorithm A requires time proportional to f(N)

we mean that given any (reasonable) implementation of the algorithm and any (reasonable) computer, there is some constant c such that A requires no more than

c$*f(N)$ *time units (such as seconds)*

to solve a problem of size N.

This notion of proportional growth rate is formally captured by the following definition.

Algorithm A is $O(f(N))$ (read A is **order** $f(N)$) if for any (reasonable) implementation of the algorithm and any (reasonable) computer, there is some constant c such that for all but a finite number of values of N, A requires no more than

$c * f(N)$ *time units*

to solve a problem of size N. We shall call such a constant c, a **constant of proportionality.**

Notice that the definition of A is $O(f(N))$ does allow A to require more than $c * f(N)$ time units for a finite number of problem sizes. This is really more of a mechanical device than a conceptual addition. It simply allows us to discount (finitely many) values of N for which $f(N)$ takes on a value less than 1. For example, the function $\log N$ takes on the value 0 when $N = 1$. If we were not allowed to discount problems of size $N = 1$, we could never conclude that an algorithm was $O(\log N)$, since for all constants c,

$c * \log 1 = 0$

and all algorithms presumably require more than 0 time units even to solve a problem of size 1 (for example, to initialize a program).

There are many important mathematical properties of "big O" that you will be exposed to in later courses. One of these properties is that *low-order terms may be dropped from an algorithm's growth rate function.* For example, if an algorithm is $O(N^3 + 4 * N^2 + 13.3 * N)$, then it is also $O(N^3)$ (see Exercise 13.3). We thus are usually able to conclude that an algorithm is $O(f(N))$, where f is a function similar to the ones listed in the table on page 602.

There is one final point to be made about the definition of the order of an algorithm. The definition states that A is $O(f(N))$ if it requires no more than

$c * f(N)$ *time units*

to solve a problem of size N (for all but a finite number of values of N).

Note that A might require varying amounts of time to solve different problems of the same size (for example, a sorting algorithm might require varying amounts of time to sort arrays of size N that contain different items). Usually we consider the *maximum* amount of time that an algorithm can require to solve a problem of size N. This **worst-case analysis** concludes that A is $O(f(N))$ if, *in the worst case*, A requires no more than

$c * f(N)$ *time units*

to solve a problem of size N (for all but a finite number of values of N).

Sometimes we also perform an **average-case analysis,** which attempts to determine an algorithm's growth rate with respect to the *average* amount of time it requires to solve problems of size N. In an average-case analysis, we would say that A is $O(f(N))$ if the *average amount of time A requires to solve a problem of size N is no more than*

$c*f(N)$ *time units*

for all but a finite number of values of N. Average-case analysis is, in general, far more difficult to perform than worst-case analysis. One of the difficulties is determining the relative probabilities of encountering the various problems of a given size. Worst-case analysis is more common, and, unless otherwise specified, an analysis is taken to mean *worst-case analysis*.

Keeping Perspective

Before applying order-of-magnitude analysis to sorting algorithms, it is appropriate to present a few words about perspective. Order-of-magnitude analysis implicitly assumes that an algorithm will be solving large problems. This allows us to focus on growth rates, since, regardless of other factors, an algorithm with a slow growth rate will require less time than an algorithm with a fast growth rate, *provided that the problems to be solved are sufficiently large.*

For example, in the next section we shall be comparing sorting algorithms that are $O(N^2)$ to ones that are $O(N*\log N)$. While it is true that an $O(N*\log N)$ sorting algorithm will require significantly less time on large arrays than an $O(N^2)$ algorithm, on small arrays ($N < 50$) the time requirements might not be significantly different at all. In fact, it is entirely possible that, because of factors such as the sizes of the constants of proportionality (the c in the definition of big O), the $O(N^2)$ algorithm will run faster on small problems. It is only on large problems that the slower growth rate of an algorithm necessarily gives it a significant advantage.

As a consequence, if we are going to be solving only small problems, it is possible that an algorithm with a higher order of magnitude is more appropriate. If the problems to be solved are not sufficiently large for the efficiency advantage of an algorithm with a lower order of magnitude to be realized, other factors such as the simplicity of the algorithms would become more significant than minor differences in efficiency.

A COMPARISON OF FOUR SORTING ALGORITHMS

In this section we shall compare the orders of magnitude of the three sorting algorithms already presented (*Insertion sort*, *Quicksort*, and *Mergesort*) and introduce the *Heapsort* algorithm.

Insertion Sort

In Chapter 3 we introduced the *Insertion sort* algorithm in the context of building a sorted linked list from data stored in a file. The *Insertion sort* strategy can also be applied to sort items that already reside in an array. This in-place version of *Insertion sort* views the array as being partitioned into two regions: Sorted and Unsorted (see Figure 13–1). At each step, *Insertion sort* takes the first item from the Unsorted region and places it into its correct position of the Sorted region. Therefore, an invariant of the algorithm is that at each step the items in the Sorted region are sorted among themselves. Since at each step the size of the Sorted region grows by one and the size of the Unsorted region shrinks by one, the entire array will be sorted when the algorithm terminates.

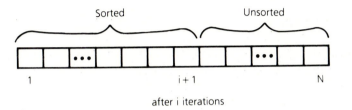

Figure 13–1

*Invariant for
Insertion sort*

The algorithm can be stated as follows.

```
InsertionSort(A)
(* Sort the elements of A[1..N] into ascending order. *)

    (* initialize the Sorted region to A[1] and the Unsorted
       region to A[2..N] - an invariant of the loop is that
       after i iterations the elements in A[1..i+1] are sorted *)
    FOR Unsorted := 2 TO N DO

        newitem := A[Unsorted]

        (* find the proper position in A[1..Unsorted]
           for newitem, shifting to make room *)
        loc := Unsorted;
        WHILE ((loc > 1) AND (newitem < A[loc-1])) DO
            A[loc] := A[loc-1]
            loc := loc - 1
        END

        A[loc] := newitem

    END
```

It can be shown that this algorithm is $O(N^2)$, where N is the number of items in the array. For small arrays (say, fewer than 50 items), *Insertion sort*'s simplicity makes it an appropriate choice. For large arrays, however, *Insertion sort* can be prohibitively inefficient.

We shall next discuss three sorting algorithms—*Quicksort*, *Mergesort*, and *Heapsort*—which, for large arrays, can require significantly less work than *Insertion sort*.

Quicksort

Since *Quicksort* is a good example of a recursive algorithm, we presented it in Chapter 5. Recall that the algorithm is:

```
Quicksort (A)
(* Sort the elements of A into ascending order. *)

    IF (size = 1) THEN
        quit

    ELSE

        choose a pivot element S from A

        partition the elements of A into three regions:
            S₁ (the elements < S)
            S₂ (the elements = S)
            S₃ (the elements > S)

        Quicksort (S₁)

        Quicksort (S₃)

    END
```

An analysis of *Quicksort*'s efficiency shows that in the worst case it, like *Insertion sort*, is $O(N^2)$. It might then seem surprising that *Quicksort* is often used to sort large arrays. The reason for *Quicksort*'s popularity is that it is usually extremely fast in practice, despite its unimpressive theoretical worst-case behavior.

The fact that *Quicksort*'s typical behavior is far better than its worst-case behavior distinguishes it from the other three sorting algorithms considered in this chapter. This makes it appropriate for us to consider *Quicksort*'s average-case behavior as well as its worst-case behavior. It can be shown that in the average case (assuming random arrangements of array items) *Quicksort* is $O(N*log\ N)$. Thus, on large arrays we can expect *Quicksort* to run significantly faster than *Insertion sort*, although in its worst case *Quicksort* will require roughly the same amount of time as *Insertion sort*.

Mergesort

The next two sorting algorithms, *Mergesort* and *Heapsort*, are $O(N*log\ N)$ in both the worst and average cases. We should point out that while the worst-case behaviors of *Mergesort* and *Heapsort* are of the same order of magnitude as *Quicksort*'s average-case behavior, in most situations *Quicksort* will run somewhat faster than either *Mergesort* or *Heapsort*. The other side, of course, is that in its worst case *Quicksort* will be significantly slower than either *Mergesort* or *Heapsort*.

In Chapter 5 we presented a *Mergesort* algorithm for sorting an array, and in Chapter 12 we modified it to sort external files. Here we shall consider only the array version:

```
Mergesort(A)
(* Sort the elements of A into ascending order. *)

    IF (size = 1)  THEN
        quit
    ELSE
        Mergesort( Lefthalf(A) )
        Mergesort( Righthalf(A) )
        Merge( Lefthalf(A), Righthalf(A) )
    END
```

While *Mergesort* is an extremely efficient algorithm with respect to time, it does have one drawback. To perform the step

```
Merge( Lefthalf(A), Righthalf(A) )
```

an auxiliary array is required of size equal to that of the original array. In situations where storage is tight, this might not be acceptable.

Heapsort

Heapsort, like *Mergesort*, is $O(N*log\ N)$ in both the worst and average cases. It has an advantage over *Mergesort* in that it does not require a second array.

As its name implies, the *Heapsort* algorithm is built around a heap, the data structure introduced in Chapter 10 as an implementation of the ADT priority queue. Recall that a heap is a complete binary tree, such that the value in the root is greater than the value in each of its children and such that both subtrees are also heaps (see Figure 10–5).

Let us suppose that we have an array of items that is already structured as a heap. Our sorting algorithm will view the array as being partitioned into two regions: the Heap region and the Sorted region. The Heap region is in $A[1..last]$ and the Sorted region is in $A[last+1..N]$. The invariant of the *Heapsort* algorithm is that, after step i:

1. The Sorted region contains the i largest values in A, and they are in sorted order—that is, $A[N]$ is the largest, $A[N-1]$ is the second largest, and so forth.

2. The items in the Heap region form a heap.

Since we assume that we are given A as a heap, the Heap region is initialized to be all of A, and the Sorted region is initialized to be empty—that is, $last=N$. At each step of the algorithm, an item I is moved from the Heap region to the Sorted region. In order for the invariant to hold, I must be the item having the largest value in the Heap region, and therefore I must be in the root of the heap. To accomplish the move, we exchange the item in the root of the heap with the last item in the heap (that is, exchange $A[1]$ with $A[last]$) and then decrement the value of $last$.

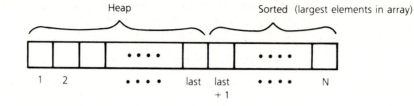

Figure 13–2

Invariant for Heapsort

The result is that the item that was just swapped from the root into $A[last]$ becomes the smallest item in the Sorted region (and is in the first position of the Sorted region). After the move, the Heap region must be transformed back into a heap since the new root may be out of place. This can be accomplished by using a procedure *Adjust* (based on the procedure in Chapter 10) to trickle down the item now in the root so that the Heap region is once again a heap.

The following algorithm summarizes the steps.

```
(*  initialize the regions *)
last := N

(* an invariant for this loop is that A[1..last] is a heap
   and A[last+1..N] is sorted and contains the largest
   elements of A *)
FOR i := N TO 2 BY -1 DO

   (* remove the largest item from the Heap region and place
      it at the beginning of the sorted region - since the Heap
      region is a heap, the largest item is at the root - to
      place it in the first position of the Sorted region, we
      swap A[1] and A[last] and decrement last *)

   Swap(A[1], A[last])

   (* expand the Sorted region - shrink the Heap region *)
   last := last - 1

   (* make the Heap region a heap again *)
   Adjust(A, 1, last)

END
```

This algorithm is the heart of *Heapsort*, but there is one other step. Recall that we have been assuming that the array A is originally structured as a heap. In general, however, the array that we are given to sort will be in no particular order at all. Thus before we can use the above algorithm, we must first transform the array A into a heap.

One way to accomplish this would be to use the priority queue's procedure *Insert* (Chapter 10) to insert the items into the heap one by one. There is, however, a more efficient method of building a heap out of the items of *A*. Suppose, for example, that the initial contents of *A* are as shown in Figure 13–3.

(a)

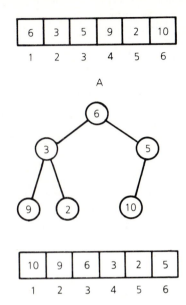

(b)

Figure 13–3

(a) Initial contents of A with corresponding tree; (b) contents of A after BuildHeap

We can transform this tree into a heap by calling *Adjust* repeatedly. *Adjust*, if you recall from Chapter 10, transforms a semiheap (a tree whose subtrees are both heaps but whose root may be out of place) into a heap. But are there any semiheaps in the above tree for *Adjust* to work on? Though *A* itself is not a semiheap, if you look at the leaves you will find semiheaps—that is, each leaf is a semiheap (in fact each leaf is a heap, but for simplicity we will choose to ignore this fact). We shall first call *Adjust* on the leaves, from right to left. We then move up the tree, knowing that by the time we reach a node i, its subtrees are heaps and thus *Adjust* will transform the semiheap rooted at i into a heap.

The following procedure is called as the first step of the *Heapsort* algorithm.

```
BuildHeap (A, N)

    FOR i := N TO 1 BY -1 DO
        (* the tree rooted at i is a semiheap -
            call Adjust to transform it into a heap *)
        Adjust (A, i, N)
    END
```

A Modula-2 implementation of *Heapsort* follows. Notice that our implementation uses open arrays, and thus arrays begin at location 0 and all subscripts are shifted by 1. This has important implications for the implementation of procedure *Adjust*. In particular, the left child of any node i is node $(2*i)+1$ and the right child is node $(2*i)+2$.

```
IMPLEMENTATION MODULE SortProc;
(* ******************************************************
    Sort an array with Heapsort.
    ************************************************** *)

(* user defined sort item *)
FROM SortType IMPORT

    sortitem;

(* ---------------------------------------------------------
    Adjust:  Convert the semiheap H rooted at position root
    into a heap.  Variable last marks the end of the heap.

    Recursively trickle the item at position root down to its
    proper position by swapping it with its larger child (if
    the child is larger than the item).

    NOTE:  In an open array, the left child of i is at (2*i)+1
    and the right child is at (2*i)+2.  This is because the
    normal heap numbering [1..size] is shifted to [0..size-1].

    If (2 * root + 1) > last then the item is at a leaf and
    nothing needs to be done.
    ------------------------------------------------------- *)
PROCEDURE Adjust(VAR H : ARRAY OF sortitem; root, last : INTEGER);

VAR

    child : INTEGER;
    temp  : sortitem;

BEGIN

    (* stop if the root is a leaf *)
    IF (2 * root + 1 <= last) THEN
        (* child is the index of the left child of root *)
        child := 2 * root + 1;

        (* child is the index of the larger child of root *)
        IF ((child + 1 <= last) AND (H[child+1] > H[child])) THEN
            INC(child);
        END;

        (* swap if the item at position root
            is smaller than the larger child *)
        IF (H[child] > H[root]) THEN
            temp := H[root];
```

```
            H[root]  := H[child];
            H[child] := temp;

            (* adjust the new subtree *)
            Adjust(H, child, last);
        END;
    END;

END Adjust;

(* -----------------------------------------------------------
    BuildHeap:  Build the initial heap H from scratch.
    ------------------------------------------------------- *)
PROCEDURE BuildHeap(VAR H : ARRAY OF sortitem);

VAR

    i : INTEGER;

BEGIN

    FOR i := HIGH(H) TO 0 BY -1 DO
        Adjust(H, i, HIGH(H));
    END;

END BuildHeap;

(* -----------------------------------------------------------
    Sort:  Array A with Heapsort.

    CALLS:  BuildHeap, Adjust
    ------------------------------------------------------- *)
PROCEDURE Sort(VAR A: ARRAY OF sortitem);

VAR

    temp : sortitem;
    i : INTEGER;

BEGIN

    (* build the initial heap *)
    BuildHeap(A);

    (* heapsort *)
    FOR i := HIGH(A) TO 1 BY -1 DO
        temp := A[0];
        A[0] := A[i];
```

```
        A[i] := temp;
        Adjust(A, 0, i-1);
    END;

END Sort;


END SortProc.
```

Approximate Growth Rates (with Respect to Time) of Four Sorting Algorithms:

	WORST CASE	AVERAGE CASE
`Insertion sort`	N^2	N^2
`Quicksort`	N^2	$N * \log N$
`Mergesort`	$N * \log N$	$N * \log N$
`Heapsort`	$N * \log N$	$N * \log N$

SUMMARY

1. When analyzing the efficiency of an algorithm, we typically focus on its proportional growth rate. This allows us to compare the inherent efficiencies of algorithms in isolation from other factors and to concentrate only on significant differences.

2. Worst-case analysis considers the maximum amount of work an algorithm will require on a problem of a given size, while average-case analysis considers the expected amount of work that it will require.

3. `Quicksort` is a sorting algorithm with an excellent average-case behavior, though its worst-case behavior is not nearly as good as either `Mergesort` or `Heapsort`.

4. `Mergesort` and `Heapsort` have very good worst- and average-case behaviors, though neither is quite as good in the average case as `Quicksort`. `Mergesort` has the disadvantage of requiring extra storage equal to the size of the array to be sorted.

EXERCISES

1. Write an iterative (nonrecursive) version of internal `Mergesort` that is based on the external version. That is, merge sorted runs that double in size at each pass of the array.

2. Implement `Insertion sort` and internal `Mergesort` (either recursive or nonrecursive—see Exercise 13.1).

   a. Run both algorithms on problems of various sizes. On what size does the difference in the time complexity (big O) of the two algorithms become "observable"?

1. In general, we should avoid analyzing an algorithm solely by studying the running times of a specific implementation. Running times are influenced by such factors as programming style, the particular computer, and the data on which the program is run.

2. If a problem is small, we should not overanalyze it. For example, if we are sorting an array containing only a small number of elements (for instance, fewer than 50) then a simple $O(N^2)$ algorithm such as *Insertion sort* is appropriate.

3. If we are sorting a very large array, an $O(N^2)$ algorithm could well be too inefficient. Since *Quicksort*'s worst-case behavior is $O(N^2)$, it might not be appropriate unless we have a high degree of confidence that the data in the array to be sorted is arranged randomly.

b. Add a counter to the two algorithms that counts the number of comparisons that are made. On what size does the difference in the number of comparisons become significant?

3. Show that any polynomial $f(x) = c_k x^k + c_{k-1} x^{k-1} + \ldots + c_1 x + c_0$ is $O(x^k)$.

4. Show that for all constants $a, b > 1$, $f(N)$ is $O(\log_a N)$ if and only if $f(N)$ is $O(\log_b N)$.

   (*Hint:* Use the identity $\log_a N = \log_b N / \log_b a$ for all constants $a, b > 1$.)

5. Show that in the pseudocode version of the *Buildheap* procedure of *Heapsort*, the **FOR** loop

   ```
   FOR i := N TO 1 BY -1 DO
   ```

   can be replaced by

   ```
   FOR i := (N DIV 2) TO 1 BY -1 DO
   ```

   How would the above modification be realized in the Modula-2 implementation that utilizes open arrays?

6. Execute *Buildheap* on the array in Figure 13–4.

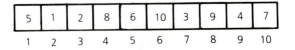

Figure 13–4

Input to Buildheap

7. One criterion used to evaluate sorting algorithms is **stability.** A sorting algorithm is stable if it does not exchange records with the same sort key. That is, records with the same sort key (possibly differing in other fields) will maintain their positions relative to each other. For example, we might want to take an array of student records that is sorted by name and produce an array that is sorted by class. Sorting the array (by class) with a stable sorting algorithm will ensure that within each class the students will remain sorted by name. Some applications mandate a stable sorting algorithm. Others do not. Which of the sorting algorithms described in this chapter are stable?

8. We want to sort a large array of elements that are restricted to be integers in the range 1..100. We can easily sort this array by *counting* the number of occurrences of each integer in the range 1..100 (using an array count[1..100]). Fill in the details of this sorting algorithm. This *Bucket sort* is the fastest sorting algorithm that we have considered. What is its big O? Why isn't it useful as a general sorting algorithm?

APPENDIX

This appendix contains the definition modules `FileIO`, `StringIO`, and `Strings`.

```
DEFINITION MODULE FileIO;
(* ************************************************************
    This module contains a collection of routines that support
    high-level I/O with files of type FixedFile.  FixedFiles
    are sequential files whose items are of a single fixed
    size (e.g., Modula-2 records of a single type).
    ********************************************************* *)

(* untyped pointer and data item *)
FROM SYSTEM IMPORT

    ADDRESS, WORD;

EXPORT QUALIFIED
    CreateFile, FixedFile, OpenRead, OpenWrite, EOF, CloseFile,
    ReadItem, WriteItem;

(* maximum length of external file name *)
CONST MaxFileName = 14;

TYPE FixedFile;

(* -----------------------------------------------------------
    Create file f for reading and writing items of size
    ItemSize.  Connect f to disk file filename.
    --------------------------------------------------------- *)
PROCEDURE CreateFile(VAR f: FixedFile;
                         filename : ARRAY OF CHAR;
                         ItemSize : CARDINAL);

    (* -----------------------------------------------------------
        Open file f for reading
        --------------------------------------------------------- *)
PROCEDURE OpenRead(VAR f: FixedFile);

    (* -----------------------------------------------------------
        Open file f for writing.
        --------------------------------------------------------- *)
PROCEDURE OpenWrite(VAR f: FixedFile);

    (* -----------------------------------------------------------
        Determine whether EOF has been read from file f.
```

```
     ---------------------------------------------------------------- *)
     PROCEDURE EOF(VAR f: FixedFile) : BOOLEAN;


   (* ----------------------------------------------------------------
      Close file f.
      ---------------------------------------------------------------- *)
     PROCEDURE CloseFile(VAR f: FixedFile);


   (* ----------------------------------------------------------------
      Read item from file f.
      ---------------------------------------------------------------- *)
     PROCEDURE ReadItem(VAR f: FixedFile; VAR item : ARRAY OF WORD);


   (* ----------------------------------------------------------------
      Write item to file f.
      ---------------------------------------------------------------- *)
     PROCEDURE WriteItem(VAR f: FixedFile; item : ARRAY OF WORD);

     END FileIO.



     DEFINITION MODULE StringIO;
   (* ****************************************************************
      Special I/O module for strings.
      **************************************************************** *)

     EXPORT QUALIFIED

        ReadString, IReadString, WriteName;

   (* ----------------------------------------------------------------
      Read a string from a file (non interactive version).
      ---------------------------------------------------------------- *)
     PROCEDURE ReadString(VAR S : ARRAY OF CHAR);


   (* ----------------------------------------------------------------
      Read a string from the terminal (interactive version).
      ---------------------------------------------------------------- *)
     PROCEDURE IReadString(VAR S : ARRAY OF CHAR);


   (* ----------------------------------------------------------------
      Write a string up through the last nonblank character.
      ---------------------------------------------------------------- *)
     PROCEDURE WriteName(S : ARRAY OF CHAR);

     END StringIO.
```

```
DEFINITION MODULE Strings;
(* **********************************************************
    Special string comparison operation.
    ****************************************************** *)

EXPORT QUALIFIED

    CompareStr;

(* ----------------------------------------------------------
    Compare two strings s1 and s2 lexicographically (based
    on the underlying character set).

    Return:     -1 if s1 < s2
                 0 if s1 = s2
                 1 if s1 > s2

    If s1 and s2 are of different lengths, the shorter string
    will be padded out with blanks to the length of the longer
    string for comparison.
    ---------------------------------------------------------- *)
PROCEDURE CompareStr (s1, s2: ARRAY OF CHAR): INTEGER;

END Strings.
```

INDEX

BUSINESS REPLY MAIL

FIRST CLASS MAIL   PERMIT NO. 174   FREMONT, CA 94555

POSTAGE WILL BE PAID BY ADDRESSEE

LOGITECH, INC.
Coupon Redemption
6505 Kaiser Drive
Fremont, CA 94555